Quick Access
Reference for Writers

SEVENTH EDITION

LYNN QUITMAN TROYKA

DOUGLAS HESSE

PEARSON

Boston   Columbus   Indianapolis   New York   San Francisco   Upper Saddle River
Amsterdam   Cape Town   Dubai   London   Madrid   Milan   Munich   Paris   Montreal   Toronto
Delhi   Mexico City   Sao Paulo   Sydney   Hong Kong   Seoul   Singapore   Taipei   Tokyo

Senior Acquisitions Editor: Lauren A. Finn
Senior Development Editor: Marion B. Castellucci
Executive Marketing Manager: Thomas DeMarco
Senior Supplements Editor: Donna Campion
Executive Digital Producer: Stefanie A. Snadjer
Digital Editor: Sara Gordus
Production Manager: Savoula Amanatidis
Project Coordination, Text Design, and Electronic Page Makeup: Laserwords
Cover Designer/Manager: John Callahan

Cover Image: *Enclosed Field with Rising Sun, Saint-Remy 1889* Vincent van Gogh (1853–1890/Dutch) Oil on canvas Private Collection, © SuperStock/SuperStock
Photo Researcher: Integra–New York
Senior Manufacturing Buyer: Dennis J. Para
Printer and Binder: R. R. Donnelley and Sons Company–Crawfordsville
Cover Printer: Lehigh-Phoenix Color Corporation–Hagerstown

For permission to use copyrighted material, grateful acknowledgment is made to the copyright holders on pp. C-1–C-2, which are hereby made part of this copyright page.

Library of Congress Cataloging-in-Publication Data
Troyka, Lynn Quitman
  Quick access reference for writers / Lynn Quitman Troyka, Douglas Hesse. — 7th ed.
    p. cm.
  Includes index.
  ISBN-13: 978-0-205-90361-0
  ISBN-10: 0-205-90361-4
  1. English language—Rhetoric—Handbooks, manuals, etc.   2. English language—Grammar—Handbooks, manuals, etc.   3. Report writing—Handbooks, manuals, etc.
I. Hesse, Douglas Dean.   II. Title.
  PE1408.T69565 2012
  808′.042—dc23

                                                          2012017712

10 9 8 7 6 5 4 3 — DOC —15 14 13

PEARSON   **www.pearsonhighered.com**   ISBN-10: 0-205-90361-4
                                                     ISBN-13: 978-0-205-90361-0

9 Sentences and Words

10 Punctuation and Mechanics

11 Tips for Multilingual Writers

12 Specific Writing Glossaries, Index

FINDING WHAT YOU NEED

Quick Access Reference for Writers will help you become a better writer by answering the questions that come up as you write. Use the following *Quick Access* tools to quickly find the information you need:

- The **Tab Directory** here lists all the tabbed parts and chapters in Quick Access.

- The **Quick View Contents** inside the back cover shows the chapter sections as well as chapters and tabbed parts.

- The **Index** lists all handbook topics covered in alphabetic order. Find your topic, note the page number, and then turn to that page to locate your information quickly.

- **Detailed Contents** for a tabbed section can be found on the back of each tab divider.

- **Quick Boxes** throughout the book give you an easy way to skim and access the most common and important issues that will come up as you write.

- The **Terms Glossary** at the end of the book defines important terms related to writing and grammar. Every word printed in SMALL CAPITAL LETTERS in *Quick Access* is defined in the glossary.

- **Proofreading Marks** and **Response Symbols** that your instructor may use to mark your writing appear on the fold of the back cover. Refer to these lists to find the section of the handbook that will help you edit and proofread your work.

- The **eText version** of the handbook provides many links to additional resources. For example,

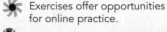 Video tutorials show key concepts in writing, grammar, and research.

 Audio podcasts explain common grammar and punctuation issues.

✳ Exercises offer opportunities for online practice.

🔍 Model documents provide examples of different kinds of writing.

Why Do You Need This New Edition?

Here are seven features that you'll find only in the new edition of *Quick Access Reference for Writers*:

- Six new chapters provide advice on writing commonly assigned papers—personal essays, informative writing, textual analysis, arguments, proposal and solution essays, and evaluations. Each chapter helps you identify your audience and purpose, gives you a Frame chart to organize your paper, provides Sentence and Paragraph Guides to help you develop common writing moves, and presents an annotated model paper (Tab 3).

- A new chapter on using sources in a research paper helps you decide what to do when your sources agree, partly agree, or disagree with one another. Sentence and Paragraph Guides demonstrate common moves you can make to transition among different sources while building your own argument (Ch. 22).

- A new chapter on evaluating sources provides five key questions to ask about each of your research sources so that you use only credible, reliable

sources in your papers. Each question includes a chart that contrasts characteristics of reliable versus questionable sources as well as examples (Ch. 21).

- A new chapter "Ten Troublesome Mistakes Writers Make" highlights the most common grammar and punctuation errors and alerts you to key areas that you might otherwise overlook. Additional examples and exercises help you identify and correct these errors in your own writing (Ch. 2).

- A new chapter, "Writing About Readings," covers the summary, response, analysis/interpretation, and synthesis essays, emphasizing how often assignments, not just in formal research papers, require writing about texts (Ch. 17).

- Completely updated MLA, APA, CM, and CSE documentation styles show you how to document and cite your sources. Examples for electronic sources like e-readers, wikis, and tweets help you accurately cite increasingly common types of new sources (Tabs 6 and 7).

- Media-rich eText versions of the handbook provide videos, animations, model documents, and exercises to create a rich, interactive learning experience. You can access additional resources online to help you write effectively and correctly.

In memory of David Troyka,
my sweetheart and
husband of 47 years

LYNN QUITMAN TROYKA

To Don and Coral Hesse

DOUG HESSE

FINDING WHAT YOU NEED ON A PAGE

The running head shows the last section on the current page.

Chapter and section

5G How can a thesis statement help me plan?

A **thesis statement** serves as the central, controlling declaration of the point being made in most essays written in reponse to typical writing assignments. A thesis statement gives readers a general preview of what they can expect to read about. The basic requirements of a thesis statement are listed in Quick Box 5.9, but you need to expect to compose many drafts of one for each essay, getting closer on successive attempts to what you want it to encapsulate.

Section heading indicates new section of a chapter.

Words in bold or SMALL CAPITAL LETTERS are discussed in various places in the book and are defined in the Terms Glossary.

Quick Boxes highlight key information.

Quick Box 5.9

Basic requirements for a thesis statement

1. It gives the essay's central message.
2. It makes an assertion or claim, which puts forth the essay's central message.
3. Its assertion or claim ties to the essay's TOPIC SENTENCES (see 7C) that start each of the essay's BODY PARAGRAPHS (see 7D).
4. It usually comes at the end of the INTRODUCTORY PARAGRAPH (see 7B).

Examples show how to apply a rule.

NO   **Approaching the island, a mountainous rock wall** was terrifying.

This sentence suggests that the mountainous wall was approaching the island.

YES   Approaching the island, **we** saw a foreboding mountainous wall.

Alert: A title stands alone. Don't open an essay with a reaction to the title or with an opening sentence that is a continuation of the title. For example, the following would be an inappropriate first sentence in student Cheryl Cusack's essay "Why We're Going Less Often to the Movies": "It's too expensive these days." Such an opening sentence is improper because it leans on the essay's title, and "It" is an unclear PRONOUN REFERENCE. ●

Alerts call attention to important rules and best practices.

ESOL Tip: If the cultural background of your readers differs from yours, you might find it difficult to estimate how much your readers know about your topic. To get a better idea of your readers' backgrounds, you might browse for information on the Internet or discuss your topic with people who might know more than you do about your readers' backgrounds. ●

ESOL icons call out information of particular use for multilingual students.

11A What is textual analysis?

A **textual analysis** essay is either (a) a content analysis that explains the meaning of a text, such as an article, a book, a Web site, a poem, a script, a song, or so on; or (b) a rhetorical analysis that explains how a text works to achieve a certain purpose or effect. Some textual analyses combine the two. Examples of textual analysis are papers that explain, for example, how women are portrayed in popular songs; what sources an historian uses to explain an event; how the images in a photo-essay create a certain meaning; what biases are evident in a politician's speech; or how characters, themes, imagery, or word choices develop meaning in a short story. To analyze a text, use this four-step process.

Watch
the Video

(((•
Listen
to the
Podcast

Section heading indicates new section of a chapter.

eText icons for video, audio, and exercise, and document resources provide links to additional instruction and practice online.

Frame for an Informative Essay

Introductory paragraph(s)

* **Capture your readers' interest** by using one of the strategies for writing effective introductory paragraphs (see 7B).
* **Present your THESIS STATEMENT**, making sure it gives the central point of the essay (see 5G).

Body paragraph(s): background information

* **Provide background** for the information in your essay. This might follow the introductory paragraph or come later in the essay at a point when the background is more relevant.
* **Start with a topic sentence** that clearly relates to your thesis statement and leads logically to the information in the paragraph (see 7C).

Frames charts show you how to organize typical college papers.

Sentence and Paragraph Guides

* People experienced with _____ advise that the public needs to know _____ so that everyone can _____.
* _____ captured my interest because _____.
* People generally consider _____, _____, and _____ as the major components of information about _____.
* In addition to _____, _____ plays a major role in _____.

Sentence and paragraph guides help you think out moves writers make.

INTRODUCTION TO STUDENTS

As writers, many of you have much in common with both of us. Sure, we've been at it longer, so we've had more practice, and most rules have become cemented in our heads. However, we share with you a common goal: to put ideas into words worthy of someone else's reading time. So that you can know us better as practicing writers, we'd each like to share a personal story with you.

From Doug: I first glimpsed the power of writing in high school, when I wrote sappy—but apparently successful—love poems. Still, when I went to college, I was surprised to discover all I didn't know about writing. Fortunately, I had good teachers and developed lots of patience. I needed it. I continue to learn from my colleagues, my students, and my coauthor, Lynn.

From Lynn: When I was an undergraduate, questions about writing nagged at me. One day, browsing in the library, I found a dust-covered book with the words *handbook* and *writing* in its title. Such books weren't common in those days, so I read it hungrily. Back then, I never imagined that someday I might write such a book myself. Now that we've completed the seventh edition of *Quick Access Reference for Writers*, I'm amazed that I ever had the nerve to begin. This proves to me—and I hope to you—that anyone can write. Students don't always believe that. I hope you will.

We welcome you as our partners in the process of writing. We hope that the pages of this handbook will help you give voice to your thoughts, in school and in life. Please know that you're welcome always to write us at troykalq@nyc.rr.com or dhesse@du.edu with comments about this handbook and about your experiences as a writer. We promise to answer.

Lynn Quitman Troyka
Doug Hesse

PREFACE

This seventh edition of *Quick Access Reference for Writers* gives "quick access" to all the information students need about writing, from writing college papers to using and documenting sources, from writing online to writing using visuals, and from mastering grammar to using correct punctuation. We designed *Quick Access* for easy use and speedy entreé into all topics, welcoming students into a conversation about becoming better writers.

WHAT'S NEW IN THE SEVENTH EDITION?

- **Six new chapters, "Frames for College Writing,"** advise students on commonly assigned papers. Guidance on the personal essay, informative writing, textual analysis, argument, proposal and solution, and evaluation includes a discussion of audience and purpose, a frames chart illustrating a typical organization, sentence/paragraph guides that help develop common writing moves, and an annotated sample student paper (Tab 3).

- **A new chapter on synthesizing researched sources** in a paper helps students decide what to do when multiple sources agree, partly agree, or disagree. Sentence and paragraph guides demonstrate common moves writers make to transition among different sources while building their arguments (Ch. 22).

- **A new chapter on evaluating sources** emphasizes five critical thinking questions for students. For each question, a chart contrasts the characteristics of reliable versus questionable sources while illustrations of sample sources show those qualities in practice (Ch. 21).

- **A new chapter "Ten Troublesome Mistakes Writers Make" with interactive online resources** highlights for students the most common grammar and punctuation mistakes, alerting them to key areas that they might otherwise overlook in what can seem a sea of grammar rules. This overview of common mistakes provides additional examples to help students identify and correct these errors in their own writing (Ch. 2). In the e-textbook, online videos and activities provide interactive instruction, practice, and remediation of the ten troublesome mistakes.

- **A new chapter on critical thinking** reinforces the fundamental importance of thinking for effective reading and writing. Sections on thinking skills, the persuasive appeals, types of reasoning, and logical fallacies help students strengthen their abilities to think deeply and develop ideas (Ch. 3).

- **More than 60 pages of new exercises** support students with opportunities to apply what they've learned about grammar and punctuation as well as thinking and writing strategies.

- **A new chapter, "Writing About Readings,"** covers the summary essay, response essay, and synthesis essay, emphasizing the importance of writing about readings in many college assignments, not just in formal research papers (Ch. 17).

- **A new chapter "Ten Top Tips for College Writers"** suggests ten fundamental writing practices and encourages students to keep basic rhetorical principles at the forefront of their writing, to record source information immediately during research, to avoid "textspeak" in college writing, and more (Ch. 1).

- **MLA, APA, CM, and CSE documentation examples** have been completely updated, and examples of electronic sources like e-readers and wikis help students accurately cite increasingly common types of new sources (Tabs 6 and 7).

- **New media enhancements in the e-textbook** link students to videos, animations, model documents, and exercises to create a rich, interactive learning experience. Resources that reinforce and extend the instructional content in *Quick Access* let students access additional help as needed and support students who have different learning styles. See E-textbook Resources on page xi for more information.

OTHER FEATURES OF *QUICK ACCESS*

- **Authoritative advice about grammar, punctuation, and mechanics** based on the comprehensive coverage of the *Simon & Schuster Handbook for Writers* provides condensed and clear explanations with plentiful examples of correct usage.

- **Quick Boxes** highlight and summarize key content throughout the text, providing quick access to important strategies, suggestions, and examples to improve student writing.

- **Extensive samples of student writing** include 12 full academic essays and 3 complete workplace documents to illustrate key elements of various types of writing and help students apply them in their own writing.

- **Annotated source illustrations** show students how to identify citation information in a range of typical sources—journal articles, web pages, and books—and how to arrange that information into correct MLA and APA citations.

- **Support for multilingual writers** includes six stand alone chapters devoted to areas of special concern as well as ESOL Tips integrated throughout the handbook and embedded within specific grammar, research, and writing topics.

- **Contemporary emphasis on visual and media literacy** includes coverage of reading visuals critically (Ch. 4), using photos and graphics to support a verbal text (Ch. 8), searching for images (Ch. 20), using multi-media in presentations (Ch. 70), and writing in online environments such as blogs and wikis (Ch. 71).

- **Thoughtful, up-to-date documentation** coverage includes more MLA, APA, and CMS example citations than most other comparable titles.

- **The Terms Glossary** provides a convenient cross-referencing system: key terms are boldfaced and defined where they first appear in this book, and are thereafter presented in small capital letters—providing visual cues to readers when more complete definitions can be found in the Terms Glossary.

PRINT AND ELECTRONIC FORMATS

The seventh edition of *Quick Access* is available both in print and as an e-textbook in the following formats:

Pearson eText. An interactive online version of *Quick Access* is available in MyCompLab. This eText brings together the many resources of MyCompLab with the instruction and content of this successful handbook to create an enriched, interactive learning experience for students. See below for more on the eText resources.

CourseSmart e-textbook. Students can subscribe to *Quick Access* at CourseSmart.com. The format of the eText allows students to search the text, bookmark passages, save their own notes, and print reading assignments that incorporate lecture notes.

Android and iPad e-textbooks. Android and iPad versions of the text provide the complete handbook and the electronic resources described below.

E-textbook resources
Marginal icons in the handbook's eText, CourseSmart, iPad, and print versions link to a wealth of electronic resources:

- Exercises from the handbook as well as additional exercises in *My-CompLab* offer ample opportunities to help students sharpen their writing, grammar, and research skills.

- Video tutorials illustrate key concepts, offering tips and guidance on critical reading, evaluating sources, avoiding plagiarism, and many other topics.

- Audio podcasts discuss common questions about grammar, usage, punctuation, and mechanics.

- Sample documents illustrate the range of writing students do in composition classes, their other courses, the workplace, and the community.

SUPPLEMENTS

- **MyCompLab®.** MyCompLab uniquely integrates proven resources and assessment tools with a student's own writing. This seamless and flexible application, built for writers by writers, helps instructors and students accomplish everyday composition tasks more easily and effectively. In addition, MyCompLab includes the eText version of *Quick Access* (see above) with additional electronic resources.

- **Instructor's Manual.** *Instructor's Resource Manual to accompany Quick Access Reference for Writers, Seventh Edition* offers practical, hands-on advice for new and experienced composition instructors for organizing their syllabi, planning, and teaching.

- *Quick Access* **Exercise Answer Key.** Contains answers to the many exercises and activities in Quick Access.

- **Student Workbook.** *Workbook for Writers* has additional instruction and exercises for the writing, research, and grammar sections.

If you would like additional information about supplements for your composition course(s), please contact your Pearson sales representative.

ACKNOWLEDGMENTS

With this seventh edition of *Quick Access Reference for Writers*, nicknamed *QA*, we heartily thank all those students who, to our great luck, have landed in our writing courses. We yearly learn from them how to stay up to date with students' needs and concerns as writers. We greatly admire how they strive to write skillfully, think critically, and communicate successfully. We especially thank the individual students who have given us permission to make them "published authors" by including their exemplary writing in this handbook.

We also are grateful to our many colleagues who have helped us with their criticisms, suggestions, and encouragement. In particular, we thank: Francesco Ancona, Sussex County Community College; Diana I. Badur, Black Hawk College; Anne Balay, Indiana University Northwest; Martin Brick, Ohio Dominican University; Ginny Buccelli, Contra Costa College; William Carney, Cameron University; Daniel J. Cleary, Lorain County Community College; Shaun D. Curran, Quincy College; Richard Davis, Grayson County College; Marya Davis Turley, Western Kentucky University; Emily Dial-Driver, Rogers State University; Envera Dukaj, The Ohio State University; Anne Dvorak, Metropolitan Community College–Longview; Ginger S. Fox, Rowan-Cabarrus Community College; Jennifer Gatto, Tunxis Community College; Kim Greenfield, Lorain County Community College; Diana Clark Grumbles, Southern Methodist University; Darin L. Hammond, Brigham

Young University–Idaho; Danielle Houck, University of Miami; Cheryl Hunter, NHTI–Concord's Community College; Roberta Kelly, Washington State University; Melinda Knight, Montclair State University; Shanon Lawson, Pikes Peak Community College; Joy Eichner Lynch, Contra Costa College; David MacWilliams, Adams State College; Brandy Meyers, The Art Institute of Philadelphia; Michael N. Morris, Eastfield College; Louise Polistena-D'Agosto, Tunxis Community College; Julie A. Ptacek-Wilkey, Northeast Community College; James Rawlins, Sussex County Community College; Jean Sorensen, Grayson County College; Virginia Tucker, Old Dominion University; and Madeline Yonker, York College of Pennsylvania.

A project as complicated as *Quick Access* cannot be completed without the expertise and dedication of many professionals. We thank all the exceptional people at Pearson who facilitated this new edition. We're especially endebted to Marion Castellucci, Senior Development Editor, for her splendid vision and disciplined leadership; we thank also Paul Sarkis, Development Editor, Lauren Finn, Senior Acquisitions Editor, and Joe Opiela, Senior Vice President and Editorial Director for English. We greatly admire the work of Michael Montagna, a fellow faculty member, for reviewing, clarifying, and streamlining our grammar sections.

Doug values Lynn Troyka's vast knowledge, skill, dedication to teaching, and patience. He appreciates the support of all his colleagues in the writing program at the University of Denver, the knowledge and dedication embodied in the memberships of CCCC and WPA, and the hardworking team at Pearson. He further states, "My children, Monica, Andrew, and Paige, amaze me with their creativity, as does the very best writer I know: Becky Bradway, my wife."

Lynn wishes first to pay tribute to David Troyka, her beloved husband of 47 years, who inspired her to enjoy teaching and writing along with their amazing adventures in barely explored parts of the world. She thanks also her coauthor Doug Hesse for his gentle friendship while working on this newest edition of the *Quick Access Reference for Writers*. For their unwavering support and love, Lynn also thanks the following: Ida Morea, her steadfast friend and Administrative Assistant for 18 years; Kristen Black, her adored daughter, Dan Black, Kristen's superb husband and their delightful children Lindsey and Ryan; Bernice Joseph, her "adopted" sister and anchor of an amazing family: Mauricia Joseph, and Rachael and Eric Thomas, along with their gifted, enchanting children Nickyla, Nicholas, and Nehemiah; Lynn's "adopted" brother Douglas Young III, his wife Anna, and young "Little" Doug IV; Michael Burns and his wife, Janelle James; and her grand pals Alice, Melanie, Avery, Jimmy, Gitam, Susan, Rose, and Amanda.

Lynn Quitman Troyka
Doug Hesse

ABOUT THE AUTHORS

Lynn Quitman Troyka

Lynn Quitman Troyka, Adjunct Professor of English in the MA Program in Language and Literature at the City College (CCNY) of the City University of New York (CUNY), taught freshman English and basic writing for many years at Queensborough Community College. Dr. Troyka is a past chair of the Conference on College Composition and Communication (CCCC); the College Section of the National Council of Teachers of English (NCTE); and the Writing Division of the Modern Language Association (MLA). She has won many awards for teaching, scholarship, and service, and has conducted hundreds of faculty workshops about teaching writing and its relation to college-level reading.

"This information," says Dr. Troyka, "tells what I've done, not who I am. I am a teacher. Teaching is my life's work, and I love it."

Doug Hesse

Doug Hesse is Professor of English and Executive Director of Writing at the University of Denver, one of only thirty writing programs to receive the CCCC Certificate of Excellence. Dr. Hesse is a past chair of the CCCC, the nation's largest association of college writing instructors. A past president, as well, of the Council of Writing Program Administrators (WPA), Dr. Hesse edited *WPA: Writing Program Administration.* He has served on the NCTE executive committee, chaired the MLA Division on Teaching as a Profession, and served on the MLA Committee on Contingent Labor. Author of nearly sixty articles and book chapters, he has been named University Distinguished Scholar at the University of Denver.

"Of various awards I've received," says Dr. Hesse, "the one that matters most is Distinguished Humanities Teacher. That one came from my students and suggests that, in however small a way, I've mattered in their education and lives."

Tab 1
Hands-On Advice
for Writers

■ ■ ■ ■ ■ ■ ■ ■ ■

CHAPTERS
1–4

Tab 1 Hands-On Advice for Writers

MyCompLab® Visit mycomplab.com for the eText and for resources for writers.

1

Ten Top Tips
for College Writers

Quick Points You will learn to

➤ Focus on ten elements to improve your college writing.

Lynn has taught writing and teachers of writing for over 36 years, and at the close of each term, she always surveyed her students by asking, "What three or four tips for writers that you've learned this term have proved most helpful?" She has seen approximately 7,200 responses. After considering the most frequent advice Doug has given thousands of writers, he found his students had a lot in common with Lynn's. We combined our lists, and the results are shown in Quick Box 1.1, starting with the top favorite tip.

Quick Box 1.1

Ten top tips for college writers

1. Be specific by thinking of RENNS: **R**easons, **E**xamples, **N**ames, **N**umbers, and the five **S**enses. (See 7D.)

2. Create a personal system to record writing ideas that pop into your head.

3. Use essay frames and sentence and paragraph guides as aids to writing. (See Chapters 9–14.)

4. Stay focused on the concepts of "purpose" and "audience" throughout your writing process. (See 5B and 5D.)

5. Weave *logos* (logic), *ethos* (credibility), and *pathos* (emotion) into your writing. (See 3B.)

6. Engage your readers by presenting and then complicating a topic. (See 7E.)

7. Play the "believing game" and the "doubting game." (See pages 7–8.)

8. Record source information the very first time you find a source, even if you're not sure you will use it. (See Chapters 18–20.)

9. Welcome feedback about your writing. (See 5E.)

10. Avoid slipping into "textspeak" in your writing.

■ TIP 1. Be specific: use RENNS.

Successful college writing moves back and forth between main ideas, usually stated in TOPIC SENTENCES,* and specific details. The letters "RENNS" start words that lead to specific details: **R**easons, **E**xamples, **N**ames, **N**umbers, and the five **S**enses (sight, sound, smell, taste, and touch). You might include emotions along with the five senses when they fit your topic. Only some RENNS need to appear as specific details in a piece of writing. Make sure topics you choose for writing assignments allow you to use sufficient details to support your generalizations. For example, the topic "Everyone deals with disappointments in their lives" is too broad to succeed.

Here's a paragraph that uses specific details to describe an environmental disaster.

> On April 20, 2010, an oil drilling rig in the Gulf of Mexico exploded, killing 11 workers and causing a huge oil spill that leaked 340,000 gallons a day of crude oil into the waters 40 miles southeast of the Louisiana coast. Because the rig, called The Deepwater Horizon, sat half submerged so that it could extract more oil per day than a surface rig, the spilled oil went into deeper water than ever in the history of oil spills. The devastation of life below, on, and above the water was unusually widespread because the Gulf's strong currents spread the oil over large areas. Coral beds that live in darker waters far below the surface died quickly as oil fell onto their

>   **Numbers**
>   **Names**
>
>   **Reasons**
>
>   **Examples**

---

* Words printed in SMALL CAPITAL LETTERS are discussed elsewhere in the text and are defined in the Terms Glossary at the back of the book.

fragile formations. Fish such as flounder and monkfish that normally live in deep water were quickly suffocated by the oil entering their gills. On the surface, microorganisms such as algae and krill, vital to oxygen in the water and food for many types of whales, were wiped out. Sea life closer to shore, such as dolphins, turtles, and seals, died slowly, coated in the thick oil that seeped into their mouths and skin. Sea grasses and kelp, near-shore nesting sites for many species, wilted and died in the oil. And who can forget photographs of oil-coated pelicans, guillemots, and other sea birds held by human hands rushing against time to wash off the thick, sticky crude oil from feathers, bills, and feet? Or the videos of people weeping silently, angry at the sight of the dead birds and turtles that could not be saved? The oil poured out of the explosion site for over a month, creating the second worst environmental disaster in the United States.

Senses and emotions

For more on RENNS with additional examples, see 7D.

■ TIP 2. Create a personal system to record writing ideas that pop into your head.

Writers often find that ideas pop into their heads while they're thinking of something else. You might be doing your laundry, driving your car or riding on a bus, or waking up in the middle of the night. Those ideas can slip through your fingers like snowflakes if you don't save them right away. We urge you to devise a recording system that suits your lifestyle. It might be a paper pad and a pencil, a cell phone, a small recording device, or a combination of these. Recording your ideas raises your awareness of how professional writers work and reminds you that in college, much of your time is spent as a writer as well as a reader.

From time to time, check what you've saved because one idea might lead you to expanded or new thoughts. And while you're writing each of your assignments, consider whether some of what you've saved might fit in well with the current project. Yes, some seemingly random ideas might turn out to be useless, but some might be just what you need to spark further thoughts as you plan, draft, and revise your writing. For more on brainstorming a topic and other techniques to help you plan your writing, see 5D–5F.

■ TIP 3. If you're unsure how to approach a writing assignment, check Tab 3, "Frames for College Writing."

The six essay frames in Tab 3 of this handbook introduce you to the different types of college writing assignments and immerse you in a variety of practical techniques to help you think clearly and write effectively. Our purpose is to give you sufficient general guidance so that you can concentrate on your own concerns: building a good THESIS STATEMENT, writing paragraphs that relate to your thesis statement and topic sentences, and making sure that you're staying on topic. For lots of information about six different essay types, see Chapters 9–14. Also, for frame information to help you write research papers, see Chapter 23.

■ TIP 4. Stay focused on the concepts of "purpose" and "audience" throughout your writing process.

All human communication starts with a PURPOSE: to explain something to someone, to describe an experience to someone, to mount an argument that you hope will persuade someone, or to inspire someone to take action or think in new ways. That "someone" is your AUDIENCE, the person or people you're reaching out to with your words. To write successfully in college, begin thinking about your topic—whether assigned by an instructor or chosen on your own—by consciously deciding from the start

- What your purpose is
- Who your audience is

Develop this habit until it flows naturally each time you start a writing assignment. When you revise your essays, always revisit your purpose and your audience. One excellent way to check yourself is to participate in class-sponsored peer reviews, which are chances for other students to read your writing and tell you whether they can discern the purpose of your writing and your intended audience.

In the following excerpt, the author's *purpose* is to give helpful advice; her *audience* is people who want to write.

> Forthwith, some advice to those of you who have always wanted to write, those with best-selling ideas, and those who really have a story. To begin, don't write about yourself. I'm not saying you're uninteresting. I realize that your life has been so crazy no one could make this stuff up. But if you want to be a writer, start by writing about other people. Observe their faces, and the way they wave their hands around. Listen to the way they talk. Replay conversations in your mind—not just the words, but the silences as well. Imagine the lives of others. If you want to be a writer, you need to get over yourself. This is not just an artistic choice; it's a moral choice. A writer attempts to understand others from the inside.
>
> —Allegra Goodman, "So You Want to Be a Writer? Here's How"

For more about the concepts of purpose and audience, see sections 5B and 5C.

▪ TIP 5. Weave logical, ethical, and emotional appeals into your writing.

The advice that Greek philosopher Aristotle gave 2300 years ago to people who wanted to persuade others is still excellent guidance for writers today. Aristotle taught that all effective communication needs three qualities:

- **Logical appeal (in Greek, *logos*).** Writers need to make statements that are logical so that the audience can accept and believe them.
- **Ethical appeal (*ethos*).** Writers need to choose words that communicate good character and integrity so their readers feel confident they're reading the ideas of someone who can be trusted and is not trying to manipulate them.
- **Emotional appeal (*pathos*).** Writers need to use words to establish an emotional connection with the audience.

Without these three qualities, readers will not accept the message being offered by the writer. Weaving all three qualities into your writing takes practice. You need to dig into yourself to make sure you're being honest, not distorting information, showing personal humility, and exhibiting an understanding of the human condition. The following paragraph uses only a few words to communicate a logical position (*logos*), engages in a bit of self-mockery that conveys humility (*pathos*), and shows that the writer is honest and forthright in accepting her position in relation to others (*ethos*).

Wearing a canvas jumpsuit zipped up to my neck, I must have looked as though I was stepping onto the set of *ET: The Extra Terrestrial*, but my actual destination was Madison Avenue, home to some of the fanciest boutiques in New York City. The bright blue jumpsuit I wore was far from high fashion; it was sized for a full-grown man, and it ballooned about my slender frame. My blonde hair was pulled back in a pony tail, and the only label I displayed was the bold-lettered logo on my back: Ready, Willing, & Able. I was suited up to collect trash from the sidewalks of New York.

Logical appeal. The author states the facts logically.

Ethical appeal. The author describes herself honestly; she isn't concerned about appearing unattractive.

Emotional appeal. The author has become a street cleaner, which many people consider undignified.

—Zoe Shewer, "Ready, Willing, and Able"

For more about the logical, ethical, and emotional appeals, see section 3B.

■ **TIP 6. Engage your readers by presenting and then complicating a topic.**

One way to capture and hold readers' attention is to present and then complicate a topic. A simple procession of details to support the generalization in a topic sentence can bore readers. When you introduce a complication into your ideas, you lure your readers to think more deeply about a topic, a habit of mind that greatly enhances the pleasure people get from reading. When you can, resolve the complication; however, sometimes complications are not easily resolved. If this is the case for you, still be sure not to ignore it at the end of your essay. You can close your discussion by acknowledging that the complication remains, and, by implication, you can invite your readers to think more about it on their own.

Here's a paragraph that contains a topic sentence as its generalization and specific details to support it. The complicating sentence is shown in boldface. By the end of the essay, the author doesn't smooth over the stark differences in worldviews that he presents, but he acknowledges them and suggests readers will see future evidence of their impact.

The world can be divided in many ways—rich and poor, democratic and authoritarian—but one of the most striking is the divide between societies with an individualistic mentality and the ones with a collectivist mentality. **This divide goes deeper than economics into the way people perceive the world.** If you show an American an image of a fish tank, the American will usually describe the biggest fish in the tank and what it is doing. If you ask a Chinese person to describe a fish tank, the Chinese will usually describe the context in which the fish swim. These experiments have been done over and over again, and the results reveal the same underlying pattern. Americans usually see individuals; Chinese and other Asians see contexts.

—David Brooks, "Harmony and the Dream"

For more about developing paragraphs by presenting and then complicating a topic, see section 7D.

■ TIP 7. Play the "believing game" and the "doubting game."

The "believing game" comes in handy when you're brainstorming and drafting. If you suddenly feel you have nothing to say, or you think your ideas aren't smart enough or your writing isn't good enough, turn on your ability to believe. Push yourself to become confident that you have something worth saying and the right to say it. Write boldly. Just get the words out. Believing can propel you to get enough on paper to start your reviewing and revising processes.

The "doubting game" is the flip side of the believing game. It's invaluable when you really don't want to bother doing any more with an essay, so you simply decide your writing is perfect and all your ideas are clear—even though you know there's room for improvement. At these times, the doubting game can jump-start your revision process. It turns up the volume of that quiet little voice, the one you'd like to ignore, that whispers maybe you had better look over your work one last time before you hand it in—perhaps you need more specific details or maybe you've cited one of your sources incorrectly. Okay, take a break. Then marshal your energy, and become your own critic. If you're like most professional writers, chances are you'll find holes that need filling or flaws you want to fix.

■ **TIP 8. Record source information the very first time you find a source, even if you're not sure you will use it.**

At the very moment you access a source, take an extra few minutes to record publication information so that you won't need to retrace your steps later on. Retracking down sources can take days, meaning wasted time and destructive stress. You can use a master checklist of the publication details you'll need for the DOCUMENTATION STYLE you'll be using. Record that information every time. Never put it off. Even if a source seems irrelevant to the focus of your topic, force yourself to note its publication information. You never know! One day as you're writing you might suddenly realize you do indeed want to use that source.

There's a related, highly important reason for recording publication information about a source from the very start: it helps you avoid unintentional PLAGIARISM. With the exact source information, you can always go back to a source to make sure that you're not claiming an author's words as your own, or that your summary or paraphrase uses too many of the author's own words. For more about what publication information to record, see section 19F.

■ **Tip 9. Welcome feedback about your writing.**

Feedback about your writing from your instructor, your classmates, and other trusted readers can be invaluable when you want to improve your writing. These readers might suggest small improvements like changing a word or large improvements like changing ideas. Avoid reacting defensively or becoming resentful when you hear constructive criticism. Receive suggestions openly and thoughtfully. If this is hard for you to tolerate or if it frightens you at first, discipline yourself to listen to the comments and consider the points made. Other readers often can help you see possibilities you didn't notice on your own. Similarly, you can help others see their writing with new eyes.

As you make decisions about the value of the others' comments, always remember that you are the author. You are the one to make the final choice about whether to use each suggestion. (Please note that because some instructors require that students to refrain from asking for feedback about their writing before handing it in, be sure to check the teacher's policy in each of your writing classes.) For more about receiving feedback on your writing and giving feedback to others about their writing, see section 5E.

■ TIP 10. Avoid slipping into "textspeak" in your writing.

Textspeak is a coined term for shortening words, mostly by omitting vowels, in informally written text and chat messages. It's quicker to type "2morrow" or "cu soon." Of course, people who text know that texting forms aren't acceptable in ACADEMIC WRITING. Yet after a while, for many people who use it frequently, textspeak starts to look normal, and it creeps without notice into their formal writing. One area where students particularly allow textspeak to slip into their writing is in blogged entries for class. Professors expect blogs for class to be written with serious, formal intent. Little will annoy your instructors and peer readers as much as assignments written in textspeak, so monitor your college writing carefully.

2 Ten Troublesome Mistakes Writers Make

■ ■ ■ ■ ■ ■ ■ ■

Quick Points   You will learn to

➤ Recognize and correct ten common errors in writing.

Ten troublesome mistakes tend to pop up frequently in college students' writing because students often forget what they learned years before. Most of these errors stand out more in written than in spoken English. We urge you to work through the quick review in this chapter to check whether any of these ten errors gives you trouble. If you see any, put aside some time right away to learn to recognize and eliminate them. Later, we include a full chapter on each error (the chapter numbers are in parentheses in Quick Box 2.1).

Quick Box 2.1   ■ ■ ■ ■ ▪ ■ ■ ■ ■

Ten troublesome mistakes in writing

1. Sentence fragments instead of complete sentences (see Chapter 37)
2. Comma-spliced sentences and run-on sentences (see Chapter 38)
3. Subject–verb disagreement (see Chapter 34)
4. Pronoun–antecedent disagreement (see Chapter 35, sections 35A–35E)
5. Pronouns unclear in what they refer to (see Chapter 35, sections 35F–35I)
6. Illogical sentence shifts (see Chapter 39)
7. Modifiers placed incorrectly (see Chapter 40)
8. Homonyms misused (see Chapter 46, section 46E)
9. Commas misused (see Chapter 47)
10. Apostrophes misused (see Chapter 50)

■ 1. Sentence fragments

Watch
the Video

A **sentence fragment** is a written mistake that looks like a sentence but isn't one. Even though it starts with a capital letter and ends with a period, it's not a sentence. It's only a group of words.

NO **When** companies show employees respect.

The fragment starts with *when*, a SUBORDINATING CONJUNCTION, and is only a group of words.

YES **When** companies show employees respect, the best workers rarely quit.

The fragment is joined with a complete sentence.

NO A positive working atmosphere most employees productive and happy.

The fragment lacks a VERB and is only a group of words.

YES A positive working atmosphere **keeps** most employees productive and happy.

Keeps, a verb, completes the sentence.

Sentence fragments are written errors created by three types of incomplete word groups. Chapter 37 lists the types and shows how to turn them into complete sentences.

■ 2. Comma splices and run-on sentences

Comma splices and run-on sentences are written mistakes that look almost alike.
A **comma-spliced sentence** uses only a comma between two complete sentences. Watch the Video
A **run-on sentence** uses no punctuation between two complete sentences. These errors disappear with any one of three fixes: placing a period or semicolon between the two sentences; writing a CONJUNCTION and any needed punctuation between the two sentences; or turning one of the sentences into a DEPENDENT CLAUSE.

COMMA SPLICES

NO Bad bosses quickly stand out in workplaces, they scream impatiently at everyone.

YES Bad bosses quickly stand out in workplaces. They scream impatiently at everyone.

A period replaces the comma, which corrects the error. A semicolon also works.

YES Bad bosses quickly stand out in workplaces, **for** they scream impatiently at everyone.

Inserting the COORDINATING CONJUNCTION *for* corrects the error.

YES Bad bosses quickly stand out in workplaces **because** they scream impatiently at everyone.

The SUBORDINATING CONJUNCTION *because* turns the second sentence into a dependent clause, which corrects the error. The comma is dropped.

YES   **Because** they scream impatiently at everyone, bad bosses quickly stand out in workplaces.

The SUBORDINATING CONJUNCTION *because* turns the second sentence into a dependent clause, which corrects the error. Now the dependent clause comes before the complete sentence, so the comma is retained.

RUN-ON SENTENCES

Watch
the Video

NO   Bad bosses quickly stand out in workplaces they scream impatiently at everyone.

YES   Bad bosses quickly stand out in workplaces. They scream impatiently at everyone.

A period or semicolon between the two sentences corrects the error.

YES   Bad bosses quickly stand out in workplaces, **for** they scream impatiently at everyone.

A comma and the COORDINATING CONJUNCTION *for* correct the error.

YES   Bad bosses quickly stand out in workplaces **because** they scream impatiently at everyone.

The SUBORDINATING CONJUNCTION *because* turns the second sentence into a dependent clause, which corrects the error.

YES   **Because** they scream impatiently at everyone, bad bosses quickly stand out in workplaces.

The SUBORDINATING CONJUNCTION *because* turns the second sentence into a dependent clause, which corrects the error. Now the dependent clause comes before the complete sentence and is followed by a comma.

Chapter 38 describes the types of comma splices and run-on sentences and explains how to revise them correctly.

■ 3. Mistakes in subject–verb agreement

Watch
the Video

A mistake in subject–verb agreement occurs when a VERB and its SUBJECT are mismatched, often within one sentence. This error, in written as well as spoken English, often occurs when singulars and plurals are mixed incorrectly.

NO   **Effective leaders** in business **knows** how to motivate people to excel.

YES   **Effective leaders** in business **know** how to motivate people to excel.

The plural subject *Effective leaders* matches the plural verb *know*.

YES   **An effective leader** in business **knows** how to motivate people to excel.

The singular subject *Effective leader* matches the singular verb *knows*.

Chapter 34 explains all the ways subject–verb agreement errors occur and shows how to correct them.

■ 4. Mistakes in pronoun–antecedent agreement

Pronoun–antecedent agreement errors occur when a PRONOUN and its ANTECEDENT
are mismatched. A pronoun—such as *it, its, they,* and *their*—takes the place of a   Watch the Video
NOUN; an antecedent is the specific noun that a pronoun replaces in the same sentence or a nearby sentence. Errors in pronoun–antecedent agreement, in written as well as spoken English, often occur when singulars and plurals are mixed incorrectly.

> **NO**   My office partner admired my new computer **monitors** for **Its** sleek design.

> **YES**   My office partner admired my new computer **monitors** for **their** sleek design.
>
> The plural antecedent *monitors* matches the plural pronoun *their*.

> **YES**   My office partner admired my new computer **monitor** for **its** sleek design.
>
> The singular subject *monitor* matches the singular pronoun *its*.

Chapter 35, sections 35A–35E, explains all the ways mistakes in pronoun–antecedent agreement occur and shows how to correct them.

■ 5. Unclear pronoun reference

Unclear pronoun reference, in written as well as spoken English, is a mistake
that happens when the noun to which a pronoun—often *it, they, them*—refers   Watch the Video
is not obvious.

> **NO**   The construction supervisors paid little attention to the bricklayers when **they** were distracted.
>
> *They* is an unclear pronoun reference. Who is distracted, the *construction supervisors* or the *bricklayers*?

> **YES**   When the construction supervisors were distracted, *they* paid little attention to the bricklayers.
>
> *They* clearly refers to the *construction supervisors*.

> **NO**   Experienced bricklayers waste little motion to preserve their energy so that they can finish an entire section of wall without taking a break. **This** creates a sturdy wall.
>
> *This* is an unclear pronoun reference. Is the wall sturdy because the bricklayers wasted little motion to preserve their energy or because the bricklayers finished an entire section without taking a break?

> **YES**   So that the wall they build is sturdy, experienced bricklayers waste little motion to preserve their energy so that they can finish an entire wall section without taking a break.
>
> *This* is eliminated when the revised sentence makes clear how bricklayers can create a sturdy wall.

Chapter 35, sections 35F–35I, describes the sentence structures that often have unclear pronoun reference problems and explains how to revise them correctly.

■ 6. Illogical shifts within sentences

**Watch
the Video**

Illogical shifts within sentences are mistakes, in written as well as spoken English, that occur midsentence when a category of word, such as the verb, changes form for no reason.

> **NO**   Our union representative **explained** the new salary schedule and then **allows** time for questions.

> **YES**   Our union representative **explained** the new salary schedule and then **allowed** time for questions.

> **YES**   Our union representative **explains** the new salary schedule and then **allows** time for questions.

> In the correct sentences, both verbs are in same tense, either PAST TENSE or PRESENT TENSE.

In addition to verb tenses, other categories of words need to remain consistent within sentences as well as in groups of sentences. Chapter 39 shows how shifts create unclear writing and how they can be avoided.

■ 7. Mistakes with modifiers

**Watch
the Video**

Mistakes with MODIFIERS are more obvious in written than spoken English. Such errors happen when a modifier is placed in the wrong spot in a sentence, thereby muddling the meaning.

MISPLACED MODIFIER

> **NO**   The consultant who observed our meeting **only** took notes with a pen.

> **YES**   The consultant who observed our meeting took notes **only** with a pen.

> Modifier *only* belongs with *pen* to clarify that nothing else was used to take notes.

> **NO**   The consultant took notes with a pen **sporting a large handlebar mustache**.

> **YES**   The consultant **sporting a large handlebar mustache** took notes with a pen.

> The mustache belongs to the consultant, not the pen.

DANGLING MODIFIER

> **NO**   Studying our company's budget projection, the numbers predicted bankruptcy.

> *Numbers* after the comma says that numbers can study.

> **YES**   Studying our company's budget projection, I saw that the numbers predicted bankruptcy.

> *I saw* after the comma says that a person is studying.

Misplaced modifiers and dangling modifiers are two of the four types of incorrect placements for modifiers. Chapter 40 explains all four and how to correct them.

■ 8. Mistakes with homonyms

Mistakes with HOMONYMS are obvious in written English more than in spoken English. Homonyms are words that sound alike, but they have different meanings and spellings.

Watch the Video

> **NO**   **Its** important **too** lock **you're** office door and **right** a note **four** the guards if you have **all ready** turned off the heat.
>
> Simply to illustrate common homonym errors, we exaggerate how many show up in one sentence.
>
> **YES**   **It's** important **to** lock **your** office door and **write** a note **for** the guards if you have **already** turned off the heat.

We advise you to compile your own personal list of the homonyms that you habitually mix up. Then set aside time to master the correct usage of each word. Although an almost overwhelming number of homonym sets turn up in any Internet search, you need be concerned only with those that give you trouble. Chapter 46, section 46E, lists the homonym sets most frequently confused.

■ 9. Comma errors

Comma errors are written, not spoken, mistakes. Commas clarify meaning for readers, especially when a sentence contains both major and minor information.

Watch the Video

Currently, commas turn up in published writing far less frequently than they did only 20 years ago. As a writer, beware of the suggestion to insert a comma whenever you pause because everyone speaks and thinks at different rates. This fact is particularly noticeable when people gather from different parts of the United States and Canada, or when a person's native language isn't English.

We suggest that you copy and carry with you the major rules for using commas, listed in Quick Box 47.1 on pages 440–441. The more you check this list of rules, the more quickly you'll know it by heart. To help you start, here's a list you'll probably master quite quickly—the five spots where a comma *never* belongs.

- Never after *such as*, but before it, it's fine: *Our office staff enjoyed perks, **such as** free coffee, tea, and hot chocolate.*
- Never before *than* in a comparison: *That company's truck was safer **than** ours.*
- Never between a subject and verb written close together: ***Our firm's maternity leave program** is **enlightened**.*
- Never immediately after a subordinating conjunction, and only after a clause that starts with one: ***Because** I developed a nasty cold, I left work early.*
- Never before an opening parenthesis, but after a closing parenthesis, it's fine: *When an office's intercom system works by public announcements **(people tend to ignore alerts by telephone)**, everyone's concentration suffers.*

Chapter 47 presents and explains all rules for comma use in written English.

■ **10. Apostrophe errors**

Watch
the Video
Apostrophe errors are written, not spoken, mistakes. Apostrophes serve only two purposes: they indicate possession (the president's car; the president's schedule), and they indicate missing letters in contractions (isn't).

NO   The main **office's** are closed for the evening.

YES   The main **offices** are closed for the evening.

Apostrophes never create plural words.

NO   The security guard **patrol's** the building every hour.

YES   The security guard **patrols** the building every hour.

Apostrophes are never involved with verbs.

NO   The security guards **do'nt** need dogs to help them.

YES   The security guards **don't** need dogs to help them.

If you write a contraction, place an apostrophe only where a letter is omitted.

For a complete chapter on apostrophes, see Chapter 50.

3   Critical Thinking

Quick Points   You will learn to

> Use critical thinking when examining ideas (section 3A).
> Recognize and use the logical, ethical, and emotional appeals (pp. 18–19).
> Reason inductively and deductively (pp. 19–22).
> Recognize logical fallacies (pp. 22–25).

3A   **What is critical thinking?**

Watch
the Video
Thinking isn't something people choose to do, any more than fish choose to live in water. To be human is to think. Thinking comes naturally. **Critical thinking**, however, demands more. To think critically, you deliberately think about your thinking by asking the questions in Quick Box 3.1.

Quick Box 3.1

Questions critical thinkers ask themselves

- Do I insist on examining an idea from all sides?
- Do I resist easy solutions that are being pushed at me?
- Do I resist facing up to uncomfortable truths?
- Do I insist on factual accuracy?
- Do I remain open to ideas that don't fit with what I'm used to believing?
- Do I insist on clarity when confronted with vague language?
- Do I insist on hearing "the whole story," not just one point of view?
- Do I resist being hurried to make up my mind?

The word *critical* here has a neutral meaning. It doesn't mean taking a negative view or finding fault, as when someone criticizes another person. For a systematic process to use when you encounter new ideas or when you want to reexamine familiar ideas more deeply, you can use the four-step sequence described in Quick Box 3.2. This process works when you evaluate your own

Quick Box 3.2

Steps in the critical thinking process: SASE

1. **S = summarize.** Whenever you encounter ideas, first make sure you understand them. Check yourself by restating the ideas accurately and objectively. Add nothing. Resist inserting your feelings or opinion into your summary.

2. **A = analyze.** Break the ideas into their component parts. Figure out how each part of the ideas contributes to the overall meaning. Move beyond your summary from Step 1 to understand what is implied by the ideas.

3. **S = synthesize.** Combine your summary from Step 1 and your analysis from Step 2 to connect them to other ideas or perspectives that you have encountered. Use other ideas you've learned, thought about, and/or experienced. Give yourself time to do this. Reflect on the connections you make, realizing that synthesis is a recursive activity that often doubles back on itself.

4. **E = evaluate.** Form your early judgment about the ideas, knowing you need to take time to reach a final conclusion. Remain resolutely open-minded about others' points of view. Examine new ideas independently and fairly, avoiding biases and prejudices you might have accepted without question before.

writing; or what you read in college, the workplace, or beyond (see 4A–4C); or in art and other types of visuals you want to see more thoroughly (see 4E).

3B How can rhetoric enhance my critical thinking?

Watch
the Video

Rhetoric is the art and skill of speaking and writing effectively. If you understand three central principles of rhetoric—the persuasive appeals—you can greatly enhance your ability to think critically. They turn up in most material you read, see in movies and on television and the Internet, and in everyday life. Often the three are called by their Greek names: *logos*, meaning logic; *ethos*, meaning credibility; and *pathos*, meaning empathy or compassion. To recognize them in action and to use them in your writing, see Quick Box 3.3.

Quick Box 3.3

Three central principles of rhetoric: the persuasive appeals

- **Use the logical appeal** (*logos*) to evoke a rational response:
  - Demonstrate sound reasoning.
  - Define terms.
  - Give accurate facts and statistics.
  - Use relevant quotations from experts and authorities.
  - Use deductive and inductive reasoning (see 3C) well.
  - Use effective evidence (see 7D and 21D).

- **Use the ethical appeal** (*ethos*) to evoke confidence in your credibility, reliability, and trustworthiness:
  - Show respect by using appropriate language and tone.
  - Be fair-minded.
  - Be well informed and sincere.
  - Be open to a variety of perspectives.
  - Use reliable sources (see Chapter 21).

- **Use the emotional appeal** (*pathos*) to evoke empathy and compassion:
  - Reflect values that call on one's "better self."
  - Use descriptive language and concrete details to create mental pictures.
  - Add a sense of humanity and reality.
  - Appeal to hearts more than minds, but never manipulate.
  - Never use biased or slanted language (see Chapter 45).
  - Use figurative language (see 44E).

These three principles of rhetoric apply to all types of thinking, writing, and reading, not just persuasion. For demonstrations and examples of these three principles in action, see Chapters 9 through 14 in this handbook: Each of the student essays in these chapters shows extensive, hands-on applications of the principles.

3C   How do I use inductive and deductive reasoning?

Two natural thought patterns, inductive reasoning and deductive reasoning, can help you think critically. **Inductive reasoning** moves from the specific to the general. In contrast, **deductive reasoning** moves from the general to the specific. Taken together, the two are major reasoning processes that help you distinguish sound reasoning from faulty reasoning.

Watch the Video

■ Inductive reasoning

Inductive reasoning moves from specific, explicit facts or instances to broad general principles. For example, suppose you go to the Registry of Motor Vehicles closest to your home to renew your driver's license, and you stand in line for 2 hours. A few months later, you return to the same location to get new license plates and again stand in a 2-hour line. A few days later, you hear a few friends talking about having had exactly the same experience. You conclude, therefore, that all offices of the Registry of Motor Vehicles serve the public inefficiently. Your conclusion is based on inductive reasoning, from your specific experiences of being in line for 2 hours twice to your general judgment about how the office is run.

As a critical thinker, however, you might ask whether the conclusion is an absolute truth. It is not. The conclusion is only a statement of probability. After all, perhaps the Registry of Motor Vehicles office farthest from your home is so well run that no one ever stands in line for more than 10 minutes. Therefore, inductive reasoning is based on probability, not absolute truth. Quick Box 3.4 on the next page lists the characteristics of inductive reasoning.

■ Deductive reasoning

Deductive reasoning moves from general claims, called premises, to a specific conclusion. The three-part structure of two premises and a conclusion is known as a **syllogism**.

> PREMISE 1   Students who don't study fail Professor Sanchez's exams.
>
> PREMISE 2   My friend didn't study.
>
> CONCLUSION   My friend failed Professor Sanchez's exams.

Premises in syllogism can be facts or **assumptions**. Assumptions need close scrutiny because they're statements assumed to be true but with no concrete

> ### Quick Box 3.4 ■ ■ ■ ■ ■ ■ ■ ■ ■
>
> #### Features of inductive reasoning
>
> - Inductive reasoning begins with specific evidence—facts, observations, or experiences—and moves to a general conclusion.
> - Inductive reasoning is based on a sampling of facts, not on the whole universe of related facts.
> - The conclusions in inductive reasoning are considered reliable or unreliable, but never true or false.
> - The advantage of inductive reasoning is that you can speculate on the unknown based on what's known.

evidence to support them. Because some assumptions are based on incorrect information, a critical thinker needs to evaluate each premise—that is, each assumption—carefully.

The conclusion in a syllogism is judged to be either valid or invalid. This means the conclusion is, or is not, "acceptable" or "well grounded." When the conclusion logically follows from the premises, a deductive argument is valid. When the conclusion doesn't logically follow from the premises, a deductive argument is invalid.

VALID—DEDUCTIVE REASONING EXAMPLE 1

PREMISE 1	When it snows, the streets get wet. [fact]
PREMISE 2	It is snowing. [fact]
CONCLUSION	Therefore, the streets are getting wet. [valid]

INVALID—DEDUCTIVE REASONING EXAMPLE 2

PREMISE 1	When it snows, the streets get wet. [fact]
PREMISE 2	The streets are getting wet. [fact]
CONCLUSION	Therefore, it is snowing. [invalid]

Deductive argument 2 is invalid because even though the two premises are facts, the conclusion is wrong. After all, the streets can be wet for many reasons other than snow: from rain, from street-cleaning trucks that spray water, or from people washing their cars.

INVALID—DEDUCTIVE REASONING EXAMPLE 3

PREMISE 1	Learning a new language takes hard work.
PREMISE 2	Nicholas has learned to speak Spanish.
CONCLUSION	Nicholas worked hard to learn Spanish.

Deductive argument 3 is invalid because it rests on a wrong assumption: not everyone has to work hard to learn a new language; some people—for example, young children—learn new languages easily. Therefore, Nicholas might have learned Spanish effortlessly.

One prime example of an invalid deductive argument like example 3 stems from people assuming that anything published in a newspaper is correct. Newspapers, however, make mistakes or even intentionally publish incorrect information. Therefore, an argument may be invalid when it's based solely on information published in a newspaper.

As a critical thinker, whenever you encounter an assumption, either stated or unstated, you need to check whether it's true. If it isn't, the reasoning is flawed. Quick Box 3.5 lists the characteristics of deductive reasoning.

Quick Box 3.5

Features of deductive reasoning

- Deductive reasoning moves from the general to the specific. Its three-part structure, called a syllogism, consists of two premises and a conclusion drawn from them.

- Deductive reasoning is valid if its conclusion follows logically from its premises.

- In deductive reasoning, if one or both premises state an assumption, the truth of the assumption needs to be proven before the truth of the reasoning can be established. However, proving assumptions to be true can be difficult or sometimes impossible.

- The conclusion in deductive reasoning can be judged either true or false.

  - If both premises are true, the conclusion is true.

  - If either premise is false, the conclusion is false.

- Deductive reasoning is based on what a person already knows, so it doesn't yield new information.

- The advantage of deductive reasoning over inductive reasoning is that it builds a stronger argument because its conclusions can be either true or false (as long as any assumptions in the premises can be proven to be true).

Explore
the
Exercise

● **EXERCISE 3-1** Working individually or with a peer-response group, determine whether each conclusion here is valid or invalid. Be ready to explain your answers. For help, consult section 3C.

1. Faddish clothes are expensive.

   This shirt is expensive.

   This shirt must be part of a fad.

2. When a storm is threatening, small-craft warnings are issued.

   A storm is threatening.

   Small-craft warnings will be issued.

3. The Pulitzer Prize is awarded to outstanding literary works.

   The Great Gatsby never won a Pulitzer Prize.

   The Great Gatsby isn't an outstanding literary work.

4. All states send representatives to the United States Congress.

   Puerto Rico sends a representative to the United States Congress.

   Puerto Rico is a state.

5. Finding a good job requires patience.

   Sherrill is patient.

   Sherrill will find a good job. ●

3D What are logical fallacies?

Watch
the Video

Logical fallacies are statements with defective reasoning based on irrational ideas. For example, suppose you see a teenage boy driving dangerously over the speed limit on a crowded highway. You would be irrational if you decided that all teenage boys drive dangerously over the speed limit on crowded highways. The label for this type of flawed statement is **hasty generalization**, which is one of the most common logical fallacies. Another very common logical fallacy occurs when, for example, people decide that someone is fit for political office because the person is a good actor or a talented chef. This fallacy is called **irrelevant argument** because one characteristic has nothing to do with the other.

Many logical fallacies aren't as obvious as the two examples just given. Critical thinking calls for analyzing statements carefully to make sure they're not based on logical fallacies. Unfortunately, many people use logical fallacies intentionally to sway audiences toward certain actions or beliefs. This often happens in debates, on public blogs, in newspaper editorials, on radio talk shows, in advertisements, in political speeches, in informal conversations, and in dozens of others places. So that you avoid falling prey to the thought manipulations of logical fallacies, you'd be wise to study the list in Quick Box 3.6 and the longer explanations that follow.

Quick Box 3.6

Common logical fallacies

FALLACIES THAT USE SHORT-SIGHTED THINKING

Either-or thinking: X and Y are the only choices.

False analogy: X and Y are completely different, but A claims they're alike.

False cause: X always causes Y, with no exceptions.

Hasty generalization: All As are the same, with no exceptions.

Stereotyping: Because A was born in B, A is no good.

FALLACIES THAT USE DISTRACTIONS

Attacking the person: A is a sloppy dresser, so A's opinions are worthless.

Bandwagon effect: A does it, so we all can do it.

Begging the question: A avoids the topic by repeating it in different words.

False authority: A is a celebrity, so A is an expert on all topics.

Irrelevant argument: What A says has nothing to do with the topic.

Red herring: A uses an emotional topic to distract everyone from the main topic.

Slippery slope: If A does one thing wrong, A will surely progress to doing much worse things.

- **Attacking the person:** Criticizing a person's appearance, personal life, or conduct instead of dealing with the merits of the individual's opinion. Example: *If Senator Williams had children of his own, he'd understand why we oppose his support of a proposed law to give short prison sentences to child abusers.* This is a fallacy because even if the man were a parent, he might still support the proposed law. (This fallacy has a Latin name: *ad hominem*, meaning "attacking a man's character rather than his argument.")

- **The bandwagon effect:** Asserting that something is right because everyone else is doing it. Example: *"Why can't we go to tonight's rap concert? All our friends are going."* This is a fallacy because "going along with the crowd" isn't a reason to justify an action. (This fallacy has a Latin name: *ad populum*, meaning "appeal to popularity.")

- **Begging the question,** also called **circular reasoning:** Restating the main issue using supporting reasons for it, instead of focusing on the main issue itself. Example: *We shouldn't increase our workers' salaries because then our payroll would be larger.* This is a fallacy because "increased salaries" means the same thing as "a larger payroll"; the issue is whether the workers deserve larger salaries or whether the company can afford to pay larger salaries.

- **Either-or thinking,** also called **false dilemma:** Limiting choices to only two alternatives when more exist. Example: *Either stop criticizing our president or move to another country.* This is a fallacy because these two extremes aren't the only options in democratic countries where people are free to criticize elected officials.

- **False analogy:** Claiming that two ideas or items are alike when they're more different than similar. Example: *If we can put someone on the moon, we should be able to find a cure for cancer.* This is a fallacy because space science is very different from biological science.

- **False authority:** Accepting the opinion of someone who isn't an expert on the topic. Example: *I want to wear XYZ running shoes because my favorite comedian says they're the best.* This is a fallacy because comedians aren't experts about running shoes; in our society, celebrities receive large sums of money to endorse products they know nothing about.

- **False cause:** Asserting that one event leads to another when the two events aren't related, even though they might happen at the same time. Example: *After we opened the new municipal park, the city's crime rate increased.* This is a fallacy because crime rates can rise for many reasons, including joblessness and gang activity. (This fallacy has a Latin name: *post hoc, ergo propter hoc,* meaning "after this, therefore because of this.")

- **Hasty generalization:** Drawing conclusions based on insufficient evidence. Example: *All college students leave bad tips at restaurants.* This is a fallacy because some students leave proper tips.

- **Irrelevant argument:** Using unrelated information to form a conclusion. Example: *Ms. Chu is a forceful speaker, so she will be an outstanding mayor.* This is a fallacy because Ms. Chu's speaking style does not reflect her administrative abilities. (This fallacy has a Latin name: *non sequitur,* meaning the premise doesn't support the conclusion.)

- **Red herring:** Sidetracking attention to an issue by bringing up unrelated issues to distract people from thinking about the core issue. Example: *Why worry about the homeless when we should really be concerned with global warming?* This is a fallacy because the topic of global warming is introduced to divert attention from the issue of the problem of homelessness.

- **Slippery slope assumption:** Believing that one small first step will inevitably lead to a chain of related actions that will terminate in a significant event. Example: *Anyone who shoplifts will soon turn to more serious crimes and eventually become a murderer.* This is a fallacy because shoplifters don't always continue to commit crimes and become murderers.

- **Stereotyping:** Holding close-minded notions about people, beliefs, or ideas based on race, religions, philosophies, etc.: *Everyone who belongs to religion X hates to dance.* This is a fallacy because (a) "everyone" excludes even one exception, and (b) "hatred" is an emotion, not part of a religious philosophy.

● **EXERCISE 3-2**   Following are comments posted to a newspaper Web site. Working alone or with a peer-response group, do a critical analysis of each, paying special attention to logical fallacies.

Explore
the
Exercise

1. I oppose the plan to convert the abandoned railroad tracks into a bicycle trail. Everyone knows that the only reason the mayor wants to do this is so that she and her wealthy friends can have a new place to play. No one I know likes this plan, and if they did, it would probably be because they're part of the wine and cheese set, too. The next thing you know, the mayor will be proposing that we turn the schools into art museums or the park into a golf course. If you're working hard to support a family, you don't have time for this bike trail nonsense. And if you're not working hard, I don't have time for you.

    —Mike1218

2. I encourage everyone to support the bicycle trail project. Good recreation facilities are the key to the success of any community. Since the bike trail will add more recreation opportunities, it will guarantee the success of our town. Remember that several years ago our neighbors over in Springfield decided not to build a new park, and look what happened to their economy, especially that city's high unemployment rate. We can't afford to let the same thing happen to us. People who oppose this plan are narrow-minded, selfish, and almost unpatriotic. As that great patriot John Paul Jones said, "I have not yet begun to fight."

    —Bikerdude ●

Reading Texts and Visuals Critically

4 ■ ■ ■ ■ ■ ■ ■ ■

Quick Points   You will learn to

➤ Use the critical reading process (see Quick Box 4.1).
➤ Use techniques for close, active reading (see pp. 31–32).
➤ Read images critically (see pp. 32–34).

4A   What is critical reading?

Watch
the Video

To read critically is to think about what you're reading, while you're reading it and afterward. You think not only about what the words say but also what they mean. Your goal is to evaluate the accuracy and truth of what you're reading, what it implies, and how it connects to other information and ideas.

4B   What steps do I use to read critically?

To read critically, use the four steps in Quick Box 4.1, which draw on the four steps for CRITICAL THINKING listed in Quick Box 3.1, Steps in the critical thinking process.

Quick Box 4.1	■ ■ ■ ■ ■ ■ ■ ■ ■ ■

Steps in the critical reading process

1. Determine **literal meaning** (read "on the line").
2. Make inferences by using analysis (read "between the lines").
3. Synthesize by associating this reading with other readings, ideas, and experiences you've encountered (read "beyond the lines").
4. Evaluate by forming your opinion of the material.

■ **Determine literal meaning**

Reading for literal meaning involves absorbing exactly what the words say, no more and no less. Your goal is to capture what's "on the lines," without injecting your related thoughts on, or opinions of, the topic. This may sound easy to

26

do, but it takes disciplined practice. For example, try this with a partner: You both read a newspaper editorial or newspaper report on an interesting story; then you tell each other exactly what it said. See if you have each filtered out what you expect or want it to say.

■ Make inferences

Making inferences involves figuring out what the words imply by reading "between the lines." In life, you make inferences many times a day. When you see people with open umbrellas, you generally infer it's raining. When you see a crowd leaving a movie theater quietly, and some people are wiping their eyes, you can generally assume the film has a sad ending.

Reading for inferential meaning isn't a casual endeavor; it takes discipline of mind to pay close attention not only to what writers are saying but also to how they're saying it. Useful strategies for making inferences during reading include

- Detecting a writer's assumptions
- Sorting facts from the writer's opinions
- Discovering the writer's bias or prejudices, if any
- Recognizing the impact of the writer's tone

DETECTING A WRITER'S ASSUMPTIONS

Watch the Video

An **assumption** is a statement or idea that writers expect readers to accept as true without proof. For example, the assumption behind this handbook is that students are open to advice about how to write successfully in college. Writers rarely state their assumptions outright, so critical readers need to take time to reflect on what they've read to uncover and examine unstated assumptions. What readers find influences how they think about the writer's ideas.

Read this passage first for its literal meaning, and then reread it for its underlying assumptions.

> Creativity is the catalyst for brilliant accomplishments, but it is also the greatest obstacle. If you examine the natural course of a new idea—from conception to execution—you'll see that nearly all new ideas die a premature death. If that seems far-fetched, just consider the ideas you have conceived on your own but never implemented: a novel you wanted to write, a business proposal you wanted to launch, a restaurant you wanted to open. For most of us, the list goes on and on. New ideas face an uphill battle from the moment they are conceived.
>
> —Scott Belsky, *Making Ideas Happen*

One underlying assumption in the preceding passage by Scott Belsky is that new ideas are always creative as well as good. Truth is, some ideas are not new, creative, or good. Two more underlying assumptions are that everyone has thought of new ideas, and if they haven't, they're less intelligent or clever than the rest of us. Truth is, these assumptions are wrong.

SORTING FACTS FROM THE WRITER'S OPINIONS

To differentiate between facts and opinion, critical readers need to think beyond the obvious. Some writers intentionally blur the difference between facts that can be verified and the opinions that they want readers to accept as facts.

- Facts are statements that can be checked objectively by observation, experiment, or research.

EXAMPLE

Abraham Lincoln was the sixteenth president of the United States.

- Opinions are statements open to debate.

EXAMPLE

Abraham Lincoln is the greatest U.S. president who ever lived.

Most statements are not so easy to discern as these about Abraham Lincoln. For example, is the statement "All people desire a steady income" a fact or an opinion? If read without reflection, it can seem a fact. However, critical readers realize that although it's common for people to equate success with a constant stream of money, some individuals prefer a more freewheeling approach to life. They may work hard, save money, and then travel for months, not working at all. Thus the statement is an opinion because although it's accurate for most people, it isn't true for all.

DISCOVERING THE WRITER'S BIAS OR PREJUDICES, IF ANY

Writers who assert strong, unwavering viewpoints but don't back them up with evidence may well be guilty of bias or prejudice. A **bias** can be a favorable or unfavorable stand about an idea, such as the value of standardized tests throughout elementary school. In contrast, prejudice always involves unfavorable opinions based on hated, fear, or ignorance: prejudice against a race, against certain books being available in schools, and so on. Critical readers want to uncover bias and prejudice so they aren't manipulated into going along with a slanted line of reasoning and or being swept up in irrational thinking. When writers make rude or cruel remarks, which are unfortunately common in online comments and some blogs, critical readers can resist being manipulated by warped points of view.

RECOGNIZING THE IMPACT OF THE WRITER'S TONE

Tone emerges from a writer's use of words and ways of presenting ideas. Just as our voices emit certain tones when we're happy, bored, sad, or excited, so do our words. Tone can be serious, respectful, friendly, humorous, slanted, sarcastic, or angry. Consider the difference you can infer about the writer between, "Would you please refrain from doing that?" and "Knock it off right now!"

A somewhat formal word choice usually imparts a tone of distant seriousness, whereas informal language is more intimate and immediate. When the tone doesn't fit the occasion, the writer may be seeking to manipulate readers rather than to have them think logically. For example, some editorial writers rely on sarcasm and strong emotional language to attempt to persuade readers and bypass their analytical censors.

■ Synthesize

By now, you've read your material on a literal level, and you've delved into it to make inferences. While you've worked through those analytic processes, you might have been aware that random thoughts as well as ideas and experiences related to your reading popped into your head. The human mind often engages in "multitasking," a process that many readers come to appreciate and value. It involves reading "beyond the lines" by associating what you've just read to other readings, ideas, and experiences you've encountered.

Watch
the Video

Now is your chance to sit quietly and bring back those thoughts that casually passed through your consciousness. As you think about them deeply, you might discover that some ideas were not as random as they seemed before. During reading for literal and inferential meaning, critical readers are highly focused and resist distractions; once it's time to engage in synthesis, they can muse freely and allow themselves rich insights into their reading. (See 17D.)

■ Evaluate the material

Critical readers evaluate what they've read only after they've worked through the literal and inferential meanings in the material and used synthesis to relate them to other thoughts. These processes provide readers with informed support for their evaluation. Based on whether you think the writer's reasoning is sound, the writer's presentation and word choice are balanced, and the material inspired you to engage a rich synthesis, you reach your opinion of it. Sometimes you might see merit in part of the material but have doubts about other parts. Above all, critical readers rarely react superficially to what they've read, and they resist jumping ahead of themselves while forming an evaluation.

Watch
the Video

Explore
the
Exercise

● **EXERCISE 4-1**   Working individually or with a collaborative group, decide which of the following statements are facts and which are opinions. For help, consult section 4B.

1. The life of people on earth is better now than it has ever been—certainly much better than it was 500 years ago.

    —Peggy Noonan, "Why Are We So Unhappy When We Have It So Good?"

2. The fast food industry pays the minimum wage to a higher proportion of its workers than any other American industry.

    —Eric Schlosser, *Fast Food Nation*

3. Grief, when it comes, is nothing we expect it to be.

    —Joan Didion, *The Year of Living Dangerously*

4. A mind is a terrible thing to waste.

    —United Negro College Fund

5. History is the branch of knowledge that deals systematically with the past.

    —*Webster's New World College Dictionary*, Fourth Edition

6. In 1927, F. E. Tylcote, an English physician, reported in the medical journal *Lancet* that in almost every case of lung cancer he had seen or known about, the patient smoked.

    —William Ecenbarger, "The Strange History of Tobacco"

7. Trucks that must travel on frozen highways in Alaska for most of the year now sometimes get stuck in the mud as the permafrost thaws.

    —Al Gore, *An Inconvenient Truth*

8. You can, Honest Abe notwithstanding, fool most of the people all of the time.

    —Stephen Jay Gould, "The Creation Myths of Cooperstown"

9. You change laws by changing lawmakers.

    —Sissy Farenthold, political activist, *Bakersfield Californian*

10. A critical task for all of the world's religions and spiritual traditions is to enrich the vision—and the reality—of the sense of community among us.

    —Joel D. Beversluis, *A Sourcebook for Earth's Community of Religions* ●

4C How do close reading and active reading work?

Close reading means **annotating** for content and meaning. When you annotate, you write notes to yourself in a text's margins, occasionally underlining or highlighting important passages or using asterisks and other special marks to focus your attention. To annotate an electronic document, you can try several strategies. You can take handwritten notes on a separate sheet of paper or type your notes in a separate computer file. You can print the document and write notes on the hard copy, as you can see in Figure 4.1. You can even annotate electronically using software functions such as underlining, highlighting, and inserting comments.

Figure 4.1 A student's annotations on an article printed from the *EBSCO Host* database.

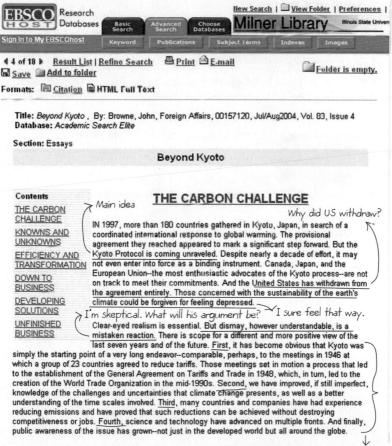

Gives four reasons for optimism.

Active reading means annotating to make connections between what you already know or have experienced and the material you're reading—in other words, synthesizing ideas. This is your chance to use your critical thinking skills to converse on paper with the writer.

4D How do I view images with a critical eye?

Watch
the Video

Images surround us, in publications, on computer screens, on smart phones. You can view images critically in the same way that you can read texts critically by using SUMMARY, ANALYSIS, SYNTHESIS, and EVALUATION (see Quick Box 3.2) or by asking the questions in Quick Box 4.2.

Quick Box 4.2   ■ ■ ■ ■ ■ ■ ■ ■ ■

Helpful questions for analyzing visual images

- What does the image show?

- What are its parts? Do the parts belong together (like a lake, trees, and mountains), or do they contrast with one another (like a woman in a fancy dress sitting on a tractor)?

- If there is a foreground and a background, what is in each?

- If the image is a scene, what seems to be going on? What might be its message?

- If the image seems to be part of a story, what might have happened before or after?

- If there are people in the image, how do they seem to relate to each other (friends, acquaintances, business associates, or strangers)?

- If there are contrasts in shading, coloring, or focus in the image, what is sharply in focus? Blurry? Bright? In shadows? Colorful? Drab? How do such differences, or their absence, call attention to various parts of the image?

- If there are words in the image, what is their relationship to it? Some words and images contrast for effect, such as a picture of a belching smokestack accompanied by a caption that says, "Fresh air."

- What connections can you make between the image and things you've experienced or learned from school, work, reading, visits to museums or other cultural sites, watching movies, plays, and television, and so on?

- What is your evaluation of the image based on your observations?

Using the four steps to critical reading in Quick Box 4.1, look at Figure 4.2 with a critical eye.

View the Model Document

On a literal level, you can see—at a minimum—a street full of older houses with modern skyscrapers in the distance.

Making inferences, you can "read between the lines" to see that it's fairly rich with layers of meaning. You can think about the meanings conveyed by the condition of the houses versus those of the modern buildings, or about the lives of the people who live and work in each place. You can focus on the message of the comparative sizes of the houses and skyscrapers; on the contrast between this street and those you imagine at the base of the skyscrapers; on why the photographer chose this perspective; on how different captions might give the picture different meanings. For example, consider the difference between three different captions: "Progress," "Inequality," or "The Neighborhood." Many possible ideas may come to mind as you study the picture critically.

View the Model Document

Synthesizing in response to the picture, you can associate "beyond the lines" to other photographs as well as other artworks you've seen, your reading, and your experiences. This imparts deeper, more richly complex connections to your thoughts about the photograph.

Evaluating the quality and impact of the message of the photograph is the last step in viewing it critically. Resist evaluating prematurely

Figure 4.2 Images help us think visually.

because by going through the earlier steps of thinking and reading critically, your evaluation becomes informed by more than a noncritical personal reaction such as "I like the picture" or "I don't like the picture." In evaluating a visual critically, you might start by speaking of how the visual "struck" you at first glance and then narrating how it did or did not gain depth of meaning as you drew inferences and engaged in synthesis within the realms of your personal experience and education.

Explore
the
Exercise

● **EXERCISE 4-2**   Working individually or with a peer-response group, use critical thinking to consider the photograph in Figure 4.3. Write either informal notes or a mini-essay, according to what your instructor requires. Use the questions in Quick Box 4.2 to generate your summary, analysis, synthesis, and evaluation of the photograph(s).

Figure 4.3   Photo of barrels in a natural setting.

Tab 2
Writing Processes

CHAPTERS
5–8

2

Writing Processes

Tab 2 Writing Processes

MyCompLab® Visit mycomplab.com for the eText and for resources on writing processes.

5 Planning Your Writing
■ ■ ■ ■ ■ ■ ■ ■

Quick Points   You will learn to

➤ Adapt the writing processes to your own needs (see 5A).
➤ Think like a writer, especially about your purpose and audience (pp. 40–43).
➤ Use different strategies to develop ideas (pp. 43–48).
➤ Write an effective thesis statement (pp. 48–50).
➤ Use outlines to help you write (pp. 50–52).

5A   What are writing processes?

Many people assume that a real writer can magically write a finished product, word by perfect word. Experienced writers know that writing is a process, a series of activities that starts the moment they begin thinking about a topic and ends when they complete a final draft. In addition, experienced writers are aware that good writing is actually rewriting—again and yet again. Their drafts contain additions, deletions, rewordings, and rearrangements. Figure 5.1 shows how Lynn drafted and revised the first few sentences of this chapter.

All writers adapt their **writing processes** to suit their personalities as well as the special demands of the different writing projects they undertake. For the customary steps in the writing process, see Quick Box 5.1. Although these steps are listed separately, few writers in the real world work in lockstep order. They know that the steps overlap and double back on themselves, as the circles and arrows in Figure 5.2 show.

Figure 5.1   Lynn's draft and revision of part of the first paragraph in 5A.

Many people assume that a real writer can *magically* write a
~~word by perfect word.~~
finished product, ~~easily.~~ Experienced writers know

~~better than that~~ that writing is a process, ~~that involves~~
the moment they begin
a series of activities that starts ~~when the writers start~~
about a topic   *when they complete*
thinking and ends ~~with~~ a final draft.

Quick Box 5.1

The writing process

- **Planning** means you think like a writer (see 5B); plan a writing port-folio (see 5C); determine your purpose and audience (see 5D and 5E); develop ideas about your topic (see 5F); compose a tentative thesis statement (see 5G); consider using an outline (see 5H).

- **Drafting** means you write a first pass by composing your ideas into sentences and paragraphs (see 6A).

- **Revising** means you rewrite your drafts, often more than once, for the purpose of expanding and/or tightening them; rearranging and/or deleting parts; checking that you've stayed on your topic; and perhaps drafting needed new material (see 6C through 6E).

- **Editing** means you check for the correctness of your surface-level features, including grammar, spelling, punctuation, and mechanics (see 6F and 6G).

- **Proofreading** means you carefully scrutinize your final draft to fix typing errors and missing/repeated small words (see 6H).

What is the major difference between weak writers and successful ones? The good ones refuse to give up. Good writing takes time. As you discover your personal preferences for your writing process, be patient with yourself. Also, remember that experienced writers sometimes struggle with ideas that are difficult to express, sentences that won't take shape, and words that aren't precise. When that becomes frustrating, they put their writing aside for a while, do something unrelated to writing, and return with the "new eyes" that only distance makes available.

Figure 5.2 Visualizing the writing process.

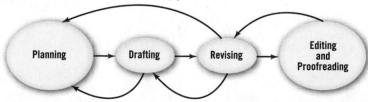

5B How do I think like a writer?

Writers begin by thinking the way writers do. As explained in Quick Box 5.2, they engage in the habits of mind of effective writers, think about each writing situation, determine their topic, decide on the purpose for each writing project, and establish who their audience will be.

Watch the Video

Quick Box 5.2 ■ ■ ■ ■ ■ ■ ■ ■ ■ ■

How to think like a writer

Think *by Engaging in Writers' Habits of Mind*
- Realize that writing takes time.
- Know that writing requires focused attention free of distractions.
- Recognize that all writing involves rewriting, often many times (see 6C through 6E).
- Believe that the physical act of writing triggers brain processes that help fresh ideas spring to mind (see 5F).
- Think critically (see Chapter 3).
- Remain self-aware by thinking about your thinking (see 3A).

Think *About Each Writing Situation*
- Read writing assignments completely. Then reread them.
- Approximate the length of a suitable final draft.
- Estimate how long you'll need for
    - Planning (see the rest of this chapter)
    - Drafting (see 6A)
    - Revising (see 6C through 6E)
    - Editing (see 6F and 6G)
    - Proofreading (see 6H)
- Calculate and set aside the total time you'll need to complete the assignment.

Think *About Your Topic*
- Does your assignment state a topic explicitly? If so, focus on it exclusively without going off the topic.
- Does your assignment give a general topic and expect you to think of a suitable subtopic? If so, make sure your chosen topic isn't too broad or too narrow:

GENERAL TOPIC	Marriage
TOO BROAD	What makes a successful marriage?
TOO NARROW	Couples can go to a municipal hall to get married.
JUST RIGHT	Compromise is vital for a happy marriage.

continued >>

Quick Box 5.2 (continued)

- Does your assignment say you're free to choose an essay topic? If so, think of one suitable for academic writing.
  - Topic needs to demonstrate your intellectual and writing abilities.
  - Topic needs sufficient specific details to back up each general statement.

Think About Typical Purposes for Your Writing (see 5D)

Think About the Audience for Your Writing (see 5E)

Think of Ways to Develop Your Topic (see 5F)

Think About Your Thesis Statement (see 5G)

Consider Outlining (see 5H)

5C   How do I plan a writing portfolio?

Many instructors require a **writing portfolio** from each student, so it's wise to plan for it from the beginning of each writing course. To do so, keep all writing you've done in response to all your assignments, including any drafts commented on during your writing process as well as your final papers and exams. Throw away nothing. Date each item. If you work on more than one computer, carry and clearly label a thumb drive set aside expressly for collecting your writing.

A writing portfolio can be paper or digital, depending on your instructor's requirements. A **paper portfolio** consists of your writings collected in a folder or a binder. A **digital portfolio** is like a paper one but in electronic format. It can contain links between—and within—individual texts. Your digital portfolio might be an upload from your work into an online course management program, such as BlackBoard. More sophisticated digital portfolios involve your own design efforts, including images, sounds, and video. Quick Box 5.3 explains how to create a writing portfolio.

Most writing portfolios include a self-reflection essay or letter. Feel free to use the first person ("I") since it's about you as a writer. Quick Box 5.4 suggests its structure. See below and page 40 for an excerpt from such a letter.

EXCERPT FROM A REFLECTIVE ESSAY

View the Model Document

During the 2013 fall semester, I completed five papers in English 101, revising each of them several times based on responses from my peers and feedback from my instructor. In the beginning, I was very frustrated. I was getting low grades, but I had been told in high school my writing was excellent. After a few weeks, I came to

Quick Box 5.3

■ ■ ■ ■ ■ ■ ■ ■ ■ ■

How to create a writing portfolio

1. Choose your writing for inclusion according your instructor's directions. Here are three typical portfolio assignments.
   - "Present three works that best display your strengths as a writer." (Here, you want to choose writings that display the range of your abilities.)
   - "Create a portfolio of three works that demonstrates how you're able to write for different AUDIENCES* and PURPOSES." (Here, you want to choose examples that respond to more than one WRITING SITUATION and one FRAME.)
   - "Select four examples of your writing from this semester that demonstrate how your writing has developed." (Here, you want to show that you've improved over the semester, so you might choose writings from the beginning, middle, and end of the course. Alternatively, you might choose a few examples of the same paper in early and revised drafts.)

2. Write an essay or letter of self-reflection in response to your specific portfolio assignment and by using the suggestions in Quick Box 5.4.

3. List all the items in your portfolio with page numbers for your instructor's reference.
   - Write a page number in the upper right corner on each sheet of paper, to conform to the list of items.
   - Make clearly visible the date of each piece of writing.

4. Use an appealing format.

Quick Box 5.4

■ ■ ■ ■ ■ ■ ■ ■ ■ ■

Self-reflection essay for a portfolio

1. An opening paragraph in which you introduce yourself as a writer and state the criteria for selecting the writings you've used in your portfolio.

2. A set of body paragraphs in which you use the title and date to refer in exact sequence to each separate piece of writing in your portfolio. Explain why you chose to include it.

3. A paragraph, either here or before the set of BODY PARAGRAPHS, that discusses how you as a writer have evolved (or have not evolved) during the course.

4. A concluding paragraph to wrap up your self-reflection, again in response to your portfolio assignment. You might also mention your future goals for yourself as a writer.

---

* Words printed in SMALL CAPITAL LETTERS are discussed elsewhere in the text and are defined in the Terms Glossary at the back of the book.

realize my critical thinking about our topics was too superficial and my peers didn't always understand what I thought was clear in my writing. I'm leaving this course with more confidence as a writer, based on the strengths the three papers in this portfolio demonstrate.

One quality apparent in these papers is my ability to adjust writings for different audiences, both academic and general. For example, "Analyzing the Merits of Organic Produce" addresses an academic readership, specifically members of the scientific community reading a review of the literature. This can be seen in my use of APA citation style and a scholarly tone suitable for experts, as in my opening sentence, "Research on the health values of organic produce over nonorganic reveals that this issue remains unresolved" (Johnson, 2006; Akule, 2007). The paper begins bluntly and directly because I decided scholars would require little orientation and would value my getting right to the point. . . . In contrast, my paper "Is That Organic Apple Really Worth It?" is aimed at a general audience, such as readers of a news magazine. That paper uses scenes and examples to engage readers with a friendly tone. On page seven, for example, I include an interview with organic grower Jane Treadway in which I describe the setting. . . .

Generalization

Specific example

Quotation

Explanation of specific example

Another specific example

5D What are typical purposes for writing?

Behind each writing project lies the reason, or **purpose**, for its being undertaken. Purposes for writing vary, and each makes its own demands on the writer. This handbook therefore includes six full chapters of targeted discussions about different writing purposes. As listed in Quick Box 5.5, each chapter discusses a different purpose for writing, ways to imagine your probable audience, a suggested essay frame along with sentence and/or paragraph guides for laying out each type of essay, and a complete annotated student essay.

⬛ **ESOL Tip:** If you're from another culture, you might be surprised— even offended—by the directness with which people speak and write in the United States. If so, we hope you'll read our open letter to multilingual writers so that you know how much we value that you honor your native culture (pp. 493–494). Some cultures might expect writing to contain elaborate,

---

Quick Box 5.5

Typical purposes for writing

- **To narrate** something about your life or ideas that's worth knowing (see Chapter 9)
- **To give information** (see Chapter 10)
- **To analyze** a text (see Chapter 11)
- **To argue or persuade**
  - In favor of a point of view on a debatable issue (see Chapter 12)
  - In favor of a proposal or a solution to a problem (see Chapter 13)
- **To evaluate** the quality of a text, object, individual, or event (see Chapter 14)

---

ceremonial language, or to wait to introduce your central point in an essay's middle, or to engage in tactful and indirect discussions. However, when you write for U.S. readers, you need to adapt to U.S. writing style to succeed. U.S. writing style is direct and straightforward, as Chapters 9 to 14 in this handbook demonstrate. ●

5E Who is the probable audience for my writing?

The **audience** for your writing consists of the people who are probably going to read it. The more specifically you can imagine who your readers will be, the more likely your chances for engaging their attention. To begin constructing a portrait of your probable readers, use the approaches listed in Quick Box 5.6.

Watch
the Video

ESOL Tip: If the cultural background of your readers differs from yours, you might find it difficult to estimate how much your readers know about your topic. To get a better idea of your readers' backgrounds, you might browse for information on the Internet or discuss your topic with people who might know more than you do about your readers' backgrounds. ●

■ Your instructor as audience

Of course, one specific audience for your college writing is always your instructor (and often your peers, as discussed later). The instructor who gave you a particular writing assignment plays three roles:

Quick Box 5.6

Ways to imagine your audience

- **Their level of knowledge.** Do your readers have a general idea of your topic, to the extent that nonspecialized educated readers might? Or are your readers specialists in your topic? The answer influences the level of information you provide in your essay.

- **Their interests.** How interested or uninterested in your topic are your readers likely to be? Can you assume your readers are probably enthusiastic about it, resistant to it, or open to it? The answer influences the techniques you use for discussing your topic.

- **Their beliefs.** Do your readers probably agree or disagree with your point of view, or have no opinion about it? The answer influences the degree to which you need to try to convince your readers to change their minds about a debatable topic. In turn, this has an impact on how you use LOGICAL APPEALS (*logos*), ETHICAL APPEALS (*ethos*), and EMOTIONAL APPEALS (*pathos*)—see 3B.

- **Their backgrounds.** Which factors are important to consider in relation to your topic and the purpose you want to achieve with your writing? How much shared background do you have with them?
  - Age, gender, economic situation, ethnic origin?
  - Roles in life, such as student, instructor, business owner, worker, parent, voter, veteran, property owner, etc.?
  - Interests or hobbies?

- **Relation to you.** Are your readers your personal friends, family, coworkers, and others you know? Or are they strangers in whom you want to build trust about your credibility, reliability, and accuracy in presenting your topic (see ETHICAL APPEAL in 3B)? The answer influences the LEVEL OF FORMALITY in the language (see 6E) you use in presenting your material.

- As a stand-in for readers with general or specialized knowledge of your topic
- As your writing coach with experience in guiding students to write well
- As the evaluator of your final draft

Although instructors know that few students are experienced writers or experts on their topics, instructors expect each writing project to show that the students took serious time to go through their writing process deliberately and respectfully. Instructors are experienced readers, so they recognize a minimal effort at once.

Be careful to avoid one misunderstanding some students bring to their college writing. Never assume that your instructor will mentally fill in information you haven't taken the time to write about. You are a learning writer, so you're expected to delve deeply into your topic and write about it fully. Always develop your material beyond its obvious, bare-bones basics. No reader will credit you with content that you "figured they already know" so you don't have to present it explicitly. For explicit advice about writing for specific audiences for specific purposes, consult Chapters 9 through 14.

■ Your peer-response group as audience

A PEER-RESPONSE GROUP consists of other students in your class. Many writing classes today assign peer groups to gather together and react to each others' writing. Participating in a peer-response group makes you part of a respected academic tradition of colleagues helping colleagues. Professional writers often seek comments from other writers to improve their rough drafts. In many business areas, final drafts almost always emerge after many people have shared their thoughts and ideas.

As a member of a peer-response group in a college writing course, you're expected to offer your peers as thorough and specific responses as you can. Hearing or reading comments from your peers can be very informative, surprising, and helpful—though such remarks need to be offered with tact and in a constructive tone. The guidelines in Quick Box 5.7 can help you do this.

5F How can I develop ideas about my topic?

When you're looking for ideas to develop your topics, try the strategies listed in Quick Box 5.8, all of which are popular with experienced writers. Experiment to find out which strategies you find most helpful, adapting to your PURPOSE and AUDIENCE for each new writing assignment.

■ Freewriting

Freewriting means using the physical act of writing to trigger brain processes that uncover ideas that don't come to mind by conscious thinking. Freewriting calls for you to write whatever comes into your mind without stopping. It means you don't think about whether your ideas are good or your spelling is correct. **Focused freewriting** means starting with a favorite word or sentence from your journal, a quotation you like, or perhaps a topic you are studying for a course, and then freewriting with that focus in mind. When you freewrite, don't interrupt the flow. Keep writing. Don't censor your thoughts or insights. Don't review or cross out. Such writing is a voyage of discovery in which you allow your thoughts to emerge as you write.

Watch
the Video

Quick Box 5.7

Guidelines for participating in peer-response writing groups

Always adopt an upbeat, constructive attitude when you participate in a peer-response writing group. This holds whether you're responding to someone else's writing or receiving responses from others.

• Think of yourself as a coach, not a judge.

• Consider all writing by your peers as "works in progress."

• Start by briefly summarizing aloud to the writer what you understood the writing to say after you hear or read a peer's writing. This helps you both make sure you read what the writer intended to write. If there's a mismatch, locate where the message is not clear.

• Begin your comments with what you think is well done. No one likes to hear criticisms right away.

• Use a constructive tone to point to places, if any, where you see problems and explain why you think improvements are needed.

• Make concrete, specific responses. Avoid "This is good" or "This is weak" because they don't tell the writer anything useful.

• Try to put your comments in writing on a separate sheet of paper so that your fellow writer can recall what you said. In listening to comments about your writing, take notes so that you can remember what people said.

• Be open to the comments of your peers about your writing. Try not to get defensive if you hear criticism, and always ask for clarification to support any reactions or advice that puzzle you.

Quick Box 5.8

Strategies for developing ideas about topics

• Freewriting and focused freewriting
• Brainstorming
• Asking and answering structured questions
• Clustering (also called "mapping")
• Writing in a journal or a blog
• Chatting with other people

After a session of freewriting, look over your material for what might be useful in your essay. At times you may find your material isn't helpful, but on other occasions, your insights may startle or delight you.

■ Brainstorming

Brainstorming means listing everything that comes to mind about your topic. Don't censor your thoughts. Let your mind roam, and jot down all ideas that flow logically or that simply pop into your head. After you've brainstormed for a while, look over your lists for patterns. If you don't have enough to work with, choose one item in your list and brainstorm from there.
Watch
the Video

Next, move the items into groups even if loosely related. Discard items that don't fit into any group. You'll probably find that the groups with the most items turn out to be most effective for developing your topic.

Here's some brainstorming by student Carol Moreno, whose essay about the benefits for women of learning to lift weights appears in Chapter 10. Carol grouped the items marked here with an asterisk and used them in her second paragraph.

*women don't want masculine-looking muscles
how much weight is safe for a woman to lift?
how long does it take?
*women's muscles grow long, not bulky
how to bend down for lifting?
*firm muscles are attractive
free weights or machines?
*exercise type—anaerobic
*exercise type—aerobic exercise
injuries
*toning the body

■ Asking and answering structured questions

Asking and answering structured questions can stimulate you to think of ideas for developing your topic. One popular question set consists of those journalists use: *Who? What? Where? When? Why? How?*

Here's how Alex Garcia used the journalists' questions to start writing about why organic foods are worth the cost, shown in Chapter 12:

Who are the people who care about the benefits of eating organic foods?

What are typical foods people prefer to be organically grown?

Where did the idea of organic foods originate?

When did organic foods become popular?

Why do organic foods cost more than nonorganic foods?

How are organic foods processed?

Another generative question set was developed years ago by rhetorician Richard Young and his colleagues.

- What are the major characteristics of the topic?
- What's the topic's history? How has the topic changed recently? How might the topic change in the future?
- To what categories does the topic belong? How does the topic fit into a larger context?
- How does the topic relate to other aspects of culture or ideas? How is the topic similar or different?

Some of these questions, in addition to the journalists' questions, helped Alex Garcia develop his essay about organic foods in Chapter 12:

What are the major characteristics of organic foods?

What's the history of growing organic food, and how has the process changed?

How might it change in the future?

What are larger contexts for organically grown food, such as being related to overall health issues?

How does interest in organically grown food connect to other aspects of our culture?

■ Clustering

Watch
the Video

Clustering, also called *mapping*, is a visual form of brainstorming. Write your topic in the middle of a sheet and then circle it. Next, move out from the middle circle by drawing lines with circles at the end of each line. Put in each circle a subtopic or detail related to the main topic. If a subtopic or detail in a given circle has further subtopics, draw lines and circles fanning out from that circle. Continue using this method as far as it can take you. Though you might not include in your essay all the subtopics and details in your map, chances are that some the material might come in handy. For example, here's the map that Miquel Sanz drew to help him think of ideas for the second paragraph of his essay about auditioning to be in a musical.

■ Writing every day in a journal or blog

Writing in a journal or blog every day for 5 to 10 minutes is like having a conversation with yourself. This gets you into the habit of productivity so that when handling a writing assignment, your routine of writing makes getting started flow more smoothly. The more you write, the more you get used to expressing yourself through words.

Watch
the Video

Write about whatever's on your mind, or start writing to see what emerges on the pages. Draw on your thoughts, experiences, observations, dreams, reactions to your course work, or responses to something you've read recently. Use a paper notebook or computer document, depending on what's most handy and pleasurable for you. One good use for your journal or blog is to serve as a source of topic for essays as well as related supporting specifics.

■ Chatting

Chatting with others means talking with them—but with a targeted purpose. Talk about your topic and toss around ideas. Keep paper, or your journal or computer, at hand so that you'll be sure to jot down the ideas as they come to mind. Research shows that new lines of thoughts and ideas slip people's minds rather quickly. Little is as frustrating as remembering you had thought of a good idea, but now you forget what is was.

"Chatting" today has come to mean more than only talking. You can chat online with instant messaging, e-mail, and other electronic forums. Exchanging ideas online not only stimulates your thinking but also acts like a warm-up for putting ideas into words.

● **EXERCISE 5-1** Here's a list brainstormed for a writing assignment. The topic was "Ways to promote a new movie." Working individually or in a peer-response group, look over the list and group the ideas. You'll find that some ideas don't fit into a group. Then, add any other ideas you have to the list.

previews in theaters	suspense	director
TV ads	book the movie was based on	topical subject
provocative	locations	special effects
movie reviews	Internet trailers	dialogue
how movie was made	adventure	excitement
sneak previews	newspaper ads	photography
word of mouth	stars	Facebook page ●

5G   How can a thesis statement help me plan?

Watch
the Video

A **thesis statement** serves as the central, controlling declaration of the point being made in most essays written in reponse to typical writing assignments. A thesis statement gives readers a general preview of what they can expect to read about. The basic requirements of a thesis statement are listed in Quick Box 5.9, but you need to expect to compose many drafts of one for each essay, getting closer on successive attempts to what you want it to encapsulate.

Quick Box 5.9   ■ ■ ■ ■ ■ ■ ■ ■ ■

Basic requirements for a thesis statement

1. It gives the essay's central message.

2. It makes an **assertion** or **claim,** which puts forth the essay's central message.

3. Its assertion or claim ties to the essay's TOPIC SENTENCES (see 7C) that start each of the essay's BODY PARAGRAPHS (see 7D).

4. It usually comes at the end of the INTRODUCTORY PARAGRAPH (see 7B).

5. It uses clear, straightforward language without IRONY or SARCASM.

6. It might lay out the major subdivisions of a topic, but a more graceful technique is to imply them rather than stating them outright.

7. Avoid these common mistakes in writing a thesis statement:

    a. Don't use it to give a fact that leads nowhere.

    b. Don't say you're not an expert in your topic; your readers expect you to have learned enough about it to write your essay.

    c. Don't announce your essay's PURPOSE with words such as "The purpose of this essay is . . ."

    d. Don't refer back to your essay's title using words such as "This is an important issue . . ." or "My essay is called 'XYZ' because . . ."

Just as a complete essay doesn't appear in full bloom in a first draft (see 6A), so too the first draft of a thesis statement is tentative. You can expect to craft a thesis statement adapted sensibly to your revised drafts only as you revise your essay by rewriting, moving, adding, deleting, and other kinds of tinkering (see 6C through 6E). "Play" with your thesis statement patiently; indeed, many writers discover their best thesis statements emerge only after they've written their concluding paragraph. As you revise your essay, continually check your thesis statement to make sure that it goes well with the content of your essay. If you find a mismatch, revise one or the other—or perhaps both.

In writing her essay "Women Can Pump Iron Too," shown in Chapter 10, Carol Moreno describes how with the right training women can become strong by lifting free weights. She uses the idiom "pumping iron," a commonly used term in gyms. Her thesis statement evolved from a thin assertion to a full one that makes her message clear.

NO   I think women can pump iron like men.

This has too little information.

NO   If trained, any woman can get strong.

The concept of lifting weights is gone; "any" is too broad.

NO   Despite thinking only men can "pump iron," women can also do it with the right training.

This repeats the essay's title rather than give its central message.

YES   With the right training, women can "pump iron" to build strength.

Captures the central message of Moreno's essay, meets the thesis statement requirements, and avoids the pitfalls listed in Quick Box 5.9.

● **EXERCISE 5-2**   Each set of the following sentences offers several versions of a thesis statement. Within each set, the thesis statements progress from weak to strong. The fourth thesis statement in each set is the best. Referring to requirements listed in Quick Box 5.9, work individually or with a group to explain why the first three choices in each set are weak and the last is best.

Explore the Exercise

A. 1. Advertising is complex.
   2. Magazine advertisements appeal to readers.
   3. Magazine advertisements must be creative and appealing to all readers.
   4. To appeal to readers, magazine advertisements must skillfully use language, color, and design.
B. 1. Soccer is a widely played sport.
   2. Playing soccer is fun.
   3. Soccer requires various skills.
   4. Playing soccer for fun and exercise requires agility, stamina, and teamwork.

C. 1. *Hamlet* is a play about revenge.
   2. Hamlet must avenge his father's murder.
   3. Some characters in the play *Hamlet* want revenge.
   4. In the play *Hamlet*, Hamlet, Fortinbras, and Laertes all seek revenge. ●

5H   How can outlining help me write?

**Watch
the Video**

An **outline** is a structured, sequential list of the contents of a text. Some instructors require an outline with assignments, but others don't. Always ask. When given a choice, some students never outline, whereas others find that outlining helps them write. Figure out what works best for you by experimenting.

For example, you might like to use outlines for some, but not all, types of writing assignments (see Chapters 9–14). Also, you might find that outlining helps at different stages of your writing process: perhaps before DRAFTING to help you flesh out, pull together, and arrange material; or perhaps during REVISION to help you check your flow of thought or make sure you haven't gone off the topic.

An **informal outline** does not follow the numbering and lettering conventions of a formal outline. It often looks like a BRAINSTORMING list, with ideas jotted down in a somewhat random order. Here's an informal outline for the second paragraph of Yanggu Cui's argument essay, "A Proposal to Improve Fan Behavior at Children's Games" (see Chapter 13).

SAMPLE INFORMAL OUTLINE

little league games

parents on sidelines

softball, baseball, soccer

parents yell at officials

insult opposing team

A **formal outline** follows long-established conventions for using numbers and letters to show relationships among ideas. No one outline format is endorsed for MLA STYLE, but instructors generally prefer the format used in Quick Box 5.10. Outlines usually don't show the content of introductory and concluding paragraphs, but some instructors want them included, so always ask.

To compose a formal outline, always use at least two subdivisions at each level—no I without a II, no A without a B, etc. If a level has only one subdivision, either integrate it into the higher level or expand it into two subdivisions. In addition, all subdivisions need to be at the same level of generality: don't pair a main idea with a subordinate idea or a subordinate idea with a supporting detail. In format, use PARALLELISM so that each outline item starts with the same PART OF SPEECH.

Quick Box 5.10

■ ■ ■ ■ ■ ■ ■ ■ ■ ■

Outline formats

FORMAT OF TRADITIONAL FORMAL OUTLINE

Thesis statement: Present the entire thesis statement.

I. First main idea

   A. First subordinate idea

      1. First reason or example

      2. Second reason or example

        a. First supporting detail

        b. Second supporting detail

   B. Second subordinate idea

II. Second main idea

EXAMPLE: FORMAL SENTENCE OUTLINE

This outline goes with the second paragraph of Yanggu Cui's argument essay, "A Proposal to Improve Fan Behavior at Children's Games" (see Chapter 13).

Thesis statement: The league organizers need to bring an end to this kind of abuse, and the best way to do so is by requiring parents to sign a code of good behavior.

I. For decades, parents have proudly watched their sons and daughters play little league softball, baseball, soccer, and other sports.

   A. In recent years, the parents who attend little league games have become more vocal on sidelines.

   B. Parents who used to shout encouragement and congratulations to their children and the teams are now rude.

      1. They scream protests about the coaches' decisions.

      2. They yell insults at the opposing team.

      3. They hurl threats at officials, many of whom are young.

EXAMPLE: FORMAL TOPIC OUTLINE

This outline goes with the second paragraph of Yanggu Cui's argument essay, "A Proposal to Improve Fan Behavior at Children's Games" (see Chapter 13).

Thesis Statement: The league organizers need to bring an end to this kind of abuse, and the best way to do so is by requiring parents to sign a code of good behavior.

continued >>

> **Quick Box 5.10** (continued)
>
> I. Parents at little league softball, baseball, soccer, and other sports
>   A. Parents more vocal on sidelines
>   B. Parents not encouraging but rude
>   1. Protest coaches' decisions
>   2. Insult the opposing team
>   3. Threaten officials

A formal outline can be a **sentence outline**, of only complete sentences, or a **topic outline**, of only words and PHRASES. Be careful never to mix the two styles in one outline. Quick Box 5.10 shows both types.

Drafting, Revising, Editing, and Proofreading

6

Quick Points   You will learn to

➤ Write a first draft (see 6A).
➤ Revise (pp. 54–57).
➤ Edit (pp. 57–58).
➤ Proofread (pp. 58–59).

6A What works in writing a first draft?

Before you draft, be sure to plan your writing (see Chapter 5). Remember that a first draft isn't a final draft, even if it looks like it's finished. Rather, it's the basis for REVISING, EDITING, and PROOFREADING, as shown in Figure 6.1. Here are three alternatives for writing a first draft.

- Write **a discovery draft**. Put aside any planning notes (see 5A–5H) and use FOCUSED FREEWRITING about your topic. Chances are you'll remember many of the ideas you thought of. When you finish the first draft, you can consult your notes.

Figure 6.1 Using a first draft for later revising, editing, and proofreading.

- Write **a structured draft**. Consult your planning notes (see 5A–5H) as you write, but don't allow yourself to stall at a part you don't like. Signal you want to return to it, and keep on going.
- Combine using a discovery draft and a structured draft. Start with a discovery draft, and when stalled, switch to a structured draft. Or do the reverse.

The direction of drafting is forward. Keep pressing ahead. If a spelling, a word choice, or a sentence bothers you, use a signal that says you want to check it later—underline it, highlight it in a color, or switch it to capital letters. Research proves that the physical act of writing without pausing makes ideas and the connections among them "pop into people's heads unbidden."

Writers vary in how they're most comfortable drafting. Some finish their first draft in one sitting. Others draft a few paragraphs, take a break, and come back later. Resist being tempted to revise before you finish the first draft. Do these drafting problems sound familiar?

MY DRAFTING PROBLEM	I open a blank document, write a few words, don't like them, delete them, and start again, repeatedly.
SOLUTION	Darken your computer screen, and type without stopping. Save your work. Then lighten your computer screen to find an early draft.
MY DRAFTING PROBLEM	I start out well, but soon I'm going off the topic.
SOLUTION	Mark the spot with a highlighter, and pull yourself back to the topic. Don't stop. You can revise later.

6B How do I get over writer's block?

Writer's block is the condition that shuts off writers from their ability to write. Even an expert writer sometimes hits a writer's block. If you get blocked, use the suggestions in Quick Box 6.1.

Watch the Video

Quick Box 6.1 ■ ■ ■ ■ ■ ■ ■ ■ ■

Ways to overcome writer's block

- **Start in the middle.** Rather than start at the beginning of your essay, start with the body paragraph you feel will be easiest or most interesting to write.

- **Visualize yourself writing, moving your fingers across the keyboard.** Top athletes always use visualizing, imagining themselves going though each motion involved in their sport. Before you start writing, visualize yourself writing easily.

- **Write an e-mail about your topic to a friend, even if you don't send it.** Write informally. Be playful with your language or ideas. Loosen up.

- **Call a friend or relative to chat about your topic.** Ask if you can chat with them a few minutes about your topic, inviting them to disagree or argue with you. Keep paper and pen at hand because this exchange can spark ideas and get your enthusiasm going.

- **Play the role of someone else and write to yourself about your topic.** Take on someone else's identity—a famous person alive now or in the past, for example—and imagine that person listening to you talk about your topic. That person might disagree or agree with you or might find it hard to understand your topic.

- **Imagine a scene or sound that relates to your topic.** Start to write by describing what you see or hear. Allow yourself to sink into the environment of that scene or sound.

6C How does revision work?

Watch
the Video

To **revise**, you work on your first draft systematically to rewrite it so that you get the content into the best shape you can. You do this by adding, cutting, replacing, and rearranging material.

During DRAFTING you suspended judgment of your writing, but for revision, you switch to making judgments. As you revise, keep all your drafts and notes as you rewrite to improve your essay. You might want to go back to an earlier revision and use part of it.

Remember during revision that although you know your topic well, your reader might be encountering it for the first time. This means you need to strive for clarity, often by defining and explaining any terms or processes that

Quick Box 6.2

■ ■ ■ ■ ■ ■ ■ ■ ■

Revision checklist

The section numbers in parentheses tell you where to go in this handbook for more information on each feature.

1. Is your introductory paragraph (see 7B) a suitable lead into your topic, thesis statement, and essay?

2. Does your thesis statement effectively focus on your topic and the purpose of your essay (see 5G)?

3. Do your topic sentences flow logically from your thesis statement (see 7C and Chapters 9–14)?

4. Are your topic sentences, which are your generalizations, supported sufficiently with reasons, examples, and other types of details (see 7D)?

5. Is the sequence of your paragraphs logically arranged (see Chapter 9–14)?

6. Have you used appropriate words of transitions to connect ideas within and between paragraphs (see 7D)?

7. Have you used deliberate repetition and parallelism, when possible, to unite your paragraphs and essay (see 7D)?

8. Does your conclusion complete your essay effectively (see 7G)?

might be unfamiliar to them. Here you work on the overarching elements of your essay. Save the last two steps—editing and proofreading—until you've finished revising the draft. This tactic is important: "premature editing" distracts writers too soon from the content of their material.

As you revise, work through the questions in Quick Box 6.2, or use revision guidelines supplied by your instructor. Every time you make a change, evaluate it on its own and also in the context of the surrounding material. As you work, check your THESIS STATEMENT so that you update it to fit well with your newly evolved essay (see 5G). Continue revising until you're satisfied that your essay is ready for editing.

In deciding whether your draft is your final one, avoid being so impressed by the clean appearance of a nicely printed and formatted paper that you avoid making changes.

Here's a section of an early draft of a paragraph in student Cheryl Cusack's essay, "Why We're Going Less Often to the Movies." Compare it to her revised draft on page 56.

FIRST DRAFT

Ticket prices are very high, with the national average at $8.00. Throw in purchasing refreshments, and a night at the movies for a couple can reach $40.00. What about a family of four? Given the recent troubles in our economy, movies are out of reach for many.

REVISED DRAFT

Cost might be a better reason. Ticket prices have continued to increase, to a national average of $8.00 and, of course, much higher many places. Throw in modest refreshments and travel costs, and a night at the movies for a couple can easily be $40. A family of four can spend almost twice that. Given recent troubles in our economy, movies may have priced themselves out of reach for many. However, at other times of financial stress, including the Great Depression of the 1930s, people still went to movies. Cost can account for some, but not all of the decline.

New topic sentence ties into thesis statement.

More specifics about ticket prices.

More specific about costs— she answers her own first draft question.

A more complete view of decline in movie going.

Clearly, Cheryl realized her earliest draft was only a beginning, and she knew that during her revision process, she could improve her work by introducing more unity and specific details throughout.

6D How do thesis statements and essay titles help with revision?

Watch the Video

To use your THESIS STATEMENT as a guide for your revision, ask at the end of each body paragraph, "Does the topic sentence and content of this paragraph relate to my thesis statement?" If it does not, revise the thesis statement, your paragraph, or both.

Your essay title is an important part of revising, so create a working title during your first draft. It helps you make sure you don't go off your topic. Use it consistently as a checkpoint as your essay evolves. Never tack on a title at the last minute.

A **direct title** tells exactly what the essay will be about: for example, "Why We're Going Less Often to the Movies." An **indirect title** hints at an essay's topic: "Can We Really Afford It?" Such an indirect title can capture a reader's interest as long as the connection is not too obscure. For example, this indirect title would not work: "Too Much and Getting Worse."

❗ Alert: A title stands alone. Don't open an essay with a reaction to the title or with an opening sentence that is a continuation of the title. For example, the following would be an inappropriate first sentence in student Cheryl Cusack's essay "Why We're Going Less Often to the Movies": "It's too expensive these days." Such an opening sentence is improper because it leans on the essay's title, and "It" is an unclear PRONOUN REFERENCE. ●

6E Why are style and tone important in revising?

As you revise your writing, you want to consider *how* you say something as well as *what* you're saying. You create the **style** of your writing by how you shape sentence structures and how you choose to address readers. **Tone** involves using the right words to deliver your meaning.

Levels of formality are expressed by your style and tone. These levels can be roughly divided into three categories.

- **Formal writing** is used for ceremonies, contracts, policies, and some literary writing.
- **Informal writing** is appropriate for e-mails, Facebook postings, and certain BLOGS, rarely for college essays.
- **Semiformal writing** is appropriate for academic writing, as well as much business and public writing. Its characteristics are
  - Tone is reasonable and evenhanded.
  - Style is clear and efficient.
  - Word choices are appropriate for readers of academic writing.

Chapters 43–45 cover matters of style and tone in greater detail.

6F How does editing work?

Editing comes after you've revised the content and organization of your paper to your critical satisfaction. Editing means finding and fixing errors you've made in grammar, spelling, punctuation, capitals, numbers, italics, and abbreviations. Some instructors call these *surface-level features*.

Watch
the Video

If you want to hand in writing that shows you've paid close attention to the small errors that can ruin a paper's clarity and shows a respectful stance toward your assignment, edit slowly and methodically. Whenever you question a rule or a writing technique, use the Index at the back of this handbook to find the page for the exact rule or technique you want to check.

You may also want to ask friends, classmates, or colleagues with a good "editing eye" to read your paper and circle anything they think you need to check for correctness.

6G Can I rely on editing software and apps?

Watch
the Video
Be very cautious if you use the editing features in word processing programs or apps. Many are wrong. For example, most versions of Microsoft Word flag correct contractions, always suggesting the alternative, when your choice is correct. Grammar- or style-check programs compare your writing to often outdated interpretations of rules of grammar, punctuation, and other conventions. Never rely on them unquestioningly.

Spell-check programs are like fire: they can help but they can also ruin your work. They spot a misspelled or mistyped word (for example, "abot" for "about"). However, they don't spot a wrong word (for example, "form" but you mean "from").

Thesaurus programs give you SYNONYMS for words. Be sure to select the ones that fit well into your particular sentences. Many synonyms have slightly different meanings, so never use one that's unfamiliar or you know only vaguely. Always look it up in your dictionary. A misused word detracts seriously from the quality of an essay because the reader assumes you do not know what you are saying and perhaps thinks you're trying to show off.

6H What strategies can I use to proofread?

PROOFREADING is a careful, line-by-line reading of a final, clean version of your writing. Always proofread for errors and correct them before you hand in a paper. If you find errors during proofreading, always print a fresh, clean copy of your work.

Almost all writers proofread more effectively on a printed page rather than on a screen, so print your pages whenever possible for proofreading purposes. If you cannot avoid working onscreen, try highlighting a small section of your writing at a time so that you are visually separating it from the rest of the screen. This helps reduce the tendency to read too quickly and overlook errors.

Here are the most effective proofreading strategies that are popular with many writers.

- Proofread with a ruler held just under the line you are reading so that you can focus on one line at a time.
- Start at the end of a paragraph or the end of your essay, and read each sentence in reverse order or word by word, to avoid being distracted by the content.

- Read your final draft aloud so that you see and/or hear errors.
- Look especially carefully for omitted letters and words.
- Watch out for repeated words ("the" or "and" are common repeats).
- Keep lists of spelling, punctuation, or grammar errors that you often make. (For example, you may have trouble keeping *to, too*, and *two* straight.) Consult your lists before you revise, edit, and proofread to look specifically for those personal troublemakers.

7 Composing Paragraphs

Quick Points   You will learn to

> Write effective introductory paragraphs (see 7B).
> Write effective body paragraphs (pp. 63–71).
> Write effective concluding paragraphs (pp. 71–72).

7A   What is a paragraph?

A **paragraph** is a group of sentences that work together to develop a unit of thought. Paragraphs help you divide material into manageable parts and arrange the parts in a unified whole. ACADEMIC WRITING typically consists of an introductory paragraph, a group of body paragraphs, and a concluding paragraph.

Watch
the Video

7B   What are effective introductory paragraphs?

Introductory paragraphs point to what lies ahead and seek to arouse readers' interest. Quick Box 7.1 suggests strategies for starting effective introductory paragraphs. The rest of the sentences then flow logically to the paragraph's final sentence, which usually presents the essay's THESIS STATEMENT (see 5G and Quick Box 5.9). Paragraphs 1 and 2 use different strategies to arouse interest; both conclude with a thesis statement.

Watch
the Video

Quick Box 7.1

Strategies for writing introductory paragraphs

STRATEGIES FOR CAPTURING YOUR READER'S INTEREST

- Provide relevant background information about your topic.
- Relate a brief, interesting anecdote that applies to your topic.
- Give pertinent, perhaps surprising statistics about your topic.
- Ask a provocative question or two to lead in to your topic.
- Use a quotation that relates closely to your topic.
- Draw an analogy to clarify or illustrate your topic.
- Define a key term you use throughout your piece of writing.

STRATEGIES TO AVOID

- Making obvious statements about the essay's topic or purpose: Not "I am going to discuss some facts about animation."
- Apologizing, as in "I'm not sure I'm right, but here's what I think."
- Using overworked expressions: "Haste does make waste, as I recently discovered."

1   Alone one is never lonely, May Sarton says in her essay "The Rewards of Living a Solitary Life." Most people, however, are terrified of living alone. They are used to living with others—children with parents, roommates with roommates, friends with friends, husbands with wives. When the statistics catch up with them, therefore, they are rarely prepared. Chances are high that most adult men and women will live alone, briefly or longer, at some time.

Paraphrase of quotation

Thesis statement

—Tara Foster, student

2   Arguably the greatest mysteries in the universe lie in the three-pound mass of cells, approximately the consistency of oatmeal, that reside in the skull of each of us. It has even been suggested that the brain is so complex that our species is smart enough to fathom everything except what makes us so smart; that is, the brain is so cunningly designed for intelligence that it is too stupid to understand itself. We now know that is not true. The mind is at last yielding its secrets to persistent

Surprising fact to arouse interest

scientific investigation. We have learned more about how the mind works in the last twenty-five years than we did in the previous twenty-five hundred.

Thesis statement

—Daniel T. Willingham, *Why don't students like school?*

7C How do topic sentences work?

A **topic sentence** contains the main idea of a BODY PARAGRAPH and controls its content. Topic sentences are usually GENERALIZATIONS containing the main idea of the paragraph. The connection between the main idea and its supporting details in the sentences that follow it needs to be clear. Topic sentences usually come at the beginning of a paragraph, but putting them at the end or implying them can be effective in some cases.

Watch the Video

■ Starting with a topic sentence

When a topic sentence starts a paragraph, readers immediately know what topic will be discussed.

3
Family businesses are discovering a new venue where they can work out their problems: the classroom. Over the past few years, more family-firm leaders have been turning to executive-education courses tailored to their needs. Instead of just teaching the best way to run a business, the courses focus on overcoming the unique obstacles that family ties can pose—such as succession planning and poor communication among relatives. Several company executives are encouraged to attend at the same time, and a large part of the courses involves getting everyone at the company on the same page, often through team exercises like role playing. The instructors act partly as professors and partly as counselors, giving advice on navigating current family conflicts as they teach business theory.

—Alina Dizik, "The Family That Goes To School Together . . ."

■ Ending with a topic sentence

When a topic sentence ends a body paragraph, all sentences leading to it need to flow into it clearly.

4
The third most popular language in America—after English and Spanish—is American Sign Language (ASL). It is a visual-gestural language composed of a collection of coded gestures based on a system developed in France in the eighteenth century. It was brought to the United States by Thomas Hopkins Gallaudet, a young Congregational minister from Connecticut. After traveling to France and learning about this system of signing, Gallaudet returned to the United States, bringing a young French deaf-signing teacher, Laurent Clerc,

with him. Together they developed a sign language system that blended French signs with American signs. As a legacy, today deaf people in both France and the United States can recognize similarities in the signs they use.

—Roger E. Axtell, *Gestures: The Do's and Taboos of Body Language around the World*

■ Implying a topic sentence

Some paragraphs convey a main idea without a specific topic sentence. This technique requires special care so that the details clearly add up to a main idea. The implied topic sentence of paragraph 5, if it were stated explicitly, might be something like "To lure buyers into the local clothing store, the manager engaged in false advertising, but not everyone caught on."

5   Customers used to wait at the cash register for minutes before a checker would finally pay attention. Of course, the wait happened only when they actually had found the item they had come to buy. Most customers went away empty-handed. The manager had a practice of running ads for products that were just about sold out. I would watch people pick through piles of shirts in a fruitless search for something other than an extra-small or an extra-extra-large.

—Armstrong Washington, student

● **EXERCISE 7-1**   Working individually or with a group, identify the topic
Explore
the
Exercise
sentences in the following paragraphs. If the topic sentence is implied, write the point the paragraph conveys. For help, consult section 7C.

A. A good college program should stress the development of high-level read-ing, writing, and mathematical skills and should provide you with a broad historical, social, and cultural perspective, no matter what subject you choose as your major. The program should teach you not only the most current knowledge in your field but also—just as important—prepare you to keep learning throughout your life. After all, you'll probably change jobs, and possibly even careers, at least six times, and you'll have other responsibilities, too—perhaps as a spouse and as a parent and certainly as a member of a community whose bounds extend beyond the workplace.

—Frank T. Rhodes, "Let the Student Decide"

B. The once majestic oak tree crashes to the ground amid the destructive flames, as its panic-stricken inhabitants attempt to flee the fiery tomb. Undergrowth that formerly flourished smolders in ashes. A family of deer darts furiously from one wall of flame to the other, without an emergency exit. On the outskirts of the inferno, firefighters try desperately to stop the destruction. Somewhere at the source of this chaos lies a former campsite containing the cause of this destruction—an untended campfire. This scene is one of many that illustrate how human apathy and carelessness destroy nature.

—Anne Bryson, student

C. Rudeness isn't a distinctive quality of our own time. People today would be shocked by how rudely our ancestors behaved. In the colonial period, a French traveler marveled that "Virginians don't use napkins, but they wear silk cravats, and instead of carrying white handkerchiefs, they blow their noses either with their fingers or with a silk handkerchief that also serves as a cravat, a napkin, and so on." In the 19th century, up to about the 1830s, even very distinguished people routinely put their knives in their mouths. And when people went to the theater, they would not just applaud politely—they would chant, jeer, and shout. So, the notion that there's been a downhill slide in manners ever since time began is just not so.

—"Horizons," *U.S. News & World Report* ●

7D   What details are effective in body paragraphs?

Body paragraphs in an essay come after the introductory paragraph. The sentences support the generalization in the TOPIC SENTENCE. What separates most good writing from bad is the writer's ability to move back and forth between generalizations and specific details. If you need help in thinking of details, try using **RENNS**, a memory device summarized in Quick Box 7.2.

Quick Box 7.2   ■ ■ ■ ■ ■ ■ ■ ■ ■ ■

RENNS: Ways to think of specific, supporting details

R = Reasons can provide support.

● Jules Verne, who wrote in the 19th century, amazes today's readers because he imagined inventions not possible back then.

E = Examples can provide support.

● For example, he predicted submarines and moon rockets.

N = Names can provide support.

● He forecast that moon rockets would take off from the state of Florida.

N = Numbers can provide support.

● He predicted the takeoffs at 27° North Latitude, 5° West Longitude.

S = Senses—sight, sound, smell, taste, touch—provide support.

● Today, NASA space vehicles blast off only 80 miles from the site Verne chose.

You can choose whichever details work in your paragraphs, and you can use them in whatever order makes the most sense.

Paragraph 6 contains many specific details that support the topic sentence at the beginning of the paragraph. Some details fit into more than one category of RENNS.

> **6** Between 1910 and 1920, "The Rubber Capital of the World" was the fastest-growing city in the nation, thanks to a booming automobile industry. Akron, Ohio, had a few crucial features that helped it thrive as a hub. It was not only located close to auto makers, it also had water power and cheap coal to draw on. During the peak years, more than 300 rubber companies called the city home, but most died off in the fierce pricing competition. Then, in the 1970s, French manufacturer Michelin introduced the longer-lasting radial tire. In Akron, profits slipped and plants closed. Goodyear Tire & Rubber Co. is now the only major tire company that still has headquarters in Akron.

Topic sentence

Reasons

Examples
Numbers
Names

—Wall Street Journal research "Akron, Ohio"

● **EXERCISE 7-2**   Working individually or with a peer-response group, look again at the paragraphs in Exercise 7-1. Identify the RENNS in each paragraph. For help, consult 7D. ●

7E   How do paragraphs become coherent?

Watch the Video

A paragraph has **coherence** when its sentences are connected in content and relate to each other in form and language. Coherence creates a smooth flow of thoughts within each paragraph as well as from one paragraph to another. Transitional words and expressions, deliberate repetition, and parallelism can help make your writing coherent.

■ Transitional expressions

Transitional expressions are words and phrases that express connections among ideas, both within and between paragraphs, as listed in Quick Box 7.3. Here are some tips for using **transitions** effectively.

- Vary the transitional expressions that you use within a category. For example, you want to avoid using *for instance* every time you give an example.
- Use each transitional expression precisely, according to its exact meaning. For example, the expression *in contrast* signals that you will be discussing something that's unlike what you just discussed.

Quick Box 7.3

Transitional words and expressions and the relationships they express

ADDITION	also, besides, equally important, furthermore, in addition, moreover, too
COMPARISON	in the same way, likewise, similarly
CONCESSION	granted, naturally, of course
CONTRAST	at the same time, certainly, despite the fact that, however, in contrast, instead, nevertheless, on the contrary, on the other hand, otherwise, still
EMPHASIS	indeed, in fact, of course
EXAMPLE	a case in point, as an illustration, for example, for instance, namely, specifically
PLACE	here, in the background, in the front, nearby, there
RESULT	accordingly, as a result, consequently, hence, then, therefore, thus
SUMMARY	finally, in conclusion, in short, in summary
TIME SEQUENCE	eventually, finally, meanwhile, next, now, once, then, today, tomorrow, subsequently, yesterday

NO The jewels were valuable. Otherwise, the carpets were not.

Otherwise makes no sense.

YES The jewels were valuable. In contrast, the carpets were not.

This comparison makes sense.

In the following paragraph, the transitional words and expressions are highlighted.

7   Jaguars, **for example**, were **once** found in the United States from southern Louisiana to California. **Today** they are rare north of the Mexican border, with no confirmed sightings since 1971. They are rare, **too,** in Mexico, where biologist Carl Koford estimated their population at fewer than a thousand in a 1972 survey. Some biologists think the number is even smaller **today. Similarly,** jaguars have disappeared from southern Argentina and Paraguay.

—Jeffrey P. Cohen, "Kings of the Wild"

■ **Deliberate repetition and parallelism**

Deliberate repetition means you intentionally repeat key words to achieve coherence within and between paragraphs. Used well, it moves readers along gracefully. Overused, its monotony dulls your impact. Paragraph 8 uses parallelism well. The word *it* is repeated throughout, each time clearly referring to the skin; midway, the word *skin* recurs once to reanchor the use of *it*.

Parallelism is another technique for achieving coherence (see Chapter 43 for a full discussion). In paragraph 8, one sentence uses the rhythm of matching phrases: *gives us, protects us, cools us, heats us.* Another sentence twice employs "of" phrasing: *organ of the body, organ of sexual attraction.*

Our skin is what stands between us and the world. If you think about it, no other part of us makes contact with something not us, but the skin. It imprisons us, but it also gives us individual shape, protects us from invaders, cools us down or heats us up as need be, produces vitamin D, holds in our body fluids. Most amazing, perhaps, is that it can mend itself when necessary, and it is constantly renewing itself.

8 Weighing from six to ten pounds, it's the largest organ of the body, and the key organ of sexual attraction. Skin can take a startling variety of shapes: claws, spines, hooves, feathers, scales, hair. It's waterproof, washable, and elastic. Although it may cascade or roam as we grow older, it lasts surprisingly well. For most cultures, it's the ideal canvas to decorate with paints, tattoos, and jewelry. But, most of all, it harbors the sense of touch.

Deliberate repetition

Parallelism

Parallelism

—Diane Ackerman, *A Natural History of the Senses*

Explore the Exercise

● **EXERCISE 7-3** Working individually or with a peer-response group, locate the coherence techniques in the following paragraph. Look for transitional expressions, deliberate repetition, and parallel structures. For help, consult 7E.

Kathy sat with her legs dangling over the edge of the side of the hood. The band of her earphones held back strands of straight copper hair that had come loose from two thick braids that hung down her back. She swayed with the music that only she could hear. Her shoulders raised, making circles in the warm air. Her arms reached out to her side; her open hands reached for the air; her closed hands brought the air back to her. Her arms reached over her head; her opened hands reached for a cloud; her closed hands brought the cloud back to her. Her head moved from side to side; her eyes opened and closed to the tempo of the tunes. Kathy was motion.

—Claire Burke, student ●

7F What types of rhetorical strategies work in developing body paragraphs?

Rhetorical strategies are patterns and techniques for presenting ideas clearly and effectively. The specific strategies that you choose to use depend on what you want to accomplish.

In this section, rhetorical strategies are presented one at a time. In real writing, however, no paragraph is isolated, so rhetorical strategies often overlap in one paragraph. For example, in a paragraph explaining how to prepare a slide to study under a microscope, you would likely use the process pattern along with definition and description.

■ Narration

Narrative writing tells what is happening or what has happened. It is storytelling.

Watch
the Video

> We walked down the path to the well-house, attracted by the fragrance of the honeysuckle with which it was covered. Someone was drawing water and my teacher placed my hand under the spout. As the cool stream gushed over one hand she spelled into the other the word *water*, first slowly, then rapidly. I stood still, my whole attention fixed upon the motions of her fingers. Suddenly I felt
> **9** a misty consciousness as of something forgotten—a thrill of returning thought; and somehow the mystery of language was revealed to me. I knew then that "water" meant the wonderful cool something that was flowing over my hand. That living word awakened my soul, gave it light, hope, joy, set it free! There were barriers still, it is true, but barriers that could in time be swept away.

> —Helen Keller, *The Story of My Life*

■ Description

Descriptive writing paints a picture in words. To impose a logical sequence on your **description**, you might work from the general to the specific, as in paragraph 10. Other effective sequences include top to bottom, left or right, and so on; from least to most important, to build to a climax; or any other organization that sits well with your topic.

Watch
the Video

> The common yo-yo is crudely made, with a thick shank between two widely spaced wooden disks. The string is knotted or stapled to the shank. With such an instrument nothing can be done except the simple up-down movement. My yo-yo, on the other hand, was a perfectly balanced construction
> **10** of hard wood, slightly weighted, flat, with only a sixteenth of an inch between the halves. The string was not attached to the shank, but looped over it in such a way as to allow the wooden part to spin freely on its own axis. The gyroscopic effect thus created kept the yo-yo stable in all attitudes.

> —Frank Conroy, *Stop Time*

■ Process

Watch
the Video

Process writing presents instructions; lays out steps in a procedure; explains how objects work; or describes human behaviors, as in paragraph 11 about people's reactions in a plane crash.

> In the precious first moments after a plane crash, when experts say a half-second head start can get you to an aisle first, the most basic elements of human character are revealed. Some instincts help survival and others hinder escape. Some people are panicked into pushing, shoving and fighting. For many, the brain shuts down and they are slow to react. That's why practice and familiarity can help. Balking at the top of a three-story evacuation slide can lead to a push, sending you cart-wheeling down and resulting in broken ankles. Research shows even practicing with the seat belt latch can help quicken escape. On average, six percent of passengers in an evacuation get delayed by seat-belt struggles, the Civil Aeronautics Administration study found.
>
> 11
>
> —Scott McCartney, "British Airways Puts Fliers in Mock Disasters:
> How to Get a Head Start"

■ Example or illustration

Watch
the Video

Examples provide concrete, specific support for the main idea. **Illustrations** provide support for the main idea of a paragraph by giving several examples. Paragraph 12 presents in rapid succession the "magical properties" of selected numbers so that examples taken together create a coherent picture.

> Certain numbers have magical properties. E, pi and the Fibonacci series come quickly to mind—if you are a mathematician, that is. For the rest of us, the magic numbers are the familiar ones that have something to do with the way we keep track of time (7, say, and 24) or something to do with the way we count (namely, on 10 fingers). The "time numbers" and the "10 numbers" hold remarkable sway over our lives. We think in these numbers (if you ask people to produce a random number between one and a hundred, their guesses will cluster around the handful that end in zero or five) and we talk in these numbers (we say we will be there in five or ten minutes, not six or 11).
>
> 12
>
> —Daniel Gilbert, "Magic by Numbers"

■ Definition

Watch
the Video

Definition calls for giving the meaning of a word or concept in more detail than a dictionary definition. Extended definitions are often part of paragraphs also developed in other ways. Paragraph 13 offers an extended definition of the term "soft skills," using examples that progress from the somewhat less important to the more dramatic crucially important point.

When it comes to soft skills, most people think they are all about those warm-and-fuzzy people skills. Yes, it's true that people skills are a part of the equation, but that's just for starters. While hard skills refer to the technical ability and the factual knowledge needed to do the job, soft skills allow you to more effectively use your technical abilities and knowledge. Soft skills encompass personal, social, communication, and self-management behaviors. They cover a wide spectrum of abilities and traits: being self-aware,

13 trustworthiness, conscientiousness, adaptability, critical thinking, attitude, initiative, empathy, confidence, integrity, self-control, organizational awareness, likeability, influence, risk taking, problem solving, leadership, time management, and then some. Quite a mouthful, eh? These so-called soft skills complement the hard ones and are essential for success in the rough-and-tumble workplace. You can have all the technical expertise in the world, but if you can't sell your ideas, get along with others, or turn your work in on time, you'll be going nowhere fast.

—Peggy Klaus, *The Hard Truth About Soft Skills*

■ Comparison and contrast

Comparisons deal with similarities; *contrasts* deal with differences. **Comparison and contrast** writing is usually organized in one of two ways. **Point-by-point organization** moves back and forth between the items being compared, as in paragraph 14. **Block organization** discusses one item completely before discussing the next, as in paragraph 15 (sporting games are covered completely before anything is said about business).

Watch the Video

The world can be divided in many ways—rich and poor, democratic and authoritarian—but one of the most striking is the divide between the societies with an individualist mentality and the ones with a collective mentality. This is a divide that goes deeper than economics into the way people perceive the world. If you show an American an image of a fish tank, the American will

14 usually describe the biggest fish in the tank and what it is doing. If you ask a Chinese person to describe a fish tank, the Chinese will usually describe the context in which the fish swim. These sorts of experiments have been done over and over again, and the results reveal the same underlying pattern. Americans usually see individuals; Chinese and other Asians see contexts.

—David Brooks, "Harmony and the Dream"

Games are of limited duration, take place on or in fixed and finite sites and are governed by openly promulgated rules that are enforced on the spot

15 by neutral professionals. Moreover, they are performed by relatively evenly matched teams that are counseled and led through every move by seasoned hands. Scores are kept, and at the end of the game, a winner is declared.

Business is usually a little different. In fact, if there is anyone out there who can say that the business is of limited duration, takes place on a fixed site, is governed by openly promulgated rules that are enforced on the spot by neutral professionals, competes only on relatively even terms, and performs in a way that can be measured in runs or points, then that person is either extraordinarily lucky or seriously deluded.

—Warren Bennis, "Time to Hang Up the Old Sports Clichés"

■ Analysis

Analysis examines and discusses separate parts of a whole. Paragraph 16 offers an analysis of how to create strong passwords for your computer's protected files.

16 For a pretty strong password, think 10. If your password contains 10 characters, you should be able to sleep well at night—perhaps for 19.24 years. That's how long it would take hackers to try every combination of 10 characters, assuming that the password is encrypted and that the hackers have enough computing power to mount a 100-billion-guesses-a-second effort to break the encryption. But if your user names and passwords are sitting unencrypted on a server, you may not be able to sleep at all if you start contemplating the potential havoc ahead.

—Randall Stross, "Digital Domain"

■ Classification

Classification groups items according to a shared characteristic. In paragraph 17, three types of signals are explained. Their commonality is that all are used by coaches.

Watch the Video

17 Many different kinds of signals are used by the coaches. There are flash signals, which are just what the name implies: The coach may flash a hand across his face or chest to indicate a bunt or hit-and-run. There are holding signals, which are held in one position for several seconds. There might be the clenched fist, bent elbow, or both hands on knees. Then there are the block signals. These divide the coach's body into different sections, or blocks. Touching a part of his body, rubbing his shirt, or touching his cap indicates a sign. Different players can be keyed to various parts of the block so the coach is actually giving several signals with the same sign.

—Rockwell Stensrud, "Who's on Third?"

■ Analogy

Analogy is a kind of comparison, identifying similarities between objects or ideas that are not usually associated with each other.

18 Casual dress, like casual speech, tends to be loose, relaxed, and colorful. It often contains what might be called "slang words": blue jeans, sneakers, baseball caps, aprons, flowered cotton housedresses, and the like. These garments could not be worn on a formal occasion without causing disapproval, but in ordinary circumstances they pass without remark. "Vulgar words" in dress, on the other hand, give emphasis and get immediate attention in almost any circumstances, just as they do in speech. Only the skillful can employ them without some loss of face, and even then they must be used in the right way. A torn, unbuttoned shirt, or wildly uncombed hair can signify strong emotions: passion, grief, rage, despair. They are most effective if people already think of you as being neatly dressed, just as the curses of well-spoken persons count for more than those of the customarily foul-mouthed.

—Alison Lurie, *The Language of Clothes*

■ Cause and effect

Cause and effect paragraphs examine outcomes and reasons for outcomes. *Causes* lead to an event or an effect; *effects* result from causes.

Watch the Video

19 Many collapses of the past appear to have been triggered, at least in part, by ecological problems: people inadvertently destroyed their environmental resources. But societies are not doomed to collapse because of environmental damage. Some societies have coped with their problems, whereas others have not. But I know of no case in which a society's collapse can be attributed simply to environmental damage; there are always complicating factors. Among them are climate change, the role of neighbors (who can be friendly or hostile), and, most important, the ways people respond to their environmental problems.

—Jared Diamond, "Collapse: Ecological Lessons in Survival"

7G How can I write effective concluding paragraphs?

The **concluding paragraph** of an essay needs to follow logically from your THESIS STATEMENT and BODY PARAGRAPHS. Never merely tack on a conclusion. Your concluding paragraph provides a sense of completion, a finishing touch that enhances the whole essay. See Quick Box 7.4 for ideas about writing

Watch the Video

Quick Box 7.4

Strategies for writing concluding paragraphs

STRATEGIES FOR CAPTURING YOUR READER'S INTEREST

- Use one of the strategies suggested for introductory paragraphs (see Quick Box 7.1), but a different one than you used in the introduction.
- Ask the reader for awareness, action, or a similar outcome.
- Project into the future.
- Summarize the main points if the essay is longer than three pages.

STRATEGIES TO AVOID

- Introducing new ideas or facts that belong in the body of the essay
- Merely rewording the introduction
- Announcing what you have done, as in "In this paper, I have explained Japanese animation"
- Making absolute claims, as in "In this essay, I have proved that anime deserves our attention"
- Apologizing, as in "Even though I am not an expert, I feel the points I have made are valid"

conclusions. The conclusion reproduced in paragraph 20 is from the essay whose introductory paragraph was reprinted in paragraph 1. It poses a challenging question and asks the reader to prepare for the future.

20 You need to ask yourself, "If I had to live alone starting tomorrow morning, would I know how?" If the answer is no, you need to become conscious of what living alone calls for. If you face up to life today, you will not have to hide from it later on.

—Tara Foster, student

8 Designing Documents

■ ■ ■ ■ ■ ■ ■ ■

Quick Points   You will learn to

- Identify the elements of good document design (see sections 8A and 8B).
- Use text and headings effectively (pp. 74–76).
- Use photographs and other visuals for a purpose (pp. 76–79).
- Lay out the pages of a document (pp. 79–80).

8A   What is document design?

DOCUMENT DESIGN refers to the physical appearance of your writing. It focuses on how a document looks rather than on what it says. Elements of document design include text, headings, visuals, white space, and layout.

👁 **Watch the Video**

🚫 **Alert:** Most instructors are very particular about the design and format of papers for their courses. They want certain margins, spacing, fonts, headings, and so on. It's disrespectful not to follow their directions—and it can also harm your grade! ●

8B   What are basic principles of design?

The basic principles of design are **unity,** variety, balance, and emphasis. Quick Box 8.1 describes how to check for these principles.

Quick Box 8.1   ■ ■ ■ ■ ■ ■ ■ ■

Checklist for document design

- **Unity:** Do all elements in my document work together visually?
- **Variety:** Have I introduced design elements, where appropriate, that break up monotony, such as headings that add to clarity or illustrations that add to content?
- **Balance:** Are the parts of my document in proportion to one another?
- **Emphasis:** Does my document design draw attention to key information?

Figure 8.1 Flyer that has unity, variety, balance, and emphasis.

The flyer that a student produced for the environmental group Sustain! in Figure 8.1 reflects the four design principles in Quick Box 8.1.

8C How do I design with text?

Text consists of letters and words. You need to decide which font, also called typeface, and what size font you'll use in your writing. Most instructors want writing to be in 12-point Times New Roman.

Fonts set a tone for your writing, so avoid using playful fonts such as **Comic Sans MS** or simulated handwriting fonts such as *Monotype Corsiva* in ACADEMIC WRITING.

■ Highlighting text

Highlighting draws attention to key words or elements of a document. You can highlight in various ways, but the one guideline that applies in all cases is this: Use moderation.

- **Boldface, italics, and underlining.** *Italics* and <u>underlining</u> have special functions in writing (for example, to indicate titles of certain works). Use them sparingly for all other purposes, such as emphasis. Reserve **boldface** for display in brochures and the like.

- **Bulleted and numbered lists.** Bulleted and numbered lists are useful when you discuss a series of items or steps in a complicated process. They're also effective when you want to summarize key points or guidelines. (Bullets are small dots or squares.)

- **Color.** In display materials such as brochures you can change the color of text for emphasis or you can highlight a text segment. Do this sparingly. For college writing, use black text.

8D   How do I use headings?

Headings clarify how you've organized your material and tell your readers what to expect in each section. For most, but not all, essay writing, headings aren't used. However, for longer documents, including reports, brochures, and Web pages, you can use headings to break content into chunks that are easier to read and understand. In ACADEMIC WRITING, APA style favors headings and MLA style tends to discourage them. Following are some guidelines for writing and formatting headings.

- **Put headings in a slightly larger type than the type size in the body of your text.**

- **Keep headings brief and informative.**

- **Change the format for headings of different levels.** Think of levels in headings the way you think of items in an OUTLINE. First-level headings show main divisions. Second-level headings divide material under first-level headings, and so on.

- **Use parallel structure.** All headings at the same level should be grammatically similar. For example, you might make all first-level headings questions and all second-level headings noun phrases. Quick Box 8.2 lists common types of headings.

Quick Box 8.2

■■■■■■■■■

Common types of headings

- **Noun phrases can cover a variety of topics.**
  - Executive Branch of Government
- **Questions can evoke reader interest.**
  - When and How Does the President Use the Veto Power?
- **Gerunds and *-ing* phrases can explain instructions or solve problems.**
  - Submitting the Congressional Budget
- **Imperative sentences can give advice or directions.**
  - Identify a Problem

8E How can I incorporate photographs?

Watch
the Video

Pictures can enhance a variety of documents. Digital cameras and the Internet have made it cheap and easy to take photographs and circulate them.

■ Finding photographs

Every Internet browser has a way to search for images, which you can then copy and paste into a document. However, note these three crucial considerations.

- **Copyright and permissions.** Just because you find something on the Web doesn't mean you can do whatever you want with it. You need to get permission from its owner or maker. Generally, you can use an image one time for class project that will not appear anywhere else, especially online. Often to find better images, consider using online "stock photo" sites (such as istockphoto.com or gettyimages.com) that have hundreds of thousands of images available for small fees or even free.

- **Quality.** Many images you find through a browser search are low resolution or poor quality. They may look fine online, but if you print them in a document they're often fuzzy. That's another reason to use stock photos.

- **Documentation.** Regardless of how you've found an image, you must document its source in your Works Cited or References page (see Chapters 25 and 28).

■ Taking photographs

Sometimes it's easier and more effective to take a picture yourself, especially if you're doing primary research or writing about people, places, or events that you've personally seen. Consider your camera as a drafting tool. Take multiple pictures of each subject, using different camera settings and zooms, so that you can choose the best one. Your main subject should fill most of the image. Avoid the common mistake of people getting lost against a background that's too large.

■ Adjusting photographs

It's fine to adjust an image by making it lighter or darker, fixing colors, and making other changes, as long as you don't distort the truth. A very useful adjustment is cropping, which means removing some parts of the image. Figure 8.2 presents two versions of the same image. There's quite a different meaning if the woman appears as part of the group or if she appears alone, as in the cropped image.

■ Placing photographs

Where you place photographs in relation to text takes planning. Your word processing program will allow you to test where to insert pictures. Often the best way is to wrap the text around it. (Look for "picture tools" or formatting commands in your word processing program.) Figure 8.3 shows a picture centered by itself, and Figure 8.4 shows a more effective version in which that same picture is wrapped by text. Digital technologies offer a third possibility, useful in posters, brochures, etc.: even placing words over the picture.

Figure 8.2 Original and cropped versions of a photograph.

Figure 8.3 Photograph simply inserted and centered.

Without a doubt, the best pitcher in baseball in 2011 was Justin Verlander of the Detroit Tigers. Verlander won the American League Cy Young and the Most Valuable Player Awards, something that almost never had happened previously. He had 250 strikeouts, won 24 games, with only five losses, and had an earned run average of 2.40.

8F How can I incorporate other visuals?

Visuals, also called **graphics**, can condense, compare, and display information more effectively than words, but only if their content is suitable.

Figure 8.4 Photograph wrapped by text.

Without a doubt, the best pitcher in baseball in 2011 was Justin Verlander of the Detroit Tigers. Verlander won the American League Cy Young and the Most Valuable Player Awards, something that almost never had happened previously. He had 250 strikeouts, won 24 games, with only five losses, and had an earned run average of 2.40.

■ Charts, graphs, and tables

- **Bar graphs** compare values, such as the number of different majors at a college, as shown in the graph at right.

- **Line graphs** indicate changes over time. For example, advertising revenue is shown over an eight-month period in the graph at left.

- **Pie charts** show the relationship of each part to a whole, such as a typical budget for a college student, as shown in the chart at right.

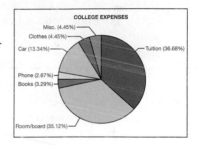

- **Tables** present data in list form, as shown in the following, to allow readers to grasp a lot of information at a glance.

TABLE 1   STUDENT RATINGS OF SUSTAINABILITY, BY TERM

Semester	Students Rating Sustainability as Important	Percentage of All Students
Fall 2011	2,321	65.8%
Spring 2012	2,892	72.3%
Fall 2012	3,425	78.1%

Quick Box 8.3 offers guidelines for using visuals in your documents.

8G What is page layout?

Layout is the arrangement of text, visuals, color, and space on a page. Arrange these elements to follow the basic principles of design (8B). **White space**, the part of your document that has neither text nor visuals, allows readers to read your document more easily and to absorb information in chunks rather than in one big block. White space also indicates breaks between ideas, thereby

Quick Box 8.3

■ ■ ■ ■ ■ ■ ■ ■ ■

Guidelines for using visuals

- Design all visuals to be simple and uncluttered.
- Include a heading or caption for each visual.
- Never use unnecessary visuals. An image or visual needs to clearly enhance your purpose, not simply decorate your document.
- Consider your audience and their sensibilities.
- Credit your source if an image or visual isn't your own. Always avoid PLAGIARISM by crediting your SOURCE. If you use a visual for anything other than a class project, you need to obtain written permission from the copyright holder. Check who owns rights to the image by looking for a copyright notice (often at the beginning or end of the document) or a credits list. For a Web page, look at the top or bottom of the document.

focusing attention on the key features of your document. Quick Box 8.4 explains how to position text and visuals. (Also see Figures 8.3 and 8.4 for some options.)

Quick Box 8.4

■ ■ ■ ■ ■ ■ ■ ■ ■

Guidelines for positioning text and visuals

- Consider the size of visuals so that they don't cluster at the top or the bottom of a page.
- Create balance in a document by imagining it as divided into halves, quarters, or eighths. As you position text or images in the spaces, see which look full, which look empty, and whether the effect seems visually balanced.
- Avoid splitting a chart or table between one page and the next. If a chart or visual runs slightly more than a page, look for ways to adjust spacing or reduce wording. If you have no choice but to continue a chart or table, on the second page, repeat the title and add the word "continued" at the top of the second page.

Tab 3
Frames for College Writing

3
Frames for
College Writing

Tab 3 Frames for College Writing

Frames for College Writing 81–134

MyCompLab® Visit mycomplab.com for the eText and for resources on college writing.

Frames for College Writing

Essay **frames** are guides that suggest how to develop and structure an effective college essay. We offer frames for six types of essays, the ones most frequently assigned in college writing courses. Each frame lays out how the elements of essays can combine to create the greatest possible unity, clarity, and impact. Each frame is followed by a complete student essay, with annotations to show how the essay works, along with the writer's thinking that includes integrating the three persuasive appeals of logical reasoning (*logos*), ethical credibility (*ethos*), and compassionate emotions (*pathos*).

Before each frame, we thoroughly explain how the writing process works for that type of essay. First, we discuss that type's PURPOSE* and probable AUDIENCE and then list specific strategies for planning and revising it. Following each frame is a collection of sentence and paragraph guides that offer hands-on experience with the language moves expected in ACADEMIC WRITING.

In using the frames and guides, you must adapt them to the specifics of each of your writing assignments. Although we place the six essay types in separate chapters, we hope you use them flexibly and creatively.

9 Personal Essays

Quick Points   You will learn to

- ➤ Describe key elements of a personal essay (see section 9A).
- ➤ Apply the writing process to a personal essay (p. 83).
- ➤ Adapt frames and guides for a personal essay to your own needs (pp. 83–84).

9A   What is a personal essay?

Personal essays narrate one or more true experiences to reveal something worth knowing about their writers' lives or ideas. Personal essays often use stories and explain what they mean. The trick in writing a personal essay

Watch
the Video

---

* Words printed in SMALL CAPITAL LETTERS are discussed elsewhere in the text and are defined in the Terms Glossary at the back of the book.

for audiences wider than your family and friends is to narrate your experiences so that readers care about not only what happened but also what you thought of it.

What makes a personal essay effective is how you present it. Your word choice, level of openness, and use of the three persuasive appeals of logic (*logos*), ethical credibility (*ethos*), and compassion and empathy (*pathos*)—see 3B—can combine to deliver an engaging essay. Consider the following example.

> **NO**   I can remember my father driving our car into a filling station at the edge of Birmingham. Two miles after we passed a particular motel, he would turn onto Callahan drive, which was a gravel road.
>
> This provides uninteresting facts and description.

> **YES**   After lunch, our father would fold up his map and tuck it in the felt visor until we pulled into the filling station on the outskirts of Birmingham. Are we there yet? We had arrived when we saw the Moon Winx Motel sign—a heart-stopping piece of American road art, a double-sided neon extravaganza; a big taxicab-yellow crescent with a man-in-the-moon on each side, a sly smile, a blue eye that winked, and that blatant misspelling that "x" that made us so happy.
>
> —Emily Hiestand, *Angela the Upside-Down Girl*

This is a detailed, thorough description about a pleasant memory from the 1950s.

■ Purpose

Personal essays mainly have an expressive or literary purpose that's designed to engage and enlighten readers. The best personal essays have a message or point. Sometimes they lead readers to learn things about their lives that they might not have otherwise recognized. Self-discovery, revealed candidly to the readers can add to the impact of personal essays. (For more about purposes for writing, see 5D.)

■ Audience

People tend to read personal essays for "serious pleasure." They want to be entertained by true stories, especially by the way the writer tells them, but they also want to encounter thoughts and ideas. Work for a mixture of scene, in which you explain the action or setting in detail, and SUMMARY, in which you cover events quickly so that you can get to the interesting stuff. (For more about audience, see 5E.)

9B How do I plan and revise personal essays?

Generating ideas

- Concentrate on getting the basic story down. Perhaps imagine you're writing to a friend who's interested in your story.
- Try creating detailed scenes. Work on describing the physical setting in detail and perhaps use some dialogue so that readers can get a sense of being there. In descriptive words, recreate the place, time, and people who were involved, to allow readers to form their opinion of the scene.

Revising

- Does your story and its details convey your impression of the experience? Be sure to "show, not tell."
- Do you need more specific details (see "RENNS" 7D)?
- Would your essay benefit if you included some dialogue?

9C What is a frame for a personal essay?

The basic shape of a personal essay is a story, but it will also probably have some commentary or reflection (when you "step back" and explain what it all means). Here is a possible frame for a personal essay to adapt to the specifics of your assignment.

Frame for a Personal Essay

Introductory paragraph(s): Dramatic scene from the story

- Capture your readers' attention with an event or significant detail.
- (1) Describe a specific scene or action at the start of your story; (2) begin with the end of the story, OR (3) begin at a dramatic point in the middle of the story. Each way creates a different kind of suspense.
- Use your THESIS STATEMENT to give readers a preview of the central point of your narrative.

Background

- Explain the background of the story, the general setting, the time and place it happened.
- Include here, if you wish, some reflection or the point of your experience.

(continued)

Personal Essay Frame (cont.)

Rest of the story

- Tell what happened in several paragraphs.
- Keep going if you started at the beginning of your story. However, if you started at the middle or end, be sure to return to the beginning so that you tell the whole story. Use a mixture of SUMMARY (covering time in a few sentences) and scene (slowing down and including details and dialogue).

Reflection or analysis

- Explain what readers can learn from this event—about you, about other people or human nature, about situations, ideas, institutions, etc.

Optional: Include related experience or event

- Include a second experience or story that relates to your main one, or an event in the news, someone else's story, or an historical situation.
- Include your reflection or analysis of the related material.
- Connect any related material to your main story.

Conclusion

- Include a final detail, a final observation, a restatement of the main message of your story, or relate what happened after your story ended as long as it flows smoothly with the rest of your paragraph.

9D What sentence and paragraph guides can help generate ideas?

Adapt these sentence and paragraph guides to your PURPOSE and AUDIENCE.

Sentence and Paragraph Guides

- One day [incident, event, experience, etc.] in particular stands out because _____.
- The experience of _____ ultimately taught me [helped me realize, illustrated how] _____.
- At first, this event might have seemed _____, but on deeper reflection it was _____.
- The most interesting [strangest, disturbing, humorous, perplexing, etc.] thing about the experience was _____. That was because _____. Furthermore, _____.

9E   A student's personal essay

View
the Model
Document

Neuchterlein 1

Samantha Neuchterlein

WRIT 1622

Dr. Hesse

2 Feb. 2012

Saved by Technology—or Distracted by It?

In the late afternoon of a cold January day, Kurt and I were struggling through deep snow. We had slung our skis over our shoulders and had spent the past hour hiking up the face of a mountain, searching for familiar territory. It would be getting dark soon, and we were lost.

I have often exaggerated that my smartphone has "saved my life." Usually these perilous moments happen when, for example, a calendar notice pops up to remind me that I have a meeting with a teacher in fifteen minutes that I had totally forgotten. Recently though, my friend and his iPhone actually saved my life. Well, maybe that's a little extreme but the phone certainly helped. In the process, however, I had a disturbing realization about the way technology has infiltrated our lives.

A few Saturdays ago, I joined two friends, Kurt and Carter, for a day of skiing. We left our dorms at the University of Denver before dawn to drive two hours west, to the Arapahoe Basin ski area. The sun came up as we neared the Continental Divide, bathing the high peaks in pink and gold light. It was a spectacular cloudless morning with temperatures in the teens, and the brilliant skies promised a great day on the slopes.

By early afternoon we had completed several runs and had just taken the lift up to the top of the mountain. Standing

Dramatic opening starts in the middle of the story, making readers wonder how the writer got there and what will happen. Embeds an emotional appeal (*pathos*).

Ethical appeal (*ethos*) hints at the character and human side of the writer. Paragraph of reflection and analysis with point at the end. Readers will wonder how writer will reach conclusion.

Paragraph explains context, introducing the people and setting the background.

continued >>

Neuchterlein 2

at 12,000 feet, we stared at the backside, considering several options in the Montezuma Bowl. One was the tempting area out of bounds, the unpatrolled and unofficial slopes where signs warned us of dangers, including death. Most skiers have a love affair with untouched powder, fluffy snow with no tracks that surrounds you in a shimmering white cocoon as you swoosh through it. Any powder had long since been packed down on Arapahoe's ski runs, but out of bounds everything was still clean and pure. So, naturally (and foolishly) the three of us ducked under the ropes and hurtled down uncharted territory.

At first it was terrific. The fresh snow squeaked with each turn that sent up white sparkling waves, as we dodged boulders and looked for a path down. We called to each other in delight. But after about fifteen turns, things changed. Carter got split off from Kurt and me, and suddenly the untouched terrain became unskiable, over sixty degrees steep, with cliffs and drop-offs. Although we had started above tree line, our path was now blocked with lodgepole pines. Going further would have been even more suicidal, so we stopped.

"What's our plan?" Kurt asked.

"Our best hope is hiking up."

So we took off our skis and began trudging back up toward the edge of the boundary. Ski boots, deep snow, and thin air are a bad combination, especially when you're trying to climb a thousand feet and it's getting late. After nearly an hour and a half, we were exhausted. It was around five o'clock, well after the lifts had closed, dusk was falling, and it was getting colder. Suddenly, Kurt's cell phone rang. He quickly ripped off his gloves thinking it was Carter. However, it was the ski

continued >>

Neuchterlein 3

patrol. Kurt told them that we had climbed back to the edge of
bounds and would be back at the bottom momentarily. Two ski
patrollers met us near the lift, which they started to get us out
of the back bowl. One said, "We got your phone numbers from
your friend. He's OK. He's skiing down with other patrollers."

Forty-five minutes later, when we finally all met at the
car, Carter explained more or less how he and his iPhone had
saved us from a cold night in the middle of the woods. When he
had realized that he was lost and much too far away from the
resort, he took out his iPhone to check if there was 3G. There
was. The first thing he Googled was when the sun would set at
his location. 5:30. He had about an hour and a half of sunlight
left. He then Googled the phone number for Arapahoe Basin
ski patrol, called them, and said he was in the middle of the
woods, split from his friends. He gave them our phone numbers,
emailed his coordinates, and sat down waiting. "So I was
sitting in the snow in the middle of the woods, waiting for them,
going through my iTunes library trying to decide which song I'd
like to die listening to." The three of us got a laugh out of this,
but later I got thinking.

Carter's comment is the epitome of how technology has
infiltrated our daily life. At all times, even a situation where
someone is contemplating his "pre-death ritual," technology
affects our decisions. Rather than thinking of his family or his
life's accomplishments, Carter was caught between Dr. Dre
and Eminem's "Forgot About Dre" and the classic by Kanye
West, "Higher." Our unique thoughts and experiences are
overshadowed by a small rectangle of plastic and metal. Even
in an extreme moment, we're not entirely in that moment.

Dialogue
creates
immediacy.
Writer
maintains
emotional
(*pathos*) and
ethical (*ethos*)
appeals.

Writer shows
the logic of
the situation
(*logos*).

Dialogue
shows Carter's
character,
rather than
telling us
about it.

This
paragraph
begins the
writer's
reflection of
thinking back
on her friend's
comment and
what it might
signify.

continued >>

Neuchterlein 4

Although this technology certainly holds the power to take us out of danger, as that day on the mountain showed, it also can distract us from our very lives.

That night on the dark drive back to Denver, we listened to music. We told each other the story of that afternoon over and over, remembering details, sharing thoughts. We knew that our irresponsibility in going out of bounds had cost others trouble and effort, but we also knew we got a great story out of it. It was a story we would tell with some guilt, but we would happily tell it anyway. Beyond that, I knew that I had seen two sides of our reliance on technology, which can both save us and distract us from ourselves.

Concluding paragraph includes both the end of the story and more reflection. It ends with a powerful sentence, a logical statement (*logos*).

10 Informative Essays

■ ■ ■ ■ ■ ■ ■

Quick Points You will learn to

➤ Describe key elements of informative essays (see section 10A).
➤ Apply the writing process to an informative essay (p. 89).
➤ Adapt frames and guides for an informative essay to your own needs (pp. 89–91).

10A What are informative essays?

Watch the Video

When you write an informative essay, you play the role of an expert on the topic you're assigned or you choose.

■ Purpose

Your PURPOSE in writing an informative essay is solely to give your readers information about your topic in a logical sequence, written clearly and engagingly. If the assignment asks only for information, don't add an argument.

Although assignments might not include the word *informative*, you can usually figure out the purpose from the wording. (For more about purposes for writing, see 5D.)

■ Audience

To give information, you want to consider whether your readers might be specialists on your topic. If you can't know this, you're safest in assuming that your audience consists of nonspecialists, which means you need to present full information for people who have no background in your topic. Your readers hope to learn not only the basics of your topic but also sufficient, interesting specifics to hold their interest. (For more about audience, see 5E.)

10B How do I plan and revise informative essays?

Generating ideas

- Do some reading or talk to people knowledgeable about your topic.
- Carefully search the Internet for useful, interesting information about your topic, remembering to use only reliable, credible sources, quote them carefully, and avoid PLAGIARISM (see Chapters 16, 20, and 21).

Revising

- Have you included the right amount of information if your audience members are specialists in your topic? Conversely, if your audience members aren't specialists on your topic, have you provided sufficient information for them?
- Have you addressed the question "Why is this information important or significant?"
- Have you used specific details to make your information come alive (for example, see 7D)?

10C What is a frame for an informative essay?

Informative essays can be organized in many ways. Here's a frame you can adapt to the specifics of your assignments.

Frame for an Informative Essay

Introductory paragraph(s)

- **Capture your readers' interest** by using one of the strategies for writing effective introductory paragraphs (see 7B).
- **Present your thesis statement**, making sure it gives the central point of the essay (see 5G).

Body paragraph(s): background information

- **Provide background** for the information in your essay. This might follow the introductory paragraph or come later in the essay at a point when the background is more relevant.
- **Start with a topic sentence** that clearly relates to your thesis statement and leads logically to the information in the paragraph (see 7C).

Body paragraph(s)

- **Present sections of information**, divided into logical groups, generally one to a paragraph.
- **Start each paragraph with a topic sentence** that clearly relates to the essay's thesis statement and leads logically to the information in the paragraph (see 7C).
- **Support each topic sentence with specific details**—use RENNS (see 7D).

Conclusion

- **Bring the essay to a logical conclusion**, using one of the strategies for writing effective concluding paragraphs (see 7G).

10D What are sentence and paragraph guides for an informative essay?

Adapt these sentence and paragraph guides to your PURPOSE and AUDIENCE.

Sentence and Paragraph Guides

- People experienced with _____ advise that the public needs to know _____ so that everyone can _____.
- _____ captured my interest because _____.
- People generally consider _____, _____, and _____ as the major components of information about _____.
- In addition to _____, _____ plays a major role in _____.

Informative Guides (cont.)

- For many people, the most compelling information about _____ is _____. However, they often overlook _____. That aspect is important because _____.
- Other important information about _____ is _____.
- In conclusion, _____.
- After considering all the information available about _____, we can conclude that _____.

10E A student's informative essay

Moreno 1

Carol Moreno

English 1122

Professor Fleming

12 Feb. 2012

Weight Lifting for Women

Last summer, after my grandmother fell and broke her hip, I wanted to help care for her. Because she was bedridden, she needed to be lifted at times. I was shocked to discover that I could not lift her fragile frame of 90 pounds without my brother's help. At least I could tend to her in other ways, especially by reading aloud to her, which she loved. Still, my pride was hurt, so I signed up for a Physical Education class at the local community college in weight lifting for women. The course brochure captured my interest immediately because it said that women can indeed "pump iron" as long as they learn how to do so properly.

What excited me the most about the weight lifting course for women was that my career goal was to be a nurse. Once my two children were old enough to go to school all day, I intended to start my studies. Nursing care for the elderly had always

*Introductory paragraph uses ethical and emotional appeals (*ethos* and *logos*), telling an anecdote to set the stage for the essay's information.*

Thesis statement presents writer's point of view about the topic.

Topic sentence ties into the thesis statement and the information in this paragraph about the writer's career goal.

continued >>

Moreno 2

Background
body
paragraph
tells how
the writer's
career goal
fits with her
experience
with her
grandmother.

appealed to me. My experience with my grandmother proved
how important physical strength would be in nursing. Although
in the United States the elderly usually are not revered as
much as they are in Asian countries, I had great respect for my
grandparents. They all lived nearby, and I would seek them out
to tell me their life stories. For example, my grandmother who
had broken her hip had lived in Nairobi, Kenya, for ten years as

Specific
details name
a location
and job.

a U.S. Trade Representative to various African countries. She
had to have been a strong, resourceful woman. Not being able
to lift her when she was ill really upset me.

Topic
sentence ties
into thesis
statement
and leads into
information
about
biology.

The first fact that I learned in my course for women
lifting weights was we can rely on our biology to protect us
from developing masculine-looking muscle mass. Women's
bodies produce only small amounts of the hormones that
enlarge muscles in men. If women want to be bodybuilders and

Specific
details name
two titles.

compete for titles such as Ms. Olympia and Ms. International,
they need to take supplements to alter their chemistry so
that their muscles become bulkier rather than longer. The
students in my class did not want that look. We wanted smooth,
firm muscles, not massive bulges. Aside from gaining nicer
looking muscles, some students said from the start that they
expected the course to help them lose weight. Our teacher had
disappointing news for them. Muscles actually weigh more

Specific
details give
factual
information.

than fat. The good news was that when our flab turned into
muscle, we would lose inches from our limbs and waist. Those
students might not weigh less, but they would look slimmer.

Striving for strength can end in injury unless weight
lifters learn the safe use of free weights and weight machines.
Free weights are barbells, the metal bars that round metal

continued >>

Moreno 3

weights can be attached to at each end. To be safe, no matter how little the weight, lifters must never raise a barbell by bending at the waist. Instead, they should squat, grasp the barbell, and then use their leg muscles to straighten into a standing position. To avoid a twist that can lead to serious injury, lifters must use this posture: head erect and facing forward, back and neck aligned. The big advantage of weight machines, which use weighted handles and bars hooked to wires and pulleys, is that lifters must use them sitting down. Therefore, machines like the Nautilus and Universal actually force lifters to keep their bodies properly aligned, which drastically reduces the chance of injury.

Writer uses logical appeal (logos).

Once a weight lifter understands how to lift safely, she needs a regimen personalized to her physical needs. Because benefits come from "resistance," which is the stress that lifting weight puts on a muscle, no one has to be strong to get started. A well-planned, progressive weight-training program begins with whatever weight a person can lift comfortably and gradually adds to the base weight as she gets stronger. What builds muscle strength is the number of repetitions, or "reps," the lifter does, not necessarily the addition of weight. Our instructor helped the women, who ranged from 18 to 43, scrawny to pudgy, and couch potato to superstar, to develop a program that was right for our individual weight, age, and overall level of conditioning. Everyone's program differed in how much weight to start out with and how many reps to do for each exercise. Our instructor urged us to not try more weight or reps than our programs called for, even if our first workouts seemed too easy. This turned out to be good advice because

Writer uses specific details for an emotional appeal (pathos).

continued >>

Moreno 4

Writer uses humor for ethical appeal (*ethos*). those of us who did not listen woke up the next day feeling as though evil forces had twisted our bodies.

Topic sentence ties back to essay's thesis statement and uses transition "in addition." In addition to fitting a program to her physical capabilities, a female weight lifter needs to design an individual routine to fit her personal goals. Most students in my class wanted to improve their upper body strength, so we focused on exercises to strengthen our arms, shoulders,

Specific details give factual information about biology. abdomens, and chests. Each student worked on specifically tailored exercises to isolate certain muscle groups. Because muscles toughen up and grow when they are rested after a workout, our instructor taught us to alternate muscle groups on different days. For example, a student might work on her

Writer uses ethical appeal (*ethos*). arms and abdomen one day and then her shoulders and chest the next day. Because I had had such trouble lifting my grandmother, I added exercises to strengthen my legs and back. Another student had hurt her neck in a car crash, so she added exercises that focused exclusively on her neck and upper shoulders. Someone else who was planning to be

Closing sentence sums up the discussion and leads into the concluding paragraph. a physical therapist added finger and hand-strengthening routines. By the middle of the term, we each had our specific, personal routine to use during class and continue once the term ended.

Opening sentence starts drawing the essay to a logical end. At the end of our 10 weeks of weight training, we had to evaluate our progress. Was I impressed! I felt ready to lift the world. If my grandmother were still bedridden, I could lift

Specific detail ties into the anecdote in the introductory paragraph. her with ease. When I started, I could not lift 10 pounds over my head twice. Midterm, I could lift that much only for four repetitions. By the end of the course, I could lift 10 pounds over

continued >>

Moreno 5

my head for 15 repetitions, and I could lift 18 pounds for two
repetitions. Also, I could swim laps for 20 sustained minutes
instead of the five I had barely managed at first. In conclusion,
I am so proud of my accomplishments that I still work out three
or four times a week. I am proof that any woman can benefit
from "pumping iron." After all, there isn't anything to lose—
except some flab.

> Specific
> details
> wrap up the
> student's
> experience.
>
> Concluding
> sentences
> tie to essay's
> thesis
> statement
> and end
> with humor.

11 Essays Analyzing a Text

■ ■ ■ ■ ■ ■ ■ ■

Quick Points   You will learn to

➤ Describe key elements of textual analysis essays (see 11A).
➤ Apply the writing process to your textual analysis (pp. 96–97).
➤ Adapt frames and guides for a textual analysis to your own needs
  (pp. 97–99).

11A What is textual analysis?

A **textual analysis** essay is either (a) a content analysis that explains the meaning of a text, such as an article, a book, a Web site, a poem, a script, a song, or so on; or (b) a rhetorical analysis that explains how a text works to achieve a certain purpose or effect. Some textual analyses combine the two. Examples of textual analysis are papers that explain, for example, how women are portrayed in popular songs; what sources an historian uses to explain an event; how the images in a photo-essay create a certain meaning; what biases are evident in a politician's speech; or how characters, themes, imagery, or word choices develop meaning in a short story. To analyze a text, use this four-step process.

Watch
the Video

1. **Make sure you understand the text** by reading or viewing it carefully and critically (see Chapter 4) and perhaps doing research to understand its context.

2. **Identify the text's separate elements or features**, such as ideas, words, figures of speech, evidence, and references. Pay attention to patterns or connections between elements.

3. **Explain the meaning of the elements** you've identified. What INFERENCES can you make from them? What effect might they have on the reader? On you?

4. **Explain the meaning that you've identified** by providing evidence and using sound reasoning.

■ Purpose

Textual analyses can have two purposes: (1) if they're descriptive analyses, they explain some features or patterns in a text, what they mean, and/or how they function; or (2) if they're evaluative analyses to describe features as well as judge them. (For more about purposes for writing, see 5D.)

■ Audience

Many audiences of textual analysis are academic: your instructors, other students, people who read scholarly journals, and so on. It is important in the humanities and social sciences including English, history, anthropology, law, marketing, and so on.

At times, textual analysis can also have a broader public audience, such as for book and movie reviews.

Whether your audience is academic or popular, take care to explain the text that's your focus, using SUMMARY or DESCRIPTION. Remember always that your readers will probably not have the text you're discussing in front of them nor will they be as familiar with the text as you are. Still, one major pitfall in writing a textual analysis is offering almost exclusively only SUMMARY and sacrificing analysis and evaluation. (For more about audience, see 5E.)

11B How do I generate ideas for a rhetorical or content analysis?

Watch
the Video

Usually, your instructors will assign a text to analyze, but sometimes you need to choose the specific text from a broad category, such as an advertisement, a newspaper editorial, or a Web site. If so, choose a text with enough features and elements to support a suitable analysis.

■ Generating ideas for a rhetorical analysis

A basic **rhetorical analysis** explains how the writer tries to influence his or her readers. It focuses on the three major rhetorical principles, also called the three persuasive appeals (see 3B): logic (*logos*), ethical credibility (*ethos*), and compassion and empathy (*pathos*). It can answer questions such as what is the text's main point? what are the text's secondary points? what support or evidence exists for the points such as expert opinions, stories, examples, analogies, or statistics? who seems to be the audience for this text and what gives you that impression?

■ Generating ideas for a content analysis

A **content analysis** focuses on the "what" of a text—its ideas or meanings—rather than on the "how." It can answer questions such as how do images or ideas in the text relate to each other, and what meanings does this create? if there are repetitions of images or phrases, why is this done? what kinds of evidence does the writer use or exclude?

■ Revising

- Do you use QUOTATION, SUMMARY, PARAPHRASE, or DESCRIPTION to explain the elements of the text you've identified?
- Do you discuss why you've identified those elements or how they tie to your THESIS STATEMENT?
- Is your analysis structured effectively? (See 11C.)
- Have you used appropriate CITATIONS? Do you have an appropriate WORKS CITED or REFERENCES page (see Chapters 24–31)?

11C What is a frame for a textual analysis?

Essays of textual analysis can be organized in many ways. Here's a possible frame you can adapt to the specifics of your assignments.

Frame for a Textual Analysis

Introductory paragraph

- **Capture your readers' interest** by using one of the strategies for writing effective introductory paragraphs (see 7B).
- **Present your thesis statement**, making sure it states the point of your analysis and offers your readers a concise preview of your essay (see 5G).

(continued)

Textual Analysis Frame (cont.)

Paragraph(s) summarizing the text

- **Characterize the text you're analyzing.** Provide information that readers will need to understand the text you're analyzing.
- **Summarize the source** and, if appropriate, information about its context: where it was published, what its purpose and audience was, etc.

Body paragraphs analyzing the text

- **Start each paragraph with a** TOPIC SENTENCE that makes a point about the text you're discussing.
- **Support each topic sentence** with specific information from the text, using quotations, summaries, or paraphrases.
- **Include discussion or explanation** that makes clear why you included the example and how it supports your topic sentence.

Evaluative paragraphs (if your assignment requires you to evaluate)

- **Start each paragraph with a topic sentence.** The topic sentence should judge the success or quality of an element you've analyzed.
- **Support topic sentences with reasons.** Include reasons and explanations that convince readers your judgment is acceptable.

Conclusion

- **Wrap up the essay.** Readers should finish the essay clearly understanding the points you've made. Most important, make clear why your analysis matters.

Works Cited or References

- **Include a Works Cited or References page.** Because you're analyzing a text, your readers will need clear information on how to find it. Follow the required style: MLA, APA, or Chicago.

11D What are some sentence and paragraph guides for textual analysis?

Adapt these guides to your PURPOSE and AUDIENCE.

Sentence and Paragraph Guides

- The writer attempts to _____ primarily by using the strategy of _____.
- The most significant feature (interesting aspect/important quality/etc.) of this text is _____ because _____.

Textual Analysis Guides (cont.)

- The writer uses emotional [or logical or ethical] appeals to create a sense of _____ in readers. Consider for example the statement that "_____" or the statement that "_____." The language of these passages suggests _____ because _____. Consider, for example, how different the emotional appeals would be if the wording had been _____.

- A noteworthy pattern in the text is _____. For example, at one point the writer states _____. At another she asserts _____. At a third, she claims _____. This pattern is significant because _____.

- Reading this text through _____'s theory that _____ reveals a key meaning.

11E A student's textual analysis

Gotlin-Sheehan 1

Matt Gotlin-Sheehan

Professor Hesse

WRIT 1622

17 Nov. 2011

Rhetorical Strategies in Two Airport Security Web Sites

Is the current level of security screening at American airports a patriotic way to safeguard travelers, or is it a ruthless assault by power-crazed bureaucrats? Most people are somewhere between these two positions; they might be annoyed by things they have to do to board a plane, but they find the experience reasonable and serving a good purpose. Other people, though, hold an extreme view. For example, the group We Won't Fly protests, "We will not be treated like criminals," while the federal government's Transportation Security Administration (TSA), soothes, "Your safety is our priority." Analyzing the web sites of these two groups reveals not only contrasting messages but also quite different rhetorical strategies for delivering them.

Opening sentence captures attention by stating two options.

Thesis statement sets up promise to discuss both the content and the strategies of two different texts.

continued >>

Gotlin-Sheehan 2

Paragraph of background information orients readers.

Airport security measures changed drastically following the September 11, 2001, attacks. Previously, private companies performed airport security and passenger screenings. However, in November 2001 the Transportation Security Administration (TSA) was created to standardize security practices and promote safer travel. In the decade that followed, a few incidents and threats persuaded the TSA to enhance their measures, culminating in full-body scanners and passenger pat downs. These practices have been the subject of intense scrutiny, criticism, and ridicule, especially over the Internet.

Topic sentence tells readers this paragraph will give arguments against the current level of airport security.

Wewontfly.com voices anger over airport security. The ultimate point of the site is to convince visitors that the TSA security procedures are invasive. Adorned with aggressive imagery, such as mock scanner images underneath a foreboding red "no" symbol, the site has bold headlines: "Act Now. Travel With Dignity" and "Stop Flying Until the Scanners and Gropers are Gone." Characterizing the screening

Writer appeals to logic (*logos*) with information and emotions (*pathos*) by quoting inflammatory language.

agents as "gropers" associates them with sex offenders and criminals, not faithful public servants, and it casts travelers as innocent victims. This strong language is reinforced by the "distressed" fonts used for the headlines on the page, as seen in Figure 1.

Inserting a screen capture of the Web site provides a helpful visual. It also confirms the writer's credibility (*ethos*) by showing an example.

Figure 1   Heading from the home page for http://wewontfly .com.

continued >>

Gotlin-Sheehan 3

The main rhetorical strategy is to arouse readers'
emotions. The page calls the TSA "ineffective and dangerous"
as well as a "health risk." The site claims that security
scanners may cause radiation poisoning, and that screeners
don't change gloves between pat-downs, increasing the chance
of spreading harmful contagion like lice. The emotional appeals
are heightened by passenger stories reported on the site's
blog. In one of them, a passenger named Elizabeth narrates
in detail how she was "a victim of a government sanctioned
sexual assault." Another anonymous poster explains that she
had once been raped, so that being touched against her will, as
during a search, was traumatic. Because physical modesty is
a strong cultural value and people regard sexual assault as a
particularly offensive crime, these stories might upset people.
They imply that, if disturbing things can happen in such graphic
detail to others, they can also happen to me, my friends, or
family.

In general, the site uses examples and stories rather than
statistics or other kinds of evidence to support its claims. As
a result, logical appeals are minimal. Consider the following
argument:

> Al-Qaeda is an agile, networked organization. It's
> peer-to-peer. The TSA is a top-down, lumbering
> bureaucracy. Al-Qaeda operatives are passionate
> and motivated. TSA employees are order-takers.
> There is simply no contest between these two types of
> organizational structures. It's like David and Goliath,
> the Viet Cong vs the US Army, Luke vs the Death Star.
> The TSA is structurally incapable of defending

Emotional appeals (pathos) are focus of this paragraph.

Two specific examples arouse readers' sense of compassion, an aspect of an emotional appeal (pathos).

To make the point most clearly, the writer includes an extended block quotation.

continued >>

Gotlin-Sheehan 4

against this threat, just as the US Army was
structurally incapable of defeating the Viet Cong.

Writer explains and analyzes the long quotation. Thus, the writer uses a logical appeal (*logos*).

Many readers will probably find the analogies between the
TSA and Goliath, the American army in Vietnam, and the
Death Star clever, perhaps even convincing. However, the site
provides no evidence to support these claims. The TSA may or
may not be a "lumbering bureaucracy," but there aren't enough
facts or evidence in this paragraph to make an informed
judgment about the truth of this claim.

Transitional sentence to the next text also serves as a topic sentence for the paragraph.

The TSA (www.tsa.gov) site also uses emotional and
ethical appeals, but to a very different effect. Featuring
smooth, clean lines, soothing shades of blue, and calming
photos of empty airports, the site implies "It's all cool. Relax!"
The site's banner features the slogan "Your Safety Is Our
Priority," and information for travelers and the media, along
with explanations of "Our Approach" suggest that the TSA has
nothing to hide. The site is easy to navigate, looks clean, and
presents visitors with extensive information, in a systematic
manner. Figure 2 shows a page from the site.

Topic sentence announces the theme of the paragraph, which provides examples, with quotations and discussion.

The TSA tries to project a personality of friendship and
common purpose. It identifies employees as "your neighbors,
friends, and relatives" who work hard so that "you and your
family can travel safely." Rather than being distant or harsh
bureaucrats, TSA workers are presented as just like us, sharing
our values and interested in our safety. The site portrays
them as hard working. They "look for bombs," "inspect rail
cars," and "patrol subways." A worker "saves a life" or "helps
a stranded motorist," suggesting that the TSA goes beyond
faithfully performing assigned duties to help people in need.

continued >>

Gotlin-Sheehan 5

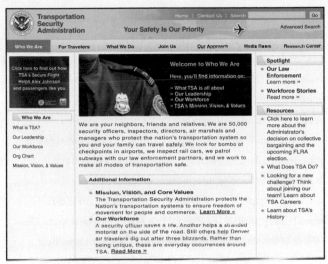

Figure 2   Page from TSA Web site: www.tsa.gov/who_we_are/
index.shtm.

These techniques are designed to provide comfort to, and instill
confidence in, the TSA.

However, the most striking rhetorical strategy on the TSA
site is the extensive use of logical appeals. The information
available ranges from poll results and surveys to news articles
and television reports from credible sources like *USA Today*.
An entire tab is devoted to "Research," which is divided into
three main headings and fourteen subheadings, each of which
lists numerous facts. "Screening Statistics," for example,
notes that, "We screened 708,400,522. The average wait time
was 3.79 minutes and the average peak wait time was 11.76
minutes." Clearly, then, the TSA site puts a strong emphasis
on knowledge. Suggesting that airline passengers understand
TSA security policies *before* they arrive at the airport seems
designed to make people less upset by surprise procedures.

Inserting a screen capture of the Web site provides a helpful visual element. It also confirms the writer's credibility (*ethos*) by showing a concrete example.

The writer saves the most important rhetorical strategy, logic (*logos*), for this paragraph, introducing it with a clear topic sentence.

Writer uses RENNS (see 7D) to give readers specific details to bring the material alive.

continued >>

Gotlin-Sheehan 6

"What to know before you go" explains various traveling scenarios, and a search bar tells passengers whether they can take particular items through a checkpoint. The strategy seems to be one of overwhelming travelers with mountains of information so that TSA looks like it's thorough, open, and cooperative, and that travelers have nothing to fear.

Once again, the writer goes beyond simply summarizing to include discussion of its meaning.

The two Web sites will succeed with different types of visitors. Chances are that an anti-government activist will distrust the extensive information on the TSA site. Likewise, a staunch supporter of U.S. security measures after 9/11 would likely scoff at *We Won't Fly's* emotional outbursts. The two sites employ rhetorical strategies that reinforce their audience's biases. Sites like *www.wewontfly*.com succeed when they make readers feel threatened, uncomfortable, and angry by using powerful slogans and anecdotes. They fail when they lack the evidence of just how legitimate and

A balanced conclusion that uses a logical appeal (*logos*) and shows the that writer is fair minded, an emotional appeal (*ethos*).

widespread concerns are. Sites like *www.tsa.gov* succeed when they reassure readers with information and facts delivered by competent and friendly people who have their interests in mind. They may be less successful when they fail to demonstrate whether they can prevent the dangerous situations they're trying to prevent.

Gotlin-Sheehan 7

Works Cited appears alone on the next page in the actual paper.

Works Cited

Transportation Security Administration. "Who We Are."
    Transportation Security Administration, 2011. Web.
    15 Nov. 2011.

Wewontfly.com. 2011. Web. 15 Nov. 2011.

12 Arguments

Quick Points You will learn to

> Describe key elements of arguments (see 12A).
> Apply the writing process to an argument (pp. 107–109).
> Adapt frames and guides for an argument to your own needs (pp. 109–111).

12A What is an argument?

A written ARGUMENT consists of

Watch the Video

- A THESIS STATEMENT (also called a *claim*) that clearly presents the topic to be debated in the essay and sets forth the writer's opinion regarding that topic
- **Support** for the writer's position on the debatable topic, consisting of reasons, with EVIDENCE, EXAMPLES, and logical explanations to back them up

If you were to judge the nature of arguments only by the popular media, you might think arguments are simply name-calling or fighting. For college-level writing, however, arguments need to demonstrate CRITICAL THINKING and sound reasoning (see Chapter 3).

■ Purpose

The goal of your argument essay is try to convince readers to believe or do something. In some instances, you can't reasonably expect to change a person's mind, especially on highly controversial issues like capital punishment or a woman's right to choose. In those cases, your purpose is to demonstrate that your point of view is thoughtful and has good reasoning behind it.

Sometimes instructors assign students a position to argue. In such cases, even if you personally disagree with it, you need to reason logically and effectively.

If instructors tell you to select your own topic, choose one suitable for college writing. For example, "Should public libraries block certain Web sites?" is worthy of a college-level essay. In contrast, "Which color is best for baseball caps?" is not. (For more about purposes for writing, see 5D.)

Arguments fall into four general categories, as explained in Quick Box 12.1.

> ### Quick Box 12.1
>
> ### Purposes and types of arguments
>
> - **Definition arguments** persuade readers to interpret a term or concept in a particular way. Is something a "work of art," or is it "obscene"? Is assisted suicide "murder" or "a medical procedure" or an "act of kindness"? What characteristics must a film have to be called a romantic comedy?
>
> - **Evaluation arguments** persuade readers that something is good or bad, worthwhile or a waste of time, or better or worse than other things like it. We explain evaluation arguments further in Chapter 14.
>
> - **Cause and effect arguments** take two different forms. One argues that a situation results from a particular cause. For example, you might argue that certain causes are most responsible for homelessness. Another argues that an action will have a specific effect. For example, you might argue that if we built more nuclear power plants, we would reduce global warming.
>
> - **Proposal or solution arguments** convince readers that a particular solution to a problem or a particular way of addressing a need is best. For more about proposal and solution arguments, see Chapter 13.

■ Audience

More than any other kind of writing, arguments require being sensitive to readers' interests and needs. You always want to analyze what your readers know and, more important, what they already believe about the topic. What are their values, viewpoints, and assumptions? As you present your argument, you want to demonstrate your command of CRITICAL THINKING, especially how you carefully avoid LOGICAL FALLACIES. The approach most commonly used for such arguments is known as CLASSICAL ARGUMENT. Section 12C offers you a frame for it.

Some readers hold extreme or one-sided opinions. Your arguments can rarely change the minds of such people. Still, you're expected to demonstrate that you can use sound reasoning and avoid logical fallacies when you address such readers. If you think that your audience is likely to read your point of view with hostility, you might consider using the approach to argument known as **Rogerian argument**. It's based on psychologist Carl Rogers's communication principles, which suggest that even hostile readers can respect your position, if you show that you understand their viewpoint and treat it with respect. Section 12C offers you a frame for a Rogerian argument.

For more about audience, see 5E.

12B How do I plan and revise arguments?

Generating ideas

- Make sure your topic is open to debate. For example, "We will eventually run out of fossil fuels" is not a debatable topic. "We should require car makers to increase mileage by 50 percent" is.

Watch
the Video

- Check that your topic is open to debate by testing whether it answers a question that could receive more than one possible answer. Here's an example of how to check.

TOPIC	Students at Mitchler College must study a foreign language.
DEBATABLE QUESTION	Should Mitchler College require students to study a foreign language?
FIRST ANSWER	Mitchler College should not require students to study a foreign language.
SECOND ANSWER	Mitchler College should require students to study a foreign language.
THIRD ANSWER	Mitchler College should require all business majors to study a foreign language.

All answers show that the topic is open to debate.

Alex Garcia, the biology major who wrote the argument essay that appears in section 12E, was interested in whether organic food was really better. Here's how Alex progressed from topic to claim to thesis statement.

DEBATABLE QUESTION	Are organic foods better than regular foods?
MY POSITION	I think people should buy organic foods when they can.
THESIS STATEMENT (FIRST DRAFT)	It is good for people to buy organic foods.
	This is a preliminary thesis statement. It clearly states the writer's position, but the word *good* is vague.
THESIS STATEMENT (SECOND DRAFT)	To achieve health benefits and improve the quality of the environment, organic foods should be purchased by consumers.
	This revised thesis statement is better because it states the writer's claim as well as a reason for the claim. However, it suffers from a lack of conciseness and from the unnecessary passive construction "should be purchased."
THESIS STATEMENT (FINAL DRAFT)	Research shows that the health and environmental benefits of organic foods outweigh their extra costs.
	This final version works well because it states the writer's claim clearly and concisely, with verbs all in the active voice. This thesis statement is suitable for the time and length given in the assignment. It also meets the requirements for a thesis statement given in Quick Box 5.9.

- Use the three principles of rhetoric, known as the persuasive appeals, explained in 3B: logical appeal (*logos*), ethical appeal (*ethos*), and emotional appeal (*pathos*).

- Use CRITICAL THINKING techniques. One strategy for generating and analyzing logical appeals was developed by philosopher Stephen Toulmin and is explained in Quick Box 12.2.

- Ask yourself *why* you take the position you do on your debatable topic. When you respond, "Because . . . ," you're ready to offer reasons.

- List the pros (in favor) and cons (against) your position.

- Consider the kinds of evidence that could be useful: facts, statistics, expert testimony, personal experience, analogies, and so on (also see RENNS, 7D).

- Arrange your possible reasons in logical order, which might suitably become TOPIC SENTENCES of your paragraphs.

- Decide whether support for your position involves research. (See Chapters 18–23.)

Revising

- Does your essay take a clear position on your debatable topic?

- Do your reasons and evidence support your argument?

- Is your evidence sufficient, representative, relevant, and accurate (see 21D)?

- Do you use logical, emotional, and ethical appeals (*logos, pathos*, and *ethos*) appropriately to convince your audience (see 3B)?

- Have you avoided logical fallacies (see 3D)?

Quick Box 12.2

Toulmin method for analyzing arguments

1. **Look for claims.** Identify all the main assertions in an argument.

2. **Identify and evaluate data (support).** The term *data* refers to evidence or support. Claims are unsupported if they have no data or if the data is weak.

3. **Identify warrants.** WARRANTS are the assumptions, often unstated, that connect data or reasons to claims. For example, in "We should not elect Daniels as mayor because she is divorced," the warrant (which is unstated) is, "Divorced people shouldn't be elected." Certainly that is open to debate. On the other hand, in "We should elect Daniels as mayor because she served in the Military," the warrant (which is stated) is "Military service is good preparation for public office." Why? The answer will help you generate reasons and support.

- Have you anticipated objections or counterarguments that others might have?
- Is your tone reasonable, thoughtful, and fair?

12C What are frames for arguments?

Successful arguments can take many forms. We present here two possible frames—one for classical argument and one for Rogerian argument—to adapt to the specifics of your assignments.

Frame for a Classical Argument

Introductory paragraph(s)

- **Capture your readers' interest** by using one of the strategies for writing effective introductory paragraphs (See 7B).
- **Present your THESIS STATEMENT**, making sure it makes the central point that you will argue.

Body paragraph(s): background information

- **Provide background** for the information in your essay. This might follow the introductory paragraph or come later in the essay at a point when the background is more relevant.
- **Start with a TOPIC SENTENCE** that clearly relates to your thesis statement and leads logically to the information in the paragraph.

Body paragraphs: Reasons to support your claim

- **Present reasons for your argument**, one to a paragraph. If a reason is very complicated, use two paragraphs divided at a logical point.
- **Start each paragraph with a topic sentence** that states your reason.
- **Support each topic sentence** with evidence, examples, and reasoning (see RENNS, 7D).

Body Paragraphs: Rebuttal

- **Present objections and answer them**. State reasons that someone might give against your position. Answer these criticisms by explaining why your position is stronger.
- **Start each paragraph with a topic sentence** that helps your readers follow your line of reasoning.

Conclusion

- **Wrap up the essay**, often with a summary of the argument.
- **Present an elaboration of the argument's significance**, or a call to action for the readers or use one of the strategies for an effective concluding paragraph listed in Quick Box 7.4.

Frame for a Rogerian Argument

Introductory paragraph(s)

- **Capture your readers' interest** by using one of the strategies for writing effective introductory paragraphs (See 7B).
- **Present your thesis statement**, making sure it makes the central point that you will argue.

Body paragraph(s): Establish common ground with readers

- **Explain the issue**, acknowledging that some readers probably don't agree with you.
- **Explain the points of agreement** you and your readers probably share concerning underlying problems or issues.
- **Summarize opposing positions** and even acknowledge ways that some of them may be desirable. This may take one paragraph or several, depending on the complexity of the issue.
- **Start each paragraph with a** TOPIC SENTENCE that ties into your thesis statement and previews the content of the paragraph.

Body paragraphs: Reasons to support your claim

- **Present reasons for your claim**, one to a paragraph.
- **Start each paragraph with a topic sentence** that states your reason.
- **Support each topic sentence** with evidence, examples, and reasoning.

Conclusion

- **Use an engaging strategy** for a concluding paragraph (see 7G).
- **Summarize why your position is preferable** to your opponent's. Use a reasonable tone.

12D What are some sentence and paragraph guides for arguments?

Adapt these guides to your PURPOSE and AUDIENCE.

Sentence and Paragraph Guides

- The main reason [the most compelling argument] is _____. Recent statistics show that _____. These statistics are important because _____.

Argument Guides (cont.)

- Many experts support this position. For example, _____, who is _____, has argued "_____." _____ makes a similar point by explaining _____. The significance of this quotation is _____.

- I understand that my opponents believe _____. I respect their reasoning that _____ and also that _____. In fact, one thing we have in common is _____.

- Some people might oppose my position by arguing that _____. They might explain that _____, and they might point to support such as _____. However, this argument fails to take into account _____. Furthermore, other evidence suggests a different conclusion, namely _____. Ultimately, this opposing argument is unconvincing because _____.

12E A student's argument essay

Garcia 1

Alex Garcia

Professor Brosnahan

WRIT 1122

4 Oct. 2012

Why Organic Foods Are Worth the Cost

Judging from cable television, many Americans apparently like talking about or watching food being made almost as much as eating it. A mainstay of these cooking programs and competitions, from Top Chef to Iron Chef, is an emphasis on fine ingredients. Beyond the caviar, truffles, and lobster, however, one small quality gets big attention: organic. Increasingly, that word matters not only on the Food Network but also in supermarkets, where displays of similar fruits and vegetables differ by cost and a tiny sticker reading "organic."

View the Model Document

Writer uses a popular reference to get readers' attention, introduces a key debatable question, and states the thesis of the paper in his last sentence.

Writer uses a logical appeal (*logos*), even though he intends to disagree with it.

continued >>

Garcia 2

Are organics worth the extra money, especially when budgets are tight? Have American consumers simply fallen victim, yet again, to peer pressure and advertising? After all, even the United States Department of Agriculture (USDA) "makes no claims that organically produced food is safer or more nutritious than conventionally produced food." Despite all the confusion, current research shows that the health and environmental benefits of organic foods outweigh their extra costs.

Organic foods are produced without using most chemical pesticides, without artificial fertilizers, without genetic engineering, and without radiation (USDA). In the case of organic meat, poultry, eggs, and dairy products, the animals are raised without antibiotics or growth hormones. As a result, people sometimes use the term "natural" instead of "organic," but "natural" is less precise. Before 2002, people could never be quite sure what they were getting when they bought supposedly organic food, unless they bought it directly from a farmer they knew personally. In 2002, the USDA established standards that food must meet in order to be labeled and sold as organic.

Organic foods do tend to cost more than nonorganic, even up to 50% more (Zelman), mainly because they are currently more difficult to mass-produce. Farmers who apply pesticides often get larger crops from the same amount of land because there is less insect damage. Artificial fertilizers tend to increase the yield, size, and uniformity of fruits and vegetables, and herbicides kill weeds that compete with desirable crops

Writer provides background information, making sure that readers understand what "organic" means.

A second paragraph of background information. Because cost is a key issue, this entire paragraph explains why organic foods are expensive.

continued >>

Garcia 3

for sun, nutrients, and moisture. Animals that routinely receive antibiotics and growth hormones tend to grow more quickly and produce more milk and eggs. In contrast, organic farmers have lower yields and, therefore, higher costs. These get passed along as higher prices to consumers.

Still, the extra cost is certainly worthwhile in terms of health benefits. Numerous studies have shown the dangers of pesticides for humans. An extensive review of research by the Ontario College of Family Physicians concludes that "Exposure to all the commonly used pesticides . . . has shown positive associations with adverse health effects" (Sanborn et al. 173). The risks include cancer, psychiatric effects, difficulties becoming pregnant, miscarriages, and dermatitis. Carefully washing fruits and vegetables can remove some of these dangerous chemicals, but according to the prestigious journal *Nature*, even this does not remove all of them (Giles 797). An extensive review of research by medical professor Denis Lairon found that "the vast majority (94–100%) of organic food does not contain any pesticide residues (38). Certainly, if there's a way to prevent these poisons from entering our bodies, we should take advantage of it. The few cents saved on cheaper food can quickly disappear in doctors' bills needed to treat conditions caused or worsened by chemicals.

Organic meat, poultry, and dairy products can address another health concern: the diminishing effectiveness of antibiotics. In the past decades, many kinds of bacteria have become resistant to drugs, making it extremely difficult to treat some kinds of tuberculosis, pneumonia, staphylococcus

Writer uses an ethical appeal (*ethos*) to arouse readers' concern for their health.

Writer uses an emotional appeal (*pathos*) and gives the first main reason in support of the thesis. Details explain the dangers of pesticides in foods, and three expert studies provide support.

A second reason in favor of organic foods. The writer uses careful reasoning to explain it.

continued >>

Garcia 4

infections, and less serious diseases ("Dangerous" 1). True, this
has happened mainly because doctors have over-prescribed
antibiotics to patients who expect a pill for every illness.
However, routinely giving antibiotics to all cows and chickens
means that these drugs enter our food chain early, giving
bacteria lots of chances to develop resistance. A person who
switches to organic meats won't suddenly experience better
results from antibiotics; the benefit is a more gradual one for
society as a whole. However, if we want to be able to fight
infections with effective drugs, we need to reserve antibiotics
for true cases of need and discourage their routine use in
animals raised for food. Buying organic is a way to persuade
more farmers to adopt this practice.

Writer uses logical, ethical, and emotional appeals (*logos, ethos,* and *pathos*).

Another benefit of organic foods is also a societal one:
Organic farming is better for the environment. In his review of
several studies, Colin Macilwain concluded that organic farms
nurture more and diverse plants and animals than regular
farms (797). Organic farms also don't release pesticides and
herbicides that can harm wildlife and run into our water
supply, with implications for people's health, too. Macilwain
notes that those farms also can generate less carbon dioxide,
which will help with global warming; also, many scientists
believe that organic farming is more sustainable because it
results in better soil quality (798). Once again, these benefits
are not ones that you will personally experience right away.
However, a better natural environment means a better quality
of living for everyone and for future generations.

Writer explains a third reason, again using an expert source in support.

By arousing the "better self" of readers, the writer uses an ethical appeal (*ethos*).

Some critics point out that organic products aren't more
nutritious than regular ones. Four years ago, media star and

continued >>

Garcia 5

physician Sanjay Gupta, for example, found the medical evidence for nutritional advantages is "thin" (60), and the *Tufts University Health and Nutrition Letter* reported that the research on nutritional benefits is mixed, ("Is Organic" 8). However, other studies differ. For example, research shows that organically raised tomatoes have higher levels of flavonoids, nutrients that have many health benefits (Mitchell et al.). More recently, both Denis Lairon and Walter J. Crinnion found higher levels of several nutrients in organic found. Nutritional value, which includes qualities such as vitamins and other beneficial substances, is a different measure than food safety. Even if the nutritional evidence is uncertain, food safety from avoiding chemicals and environmental quality remain convincing reasons to purchase organic food.

> Writer acknowledges an objection and even cites expert opinions that contradict his argument. However, he counters those objections and concludes with a strong comment in support of organic foods.

> Writer uses logical and emotional appeals (*logos* and *pathos*) to try to convince his readers.

One point has to be conceded. Claims that organic foods taste better are probably groundless. Researchers at Cornell University gave people identical chips, yogurt, and cookies but labeled some of them "organic" and others "regular." People rated the organic ones as better tasting even though there was no difference ("Even Organic"). Labels clearly shape our perceptions.

> Writer concedes a possible objection. This builds an ethical case (*ethos*) by showing writer is open-minded.

Despite considerable benefits for purchasing organic products, consumers have to make individual purchasing decisions. There are no simple ways to measure that spending fifty cents more on a cantaloupe will improve my quality of life by fifty cents. However, there is a position between all organics and none. The nonprofit Environmental Working Group identifies a dozen types of organic produce (including apples, strawberries, and spinach) as safer and worth the extra cost,

> Concluding paragraph returns to issues of cost in the thesis statement, summarizes the reasons the paper has provided, and ends with a strong call for action.

continued >>

Garcia 6

but they conclude another dozen are not, including bananas, pineapples, and onions (Zelman). The bottom line is that countless people are rightly concerned these days about our personal health and the health of the world in which we live. It's nearly impossible to put a value on a sustainable, diverse natural environment and having the physical health to enjoy it. The long-term benefits of buying organic, for anyone who can reasonably afford to, far outweigh the short-term savings in the checkout line.

The writer ends by appealing to logic, ethics, and emotions (*logos, ethos,* and *pathos*).

Garcia 7

Works Cited

In an actual paper, the Works Cited appears alone on a new page.

"Dangerous Bacterial Infections Are on the Rise." *Consumer Reports on Health* (Nov. 2007): 1-4. Print.

Crinnion, Walter J. "Organic Foods Contain Higher Levels of Certain Nutrients, Lower Levels of Pesticides, and May Provide Health Benefits for the Consumer." *Alternative Medicine Review* 15.1 (Apr. 2010): 4-12. Web. 14 Sept. 2011.

"Even Organic Cookies and Chips Enjoy Health 'Halo'." *Tufts University Health and Nutrition Letter* 29.5 (July 2011): 3. Web. 12 Sept. 2011.

Giles, Jim. "Is Organic Food Better for Us?" *Nature* 428.6985 (2004): 796-97. Print.

continued >>

Garcia 8

Gupta, Sanjay, and Shahreen Abedin. "Rethinking Organics."
   Time (20 Aug. 2007): 60. Print.

"Is Organic Food Really More Nutritious?" *Tufts University Health and Nutrition Letter* (Sept. 2007): 8. Web. 25 Sept. 2011.

Lairon, Denis. "Nutritional Quality and Safety of Organic Food. A Review." *Agronomy for Sustainable Development* 30 (2010): 33-41. Web. 14 Sept. 2011.

Macilwain, Colin. "Is Organic Farming Better for the Environment?" *Nature* 428.6985 (2004): 797-98. Print.

Mitchell, Alyson E., et al. "Ten-Year Comparison of the Influence of Organic and Conventional Crop Management Practices on the Content of Flavonoids in Tomatoes." *Journal of Agricultural Food Chemistry* 55.15 (2007): 6154-59. Web. 30 Sept. 2011.

United States. Dept. of Agriculture. "Organic Food Labels and Standards: The Facts." National Organic Program. Jan. 2007. Web. 26 Sept. 2011.

Sanborn, Margaret, et al. *Pesticides Literature Review: Systematic Review of Pesticide Human Health Effects.* Toronto: Ontario College of Family Physicians, 2004. Web. 28 Sept. 2011.

Zelman, Kathleen M. "Organic Food—Is 'Natural' Worth the Extra Cost?" *WebMD*. 2007. Web. 17 Sept. 2011.

Quick Points   You will learn to

> Describe key elements of a proposal or solution essay (see 13A).
> Apply the writing process to a proposal or solution essay (pp. 119–120).
> Adapt frames and guides for a proposal or solution essay to your own needs (pp. 120–122).

13A   What are proposal or solution essays?

Watch the Video

Proposal or **solution essays** are specific types of ARGUMENTS (see Chapter 12) that require you to do three things:

1. Convince readers that a particular problem or opportunity exists and requires action.

2. Propose a specific solution or course of action and offer reasons for proposing it.

3. Defend your solution or proposal as better than others.

■ Purpose

Proposal or solution essays seek to persuade readers to act on a solution. In your essay, you need to address the problem you want to write about, your proposed solution(s), and the beliefs your readers hold about them. Here are two examples:

A. Problem: Students can't get the classes they need to graduate on time.

   Solution 1: The college should offer more courses by either (a) hiring more faculty, or (b) having faculty teach more students.

   Solution 2: The college should increase the number of popular or required courses it offers by cutting unpopular or elective courses.

   Solution 3: The college should change graduation requirements.

B. Problem: Unemployment is high.

   Solution 1: The government should hire unemployed people to build roads, bridges, parks, and other public projects.

   Solution 2: The government should reward businesses that hire people to work in this country or penalize businesses that send jobs overseas.

   Solution 3: Workers should be less choosey about the jobs they will accept, or they should start their own businesses.

In both examples, some people may deny a problem exists. They might think students are graduating on time or that delays for graduation aren't a problem. They might not realize how many people are unemployed or consider high unemployment troublesome.

The preceding examples list several possible solutions, but no doubt you can think of others. Which solution would be best? Why? (For more about purposes for writing, see 5D.)

▪ Audience

Audiences for proposal or solution essays can range in size from small and immediate (such as a club to which you belong for which you write a fund-raising proposal) to large and distant (such as the U.S. Congress, for which you propose a law that solves a national problem).

In addition, consult Quick Box 13.1 for four other considerations of audience specifically for problem or solution essays. For more about audience, see 5E.

13B How do I plan and revise proposal or solution arguments?

Consult secton 12B for advice useful for generating arguments and their support, or use these questions for proposal or solution essays.

- **What caused the problem?** Complex problems usually have many possible causes so take time to brainstorm a list.

- **What are possible solutions?** Because each cause might have a different solution, don't rush into settling on one of them. Allow yourself time to be creative.

- **Why is your solution effective?** Who needs to be involved? What do they need to do? When? How? Why?

Quick Box 13.1

■ ■ ■ ■ ■ ■ ■ ■ ■

Four aspects of audience for problem or solution essays

1. **The audience doesn't know or agree that a problem exists.** Here explaining the problem is your most important task. You want to increase public awareness so that the desperate need for solutions becomes obvious, but your solution isn't your central concern.

2. **The audience generally agrees on a problem—but not on a solution.** Here you explain the problem briefly and spend your time and energy on writing about the value of your solution.

3. **The audience believes there's a problem, but it favors a different solution.** Here you emphasize why your solution is better (for instance, more practical, easier to achieve, less expensive) than theirs.

4. **The audience is in a direct position to act versus an indirect position.** Here you target your argument to the audience that has direct power to act or indirect power to influence. Sometimes both.

- **Why is your solution feasible?** A solution is feasible when it is practical and affordable. For example, we could solve poverty by giving every poor person $50,000 a year, but that's not feasible.

- **What are drawbacks of other solutions?** Apply questions of effectiveness and feasibility to all solutions to reveal weaknesses in alternative proposals. Also, you might consider unintended effects or results.

- **What will happen if people don't act?** This question can generate an effective conclusion and be a good source of emotional appeals (*pathos*).

Revising

- Have you established that there's a problem that needs a solution?
- Is your solution effective, feasible, and better than others?
- Have you used evidence that is sufficient, representative, relevant, and accurate (see 21D)?
- Have you used appropriate logical, emotional, and ethical appeals (*logos, pathos,* and *ethos;* see 3B)?
- Is your TONE reasonable, thoughtful, and fair?

13C What is a frame for a proposal or solution essay?

Here is a possible proposal/solution essay frame to adapt to the specifics of your assignments.

Frame for a Proposal or Solution Essay

Introductory paragraph(s)

- **Capture your readers' interest** in your topic by using one of the strategies for writing effective introductory paragraphs (see 7B).
- **Introduce** a problem or opportunity.
- **Present your THESIS STATEMENT**, making sure it proposes an action or solution (see 5G).

Body paragraph(s): Background information

- **Provide background information.** Note: If the background isn't complicated, your essay might move directly to persuading readers that a problem exists.
- **Start each paragraph with a TOPIC SENTENCE** that clearly relates to your thesis statement and leads logically to the information in the paragraph (see 7C).

Body paragraphs: Persuade readers that a problem exists

- **Explain the problem that exists**, grouping the parts of the problem effectively within separate paragraphs.
- **Start each paragraph with a TOPIC SENTENCE** that makes clear what you will explain in the paragraph.
- **Support each topic sentence** with evidence, examples, and reasoning.
- **If your emphasis is on the solution** because the problem is well known, keep this section short.

Solution paragraph(s)

- **Explain why your solution will be effective and feasible**.
- **Divide parts of your solution** into sensible paragraphs, starting each one with a topic sentence that leads into the point you are making.
- **If your emphasis is on the problem**, keep this section short.

Rebuttal paragraph(s): Place here or immediately before your solution

- **Present alternative solutions and refute them**. State other possible solutions and explain why they aren't as good as yours. Answer possible criticisms.
- **Again, if your emphasis is on the problem**, keep this section short.

Conclusion

- **Wrap up the essay** with one of the strategies for concluding paragraphs in 7G.
- **Summarize** your problem or solution.
- **Make a call to action** or portray the negative consequences of not acting or the clear benefits of adopting your solution.

13D What are some sentence and paragraph guides for proposal/solution essays?

Adapt these guides to your PURPOSE and AUDIENCE.

Sentence and Paragraph Guides

- The best way to solve the problem of _____ is by _____.
- To address the problem of _____, _____ (we, you, the city council, the board, parking services, etc.) should _____.
- There are _____ reasons the current situation is a problem. The first is _____. The second is _____. However, the most important is _____.
- The most effective and practical solution to this problem is _____. One result of implementing this solution would be _____. That's because _____. Another outcome would be _____. A potential difficulty of this solution is _____. However, we can overcome that difficulty by _____.
- Some other possible solutions would be to _____ or to _____. The first is problematic because _____. The second is impractical because _____. My solution is preferable to both alternatives because _____.
- Failing to take this action will have several negative consequences. First, _____. Furthermore, _____.

13E A student's solution essay

**View
the Model
Document**

Cui 1

Yanggu Cui

Professor Leade

Writing 102

10 Dec. 2012

**Quotations
get readers'
attention and
lead to the
introduction.**

A Proposal to Improve Fan Behavior at Children's Games

"Ref, you're an idiot!"

"You're blind as a bat and twice as stupid!"

continued >>

Cui 2

"Get a life, ref!"

"I'll see you after the game!"

Those were just a few yells I heard from the sidelines of a soccer game last Saturday. I wasn't watching a professional match or even a high school one. Instead, it was my eight year old cousin's game in the Arapahoe Recreation League. The referee wasn't a 30 year old professional but, rather, a skinny high school girl who seemed to be fifteen or sixteen. The people yelling weren't drunken guys in sweatshirts or even coaches with red faces and bulging neck veins; instead, they were moms and dads drinking lattes. The league organizers need to bring an end to this kind of abuse, and the best way to do so is by requiring all parents to sign a code of good behavior.

Parents for decades have proudly watched their sons and daughters play little league softball, baseball, soccer, and other sports. In recent years, these sports have gotten more competitive, with more games, longer seasons, more practices, and greater expectations for winning. One result is that parents have gotten more vocal on the sidelines, not only yelling encouragement for Julio and Jenny but also screaming protests at coaches, the opposing team, and officials. Almost every call against their team is greeted by a loud disbelief, at best, and insults or threats, at worst.

The current level of fan abuse is troubling for at least four reasons. First, it discourages officials, especially younger ones who are just learning the job themselves. No one fears making a wrong call more than someone who is just gaining experience as a referee. If parents make the job so unpleasant

Details create emotional appeals (*pathos*) by giving a picture of the events.

Introductory paragraph sets up the problem. In the thesis sentence at the end of the paragraph, the writer presents a solution.

By invoking parents with children, the writer appeals to emotions (*pathos*) and provides context about the issue.

Topic sentence announces four reasons for convincing readers that a problem exists and is a logical appeal (*logos*).

continued >>

Cui 3

that kids making minimum wage stop doing it, the games will come to a halt. Second, it makes what should be a fun recreational experience for all into an ordeal. Rather than paying attention to the game, players and spectators alike get distracted by the drama on the sidelines, even getting nervous that a physical confrontation or fight might occur. Third, it embarrasses the kids themselves. Parents might feel like their kids appreciate and value someone sticking up for them, but the truth of the matter is that most children would rather not have that particular kind of attention.

Each reason receives a brief explanation. Numbering creates clarity.

The fourth, and most distressing, problem is that fan abuse warps the nature of the game itself. At a time when participating, having fun, and learning new skills should be primary, young players get the clear message that only winning matters, winning at all costs. Rather than assuming that officials and others are trying their best to be impartial and fair, kids are being taught that people are incompetent and malicious. Rather than assuming that sometimes in life we make mistakes that get penalized, but life goes on, kids learn that they are rarely, if ever at fault. Rather than accepting adversity, even if sometimes it's wrong, kids learn to dwell on every hardship. The result is that, instead of learning lessons valuable for a happy life, kids learn to be intolerant and bitter, and they learn it from their parents.

The writer keeps the most important reason for last and devotes an entire paragraph to explaining it in detail.

Writer uses ethical and emotional appeals (*ethos* and *pathos*) by showing the negative influence on children.

It would be nice to assume that merely talking to parents would control the situation, but the situation actually requires a more active solution. The Arapahoe Recreational League should adopt a code of conduct for all parents, in the form of an agreement they must sign. This code should indicate

Writer introduces the solution and provides an explanation using a logical appeal (*logos*).

continued >>

Cui 4

fan behaviors that are approved and encouraged; these would include yelling encouragement or congratulations for all players. The code would also specify behaviors that are banned; these would include taunting or criticizing players, coaches, and officials. Children whose parents refuse to sign would not be allowed to participate.

Granted, merely signing a code of conduct will not prevent all abuse. However, it gives a clear mechanism to end it once it happens. If there's a violation, officials can stop the game, and ask the coach of the team with offending parents to remind them of the code they signed. If extreme behavior continues, the official can stop the game for an extended period, and if it still persists, he or she can declare a forfeit and end the game. This series of events puts responsibility on the parents, who cannot claim they didn't understand the consequences, and it puts a clear end to the abuse.

Other solutions have been proposed in different leagues. The most extreme is to ban spectators from even attending games. While a ban would surely prevent fan abuse, it would unfairly penalize those many parents who are good sports and supportive spectators. Plus, who wants to deprive people from seeing an important part of their children, grandchildren, and friends' childhood? Another solution has been to require spectators to be absolutely silent during games. This solution, while also potentially successful, deprives players and parents alike of the joys of praise and encouragement.

I urge you, then, to adopt my solution. Having a code of conduct will reduce fan abuse, restore some of the fun to

> Writer strengthens her ethical appeal (*ethos*) by recognizing some limitations. She goes on to explain how the solution would be effective.

> Topic sentence acknowledges other possible solutions and explains their shortcomings.

continued >>

Cui 5

The essay concludes with a call to action that has a logical appeal (*logos*). It shows the benefits of the solution and portrays the consequences of not adopting it.

our games, and keep them in perspective as fun, not battles. Failing to take this action would worsen the attitude that winning is everything and leave children even less prepared for the inevitable disappointments and struggles of life. Ultimately, it might eventually result in empty fields with no one willing to endure threats and insults from spectators who lack the discipline and perspective to behave in ways that their own children deserve.

14 Evaluation Essays

Quick Points   You will learn to

- Describe key elements of an evaluation (see 14A).
- Apply the writing process to an evaluation (pp. 128–129).
- Adapt frames and guides for an evaluation to your own needs (pp. 129–131).

14A   What are evaluation essays?

Watch the Video

Evaluation essays judge the quality of a text, object, individual, or event by providing reasons and support for that judgment. Here are typical categories of evaluations:

- **Reviews.** Movie, concert, book, theater, television, architecture, restaurant, product, or art reviews are all evaluations. They answer questions such as: Is that play worth seeing? Will certain readers like that book? Is the current season of this television series as good as last year's?

- **Recommendations or performance reviews.** Letters of recommendation and/or reviews of performances evaluate peoples' qualifications for a particular job or how well they've done it. Examples include editorials about an elected official's job performance or articles about whether a candidate should be elected.

- **Critical analyses.** A critical analysis judges ideas, recommendations, or proposals. It assesses whether an argument is sound or whether an informative text is accurate or useful. It answers questions such as, "Do the facts support the writer's claims? Is the writer fair and reasonable? Is the recommended action practical and more effective than other actions?"

■ Purpose

Evaluations have mainly an argumentative purpose and inform readers about what is being evaluated. You make claims about the quality of something or someone, and you provide evidence and reasoning to convince readers that your judgment is sound. (For more about purpose, see 5D.)

■ Audience

Audiences for evaluations can be as small as a single person (such as an employee's annual job evaluation) or as large as the general public who reads a magazine or blog. The narrower the audience, the more specifically you can address its needs and expectations. If your audience is general, these questions will help you.

- **What will readers already know about your subject?** Are they familiar with the text, object, individual, or event being evaluated? Do you need to explain your subject in detail, or is a brief explanation sufficient?

- **What might readers already believe about your subject?** Most people think fondly of *The Wizard of Oz* so if you argue that Judy Garland played Dorothy poorly, you need to be aware that your readers might disagree with your opinion.

- **What are the circumstances in which your readers will read your evaluation?** For an academic audience, including scholars like your instructor, you need to be scholarly and your TONE relatively formal. You might need research to support your position. On the other hand, for a popular blog, your tone can be more informal, but you still need sound reasons for your position.

For more about audience, see 5E.

14B How do I plan and revise evaluation essays?

Several questions can generate ideas for evaluations. Although we've arranged them here according to types, they can be mixed in the order you find most effective.

Generating ideas for reviews

- What seems to be the main purpose of the author, director, artist, etc.? How well was it achieved? Is that purpose worthwhile?
- Was the plot plausible? Interesting? Original?
- Were characters interesting and effective? In other words, if you infer that viewers are supposed to like, hate, or sympathize with them, can they?
- How well did the setting work, including what it looked like, its lighting, sounds, any music, etc.? (These questions apply to restaurants, galleries, or other settings, too.)
- What other works does this particular one resemble? Does it compare well? Why or why not?

Generating ideas for performance evaluations

- What specific qualities are needed to perform a particular job? Does the individual have those qualities? How can you tell?
- What are examples of the person's main strengths? Main weaknesses?
- How does this person compare with others in similar positions?
- What advice do you have for this person or anyone working with him or her?

Generating ideas for critical analyses

- Is the support the writer gives for his or her claims reasonable? Sufficient?
- Are there missing facts, viewpoints, or interpretations?
- Who would agree and who would disagree with the text? On what basis? How right would people be who disagree?
- If the text proposes an action, would it work? Is it practical? Is it the best one available?

Revising

- Does your THESIS STATEMENT present a clear judgment of the text, object, person, or event you're evaluating?
- Will your readers have a clear understanding of the text, object, person, or event you're summarizing? Have you given enough detail but not too much?

- Do you give and support reasons for your evaluation?
- Do you take into account your audience's knowledge, belief, and expectations?
- If your evaluation is mostly negative, have you tried to acknowledge possible strengths? If your evaluation is mostly positive, have you tried to acknowledge possible critiques?
- Do you need to include a WORKS CITED or REFERENCES page? If so, it is formatted correctly, with proper in-text citations?

14C What is a frame for an evaluation essay?

Here is a possible frame for an evaluation essay to adapt to your assignments.

Frame for an Evaluation Essay

Introductory paragraph(s)

- **Capture your readers' interest** in your topic by using one of the strategies for writing effective introductory paragraphs (see 7B).
- **Present your THESIS STATEMENT**, making sure it states your overall evaluation (see 5G).

Background paragraph(s):

- **Clearly explain what you're evaluating.** Give a brief objective overview by providing a brief plot summary if you're evaluating a book, play, movie, etc.; providing a description of an event or object; introducing the person if you're writing a recommendation.

Body paragraphs: Stating evaluations

- **Start each paragraph with a TOPIC SENTENCE** that states a reason that ties in logically to your thesis statement.
- **Support each topic sentence** with examples, evidence, and reasoning (including SUMMARIES or QUOTATIONS, if appropriate).
- **Include as many paragraphs as there are reasons** for your evaluation. If a reason is especially complicated, or if you have extensive examples or explanations, you might divide it into two or more paragraphs.
- **Save your most important evaluation for last.** Building toward your most powerful judgment will leave readers with the best reason for believing you.

(continued)

Evaluation Frame (cont.)

Rebuttal or "conceding" paragraph(s): Place either after your evaluating paragraphs, as in this frame; or immediately after your background paragraph(s) above.

- **Present alternative evaluations and refute them.** If it seems practical, state some reasons why others might disagree with your evaluations, and explain why your evaluation is still strong.
- **[optional] Concede some points.** To concede a point means to admit that it's valid. If it seems practical and honest, and you think it will make your readers more receptive to your evaluation, concede a positive point or two (if your overall evaluation is negative) or concede a negative point or two (if you're positive). Still, explain why your overall evaluation is reasonable.

Conclusion

- **Wrap up the essay with an engaging strategy** for concluding paragraphs (see 7G).
- **Summarize your point of view.**
- **Give your readers a recommendation,** such as buy this, don't attend that, hire this person, don't accept this argument, etc.

14D What are some sentence and paragraph guides for evaluations?

Adapt these guides to your PURPOSE and AUDIENCE.

Sentence and Paragraph Guides

- Despite a few redeeming qualities, this _____ (book, movie, CD, etc.) is ultimately _____ (disappointing, frustrating, infuriating, etc.).
- Four qualities are especially strong. First, _____. Second, _____. Third, _____. Most important, however, is _____.
- Admittedly, _____ has a couple of strong features. For example, _____. In addition, _____. However, even taking these into consideration, the total effect is not enough to overcome an overall weakness. That is primarily because _____.

Evaluation Guides (cont.)

- The author's strongest point is _____. The idea is effective because _____. For example, she _____, as is clear from the statement that "_____."
- _____'s most impressive quality is her [or his] ability to _____. That quality came through most clearly when _____. Although other employees might have _____, _____ instead chose to _____.

14E A student's evaluation essay

View
the Model
Document

Pietruszynski 1

Kelly Pietruszynski

Communications 100

Professor Moeller

12 Nov. 2012

The Worthy *Rise of the Planet of the Apes*

In the famous scene at the end of the 1968 movie *The Planet of the Apes*, Charlton Heston rides along a desolate beach until he comes across the top of the Statue of Liberty buried in the sand. At that moment, he and the movie's audience realize that the planet on which he's been stranded, where apes rule humans, is actually Earth in the future. That successful original movie led to sequels and even a remake in 2001, starring Mark Wahlberg. But not until the 2011 film *Rise of the Planet of the Apes* did we get any explanation of how the strange future came to be. The result is a satisfying film well worth seeing.

Rise of the Planet of the Apes is set in contemporary San Francisco. Will Rodman (played by James Franco) is a scientist who develops a drug meant to grow new brain cells and, as

Opening paragraph stirs interest by giving some background, ending with a thesis sentence that states the evaluation the writer will support.

continued >>

Pietruszynski 2

a result, cure diseases like Alzheimer's. Through a series of
events, Rodman adopts and raises an ape exposed to that
drug. Caesar (the ape) demonstrates human-like intelligence

The writer summarizes the movie's plot so that readers have a clear context for the writer's arguments. that eventually gets him in trouble, resulting in his being
imprisoned with a number of apes, gorillas, and orangutans in
a medical testing facility. After being exposed to another drug,
the entire colony of apes develops intelligence and escapes,
led by Caesar.

Topic sentence gives one reason for the evaluation. The rest of this paragraph supports the topic sentence. One impressive quality of this movie is the plot.
Admittedly, any attempt to explain how apes become
intelligent and humans stupid is finally going to stretch
credibility. However, *Rise of the Planet of the Apes* is fairly
plausible. Because finding a cure for Alzheimer's and related
diseases is such a strong interest in our society, we can easily
imagine extensive research and animal testing. To the plot's
credit, the ape's intelligence breakthrough isn't sudden and

An appeal to logic as well as ethics (*logos* and *ethos*). miraculous. Even after Caesar is exposed to the drug, years
pass while he lives with Will, allowing him to accumulate
human experiences and intelligence. We see conflict
development in Caesar between the world of nature and the
world of human society, and his mistreatment at the hands of
cruel humans, especially a keeper named Dodge explains why
the apes eventually turn against humans.

Topic sentence gives a second reason for the evaluation. Note the transitional connection to the previous paragraph. This plot benefits from exceptional camera work and
special effects. There are powerfully breathtaking scenes. For
example, when Will takes Caesar to play in a redwood forest,
the size and scope of the trees as Caesar climbs through them
is stunning. When the apes later escape, we see them swarm
through the trees on San Francisco streets; or, rather, we see

continued >>

Pietruszynski 3

the trees shuddering, as the apes are invisible among them, which is a more suggestive effect. The final battle takes place with dramatic fury on Golden Gate Bridge. But some of the best camera work depicts quiet scenes, not energetic ones. In one profound scene, Caesar is alone in the attic. Through a small window, he watches children play on the street far below, and the camera angle and distance creates a powerful sense of isolation and loneliness.

> The writer uses an emotional appeal here (*pathos*).

　　The best special effect is Caesar himself. While the original movie had actors wearing masks and makeup that won an Academy Award in 1969, *Rise of the Planet of the Apes* uses motion capture computer graphics. Andy Serkis (who played Gollum in *Lord of the Rings*) wore multiple computer sensors while acting the role of Caesar. The results were translated by skilled technicians and powerful computers into extraordinarily realistic images. The apes look like real animals, not actors in costumes. Most impressive are the emotions conveyed. At various times, Caesar looks happy, sad, confused, scheming, and so on. The effects alone are worth seeing.

> Topic sentence ties back to the previous paragraph and explains one effect in detail.

> Writer uses an emotional appeal (*pathos*) to urge readers to see the movie.

　　The movie's most impressive quality, however, is the way it establishes relationships between its characters. Will lives with his father, played by John Lithgow, who has Alzheimer's, and you can see not only the loving relationship between the two of them, but also Lithgow and Caesar. Indeed, Caesar gets into trouble at one point because he comes to the ailing man's defense. The most important relationship, of course, is between Will and Caesar, which develops fairly convincingly as identical to one between father and son. The relationship is

> Topic sentence states the third reason in support of the thesis. Note that the writer saved what she thought was the best reason for last.

continued >>

Pietruszynski 4

Writer uses an ethical and emotional appeal (*ethos* and *pathos*).

complete with struggles for autonomy that characterize human families, as children move through adolescence and parents try to find the right combination of discipline and independence. As a result, we identify with and care about Will and Caesar. Instead of just being an action flick, *Rise* has emotional depth.

Transitional sentence moves into some counterarguments.

There are silly relationships, too. It's hard to imagine what Will's love interest, an attractive veterinarian played by Frieda Pinto, sees in him. He's so obsessed with his work and his family situation, that I can't see her putting up with him

Topic sentence for this paragraph comes in the middle to connect the opening three sentences to three sentences that acknowledge why some might disagree with the writer's evaluation.

through the several years in which the movie unfolds. This is just one of several negative elements of the film. Critics can accurately point out that the villains in the film are just too extreme, from the evil animal keepers, to an angry neighbor, to the ultimate bad guy, the director of Will's lab who pursues profits at any cost. Also, the final battle scenes clash a little with the rest of the movie. The director seems to trade subtle relationships and characterizations for chases and explosions.

Concluding paragraph uses a logical appeal (*logos*) by saying this isn't a perfect movie, summarizes the writer's positive review, and ends on a strong recommendation.

Rise of the Planet of the Apes, then, is hardly a perfect movie. However, it is an entertaining and thoughtful one. It provides a plausible origin story for the entire series of films, delivering a solid plot, great special effects, and engaging relationships. As with any science fiction, viewers have to go along with certain premises. Because this movie makes you willing to do so, it's well worth seeing.

Tab 4
Using Sources
in Your Writing

■ ■ ■ ■ ■ ■ ■ ■ ■

CHAPTERS
15–17

Tab 4 Using Sources in Your Writing

MyCompLab® Visit mycomplab.com for the eText and for resources on using sources in your writing.

15 Quoting, Paraphrasing, and Summarizing

Quick Points You will learn to

➤ Use quotations effectively (see 15B).
➤ Integrate sources using paraphrasing and summarizing (pp. 140–146).

15A How can I integrate sources into my writing?

You integrate sources into your writing when you combine information or ideas from other writers with your own. To do this well, you use three techniques: QUOTATION (see 15B), PARAPHRASE (see 15C), and SUMMARY (see 15D). Mastering these techniques allows you to write smooth, effective papers that avoid **plagiarism:** stealing or representing someone else's words or ideas as your own (see Ch. 16).

15B How can I use quotations effectively?

A QUOTATION is the exact words of a source enclosed in quotation marks (see Chapter 51). Well-chosen quotations can lend a note of authority and enliven a document with someone else's voice.

Watch
the Video

Avoid adding too many quotations, however. If more than a quarter of your paper consists of quotations, you've probably written what some people call a "cut-and-paste special." Doing so gives your readers—including instructors—the impression that you haven't bothered to develop your own thinking and that you're letting other people do your talking. Quick Box 15.1 provides guidelines for using quotations.

■ Making quotations fit smoothly with your sentences

When you use quotations, the greatest risk you take is that you'll end up with incoherent, choppy sentences. You can avoid this problem by making the words you quote fit smoothly with three aspects of your writing: grammar, style, and logic. Here are some examples of sentences that don't mesh well with quotations, followed by a revised version. All examples are in MLA documentation style.

SOURCE

Turkle, Sherry. *Alone Together: Why We Expect More from Technology and Less from Each Other.* New York: Basic Books, 2011. Print.

Quick Box 15.1

Guidelines for using quotations

- Use quotations from authorities on your subject to support or refute what you've written.
- Never use a quotation to present your THESIS STATEMENT or a TOPIC SENTENCE.
- Select quotations that fit your message. Choose a quotation only for the following reasons.

    Its language is particularly appropriate or distinctive.

    Its idea is particularly hard to paraphrase accurately.

    The source's authority is especially important for support.

    The source's words are open to interpretation.

- Never allow quotations to make up a quarter or more of your paper. Instead, rely on paraphrase (see 15C) and summary (see 15D).
- Quote accurately. Always check a quotation against the original source—and then recheck it.
- Integrate quotations smoothly into your writing.
- Avoid plagiarism (Chapter 16).
- Document quotations carefully.

ORIGINAL (TURKLE'S EXACT WORDS)

Digital connections and the sociable robot may offer the illusion of companionship without the demands of friendship. Our networked life allows us to hide from each other, even as we are tethered to each other.   [from page 1]

GRAMMAR PROBLEM

Turkle explains how relying on network communication "illusion of companionship without the demands of friendship" (1).

STYLE PROBLEM

Turkle explains that the digital connections and lives of robots "offer the illusion of companionship without the demands of friendship" (1).

LOGIC PROBLEM

Turkle explains networked connections "without the demands of friendship" (1).

ACCEPTABLE USE OF THE QUOTATION

Turkle explains that networked connections "may offer the illusion of companionship without the demands of friendship" (1).

■ Using brackets to add words

What do you do when a quotation doesn't fit smoothly with your writing? You can add a word or very brief phrase to the quotation, in brackets—[ ]—so that it fits seamlessly with the rest of your sentence. Make sure, however, that your bracketed additions don't distort the meaning of the quotation.

ORIGINAL (TURKLE'S EXACT WORDS)

If we divest ourselves of such things, we risk being coarsened, reduced.   [from page 292]

QUOTATION WITH EXPLANATORY BRACKETS

"If we divest ourselves of such things [as caring for the sick], we risk being coarsened, reduced" (Turkle 292).

■ Using ellipsis to delete words

Another way to fit a quotation smoothly into your sentence is to use ellipsis. Delete the part of the quotation that seems to be causing the problem, and mark the omission by using ELLIPSIS POINTS. When you use ellipses to delete troublesome words, make sure that the remaining words accurately reflect the source's meaning and that your sentence still flows smoothly.

ORIGINAL (TURKLE'S EXACT WORDS)

The idea of addiction, with its one solution that we know we won't take, makes us feel hopeless.   [from page 294]

QUOTATION USING ELLIPSIS

Turkle notes that "the idea of addiction . . . makes us feel hopeless" (294).

■ Integrating author names, source titles, and other information

A huge complaint instructors have about student papers is that sometimes quotations are simply stuck in, for no apparent reason. Without context-setting information, your readers can't know exactly why you included a particular quotation. Furthermore, your readers need to know who said each group of quoted words.

SOURCE

Wright, Karen. "Times of Our Lives." *Scientific American* Sept. 2002: 58–66.
   Print.

ORIGINAL (WRIGHT'S EXACT WORDS)

In human bodies, biological clocks keep track of seconds, minutes, days, months and years.   [from page 66]

INCORRECT (DISCONNECTED QUOTATION)

The human body has many subconscious processes. People don't have to make their hearts beat or remind themselves to breathe. "In human bodies, biological clocks keep track of seconds, minutes, days, months and years" (Wright 66).

CORRECT

The human body has many subconscious processes. People don't have to make their hearts beat or remind themselves to breathe. However, other processes are less obvious and perhaps more surprising. Karen Wright observes, for example, "In human bodies, biological clocks keep track of seconds, minutes, days, months and years" (66).

Another strategy for working quotations smoothly into your paper is to integrate the author's name, the source title, or other information, as shown in Quick Box 15.2.

Here are some examples, using a quotation from Karen Wright, that apply techniques from Quick Box 15.2.

AUTHOR'S NAME

Karen Wright explains that "in human bodies, biological clocks keep track of seconds, minutes, days, months and years" (66).

Quick Box 15.2

■ ■ ■ ■ ■ ■ ■ ■ ■ ■

Strategies for introducing quotations

- Mention in your sentence (before or after the quotation) the name of the author you're quoting.
- Mention in your sentence the title of the work you're quoting from.
- Give additional authority to your material. If the author of a quotation is a noteworthy figure, refer to his or her credentials.
- Add your own introductory analysis to the quotation, along with the name of the author, the title of the source, and/or the author's credentials.

AUTHOR'S NAME AND SOURCE TITLE

Karen Wright explains in "Times of Our Lives" that "in human bodies, biological clocks keep track of seconds, minutes, days, months and years" (66).

AUTHOR'S NAME AND CREDENTIALS

Karen Wright, an award-winning science journalist, explains that "in human bodies, biological clocks keep track of seconds, minutes, days, months and years" (66).

AUTHOR'S NAME WITH STUDENT'S INTRODUCTORY ANALYSIS

Karen Wright reviews evidence of surprising subconscious processes, explaining that "in human bodies, biological clocks keep track of seconds, minutes, days, months and years" (66).

● **EXERCISE 15-1** Working individually or with a group, read the following original material, from page 295 of *Deep Water: The Gulf Oil Disaster and the Future of Offshore Drilling*, published in 2011 by the National Commission on the BP Deepwater Horizon Oil Spill and Offshore Drilling. Then, read items 1 through 4 and explain why each is an incorrect use of a quotation. Next, revise each numbered sentence so that it correctly uses a quotation. End each quotation with this MLA-style parenthetical reference: (National 295).

Explore the Exercise

Yet growing demand for oil around the world, particularly in the huge and rapidly developing economies of Asia, ensures heightened competition for supplies, putting upward pressure on oil prices. That poses a long-term challenge for the United States, which is not and cannot be self-sufficient in oil supply.

UNACCEPTABLE USES OF QUOTATIONS

1. Demand for oil is increasing globally. "That poses a long-term challenge for the United States, which is not and cannot be self-sufficient in oil supply" (National 295).
2. One obvious cause is that "the huge economies of Asia are putting upward pressure on prices" (National 295).
3. A difficult situation, "that poses a long-term challenge for the United States" (National 295).
4. In the 1990s, "that poses a long-term challenge for the United States" (National 295). ●

15C How can I write a good paraphrase?

Watch
the Video
A PARAPHRASE precisely restates in your own words the written or spoken words of someone else. Paraphrase only passages that carry ideas you need to reproduce in detail to explain a point or support an argument. Avoid trying to paraphrase more than a paragraph or two; for longer passages, use summary (see 15D). Quick Box 15.3 offers advice for paraphrasing.

Here is an example of an unacceptable paraphrase and an acceptable one.

SOURCE

Hulbert, Ann. "Post-Teenage Wasteland?" *New York Times Magazine*
    9 Oct. 2005: 11–12. Print.

ORIGINAL (HULBERT'S EXACT WORDS)

[T]he available data suggest that the road to maturity hasn't become as drastically different as people think—or as drawn out, either. It's true that the median age of marriage rose to 25 for women and almost 27 for men in 2000, from 20 and 23, respectively, in 1960. Yet those midcentury figures were record lows (earnestly analyzed in their time). Moreover, Americans of all ages have ceased to view starting a family as the major benchmark of grown-up status. When asked to rank the importance of traditional milestones in defining the arrival of adulthood, poll respondents place completing school,

---

Quick Box 15.3 ■ ■ ■ ■ ■ ■ ■ ■ ■ ■

Guidelines for writing paraphrases

- Never use a paraphrase to present your THESIS STATEMENT or a TOPIC SENTENCE.
- Say what the source says, but no more.
- Reproduce the source's sequence of ideas and emphases.
- Use your own words, phrasing, and sentence structure to restate the material. If some technical words in the original have only awkward synonyms, quote the original words—but do so sparingly.
- Read your sentences over to make sure they don't distort the source's meaning.
- Expect your material to be as long as the original or even slightly longer.
- Integrate your paraphrase into your writing so that it fits smoothly.
- Avoid PLAGIARISM (Chapter 16).
- Document your paraphrase carefully.

finding full-time employment, achieving financial independence and being able to support a family far above actually wedding a spouse or having kids. The new perspective isn't merely an immature swerve into selfishness; postponing those last two steps is good for the future of the whole family. [from page 11]

UNACCEPTABLE PARAPHRASE (HIGHLIGHTED WORDS ARE PLAGIARIZED)

Data suggest that the road to maturity hasn't changed as much as people think. True, the median age of marriage was 25 for women and 27 for men in 2000, up from 20 and 23 in 1960. Yet those 1960 figures were record lows. Furthermore, Americans have stopped regarding beginning a family as the signpost of grown-up status. When they were asked to rank the importance of traditional benchmarks for deciding the arrival of adulthood, people rated graduating from school, finding a full-time job, gaining financial status, and being a breadwinner far above marrying or having kids. This new belief isn't merely immature selfishness; delaying those last two steps is good for the future of the whole family (Hulbert 11).

ACCEPTABLE PARAPHRASE

According to Ann Hulbert, statistics show that people are wrong when they believe our society is delaying maturity. She acknowledges that between 1960 and 2000, the median age at which women married rose from 20 to 25 (for men it went from 23 to 27), but points out that the early figures were extreme lows. Hulbert finds that Americans no longer equate adulthood with starting a family. Polls show that people rank several other "milestones" above marriage and children as signaling adulthood. These include finishing school, securing a full-time job, and earning enough to be independent and to support a family. Hulbert concludes that we should regard postponing marriage and children not as being selfish or immature but as investing in the family's future (11).

The first attempt to paraphrase is unacceptable because the writer has simply changed a few words. What remains is plagiarized.

The second paraphrase is acceptable because it captures the meaning of the original in the student's own words.

● **EXERCISE 15-2** Working individually or with your peer-response group, read the original material, a paragraph from page 49 of *Uniforms: Why We Are What We Wear* by Paul Fussell (Boston: Houghton, 2002). Then, read the unacceptable paraphrase, and point out each example of plagiarism. Finally, write your own paraphrase, starting it with a phrase naming Fussell and ending it with this parenthetical reference: (49).

ORIGINAL (FUSSELL'S EXACT WORDS)

Until around 1963, part of the routine for Levi's wearers was shrinking the trousers to fit, and the best way to do that was to put them on wet and let them dry on your body. This gave the wearer the impression that he or she was actually creating the garment, or at least emphasizing one's precious individuality, and that conviction did nothing to oppose the illusion of uniqueness precious to all American young people.   [from page 49]

UNACCEPTABLE PARAPHRASE

Paul Fussell says that until around 1963 Levi's wearers used to shrink new trousers to fit. The best way to do that was to put them on wet and let them dry while wearing them. Doing this created the impression that wearers were actually creating the garment or emphasizing their precious individuality. It reinforced the illusion of uniqueness precious to all American teens (49). ●

15D How can I write a good summary?

Watch
the Video

A SUMMARY differs from a paraphrase (see 15C) in an important way: Whereas a paraphrase restates the original material in its entirety, a summary states only the main points of the original source in a much briefer fashion. A summary doesn't include supporting evidence or details. It's the gist, the hub, the seed of what the author is saying. As a result, a summary is much shorter than a paraphrase. Summarizing is the technique you'll probably use most frequently to integrate sources. Quick Box 15.4 explains how to summarize effectively.

Here's an example of an unacceptable summary and an acceptable one.

SOURCE

Tanenbaum, Leora. *Catfight: Women and Competition.* New York: Seven Stories, 2002. Print.

ORIGINAL (TANENBAUM'S EXACT WORDS)

Until recently, most Americans disapproved of cosmetic surgery, but today the stigma is disappearing. Average Americans are lining up for procedures—two-thirds of patients report family incomes of less than $50,000 a year—and many of them return for more. Younger women undergo "maintenance" surgeries

Quick Box 15.4

∎ ∎ ∎ ∎ ∎ ∎ ∎ ∎ ∎

Guidelines for summarizing

- Identify the main points, and take care not to alter the meaning of the original source.
- Don't be tempted to include your opinions; they don't belong in a summary.
- Never use a summary to present your THESIS STATEMENT or a TOPIC SENTENCE.
- Keep your summary as short as possible to accomplish your purpose.
- Integrate summarized material smoothly into your writing.
- Use your own words. If you need to use key terms or phrases from the source, include them in quotation marks, but otherwise put everything into your own words.
- Document the original source accurately.
- Avoid PLAGIARISM (Chapter 16).

in a futile attempt to halt time. The latest fad is Botox, a purified and diluted form of botulinum toxin that is injected between the eyebrows to eliminate frown lines. Although the procedure costs between $300 and $1000 and must be repeated every few months, roughly 850,000 patients have had it performed on them. That number will undoubtedly shoot up now that the FDA has approved Botox for cosmetic use. Even teenagers are making appointments with plastic surgeons. More than 14,000 adolescents had plastic surgery in 1996, and many of them are choosing controversial procedures such as breast implants, liposuction, and tummy tucks, rather than the rhinoplasties of previous generations.   [from pages 117–118]

UNACCEPTABLE SUMMARY (HIGHLIGHTED WORDS ARE PLAGIARIZED)

Average Americans are lining up for surgical procedures. The latest fad is Botox, a toxin injected to eliminate frown lines. This is an insanely foolish waste of money. Even teenagers are making appointments with plastic surgeons, many of them for controversial procedures such as breast implants, liposuction, and tummy tucks (Tanenbaum 117–18).

ACCEPTABLE SUMMARY

Tanenbaum explains that plastic surgery is becoming widely acceptable, even for Americans with modest incomes and for younger women. Most popular is injecting the toxin Botox to smooth wrinkles.

> She notes that thousands of adolescents are even requesting
> controversial surgeries (117–18).

The unacceptable summary has several major problems: It doesn't isolate the main point. It plagiarizes by taking much of its language directly from the source. It includes the writer's interpretation ("This is an insanely foolish waste of money") rather than objectively representing the original. The acceptable summary concisely isolates the main point, puts the source into the writer's own words, calls attention to the author by including her name in the summary, and remains objective throughout.

■ Degrees of summary

The degree to which your summary compresses the original source depends on your situation and assignment. For example, you can summarize an entire 500-page book in a single sentence, in a single page, or in five or six pages. Following are two different levels of summary based on the same source, a 3,000-word article too long to reprint here.

SOURCE

Schwartz, Barry. "The Tyranny of Choice." *Chronicle of Higher Education*
(23 Jan. 2004): B6. Web. 3 Apr. 2011.

SUMMARY IN A SINGLE SENTENCE

Research finds that people with large numbers of choices are actually less happy than people with fewer choices (Schwartz).

SUMMARY IN 50 TO 100 WORDS

Research finds that people with large numbers of choices are actually less happy than people with fewer choices. Although the amount of wealth and number of choices have increased during the past thirty years, fewer Americans report themselves as being happy, and depression, suicide, and mental health problems have increased. Although some choice is good, having too many choices hinders decision making, especially among "maximizers," who try to make the best possible choices. Research in shopping, education, and medical settings shows that even when people eventually decide, they experience regret, worrying that the options they didn't choose might have been better (Schwartz).

Notice that the longer summary begins with the same sentence as the short one; leading a summary with the reading's main idea is effective. Notice that both summaries put ideas in the writer's own words and capture only the main idea.

Explore the Exercise

● **EXERCISE 15-3** Working individually or with your peer-response group, read the original material from pages 23–24 of *Diversity: The Invention of a Concept* by Peter Wood (San Francisco: Encounter, 2003). Then, read the unacceptable summary. Point out each example of plagiarism. Finally, write your own summary, starting it with a phrase mentioning Wood and ending it with this parenthetical reference: (23–24).

ORIGINAL (WOOD'S EXACT WORDS)

Among the many meanings of diversity, let's for the moment distinguish two: the actual racial and ethnic condition of America, which I will call *diversity I*, and the diversiphile ideal of how American society should recognize and respond to its racial and ethnic composition, which I will call *diversity II*. In principle, it ought to be easy to distinguish between these two meanings. One refers to the facts, the other to hopes or wishes. *Diversity I* is the sort of thing that we might expect could be counted, or at least approximated, with wide agreement. We know with reasonable certainty, for example, that about 13 percent of the U.S. population considers itself of African descent. We can and do argue with one another over the significance of this fact, but the fact itself is not seriously in dispute.

Diversity II, by contrast, is an ideal. It expresses a vision of society in which people divide themselves into separate groups, each with profound traditions of its own, but held together by mutual esteem, respect and tolerance. It would be futile, however, to look for general agreement about the exact details of this ideal.

UNACCEPTABLE, PLAGIARIZED SUMMARY

Peter Wood distinguishes between diversity I, the actual racial and ethnic condition of America, and diversity II, the diversiphile ideal of how American society should recognize and respond to its racial and ethnic composition. Diversity I could be counted or approximated with wide agreement. Diversity II is an ideal vision of society, but there can be no general agreement about the exact nature of this ideal (23–24). ●

15E Which verbs help weave source material into sentences?

Use the verbs in Quick Box 15.5 appropriately according to their meanings in your sentences. For example, *says* and *states* are fairly neutral introductory verbs; you're just reporting the source's words. On the other hand, while still fairly neutral, *claims* or *contends* introduces a slight skepticism; you're suggesting that you may not share the source's certainty. *Demonstrates* or, even stronger, *proves* indicates that you find the source conclusive on a particular point.

Quick Box 15.5

■ ■ ■ ■ ■ ■ ■ ■ ■

Useful verbs for integrating quotations, paraphrases, and summaries

acknowledges	contrasts	illustrates	recommends
agrees	declares	implies	refutes
analyzes	demonstrates	indicates	rejects
argues	denies	insists	remarks
asserts	describes	introduces	reports
begins	develops	maintains	reveals
believes	discusses	means	says
claims	distinguishes	notes	shows
comments	between	notices	specifies
compares	among	observes	speculates
complains	emphasizes	offers	states
concedes	establishes	points out	suggests
concludes	explains	prepares	supports
confirms	expresses	promises	supposes
considers	finds	proves	wishes
contends	focuses on	questions	writes
contradicts	grants	recognizes	

Avoiding Plagiarism

16

■ ■ ■ ■ ■ ■ ■ ■ ■

Quick Points You will learn to

➤ Identify plagiarism (see 16A).
➤ Use techniques to avoid the different types of plagiarism (see 16B).

16A What is plagiarism?

Watch
the Video

To use SOURCES well, you need to learn how to incorporate others' words and ideas into your own papers accurately, effectively, and honestly. This last skill is especially important, so that you avoid PLAGIARISM, which is presenting another person's words, ideas, or visual images as if they were your own. Plagiarizing, like stealing, is a form of academic dishonesty or cheating. It's a serious offense that can be grounds for a failing grade or expulsion from a college. Beyond that, you're hurting yourself. If you're plagiarizing, you're not learning.

Plagiarism isn't just something that college instructors get fussy about. In the workplace, it can get you fired. Plagiarism at work also has legal implications; using someone else's intellectual property without permission or credit is a form of theft that may land you in court. Furthermore, plagiarism in any setting—academic, business, or civic—hurts your credibility and reputation. Quick Box 16.1 lists the major types of plagiarism.

Quick Box 16.1

Types of plagiarism

You're plagiarizing if you . . .

- Buy a paper from an Internet site, another student or writer, or any other source.

- Turn in any paper that someone else has written, whether the person has given it to you, you've downloaded it from the Internet, or you've copied it from any other source.

- Change selected parts of an existing paper and claim the paper as your own.

- Neglect to put quotation marks around words that you quote directly from a source, even if you list the source in your Works Cited or References.

- Type or paste into your paper any key terms, phrases, sentences, or longer passages from another source without using documentation to tell precisely where the material came from.

- Use ideas or reasoning from a source without correctly citing and documenting that source, even if you put the ideas into your own words. (See 16E.)

- Combine ideas from many sources and pass them off as your own without correctly citing and documenting the sources.

- Use photographs, charts, figures, or other visual images from anyone (colleagues, organizations, Web sites, and so on) without crediting and documenting them.

ESOL Tip: Perhaps you come from a country or culture that considers it acceptable for students to copy the writing of experts and authorities. Some cultures, in fact, believe that using another's words, even without citing them, is a sign of respect or learning. However, this practice is unacceptable in American colleges. ●

16B How do I avoid plagiarism?

Watch
the Video

The first step in avoiding plagiarism is to learn the techniques of quoting (see 15B), paraphrasing (see 15C), and summarizing (see 15D) source materials. The second step is to document sources correctly. A third step is to take advantage of the learning opportunities your instructor may build into assignments. Many instructors require students to hand in a WORKING BIBLIOGRAPHY (see 19F) or ANNOTATED BIBLIOGRAPHY (see 19H). Your instructor may ask to see your research log (see 19E), your working notes, copies of your sources, or working drafts of your paper. Quick Box 16.2 suggests some practical steps you can take to avoid plagiarism.

Quick Box 16.2   ■ ■ ■ ■ ■ ■ ■ ■

Strategies for avoiding plagiarism

- Acknowledge when you're using the ideas, words, or images of others. Always document the sources.

- Become thoroughly familiar with the documentation style your instructor requires you to use (see Chs. 24–31).

- Follow a consistent notetaking system. Use different colors, or some other coding system, to distinguish three different types of material.
    1. **Quotations** from a source; write clear, even oversized quotation marks so you can't miss them later (documentation required)
    2. **Material you have paraphrased, summarized**, or otherwise drawn from a source (documentation required)
    3. **Your own thoughts**, triggered by what you have read or experienced (no documentation required; see 16D)

- Immediately when you quote, paraphrase, or summarize in your draft, include the appropriate in-text citation, and add the source to your Works Cited or References. Don't wait to do this later. The danger of forgetting or making a mistake is too great.

- As part of editing and proofreading, look carefully at your paper for any places that might need documentation.

- Consult your instructor if you're unsure about any aspect of the documentation process.

16C How do I avoid plagiarism when using Internet sources?

You might be tempted to download a paper from the Internet. Don't. That kind of intellectual dishonesty can get you into real trouble. We've been dismayed to hear that some students believe if they buy a paper or hire someone else to write it, the paper is "theirs." No. It's not. This is clearly plagiarism.

Watch
the Video

Even if you have absolutely no intention of plagiarizing, being careless can easily lead to trouble. Quick Box 16.3 suggests some ways you can avoid plagiarism when you're working on the Internet.

Quick Box 16.3

Guidelines for avoiding plagiarism when using Internet sources

- Never copy material from an online source and paste it directly into your paper without taking great care. You can too easily lose track of which language is your own and which comes from a source.

- Keep material that you downloaded or printed from the Internet separate from your own writing, whether you intend to quote, summarize, or paraphrase the material. Be careful how you manage copied files. Use another color or a much larger font as a visual reminder that this isn't your work.

- Copy or paste downloaded or printed material into your paper only when you intend to use it as a direct quotation or visual. Immediately place quotation marks around the material (later you may decide to set off a long passage as a block quotation; only then would you remove the quotation marks). Be sure to document the source at the same time as you're copying or pasting the quotation into your paper, or you may forget to do it later or do it incorrectly.

- Summarize or paraphrase materials *before* you include them in your paper. Document the sources of summarized passages at the same time as you insert them in your paper.

- Use an Internet service to check a passage you're not sure about. If you're concerned that you may have plagiarized by mistake, use Google to search one or two sentences that concern you. To make this work, always place quotation marks around the sentences you want to check when you type them into the search window.

16D What don't I have to document?

You don't have to document common knowledge or your own thinking. Common knowledge is information that most educated people know, although they might need to remind themselves of certain facts by looking them up in a reference book. For example, you would not need to document statements like these:

- George W. Bush was the U.S. president before Barack Obama.
- Mercury is the planet closest to the sun.
- Water boils at 212°F.
- All the oceans on our planet contain saltwater.

16E How do I document ideas?

You need to document everything that you learn from a source, including ideas or reasoning. Expressing others' ideas in your own words doesn't release you from the obligation to tell exactly where you got them. Consider the following example.

SOURCE

Silberman, Steve. "The Placebo Problem." *The Best American Science Writing 2010*. Ed. Jerome Groopman and Jesse Cohen. New York: Ecco, 2010. 31–44. Print.

ORIGINAL (SILBERMAN'S EXACT WORDS)

The fact that an increasing number of medications are unable to beat sugar pills has thrown the industry into crisis. The stakes could hardly be higher. In today's economy, the fate of a long-established company can hang on the outcome of a handful of tests.   [from page 33]

PLAGIARISM EXAMPLE

The fact that more and more drugs are unable to beat sugar pills has caused problems. Much is at stake. Currently, the future of established companies can depend on the outcome of a handful of tests.

Even though the writer changed some wording in the preceding example, the ideas aren't original. The highlighted phrases are especially problematic examples of plagiarism because they're Silberman's exact wording. To avoid plagiarism the student needs both to document the source and to use quotation marks to show Silberman's wording.

1. CORRECT EXAMPLE USING QUOTATION, PARAPHRASE, AND DOCUMENTATION

Steve Silberman claims that the increasing success of placebos "has thrown the [drug] industry into crisis." The market is so competitive that even "a handful of tests" can determine whether a company survives (33).

2. CORRECT EXAMPLES USING SUMMARY AND DOCUMENTATION

A. Steve Silberman argues that the success of placebos challenges drug company profits (33).

B. The success of placebos challenges drug company profits (Silberman 33).

In correct example 1, the writer has properly integrated Silberman's ideas through quotation and paraphrase, and she has included an in-text citation that points to her Works Cited page. In correct example 2A, the writer summarizes the idea, including the author's name in the sentence and a parenthetic citation. In correct example 2B, she also summarizes, but here she includes the author's name as part of the parenthetical citation.

17 Writing About Readings ■ ■ ■ ■ ■ ■ ■ ■

Quick Points You will learn to

➤ Write summary and response essays (see 17B and 17C).
➤ Use analysis and synthesis in your writing (pp. 157–159).

17A What are typical assignments for writing about readings?

Although much college writing requires using techniques for integrating sources (QUOTATION, PARAPHRASE, and SUMMARY, which we explained in Chapter 15), some assignments focus entirely on writing about reading. Some common types of papers are summary essays (see 17B), response essays (see 17C), analysis essays (see Chapter 11), and synthesis essays (see 17D). Research paper assignments require finding and synthesizing multiple sources. Chapters 18–23 give extensive advice about RESEARCH writing.

17B How do I write a summary essay?

Watch
the Video

For papers that consist entirely of summary, you might get an assignment like "Write a 500-word summary of the article by Newmann," or "Write a one-page summary of Chapter 7." Writing summary essays takes practice and skill to do them well.

We offered several techniques for summarizing within a longer essay in 15D. Following is specific advice for writing a summary paper.

Generating ideas for a summary essay

- Identify TOPIC SENTENCES or main ideas, separating them from examples or illustrations. You want to focus on the main ideas.
- Take notes in your own words, then put the source away. Write from your notes, going back to check the original only after you've written a first draft.

Shaping and drafting a summary essay

- Begin with a sentence that summarizes the entire reading, unless you're writing a particularly long summary.
- Follow the order of the original.
- Summarize proportionally. Longer and more important aspects of the original source need to get more space and attention in your summary.
- Include a Works Cited (Ch. 25) or References (Ch. 28) page, depending on the required DOCUMENTATION STYLE.

■ A student's summary essay

Brian Jirak received the assignment to write a 200-word summary of an article.

Jirak 1

Brian Jirak

Economics 101

Professor Connolly

15 Jan. 2012

Summary of "Living by Default"

In "Living by Default," James Surowiecki argues that there is a double standard regarding defaulting on loans.

Jirak 2

When corporations like American Airlines do so, analysts call them "very smart" (44). However, when homeowners don't pay mortgages, they are called deadbeats.

Surowiecki notes that millions of American homeowners owe far more than their homes are worth, so that paying the mortgage is "like setting a pile of money on fire every month" (44). Still, most people keep doing so. Why? Although one reason is worry about damaging their credit ratings, the more important reason is that people feel ashamed not to pay.

While Surowieki generally agrees that people should pay debts, he believes that if we consider it reasonable for corporations to walk away from loans, we should think the same for homeowners. Of course, banks and corporations could help by changing loans or modifying debts, but they choose not to. Surowieki calls them hypocritical for scolding homeowners when they have done worse. In the end, he suggests it might make sense for people just to stop paying on bad mortgages, because it may force banks to change their ways.

Jirak 3

Work Cited

Surowiecki, James. "Living by Default." *The New Yorker*. 19 and
        26 Dec. 2011. 44. Print.

17C How do I write a response essay?

Watch
the Video

A RESPONSE essay has two missions: to provide a SUMMARY of a source and to make statements—supported by reasons—about the source's ideas or quality. Responses may

1. Comment on a work's accuracy, logic, or conclusions ("Is this history of hip-hop music accurate?" "Is this argument about requiring military service convincing?")

2. Present the writer's reaction to a source ("I found the ideas in the reading shocking/intriguing/confusing/promising, etc.") (See Ch. 14.)

3. Focus on a work's form, or genre ("How well does this poem satisfy the requirements of a sonnet?")

4. Explain a reading's relation to other works ("Is this novel better than that novel?") or to the "real" world ("To what extent does this article accurately portray student life?")

Quick Box 17.1 explains additional elements of effective response essays.

Generating ideas for a response essay

• Use ACTIVE READING (see 4C) and CRITICAL READING (see 4A) to identify the main points and generate reactions to the source.

• Use techniques for ANALYZING (see 4B), drawing INFERENCES (see 4B), and assessing reasoning processes (see 3A).

• Discuss the source with another person. Summarize its content and ask the other person's opinion or ideas. Deliberately debate that opinion or challenge their ideas. Discussions and debates can get your mind moving. (If in your writing you use that other person's ideas, be sure to give the person credit as a source.)

• Respond to the source based on your prior knowledge and experience, your reading, or your research.

Quick Box 17.1 ■ ■ ■ ■ ■ ■ ■ ■ ■

Effective response essays

• Include a clear and concise summary of the source.

• State agreements, disagreements, or qualified agreements. (In a qualified agreement, you accept some points but not others.)

• Provide reasons and evidence for your statements.

■ A student's response essay

Here is student Kristin Boshoven's short response to Barry Schwartz's essay, "The Tyranny of Choice"; we included Kristin's summary of that essay in 15D, on page 144. Note that she incorporates the summary before using her own experience and her general knowledge to respond.

Boshoven 1

Kristin Boshoven

English 101

Professor Lequire

12 Apr. 2011

Too Much Choice: Disturbing but Not Destructive

Barry Schwartz argues that people with large numbers of choices are actually less happy than people with fewer choices. Although the amount of wealth and choice has increased during the past thirty years, studies show that fewer Americans report themselves as being happy. Depression, suicide, and mental health problems have increased. While some choice is good, too many choices hinder decision making, especially among people who Schwartz calls "maximizers," people who try to make the best possible choices. Research in shopping, education, and medical settings shows that even when people eventually decide, they experience regret, worrying that the options they didn't choose might have been better.

Although Schwartz cites convincing evidence for his claims, he ultimately goes too far in his conclusions. Excessive choice does seem to make life harder, not easier, but it alone can't be blamed for whatever unhappiness exists in our society.

My own experience supports Schwartz's finding that people who have thirty choices of jam as opposed to six often don't purchase any. A week ago I decided to buy a new smart

---

continued >>

phone. When we went to the store, we were confronted with twenty different models, and even though a helpful salesperson explained the various features, I couldn't make up my mind. I decided to do more research, which was a mistake. After reading reviews in everything from *Consumer Reports* to the *New York Times*, I am close to making a decision. However, I have a sinking feeling that as soon as I buy a phone, I'll learn that another choice would have been better, or mine will drop $50 in price. I could relate similar experiences trying to choose which movie to see, which dentist to visit, and so on. I suspect others could, too, which is why I find Schwartz's argument convincing at this level.

However, when he suggests that the increase of choice is a source of things like depression and suicide, he goes too far. Our society has undergone tremendous changes in the past forty or fifty years, and many of those changes are more likely to cause problems than the existence of too much choice. For example, workers in the 1950s through the 1970s could generally count on holding jobs with one company as long as they wanted, even through retirement. A 1950s autoworker, for example, might not have been thrilled with his job (and these were jobs held almost exclusively by men), but at least he could count on it, and it paid enough to buy a house and education for his family. The economic uncertainties of the past decade have meant that workers—and now women as well as men—do not have the same job stability they once did.

Although I agree that too many choices can lead to anxiety and even unhappiness, there are larger factors. If Americans report more depression and suicide than previously, a more likely candidate is economic and social uncertainty, not having too many kinds of cereal on the grocery store shelves.

Boshoven 3

Work Cited

Schwartz, Barry. "The Tyranny of Choice." *Chronicle of Higher Education* (23 Jan. 2004): B6. Web. 3 April 2011.

17D How do I write synthesis essays?

A SYNTHESIS weaves ideas together. Unsynthesized ideas and information are like separate spools of thread, neatly lined up, possibly coordinated, but not woven together or integrated. Synthesized ideas and information are like threads woven into a tapestry. By synthesizing, you show evidence of your ability to bring ideas together.

One common synthesizing task is to connect two or more readings or source materials into a single piece of writing. Another common type of synthesis is to connect material to what you already know, as the student did in 17C.

Your goal in synthesizing multiple sources is to join two or more texts together into a single piece of writing that is your own. The resulting text needs to be more than just a succession of summaries. That is, avoid merely listing who said what about a topic. Such a list isn't a synthesis—it doesn't create new connections.

Quick Box 17.4 suggests additional approaches for writing a synthesis.

Quick Box 17.4

Effective syntheses

- Make comparisons with—or contrasts between—ideas and information. Do the sources generally agree or generally disagree? What are the bases of their agreement or disagreement? Are there subtle differences or shades of meaning or emphasis?

- Create definitions that combine and extend definitions you encounter in the separate sources.

- Use examples or descriptions from one source to illustrate ideas in another.

- Use processes described in one source to explain those in others.

- Truly synthesize the sources, not just write about one source and then the other.

The following example shows how a student synthesized two sources. Read source 1 and source 2 to familiarize yourself with the information the student read.

SOURCE 1

Shishmaref is melting into the ocean. Over the past 30 years, the Inupiaq Eskimo village, perched on a slender barrier island 625 miles north of Anchorage, has lost 100 ft. to 300 ft. of coastline—half of it since 1997. As Alaska's climate warms, the permafrost beneath the beaches is thawing and the sea ice is thinning, leaving its 600 residents increasingly vulnerable to violent storms. One house has collapsed, and 18 others had to be moved to higher ground, along with the town's bulk-fuel tanks.   [from page 68]
—Margot Roosevelt, "Vanishing Alaska"

SOURCE 2

Since 2000 more than 6.5 million acres have perished in the U.S., turning forests into meadows in almost a dozen states. The culprit: the pine beetle, a fingernail-size bug that's become more voracious as the planet warms. Once a balanced part of forest life, the tree-eating insect now usually survives the winter, starts feeding earlier in the spring, and continues to plunder late into the fall.   [from page 8]
—Jim Robbins, "Global Warming Kills Forests in Colorado"

EXAMPLE OF A SYNTHESIS OF TWO SOURCES

Global warming is affecting both the natural and artificial worlds. Rising temperatures have allowed pine beetles to survive winters and thrive, killing over 6.5 million acres of forests (Robbins 8). Climate change has also altered life for residents of Arctic regions. For example, eighteen families in Shishmaref, Alaska, had to move their houses away from the coast because the permafrost under the beaches had thawed (Roosevelt 68).

—Devon Harris, student

Notice in the student's synthesis, how he used summary (see 15D) and paraphrase (see 15C) to synthesize the two sources. Also observe how the first sentence in his synthesis weaves the sources together with a new concept. The student also used in-text citations (in MLA STYLE) to signal to the reader which information he borrowed from the two sources. In his Works Cited list at the end of his paper, he listed full source information for both sources.

SOURCES LISTED ON DEVON'S WORKS CITED PAGE

Robbins, Jim. "Global Warming Kills Forests in Colorado." *Newsweek* 19 Apr. 2010: 8. Web. 5 May 2011.

Roosevelt, Margot. "Vanishing Alaska." *Time* 4 Oct. 2004: 68-70. Print.

● **EXERCISE 17-1**   Write a one-paragraph synthesis of the summary of the Barry Schwartz passage (on page 144) and the following opening to a short online article by Ronni Sandroff, editor of *Consumer Reports on Health.*

Last time I dropped by my pharmacy in search of a decongestant, I was stopped cold by the wall-sized display of remedies. The brands I had used in the past had multiplied into extended families of products. Yes, I saw *Contac, Excedrin, Tylenol,* and *Vicks,* but each brand came in multiple versions. Products for severe colds, coughs and colds, and headache and flu abounded, and there were further choices: gels, tablets, capsules, extended release, extra strength. I was eager to just grab a product and go, but to find the right one I had to dig out my reading glasses and examine the fine print.   [from page 3]

—Ronni Sandroff, "Too Many Choices" ●

Tab 5
Research Writing

Tab 5 Research Writing

MyCompLab® Visit mycomplab.com for the eText and for resources on research writing.

Quick Points   You will learn to

> Choose a research topic and refine a research question (see 18B and 18C).
> Identify two main types of research papers (p. 164).

18A What is research?

Research is a systematic process of gathering information to answer a question. You're doing research when you're trying to decide which college to attend or which smartphone to buy. Even these everyday tasks have things in common with college research: finding, evaluating, and synthesizing information. Research is an absorbing, creative activity. It lets you come to know a subject deeply, leads to fresh insights, and shapes you into a self-reliant learner.

How much research you will do for a writing assignment can vary, depending on your AUDIENCE, PURPOSE, and type of writing (Chapter 5; Chapters 9–14). Commonly, you might need to write a RESEARCH OR TERM PAPER,* and Chapter 23 will help you with such long projects. However, any writing might benefit from a little research. Consider the original and revised sentences that follow.

> ORIGINAL   Most people own a cell phone these days.
>
> RESEARCHED   According to the Pew Research Center, 84% of American adults owned a cell phone in 2011 (Purcell 2).

WORK CITED

Purcell, Kristen, Lee Rainie, Tom Rosenstiel, and Amy Mitchell. "How Mobile Devices are Changing Community Information Environments." *Pew Internet Project*. Pew Research Center, 14 Mar. 2011. Web. 20 Apr. 2011.

In the second version, the writer specifically answers the question, "How many people own cell phones?" Whenever writing has a vague language like "a lot" or "many" or "some," research can improve it with more precise information. Your ETHICAL APPEALS (Ch. 3) are stronger because readers respect you as someone who takes the time to find facts. Specific details persuade readers.

---

* Words printed in SMALL CAPITAL LETTERS are discussed elsewhere in the text and are defined in the Terms Glossary at the back of the book.

Here are major reasons writers do research:

- **To find a single fact.** Sometimes you simply need to answer a direct question of "How much?" or "When?" or "Where?" or "Who?"

  - How does the cost of college today compare to the cost twenty years ago?

- **To understand an issue or situation more broadly.** Sometimes you need to learn basic information as well as the range of viewpoints or opinions on a particular topic.

  - What are the effects of globalization?

- **To gather current information.** You may need to bring together the most current information. A **review of the literature** is a comprehensive synthesis of the latest knowledge on a particular topic.

  - What treatments are possible for diabetes?

- **To identify a specific opinion or point of view.** You might want to find out what the people who disagree with you believe—and why. You can then defend your position. You might also look for experts who support your view.

  - What are the arguments for colleges restricting student Internet downloads?

- **To create new knowledge.** Researchers can also make new knowledge. Chemists and biologists do this kind of research, of course, but so do psychologists, sociologists, journalists, and others. They do experiments, surveys, interviews, and observations. For instance, if you were writing a guide to coffeehouses in a certain area, you'd need to visit all of them, take notes, and present your findings to readers. Field research (see 19C) is a general name for research that creates new knowledge.

  - What are the current political views of 18- to 25-year-olds?

18B How do I choose a research topic?

Watch
the Video Sometimes college instructors assign specific topics; other times you get to choose (see 5F). When you need to select your own research topic:

- Select a topic that interests you. It will be your companion for quite a while, perhaps most of a term.

- Choose a sufficiently narrow topic that will allow you to be successful within the time and length given by the assignment. Avoid topics that are too broad.

  NO Emotions

  YES How people respond to anger in others

NO Social networking

YES The effect of Facebook on job applications

- Choose a topic that your readers will perceive as significant. Avoid trivial topics that prevent you from investigating ideas, analyzing them critically, or synthesizing complex concepts.

NO Kinds of fast food

YES The relation between fast food and obesity

If the freedom to choose any topic leads to research–topic block, don't panic. Instead, try some of the following strategies for generating ideas.

- **Talk with others.** Ask instructors or other experts in your area of interest what issues currently seem important to them. Ask them to recommend readings or the names of authorities on those issues.
- **Browse the Internet.** Some Web search engines provide SUBJECT DIRECTORIES (see 20E). Browsing those, their categories and subcategories can turn up an interesting topic.
- **Pay attention to news and current events.** Regularly browsing newspapers or magazines (print or online), blogs, or social network channels can furnish a wealth of issues and topics.
- **Browse textbooks in your area of interest.** Read the table of contents and major headings in a textbook related to your topic. Note the names of important books and experts, often mentioned in reference lists at the end of chapters or at the back of the book.
- **Read encyclopedia articles.** Read online and, if available, print encyclopedias about your area of interest. Notice its subcategories for possible ideas for investigation. Never, however, stop with encyclopedias—they are too basic for college-level research. Be very cautious about using information from Wikipedia because it can be seriously unreliable (see the Alert in 20H).
- **Browse the library or a good bookstore.** Stroll through the shelves to find subjects that interest you. Look at books as well as popular magazines. Skim academic journals in fields that interest you.

18C What is a research question?

A **research question** provides a clear focus for your research and a goal for your WRITING PROCESS. Without such a question, your research writing can become an aimless search for a haphazard collection of facts and opinions. For example, you can more successfully research the question "How do people become homeless?" than you can research the broad topic of "homelessness." Some questions can lead to a final, definitive answer (for example, "How does penicillin destroy bacteria?"). Others can't because they involve an argument that has two or more sides (for example, "Is softball a better sport than volleyball?").

The answer to your research question usually, but not always, appears in your THESIS STATEMENT (see 5G) of your research essay. Sometimes the thesis statement simply alludes to your answer, especially when the answer is long or complicated.

18D What are two main types of research papers?

Most research papers are either informative or argumentative. Informative research papers explain a topic by SYNTHESIZING several sources (see 17D). Your goal is to gather and clarify scattered information for your readers. Informative research papers answer questions like "What is the current state of knowledge about X?" or "What are the current controversies or positions about Y?" We devote Chapter 22 to synthesizing and integrating sources in research papers.

In section 23C, we present a FRAME for writing an informative research paper. It is much like the frame for an informative essay in Chapter 10, and the sample student essay in section 10E serves as a useful example of informative writing.

Argumentative research papers go a step further to argue a point. In these papers, you choose a topic on which intelligent people have different positions, identify and analyze sources, and argue the position that appears best. You back reasons with support. Argumentative research papers answer questions like, "What is the best course of action regarding X?" or "Why should I believe Y?"

In section 23C, we present a frame for an argumentative research paper along with a sample student paper. That example is a companion to the frame and sample argumentative student essay in Chapter 12, as well as to the frame and sample proposal–solution student essay in Chapter 13.

19 Developing a Search Strategy

■ ■ ■ ■ ■ ■ ■

Quick Points   You will learn to

➤ Use search strategies appropriate for your research project (see 19A–19C).
➤ Do field research (pp. 166–169).
➤ Maintain a research log and bibliographies (pp. 170–173).
➤ Take effective notes (pp. 174–175).

19A   What is a search strategy?

A SEARCH STRATEGY is an organized procedure for locating and gathering sources to answer your research question. Using a search strategy helps you work more systematically and quickly. Following are three frequently used search strategies. You can switch or combine strategies or create your own.

QUESTIONING METHOD
Useful when you have a topic. Think of a research question and brainstorm to break it into several smaller questions. Then find sources to answer each of them. This allows you to see if your sources cover all the areas important to your research question. This can give your search a direction and purpose.

EXPERT METHOD
Useful when your topic is specific and narrow. Start with articles or books by an expert in the field. You might want to interview an expert on the topic. Then pursue key sources mentioned.

CHAINING METHOD
Useful when your topic is general. Start with reference books and bibliographies in current articles or WEB SITES. Use them to link to additional sources. Keep following the links until you reach increasingly expert sources. You might also talk with people who have some general knowledge of your topic and ask them to refer you to experts and/or sources they might know.

Start and complete your search as soon as possible after you get your assignment. This gives you time early in your process to discover sources that take time to obtain (for example, through an interlibrary loan).

One more piece of advice: Rather than spend endless hours simply gathering sources, take time to read and analyze some of your materials to make sure your topic will work. Your research log (see 19E) can be useful for this purpose.

19B   What is a source?

Watch the Video

A SOURCE is any form of information that provides ideas, examples, or evidence. Sources are either primary or secondary.

- A PRIMARY SOURCE is original work that can take one of two forms. One is FIELD RESEARCH (see 19C) that you carry out yourself, such as experiments, observations, interviews, or surveys. Another form is original documents such as letters, diaries, novels, poems, short stories, autobiographies, original reporting, findings from a research study, speeches, journals, or so on. In addition to physical copies in libraries or elsewhere, copies of original documents often exist online in digital form.

- A SECONDARY SOURCE reports, describes, comments on, or analyzes someone's original work. That is, someone other than the primary source relays the information, adding a layer between you and the original material. This happens online all the time; someone summarizes a news article in a blog (or maybe only includes a link) but then comments on it. Secondary sources aren't necessarily weak, but be sure to evaluate them to check what's being reported to you isn't distorted or biased.

Suppose you wish to research student attitudes toward American policy in the Middle East. Surveying several students would be primary research. Consulting scholars' books and articles about student attitudes toward the Middle East would be secondary research. Your decision to use primary and/or secondary sources depends on your research question or the nature of your assignment. For her paper in Chapter 29, Leslie Palm conducted primary research by analyzing several video games and secondary research by reading scholarly articles about them.

19C   What is field research?

Field research involves going into real-life situations to observe, survey, interview, or participate in some activity firsthand. As a field researcher, you might go to a factory, a lecture, a day-care center, or a mall—anywhere that people engage in everyday activities. You might also interview experts and other relevant individuals. Finally, you might observe and describe objects, such as paintings or buildings, or performances and events, such as concerts or television shows. Field research yields original data.

■ Surveying

Surveys use questions to gather information about peoples' experiences, situations, or opinions. Multiple-choice or true/false questions are easy for people to complete and for researchers to summarize and report. Open-ended questions, in which people are asked to write responses, require more effort to summarize. However, they sometimes provide more complete or accurate information. For advice on developing a survey, see Quick Box 19.1.

Watch the Video

When you report findings from a survey, keep within your limitations. For example, if the only people who answer your survey are students at a particular campus, you can't claim they represent "all college students."

🚯 **Alert:** Online tools can help you distribute and analyze surveys easily. Two popular free services for small surveys are Zoomerang and Survey-Monkey. You go to the service's Web site, enter your survey questions, and then receive a URL to send to participants. After you receive responses, you can go back to the Web site to download the results or do some analysis. ●

Quick Box 19.1   ■ ■ ■ ■ ■ ■ ■ ■ ■

Guidelines for developing a survey

1. Define what you want to learn.
2. Identify the appropriate types and numbers of people to answer your survey so that you get the information you need.
3. Write questions to elicit the information.
4. Phrase questions so that they are easy to understand.

   NO   Recognizing several complex variables, what age generally do you perceive as most advantageous for matrimony?

   YES   What do you think is the ideal age for getting married?

5. Make sure that your wording doesn't imply what you want to hear.

   NO   Do irresponsible and lazy deadbeats deserve support from hardworking and honest taxpayers?

   YES   Should we provide benefits to unemployed people?

6. Decide whether to include open-ended questions that allow people to write their own answers.
7. Test a draft of the questionnaire on a small group of people. If any question is misinterpreted or difficult to understand, revise and retest it.

■ Interviewing

Watch
the Video

Instead of surveying, you might interview people in the general population to gather data or opinions. You might also interview experts, who can offer valuable information and viewpoints. One good place to start is with the faculty at your college, who may also suggest additional sources. Also, corporations, institutions, or professional organizations often have public relations offices that can answer questions or make referrals.

Make every attempt to conduct interviews in person so that you can observe body language and facial expressions. However, if distance is a problem, you can conduct interviews over the phone or online. Quick Box 19.2 provides suggestions for conducting interviews.

■ Observing people and situations

Anthropologists, education and marketing researchers, sociologists, and other scholars conduct research by observing people and situations. For observations of behavior (for example, fans at a game or tourists at a museum), take notes during the activity. Try to remain objective so that you can see things clearly.

Quick Box 19.2

Conducting research interviews

- Arrange the interview well in advance, do background research, prepare specific questions, and arrive on time.

- Rehearse how to ask your questions without reading them (perhaps highlight the key words). Looking your interviewee in the eye as you ask questions establishes ease and trust. If you're interviewing on the telephone, be organized and precise.

- Take careful notes, listening especially for key names, books, Web sites, or other sources.

- Create a shortcut symbol or letter for key terms you expect to hear during the interview. This cuts down on the time needed to look away from your interviewee.

- Use standard paper so that you have room to write. (Many people are annoyed when others type while they're talking.)

- Bring extra pens or pencils.

- Never depend on recording an interview because people have become reluctant to be recorded.

Figure 19.1 A double-column set of notes.

Notes	Comment/Analyses
Small conference room; round table covered with papers	
JP suggests fundraising plan	JP seems nervous. Her normal behavior, or is it this situation?
AR and CT lean forward; SM leans back	
SM interrupts JP's plan, asks for more; CT silent	The fact that JP and AR are women might explain SM's response. Or is it that he's more senior?
JP continues proposal	
SM looks out window, taps pencil	Seems to have made up his mind. A power move?

One strategy is to take notes in a two-column format. On the left, record only objective observations; on the right, record your comments or possible interpretations. Figure 19.1 is an example of a double-column note strategy.

19D What documentation style should I use?

A DOCUMENTATION STYLE is a system for providing information to your readers about each source you use. Documentation styles vary from one academic discipline to another.

MLA (Modern Language Association) STYLE (Chapter 24): Humanities

APA (American Psychological Association) STYLE (Chapter 27): Social sciences

CM (*Chicago Manual*) STYLE (Chapter 30): Various disciplines, generally in the humanities

CSE (Council of Science Editors) STYLE (Chapter 31): Many natural sciences

If you don't know which style to use, ask your instructor. Use only one documentation style in each piece of writing.

Determine the required documentation style at the start so that you keep a list of the exact details you need to document your sources. You need to document all PRIMARY SOURCES and SECONDARY SOURCES. If you're doing primary research, your instructor may ask you to submit notes or results from observations, questionnaires, surveys, or interviews.

19E What is a research log?

A **research log**—a diary of your research process—can be useful for keeping yourself organized and on track. With long projects it's easy to waste time retracing what you've done and figuring out where you're headed next. Research logs can also show instructors and others how carefully you've worked. Here's how to set one up:

- Create a "Research Log" file or folder on your computer or notebook.
- Record each step in your search for information. Enter the date, your search strategies, the gist of the information you discovered, the documentation details of exactly where you found it, and exactly where you have filed your detailed notes, if any, on the source.
- Decide on the next step you should take with your research.
- Realize when you're ready to move away from gathering material to organizing it or writing about it.
- Keep notes on your thoughts and insights as you move through the research, organizing, and writing processes.

Although much of what you write in your research log will never find its way into your paper, it will greatly increase your efficiency. Figure 19.2 shows a page from Andrei Gurov's research log for his paper in Chapter 26.

Figure 19.2 A selection from the research log of Andrei Gurov, who wrote the paper in 26B.

November 17: Finished reading Brown's book, The Déjà Vu Experience. Great source. I wonder if he's published anything more recently. Will meet with reference librarian this afternoon to identify sources.

November 18: Followed librarian's suggestion and searched the PsycINFO database for more recent articles. Found a chapter by Brown in a 2010 book that looks promising.

19F What is a working bibliography?

A WORKING BIBLIOGRAPHY is a preliminary list of the sources you gather in your research. It contains information about each source and where your readers can find it. As a rough estimate, your working bibliography needs to be about twice as long as the list of sources you end up using. Following is a list of basic elements to include (for more detailed information about documenting specific types of sources, see Chapters 24–31).

ELEMENTS OF A CITATION TO RECORD

Books	Periodical Articles	Online Sources
Author(s)	Author(s)	Author(s) (if available)
Title of book	Title of article; digital object identifier (doi), if any	Title of document
Publisher and place of publication	Name of periodical, volume number, issue number	Name of Web site or database; editor or sponsor of site
Year of publication	Date of issue	Date of electronic publication
Call number	Page numbers of article	Electronic address (URL)
Print or Web version?	Print or Web version?	Date you accessed the source

Begin your working bibliography as soon as you start identifying sources. If your search turns up only a very few sources, you may want to change your topic. If it reveals a vast number, you'll want to narrow your topic or choose a different one. Expect to add and drop sources throughout the research process.

You can record your working bibliography on note cards or on a computer. On the one hand, note cards are easy to sift through and rearrange. At the end of your WRITING PROCESS, you can easily alphabetize them to prepare your final bibliography. Write only one source on each card (see Figure 19.3).

On the other hand, putting your working bibliography on a computer saves having to type your list of sources later. If you do this, clearly separate one entry from another alphabetically, by author, or by subtopics.

Figure 19.3 Bibliographic entry in MLA format.

> Brown, Alan S. and Elizabeth J. Marsh. "Digging into Déjà Vu:
> Recent Research on Possible Mechanisms." The Psychology of
> Learning and Motivation: Advances in Research and Theory.
> Ed. Brian H. Ross. Burlington: Academic P, 2010, 33–62. Web.
> 20 Nov. 2011.

Whichever method you use, when you come across a potential source, immediately record the information exactly as you need it to fulfill the requirements of the DOCUMENTATION STYLE your assignment requires. Spending a few extra moments at this stage can save you hours of work and frustration retracing your steps later on.

19G   Can social networking software help me create or organize bibliographies?

Several software programs allow you to store bibliographic information about your sources and then access this information to organize it in many ways. For example, a program like NoodleBib or RefWorks lets you type in information (author, title, publisher, and so on) about each source you find. Then, with a click of a button, you can generate an MLA-style "Works Cited" page, an APA-style "References" page, or a bibliography in many other formats. You can export the bibliography into the paper you're writing, without having to retype. Of course, you're still responsible for the accuracy of any bibliography you generate with this software.

These programs also allow you to import citations directly from many databases, which means you never have to type them. Because you store your source information online, you can access it from any computer. Check to see if your library gives you access to bibliographic software. See Figure 19.4 for an example of one of these programs.

Other online tools can help you collect, store, access, and organize materials you find on the Web. For example, Diigo (http://www.diigo.com/) allows you to store URLs or even copies of Web pages so you always have access to them from any device that connects to the Internet. You can tag each entry by adding descriptive words so that you can search for particular topics later.

Figure 19.4 Web page showing the start of a project in NoodleBib.

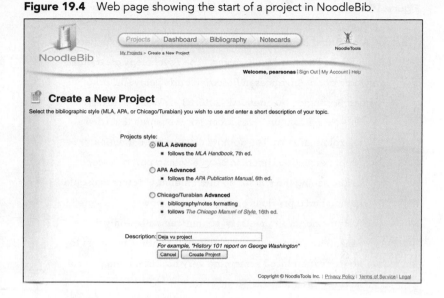

You can also highlight or add notes. You can share your bibliographies with others, which can be helpful for group projects.

There's one disadvantage, however. Because this software makes it so easy to gather materials, it can be tempting to merely record information and avoid analysis. Analysis is vital to making sources your own (see Chapters 4 and 11).

19H What is an annotated bibliography?

An ANNOTATED BIBLIOGRAPHY includes not only documentation information about your sources but also a commentary. Instructors sometimes require annotated bibliographies as a step in research projects, or they sometimes assign them as separate projects in their own right.

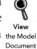

View the Model Document

Most annotations contain

1. The thesis or a one-sentence summary

2. The main points or arguments in support of the thesis

3. The kinds of evidence used in the source (For example, does the source report facts or results from formal studies? Are these primary or secondary? Does source contain stories? Interviews?)

Figure 19.5 shows part of an annotated bibliography using MLA-style documentation.

Figure 19.5 Section from an annotated bibliography in MLA style.

Brown, Alan S. and Elizabeth J. Marsh. "Digging into Déjà Vu: Recent
Research on Possible Mechanisms." *The Psychology of Learning
and Motivation: Advances in Research and Theory.* Ed. Brian
H. Ross. Burlington: Academic P, 2010, 33-62. Web. 20 Nov.2011.

This chapter summarizes laboratory research that tried
to explain déjà vu. The authors discuss three theories.
"Split perception" refers to people seeing part of a scene
before seeing the whole. "Implicit memory" refers to people
having had a previous experience that, however, is stored in
their memories imprecisely, so they remember only the
sensation and not the scene. "Gestalt familiarity" refers to
having experienced something very familiar to the present
setting.

Carey, Benedict. "Déjà Vu: If It All Seems Familiar, There May Be
a Reason." *New York Times* 14 Sept. 2004: F1+. *LexisNexis.*
Web. 11 Nov. 2011.

Scientific research shows that déjà vu is a common and real
phenomenon, even if its causes are unclear. Perhaps the best
explanation is that people have had a similar previous
experience that they have since forgotten.

191 How do I take content notes?

Watch
the Video

When you write **content notes**, you record information from your sources.

- For content notes on index cards, put a heading (title and author) on each
  card that gives a precise link to one of your bibliography items.

- For content notes on your computer, keep careful track of what ideas came
  from each source. One strategy is to open a new file for each source. Later,
  after you determine what topics are important for your paper, open a new
  file and type a heading for each topic. Copy and paste notes from all your
  sources under the headings they best fit.

Figure 19.6 Handwritten content note card in MLA style.

Brown, Alan S. "The Déjà Vu Illusion." <u>Current Directions in</u>
  <u>Psychological Science</u> 13.6 (2004): 256–59. Print.

Summary: Recent advances in neurology and the study of cognitive illusions
reveal that two seemingly separate perceptual events are indeed one.

Comment: This is the part that grabs my attention. How could this be?

- For all content notes, always include the page numbers from which you're taking notes. If an electronic source has no page numbers, use chapter, section, or paragraph numbers, if any.

- For every note, do one of three things: (1) copy the exact words from a source, enclosing them in quotation marks; (2) write a paraphrase; or (3) write a summary. Keep track of the kind of note you're taking to avoid PLAGIARISM. You might use the code *Q* for QUOTATION, *P* for PARAPHRASE, and *S* for SUMMARY.

- As you take notes, separately record your own reactions and ideas. Use critical thinking skills. For example, what are the strengths and weaknesses of the source? What are its implications? Also include a note about what might be useful from the source. Does it provide an example? An idea? A fact? Take care to differentiate your ideas from those in your sources. You might write your own thoughts in a different color ink (note card) or font (computer); you might use a computer's "Comment" feature.

Figure 19.6 shows one of Andrei Gurov's note cards for his research paper in 26B.

19J   How do I plan a research project?

If you feel overwhelmed by the prospect of research writing, you're not alone. Dividing your project into steps makes the process less intimidating, and target deadlines along the way keeps you on track. Quick Box 19.3 suggests how to plan a research project. (The numbers in parentheses tell you where to find more information in this book.)

Quick Box 19.3

■ ■ ■ ■ ■ ■ ■ ■ ■

Sample schedule for a research project

Assignment received _____
Assignment due date _____

PLANNING	FINISH BY (DATE)

1. Start my research log (19E).   _____

2. Choose a topic suitable for research (18B).   _____

3. Draft my research question (18C).   _____

4. Understand my writing situation and type   _____
   of research paper (5D and 19D).

5. Determine what documentation style I need   _____
   to use (19D).

RESEARCHING

6. Plan my SEARCH STRATEGY, but modify as   _____
   necessary (19A).

7. Decide the kinds of research I need to do:

   a. Conduct FIELD RESEARCH (19C)? If yes,   _____
      schedule tasks.
   b. Find published sources?   _____

8. Locate and evaluate sources (20, 21).   _____

9. Compile a working bibliography (19F) and/or   _____
   annotated bibliography (19H).

10. Take content notes from sources I find   _____
    useful (19I).

WRITING

11. Draft my thesis statement (5G).   _____

12. Review content notes and determine relations   _____
    between sources (22).

13. Create an outline, as required or useful (5H).   _____

14. Draft my paper (23B).   _____

15. Use correct in-text citations (24B–C,   _____
    27B–C, 30A, 31A).

continued >>

Quick Box 19.3 (continued)

16. Compile my final bibliography (Works Cited for MLA; References for APA) or any other documentation style required (25A–B, 28A–B, 30B, 31B). _____

17. Revise my paper (23E). _____

18. Edit and proofread my paper for content, plagiarism, in-text citations, bibliography, and format. (23E, 23F)

20 Finding Published Sources

■ ■ ■ ■ ■ ■ ■ ■

Quick Points You will learn to

➤ Identify the different types of published sources (see 20A).

➤ Locate sources using libraries, databases, and online tools (pp. 178–195).

20A What kinds of published sources are there?

Published sources refer to books, articles, documents, and other writings that appear online or in print. Because most college researched writing relies on published sources—material for you to read—we've written this chapter to explain how to find them. The sheer number and types of published sources today can be confusing. However, you can clarify your research by asking two questions: Is the source "scholarly" or "popular"? Quick Box 20.1 helps you decide. Is the source "edited" or "unedited"? Quick Box 20.2 explains the differences.

Popular sources can be high quality, especially if they're edited and from serious publishers or periodicals (such as *The New York Times* or *The Atlantic Monthly*). Unedited sources can be useful, too, but because no editor has selected or reviewed them, you should judge them carefully before you use them. Chapter 21 explains how to evaluate all your sources.

Quick Box 20.1

Scholarly sources versus popular sources

Scholarly Sources	Popular Sources
Examples: Journal articles; books published by university presses; professional organization Web sites	**Examples:** Newspapers and magazines; general Web sites and blogs
Audience: Scholars, experts, researchers, students	**Audience:** General readers; people who may be interested but don't necessarily have specific knowledge or expertise
Purpose: To provide cutting-edge ideas and information supported by research	**Purpose:** To entertain; to translate expert information for general readers; to persuade
Authors: Researchers; professors; content experts; professionals	**Authors:** Journalists or freelance writers; hobbyists or enthusiasts; people from all walks of life
Characteristics: Citations and bibliographies show sources of ideas; sources explain research methods and limitations of conclusions	**Characteristics:** Rarely include citations or bibliographies; might refer to people or sources in the body of the work
Where published: Appear in scholarly books and periodicals or on Web sites maintained by professional organizations	**Where published:** Appear in popular books and periodicals; blogs; personal or informal Web sites
How you find them: Mainly through DATABASES	**How you find them:** Sometimes through databases; often through SEARCH ENGINES

20B How can libraries help me?

Watch the Video

In an age when the Web contains billions of pages of information, it might seem almost prehistoric to talk about libraries. After all, the library is where generations of college students have traditionally gone to find books and PERIODICALS organized by CATALOGS, INDEXES, and DATABASES, but today so much is now available online. Still, many sources, especially scholarly ones, are available only through the library. Notice that we've said "through" the library, not necessarily "in" it. That's because many library sources and services are available through the Internet to students or registered users.

Quick Box 20.2

■ ■ ■ ■ ■ ■ ■ ■ ■

Edited versus unedited sources

Edited	Unedited
Examples: Periodicals; books from a publisher; organizational or professional Web site	**Examples:** Personal blogs and Web sites; online comments or discussion postings; self-published books
Selection: An editor or other professional has evaluated and chosen the work to publish	**Selection:** The individual publishes his or her work (for example, in a blog)
Accuracy/Quality: Reviewed by an editor or expert readers	**Accuracy/Quality:** Not reviewed by others before publication
Publisher: A periodical, book publisher, or professional organization	**Publisher:** The author him- or herself (as in blogs or discussion posts) or perhaps a special-interest group
How you find them: Mainly through databases or catalogs	**How you find them:** Mainly through search engines; unedited works almost never appear in databases

In many respects, the function that a library performs is even more important than the physical building. Librarians and scholars have systematically gathered and organized sources so that you can find the best ones efficiently and reliably. You can access and search electronic catalogs, indexes, and databases from computers with the library itself or, in many cases, by connecting to the library via the Internet. If you have remote access, you'll probably need to log in with an ID and password. In fact, you might be able use library-based sources without ever setting foot in the building.

Still, the building itself continues to be a vital place for all research. One key advantage of going to the library is your chance to consult with librarians face-to-face. Helping is their profession. Never hesitate to ask how to proceed or where to find a resource. Quick Box 20.3 lists ten useful questions librarians are used to answering.

20C What are search engines and databases?

Using search engines and using databases are two related, but different, ways to find published sources.

Quick Box 20.3

■ ■ ■ ■ ■ ■ ■ ■ ■ ■

Top ten questions to ask a librarian

1. Do I need to log in to use the library's computer system? If so, how?

2. Can I access the library's computer system from home or off campus?

3. How do I search the library's catalog?

4. Can I look for books directly on the shelves, or do I need to request them from a central place? How do I check out materials?

5. How do I use an electronic version of a library book?

6. What databases would you recommend if I'm looking for scholarly sources on topic X?

7. What might be the best keywords or search strategy to use when I'm searching databases for sources on topic X?

8. How can I best keep track of sources I find? Can I e-mail them to myself? Print a list of citations?

9. How can I get copies of articles or other sources I need?

10. If our library doesn't own a source I need, is there a way for me to access or order a copy?

■ Search engines

Watch the Video

Search engines are programs designed to hunt the Web for sources on specific topics by using KEYWORDS (see 20D) or subject directories (see 20E). Once you use a BROWSER (a program like Internet Explorer, Firefox, or Safari) to get on the Web, you can use a search engine like Google (www.google.com) or Yahoo! (www.yahoo.com). Of course, if you know a specific Web address—called a **URL**, for Universal (or Uniform) Resource Locator—you can type it directly in a search box. Quick Box 20.4 offers tips for using search engines.

Anyone can put anything on the Web. This makes the Web a rich source of information, but it also makes finding what you need difficult, and it opens the possibility of encountering inaccurate or biased materials. Searching the Web will produce hits: links to specific sites or materials. However, many articles and documents, especially those published in scholarly journals or some edited periodicals, can't be found on the Web through search engines. To find them, you need to use databases.

■ Databases

Watch the Video

DATABASES are collections of sources that experts or librarians have gathered. You find databases mostly in libraries or through library Web sites, and you search them mainly by using keywords. We explain how in section 20D.

Quick Box 20.4

■ ■ ■ ■ ■ ■ ■ ■ ■

Tips on using Web search engines

- Use keyword combinations or BOOLEAN EXPRESSIONS if you need to narrow your search (see Quick Box 20.5).

- Try using more than one search engine because different search engines will provide different results for the same search.

- To be able to return to a good source easily, go to the toolbar at the top of the screen, click on "Bookmark," and then click on "Add." Or use social networking software (see 19G) to gather your sources.

- Use the "History" function in your search engine to revisit sites you've been to before.

- Be prepared to find sources in various formats. Most common are Web pages in html (Hypertext Markup Language) format. However, you may also encounter Word or Excel documents, PowerPoint slides, or PDF (portable document format) files.

Sources that you identify through databases are usually more reliable and appropriate than sources you find by simply browsing the Web. Therefore, we recommend that you search a database as part of any college research project.

Alert: Google Scholar is a site within Google that does pretty much what it announces: lists scholarly sources, including books and articles, that are on the Web. It functions somewhat like a database. ●

Most college libraries subscribe to one or more database services, such as EBSCO, ProQuest, and FirstSearch. Your library's Web site will show the resources it has available. Because the college pays for these services, you don't have to, but you'll need an ID or password to use them. Commonly, your student number serves as your ID, but check with a librarian to see what's required at your college.

GENERAL DATABASES include sources from a broad range of periodicals and books, both popular and scholarly. General databases are suitable for academic research projects. However, take care to focus on scholarly sources and well-regarded popular publications. Large libraries have many general databases. A common one is *Academic Search Premier*.

SPECIALIZED DATABASES focus on specific subject areas or disciplines. They list books and articles published by and for expert readers. Some examples include *Art Abstracts*, *MLA International Bibliography*, *PsycINFO*, and *Business*

Abstracts. Many specialized databases include the abstract, or summary, that is printed at the beginning of each scholarly article.

Each source in a DATABASE contains bibliographic information, including a title, author, date of publication, and publisher (in the case of books or reports) or periodical (in the case of articles). The entry might also provide a summary or list of contents.

20D How do I use search engines and databases?

Watch
the Video

KEYWORDS (also called *descriptors* or *identifiers*) are your pathways to finding sources in databases, catalogs, and Web sites. Keywords are the main words in a source's title or words that an author or editor has identified as most important to its topic and content. Figure 20.1 shows three screens from a keyword search

Figure 20.1 Keyword search of *déjà vu* in a database.

Keyword Search

Searching: PaycINFO | Choose Databases >>

deja vu   in Select a Field (optional)   Search   Clear

AND   in Select a Field (optional)

AND   in Select a Field (optional)   Add Row

Basic

95 Results for...

Refine your resul

☐ Linked Full Text
☐ References Availabl
☐ Scholarly (Peer Revi
   Journals

2005 Publication
     Date

Partial
search
result

One article
selected from
the database

7. Déjà vu: Origins and phenomenology: Implications of the four subtypes for future research.
Neppe, Vernon M.; Journal of Parapsychology, Vol 74(1), Spr. 2010. pp. 61-97. [Journal Article]
An analysis of déjà vu subtypes is done in accordance with Neppe's universally accepted operational definition of déjà vu (any subjectively inappropriate impression of familiarity of the present ...
Subjects: Consciousness States; Etiology; Parapsychology; Phenomenology
Database: PsycINFO
Add to folder Relevancy: ▪▪▪▪▪▪▪▪▪ | Cited References: (71)
Find this item in Penrose Library   ARTICLE   Check Article Linker

8. **Novel insights into false recollection: A model of déjà vécu.**

Authors: O'Connor, Akira R., Washington University in St. Louis, St. Louis, MO, US
Lever, Colin, Institute of Psychological Sciences, University of Leeds, Leeds, United Kingdom
Moulin, Chris J. A., Leeds Memory Group, Institute of Psychological Sciences, University of Leeds, Leeds, United Kingdom, c.j.a.moulin@leeds.ac.uk

Address: Moulin, Chris J. A., Institute of Psychological Sciences, University of Leeds, Leeds, United Kingdom, LS2 9JT, c.j.a.moulin@leeds.ac.uk

Source: Cognitive Neuropsychiatry, Vol 15(1-3), Jan, 2010. pp. 118-144.

Page Count: 27

Publisher: United Kingdom: Taylor & Francis.

ISSN: 1354-6805 (Print)
1464-0619 (Electronic)

Language: English

Keywords: false recollection; cognitive neurosciences; hippocampus; familiarity; dementia; **deja vu**

Abstract: The thesis of this paper is that **déjà** experiences can be separated into two forms: **déjà vu**, arising from the erroneous sensation of familiarity, and **déjà** vécu, arising from the erroneous sensation of recollection. We summarise a series of cases for of *PsycINFO* on *déjà vu*. While working on the research paper that appears in section 26B the student consulted this database.

You can search the Web with a single keyword, but usually that generates far too many or far too few "hits." Combinations of keywords using BOOLEAN EXPRESSIONS or ADVANCED SEARCHES can solve both problems.

Using Boolean expressions

Using BOOLEAN EXPRESSIONS means that you search a database or search engine by typing keyword combinations that narrow and refine your search. To combine keywords, use the words *AND, OR,* and *NOT* (or symbols that represent those words). Quick Box 20.5 explains how.

Quick Box 20.5   ■ ■ ■ ■ ■ ■ ■ ■ ■

Boolean expressions for refining keyword searches

AND or the + ("plus") symbol: Narrows the focus of your search because both keywords must be found. If you research the topic of the APA paper in 29B (how women characters are depicted in video games), the expression *video games AND women AND characters* works. Many search engines and databases don't require the word *AND* between terms. Figure 20.2 illustrates the results.

NOT or the – ("minus") symbol: Narrows a search by excluding texts containing the specified word or phrase. If you want to eliminate women playing games from your search, type *video games AND women AND characters NOT players*.

OR: Expands a search's boundaries by including more than one keyword. If you want to expand your search to include sources about women characters who are either heroes or villains in games, try the expression *video games AND women AND characters OR heroes OR villains*.

Quotation marks (" "): Direct the search to match your exact word order. For example, a search for *"role playing games"* will find sources that contain the exact phrase "role playing games." Also, if you search for *James Joyce* without using quotation marks, search engines will return all pages containing the words *James* and *Joyce* anywhere in the document; however, a search using "James Joyce" brings you closer to finding Web sites about the Irish writer.

Figure 20.2 A Venn diagram showing overlaps among video games, women, and characters.

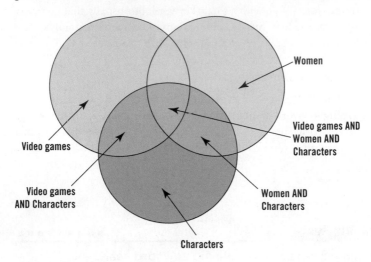

Women

Video games AND
Women AND
Characters

Video games

Video games
AND Characters

Women AND
Characters

Characters

Using advanced searches

Advanced searches (sometimes called *guided searches*) allow you to search by entering information in a form online. A typical search involves selecting a range of dates of publication (for example, after 2010 or between 1990 and 1995) and specifying only a certain language (such as English) or a certain format (such as books). Figure 20.3 shows an example of a search for sources that have *déjà vu* in their titles and use *false memory* as another keyword but are not about *crime*.

Figure 20.3 Advanced keyword search.

20E How do I use subject directories?

Subject directories provide an alternative to keyword searches. These directories are lists of topics (education, computing, entertainment, and so on) or resources and services (shopping, travel, and so on), with links to sources on those topics and resources. Most search engines, and some library catalogs or databases, have one or more subject directories. In addition, there are independent subject directories. Some examples are

> *Educator's Reference Desk* (http://www.eduref.org)
>
> *Librarians' Index to the Internet* (http://lii.org)
>
> *Library of Congress* (http://www.loc.gov)
>
> *Refdesk.com* (http://www.refdesk.com).

Clicking on a general category in a subject directory will take you to lists of increasingly specific categories. Eventually, you'll get a list of Web pages on the most specific subtopic you select. These search engines also allow you to click on a category and enter keywords. For example, suppose you're using Google.com to search for information on organic food. You would first go to Google's general category of "Health" and find the category of "Nutrition." Within "Nutrition" you would find a link to "Organic Food," a page that lists dozens of additional categories and sources.

20F How do I find books?

A library's CATALOG, which lists its holdings (its entire collection), exists as a computer database in almost every modern library. To find a book, you can search by author, by title, by subject, or by keyword. Figure 20.4 shows the home page for a typical **book catalog**, this one at the Library of Congress. Note that it allows you to search by title, author, subject, CALL NUMBER, or keyword; to search particular indexes; or to search using Boolean expressions.

Suppose a source recommends that you find a book by the author Tim Wu, but you don't know its title. A screen on your library's computer will have a place for you to type *Wu, Tim* in a space for "author." (Usually, you enter last name, then first name, but check which system your library uses.) If your library owns any books by Tim Wu, the computer will display their titles and other bibliographic information, such as the library call number. Then you can use the call number to request the book or to find it yourself. Figure 20.5 shows results from search for books by author Tim Wu.

Among the books you might find when searching for "Wu, Tim" is *The Master Switch: The Rise and Fall of Information Empires* (New York: Knopf, 2010. Print.). Suppose you know that book's title but not its author and want to see if your library owns a copy. Find the place to type in the title. In some

Figure 20.4 Library of Congress online catalog.

Figure 20.5 Results of an author search for Tim Wu.

systems, you don't type articles (*a, an, the*), so you would type in only *"Master Switch Rise Fall Information Empires."*

Suppose, however, you don't know an author's name or a book title. You have only a research topic. In this case, you need to search by subject, using the terms listed in the *Library of Congress Subject Headings* (*LCSH*). The *LCSH* is a multivolume catalog available, primarily in book form, in the reference section of every library. An abridged version of the information in the *LCSH* is online at http://authorities.loc.gov.

Finally, you may wish to search by keyword in your library's holdings. You could find Wu's book using the keywords *information, media, technology*, and so on. A sample book catalog keyword search is shown in Figure 20.6.

Scan the results to identify promising sources. When you select a record (usually by clicking on it or a box next to it), you encounter detailed information about the source, as we illustrate in Figure 20.7.

Some libraries allow you to print out this information, send it to your e-mail account, download it, or use social networking (see 19G). Whether you choose one of these options or copy the information directly into your WORKING BIBLIOGRAPHY, it's crucial to record the CALL NUMBER exactly as it

Figure 20.6 A catalog search using keywords.

Figure 20.7 Detailed book record in a library catalog.

This book is on the library's upper level, at the call number listed. However, the book is currently checked out.

appears, with all numbers, letters, and decimal points. The call number tells where the book is located in the library's stacks (storage shelves). If you're researching in a library with open stacks (shelves that are accessible without special permission), the call number leads you to the area in the library where all books on the same subject can be found.

A call number is especially crucial in a library or special collection with closed stacks, which is a library where you hand in a slip at the call desk (or submit a request online) and wait for the book to arrive. Such libraries don't permit you to browse the stacks, so you have to rely entirely on the book catalog.

Figure 20.8 Book available only online.

Author	Clarke, Bruce.
Title	**The Routledge Companion to Literature and Science [electronic resource].**
Publ Info	Hoboken : Taylor & Francis, 2010.

The links below are for electronic versions of this publication:
Access online: Individual login with EBL required

LOCATION	CALL #	STATUS
Internet	PN55.R68 2010eb	ONLINE

Description	1 online resource (569 p.)
Series	Routledge Literature Companions.
	Routledge Literature Companions.
	Routledge Literature Companions.
Note	Book preview interface supplies PDF, image or read-aloud access. Adobe Digital Editions software required for book downloads.
	Mode of access. World Wide Web.
Note(S)	Description based upon print version of record.
Contents	BOOK COVER; TITLE; COPYRIGHT; CONTENTS; FIGURES; CONTRIBUTORS; PREFAE; PART I: LITERATURES AND SCIENCES; 1 AI AND ALIFE; 2 ALCHEMY; 3 BIOLOGY; 4 CHAOS AND COMPLEXITY THEORY; 5 CHEMISTRY; 6 CLIMATE SCIENCE; 7 COGNITIVE SCIENCE; 8 CYBERNETICS; 9 ECOLOGY; 10 EVOLUTION; 11 GENETICS; 12 GEOLOGY; 13 **INFORMATION** THEORY; 14 MATHEMATICS; 15 MEDICINE; 16 NANOTECHNOLOGY; 17 PHYSICS; 18 PSYCHOANALYSIS; 19 SYSTEMS THEORY; 20 THERMODYNAMICS; PART II: DISCIPLINARY AND THEORETICAL APPROACHES; 21 AGRICULTURAL STUDIES; 22 ANIMAL STUDES; 23 ART CONNECTIONS; 24 CULTURAL SCIENCE STUDIES; 25 DECONSTRUCTION

Electronic books

You're probably familiar with electronic books and readers like the Kindle, Nook, or iPad. Many books have electronic versions that you can access—and without paying, if you go through a library. Figure 20.8 shows one book found in a library catalog that's available only in an electronic format. Students at this school can log in to read the book online.

Google has scanned many books and put them on the Web. You can find them by searching Google Books. Even if you find a book you want online, unless it's very old, only a portion of it will be available. If you're lucky, it will be the part you want; otherwise, you'll need to find the book through other means such as Interlibrary Loan. Figure 20.9 shows the Google Books contents for *The Master Switch*.

20G How do I find periodicals?

PERIODICALS are edited magazines, journals, and newspapers published periodically, that is, at set intervals. Periodicals used to appear only in print. Many of them now have Web sites or publish electronic versions. An increasing number of periodicals appear only online. You find periodicals by searching databases. Quick Box 20.6, p. 191, describes several types of periodicals.

Figure 20.9 Google Books contents for *The Master Switch*.

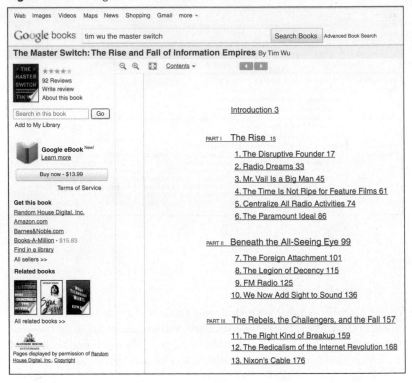

■ Locating articles themselves

Databases help you find information about sources, but how do you get your hands on the source itself? Often you can find an online full-text version of the article to read, download, or print. A full-text version may be either in HTML format or PDF; the listing will tell you which one. If you have a choice, we recommend using the PDF version, which is easier to cite because it has the layout of a print article. However, if you want to copy a section and paste it in your notes, only HTML allows this (but be careful to avoid plagiarism).

Sometimes, however, you need to find a print copy of the periodical. Often the listing in the database will say whether your library owns a copy and what its call number is. Otherwise, you'll need to check if the periodical is listed in the library's CATALOG.

In either case, search for the periodical by name (for example, *American Literature* or *The Economist*), not the article's author or title. Then use its call number to find it in the library. To find the specific article you want, look for the issue in which the article you need appears. For advice on locating sources that your library doesn't own, see the alert on page 195.

Quick Box 20.6

Types of periodicals

Type	Characteristics	Useful for
Journal	Scholarly articles written by experts for other experts; usually focus on one academic discipline; published relatively infrequently; examples are *College Composition and Communication* and *American Journal of Public Health*.	The most reliable expert research on a particular subject; detailed articles and extensive bibliographies that can point to other sources or experts; may also have book reviews
News magazines	Short to modest-length articles on current events or topics of interest to a broad readership; lots of photos and graphics; may have opinions or editorials, as well as reviews; generally are published weekly; examples are *Time* and *Newsweek*	Easily understandable and timely introductions to current topics; often can point to more expert sources, topics, and keywords
Special-interest or "lifestyle" magazines	Written for audiences (including fans and hobbyists) interested in a particular topic; include news and features on that topic; generally published monthly, with entertainment as an important goal; examples include *Outside*, *Rolling Stone*, *Wired*	Providing "how-to" information on their topics of focus, as well as technical information or in-depth profiles of individuals, products, or events; many include reviews related to emphasis; the more serious examples are well written and reliable
"Intellectual" or literary magazines	Publish relatively longer articles that provide in-depth analysis of issues, events, or people; may include creative work as well as nonfiction; aimed at a general, well-educated audience; usually published monthly; examples include *The Atlantic*, *Harper's*, *The New Yorker*	Learning about a topic in depth but in a way more accessible than scholarly journals; becoming aware of major controversies and positions; learning who experts are and what books or other sources have been published; reading arguments on topics

continued >>

Quick Box 20.6 (continued)

Type	Characteristics	Useful for
Trade magazines	Focus on particular businesses, industries, and trade groups; discuss new products, legislation, or events that will influence individuals or businesses in that area; examples include *National Hog Farmer, Sound and Video Contractor*	Specialized information focusing on applying information or research in particular settings; seeing how specific audiences or interest groups may respond to a particular position
Newspapers	Publish articles about current news, sports, and cultural events; contain several sections, including opinions and editorials, lifestyle, sports; most appear daily; examples are *The Washington Post, The DeWitt, Iowa, Observer*	Very current information; national newspapers (such as *The New York Times*) cover world events and frequently have analysis and commentary; local newspapers cover small happenings you likely won't find elsewhere; opinion sections and reviews are sources of ideas and positions

20H How do I use reference works?

Reference works include encyclopedias, almanacs, yearbooks, fact books, atlases, dictionaries, biographical reference works, and bibliographies. *General* reference works provide information on a vast number of subjects, but without much depth. *Specialized* reference works provide information on selected topics, often for more expert or professional audiences.

■ General reference works

GENERAL REFERENCE WORKS are the starting point for many college researchers—but they're no more than a starting point. They help researchers identify useful keywords to use to search for subject headings and online catalogs. They're also good for finding examples and verifying facts.

Most widely used general reference works are available online. Check your library's Web site to see what it has subscribed to. For example, you may find a subscription to the *Gale Virtual Reference Library*, which gives libraries access to up to 1,000 reference books online. Alternatively, you can search the Web on your own. (For example, *Encyclopaedia Britannica* is at http:// www.britannica.com.) Be aware that often you have to pay a fee for works you don't access through a library.

GENERAL ENCYCLOPEDIAS

Articles in multivolume general encyclopedias, such as the *Encyclopaedia Britannica*, can give you helpful background information, the names of major experts in the field, and, often, a brief BIBLIOGRAPHY on the subject.

❶ Alert: A Note on *Wikipedia*. *Wikipedia* is an unedited source that almost anyone can modify. Obviously, then, the accuracy and quality of information it contains isn't always reliable. There's always the possibility that a *Wikipedia* source is flawed. Still, *Wikipedia* can be a useful starting place for some quick information on a topic. For example, like many professionals and professors, we occasionally check *Wikipedia* to learn names, concepts, or basic information on a particular topic. But we know *Wikipedia* is only a starting place, a way to get oriented. Other sources serve us—and you—better for college-level research. When students use *Wikipedia* extensively, readers realize they haven't taken the time or responsibility to find more scholarly sources. ●

ALMANACS, YEARBOOKS, AND FACT BOOKS

Often available both in print and online, almanacs, yearbooks, and fact books are huge compilations of facts and figures. Examples include the *World Almanac, Facts on File*, and the annual *Statistical Abstract of the United States* (accessed online through http://www.census.gov).

ATLASES AND GAZETTEERS

Atlases, such as the *Times Atlas of the World*, contain maps of our planet's continents, seas, and skies. Gazetteers, such as the *Columbia Gazetteer of the World*, provide comprehensive geographical information on topography, climates, populations, migrations, natural resources, and so on.

DICTIONARIES

Dictionaries define words and terms. In addition to general dictionaries, specialized dictionaries focus exclusively on many academic disciplines.

BIOGRAPHICAL REFERENCE WORKS

Biographical reference books, such as the *Who's Who* series and the *Dictionary of American Biography*, give brief factual information about famous people—their accomplishments along with pertinent events and dates in their lives.

BIBLIOGRAPHIES

BIBLIOGRAPHIES are guides to sources on particular topics. They list books, articles, documents, films, and other resources along with publication information so that you can find them. Annotated or critical bibliographies describe and evaluate the works that they list.

■ Specialized reference works

SPECIALIZED REFERENCE WORKS provide authoritative, specific information on selected topics, often for more expert researchers. These works are usually appropriate for college-level research because the information is more advanced and detailed. Examples include the *Dictionary of American Biography, Encyclopedia of Banking and Finance, Encyclopedia of Chemistry, Encyclopedia of Religion, Encyclopedia of the Biological Sciences, International Encyclopedia of Film, New Grove Dictionary of Music and Musicians,* and *Oxford Companion to the Theatre.*

20l How can I find images?

If you need or want to include images in a research paper, you have three options. A keyword search through the "Images" menu on Google or Yahoo! will generate links to images as they appear in sites and documents across the Internet. However, there are ethical and, sometimes, even legal concerns in using what you find this way. Although "fair use" means that students can usually use sources once for a classroom project, you are behaving ethically if you get written permission from the photographer or site where you found the image. Always be sure to cite the source properly.

A good alternative is to use a "stock photo" Web site. These are services like iStockphoto.com or GettyImages.com that have gathered thousands, even millions, of photographs, which you can browse by category or keyword. For a small fee you can purchase the one-time use of an image from these sites. (There are a few "free" sites, too.)

Finally, your library may provide access to image archives or databases. Ask a librarian. Once again, always cite images properly.

20J How do I find government documents?

Government publications are available in astounding variety. You can find information on laws and legal decisions, regulations, population, weather patterns, agriculture, national parks, education, and health, to name just a few topics. Most are available online.

- The Government Printing Office maintains its searchable *Catalog of U.S. Government Publications* at http://www.gpoaccess.gov/index.html.

- THOMAS, a service of the Library of Congress, offers information about legislation at http://thomas.loc.gov/.

- A directory of all U.S. federal government sites, at http://www.fedstats.gov, provides statistical information.

- The LexisNexis database service provides access to a huge number of other governmental reports and documents. For example, the Congressional Information Service indexes all papers produced by congressional panels and committees.

! Alert: Almost no library will contain every source that you need. However, many libraries are connected electronically to other libraries' book catalogs, giving you access to additional holdings. Often you or a librarian can request materials from other libraries through interlibrary loan (generally free of charge). ●

21 Evaluating Sources

Quick Points You will learn to

➤ Identify reliable sources.

Not all sources are created equal. We don't only mean the differences explained in Chapter 20 between books, PERIODICALS, and Web sites, or between scholarly and popular sources. Sources differ also in quality. Some present information that has been carefully gathered and checked. Others report information, Watch the Video

> ### Quick Box 21.1
>
> ■■■■■■■■■■■
>
> **Five questions for evaluating sources**
>
> 1. How did you find the source? (See 21A.)
> 2. Is the publisher authoritative? (See 21B.)
> 3. Is the author qualified to write about the topic? (See 21C.)
> 4. Does the source have sufficient and credible evidence? (See 21D.)
> 5. Does the source pass other critical thinking tests? (See 21E.)

even rumor, that is second- or thirdhand or, worse, perhaps not even based in fact.

Some sources make claims that are accompanied by strong evidence and reasoning. Others make claims based only on opinion, or they use information illogically. Some are written by experts wanting to advance knowledge. Others are produced by people wanting to promote special interests however they can, even if it means ignoring data, oversimplifying issues, or overpromising results. Some sources have been reviewed by experts and published only after passing standards. Others appear without anyone judging their quality.

As a college writer, you don't want to use weak sources that hurt your ETHOS and ruin your paper. Therefore, evaluate each source you find by asking the questions in Quick Box 21.1.

21A How did you find the source?

Sources that you find through DATABASES, especially databases you access through a library Web site (see Chapter 20), are more likely to be useful than sources found through a general Google or Yahoo! search. A source in a database has been edited and checked for quality. The more scholarly a database is, the more confident you can be that its sources are reliable.

For example, suppose you want to research the safety of vaccines. (We illustrate the range of options on this topic in Figure 21.1, where a student has done four different searches.) A Google search produces thousands of sources. Some of them are reliable; many are not. If you search a library database like Academic Search Premier, you'll find hundreds of sources, mainly of higher quality. Still, the most authoritative sources come from a college library's CATALOG or a scholarly database like Medlines, which is created for physicians, researchers, and other medical professionals. (Of course, some highly advanced expert sources can be hard to understand.)

Figure 21.1 Four searches with less to more reliable results.

A. Least Reliable:
A general Google search

A site that expresses the strong opinion that doctors cause autism. You'd have to check this one carefully.

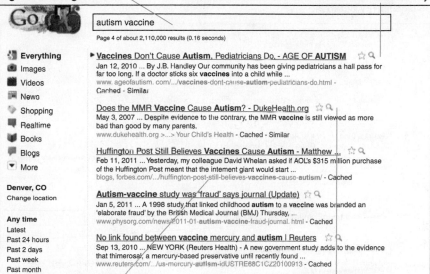

Blogs can have opinions unsupported by facts. Check carefully.

The name and the .org domain suggests that it might be associated with Duke University.

B. More Reliable:
A Google Scholar Search

Sources on this page come from journals in the field, which are edited and written by experts.

Full text versions show that these are articles, not Web sites.

The sources are somewhat old, however, for medical research.

(continued)

Figure 21.1 Four searches with less to more reliable results (continued).

C. Also Reliable: A search using a common college library database

Database includes popular sources like newspaper articles, which will be easier to understand.

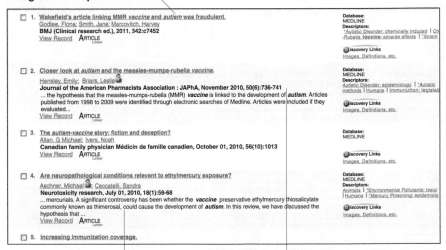

> EBSCOhost: Result List: autism va...
>
> 5. **Refusing kids' vaccine more common**
>   By: Liz Szabo, *USA Today*, 05/04/2010
>   Database: Academic Search Complete
>
>   Add to folder
>
>   HTML Full Text   Find this items in Penrose Library   ARTICLE Linker   Check Article Linker
>
> 6. **3 Rulings Find No Link to Autism in a Mercury Preservative in Vaccines.**
>   By: McNEIL, Jr., DONALD G., *New York Times*, 3/13/2010, p11, 0p
>   Subjects: VACCINATION; AUTISM; DEVELOPMENTAL disabilities; UNITED States; UNITED States. Court of Federal Claims; Administration of Public Health Programs
>
>   Database: Academic Search Complete
>
>   Add to folder
>
>   Find this items in Penrose Library   ARTICLE Linker   Check Article Linker
>
> 7. **Lancet retracts 12-year-old article linking autism to MMR vaccines.**
>   By: Eggertson, Laura, *CMAJ: Canadian Medical Association Journal*, 3/9/2010 Supplement, Vol. 182, pE199-E200, 2p, 1 Color Photograph; DOI: 10.1503/cmaj.109-3179
>   Subjects: VACCINATION of children; AUTISM in children; GREAT Britain; LANCET, The (Periodical); MMR vaccine; WAKEFIELD, Andrew
>
>   Database: Academic Search Complete

Database also includes scholarly sources like journal articles. These PRIMARY SOURCES will have most authoritative research but can sometimes be difficult.

D. Expert: A search using a database designed for experts in a field

> ☐ 1. Wakefield's article linking MMR *vaccine* and *autism* was fraudulent.
>   Godlee, Fiona; Smith, Jane; Marcovitch, Harvey
>   **BMJ (Clinical research ed.), 2011, 342:c7452**
>   View Record ARTICLE Linker
>   Database: MEDLINE
>   Descriptors: *Autistic Disorder: chemically induced | Ch *Rubella Vaccine: adverse effects | *Scient
>   Discovery Links
>   Images, Definitions, etc.
>
> ☐ 2. Closer look at *autism* and the measles-mumps-rubella *vaccine*.
>   Hensley, Emily; Briars, Leslie
>   **Journal of the American Pharmacists Association : JAPhA, November 2010, 50(6):736-741**
>   ... the hypothesis that the measles-mumps-rubella (MMR) *vaccine* is linked to the development of *autism*. Articles published from 1998 to 2009 were identified through electronic searches of Medline. Articles were included if they evaluated...
>   View Record ARTICLE Linker
>   Database: MEDLINE
>   Descriptors: Autistic Disorder: epidemiology | *Autistic methods | Humans | Immunization: legislat
>   Discovery Links
>   Images, Definitions, etc.
>
> ☐ 3. The *autism-vaccine* story: fiction and deception?
>   Allan, G Michael; Ivers, Noah
>   **Canadian family physician Médicin de famille canadien, October 01, 2010, 56(10):1013**
>   View Record ARTICLE Linker
>   Database: MEDLINE
>   Discovery Links
>   Images, Definitions, etc.
>
> ☐ 4. Are neuropathological conditions relevant to ethylmercury exposure?
>   Aschner, Michael; Ceccatelli, Sandra
>   **Neurotoxicity research, July 01, 2010, 18(1):59-68**
>   ... mercurials. A significant controversy has been whether the *vaccine* preservative ethylmercury thiosalicylate commonly known as thimerosal, could cause the development of *autism*. In this review, we have discussed the hypothesis that ...
>   View Record ARTICLE Linker
>   Database: MEDLINE
>   Descriptors: Animals | *Environmental Pollutants: toxic | Humans | *Mercury Poisoning: epidemiolo
>   Discovery Links
>   Images, Definitions, etc.
>
> ☐ 5. Increasing immunization coverage.

Short descriptions provide some information about article contents.

All articles in this database come from scholarly journals, and many report research.

21B Is the publisher authoritative?

The publisher is the company or group ultimately responsible for a book, periodical, or Web site.

Is the Publisher Authorative?

Reliable sources are . . .	Questionable sources are . . .
• **From reputable publishers.** Generally, encyclopedias, textbooks, and academic journals, such as the *Journal of Counseling and Development*, are authoritative. Books from university and other established presses are authoritative. Sources published in major newspapers, such as *The Washington Post*; in general-readership magazines such as *Time, Harper's*, and textbooks, such as those from Pearson, are reliable, too. See Figure 21.2.	• **From special-interest groups.** Some groups exist only to advance a narrow interest or political viewpoint. Examples would be a group existing only to legalize marijuana or one to stop all immigration. Special-interest groups might publish useful sources, but you want to check their facts and reasoning by asking "Why does the group exist?" Be sure to question its motives, especially if it asks you to take a specific action, such as donate money. See if materials published by the group are included in scholarly databases, and apply other tests listed in this chapter.
• **Web sites from educational, not-for-profit, or government organizations.** Web sites from professional associations, such as the National Council of Teachers of English or The American Medical Association, are reliable. If you don't recognize an organization, you need to investigate how long it has existed, whether it is not-for-profit, who its members and leaders are, and so on.	• **Web sites from commercial enterprises** may or may not provide evidence or list sources for claims they make. If they fail to do so, or if the evidence and sources seem weak, don't use them. Be sure the Web site is not one that encourages illegal activities. See Figure 21.3.
• **Direct online versions of authoritative print sources.** Many journals, newspapers, and book publishers release online versions of print publications. Online versions of authoritative publications are reliable.	• **Secondhand excerpts, quotations, and references.** Materials that appear in a source that is not the official site of the publisher (such as a quotation taken from a magazine) may have been edited in a biased or inaccurate manner. Always check the original. Figure 21.4 illustrates a problem that can occur with secondhand materials.

Figure 21.2 A commercial (nonscholarly) book and a scholarly book.

Commercial Book

A self-help book that gives diet and relationship advice and promises results. The publisher also sponsors a commercial Web site focusing on spin-off products. This is not a scholarly source.

McIntire, Marilyn. *Love Yourself Thin!* Ankeny, IA: Maddie, 2012. Print.

Scholarly Book

A scholarly book that reports findings from a research study of body image and relationships among young college graduates. The publisher is a university press.

Neufeld, Sarah. *Body Image, Relationships, and the Influence of Popular Culture.* Evergreen, CO: Evans UP, 2012. Print.

21C Is the author qualified to write about the topic?

Anyone can express an opinion or argue for an action, but the only writers worth your quoting or summarizing in your writing have knowledge and expertise about their topics. Often, their credentials appear in a note in an

Figure 21.3 An authoritative Web site and a questionable Web site.

An authoritative Web site

A .gov URL signals government sponsorship.

Site points to a wide range of information.

Site emphasizes facts.

Site is current.

A questionable Web site

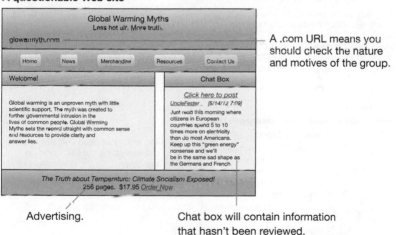

A .com URL means you should check the nature and motives of the group.

Advertising.

Chat box will contain information that hasn't been reviewed.

Note: Site might have worthy information, but it needs checking.

introduction, at the bottom of the first page, or at the end of an article. In a book, look for an "About the Author" statement, on a Web site a short biography or a "Contributors" note (see Figure 21.5). Sometimes you might need to do some research to learn about the author.

Figure 21.4 A section from an original article and a misused quotation from that article.

THURSDAY, MARCH 10, 2011 SEARCH OUR SITE

the **Atlantic**

POLITICS | BUSINESS | CULTURE | INTERNATIONAL |

APRIL 2011 ATLANTIC MAGAZINE

At an individual level, I think the "distracted Americans" scare will pass. Either people who manage to unplug, focus, and fully direct their attention will have an advantage over those constantly checking Facebook and their smart phone, in which case they'll earn more money, get into better colleges, start more successful companies, and win more Nobel Prizes. Or they won't, in which case distraction will be a trait of modern life but not necessarily a defect. At the level of national politics, America is badly distracted, but that problem long predates Facebook and requires more than a media solution.

Fallows, James. "Learning to Love the (Shallow, Divisive, Unreliable) New Media." *The Atlantic,* April 2011. Web. 10 Mar. 2011.

Comment on original: In the original full article from *The Atlantic*, a serious magazine for general readers, James Fallows agrees that Americans are distracted when it comes to politics, but he does not blame the Internet for that situation.

CIVILIZATION
The Truth about Our Declining World
About / Links / Campaigns / Donations

James Fallows complains about the effects of the internet on democracy when he says that, "At the level of national politics, America is badly distracted."

Comment on misused quotation: The Civilization Web site misrepresents Fallows. By using only part of his quotation, it makes him express exactly the opposite of what he actually wrote. It would be a serious mistake to quote this site.

Figure 21.5 An author without scholarly credentials and an author with.

Start Loving Life!

Hi! I'm **Marilyn McIntire**, motivational speaker, fitness guru, relationship coach, and author. My life has been an astonishing adventure, and yours can be, too. Let's walk this journey together! Check me out whenever you need inspiration, advice, and a good laugh. —Rainbow joys, Marilyn

If you were writing an academic paper on dieting and evaluating the two books in Figure 21.2 (page 200), the credentials of Sarah Neufeld would be much more credible. (Marilyn McIntire's credentials would be suitable for other purposes, perhaps, but not for an academic paper.)

Sarah Neufeld

Psychology Department Chair

Dr. Sarah Neufeld, Professor of Psychology at Evans University, was named chair of the department in 2011. She joined the faculty after receiving her Ph.D. from New York University in 1998 and has published over 35 articles in her area of research: the effects of popular culture on self-esteem and interpersonal behavior.

Is the Author Qualified to Write About the Topic?

Reliable sources are . . .	Questionable sources are . . .
• **From expert authors.** Experts have degrees or credentials in their field. Biographical material in the source may list these credentials. If in doubt, look up the author in a biographical dictionary, search online for a resume or bio, or search a database. Check if the author's name appears in other reliable sources. Check whether there is contact information for questions or comments.	• **From authors with fuzzy credentials.** A warning sign should flash when you can't identify who has produced a source. Discussion threads, anonymous blogs, and similar online postings are questionable when they don't give information about the writer's qualifications. Check to make sure that listed credentials fit the topic. Just because someone has a graduate degree in history, for example, doesn't qualify the person to give medical advice.

ESOL Tip: The definition of "authority" can differ across cultures. In the United States, a source has authority only if it meets specific criteria. It must appear in a scholarly book or journal; its author must have a degree, title, or license; or other authorities must seek his or her knowledge. A source is not reliable simply because the author or speaker is an influential or well-known member of the community; claims to have knowledge about a topic but has no credentials related to the topic; or publishes material in print or online on the topic without being qualified to do so. You are expected to judge the authority of sources in a U.S. college. ●

21D Does the source have sufficient and accurate evidence?

If an author expresses a point of view but offers little evidence to back up that position, reject the source. See Figure 21.6 for an example of how sources use evidence.

Figure 21.6 Source that cites evidence and source that does not.

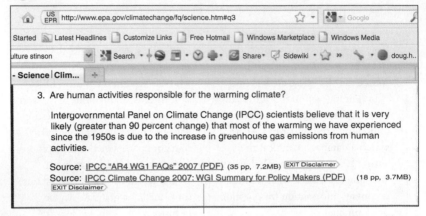

The Environmental Protection Agency provides specific facts, and the source of those facts.

RedDawn [6/13/2012]
So it's been hot and the global warming clones are screaming again. Big deal. many scientists show that theres no proof we're making the world warmer, just google it if you want to know the truth. If the temperatures increasing, its because of natural causes not pollution, smoke, etc. Politicians wont give money to real scientists to prove it. Common sense, people!

This posting, from a blog, makes claims but provides no evidence, simply telling readers to "just google it."

The source has some proofreading errors, substitutes name-calling for reasoning, and has other logical fallacies.

Does the Source Have Sufficient and Accurate Evidence?

Reliable sources are . . .	Questionable sources are . . .
• **Well supported with evidence.** The source's writer provides clear and plentiful facts and reasons to support assertions.	• **Unsupported or biased.** They carry assertions that have little or no supporting evidence.
• **Factually accurate.** The sources for statistics, quotations, and other information are listed. You or anyone can look them up to check their accuracy.	• **Factually questionable.** They may include statistics or other information, but they fail to identify who generated it. You have no way to check facts.
• **Current.** Information is recent or, in the case of Web sites, regularly updated.	• **Outdated.** This is 20-year-old medical advice. The political situation is based on a Web site last updated in 2009.

21E Does the source pass other critical thinking tests?

Use CRITICAL THINKING skills when you evaluate a source (see Chapter 3). Figure 21.7 shows a Web site that shows critical thinking in its fairly balanced tone and one that is more biased in tone.

Figure 21.7 A source with balanced tone and a source with biased tone.

Balanced tone

The writer acknowledges there is a difference of opinion.

The writer summarizes the point of view with which he or she disagrees.

There is a slight element of bias in saying that people have an ideology.

Biased tone

The writer relies on name-calling rather than acknowledging others.

The comparison to "vampires avoid silver bullets" gets readers' attention, but it's hardly respectful.

At least the writer promises to send readers to a "rigorous but accessible" informational site. You would have to evaluate that site to be sure.

Does the Source Pass Other Critical Thinking Tests?

Reliable sources are . . .	Questionable sources are . . .
• **Balanced in tone.** The source is respectful of others and creates a sense of fairness.	• **Biased in tone.** Some warning signs of biased tone are name-calling, sarcasm, stereotyping, or absolute assertions about matters that are open to interpretation. For example, if a source declares, "Television programs are never worth watching" or that "women are always better than men at writing," you are encountering bias.
• **Balanced in treatment.** The author advocates a credible position but also acknowledges different viewpoints. For example, they summarize contradictory evidence.	• **One-sided.** The author omits any mention or fair summary of competing views or gives unreliable information especially if openly ridiculing competing positions.
• **Logical.** The source draws fair conclusions from evidence. The reasoning is clear.	• **Full of logical fallacies.**
• **Well-edited.** The source has been proofread and is free of grammatical errors.	• **Marked by errors.** Beware of any source that has typos or sloppy errors.

Synthesizing Sources in Research Papers

22 ▪ ▪ ▪ ▪ ▪ ▪ ▪

Quick Points You will learn to

➤ Connect the different sources you use in your writing.
➤ Synthesize source material and integrate it into your writing (pp. 207–216).

22A What is synthesizing sources in research papers?

When you SYNTHESIZE sources, you connect them to one another and to your own thinking, in an original paper that answers your research question. Your CRITICAL THINKING (Chapter 3) skills help you synthesize, as do QUOTING, SUMMARIZING, and PARAPHRASING (Chapter 15). We also explained synthesizing in 17E. We've found that a useful question to help you synthesize multiple sources in a research paper is "How do the sources I've found relate to one another?" The rest of Chapter 22 explains how to define relationships between sources.

Watch the Video

22B What are possible relationships between sources?

Knowing five relationships can help you go beyond simply listing or summarizing your sources, a strategy that usually results in a weak paper. Those relationships are

- **Different Subtopic:** Sources are on same broad subject but about different subtopics.
- **Agreement:** Two sources make the same basic point, though perhaps in different words.
- **Part Agreement:** Two sources mostly agree but differ a little bit.
- **Disagreement:** Two sources disagree.
- **General and Specific:** One source offers specific information that either supports or contradicts a more general point in another source.

We suggest that you begin by reading through your content notes and sorting them into groups by subtopic. Next, within each group, choose one pair of sources and ask which relationship in the list just given best describes them. Repeat this process with additional sources until you've identified the relationships between all of them.

22C What can I do when sources are about different subtopics?

You will likely find sources that present different subtopics of the same broad subject. For example, as you research career options, one source might discuss salaries, another might discuss workplace environments, and a third might discuss expectations for job openings. When Matthew Yan was researching how the Internet has affected the way we get information (part of his paper appears in Chapter 23), among the sources he found were these.

Source A	Source B
"While new technology eases connections between people, it also, paradoxically, facilitates a closeted view of the world, keeping us coiled tightly with those who share our ideas. In a world that lacks real gatekeepers and authority figures . . . conspiracy theories, myths, and outright lies may get the better of many of us." (17–18)	"CNN used to be a twenty-four-hour news outlet shown only on TV. The *New York Times* and the *Wall Street Journal* were simply newspapers. But on the Internet today, they are surprisingly similar. . . . Online, the lines between television and newspapers have blurred—and soon the same will be said about books, movies, TV shows, and more." (14)
Manjoo, Farhad. *True Enough: Learning to Live in a Post-Fact Society.* Hoboken, NJ: Wiley. 2008. Print.	Bilton, Nick. *I Live in the Future & Here's How It Works.* New York: Crown Business, 2010. Print.
Student's Content Note	**Student's Content Note**
Manjoo 17-18	Bilton 14
—although technology can connect us to others, it can also allow us to communicate only with people that agree with us; we might be susceptible to lies [paraphrase]	—TV network and newspaper sites have become similar on the Internet. Examples: CNN and *NY Times*, *WSJ* [summary]

Notice how in the student's content notes, he included the kind of note he took in brackets (see 19I). Here is a possible sentence/paragraph guide for sources on different subtopics:

Sentence and Paragraph Guides

There are (one, two, or however many) important considerations for (aspects of, reasons for, etc.) _____. One is _____ [from Source A] _____. A second is _____ [from Source B] _____.

EXAMPLE

There are two important developments in the way we receive news online. One is that, even though it is easier to connect to information, we tend to seek people with whom we already agree (Manjoo 17-18). A second, as Nick Bilton notes, is that distinctions between types of news sources on the Internet are disappearing (14).

As you write your content notes, consider making each source a separate section, paragraph, or sentence of your paper, depending on how much information each source contains.

22D What can I do when sources agree?

Sources agree when they present similar information or make the same point. If sources are truly repetitious, you might use only one. Sometimes, however, including multiple similar sources strengthens your point. Here is an example:

Source A	Source B
"Our study confirmed the well-known gender gap in gaming, verifying that this overall trend also occurs among college students. Seventy percent of male undergraduates had played a digital game the week of the survey, compared to only one quarter of the females. The majority of women fell in the category of non-gamers, those who had not played a game in over 6 months, or never." (Winn 10)	"Women proportionally were more likely than men to only play an hour or less per week. . . . Twenty-one percent of the women and 68% of the men played two or more hours per week." (Ogletree 539)
Winn, Jillian, and Carrie Heeter. "Gaming, Gender, and Time: Who Makes Time to Play?" *Sex Roles* 61 (2009): 1–13. Web. 9 May 2011.	Ogletree, Shirley Matile, and Ryan Drake. "College Students' Video Game Participation and Perceptions: Gender Differences and Implications." *Sex Roles* 56 (2007): 537–42. Web. 9 May 2011.
Student's Content Notes	Student's Content Notes
Winn 10	Ogletree
—70% of male students played video games; 25% of female [summary]	—68% of men and 21% of women played 2 or more hours per week [summary]

Here is a possible sentence/paragraph guide for synthesizing sources that agree:

> ### Sentence and Paragraph Guides
>
> A and B reach the same conclusion (provide similar information, argue the same point, reach the same conclusion etc.) about _____.
> A explains that _____. B found that _____.

EXAMPLE

Researchers Winn and Heeter and researchers Ogletree and Drake reached the same conclusion that men play video games more extensively than women. Winn and Heeter found that 70% of male students but only 25% of females regularly play games (10). In a study of how many hours per week students play, Ogletree and Drake learned that 68% of men and only 21% of women play two or more hours per week (539).

A REVISION (TO MAKE THE WRITING MORE CONCISE AND MORE EFFECTIVE)

Two studies show that men play video games more extensively than women. Winn and Heeter found that 70% of male students but only 25% of females regularly play games (10). In a study of how many hours per week students play, Ogletree learned that 68% of men and only 21% of women play two or more hours per week (539).

22E   What can I do when sources partly agree?

Often sources generally agree with each other but use different evidence or emphasize slightly different conclusions. Here is an example:

Source A	Source B
"[M]ore males reportedly developed leadership skills as a result of playing video games as opposed to females. More males also reported that playing video games helped them develop skills that will help them in the workplace, such as the ability to work as a team member, to collaborate with others and the ability to provide directions to others." (Thirunarayanan, 324)	"Games make it easy to build stronger social bonds with our friends and family. Studies show that we like and trust someone better after we play a game with them—even if they beat us. And we're more likely to help someone in real life after we've helped them in an online game." (McGonigal)

Source A	Source B
Thirunarayanan, M. O., Manuel Vilchez, Liala Abreu, Cyntianna Ledesma, and Sandra Lopez. "A Survey of Video Game Players in a Public, Urban Research University." *Educational Media International* 47.4 (2009): 311–27. Web. 9 May 2011.	McGonigal, Jane. "Be a Gamer, Save the World." wsj.com. *Wall Street Journal*, 22 Jan 2011. Web. 9 May 2011.
Student's Content Note	**Student's Content Note**
Thirunarayanan, 324 —more men said they learn leadership and team member skills than women said they did [summary]	McGonigal —games build social connections like trust and willingness to help others [summary]

Here is a possible sentence or paragraph guide to use when sources partly agree:

Sentence and Paragraph Guides

Scholars generally agree (conclude, share the opinion, or demonstrate, etc.) that _____. However, a difference between them is _____ ___. A emphasizes (asserts, believes, etc.) _____. B, on the other hand, emphasizes _____.

EXAMPLE

Scholars generally agree that playing video games can have some positive social effects. However, they differ as to who benefits most. Jane McGonigal asserts that games build social connections such as trust and the willingness to help others, suggesting this is true for all players. Thirunarayanan et al., on the other hand, found that men believe they learn leadership and team member skills more than women say they do (324).

22F What can I do when sources disagree?

Because people can disagree on everything from whether certain laws should be passed to whether certain movies are any good, it's no surprise that sources can disagree, too. Here is an example:

Source A	Source B
"Imagine that everything stays 99 percent the same, that people continue to consume 99 percent of the television they used to, but 1 percent of that time gets carved out for producing and sharing. The connected population still watches well over a trillion hours of TV a year; 1 percent of that is more than one hundred Wikipedias' worth of participation per year." (Shirky 23)	"With hundreds of thousands of visitors a day, Wikipedia has become the third most visited site for information and current events; a more trusted source for news than the CNN or BBC Web sites, even though Wikipedia has no reporters, no editorial staff, and no experience in news-gathering. It's the blind leading the blind— infinite monkeys providing infinite information for infinite readers, perpetuating the cycle of misinformation and ignorance." (Keen 4)
Shirky, Clay. *Cognitive Surplus, Creativity and Generosity in a Connected Age.* New York: Penguin, 2010. Print.	Keen, Andrew. *The Cult of the Amateur.* New York: Doubleday, 2007. Print.
Student's Content Note	*Student's Content Note*
Shirky 23 —If people used even 1% of time they spend watching TV instead to produce content for the Web they'd create "one hundred Wikipedia's worth" each year [paraphrase and quotation]	Keen 4 —Wikipedia used more for information and current events than CNN or the BBC —no professionals writing for W. —writers are "infinite monkeys" who create "misinformation and ignorance" [summary and quotation]

Here is a possible sentence/paragraph guide to use for sources that disagree:

Sentence and Paragraph Guides

There are two different perspectives (positions, interpretations, or opinions, etc.) about _____. A says _____. B, on the other hand, says _____.

However, your writing will be stronger if you go a step further and use critical thinking to understand the nature of the disagreement. For example:

- Writers might disagree because they use different facts or information (or no information at all!).
- Writers might disagree when they use the same information but interpret it differently.
- Writers might operate with different assumptions or perspectives.

Here is a stronger sentence/paragraph guide for sources that disagree:

Sentence and Paragraph Guides

There are two different perspectives (positions, interpretations, or opinions, etc.) about _____. A says _____. B, on the other hand, says _____. They disagree mainly because they cite different facts (interpret information differently, operate with different assumptions). A points to _____, while B _____ _____. On this point, B's [or A's] perspective is more convincing because _____.

EXAMPLE

There are two different opinions about Wikipedia. Clay Shirky is enthusiastic and notes that if people diverted just 1% of their TV watching time to writing for the Web, they could generate "one hundred Wikipedia's worth" of content each year (23). Andrew Keen, on the other hand, sees Wikipedia writers as "infinite monkeys" who only spread "misinformation and ignorance" (4). They disagree mainly because they have different assumptions about the quality of Wikipedia entries. Shirky believes it is generally fine, while Keen sees almost nothing of value.

Here is a revised version, with more effective wording:

Some writers find Wikipedia a reason for celebration, while others declare it a cause for despair. Clay Shirky hopes people will divert just 1% of their TV watching time to writing for the Web, which could generate "one hundred Wikipedia's worth" of content each year (23). That possibility would trouble Andrew Keen, who characterizes those writers as "infinite monkeys" who only spread "misinformation and ignorance" (4). They assume quite different things about quality of knowledge on Wikipedia. Keen has considerably less faith in the ability of people to write accurate information.

22G What can I do when sources aren't equally specific?

■ 1. When a specific source supports a more general idea in another source.

Sometimes a source provides examples, illustrations, or evidence that support a more general point in another. Here is an example:

Source A	Source B
"Old media is facing extinction." (Keen 9)	"In 2008, paid newspaper circulation in the United States fell to 49.1 million, the lowest number since the late 1960s and well below the peak of 60 million reached in the 1990s, when the internet was just starting to come into its own." (Bilton 6)
Keen, Andrew. *The Cult of the Amateur*. New York: Doubleday, 2007. Print.	Bilton, Nick. *I Live in the Future & Here's How It Works*. New York: Crown Business, 2010. Print.
Student's Content Note	Student's Content Note
Keen 9 "Old media is facing extinction" [quotation]	Bilton 6 —newspaper circulation was 60 million in the 1990s, 49.1 million in 2008 [summary]

Here are useful sentence/paragraph guides when a specific source supports a general one:

Sentence and Paragraph Guides

A observes (claims, argues, concludes, etc.) that _____.
B provides an example (a set of data, some information, etc.) to support this observation. B states that _____.

or

According to B, _____. This illustrates A's concept (point, claim, conclusion) that _____.

EXAMPLE

According to Nick Bilton, newspaper circulation declined over ten million between the 1990s and 2008, from 60 million to 49.1 million subscribers (6). His figures illustrate Andrew Keen's observation that "Old media is facing extinction" (9).

■ 2. When a specific source contradicts a more general idea in another source.

Sources can disagree with each other at the level of ideas or claims. Sometimes, however, the disagreement is more subtle. Specific information in one source can contradict a more general point made in another. This can happen when writers make a claim but offer no proof or when they offer partial or different evidence. Here's an example:

Source A	Source B
"But college students are, in fact, getting lazier. 'Aggregate time spent studying by full-time college students declined from about 24 hours per week in 1961 to about 14 hours per week in 2004,' Babcock writes, citing his own research." (de Vise)	"Nationally, approximately 80 percent of community college students work, and they work an average of 32 hours per week. Research indicates that working a few hours each week is actually beneficial to students' persistence and success, provided that they are in school full time and attending consistently. However, to succeed academically, experts suggest working no more than 15–20 hours per week." (Zomer 2)
de Vise, Daniel. "Grade Inflation is Making Students Lazier." washingtonpost.com/college-inc. *Washington Post*, 22 July 2010. Web. 9 May 2011.	Zomer, Saffron. *Working Too Hard to Make the Grade*. Sacramento, CA: California Public Interest Research Group, 2009. Web. 9 May 2011.
Student's Content Note	Student's Content Note
de Vise —college students getting "lazier"; they studied 7 hours a week less in 2004 than in 1961 [summary]	Zomer 2 —80% of CC students work average of 32 hours/week —some work is good, but should be no more than 15–20 hours [summary]

Here is a useful sentence/paragraph guide when specific information contradicts a general claim:

Sentence and Paragraph Guides

Evidence suggests (proves, demonstrates, etc.) that A's claim that
_____ is wrong (incomplete, overstated, etc.). B shows that
_____.

EXAMPLE

Daniel de Vise's claim that college students are getting lazier fails to recognize complete information. De Vise points to students studying seven hours per week less in 2004 than in 1961. However, he fails to take into account how much students are now working. For example, 80% of community college students now work an average of 32 hours per week, even though experts recommend working no more than 20 hours per week (Zomer 2). Far from being lazy, college students are working hard, perhaps with less time for studying.

Drafting and Revising a Research Paper

23

■ ■ ■ ■ ■ ■ ■ ■

Quick Points   You will learn to

➤ Write and refine a research paper.

23A   How does the writing process apply to research papers?

DRAFTING and REVISING a research paper is like drafting and revising any piece of writing (see Chapter 6). Yet to write a research paper, you need extra time because you need to demonstrate that:

- You've followed the steps of the research process (see Chapters 18–20).
- You've evaluated your SOURCES (see Chapter 21).

- You haven't plagiarized (see Chapter 16).

- You've correctly employed QUOTATIONS, PARAPHRASES, and SUMMARIES (see Chapter 15).

- You've moved beyond summary to SYNTHESIS so that your sources are interwoven with each other and with your own thinking, not merely listed one by one (see Chapter 22).

- You've used DOCUMENTATION accurately. (For MLA STYLE, see Chapters 24–26; for APA STYLE, see Chapters 27–29; for other documentation styles, see Chapters 30–31.)

23B How do I draft a research paper?

Expect to write several drafts of your research paper. The first draft is a chance to discover new insights and fresh connections. Here are some ways to write your first draft.

Watch
the Video

- **Some researchers work from a source map or cluster diagram.** They organize their notes into topics and determine the relationship between sources. They use frames and sentence and paragraph guides to generate a first draft.

- **Some research writers work with their notes at hand.** They organize the notes into broad categories so that each category becomes a section of the first draft. This method can reveal any gaps in information that call for additional research. It can also show that some of your research doesn't fit into your paper. However, don't throw it out because it might be useful in a later draft.

- **Some research writers generate a list of questions that their paper needs to address.** Then they answer each question, one at a time, looking for the content notes that will help them. For example, on the topic of déjà vu, some possible questions might be, "What is déjà vu? What are possible explanations for it? Does everyone experience it the same way or with the same frequency?" Generating and answering questions can turn a mass of information into manageable groupings.

- **Some research writers stop at various points and use FREEWRITING to get their ideas into words.** They say that it helps them to recognize when they need to adjust their research question or adjust their search. After a number of rounds of researching and freewriting, they find that they can write their complete first draft relatively easily.

- **Some research writers review their sources and create an OUTLINE before drafting.** Some find a FORMAL OUTLINE helpful, whereas others use a less formal approach.

23C What are frames for research papers?

Although all research papers seek to answer a question, some are mainly informative, others are mainly persuasive, and still others are a mix. We offer here two possible frames to adapt to the specifics of your assignment. The first frame is for an informative research paper; the second for an argumentative research paper.

Frame for an Informative Research Paper

Introductory paragraph(s)

- **Establish why your topic is important or interesting**. Consider, "Why does this matter? To whom does this matter? What might happen if we resolve this issue one way versus another?"
- **Your** THESIS STATEMENT needs to make clear how you will answer your research question.

Body paragraph(s): Background information

- **Provide the history or background of your topic**. Why is it a problem or concern at this time?

Body paragraphs: Explanations of topics

- **Discuss the main subtopics** of your general topic in a paragraph with a clear TOPIC SENTENCE.
- If a subtopic is lengthy, it may require more than one paragraph.

Body Paragraphs: Complications

- **Discuss what is controversial or in dispute**. What do people disagree about? Why? Do they dispute facts? Interpretations? Causes? Effects or implications? Solutions?

Conclusion

- **Wrap up your topic.** What questions or issues remain? What are areas for further research or investigation? What might readers do with this information?

Works Cited or References

- If you are using MLA style, include a list of Works Cited (Chapter 25); if you are using APA style, include a References list (Chapter 28).

Frame for an Argumentative Research Paper

Introductory paragraph(s)

- **Establish why your topic is important or interesting.** Consider, "Why does this matter? To whom does this matter? What might happen if we resolve this issue one way versus another?"
- **Your THESIS STATEMENT** needs to make clear how you will answer your research question.

Body paragraph(s): Background information

- **Provide the history or background of your topic.** Why is it a problem or concern at this time?

Body paragraph(s): Agreement among sources

- **Discuss points of agreement.** What is uncontroversial or widely accepted?
- Depending on the size or nature of the topic, this may be one or several paragraphs.

Body paragraph(s): Complications

- **Discuss what is controversial or in dispute.** What do people disagree about? Why? Do they dispute facts? Interpretations? Causes? Effects or implications? Solutions?

Body paragraph(s): Arguments

- **Present your arguments.** What reasons do you have for your position or proposed action? State each reason as a TOPIC SENTENCE, and provide evidence and support in the paragraph.
- If you have extensive support for a particular reason, you might need more than one paragraph.

Conclusion

- **Wrap up your argument.** Why is your position or proposal best? What actions should follow?

Works Cited or References

- If you are using MLA style, include a list of Works Cited (Chapter 25); if you are using APA style, include a References list (Chapter 28).

23D A student's argumentative research paper

Here's a short research paper in which a student uses the argumentative frame to organize his argument about the effects of digital information on democracy. For a complete argumentative research paper in MLA STYLE, see 12E. For a complete informative research paper in MLA STYLE, see 26B.

View the Model Document

Yan 1

Matthew Yan

Professor Daniels

WRIT 1133

5 May 2011

Cautions about Information in the Digital Age

Consider how typical middle class Americans in the 1970's learned about the world around them. A newspaper arrived on the doorstep each morning, and the three major television networks summarized major events each evening. After dinner people might have read a magazine, perhaps checking background information in a family encyclopedia. Occasionally they visited the library to consult expert materials housed there.

Forty years later this daily pattern would still be true for a small group of people—a very small group. Most of us now get news from a wide range of digital sources, from online Web sites to social networks to on-demand television networks, and they get it 24/7. Paul Sagan and Tom Leighton point out that people now "listen to podcasts on their way to work; check for news updates on their cell phones; watch, pause, and rewind live video newsfeeds on the Internet; and read and comment on blogs at the office, the gym, or the corner coffee shop" (119). Clearly the amount of easily-accessed information is useful

This two-paragraph INTRODUCTION explains the topic, points to an important question, and ends with the paper's thesis statement.

continued >>

Yan 2

and convenient. However, there are troubling signs that the nature of digital information is eroding important aspects of our democracy.

There is wide agreement on the lessening popularity of traditional print media. Nick Bilton, a *New York Times* writer, notes that American newspaper circulation was 60 million in the 1990s but had declined to 49.1 million in 2008 (6). These declines have continued, with nearly 9% fewer subscribers in early 2010 compared to the previous year (Plambeck). While people continue to get their news from television, viewership from traditional network programs such as "The NBC Nightly News" continues to drop. A study by the Pew Research Center characterizes Americans' news habits as "foraging and opportunism. They seem to access news when the spirit moves them or they have a chance to check up on headlines" (Purcell 2). Andrew Keen summarizes the current situation briefly: "Old media is facing extinction" (9).

· ·

Although everyone agrees that people are getting less information through professional reporters through traditional pipelines, there is a heated debate whether this is positive or negative, especially when it comes to the Internet. Clay Shirky is a strong advocate for common people generating knowledge. He hopes people might divert just 1% of their TV watching time to writing for the Web, which could generate "one hundred Wikipedia's worth" of content each year (23). That possibility would trouble Andrew Keen, who characterizes those writers as "infinite monkeys" who only spread "misinformation and ignorance" (4). These two men assume quite different

paraphrases

quotations

This section of the essay is not shown here to conserve space.

Combination of para-phrases and quotations, worked smoothly into the sentences.

continued >>

Yan 3

The writer presents COMPLICATIONS, points on which people disagree about this subject.

things about quality of knowledge on Wikipedia. Keen has considerably less faith than Sharky in the ability of people to write accurately. James Fallows points out common fears that ours will become "an age of lies and idiocy," although he ultimately decides that common people posting tweets and blogs and videos strengthens our knowledge of emerging events (44).

The writer presents ARGUMENTS to persuade readers to accept his point of view.

Despite the positive contributions of amateur reporters, there are three reasons why traditional sources of expert information are important. First, the amount of misinformation online is extensive and troubling. Second, many internet postings tend to reduce complex ideas to slogans or oversimplifications. Last, people increasingly tend to select themselves into interest groups, which makes it harder to understand other points of view and to consider ideas rationally.

To conserve space, we do not show here the student's lengthy paragraphs about each of the three arguments announced in the previous paragraph.

CONCLUSION that calls for specific actions as a result of the arguments the student has presented.

There is convincing evidence that the nature of digital information and how people read it have the potential to erode our democracy. What, then, should we do? Obviously, it would be impossible to restrict online publishing only to experts. It would be undesirable, too; the Internet contains huge amounts of good information, and access for all to contribute means that diverse voices and experiences can be heard. Instead of restricting readers and writers, the answer is to educate them. With such a flood of information coming from so many channels, schools now need more than ever to teach students how to recognize information that is questionable or biased. Beyond that, however, is the personal responsibility that

continued >>

Yan 4

each of us has as readers and writers. We need to pursue the truth and to form judgments based on sound evidence and reasoning, especially when important issues are at stake. This can take effort, but it leaves plenty of time for online entertainment, for silly pictures of cats and Facebook stories of last night's celebration.

Yan 5

Works Cited

Bilton, Nick. *I Live in the Future & Here's How It Works*. New York: Crown Business, 2010. Print.

Fallows, James. "Learning to Love the (Shallow, Divisive, Unreliable) New Media." *Atlantic*. Atlantic Monthly Group, April 2011: 34-49. Web.

Keen, Andrew. *The Cult of the Amateur*. New York: Doubleday, 2007. Print.

Plambeck, Joseph. "Newspaper Circulation Falls Nearly 9%." *New York Times*. New York Times, 26 Apr. 2010. Web. 26 Apr. 2011.

Purcell, Kristen, Lee Rainie, Amy Mitchell, Tom Rosenstiel, and Kenny Olmstead. "Understanding the Participatory News Consumer: How Internet and Cell Phone Users Have Turned News into a Social Experience." *Pew Internet and American Life Project*. Pew Research Center, 1 Mar. 2010. Web. 24 Apr. 2011.

continued >>

Yan 6

Sagan, Paul, and Tom Leighton. "The Internet & the
    Future of News." *Daedalus* 139.2 (2010): 119–125.
    Academic Search Premier, Web. 24 Apr. 2011.
Shirky, Clay. *Cognitive Surplus, Creativity and Generosity in a*
    Connected Age. New York: Penguin, 2010. Print.

23E How do I revise a research paper?

Before you write each new draft, read your previous draft with a sharp eye.
Assess all the features listed in Quick Box 6.2 (see 6C) and Quick Box 23.1.
For best results, take a break of a few days (or at least a few hours) before
beginning this process to get some distance from your material and a clearer
vision of what you need to revise. You might consider asking a few people you
respect to read and react to a draft.

One key to revising any research paper is to examine carefully the evidence you've included. EVIDENCE consists of facts, statistics, expert studies
and opinions, examples, and stories. Use RENNS (see 7D) to see if you can
develop paragraphs more fully. Identify each of the points you have made in
your paper, including your THESIS STATEMENT and all your subpoints. Then
ask yourself the following questions.

- **Is the evidence sufficient?** To be sufficient, evidence can't be thin or
  trivial. As a rule, the more evidence you present, the more convincing your
  thesis will be to readers.

- **Is the evidence representative?** Representative evidence is customary and
  normal, not based on exceptions.

- **Is the evidence relevant?** Relevant evidence relates directly to your thesis
  or topic sentence. It illustrates your reasons straightforwardly and never
  introduces unrelated material.

- **Is the evidence accurate?** Accurate evidence is correct, complete, and up
  to date. It comes from a reliable source. Equally important, you present it
  honestly, without distorting or misrepresenting it.

- **Is the evidence reasonable?** Reasonable evidence is not phrased in extreme
  language and avoids sweeping generalizations. Reasonable evidence is free
  of LOGICAL FALLACIES (see 3D).

Quick Box 23.1 ■ ■ ■ ■ ■ ■ ■ ■ ■

Revision checklist for a research paper

WRITING

✓ Do your one or two introductory paragraphs lead effectively into the material? (7A)

✓ Have you met the basic requirements for a thesis statement? (5G)

✓ Do your thesis statement and the content of your paper address your research question(s)? (18C)

✓ Have you developed effective body paragraphs? (7F)

✓ Do your ideas follow sensibly and logically within each paragraph and from one paragraph to the next? (7E)

✓ Does the concluding paragraph end your paper effectively? (7G)

RESEARCH

✓ Have you fully answered your research question? (18C)

✓ Have you evaluated the quality of your sources? Have you used sources that are appropriate for ACADEMIC WRITING? (21)

✓ Have you used QUOTATIONS, PARAPHRASES, and SUMMARIES well? (15)

✓ Have you integrated your source material well without PLAGIARIZING? (16)

23F How do I edit and format a research paper?

Quick Box 23.2 lists questions to ask when you edit your research paper.

Quick Box 23.2 ■ ■ ■ ■ ■ ■ ■ ■ ■

Editing checklist for a research paper

✓ Is the paper free of errors in grammar, punctuation, and mechanics?

✓ Are your style and tone effective?

✓ Is your format correct in your parenthetical references? (Chapter 24 or 27)

✓ Does each of your parenthetical references tie into an item in your Works Cited list (MLA style) or References list (APA style) at the end of your paper or follow CM or CSE styles? (Chapter 25, 28, 30, or 31)

✓ Does your format exactly match what you've been assigned to follow? Check margins, spacing, title, headings, page numbers, font, and so on. (Chapter 26 or 29)

Tab 6
MLA Documentation

CHAPTERS
24–26

Tab 6 MLA Documentation

MyCompLab® Visit mycomplab.com for the eText and for resources on MLA documentation and format.

24 MLA In-Text Citations

■ ■ ■ ■ ■ ■ ■ ■

Quick Points   You will learn to

➤ Cite sources in your writing using MLA style.

24A   What is MLA documentation style?

A DOCUMENTATION STYLE* is a standard format that writers follow to tell readers what SOURCES they used and how to find them. Different disciplines follow different documentation styles. The one most frequently used in the humanities is from the Modern Language Association (MLA).

MLA STYLE requires you to document your sources in two connected, equally important ways.

1. Within the body of the paper, use parenthetical documentation, as described in this chapter.

2. At the end of the paper, provide a list of the sources you used in your paper. Title this list "Works Cited," as described in Chapter 25.

The guidelines and examples in this chapter are based on the Seventh Edition of *The MLA Handbook for Writers of Research Papers* (2009), which is the most current edition. If you need more information regarding MLA style updates, check http://www.mla.org. See Quick Box 25.1 on pages 234–236 for more guidance on these requirements.

24B   What is MLA in-text parenthetical documentation?

MLA-style PARENTHETICAL DOCUMENTATION (also called IN-TEXT CITATIONS) places source information in parentheses within the sentences of your research papers. This information—given each time that you quote, summarize, or paraphrase source materials—signals materials used from outside sources and enables readers to find the originals. (See Chapter 15 for information on how to quote, paraphrase, and summarize.)

Author name cited in text; page number cited in parentheses   If you include an author's name (or, if none, the title of the work) in the sentence

---

* Words printed in SMALL CAPITAL LETTERS are discussed elsewhere in the text and are defined in the Terms Glossary at the back of the book.

to introduce the source material, you include in parentheses only the page number where you found the material:

> According to Brent Staples, IQ tests give scientists little insight into intelligence (293).

For readability and good writing technique, try to introduce the names of authors (or titles of sources) in your own sentences.

Author name and page number cited in parentheses If you don't include the author's name in your sentence, you need to insert it in the parentheses, before the page number. There is no punctuation between the author's name and the page number:

> IQ tests give scientists little insight into intelligence (Staples 293).

■ Placement of parenthetical reference

When possible, position a parenthetical reference at the end of the quotation, summary, or paraphrase it refers to—preferably at the end of a sentence, unless that would place it too far from the source's material. When you place the parenthetical reference at the end of a sentence, insert it before the sentence-ending period.

If you're citing a quotation enclosed in quotation marks, place the parenthetical information after the closing quotation mark but before sentence-ending punctuation.

> Coleman summarizes research that shows that "the number, rate, and direction of time-zone changes are the critical factors in determining the extent and degree of jet lag symptoms" (67).

Block quotations: Longer than four lines The one exception to the rule of putting parenthetical information before sentence-ending punctuation concerns quotations that you set off in block style, meaning one inch from the left margin. (MLA requires that quotations longer than four typed lines be handled this way.) For block quotations, place the parenthetical reference after the period.

> Bruce Sterling worries that people are pursuing less conventional medical treatments, and not always for good reasons:
>
>> Medical tourism is already in full swing. Thailand is the golden shore for wealthy, sickly Asians and Australians. Fashionable Europeans head to South Africa for embarrassing plastic surgery. Crowds of scrip-waving Americans buy prescription drugs in Canada and Mexico. (92)

If you're quoting part of a paragraph or one complete paragraph, don't indent the first line of quoted words more than an inch. But if you quote more than one paragraph, indent the first line of each paragraph—including the first if it's a complete paragraph from the source—an additional quarter inch.

24C What are MLA examples for parenthetical citations?

The directory at the beginning of this tab corresponds to the numbered examples in this section. Most of these examples show the author's name or the title included in the parenthetical citation, but remember that it's usually more effective to include that information in your sentence.

1. One Author—MLA

Give an author's name as it appears on the source: for a book, on the title page; for an article, directly below the title or at the end of the article.

> IQ tests give scientists little insight into intelligence (Staples 293).

2. Two or Three Authors—MLA

Give the names in the same order as in the source. Spell out *and*. For three authors, use commas to separate the authors' names.

> As children get older, they begin to express several different kinds of intelligence (Todd and Taylor 23).

> Another measure of emotional intelligence is the success of inter- and intrapersonal relationships (Voigt, Dees, and Prigoff 14).

3. More Than Three Authors—MLA

If your source has more than three authors, you can name them all or use the first author's name only, followed by *et al.*, either in a parenthetical reference or in your sentence. *Et al.* is an abbreviation of the Latin *et alii*, meaning "and others." In MLA citations, don't underline or italicize *et al.* No period follows *et*, but one follows *al.*

> Emotional security varies, depending on the circumstances of the social interaction (Carter et al. 158).

4. More Than One Source by an Author—MLA

When you use two or more sources by the same author, include the relevant title in each citation. In parenthetical citations, use a shortened version of the title. For example, in a paper using two of Howard Gardner's works, *Frames of Mind: The Theory of Multiple Intelligences* and "Reflections on Multiple Intelligences: Myths and Messages," use *Frames* and "Reflections." Shorten the titles as much as you can without making them ambiguous to readers, and start with the word by which the work is alphabetized in your WORKS CITED list. Separate the author's name and the title with a comma, but don't use punctuation between the title and page number.

> Although it seems straightforward to think of multiple intelligences as multiple approaches to learning (Gardner, *Frames* 60–61), an intelligence is not a learning style (Gardner, "Reflections" 202–03).

When you incorporate the title into your own sentences, you can omit a subtitle. After the first mention, you can shorten the main title as well.

5. Two or More Authors with the Same Last Name—MLA

Use each author's first initial and full last name in each parenthetical citation. If both authors have the same first initial, use the full name in all instances.

> According to Anne Cates, psychologists can predict how empathetic an adult will be from his or her behavior at age two (41), but other researchers disagree (T. Cates 171).

6. Group or Corporate Author—MLA

Use the corporate name just as you would an individual's name.

> A five-year study shows that these tests are usually unreliable (Boston Women's Health Collective 11).

7. Work Cited by Title—MLA

If no author is named, use only the title. If the title is long, shorten it. Here's an in-text citation for an article titled "Are You a Day or Night Person?"

> The "morning lark" and "night owl" descriptions typically are used to categorize the human extremes ("Are You" 11).

8. Multivolume Work—MLA

If you use more than one volume of a multivolume work, include the relevant volume number in each citation. Separate the volume number and page number with a colon followed by a space.

> Although Amazon forest dwellers had been exposed to these viruses by 1900 (Rand 3: 202), Borneo forest dwellers escaped them until the 1960s (Rand 1: 543).

9. Novel, Play, Short Story, or Poem—MLA

Literary works frequently appear in different editions. When you cite material from literary works, providing the part, chapter, act, scene, canto, stanza, or line numbers usually helps readers locate what you are referring to better than page numbers alone. Unless your instructor tells you not to, use arabic numerals for these references, even if the literary work uses roman numerals. For novels that use them, give part and/or chapter numbers after page numbers. Use a semicolon after the page number but a comma to separate a part from a chapter.

> Flannery O'Connor describes one character in *The Violent Bear It Away* as "divided in two—a violent and a rational self" (139; pt. 2, ch. 6).

For plays that use them, give act, scene, and line numbers. Use periods between these numbers. For short stories, use page numbers.

> Among the most quoted of Shakespeare's lines is Hamlet's soliloquy beginning "To be, or not to be: that is the question" (3.1.56).

> The old man in John Collier's "The Chaser" says about his potions, "I don't deal in laxatives and teething mixtures . . . " (79).

For poems and songs, give canto, stanza, and/or line numbers. Use periods between these numbers.

> In "To Autumn," Keats's most melancholy image occurs in the lines "Then in a wailful choir the small gnats mourn / Among the river swallows" (3.27–28).

10. Bible or Sacred Text—MLA

Give the title of the edition you're using, the book (in the case of the Bible), and the chapter and verse. Spell out the names of books in sentences, but use abbreviations in parenthetical references.

> He would certainly benefit from the advice in Ephesians to "get rid of all bitterness, rage, and anger" (*New International Version Bible*, 4.31).

> He would certainly benefit from the advice to "get rid of all bitterness, rage, and anger" (*New International Version Bible*, Eph. 4.31).

11. Work in an Anthology or Other Collection—MLA

You may want to cite a work you have read in a book that contains many works by various authors and that was compiled or edited by someone other than the person you're citing. Your in-text citation should include the author of the selection you're citing and the page number. For example, suppose you want to cite the poem "Several Things" by Martha Collins, in a literature text edited by Pamela Annas and Robert Rosen. Use Collins's name and the title of her work in the sentence and the line numbers (see item 9) in a parenthetical citation.

> In "Several Things," Martha Collins enumerates what could take place in the lines of her poem: "Plums could appear, on a pewter plate / A dead red hare, hung by one foot. / A vase of flowers. Three shallots" (2–4).

12. Indirect Source—MLA

When you want to quote words that you found quoted in someone else's work, put the name of the person whose words you're quoting into your own sentence. Give the work where you found the quotation either in your sentence or in a parenthetical citation beginning with *qtd. in.*

> Martin Scorsese acknowledges the link between himself and his films: "I realize that all my life, I've been an outsider. I splatter bits of myself all over the screen" (qtd. in Giannetti and Eyman 397).

13. Two or More Sources in One Reference—MLA

If more than one source has contributed to an idea, opinion, or fact in your paper, cite them all. An efficient way to credit all is to include them in a single parenthetical citation, with a semicolon separating each block of information.

> Once researchers agreed that multiple intelligences existed, their next step was to try to measure or define them (West 17; Arturi 477; Gibbs 68).

14. An Entire Work—MLA

References to an entire work usually fit best into your own sentences.

> In *Convergence Culture*, Henry Jenkins explores how new digital media create a culture of active participation rather than passive reception.

15. Electronic Source with Page Numbers—MLA

The principles that govern in-text citations of electronic sources are exactly the same as the ones that apply to books, articles, or other sources. When an electronically accessed source identifies its author, use the author's name for parentherical references. If no author is named, use the title of the source. When an electronic source has page numbers, use them exactly as you would the page numbers of a print source.

> Learning happens best when teachers truly care about their students' complete well-being (Anderson 7).

16. Electronic Source without Page Numbers—MLA

Many online sources don't number pages. Simply refer to those works in their entirety. Include the name of the author, if any, in your sentence.

> In "What Is Artificial Intelligence?" John McCarthy notes that the science of artificial intelligence includes efforts beyond trying to simulate human intelligence.

25 ■ MLA Works Cited List

Quick Points   You will learn to

➤ Cite your sources at the end of your paper in an MLA Works Cited list.

25A   What are MLA guidelines for a Works Cited list?

Watch
the Video

In MLA-style DOCUMENTATION, the WORKS CITED list gives complete bibliographic information for each SOURCE used in your paper. Include only the sources from which you quote, paraphrase, or summarize. Quick Box 25.1 gives general information about the Works Cited list. The rest of this chapter gives models of many specific kinds of Works Cited entries.

Quick Box 25.1   ■ ■ ■ ■ ■ ■ ■ ■ ■ ■

Guidelines for an MLA-style Works Cited list

See Chapter 26, pages 258–271, for a sample student Works Cited list.

TITLE
Use "Works Cited" (without quotation marks), centered, as the title.

PLACEMENT OF LIST
Start a new page numbered sequentially with the rest of the paper, following the Notes pages, if any.

CONTENT AND FORMAT
Include all sources quoted from, paraphrased, or summarized in your paper. Start each entry on a new line and at the regular left margin. If the entry uses more than one line, indent the second and all following lines one-half inch from the left margin. Double-space all lines.

SPACING AFTER PUNCTUATION
Use one space after a period, unless your instructor asks you to use two. Always put only one space after a comma or a colon.

ARRANGEMENT OF ENTRIES
Alphabetize by author's last name. If no author is named, alphabetize by the title's first significant word (ignore *A*, *An*, or *The*).

continued >>

234

Quick Box 25.1 (continued)

AUTHORS' NAMES
Use first names and middle names or middle initials, if any, as given in the source. Don't reduce to initials any name that is given in full. For one author or the first-named author in multiauthor works, give the last name first. Use the word *and* with two or more authors. List multiple authors in the order given in the source. Use a comma between the first author's last and first names and after each complete author name except the last, which ends with a period: Fein, Ethel Andrea, Bert Griggs, and Delaware Rogash.

Include *Jr., Sr., II,* or *III* but no other titles or degrees before or after a name. For example, an entry for a work by Edward Meep III, MD, and Sir Richard Bolton would start like this: Meep, Edward, III, and Richard Bolton.

CAPITALIZATION OF TITLES
Capitalize all major words and the first and last words of all titles and sub-titles. Don't capitalize ARTICLES (*a, an, the*), PREPOSITIONS, COORDINATING CONJUNCTIONS, or *to* in INFINITIVES in the middle of a title.

SPECIAL TREATMENT OF TITLES
Use quotation marks around titles of shorter works (poems, short stories, essays, articles). Use italics for the titles of longer works (books, periodicals, plays).

When a book title includes the title of another work that is usually in italics (such as a novel, play, or long poem), the preferred MLA style is not to italicize the incorporated title: *Decoding* Jane Eyre.

If the incorporated title is usually enclosed in quotation marks (such as a short story or short poem), keep the quotation marks and italicize the complete title of the book: *Theme and Form in "I Shall Laugh Purely": A Brief Study*.

Drop *A, An,* or *The* as the first word of a periodical title.

PLACE OF PUBLICATION
If several cities are listed for the place of publication, give only the first. MLA doesn't require US state names. For an unfamiliar city outside the United States, include an abbreviated name of the country or Canadian province.

PUBLISHER
Use shortened names as long as they're clear: *Random* for *Random House*. For companies named for more than one person, name only the first: *Prentice* for *Prentice Hall*. For university presses, use the capital letters *U* and *P* (without periods): Oxford UP, U of Chicago P. If there is no publisher, use "N.p."

PUBLICATION MONTH ABBREVIATIONS
Abbreviate all publication months except *May, June,* and *July*. Use the first three letters followed by a period (*Dec., Feb.*) except for *Sept*.

continued >>

Quick Box 25.1 (continued)

PAGE RANGES

Give the page range—the starting page number and the ending page number, connected by a hyphen—of any paginated electronic source and any paginated print source that is part of a longer work (for example, a chapter in a book, an article in a journal). A range indicates that the cited work is on those pages and all pages in between. If that is not the case, use the style shown next for discontinuous pages. In either case, use numerals only, without the word *page* or *pages* or the abbreviation *p.* or *pp.*

Use the full second number through 99. Above that, use only the last two digits for the second number unless it would be unclear: 103-04 is clear, but 567-602 requires full numbers.

DISCONTINUOUS PAGES

When the source is interrupted by material that's not part of the source (for example, an article beginning on page 32 but continued on page 54), use the starting page number followed by a plus sign (+): 32+.

MEDIUM OF PUBLICATION

Include the medium of publication for each Works Cited entry. For example, every entry for a print source must include "Print" at the end, followed by a period. Supplementary bibliographic information like the original publication information for a work cited in translation, name of a book series, or the number of volumes in a set should follow the medium of publication. Every source from the World Wide Web must include *Web* at the end, followed by a period and the date of access. The medium of publication also needs to be included for broadcast sources (*Television*, *Radio*), sound recordings (*CD*, *Podcast*, *LP*, *Audiocassette*), as well as films, DVDs, live performances, musical scores, works of visual art, and so on.

ISSUE AND VOLUME NUMBERS FOR SCHOLARLY JOURNALS

Include both an issue and volume number for each Works Cited entry for scholarly journals. This applies both to journals that are continuously paginated and those that are not.

URLs IN ELECTRONIC SOURCES

Entries for online citations should include the URL *only when the reader probably could not locate the source without it.* If the entry requires a URL, enclose the URL in angle brackets <like this>. Put the URL before the access date, and end it with a period. If your computer automatically creates a hyperlink when you type a URL, format the URL to look the same as the rest of the entry. If a URL must be divided between two lines, break the URL only after a slash and do not use a hyphen.

25B What are MLA examples for sources in a Works Cited list?

The directory at the beginning of this tab corresponds to the numbered examples in this section. Not every possible documentation model is here. You may find that you have to combine features of models to document a particular source. You will also find more information in the *MLA Handbook for Writers of Research Papers*. Figure 25.1 provides another tool to help you find the Works Cited model you need: a decision-making flowchart.

Figure 25.1 Decision-making flowchart for finding the right MLA citation format.

1. Is the source an article from a **periodical?** (A periodical is a magazine, journal, or newspaper that is published at regular intervals, either in print or online.) — Yes → See examples 1–22.

No ↓

2. Is the source a book or part of a **book?** — Yes → See examples 23–48.

No ↓

3. Is the source an image, audio item, film, or video? — Yes → See examples 49–67.

No ↓

4. Is the source available **online but not a periodical** (for example, Web pages, e-mails, chats, other kinds of documents)? — Yes → See examples 68–80.

No ↓

5. Is the source in any **other print, nonprint, or electronic form** not accessed through the Internet (for example, letters, brochures, performances, advertisements, and so on)? — Yes → See examples 81–94.

PERIODICALS

You can read periodical articles in four different formats. Some articles appear in all print and electronic versions; others are published in only one or two formats.

1. **Print**

2. **Digital version in a database.** You most commonly access these sources through a DATABASE such as EBSCO or Academic Search Premier, which your library purchases.

3. **Digital version with direct online access.** Without going through a database, you access these sources directly on the Web, either by entering a specific URL or clicking on links provided by a search. Of course, many other Web sources are not from periodicals; we explain them in examples 68–80.

4. **Digital version on a digital reader.** Many devices allow you to access online content. These include e-readers like Kindle or Nook, tablet computers (like iPads), or smart phones (like Android).

A citation for a periodical title contains three major parts: author, title of article, and publication information, including the medium in which you access the source—usually print or Web—and for Web sources, your date of access as well. MLA also identifies some types of sources, such as editorials or letters, in citations.

Figure 25.2 shows how to cite a print article from a scholarly journal.

Figure 25.3, p. 240, shows how to cite an article from a scholarly journal that was accessed in a database.

1. Article in a Scholarly Journal: Print

Williams, Bronwyn T. "Seeking New Worlds: The Study of Writing beyond Our Classrooms." *College Composition and Communication* 62.1 (2010): 127–46. Print.

Provide both volume and issue number, if available.

2. Article in Scholarly Journal with a Print Version: Database

Williams, Bronwyn T. "Seeking New Worlds: The Study of Writing beyond Our Classrooms." *College Composition and Communication.* 62.1 (2010): 127–46. Proquest. Web. 24 Oct. 2011.

The final date (24 Oct. 2011) is the date you accessed the article on the Web.

3. Article in a Scholarly Journal with a Print Version: Direct online access

Hoge, Charles W., et al. "Mild Traumatic Brain Injury in U.S. Soldiers Returning from Iraq." *New England Journal of Medicine* 358.5 (2008): 453–63. Web. 10 Sept. 2008.

Figure 25.2 Print article from a scholarly journal, accessed in print.

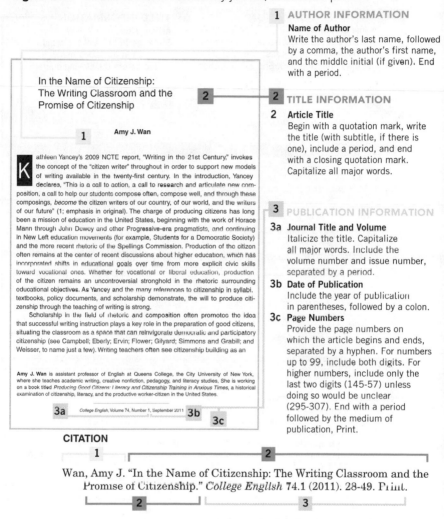

1 AUTHOR INFORMATION

Name of Author
Write the author's last name, followed by a comma, the author's first name, and the middle initial (if given). End with a period.

2 TITLE INFORMATION

2 Article Title
Begin with a quotation mark, write the title (with subtitle, if there is one), include a period, and end with a closing quotation mark. Capitalize all major words.

3 PUBLICATION INFORMATION

3a Journal Title and Volume
Italicize the title. Capitalize all major words. Include the volume number and issue number, separated by a period.

3b Date of Publication
Include the year of publication in parentheses, followed by a colon.

3c Page Numbers
Provide the page numbers on which the article begins and ends, separated by a hyphen. For numbers up to 99, include both digits. For higher numbers, include only the last two digits (145-57) unless doing so would be unclear (295-307). End with a period followed by the medium of publication, Print.

In the Name of Citizenship: The Writing Classroom and the Promise of Citizenship

Amy J. Wan

Kathleen Yancey's 2009 NCTE report, "Writing in the 21st Century," invokes the concept of the "citizen writer" throughout in order to support new models of writing available in the twenty-first century. In the introduction, Yancey declares, "This is a call to action, a call to research and articulate new composition, a call to help our students compose often, compose well, and through these composings, *become* the citizen writers of our country, of our world, and the writers of our future" (1; emphasis in original). The charge of producing citizens has long been a mission of education in the United States, beginning with the work of Horace Mann through John Dewey and other Progressive-era pragmatists, and continuing in New Left education movements (for example, Students for a Democratic Society) and the more recent rhetoric of the Spellings Commission. Production of the citizen often remains at the center of recent discussions about higher education, which has incorporated shifts in educational goals over time from more explicit civic skills toward vocational or liberal education. Whether for vocational or liberal education, production of the citizen remains an uncontroversial stronghold in the rhetoric surrounding educational objectives. As Yancey and the many references to citizenship in syllabi, textbooks, policy documents, pedagogy, and scholarship demonstrate, the will to produce citizenship through the teaching of writing is strong.

Scholarship in the field of rhetoric and composition often promotes the idea that successful writing instruction plays a key role in the preparation of good citizens, situating the classroom as a space that can reinvigorate democratic and participatory citizenship (see Campbell; Eberly; Ervin; Flower; Gilyard; Simmons and Grabill; and Weisser, to name just a few). Writing teachers often see citizenship building as an

Amy J. Wan is assistant professor of English at Queens College, the City University of New York, where she teaches academic writing, creative nonfiction, pedagogy, and literacy studies. She is working on a book titled *Producing Good Citizens: Literacy and Citizenship Training in Anxious Times*, a historical examination of citizenship, literacy, and the productive worker-citizen in the United States.

3a *College English,* Volume 74, Number 1, September 2011 **3b** **3c**

CITATION

Wan, Amy J. "In the Name of Citizenship: The Writing Classroom and the Promise of Citizenship." *College English* 74.1 (2011). 28-49. Print.

4. Article in a Scholarly Journal Published Only Online: Direct online access

Rutz, Paul X. "What a Painter of 'Historical Narrative' Can Tell Us about War Photography." *Kairos* 14.3 (2010). Web. 11 Nov. 2010.

Some periodicals appear only online and publish no print version.

5. Article in a Weekly or Biweekly Magazine: Print

Foroohar, Rana. "Why the World Isn't Getting Smaller." *Time* 27 June 2011: 20. Print.

MLA
25B

240

Author. Title. Type of source. Publication information.
MLA WORKS CITED LIST

Figure 25.3 Article from a scholarly journal accessed in a database.

1 AUTHOR INFORMATION
Name of Author
Write the author's last name, followed by a comma, the author's first name, and the middle initial (if given). End with a period.

2 TITLE INFORMATION
Article Title
State the full title of the article, enclosed in quotation marks. Use a period before the closing quotation mark.

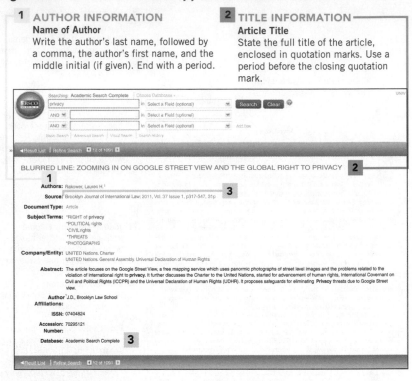

3 PUBLICATION INFORMATION

3a Name of Periodical
Provide the journal title (italicized).

3b Volume and Issue Numbers
Leave one space after the journal title and provide the volume and issue numbers, separated by a period.

3c Date of Publication
Provide the year of publication, in parentheses, followed by a colon.

3d Page Numbers
Provide the inclusive page numbers for the complete article, not just the portion you used. End with a period.

3e Title of Database
Italicize the name of the database. End with a period.

3f Medium of Publication
Provide the medium of publication consulted (Web), followed by a period.

3g Date of Access
Provide the day, month, and year that you accessed the article online. End with a period.

CITATION

Rakower, Lauren H. "Blurred Line: Zooming in on Google Street View and the Global Right to Privacy." *Brooklyn Journal of International Law* 37.1 (2011): 317-47. *Academic Search Complete*. Web. 21 Feb. 2012.

If there is no author given, begin with the title of the article.

"The Price Is Wrong." *Economist* 2 Aug. 2003: 58–59. Print.

6. Article in a Weekly or Biweekly Magazine: Database

Foroohar, Rana. "Why the World Isn't Getting Smaller." *Time* 19 June 2011.
    Academic Search Complete. Web. 28 Aug. 2011.

7. Article in a Weekly or Biweekly Magazine: Direct online access

Foroohar, Rana. "Why the World Isn't Getting Smaller." *Time.* Time, 19 June
    2011. Web. 27 Aug. 2011.

The name of the Web site is italicized. The sponsor (owner) of the Web site
precedes the date of publication.

8. Article in a Monthly or Bimonthly Magazine: Print

Goetz, Thomas. "The Feedback Loop." *Wired* July 2011: 126–33. Print.

9. Article in a Monthly or Bimonthly Magazine: Database

Goetz, Thomas. "The Feedback Loop." *Wired* July 2011: 126–33. *ProQuest.*
    Web. 16 Sept. 2011.

10. Article in a Monthly or Bimonthly Magazine: Direct online access

Goetz, Thomas. "The Feedback Loop." *Wired.* Conde Nast, 19 June 2011. Web.
    16 Sept. 2011.

11. Article Published Only Online: Direct online access

Ramirez, Eddy. "Comparing American Students with Those in China and
    India." *U.S. News and World Report.* U.S. News and World Report, 30 Jan.
    2008. Web. 4 Mar. 2008.

12. Article in a Newspaper: Print

Hesse, Monica. "Love among the Ruins." *Washington Post* 24 Apr. 2011: F1+. Print.

Omit *A, An,* or *The* as the first word in a newspaper title. Give the day, month,
and year of the issue (and the edition, if applicable). If sections are designated,
give the section letter as well as the page number. If an article runs on non-
consecutive pages, give the starting page number followed by a plus sign (for
example, 1+ for an article that starts on page 1 and continues on a later page).

If no author is listed, begin with the title of the article.

"Prepping for Uranium Work." *Denver Post* 18 June 2011: B2. Print.

If the city of publication is not part of the newspaper's name, put it in square
brackets after the name, not italicized.

13. Article in a Newspaper: Database

Hesse, Monica. "Falling in Love with St. Andrews, Scotland." *Washington Post*
    24 Apr. 2011. *LexisNexis Academic.* Web. 3 Oct. 2011.

MLA
25B

242

Author. Title. Type of source. Publication information.
MLA WORKS CITED LIST

14. Article in a Newspaper: Direct online access

Hesse, Monica. "Falling in Love with St. Andrews, Scotland." *Washington Post*.
Washington Post, 22 Apr. 2011. Web. 3 Oct. 2011.

15. Article from a News Site Published Only Online: Direct online access

Katz, David. "What to Do about Flu? Get Vaccinated." *Huffington Post*.
Huffington Post, 28 Oct. 2010. Web. 25 May 2011.

16. Editorial

"Primary Considerations." Editorial. *Washington Post* 27 Jan. 2008: B6. Print.

If an author is listed, include her or his name before the title, then provide the
title and information about the type of publication.

17. Letter to the Editor: Print

Goldstein, Lester. "Roach Coaches: The Upside." Letter. *Sierra* May/June 2011:
2. Print.

If there is no title, include just the type, as in example 18.

18. Letter to the Editor: Direct online access

Ennis, Heather B. Letter. *U.S. News and World Report*. U.S. News and World
Report, 20 Dec. 2007. Web. 22 Dec. 2007.

19. Review

Shenk, David. "Toolmaker, Brain Builder." Rev. of *Beyond Big Blue: Building
the Computer That Defeated the World Chess Champion*, by Feng-Hsiung
Hsu. *American Scholar* 72 (2003): 150–52. Print.

20. Article in a Collection of Reprinted Articles: Print

Brumberg, Abraham. "Russia after Perestroika." *New York Review of Books*
27 June 1991: 53–62. Rpt. in *Russian and Soviet History*. Ed. Alexander
Dallin. Vol. 14. New York: Garland, 1992. 300–20. Print.

Textbooks used in college writing courses often collect previously printed
articles.

Wallace, David Foster. "Consider the Lobster." *Gourmet* Aug. 2004: 50–55. Rpt.
in *Creating Nonfiction: A Guide and Anthology*. By Becky Bradway and
Doug Hesse. Boston: Bedford, 2009. 755–69. Print.

21. Abstract: Print

Marcus, Hazel R., and Shinobu Kitayamo. "Culture and the Self: Implications
for Cognition, Emotion, and Motivation." *Psychological Review* 88 (1991):
224–53. Abstract. *Psychological Abstracts* 78 (1991): item 23878. Print.

For abstracts identified by item numbers rather than page numbers, use the
word *item* before the item number.

22. Abstract: Database

Marcus, Hazel R., and Shinobu Kitayamo. "Culture and the Self: Implications for Cognition, Emotion, and Motivation." Abstract. *Psychological Abstracts* 78 (1991): item 23878. *PsycINFO*. Web. 10 Apr. 2004.

BOOKS

You can read books these days in four different formats.

1. **Print**

2. **Digital version through an e-book.** E-books are electronic versions of books for digital readers like the Kindle, Nook, iPad, and so on.

3. **Digital version from a database.** Some books are available through library databases; in a sense, you're "checking out the books" online.

4. **Digital version through direct online access.** Versions of some older books, whose copyrights have expired because their authors died more than 70 years ago, are available directly on the Web. Portions of several more recent books are also available directly on the Web, through sites like Google Books. However, the section you might need for your research is frequently not available.

Figure 25.4 shows how to cite a single-author print book.

We provide examples of all formats in examples 23–26. The same principles apply to all books, so you can adapt these basic models as needed. We also note that there are audio versions of some books: recordings of an actor (or sometimes, the author) reading the book. We explain how to cite audio books in example 59.

23. Book by One Author: Print

Turkle, Sherry. *Alone Together: Why We Expect More from Technology and Less from Each Other*. New York: Basic, 2011. Print.

24. Book by One Author: E-Book

Turkle, Sherry. *Alone Together: Why We Expect More from Technology and Less from Each Other*. New York: Basic, 2011. Kindle file.

25. Book by One Author: Database

Turkle, Sherry. *Evocative Objects: Things We Think With*. Cambridge: MIT P, 2007. *Ebrary*. Web. 3 May 2011.

26. Book by One Author: Direct online access

Turkle, Sherry. *Alone Together: Why We Expect More from Technology and Less from Each Other*. New York: Basic, 2011. *Google Books*. Google, 2011. Web. 25 July 2011.

Chopin, Kate. *The Awakening*. 1899. *PBS Electronic Library*. PBS, 10 Dec. 1998. Web. 13 Nov. 2004.

MLA
25B
244

Author. Title. <mark>Type of source.</mark> Publication information.
MLA WORKS CITED LIST

Figure 25.4 Single-author print book.

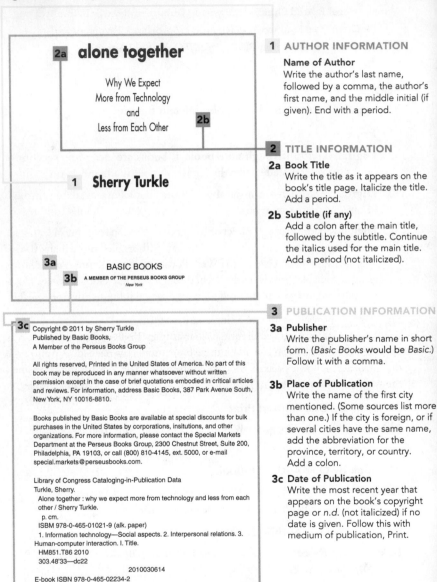

1 AUTHOR INFORMATION

Name of Author
Write the author's last name, followed by a comma, the author's first name, and the middle initial (if given). End with a period.

2 TITLE INFORMATION

2a Book Title
Write the title as it appears on the book's title page. Italicize the title. Add a period.

2b Subtitle (if any)
Add a colon after the main title, followed by the subtitle. Continue the italics used for the main title. Add a period (not italicized).

3 PUBLICATION INFORMATION

3a Publisher
Write the publisher's name in short form. (*Basic Books* would be *Basic.*) Follow it with a comma.

3b Place of Publication
Write the name of the first city mentioned. (Some sources list more than one.) If the city is foreign, or if several cities have the same name, add the abbreviation for the province, territory, or country. Add a colon.

3c Date of Publication
Write the most recent year that appears on the book's copyright page or *n.d.* (not italicized) if no date is given. Follow this with medium of publication, Print.

CITATION

Turkle, Sherry. *Alone Together: Why We Expect More from Technology and Less from Each Other.* New York: Basic, 2004. Print.

27. Book by Two or Three Authors

Edin, Kathryn, and Maria Kefalas. *Promises I Can Keep: Why Poor Women Put Motherhood before Marriage*. Berkeley: U of California P, 2005. Print.

Lynam, John K., Cyrus G. Ndiritu, and Adiel N. Mbabu. *Transformation of Agricultural Research Systems in Africa: Lessons from Kenya*. East Lansing: Michigan State UP, 2004. Print.

For these and the following citations, you can adapt the elements to examples 24–26. For e-books, adapt the model to example 24. For a book in a database, see example 25. For a book accessed directly online, see example 26.

28. Book by More Than Three Authors

Saul, Wendy, et al. *Beyond the Science Fair: Creating a Kids' Inquiry Conference*. Portsmouth: Heinemann, 2005. Print.

Give only the first author's name, followed by a comma and the phrase *et al.* (abbreviated from the Latin *et alii*, meaning "and others"), or list all names in full in the order in which they appear on the title page.

29. Two or More Works by the Same Author(s)

Jenkins, Henry. *Convergence Culture: Where Old and New Media Collide*. New York: New York UP, 2006. Print.

---. *Fans, Bloggers, and Gamers: Exploring Participatory Culture*. New York: New York UP, 2006. Print.

Give author name(s) in the first entry only. In the second and subsequent entries, use three hyphens and a period to stand for exactly the same name(s). Arrange the works in alphabetical (not chronological) order according to title.

30. Book by a Group or Corporate Author

American Psychological Association. *Publication Manual of the American Psychological Association*. 6th ed. Washington: APA, 2010. Print.

When a corporate author is also the publisher, use a shortened form of the corporate name at the publisher position.

31. Book with No Author Named

The Chicago Manual of Style. 16th ed. Chicago: U of Chicago P, 2010. Print.

If there is no author's name on the title page, begin the citation with the title. Alphabetize the entry according to the first significant word of the title (ignore *A*, *An*, or *The*).

32. Book with an Author and an Editor

Stowe, Harriet Beecher. *Uncle Tom's Cabin*. Ed. Elizabeth Ammons. New York: Norton, 2010. Print.

MLA

25B

246

Author. Title. Type of source. Publication information.
MLA WORKS CITED LIST

If your paper refers to the work of the book's author, put the author's name first. If your paper refers to the work of the editor, put the editor's name first.

Ammons, Elizabeth, ed. *Uncle Tom's Cabin*. By Harriet Beecher Stowe. New York: Norton, 2010. Print.

33. Translation

Nesbo, Jo. *The Leopard*. Trans. Don Bartlett. New York: Vintage, 2011.

34. Work in Several Volumes or Parts

Chrisley, Ronald, ed. *Artificial Intelligence: Critical Concepts*. Vol. 1. London: Routledge, 2000. Print. 4 vols.

If you are citing only one volume, put the volume number before the publication information. If you wish, you can give the total number of volumes at the end of the entry. MLA recommends using arabic numerals, even if the source uses roman numerals (*Vol. 6* rather than *Vol. VI*).

35. Anthology or Edited Book

Purdy, John L., and James Ruppert, eds. *Nothing but the Truth: An Anthology of Native American Literature*. Upper Saddle River: Prentice, 2001. Print.

Use this model if you are citing an entire anthology. In the example above, *ed.* stands for "editor," so use *eds.* when more than one editor is named.

36. One Selection from an Anthology or an Edited Book

Trujillo, Laura. "Balancing Act." *Border-Line Personalities: A New Generation of Latinas Dish on Sex, Sass, and Cultural Shifting*. Ed. Robyn Moreno and Michelle Herrera Mulligan. New York: Harper, 2004. 61–72. Print.

Teasdale, Sara. "Driftwood." *Flame and Shadow*. Ed. A. Light. N.p., 1920. *Project Gutenberg*. 1 July 1996. Web. 18 Aug. 2008.

Give the author and title of the selection first and then the full title of the anthology. Information about the editor starts with *Ed.* (for "Edited by"), so don't use *Eds.* when there is more than one editor. Give the name(s) of the editor(s) in normal order rather than reversing first and last names. Give the page range of the selection at the end.

37. More Than One Selection from the Same Anthology or Edited Book

Bond, Ruskin. "The Night Train at Deoli." Chaudhuri 415–18.

Chaudhuri, Amit, ed. *The Vintage Book of Modern Indian Literature*. New York: Vintage, 2004. Print.

Vijayan, O.V. "The Rocks." Chaudhuri 291–96.

If you cite more than one selection from the same anthology, you can list the anthology as a separate entry with all of the publication information. Also list each selection from the anthology by author and title of the selection, but give only the name(s) of the editor(s) of the anthology and the page number(s) for each selection. Here, *ed.* stands for "editor," so it is correct to use *eds.* when more than one editor is named. List selections separately in alphabetical order by author's last name.

38. Article in a Reference Book

Burnbam, John C. "Freud, Sigmund." *The Encyclopedia of Psychiatry, Psychology, and Psychoanalysis.* Ed. Benjamin B. Wolman. New York: Holt, 1996. Print.

If the articles are alphabetically arranged, you don't need to give volume and page numbers.

If no author is listed, begin with the title of the article.

"Ireland." *The New Encyclopaedia Britannica: Macropaedia.* 15th ed. 2002. Print.

If you're citing a widely used reference work, don't give full publication information. Instead, give only the edition and year of publication.

39. Second or Later Edition

MLA Handbook for Writers of Research Papers. 7th ed. New York: MLA, 2009. Print.

If a book is not a first edition, the edition number is on the title page. Place the abbreviated information (*2nd ed., 3rd ed.,* etc.) between the title and the publication information. Give only the latest copyright date for the edition you are using.

40. Introduction, Preface, Foreword, or Afterword

Hesse, Doug. Foreword. *The End of Composition Studies.* By David W. Smit. Carbondale: Southern Illinois UP, 2004. ix–xiii. Print.

Give first the name of the writer of the part you're citing and then the name of the cited part, capitalized. After the book title, put *By* and the book author's full name, if different from the writer of the cited material. If the writer of the cited material is the same as the book author, use a separate entry only when there is also an editor or translator of the book. After the publication information, give inclusive page numbers for the cited part. When the introduction, preface, foreword, or afterword has a title, include it in the citation before the section name, as in the following example:

Fox-Genovese, Elizabeth. "Mothers and Daughters: The Ties That Bind." Foreword. *Southern Mothers.* Ed. Nagueyalti Warren and Sally Wolff. Baton Rouge: Louisiana State UP, 1999. iv–xviii. Print.

41. Unpublished Dissertation or Essay

Stuart, Gina Anne. "Exploring the Harry Potter Book Series: A Study of Adolescent Reading Motivation." Diss. Utah State U, 2006. Print.

Treat published dissertations as books.

MLA
25B
248

Author. Title. Type of source. Publication information.
MLA WORKS CITED LIST

42. Reprint of an Older Book

Coover, Robert. *A Night at the Movies, Or, You Must Remember This.* 1987.
Champaign: Dalkey Archive, 2007.

Republishing information can be found on the copyright page.

43. Book in a Series or Scholarly Project

Ardell, Jean Hastings. *Breaking into Baseball: Women and the National Pastime.*
Carbondale: Southern Illinois UP, 2005. Print. Writing Baseball Series.

44. Book with a Title within a Title

Lumiansky, Robert M., and Herschel Baker, eds. *Critical Approaches to Six
Major English Works:* Beowulf *through* Paradise Lost. Philadelphia:
U of Pennsylvania P, 1968. Print.

MLA also accepts a second style for embedded titles:

Lumiansky, Robert M., and Herschel Baker, eds. *Critical Approaches to Six
Major English Works: "Beowulf" through "Paradise Lost."* Philadelphia:
U of Pennsylvania P, 1968. Print.

45. Bible or Sacred Text

Bhagavad Gita. Trans. Juan Mascaro. Rev. ed. New York: Penguin, 2003. Print.

The Holy Bible: New International Version. New York: Harper, 1983. Print.

The Qur'an. Trans. M.A.S. Abdel Haleem. New York: Oxford UP, 2004. Print.

46. Government Publication with No Author

United States. Cong. Senate. Select Committee on Intelligence. *Report on the
U.S. Intelligence Community's Prewar Intelligence Assessment of Iraq.*
108th Cong., 1st sess. Washington: GPO, 2004. Print.

Start with the name of the government. Then name the government agency.
(*GPO* stands for *Government Printing Office.*) Then include the title, any series
information, the publication date, and the medium of publication.

47. Government Publication with Named Author

Wallace, David Rains. *Yellowstone: A Natural and Human History, Yellowstone
National Park, Idaho, Montana, and Wyoming.* US Interior Dept. National
Park Service. Official National Park Handbook 150. Washington: GPO, 2001.
Print.

MLA also permits an alternative format:

United States. Interior Dept. National Park Service. *Yellowstone: A Natural and
Human History, Yellowstone National Park, Idaho, Montana, and Wyoming.*
By David Rains Wallace. Official National Park Handbook 150. Washington:
GPO, 2001. Print.

48. Published Proceedings of a Conference

Rocha, Luis Mateus, et al., eds. *Artificial Life X: Proceedings of the Tenth International Conference on the Simulation and Synthesis of Living Systems.* 3–7 June 2006, Bloomington, IN. Cambridge: MIT P, 2006. Print.

IMAGES, AUDIO, FILM, AND VIDEO

49. Photograph, Painting, Drawing, Illustration, etc. (Original)

Mydans, Carl. *General Douglas MacArthur Landing at Luzon, 1945.* Gelatin silver print. Soho Triad Fine Art Gallery, New York. 21 Oct.–28 Nov. 1999.

If the image has no title, provide a brief description.

50. Photograph, Painting, Drawing, Illustration, etc. in a Periodical: Print

Greene, Herb. *Grace Slick.* Photograph. *Rolling Stone* 30 Sept. 2004: 102. Print.

Include maker, title, and type as in example 49, but include publication information as for a print article.

51. Photograph, Painting, Drawing, Illustration, etc. in a Periodical: Direct online access

Morris, Christopher. *Man in Camouflage.* Photograph. *Atlantic.* The Atlantic Monthly Group, July/Aug. 2011. Web. 5 Aug. 2011.

52. Photograph, Painting, Drawing, Illustration, etc. in a Book: Print

The World's Most Populous Countries. Illustration. *Maps of the Imagination: The Writer as Cartographer.* By Peter Turchi. San Antonio: Trinity UP, 2004. 116–17. Print.

53. Photograph, Painting, Drawing, Illustration, etc.: Direct online access

Bourke-White, Margaret. *Fort Peck Dam, Montana.* 1936. Gelatin silver print. *Metropolitan Museum of Art.* Web. 5 Aug. 2008.

54. Comic or Cartoon

Sutton, Ward. "Ryan's a Late Adopter." Cartoon. *New Yorker* 2 May 2011: 64. Print.

55. Photo Essay: Direct online access

Nachtwey, James. "Crime in Middle America." *Time.* Time, 2 Dec. 2006. Web. 5 May 2007.

56. Image from a Social Networking Site

Gristellar, Ferdinand. *The Gateway Arch.* Photograph. Ferdinand Gristellar. Facebook, 7 Aug. 2009. Web. 3 Sept. 2009.

MLA

25B

250

Author. Title. Type of source. Publication information.
MLA WORKS CITED LIST

57. Image from a Service or Distributor

World Perspectives. *Launching of the Space Shuttle Columbia, Florida, USA, 1998.* Photograph. Getty Images #AT3775-001. Web. 3 Mar. 2011.

In this example, the photographer was listed as "World Perspectives."

58. Map, Chart, or Other Graphic: Direct online access

"Hurricane Rita." Graphic. *New York Times Online.* New York Times, 24 Sept. 2005. Web. 24 Sept. 2005.

59. Audio Book

Turkle, Sherry. *Alone Together: Why We Expect More from Technology and Less from Each Other.* Narr. Laural Merlington. Tantor Media, 2011. CD.

60. Sound Recording: CD, DVD

Verdi, Giuseppe. *Requiem.* Chicago Symphony Orchestra and Chorus. Cond. Ricardo Muti. CSO Resound, 2010. CD.

Put first the name most relevant to what you discuss in your paper (performer, conductor, work performed). Include the recording's title, the medium for any recording other than a CD (*LP, Audiocassette*), the name of the issuer, and the year the work was issued.

61. Sound Recording: MP3

Radiohead. "Jigsaw Falling into Place." *In Rainbows.* Radiohead, 2007. MP3 file.

62. Sound Recording: Direct online access

Komunyakaa, Yusef. "My Father's Love Letters." *Poets.org Listening Booth.* Academy of American Poets, 5 May 1993. Web. 19 Aug. 2008.

63. Podcast: Direct online access

Blumberg, Alex, and Adam Davidson. "The Giant Pool of Money." *This American Life.* NPR, 9 May 2008. Web. 19 Oct. 2009.

A podcast is an audio recording that is posted online. Thus, the publication medium is *Web*.

64. Film, Video, or DVD

It Happened One Night. Screenplay by Robert Riskin. Dir. and Prod. Frank Capra. Perf. Clark Gable and Claudette Colbert. 1934. Sony Pictures, 1999. DVD.

Give the title first, and include the director, the distributor, and the year. For films that were subsequently released on tape or DVD, provide the original release date of the movie *before* the type of medium. Other information (writer, producer, major actors) is optional but helpful. Put first names first.

65. Video or Film: Direct online access

For video downloads, include the download date and the source.

It Happened One Night. Screenplay by Robert Riskin. Dir. and Prod. Frank Capra.
    Perf. Clark Gable and Claudette Colbert. 1934. *Netflix*. Web. 15. Dec. 2011.

CNN. *Challenger Disaster Live on CNN*. *YouTube.com*. YouTube, 27 Jan. 2011.
    Web. 4 Mar. 2011.

66. Broadcast Television or Radio Program

Include at least the title of the program (in italics), the network, the local
station and its city, and the date of the broadcast.

Not for Ourselves Alone: The Story of Elizabeth Cady Stanton and Susan B.
    Anthony. By Ken Burns. Perf. Julie Harris, Ronnie Gilbert, and Sally
    Kellerman. Prod. Paul Barnes and Ken Burns. PBS. WNET, New York.
    8 Nov. 1999. Television.

The Madeleine Brand Show. SCPR. KPCC, Pasadena. 20 June 2011. Radio.

For a series, also supply the title of the specific episode (in quotation marks)
before the title of the program (italicized).

"The Bruce-Partington Plans." *Sherlock Holmes*. RMPBS. KRMA, Denver.
    30 June 2011. Television.

67. Television or Radio Program: Direct online access

"Bill Moyer." *The Daily Show*. Perf. Jon Stewart. Comedy Central. *Hulu.com*.
    Hulu, 1 June 2011. Web. 22 Sept. 2011.

"The Disappearing Incandescent Bulb." *The Madeleine Brand*
    Show. SCPR. KPCC, Pasadena. 20 June 2011. Web. 6 Oct. 2011.
    <http://www.scpr.org/programs/madeleine-brand/2011/06/20/
    the-disappearing-incandescent-bulb/>.

Because this source may be difficult to find, the URL is listed.

OTHER INTERNET SOURCES

This section shows models for other online sources. For such sources, provide
as much of the following information as you can.

1. The author's name, if given

2. In quotation marks, the title of a short work (Web page, brief document,
   essay, article, message, and so on); or italicized, the title of a book

3. Publication information for any print version, if it exists

4. The name of an editor, translator, or compiler, if any, with an abbreviation such as *Ed., Trans.,* or *Comp.* before the name

5. Publication information for the Web:

  a. The italicized title of the Internet site (scholarly project, database, online periodical, professional or personal Web site). If the site has no title, describe it: for example, Home page.
  b. The date of electronic publication or posting or the most recent update.
  c. The name of a sponsoring organization, if any.
  d. The medium of publication: Web.
  e. The date you accessed the material.
  f. The URL in angle brackets (< >), only when the reader probably could not locate the source without it. If you must break a URL at the end of a line, break only after a slash and do not use a hyphen.

Figure 25.5 shows how to cite a page from a Web site.

68. Entire Web Site

WebdelSol.Com. Ed. Michael Neff. 2011. Web. 4 Aug. 2011.

69. Home Page (Organization or Company)

Association for the Advancement of Artificial Intelligence. AAAI, n.d. Web.
    17 Oct. 2011.

70. Personal Home Page

Hesse, Doug. Home page. Web. 1 Nov. 2011. *<http://portfolio.du.edu/dhesse>.*

Provide the URL if the page might be difficult to find.

71. Page from a Web Site

"Protecting Whales from Dangerous Sonar." *National Resources Defense
    Council.* NRDC, 9 Nov. 2005. Web. 12 Dec. 2005.

"Ethical and Social Implications of AI for Society." *Association for the
    Advancement of Artificial Intelligence.* AAAI, 3 May 2012. Web. 19 May 2012.

Provide as much information as you can, starting with the author, if available, and the title of the page, followed by the site information.

72. Academic Department Home Page

Writing. Dept. home page. Grand Valley State U. Web. 26 Feb. 2010.

73. Course Home Page

St. Germain, Sheryl. Myths and Fairytales: From *Inanna* to *Edward
    Scissorhands.* Course home page. Summer 2003. Dept. of English,
    Iowa State U. Web. 20 Feb. 2005. <http://www.public.iastate.edu/
    ~sgermain/531.homepage.html>.

74. Government or Institutional Web Site

Home Education and Private Tutoring. Pennsylvania Department of Education,
    2005. Web. 5 Aug. 2008.

Figure 25.5 Page from a Web site.

1 TITLE

Title of the Work
State the full title of the work cited, enclosed in quotation marks. Use a period before the closing quotation mark.

2 PUBLICATION INFORMATION

2a Title of the Overall Web Site
Provide the title of the Web site (italicized), followed by a period.

2b Publisher or Sponsor of the Web Site
Leave one space after the title of the overall Web site and provide the publisher or sponsor of the Web site. If this information is not available, use *N.p.* End with a comma.

2c Date of Publication
Provide the available date (day, month, and year) of publication, followed by a period. If no date is available, use *n.d.*

2d Medium of Publication
Provide the medium of publication consulted (*Web*), followed by a period.

2e Date of Access
Provide the day, month, and year that you accessed the article online. End with a period.

CITATION

"Agriculture and Food Supply." *U.S. Environmental Protection Agency.* US Environmental Protection Agency, 2012. Web. 5 Mar. 2012.

75. Online Discussion Posting

Firrantello, Larry. "Van Gogh on Prozac." Online posting. 23 May 2005. *Salon Table Talk.* Web. 7 June 2005.

Give the date of the posting and the name of the bulletin board, if any. Then give the publication medium, the access date and, in angle brackets, the URL if needed.

MLA

25B

254

Author. Title. Type of source. Publication information.
MLA WORKS CITED LIST

76. Chat or Real-Time Communication

Berzsenyi, Christyne. Online discussion of "Writing to Meet Your Match:
Rhetoric, Perceptions, and Self-Presentation for Four Online Daters."
Computers and Writing Online. AcadianaMoo, 13 May 2007. Web.
13 May 2007.

Glenn, Maria. Chat. *Laurence Smith.* Facebook, 9 Sept. 2010. Web. 9 Sept. 2010.

Give the name of the speaker or writer, a title for the event (if any), the Web
page or forum, date, publication medium, access date, and URL if needed.

77. E-Mail Message

Martin, Tara. "Visit to Los Alamos." Message to David Sanz. 25 July 2010.
E-mail.

Start with the name of the person who wrote the e-mail message. Give the title
or subject line in quotation marks. Then describe the message, including the
recipient's name. Add the date. Finally, write the medium of delivery (e-mail).

78. Posting on a Blog

Phillips, Matthew. "Need to Go to the ER? Not Until the Game's Over."
Freakonomics. Freakonomics, LLC, 15 June 2011. Web. 14 Aug. 2011.

79. Wiki

"NASCAR Sprint Cup Series." *NASCAR Wiki.* Wikia, 11 Jan. 2011. Web. 6 Apr. 2011.

80. Posting on Facebook or Twitter

Adler-Kassner, Linda. "Conversations toward Action." *Council of Writing
Program Administrators.* Facebook, 5 Feb. 2010. Web. 6 May 2011.

Adams, John Quincy (JQ Adams_MHS). "3|12|1812: Brancia called and read me
all the official Correspondence concerning the duels at Naples. An idle
day." 20 Mar. 2012, 2:09 p.m. Tweet.

Reproduce the entire tweet and the time you accessed it.

OTHER PRINT, NONPRINT, AND ELECTRONIC SOURCES

81. Published or Unpublished Letter

Irvin, William. Letter to Lesley Osburn. 7 Dec. 2011. MS.

Williams, William Carlos. Letter to his son. 13 Mar. 1935. *Letters of the Century:
America 1900–1999.* Ed. Lisa Grunwald and Stephen J. Adler. New York:
Dial, 1999: 225–26. Print.

Begin the entry with the the author of the letter. Note the recipient, too. If
the letter is published in a periodical, a book, or online, follow the appropriate
citation format, shown here.

82. Microfiche Collection of Articles

Wenzell, Ron. "Businesses Prepare for a More Diverse Work Force." *St. Louis Post Dispatch* 3 Feb. 1990: 17. Microform. *NewsBank: Employment* 27 (1990): fiche 2, grid D12.

A microfiche is a transparent sheet of film (a *fiche*) with microscopic printing that needs to be read through a special magnifier.

83. Report or Pamphlet

National Commission on Writing in America's Schools and Colleges. *The Neglected "R": The Need for a Writing Revolution.* New York: College Board, 2003. Print.

Use the format for books, to the extent possible, including whether you're citing a print or digital version.

84. Legal Source

Brown v. Board of Educ. 347 US 483-96. Supreme Court of the US. 1954. Print.

Include the name of the case, the number of the case (preceded by *No.*), the name of the court deciding the case, and the date of the decision. Legal sources can frequently be accessed through a database:

Brown v. Board of Educ. 347 US 483-96. Supreme Court of the US. 1954. *LexisNexis Academic.* Web. 25 Jan. 2010.

85. Interview

Friedman, Randi. Telephone interview. 30 Aug. 2008.

Winfrey, Oprah. "Ten Questions for Oprah Winfrey." By Richard Zoglin. *Time* 15 Dec. 2003: 8. Print.

Pope, Carl. Interview by Amy Standen. *Salon.com.* Salon Media Group, 29 Apr. 2002. Web. 27 Jan. 2005.

Note the type of interview, for example "Telephone" or "Personal" (face-to-face). For a published interview, give the name of the interviewed person first, identify the source as an interview, and then give details as for any published source: title; author (preceded by the word *By*); and publication details. Follow the citation format for a periodical, book, or Web source, as appropriate.

86. Lecture or Speech

Kennedy, John Fitzgerald. Greater Houston Ministerial Assn. Rice Hotel, Houston. 12 Sept. 1960. Speech.

Katz, Jennifer. "Spiral Galaxies." Astronomy 1000. University of Denver, Denver. 7 Feb. 2011. Lecture.

MLA

256 **25B**

Author. Title. Type of source. Publication information.
MLA WORKS CITED LIST

87. Live Performance (Play, Concert, Dance, etc.)

All My Sons. By Arthur Miller. Dir. Calvin McLean. Center for the Performing
Arts, Normal, IL. 27 Sept. 2005. Performance.

Nelson, Willie. Concert. Red Rocks Amphitheater, Denver. 22 June 2011.
Performance.

88. Work of Art, Original

Cassatt, Mary. *La Toilette*. 1890. Oil on canvas. Art Institute of Chicago.

Fourquet, Léon. *The Man with the Broken Nose*. 1865. Marble. Musée Rodin, Paris.

89. Musical Score

Schubert, Franz. *Unfinished Symphony*. 1822. Print.

Italicize any musical work that has a title, such as an opera, a ballet, or a named
symphony. Don't underline or put in quotation marks music identified only
by form, number, and key, as follows.

Schubert, Franz. Symphony no. 8 in B minor. 1822. Print.

To cite a published score, use the following format.

Schubert, Franz. *Symphony in B Minor (Unfinished)*. 1822. Ed. Martin Cusid.
New York: Norton, 1971. Print.

90. Advertisement

Southwest Airlines. Advertisement. ABC. 24 Aug. 2010. Television.

Canon Digital Cameras. Advertisement. *Time* 2 June 2003: 77. Print.

Samsung. Advertisement. *RollingStone*. Wenner Media, 8 Nov. 2005. Web. 11
Nov. 2005.

91. Video Game or Software

The Island: Castaway. N.p.: Awem Studio, 2010. Game.

"N.p." indicates that the place of publication is unknown.

92. Nonperiodical Publications on CD, DVD, or Magnetic Tape

Perl, Sondra. *Felt Sense: Guidelines for Composing*. Portsmouth: Boynton,
2004. CD.

Citations for publications on DVD, CD-ROM, or other recording formats
follow guidelines for print publications, with two additions: list the publication medium (for example, *CD*), and give the vendor's name and date of issue.

93. PowerPoint or Similar Presentation

Delyser, Ariel. "Political Movements in the Philippines." University of Denver,
7 Feb. 2010. PowerPoint.

94. Work in More Than One Publication Medium

Shamoon, Linda, et al., eds. *Coming of Age: The Advanced Writing Curriculum.*
   Coming of Age Course Descriptions. Portsmouth: Boynton, 2000. Print,
   CD-ROM.

This book and CD-ROM come together. Each has its own title, but the publication information—Portsmouth: Boynton, 2000—applies to both.

25C What are MLA guidelines for content or bibliographic notes?

In MLA STYLE, footnotes or endnotes serve two specific purposes: (1) You can use them for ideas and information that do not fit into your paper but are still worth relating; and (2) you can use them for bibliographic information that would intrude if you were to include it in your text. See 26A for advice about formatting notes.

TEXT OF PAPER

Eudora Welty's literary biography, *One Writer's Beginnings*, shows us how both the inner world of self and the outer world of family and place form a writer's imagination.[1]

CONTENT NOTE—MLA

1. Welty, who valued her privacy, resisted investigation of her life. However, at the age of seventy-four, she chose to present her own autobiographical reflections in a series of lectures at Harvard University.

TEXT OF PAPER

Barbara Randolph believes that enthusiasm is contagious (65).[1] Many psychologists have found that panic, fear, and rage spread more quickly in crowds than positive emotions do, however.

BIBLIOGRAPHIC NOTE—MLA

1. Others who agree with Randolph include Thurman 21, 84, 155; Kelley 421–25; and Brookes 65–76.

A Student's MLA-Style Research Paper

Quick Points You will learn to

➤ Format your paper according to MLA guidelines.

26A What are MLA format guidelines for research papers?

Watch the Video

Check whether your instructor has special instructions for the final draft of your research paper. If there are no special instructions, you can use the MLA STYLE guidelines here. The student paper in 26B was prepared according to MLA guidelines.

■ General formatting instructions—MLA

Use 8½-by-11-inch white paper. Double-space throughout. Use a one-inch margin on the left, right, top, and bottom. Don't justify the type.

Drop down ½ inch from the top edge of the paper to the name-and-page-number line described below. Then drop down another ½ inch to the first line, whether that is a heading, a title, or a line of the text of your paper. For an example, see page 262.

Paragraph indents in the body of the paper and indents in Notes and Works Cited are ½ inch, or about five characters. The indent in Microsoft Word is a hanging indent of ½ inch for "first line." The indent for a set-off quotation (p. 263) is 1 inch, or about ten characters.

■ Order of parts—MLA

Use this order for the parts of your paper: body of the paper; endnotes, if any (headed "Notes," without quotation marks); Works Cited list; and attachments, if any (such as questionnaires, data sheets, or any other material your instructor tells you to include). Number all pages consecutively.

■ Name-and-page-number header for all pages—MLA

Use a header consisting of a name-and-page-number line on every page of your paper, including the first, unless your instructor requires otherwise. Most word-processing programs have an "insert header" or "view header" function that automatically places a header ½ inch from the top edge of the page. In the header, type your last name, then a one-character space, and then the page number. Align the header an inch from the right edge of the paper; in most word-processing programs, this is a "flush right" setting.

First page—MLA

Use a name-and-page number line. MLA doesn't require a cover page but understands that some instructors do, in which case you should follow your instructor's prescribed format.

If your instructor does not require a cover page, use a four-line heading at the top of the first page. Drop down 1 inch from the top of the page. Start each line at the left margin, and include the following information.

Your name (first line)

Your instructor's name (second line)

Your course name and section (third line)

The date you hand in your paper (fourth line)

For the submission date, use either day-month-year form (26 Nov. 2012) or month-day-year style (Nov. 26, 2012) if your instructor prefers it.

On the line below this heading, center the title of your paper. Don't underline the title or enclose it in quotation marks. On the line below the title, start your paper.

⚠ Capitalization Alerts: (1) Use a capital letter for the first word of your title and the first word of a subtitle, if you use one. Start every NOUN, PRONOUN, VERB, ADVERB, ADJECTIVE, and SUBORDINATING CONJUNCTION with a capital letter. Capitalize the last word of your title, no matter what part of speech it is. In a hyphenated compound word (two or more words used together to express one idea), capitalize every word that you would normally capitalize: Father-in-Law.

(2) Don't capitalize an article (*a, an, the*) unless one of the preceding capitalization rules applies to it. Don't capitalize any PREPOSITIONS, no matter how many letters they contain. Don't capitalize COORDINATING CONJUNCTIONS. Don't capitalize the word *to* used in an INFINITIVE. ●

Notes—MLA

If you use a note in your paper (p. 257), try to structure the sentence so that the note number falls at the end. The ideal place for a note number, which appears slightly raised above the line of words, is after the sentence-ending punctuation. Don't leave a space before the number. Word processing programs have commands for inserting "references" such as notes, and you'll want to choose endnotes rather than footnotes. If you use the references feature to insert a note, the program will generally open a box in which you type the words of your note. The program then saves all your notes together, in order.

Your notes should come on a separate page after the last page of the body of your paper and before the Works Cited list. You may have to cut and paste your notes file into the proper position. Center the word *Notes* at the top of the page, using the same 1-inch margin; don't underline it or enclose it in quotation marks.

Number the notes consecutively throughout the paper, except for notes accompanying tables or figures. Place table or figure notes below the table or illustration. Instead of note numbers, use raised lowercase letters: a, b, c.

■ Works Cited list—MLA

The Works Cited list starts on a new page that has the same name-and-page-number heading as the previous pages. One inch below the top edge of the page, center the words "Works Cited." Don't underline them or put them in quotation marks.

One double space after the Works Cited heading, start the first entry in your list at the left margin. If an entry takes more than one line, indent each subsequent line after the first by ½ inch. Use no extra spacing between entries.

26B A student's MLA-style research paper

MLA style doesn't require an outline before a research paper. Nevertheless, many instructors want students to submit them. Most instructors prefer the standard traditional outline format that we discuss in 5H. Unless you're told otherwise, use that format.

Some instructors prefer what they consider a more contemporary outline format. Never use it unless it's explicitly assigned. It differs because it outlines the content of the INTRODUCTORY and CONCLUDING PARAGRAPHS, and full wording of the THESIS STATEMENT is placed in the outline of the introductory paragraph. We show an example of this type in the topic outline of Andrei Gurov's paper that follows.

View
the Model
Document

1"   ½"

Gurov i

Outline ——— Double-space

I. Introduction

    A. The meaning of the term déjà vu

    B. Thesis statement: Although a few people today still believe that feelings of déjà vu have mysterious and supernatural origins, recent research in cognitive psychology and the neurosciences has shed much rational light on the phenomenon.

1"

II. Percentage of people who report experiencing déjà vu

III. Misunderstandings of the phenomenon of déjà vu

    A. Precognition

    B. False memory

IV. New psychological and medical theories of déjà vu

    A. Human sight's two pathways

    B. Implanted memories

       1. Natural: from old memories long forgotten

       2. Manipulated: from subliminal stimulation

       3. Inattentional blindness

V. Conclusion

    A. Many years of paranormal explanations of déjà vu

    B. Scientific research after 1980

    C. Much promise for further research

↕ 1"

Use ½-inch top margin, 1-inch bottom and side margins; double-space throughout.

Gurov 1

↕ ½"

Andrei Gurov

Professor Ryan

English 101, Section A4

12 Dec. 2011

Put identifying information in upper left corner.

Center title.

Déjà Vu: At Last a Subject for Serious Study

"Brain hiccup" might be another name for *déjà vu*, French for "already seen." During a moment of déjà vu, a person relives an event that in reality is happening for the first time. The hiccup metaphor seems apt because each modern scientific explanation of the déjà vu phenomenon involves a doubled event, as this paper will demonstrate. However, such modern scientific work was long in coming. In his article "The Déjà Vu Illusion," today's leading researcher in the field, Alan S. Brown at Southern Methodist University, states that "for over 170 years, this most puzzling of memory illusions has intrigued scholars" but was hampered when "during the behaviorist era . . . the plethora of parapsychological and psychodynamic interpretations" multiplied rapidly (256). Thus, notions of the supernatural and magic halted the scientific study of déjà vu for almost two centuries. By the first quarter of the twentieth century, it began again slowly. Although a few people today still believe that feelings of déjà vu have mysterious or supernatural origins, recent research in cognitive psychology and the neurosciences has shed much rational light on the phenomenon.

Quotation marks around phrases show they appeared separately in the source.

The ellipsis indicates words omitted from a quotation.

continued >>

(Proportions shown in this paper are adjusted to fit space limitations of this book. Follow actual dimensions discussed in this book and your instructor's directions.)

Gurov 2 Header has student's last name and page number.

Some people report never having experienced déjà vu, and the percentages vary for the number of people who report having lived through at least one episode of it. In 2004, Brown reports that of the subjects he has interviewed, an average of 66 percent say that they have had one or more déjà vu experiences during their lives (*Experience* 33). However, in early 2005 in "Strangely Familiar," Uwe Wolfradt reports that "various studies indicate that from 50 to 90 percent of the people [studied] can recall having had at least one such déjà vu incident in their lives."

This Web source has no page numbers or paragraph numbers.

Perhaps part of the reason for this variation in the range of percentages stems from a general misunderstanding of the phrase *déjà vu*, even by some of the earlier scientific researchers twenty or more years ago. Indeed, in today's society, people throw around the term *déjà vu* without much thought. For example, it is fairly common for someone to see or hear about an event and then say, "Wow. This is déjà vu. I had a dream that this exact same thing happened." However, dreaming about an event ahead of time is a different phenomenon known as *precognition*, which relates to the paranormal experience of extrasensory perception. To date, precognition has never been scientifically demonstrated. As Johnson explains about dreams, however,

> . . . there is usually very little "data," evidence, or
> documentation to confirm that a Precognition has
> taken place. If a person learns about some disaster
> and THEN [author's emphasis] tells people that
> he/she has foreseen it the day before, that may
> or may not be true, because there is usually not
> corroborative confirmation of what the person claims.

Use block indent of 1-inch (about ten spaces) for a quotation longer than four typed lines.

continued >>

Gurov 3

Thus, precognition, a phenomenon talked about frequently but one that has never held up under scientific scrutiny, is definitely not the same as déjà vu.

False memory is another phenomenon mislabeled *déjà vu*. It happens when people are convinced that certain events took place in their lives, even though the events never happened. This occurs when people have strong memories of many unrelated occurrences that suddenly come together into a whole that's very close to the current experience. It seems like a déjà vu experience. This occurs from the

> converging elements of many different but related experiences. When this abstract representation, which has emerged strictly from the melding together of strongly associated elements, happens to correspond to the present experience, a déjà vu may be the outcome. (Brown, *Experience* 160)

To illustrate lab-induced false memory, Brown in *The Déjà Vu Experience* cites investigations in which subjects are shown lists of words related to sleep; however, the word *sleep* itself is not on the list. In recalling the list of words, most subjects insist that the word *sleep* was indeed on the list, which means that the memory of a word that was never there is false memory. This is exactly what happens when well-intentioned eyewitnesses believe they recall certain criminal acts even though, in fact, they never saw or experienced the events at all (159).

In the last twenty years especially, new theories have come to the fore as a result of rigorous work from psychological and medical points of view. In *Experience*, Brown surveys the literature and concludes that this relatively young field of investigation is dividing itself into four categories: (1) dual

Introductory phrase smoothly leads into direct quotation.

Put only page number in parentheses when author is named in text.

continued >>

Gurov 4

processing, (2) memory, (3) neurological, and (4) attentional. This paper briefly discusses the first and second as each relates to the third. Next, I discuss the first as it relates to the second.

Brain-based studies of the human sense of sight are one heavily researched theory of déjà vu that has been partially explained in the last two decades. Such studies focus on the dual pathways by which the sight of an event reaches the brain (Glenn; Carey F1). For example, the left hemisphere processes information from the right eye and the right hemisphere processes information from the left eye. The brain is incapable of storing data with respect to time and is only able to "see" events in relation to others. Each eye interprets data separately, at the same precise time. According to research, the human brain can perceive two visual stimuli at one instant as long as they are "seen" less than 25 milliseconds apart. Since the human brain is capable of interpreting both signals within this time, when events are perceived normally, they are seen and recognized by the brain as one single event (Weiten 69, 97–99, 211).

Put author and page number in parentheses when author is not named in the sentence.

Occasionally, however, the neurological impulses that carry data from each eye to the brain are delayed. As Johnson explains, the person might be fatigued or have had his or her attention seriously distracted (as when crossing the street at a dangerous intersection). As a result, one signal may reach the brain in under 25 milliseconds, while the other signal is slowed and reaches the brain slightly more than 25 milliseconds later. Even a few milliseconds' delay makes the second incoming signal arrive late—and, without fail, the brain interprets the stimuli as two separate events rather than one event. The person thus has the sensation of having seen the event before because the brain has recognized the milliseconds-later event as a memory.

Paragraph summarizes several pages of source material, as parenthetical citation shows.

continued >>

Gurov 5

Implanted memories are another well-researched explanation for the déjà vu phenomenon. Examples of implanted memories originate in both the natural and the lab-induced experiences of people. For instance, perhaps a person walks into the kitchen of a new friend for the first time and, although the person has never been there before, the person feels certain that he or she has. With hypnosis and other techniques, researchers could uncover that the cupboards are almost exactly like those that the person had forgotten were in the kitchen of the person's grandparents' house and that the scent of baking apple pie is identical to the smell the person loved when walking into the grandparents' home during holidays (Carey F1). Colorado State University Professor Anne Cleary and her colleagues conducted an experiment in which students studied images of simple scenes and then were shown a second set of images. Some of the second set were made to resemble the original study images. Students tended to "remember" those scenes that had elements in common, even if they were not identical (1083).

Thomas McHugh, a researcher at MIT, believes he has even discovered the specific "memory circuit" in the brain that is the source of this kind of déjà vu (Lemonick). This circuit allows people to complete memories with just a single cue. For example, you can remember much about a football game you saw even if someone just mentions the two teams involved. Sometimes, however, the circuit "misfires," and it signals that a new memory is actually part of the pattern of an old one. Researchers Akira O'Connor, Colin Lever, and Chris Moulin claim that the false sensations of memory differ from those of familiarity. They call the former "déjà vécue," and

continued >>

note serious cases in which people live much of their life in this state. It remains to be seen whether their distinction will be confirmed.

Wolfradt describes a lab-induced experiment in which psychologist Larry L. Jacoby in 1989 manipulated a group of subjects so that he could implant a memory that would lead to a déjà vu experience for each of them. He arranged for his subjects to assemble in a room equipped with a screen in front. He flashed on the screen one word so quickly that no one was consciously aware they had seen the word. Jacoby was certain, however, that the visual centers of the brain of each subject had indeed "seen" the word. Later, when he flashed the word leaving it on the screen long enough for the subjects to consciously see it, everyone indicated they had seen the word somewhere before. All the subjects were firmly convinced that the first time they had seen the word, it absolutely was not on the screen at the front of the room they were in. Some became annoyed at being asked over and over. Since Jacoby's work, lab-induced memory research has become very popular in psychology. In fact, it has been given its own name: *priming*. Alan Brown and Elizabeth Marsh confirmed Jacoby's findings in three follow-up studies (38–41).

Inattention, or what some researchers call "inattentional blindness," is also an extensively researched explanation for the déjà vu experience. Sometimes people can see objects without any impediment right before them but still not process the objects because they're paying attention to something else (Brown, *Experience* 181). The distraction might be daydreaming, a sudden lowering of energy, or simply being drawn to another

continued >>

Gurov 7

object in the environment. As David Glenn explains in "The Tease of Memory":

> Imagine that you drive through an unfamiliar town but pay little attention because you're talking on a cellphone [sic]. If you then drive back down the same streets a few moments later, this time focusing on the landscape, you might be prone to experience déjà vu. During your second pass, the visual information is consciously processed in the hippocampus [of the brain] but feels falsely "old" because the images from your earlier drive still linger in your short term memory.

The busy lifestyle today would seem to lead to many distractions of perception and thus to frequent experiences of déjà vu; however, these are no more frequently reported than any other causes reported concerning déjà vu.

One compelling laboratory experiment studying inattention is described by Carey in "Déjà Vu: If It All Seems Familiar, There May Be a Reason." He recounts a test with many college students from Duke University in Durham, North Carolina. The students were asked to look at a group of photographs of the campus of Southern Methodist University in Dallas, Texas, that were flashed before them at a very quick speed. A small black or white cross was superimposed on each photograph, and the students were instructed to find the cross and focus on it (F6). Brown in *Experience* explains that the researchers assumed that the quick speed at which the photographs had been shown would result in no one's having noticed the background scenes. A week's time passed, and the same students were shown the pictures again, this

continued >>

Gurov 8

time without the crosses. Almost all insisted that they had been to the college campus shown in the photos, which was physically impossible for that many students since they lived in Durham, North Carolina, and the college in the photographs was in Dallas, Texas (182–83). This means that the scenes in the photographs did indeed register in the visual memories of the students in spite of the quick speed and the distraction of looking only for the crosses.

The worlds of psychology and neurology have learned much since the age of paranormal interpretations of déjà vu experiences, starting around 1935. That is when rational science energetically began its disciplined investigations of brain-based origins of the déjà vu phenomenon. Concepts such as dual processing of sight, implanted memories, and inattentional blindness, among other theories, have gone far in opening the door to the possibilities of many more inventive theories to explain incidents of déjà vu. The leading researcher in the field today, Alan S. Brown, is among the strongest voices urging a vast expansion of investigations into this still relatively unexplored phenomenon. He is optimistic this will happen, given his whimsical remark to Carlin Flora of *Psychology Today:* "We are always fascinated when the brain goes haywire." Researchers conducting these studies might watch for the unsettling experiences of other investigators who "have had déjà vu about having déjà vu" (Phillips 29).

> Concluding paragraph summarizes paper.

continued >>

Gurov 9

Works Cited

Works Cited
begins on a
new page.
Note that
heading is
centered.

Brown, Alan S. *The Déjà Vu Experience: Essays in Cognitive Psychology.* New York: Psychology, 2004. Print.

---. "The Déjà Vu Illusion." *Current Directions in Psychological Science* 13.6 (2004): 256–59. Print.

Three
hyphens
indicate
same author
as entry
above.

--- and Elizabeth J. Marsh. "Digging into Deja Vu: Recent Research on Possible Mechanisms." *The Psychology of Learning and Motivation: Advances in Research and Theory.* Ed. Brian H. Ross. Burlington: Academic, 2010, 33–62. *LexisNexis.* Web. 20 Nov. 2011.

Double-
space
throughout.

Carey, Benedict. "Déjà Vu: If It All Seems Familiar, There May Be a Reason." *New York Times* 14 Sept. 2004: F1+. *LexisNexis.* Web. 11 Nov. 2011.

List
sources in
alphabetical
order.

Cleary, Anne M., Anthony J. Ryals, and Jason S. Nomi. "Can Déjà Vu Result from Similarity to a Prior Experience? Support for the Similarity Hypothesis of Déjà Vu." *Psychonomic Bulletin & Review* 16.6 (2009): 1082–88. Web. 3 Dec. 2011.

Flora, Carlin. "Giving Déjà Vu Its Due." *Psychology Today* Mar.–Apr. 2005: 27. *Academic Search Premier.* Web. 7 Nov. 2011.

Glenn, David. "The Tease of Memory." *Chronicle of Higher Education* 23 July 2004: A12. Print.

Johnson, C. "A Theory on the Déjà Vu Phenomenon." *MB-soft.com,* 8 Dec. 2001. Web. 20 Nov. 2011.

Lemonick, Michael D. "Explaining Déjà Vu." *Time* 20 Aug. 2007. *Academic Search Premier.* Web. 5 Dec. 2011.

O'Connor, Akira R., Colin Lever, and Chris J.A. Moulin. "Novel Insights into False Recollection: A Model of Déjà Vécue." *Cognitive Neuropsychiatry* 15.1–3 (2010): 118–44. Web. 14 Nov. 2011.

continued >>

Phillips, Helen. "Looks Familiar." *New Scientist* 201.2701 (2009): 28–31. Web. 20 Nov. 2011.

Weiten, Wayne. *Psychology: Themes and Variations.* Belmont: Wadsworth, 2005. Print.

Wolfradt, Uwe. "Strangely Familiar." *Scientific American Mind* 16.1 (2005): 32–37. *Academic Search Elite.* Web. 7 Nov. 2011.

Tab 7
APA, CM, and CSE Documentation

Tab 7 APA, CM, and CSE Documentation

MyCompLab® Visit mycomplab.com for the eText and for resources on APA, CM, and CSE documentation and format.

27 APA In-Text Citations
■ ■ ■ ■ ■ ■ ■ ■

Quick Points   You will learn to

➤ Cite sources in your writing using APA style.

27A What is APA documentation style?

The American Psychological Association (APA) sponsors the APA STYLE,* a DOCUMENTATION system widely used in the social sciences. APA style has two equally important features that need to appear in research papers.

1. Within the body of your paper, use IN-TEXT CITATIONS, in parentheses, to acknowledge your SOURCES. Sections 27B and 27C explain the proper way to provide in-text citations.

2. At the end of the paper, provide a list of the sources you used—and only those sources. Title this list, which contains complete bibliographic information about each source, "References." Chapter 28 provides examples.

See Chapter 29 for a sample student paper in APA style.

27B What are APA in-text parenthetical citations?

APA style requires parenthetical in-text citations that identify a source by the author's name and the copyright year. If there is no author, use a shortened version of the title. In addition, APA style requires page numbers for DIRECT QUOTATIONS, but it recommends using them also for PARAPHRASES and SUMMARIES. Find out your instructor's preference to avoid any problems. Put page numbers in parentheses, using the abbreviation *p.* before a single page number and *pp.* when the material you're citing falls on more than one page. Separate the parts of a parenthetical citation with commas. End punctuation always follows the citation unless it's a long quotation set in block style.

If you refer to a work more than once in a paragraph, APA style recommends giving the author's name and the date at the first mention and then using only the name after that. However, if you're citing two or more works by the same author, include the date in each citation to identify which work you're citing. When two or more sources have the same last name, keep them clear by using both first and last names in the text or first initial(s) and last names in parentheses.

---

* Words printed in SMALL CAPITAL LETTERS are discussed elsewhere in the text and are defined in the Terms Glossary at the back of the book.

27C What are APA guidelines for in-text citations?

This section shows how to cite various kinds of sources in the body of your paper. The directory at the beginning of this tab corresponds to the numbered examples in this section.

1. Paraphrased or Summarized Source

> Modern technologies and social media tend to fragment individual identities (Conley, 2009).

Author name and date cited in parentheses.

> Dalton Conley (2009) contends that modern technologies and social media fragment individual identities.

Author name cited in text; date cited in parentheses.

2. Source of a Short Quotation

> Approaches adopted from business to treat students as consumers "do not necessarily yield improved outcomes in terms of student learning" (Arum & Roksa, 2011, p. 137).

Author names, date, and page reference cited in parentheses.

> Arum & Roksa (2011) find that approaches adopted from business to treat students as consumers "do not necessarily yield improved outcomes in terms of student learning" (p. 137).

Author names cited in text, followed by the date cited in parentheses incorporated into the words introducing the quotation; page number in parentheses immediately following the quotation.

3. Source of a Long Quotation

When you use a quotation of forty or more words, set it off in block style indented ½ inch from the left margin. Don't use quotation marks. Place the parenthetical reference one space after the end punctuation of the quotation's last sentence.

> Although some have called for regulating online games, others see such actions as unwarranted:
>
> > Any activity when taken to excess can cause problems in a person's life, but it is unlikely that there would be legislation against, for example, people excessively reading or exercising. There is no argument that online gaming should be treated any differently. (Griffiths, 2010, pp. 38–39)

Author name, date, and page reference are cited in parentheses following the end punctuation.

4. One Author

> One of his questions is, "What binds together a Mormon banker in Utah
> with his brother or other coreligionists in Illinois or Massachusetts?"
> (Coles, 1993, p. 2).

In a parenthetical reference in APA style, a comma and a space separate a name
from a year and a year from a page reference.

5. Two Authors

Give both names in each citation.

> One report describes 2,123 occurrences (Krait & Cooper, 2003).

> The results that Krait and Cooper (2003) report would not support the
> conclusions Davis and Sherman (1999) draw in their review of the
> literature.

When you write a parenthetical in-text citation naming two (or more) authors,
use an ampersand (&) between the final two names, but write out the word
and for any reference in your own sentence.

6. Three, Four, or Five Authors

Use all the authors' last names in the first reference. In all subsequent references, use only the first author's last name followed by *et al.* (meaning "and
others"). No period follows *et*, but one always follows *al.*

FIRST REFERENCE

> In one study, only 30% of the survey population could name the most
> commonly spoken languages in five Middle Eastern countries (Ludwig,
> Rodriquez, Novak, & Ehlers, 2008).

SUBSEQUENT REFERENCE

> Ludwig et al. (2008) found that most Americans could identify the language
> spoken in Saudi Arabia.

7. Six or More Authors

Name the first author followed by *et al.* in all in-text references, including the first.

> These injuries can lead to an inability to perform athletically, in addition
> to initiating degenerative changes at the joint level (Mandelbaum et al.,
> 2005).

8. Author(s) with Two or More Works in the Same Year

If you use more than one source written in the same year by the same author(s),
alphabetize the works by title for the REFERENCES list, and assign letters in
alphabetical order to each work: (2007a), (2007b), (2007c). Use the year–letter

combination in parenthetical references. Note that a citation of two or more such works lists the year extensions in alphabetical order.

> Most recently, Torrevillas (2007c) draws new conclusions from the results of eight experiments conducted with experienced readers (Torrevillas, 2007a, 2007b).

9. Two or More Authors with the Same Last Name

Include first initials for every in-text citation of authors who share a last name. Use the initials appearing in the References list. (In the second example, a parenthetical citation, the name order is alphabetical, as explained in item 12.)

> R. A. Smith (2008) and C. Smith (1999) both confirm these results.

> These results have been confirmed independently (C. Smith, 1999; R. A. Smith, 2008).

10. Group or Corporate Author

If you use a source in which the "author" is a corporation, agency, or group, an in-text reference gives that name as author. Use the full name in each citation, unless an abbreviated version of the name is likely to be familiar to your audience. In that case, use the full name and give its abbreviation at the first citation; then, use the abbreviation for subsequent citations.

> Although the space shuttle program has ended, other programs will continue to send Americans into space (National Aeronautics and Space Administration [NASA], 2011).

> In subsequent citations, use the abbreviated form alone.

11. Work Listed by Title

If no author is named, use a shortened form of the title for in-text citations. Ignoring *A, An,* or *The,* make the first word the one by which you alphabetize the title in your References list. The following example refers to an article fully titled "Are You a Day or Night Person?"

> Scientists group people as "larks" or "owls" on the basis of whether individuals are more efficient in the morning or at night ("Are You," 1989).

12. Two or More Sources in One Reference

If more than one source has contributed to an idea or opinion in your paper, cite them alphabetically by author in one set of parentheses; separate each source of information with a semicolon.

> Conceptions of personal space vary among cultures (Morris, 1977; Worchel & Cooper, 1983).

13. Personal Communication, Including E-Mail and Other Nonretrievable Sources

Telephone calls, personal letters, interviews, and e-mail messages are "personal communications" that your readers can't access or retrieve. Acknowledge personal communications in parenthetical references, but never include them in your References list at the end of your paper.

> Recalling his first summer at camp, one person said, "The proximity of 12 other kids made me—an only child with older, quiet parents—frantic for eight weeks" (A. Weiss, personal communication, January 12, 2011).

14. Retrievable Online Sources

When you quote, paraphrase, or summarize an online source that is available to others, cite the author (if any) or title and the date as you would for a print source, and include the work in your References list.

> It is possible that similarity in personality is important in having a happy marriage (Luo & Clonen, 2005, p. 324).

15. Sources with No Page Numbers

If a source doesn't provide page numbers, use the paragraph number preceded by the abbreviation *para.* If there are no printed paragraph numbers, count down from the beginning of the document, or cite the closest subheading and count down paragraphs from that.

> (Daniels, 2010, para. 4)

> (Sanz, 2009, Introduction)

> (Herring, 2011)

16. Source Lines for Graphics and Table Data

If you use a graphic from another source or create a table using data from another source, provide a note at the bottom of the table or graphic, crediting the original author and the copyright holder. Here are examples of two source notes, one for a graphic using data from an article, the other for a graphic reprinted from a book.

GRAPHIC USING DATA FROM AN ARTICLE

Note. The data in columns 1 and 2 are from "Advance Organizers in Advisory Reports: Selective Reading, Recall, and Perception," by L. Lagerwerf et al., 2008, *Written Communication, 25*(1), p. 68. Copyright 2008 by Sage Publications.

GRAPHIC FROM A BOOK

Note. From *Academically Adrift: Limited Learning on College Campuses* (p. 97), by R. Arum and J. Roksa, 2011, Chicago: University of Chicago Press. Copyright 2011 by The University of Chicago.

28 APA References List

■ ■ ■ ■ ■ ■ ■ ■

Quick Points You will learn to

➤ Cite your sources at the end of your paper in an APA References list.

The REFERENCES list at the end of your research paper provides complete bibliographic information for readers who may want to access the SOURCES you drew on to write your paper.

Include in the References list all the sources you quote, paraphrase, or summarize in your paper so that readers can find the same sources with reasonable effort. Never include in your References list any source that's not generally available to other people (see item 13 in 27C).

28A What are APA guidelines for a References list?

An APA References list needs to meet specific requirements in terms of its title, placement, contents and format, spacing, arrangement, type and order of elements included for each kind of entry, punctuation, capitalization, and so on. Quick Box 28.1 provides details.

Quick Box 28.1   ■ ■ ■ ■ ■ ■ ■ ■

Guidelines for an APA-style References list

TITLE
The title is "References," centered, without quotation marks, italics, or underlining.

PLACEMENT OF LIST
Start a new page numbered sequentially with the rest of the paper, immediately after the body of the paper.

CONTENTS AND FORMAT
Include all quoted, paraphrased, or summarized sources in your paper that are not personal communications; however, if your instructor tells you also to include all the references you have simply consulted, please do so. Start each entry on a new line, and double-space all lines. Use a *hanging indent*

continued >>

Quick Box 28.1 (continued)

style: The first line of each entry begins flush left at the margin, and all other lines are indented ½ inch.

Wolfe, C. R. (2011). Argumentation across the curriculum. *Written Communication, 28,* 193–218.

SPACING AFTER PUNCTUATION
APA calls for one space after commas, periods, question marks, and colons.

ARRANGEMENT OF ENTRIES
Alphabetize by the author's last name. If no author is named, alphabetize by the first significant word (ignore *A, An,* or *The*) in the title of the work.

AUTHORS' NAMES
Use last names, first initials, and middle initials, if any. Reverse the order for all authors' names, and use an ampersand (&) before the last author's name: Mills, J. F., & Holahan, R. H.

Give names in the order in which they appear on the work. Use a comma between each author's last name and first initial and after each complete name except the last. Use a period after the last author's name. When the author name is the same as the publisher, write "author" at the end of the citation.

DATES
Date information follows the name information and is enclosed in parentheses. Place a period followed by one space after the closing parenthesis.

For books, articles in journals that have volume numbers, and many other print and nonprint sources, the year of publication or production is the date to use. For articles from most general-circulation magazines and newspapers, use the year followed by a comma and then the exact date that appears on the issue (month, month and day, or season, depending on the frequency of the publication). Capitalize any words in dates, and use no abbreviations.

CAPITALIZATION OF TITLES
For book, article, and chapter titles, capitalize the first word, the first word after a colon between a title and subtitle, and any proper nouns. For names of journals and proceedings of meetings, capitalize the first word; all NOUNS, VERBS, ADVERBS, and ADJECTIVES; and any other words four or more letters long.

SPECIAL TREATMENT OF TITLES
Use no special treatment for titles of shorter works (poems, short stories, essays, articles, Web pages). Italicize titles of longer works (books, newspapers, journals, or Web sites). If an italic typeface is unavailable, underline the title and the end punctuation using one unbroken line.

Do not drop any words (such as *A, An,* or *The*) from the titles of periodicals such as newspapers, magazines, and journals.

continued >>

Quick Box 28.1 (continued)

ABBREVIATIONS OF MONTHS
Do not abbreviate the names of months in any context.

PAGE NUMBERS
Use all digits, omitting none. For references to books and newspapers only, use *p.* and *pp.* before page numbers. List all discontinuous pages, with numbers separated by commas: pp. 32, 44–45, 47–49, 53.

PUBLICATION INFORMATION
See 28B for how to cite articles from periodicals (both print or online), books (both print or digital), images and video, other Web sources, and miscellaneous sources.

28B What are APA examples for sources in a References list?

The directory at the beginning of this tab corresponds to the numbered examples in this section. For quick help deciding which example you should follow, see the decision flowchart in Figure 28.1 (page 283). You can find other examples in the *Publication Manual of the American Psychological Association* (6th edition) or at the APA Web site, http://www.apastyle.org.

Citations for periodical articles contain four major parts: author, date, title of article, and publication information (usually, the periodical title, volume number, page numbers, and sometimes a digital object identifier).

Quick Box 28.2 summarizes the basic entries for periodical entries. Variations on the basic entries follow the Quick Box.

Quick Box 28.2 ■ ■ ■ ■ ■ ■ ■ ■ ■

Basic entries for periodical articles—APA

1. Articles with a DOI: Print or online

A **DOI** (digital object identifier) is a numerical code sometimes assigned to journal articles. The DOI for an article will be the same even if the article appears in different versions, including print and online. (To see where you can find an article's DOI, refer to Figure 28.2.) If a source contains a DOI, simply conclude the citation with the letters "doi" followed by a colon, then the number. If a source has a DOI, always use this citation method.

continued >>

Quick Box 28.2 (continued)

AUTHOR   DATE   ARTICLE TITLE

Agliata, A. K., Tantelff-Dunn, S., & Renk, K. (2007). Interpretation of

PUBLICATION INFORMATION

teasing during early adolescence. *Journal of Clinical Psychology,*

DOI

63(1), 23–30. doi: 10.1002/jclp.20302

2. Articles with no DOI: Print

For print articles without a DOI, use this format.

AUTHOR   DATE   ARTICLE TITLE

Wood, W., Witt, M. G., & Tam, L. (2005). Changing circumstances,

PERIODICAL TITLE

disrupting habits. *Journal of Personality and Social Psychology,*

VOLUME PAGE
NUMBER RANGE

88, 918–933.

3. Articles with no DOI: Online

For online articles without a DOI, retrieval information begins with the words "Retrieved from," then the URL of the periodical's Web home page, and, occasionally, additional information. If you found the article through an online subscription database, do a Web search for the URL of the periodical's home page on the Web, and include the home page URL. If you can't find the periodical's Web home page, then name the database in your retrieval statement: Retrieved from Academic Search Premier database. (See citation 20.) If a URL must be divided between two or more lines, only break the address before slashes or punctuation marks.

Retrieval date: Include the date you retrieved the information only if the item does not have a publication date, is from an online reference book, or is likely to be changed in the future (such as a prepublication version of an article, a Web page, or a Wiki; see citation 72).

AUTHOR   DATE   ARTICLE TITLE

Eagleman, D. (2011, July/August). The brain on trial.

MAGAZINE TITLE   ONLINE RETRIEVAL INFORMATION

The Atlantic. Retrieved from http://www.theatlantic.com

Notice that the only punctuation in the URL is part of the address. Do not add a period after a URL. APA keeps *The, A,* and *An* in titles.

Figure 28.1 Decision-making flowchart for APA References citations.

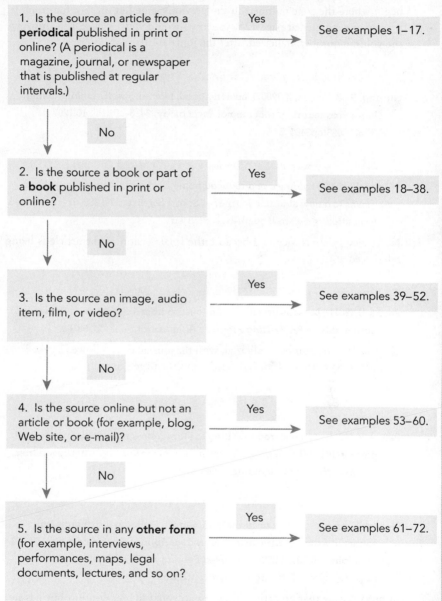

1. Is the source an article from a **periodical** published in print or online? (A periodical is a magazine, journal, or newspaper that is published at regular intervals.)

Yes → See examples 1–17.

No ↓

2. Is the source a book or part of a **book** published in print or online?

Yes → See examples 18–38.

No ↓

3. Is the source an image, audio item, film, or video?

Yes → See examples 39–52.

No ↓

4. Is the source online but not an article or book (for example, blog, Web site, or e-mail)?

Yes → See examples 53–60.

No ↓

5. Is the source in any **other form** (for example, interviews, performances, maps, legal documents, lectures, and so on?

Yes → See examples 61–72.

PERIODICALS—APA REFERENCES

1. Article in a Journal with Continuous Pagination: Print

Williams, B. T. (2010). Seeking new worlds: The study of writing beyond our classrooms. *College Composition and Communication, 62,* 127–146.

Continuous pagination means that page numbers in each issue of a volume begin where the page numbers in the previous issue left off. So, for example, if issue one stopped at page 125, issue two would start at page 126. Just give the volume number, italicized, after the journal title.

2. Article in a Journal with Continuous Pagination: Online, with DOI

Gurung, R., & Vespia, K. (2007). Looking good, teaching well? Linking liking, looks, and learning. *Teaching of Psychology, 34,* 5–10. doi: 10.1207 /s15328023top3401_2

3. Article in a Journal with Continuous Pagination: Online, no DOI

Pollard, R. (2002). Evidence of a reduced home field advantage when a team moves to a new stadium. *Journal of Sports Sciences, 20,* 969–974. Retrieved from http://www.tandf.co.uk/journals/rjsp

No retrieval date is included because the final version of the article is being referenced.

4. Article in a Journal That Pages Each Issue Separately: Print

Peters, B. (2011). Lessons about writing to learn from a university–high school partnership. *WPA: Writing Program Administration, 34*(2), 59–88.

Give the volume number, italicized, with the journal title, followed by the issue number in parentheses (not italicized), and the page number(s).

5. Article in a Journal That Pages Each Issue Separately: Online, with no DOI

Peters, B. (2011). Lessons about writing to learn from a university–high school partnership. *WPA: Writing Program Administration, 34*(2). Retrieved from http://wpacouncil.org/journal/index.html

6. In-press Article: Online

George, S. (in press). How accurately should we estimate the anatomical source of exhaled nitric oxide? *Journal of Applied Physiology.* doi:10.1152 /japplphysiol.00111.2008. Retrieved February 2008 from http://jap.physiology.org/papbyrecent.shtml

In press means that an article has been accepted for publication but has not yet been published in its final form. Therefore, there is no publication date, so although the article has a DOI, it also has a "retrieved from" statement that includes a date, in case anything changes.

Figure 28.2 Journal article available (a) online and (b) in print, with a DOI.

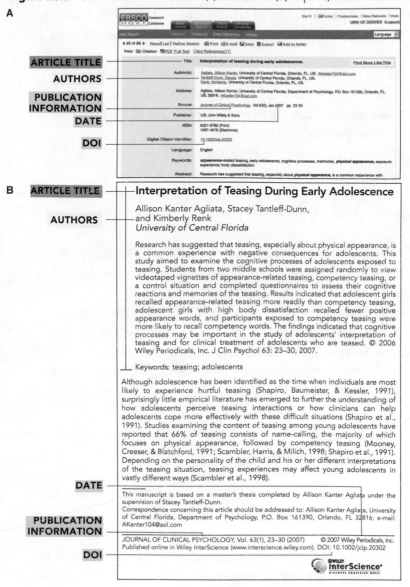

A

ARTICLE TITLE
AUTHORS
PUBLICATION INFORMATION
DATE
DOI

B

ARTICLE TITLE — Interpretation of Teasing During Early Adolescence

AUTHORS — Allison Kanter Agliata, Stacey Tantleff-Dunn, and Kimberly Renk
University of Central Florida

Research has suggested that teasing, especially about physical appearance, is a common experience with negative consequences for adolescents. This study aimed to examine the cognitive processes of adolescents exposed to teasing. Students from two middle schools were assigned randomly to view videotaped vignettes of appearance-related teasing, competency teasing, or a control situation and completed questionnaires to assess their cognitive reactions and memories of the teasing. Results indicated that adolescent girls recalled appearance-related teasing more readily than competency teasing, adolescent girls with high body dissatisfaction recalled fewer positive appearance words, and participants exposed to competency teasing were more likely to recall competency words. The findings indicated that cognitive processes may be important in the study of adolescents' interpretation of teasing and for clinical treatment of adolescents who are teased. © 2006 Wiley Periodicals, Inc. J Clin Psychol 63: 23–30, 2007.

Keywords: teasing; adolescents

Although adolescence has been identified as the time when individuals are most likely to experience hurtful teasing (Shapiro, Baumeister, & Kessler, 1991), surprisingly little empirical literature has emerged to further the understanding of how adolescents perceive teasing interactions or how clinicians can help adolescents cope more effectively with these difficult situations (Shapiro et al., 1991). Studies examining the content of teasing among young adolescents have reported that 66% of teasing consists of name-calling, the majority of which focuses on physical appearance, followed by competency teasing (Mooney, Creeser, & Blatchford, 1991; Scambler, Harris, & Milich, 1998; Shapiro et al., 1991). Depending on the personality of the child and his or her different interpretations of the teasing situation, teasing experiences may affect young adolescents in vastly different ways (Scambler et al., 1998).

DATE — This manuscript is based on a master's thesis completed by Allison Kanter Agliata under the supervision of Stacey Tantleff-Dunn.
Correspondence concerning this article should be addressed to: Allison Kanter Agliata, University of Central Florida, Department of Psychology, P.O. Box 161390, Orlando, FL 32816; e-mail: AKanter104@aol.com

PUBLICATION INFORMATION — JOURNAL OF CLINICAL PSYCHOLOGY, Vol. 63(1), 23–30 (2007)   © 2007 Wiley Periodicals, Inc.
Published online in Wiley InterScience (www.interscience.wiley.com). DOI: 10.1002/jclp.20302

DOI

CITATION

Agliata, A.K., Tantleff-Dunn, S., & Renk, K. (2007). Interpretation of teasing during

early adolescence. *Journal of Clinical Psychology, 63*(1). 23–30. doi: 10.1002/jcpl.2302

7. Article in a Weekly or Biweekly Magazine: Print

Foroohar, R. (2011, June 27). Why the world isn't getting smaller. *Time*, 20.

Give the year, month, and date. If no author is listed, begin with the title of the article.

The price is wrong. (2003, August 2). *The Economist, 368,* 58–59.

8. Article in a Weekly or Biweekly Magazine: Online

Foroohar, R. (2011, June 27). Why the world isn't getting smaller. *Time.*
   Retrieved from http://www.time.com/time/

9. Article in a Monthly or Bimonthly Periodical: Print

Goetz, T. (2011, July). The feedback loop. *Wired, 19*(7), 126–133.

Give the year and month(s). Insert the volume number, italicized with the periodical title. Put the issue number in parentheses; do not italicize it.

10. Article in a Newspaper: Print

Hesse, M. (2011, April 24). Love among the ruins. *The Washington Post,* p. F1.

Use the abbreviation *p.* (or *pp.* for more than one page) for newspapers. If no author is listed, begin with the title of the article.

Prepping for uranium work. (2011, June 18). *The Denver Post,* p. B2.

11. Article in a Newspaper: Online

Hesse, M. (2011, April 22). Falling in love with St. Andrews, Scotland. *The Washington Post.* Retrieved from http://www.washingtonpost.com/

Give the URL from the newspaper's Web site.

12. Unsigned Editorial

Editorial: Primary considerations. [Editorial]. (2008, January 27). *The Washington Post,* p. B6.

13. Letter to the Editor

Ennis, H. B. (2007, December 22). [Letter to the editor]. *U.S. News and World Report.* Retrieved from http://www.usnews.com

14. Book Review

Shenk, D. (2003, Spring). Toolmaker, brain builder. [Review of the book *Beyond Deep Blue: Building the computer that defeated the world chess champion* by Feng-Hsiung Hsu]. *The American Scholar, 72,* 150–152.

15. Article in a Looseleaf Collection of Reprinted Articles

Hayden, T. (2002). The age of robots. In E. Goldstein (Ed.), *Applied Science 2002. SIRS 2002,* Article 66. (Reprinted from *U.S. News & World Report,* pp. 44–50, 2001, April 23).

16. Online Magazine Content Not Found in Print Version

Shulman, M. (2008, January 3). 12 diseases that altered history. [Supplemental material]. *U.S. News & World Report*. Retrieved from http://health.usnews.com/

17. Abstract as a Secondary Source: Online

Walther, J. B., Van Der Heide, B., Kim, S., Westerman, D., & Tong, S. (2008). The role of friends' appearance and behavior on evaluations of individuals on Facebook: Are we known by the company we keep? *Human Communication Research 34*(1), 28–49. Abstract retrieved from PsycINFO database.

BOOKS—APA REFERENCES

Quick Box 28.3 summarizes the basic entry for books, both print and electronic. Variations on the basic entries follow. Where to locate a book's citation information is shown in Figure 28.3 (page 289).

Quick Box 28.3

■ ■ ■ ■ ■ ■ ■ ■ ■ ■

Basic entries for books—APA

All citations for books have four main parts: author, date, title, and publication information. For traditional print books, publication information includes place of publication and the name of the publisher. For electronic versions of books, publication information also includes retrieval information.

PLACE OF PUBLICATION
For US publishers, give the city and state, using two-letter postal abbreviations listed in most dictionaries. For publishers in other countries, give city and country spelled out. However, if the state or country is part of the publisher's name, omit it after the name of the city.

PUBLISHERS
Use a shortened version of the publisher's name except for an association, corporation, or university press. Drop *Co., Inc., Publishers*, and the like, but retain *Books* or *Press*.

AUTHOR   DATE   TITLE

Wood, G. S. (2011). *The idea of America: Reflections on the birth of the*

PUBLICATION INFORMATION

United States. New York, NY: Penguin Press.

continued >>

Quick Box 28.3 (continued)

RETRIEVAL INFORMATION FOR ELECTRONIC BOOKS

If a book has a DOI (Digital Object Identifier), include that number after the title, preceded by doi and a colon. Most electronic books do not have a DOI. When there is no DOI, use "Retrieved from" followed by the URL where you accessed the book.

18. Book by One Author: Print

Turkle, S. (2011). *Alone together: Why we expect more from technology and less from each other.* New York: Basic Books.

19. Book by One Author: Online

Turkle, S. (2007). *Evocative objects: Things we think with.* Retrieved from http://0-site.ebrary.com.bianca.penlib.du.edu/

Some books are increasingly available through library databases. APA does not include the name or location of the publisher in citations for online books.

20. Book by One Author: E-book or E-reader

Hertsgaard, M. (2011). *Hot: Living through the next fifty years on Earth.* [Kindle version]. Retrieved from http://amazon.com

The name of the version appears in brackets following the title, for example [Kindle version] or [Nook version]. "Retrieved from" precedes the URL of the site from which you downloaded the book.

21. Book by Two Authors

Edin, K., & Kefalas, M. (2005). *Promises I can keep: Why poor women put motherhood before marriage.* Berkeley: University of California Press.

22. Book by Three to Seven Authors

Lynam, J. K., Ndiritu, C. G., & Mbabu, A. N. (2004). *Transformation of agricultural research systems in Africa: Lessons from Kenya.* East Lansing: Michigan State University Press.

For a book by three to seven authors, include all the names. For a book by eight or more authors, use the first six names followed by three ellipsis points and then the last author's name: Smith, A., Jones, B., Ramos, C., Abrams, D., Sagan, E., Chin, F. . . . Havel, J.

23. Two or More Books by the Same Author(s)

Jenkins, H. (1992). *Textual poachers: Television fans and participatory culture.* New York, NY: Routledge.

Figure 28.3 Citation information for a print book—APA.

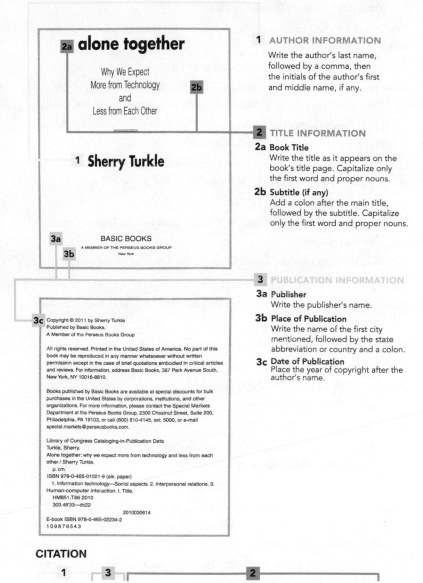

CITATION

Turkle, S. (2011). *Alone together: Why we expect more from technology and less from each other.* New York, NY: Basic Books.

Jenkins, H. (2006). *Convergence culture: Where old and new media collide*. New York, NY: New York University Press.

References by the same author are arranged chronologically, with the earlier date of publication listed first.

24. Book by a Group or Corporate Author

American Psychological Association. (2010). *Publication manual of the American Psychological Association* (6th ed.). Washington, DC: Author.

Boston Women's Health Collective. (1998). *Our bodies, ourselves for the new century*. New York: Simon & Schuster.

Cite the full name of the corporate author first. If the author is also the publisher, use the word *Author* as the name of the publisher.

25. Book with No Author Named

The Chicago manual of style (16th ed.). (2010). Chicago, IL: University of Chicago Press.

This would be alphabetized under *Chicago*, the first important word in the title.

26. Book with an Author and an Editor

Stowe, H. B. (2010). *Uncle Tom's cabin* (E. Ammons, Ed.). New York, NY: Norton.

27. Translation

Nesbo, J. (2011). *The leopard* (D. Bartlett, Trans.) New York, NY: Vintage.

28. Work in Several Volumes or Parts

Chrisley, R. (Ed.). (2000). *Artificial intelligence: Critical concepts* (Vols. 1–4). London, England: Routledge.

29. Anthology or Edited Book

Purdy, J. L., & Ruppert, J. (Eds.). (2001). *Nothing but the truth: An anthology of Native American literature*. Upper Saddle River, NJ: Prentice Hall.

30. Selection in an Anthology or an Edited Book

Trujillo, L. (2004). Balancing act. In R. Moreno & M. H. Mulligan (Eds.), *Borderline personalities: A new generation of Latinas dish on sex, sass, and cultural shifting* (pp. 61–72). New York, NY: HarperCollins.

To refer to an anthology, see example 29 or the Chaudhuri citation in example 31.

31. Selection in a Work Already Listed in References

Bond, R. (2004). The night train at Deoli. In A. Chaudhuri (Ed.), *The Vintage book of modern Indian literature* (pp. 415–418). New York, NY: Vintage Books.

Chaudhuri, A. (Ed.). (2004). *The Vintage book of modern Indian literature*. New York, NY: Vintage Books.

Provide full information for the already cited anthology (first example), along with information about the individual selection. Put entries in alphabetical order.

32. Second or Later Edition

Modern Language Association. (2009). *MLA handbook for writers of research papers* (7th ed.). New York, NY: Author.

Any edition number appears on the title page.

33. Introduction, Preface, Foreword, or Afterword

Hesse, D. (2004). Foreword. In D. Smit, *The end of composition studies* (pp. ix–xiii). Carbondale: Southern Illinois University Press.

If you're citing an introduction, preface, foreword, or afterword, give its author's name first. After the year, give the name of the part cited. If the writer of the material you're citing isn't the author of the book, use the word *In* and the author's name before the title of the book.

34. Reprint of an Older Book

Coover, R. (2007). *A night at the movies, or, you must remember this.* Champaign: Dalkey Archive, 2007. (Original work published 1987)

35. Government Publication

U.S. Congress. House Subcommittee on Health and Environment of the Committee on Commerce. (1999). *The nursing home resident protection amendments of 1999* (99-0266-P). Washington, DC: U.S. Government Printing Office.

36. Published Proceedings of a Conference

Rocha, L., Yaeger, L., Bedau, M., Floreano, D., Goldstone, R., & Vespignani, A. (Eds.). (2006, June). *Artificial Life X: Proceedings of the Tenth International Conference on the Simulation and Synthesis of Living Systems.* Bloomington, IN. Cambridge, MA: MIT Press.

37. Thesis or Dissertation

Stuart, G. A. (2006). *Exploring the Harry Potter book series: A study of adolescent reading motivation.* Retrieved from ProQuest Digital Dissertations. (AAT 3246355)

The number in parentheses at the end is the accession number.

38. Entry from Encyclopedia: Print or Online

Ireland. (2002). In *The new encyclopaedia Britannica: Macropaedia* (15th ed., Vol. 21, pp. 997–1018). Chicago, IL: Encyclopaedia Britannica.

Turing test. (2008). In *Encyclopædia Britannica.* Retrieved February 9, 2008, from http://www.britannica.com/bps/topic/609757/Turing-test

Because the reference is to a work that may change, a retrieval date is included.

IMAGES, AUDIO, FILM, AND VIDEO

39. Photograph, Painting, Drawing, Illustration, etc.: Original

Cassatt, Mary. (1890). *La toilette*. [Painting]. Art Institute of Chicago.

Fourquet, Léon. (1865). *The man with the broken nose*. [Sculpture]. Paris, France: Musée Rodin.

Mydans, C. (1999, October 21–November 28). *General Douglas MacArthur landing at Luzon, 1945* [Photograph]. New York, NY: Soho Triad Fine Art Gallery.

This form is for original works appearing in a gallery, museum, private collection, etc. The date in the third example shows that the work appeared only for a brief period, in this case at the Soho Triad Fine Art Gallery.

40. Photograph, Painting, Drawing, Illustration, etc. in a Periodical

Greene, H. *Grace Slick*. (2004, September 30). [Photograph]. *Rolling Stone*, 102.

41. Photograph, Painting, Drawing, Illustration, etc. in a Book

The world's most populous countries. (2004). [Illustration]. In P. Turchi, *Maps of the imagination: The writer as cartographer* (pp. 116–117). San Antonio, TX: Trinity University Press.

Indicate the type of image in brackets following the title or, as in this example, the date.

42. Comic or Cartoon

Sutton, W. (2011, May 2). *Ryan's a Late Adopter*. [Cartoon]. *The New Yorker*, *87*(11), 64.

43. Photo Essay

Nachtwey, J. (2006, December 2). *Crime in middle America*. [Photo essay]. *Time*. Retrieved from http:/www./time.com

44. Image from a Social Networking Site

Gristellar, F. (2009, August 7). *The Gateway Arch*. [Photograph]. Retrieved from https://www.facebook.com/qzprofile.php?id=7716zf92444

45. Map, Chart, or Other Graphic: Online

Hurricane Rita. (2005, September 24) [Graphic]. *New York Times Online*. Retrieved from http://www.nytimes.com/packages/html/national/20050923_RITA_GRAPHIC/index.html

46. Audio Book

Turkle, S. (2011). *Alone together: Why we expect more from technology and less from each other*. [MP3-CD]. Old Saybrook, CT: Tantor Media.

47. Sound Recording

Verdi, G. (1874). Requiem. [Recorded by R. Muti (Conductor) and the Chicago
    Symphony Orchestra and Chorus]. On *Requiem* [CD]. Chicago: CSO
    Resound. (2010)

Winehouse, A. (2007). Rehab. On *Back to Black* [MP3]. Universal Republic
    Records. Retrieved from http://amazon.com

48. Audio Podcast

Blumberg, A., & Davidson, D. (Producers). (2008, May 9). *The giant pool of
    money.* [Audio podcast]. Retrieved from http://thisamericanlife.org

49. Film, Videotape, or DVD

Capra, F. (Director/Producer). (1934). *It happened one night* [Motion Picture].
    United States: Columbia Pictures.

Madden, J. (Director), Parfitt, D., Gigliotti, D., Weinstein, H., Zwick, E., & Norman,
    M. (Producers). (2003). *Shakespeare in love* [DVD]. United States: Miramax.
    (Original motion picture released 1998)

50. Video: Online

For video downloads, include the download date and the source.

Capra, F. (Director/Producer). (2010). *It happened one night* [Motion Picture].
    United States: Columbia Pictures. Retrieved from Netflix. (Original
    motion picture released 1934)

Wesch, M. (2007, January 31). *Web 2.0 . . . the machine is us/ing us*
    [Video file]. Retrieved from http://www.youtube.com
    /watch?v=6gmP4nk0EOE

51. Broadcast Television or Radio Program

Burns, K. (Writer/Producer), & Barnes, P. (Producer). (1999, November 8). *Not
    for ourselves alone: The story of Elizabeth Cady Stanton and Susan B.
    Anthony* [Television broadcast]. New York, NY: Public Broadcasting
    Service.

52. Television or Radio Program: Online

Stewart, J. (Performer). (2011, June 1). Bill Moyers. *The Daily Show.* [Video file].
    Retrieved from http://www.hulu.com

The disappearing incandescent bulb. (2011, June 20). *The Madeleine
    Brand Show.* [Radio recording]. KPCC, Pasadena. Retrieved from
    http://www.scpr.org/programs/madeleine-brand/2011/06/20
    /the-disappearing-incandescent-bulb/

Give the name of the writer, director, or performer, if available; the date; the title of the episode; the title of the program or series; the type of recording; and retrieval information. Because the second source may be difficult to find, the URL is listed.

OTHER ONLINE SOURCES

Because Web sites may change, the retrieval statement includes the date retrieved as well as the URL. This example has no author.

ARTICLE TITLE   DATE

Think again: Men and women share cognitive skills. (2006).

PUBLICATION INFORMATION   RETRIEVAL INFORMATION

American Psychological Association. Retrieved January 18, 2006,

URL

from http://www.psychologymatters.org/thinkagain.html

53. Entire Web Site

Association for the Advancement of Artificial Intelligence. (2008, March). Retrieved March 17, 2008, from http://www.aaai.org

Neff, M. (Ed.). (2011). WebdelSol. Retrieved August 4, 2011, from http://webdelsol.com

Because material on a Web site may change, use a "retrieved from" date.

54. Page from a Web Site

Think again: Men and women share cognitive skills. (2006). American Psychological Association. Retrieved January 18, 2011, from http://www.psychologymatters.org/thinkagain.html

Pennsylvania Department of Education. (n.d.). Home education and private tutoring. Retrieved March 4, 2011, from http:// www.education.state.pa.us/portal/server.pt/community /home_education_and_private_tutoring/20311

In the second example, "n.d." indicates there was no date given. The retrieval information, however, contains a date.

55. Real-Time Online Communication

Berzsenyi, C. (2007, May 13). Writing to meet your match: Rhetoric, perceptions, and self-presentation for four online daters. *Computers*

and Writing Online. [Synchronous discussion]. Retrieved from
http://acadianamoo.org

If a chat, discussion, or synchronous (meaning available as it is happening)
online-presentation can be retrieved by others, include it in your References
list.

56. E-Mail Message

Because e-mails to individuals cannot be retrieved by others, they should not
appear on the References list. Cite them in the body of your paper, as in this
example:

> The wildfires threatened several of the laboratory facilities at Los Alamos
> (T. Martin, personal communication, June 20, 2011).

57. Posting on a Blog

Phillips, M. (2011, June 15). Need to go to the ER? Not until the game's over.
[Web log post]. Retrieved from http://www.freakonomics.com/2011/06/15
/need-to-go-to-the-er-not-until-the-games-over/

58. Wiki

NASCAR Sprint Cup series. (2011). [Wiki]. Retrieved April 6, 2011, from
http://nascarwiki.com

Machine learning. (n.d.) Retrieved January 5, 2008, from Artificial Intelligence
Wiki: http://www.ifi.unizh.ch/ailab/aiwiki/aiw.cgi

N.d. means "no date." Because a Wiki can change by its very nature, always
include a retrieval date.

59. Posting on Facebook

Adler-Kassner, L. (2011, May 6). Conversations toward action. [Facebook
group]. Retrieved from Council of Writing Program Administrators at
https://www.facebook.com/groups/106575940874

Include the citation in your References list only if it is retrievable by others. If
it's not, cite it only in the body of your paper, as in example 56.

60. Message on a Online Forum, Discussion Group, or Electronic Mailing List

Firrantello, L. (2005, May 23). Van Gogh on Prozac. *Salon Table Talk.*
[Online forum posting]. Retrieved February 15, 2009, from
http://www.salon.com

Boyle, F. (2002, October 11). Psyche: Cemi field theory: The hard problem
made easy [Discussion group posting]. Retrieved from
news://sci.psychology.consciousness

Haswell, R. (2005, October 17). A new graphic/text interface. [Electronic mailing list message]. Retrieved May 20, 2011, from http://lists.asu.edu/archives /wpa-l.html

APA advises using *electronic mailing list*, as Listserv is the name of specific software.

OTHER SOURCES

61. Letters

Williams, W. C. (1935). [Letter to his son]. In L. Grunwald & S. J. Adler (Eds.), *Letters of the century: America 1900–1999* (pp. 225–226). New York, NY: Dial Press.

In the APA system, unpublished letters are considered personal communications inaccessible to general readers, so they do not appear in the References list. They are cited only in the body of the paper (see example 56). Letters that have been published or can be retrieved by others are cited as above.

62. Report, Pamphlet, or Brochure

National Commission on Writing in America's Schools and Colleges. (2003). *The neglected "R": The need for a writing revolution* (Report No. 2). New York, NY: College Board.

U.S. Department of Agriculture. (2007). *Organic foods and labels* [Brochure]. Retrieved December 8, 2008, from http://www.ams.usda.gov/nop /Consumers/brochure.html

63. Legal Source

Brown v. Board of Educ., 347 U.S. 483 (1954).

For Supreme Court cases, give the name of the case, volume number, source, page number, and date of the decision. For other courts, add the court with the date: (E.D. Wisc. 1985) for "Eastern District of Wisconsin."

64. Advertisement

Swim at home. (2005). [Advertisement]. *The American Scholar* 74(2), 2.

Nikon D7000. (2010, November). [Advertisement]. Retrieved December 12, 2010, from http://rollingstone.com

65. Computer Software or Video Game

The Island: Castaway. (2010). [Video game]. N.p.: Awem Studio.

"N.p." indicates that the place of publication is unknown.

Guitar hero III: Legends of rock. (2007). [Video game]. Santa Monica, CA: Activision.

Provide an author name, if available. Standard software (Microsoft Word) and program languages (C++) don't need to be given in the References list.

66. Presentation Slides or Images

Alaska Conservation Solutions. (2006). *Montana global warming* [PowerPoint slides]. Retrieved from http://www.alaskaconservationsolutions.com/acs /presentations.html

67. Interview

In APA style, a personal interview is not included in the References list. Cite the interview in the text as a personal communication.

> Randi Friedman (personal communication, June 30, 2010) endorses this view.

If the interview is published or can be retrieved by others, cite it as an article.

68. Lecture, Speech, or Address

Kennedy, J. F. (1960, September 12). Speech to the Greater Houston Ministerial Association, Rice Hotel, Houston, TX.

69. Live Performance

Miller, A. (Author), & McLean, C. (Director). (2005, September 27). *All my sons* [Theatrical performance]. Center for the Performing Arts, Normal, IL.

Nelson, W. (2011, June 22). *Country Throwdown Tour* [Concert]. Red Rocks Amphitheater, Denver, CO.

70. Microfiche Collection of Articles

Wenzell, R. (1990, February 3). Businesses prepare for a more diverse work force [Microform]. *St. Louis Post Dispatch*, p. 17. *NewsBank: Employment* 27, fiche 2, grid D12.

A microfiche is a transparent sheet of film (a *fiche*) with microscopic printing that needs to be read through a special magnifier. Each fiche holds several pages, with each page designated by a grid position. A long document may appear on more than one fiche.

71. Musical Score

Schubert, F. (1971). *Symphony in B Minor (Unfinished)*. M. Cusid (Ed.). [Musical score]. New York, NY: Norton. (Original work composed 1822)

72. Nonperiodical Publications on CD, DVD, or Magnetic Tape

Perl, S. (2004). *Felt Sense: Guidelines for Composing*. [CD]. Portsmouth, NH: Boynton.

Quick Points   You will learn to

➤ Format your paper according to APA guidelines.

29A   What are APA format guidelines for research papers?

Watch
the Video

Ask whether your instructor has instructions for preparing a final draft. If not, you can use the APA guidelines here. For an illustration of these guidelines, see the student paper in 29B.

■ General instructions—APA

Print on 8½-by-11-inch white paper and double space. Set at least a 1-inch margin on the left, and leave no less than 1 inch on the right and at the bottom.

Leave ½ inch from the top edge of the paper to the title-and-page-number line (also known as a running head). Leave another ½ inch (or 1 inch from the top edge of the paper) before the next line on the page, whether that's a heading (such as "Abstract" or "Notes") or a line of your paper.

Indent the first line of all paragraphs ½ inch, except in an abstract, the first line of which isn't indented. Do not justify the right margin. Indent footnotes ½ inch.

■ Order of parts—APA

Number all pages consecutively. Use this order for the parts of your paper:

1. Title page
2. Abstract (if required)
3. Body of the paper
4. References
5. Footnotes, if any
6. Appendixes, if any (questionnaires, data sheets, or other material your instructor asks you to include)

■ Title-and-page-number line (running head) for all pages—APA

Use a title-and-page-number line on all pages of your paper. Place it ½ inch from the top edge of the paper, typing the title (use a shortened version if necessary). Place the page number 1 inch from the right edge of the paper. Ask whether your instructor wants you to include your last name in the running head. The "header" tool on a word processing program will help you create the title-and-page-number line easily. See the sample student paper on page 301.

■ Title page—APA

Use a separate title page. Include your running head. Center your complete title horizontally and place it in the top half of the page. (Don't italicize, underline, or enclose your title in quotation marks.) On the next line, center your name, and below that center the course title and section, your professor's name, and the date. See the sample student paper on page 301.

🛈 **Alerts:** (1) Use the guidelines here for capitalizing the title of your own paper and for capitalizing titles you mention in the body of your paper, but not in the REFERENCES list; see Quick Box 28.1.

(2) Use a capital letter for the first word of your title and for the first word of a subtitle, if any. Start every NOUN, PRONOUN, VERB, ADVERB, and ADJECTIVE with a capital letter. Capitalize each main word in a hyphenated compound word (two or more words used together to express one idea): *Father-in-Law, Self-Consciousness.*

(3) Do not capitalize ARTICLES (*a, an, the*) unless one of the other capitalization rules applies to them. Do not capitalize PREPOSITIONS and CONJUNCTIONS unless they're four or more letters long. Do not capitalize the word *to* used in an INFINITIVE. ●

■ Abstract—APA

An abstract is a summary of your paper in 150 to 250 words. Type the abstract on a separate page, using the numeral 2 in the title-and-page-number line. Center the word *Abstract* 1 inch from the top of the paper. Do not italicize or underline it or enclose it in quotation marks. Double-space below this title, and then start your abstract, double-spacing it. Do not indent the first line.

■ Set-off quotations—APA

Set off (display in block style) quotations of forty words or more. See 27C for a detailed explanation and example.

■ References list—APA

Start a new page for your References list immediately after the end of the body of your paper. One inch from the top of the paper center the word *References*. Don't italicize, underline, or put it in quotation marks. Double-space below it. Start the first line of each entry at the left margin, and indent any subsequent lines five spaces or ½ inch from the left margin. Use this hanging indent style unless your instructor prefers a different one. Double-space within each entry and between entries.

■ Notes—APA

Put any notes on a separate page after the last page of your References list. Center the word *Footnotes* one inch from the top of the paper. Do not italicize or underline it or put it in quotation marks.

On the next line, indent ½ inch and begin the note. Raise the note number slightly (you can use the superscript feature in your word processing program), and then start the words of your note, leaving no space after the number. If the note is more than one typed line, do not indent any line after the first. Double-space throughout.

29B A student's APA-style research paper

View
the Model
Document

Leslie Palm wrote the following paper in response to an assignment that asked students to research how gender was portrayed in a specific circumstance.

↑ ½"
Running head: WOMEN IN VIDEO GAMES   1 ←→
1"

Put a short version of your title, followed by the page number, as a header on each page.

Use the first page for the title page.

Center the title, your name, course, instructor and date in the top half of the page. Use double spacing.

The Troubling Roles of Women in Video Games

Leslie Palm

Sociology 200

Professor K. Thetard

May 9, 2011

↑ ½"
WOMEN IN VIDEO GAMES   ↓ 1"   2 ←→
1"

Abstract

Double-space → Despite the fact that 40% of video game players are women, female characters and players are treated in ways that are problematic. Video games often portray unrealistic physical characteristics of female characters, exaggerating certain body features. Many games portray women either as vulnerable "damsels in distress" or as sexually aggressive. Women game players often experience stereotyping or harassment. Recent games are changing the way they present female characters.

Place your abstract, if required, on the second page.

1"

continued >>

WOMEN IN VIDEO GAMES   3

The Troubling Roles of Women in Video Games

Lady Reagan Cousland the First jogs across a virtual

pastoral landscape with a two-handed battleax strapped

across her shoulders. She is the Player Character in a play

through of *Dragon Age: Origins*, a 2009 single-player role-play

game, and she is trying to progress through the main quest.

However, other characters taunt her. "I have never seen a

woman Grey Warden before," says one skeptically. Lady rolls

her eyes before sharply answering, "That's because women are

too smart to join."

"So what does that make you?" asks the interrupter.

"Insane," she replies.

This exchange exemplifies how women have frequently

been portrayed and treated in videogames for over two decades.

Gaming has long been inaccurately considered an activity

pursued almost solely by reclusive males caricatured as "pale

loners crouched in the dark among Mountain Dew bottles and

pizza boxes" (Wong, 2010). Game producers have mostly catered

to this stereotypical player, with discouraging results. Despite

evidence that large numbers of women play video games, and

despite some important changes, women game characters

continue to be physically objectified, represented either as

passive or sexually aggressive, and even harassed.

According to data from the Entertainment Software

Association (2011), 67% of American households own a video

game console of some variety—and 40% of all players are

women. In fact, "Women over 18 years of age are one of the

industry's fastest growing demographics, [representing] a

greater portion of the game-playing population (33 percent)

than boys age 17 or younger (20 percent)" (Entertainment

Begin the body of your paper on page 2 if you have no abstract, on page 3 if you do.

Introductory paragraphs create interest.

Paragraph 2 provides background information.

Thesis statement gives paper's focus.

Paragraph 3 gives data.

Brackets show the writer added language.

continued >>

WOMEN IN VIDEO GAMES   4

Software Association, 2011). And yet, studies show that both
male and female gamers believe games to be a "particularly
masculine pursuit" (Selwyn, 2007, p. 533).

Physical Characteristics of Female Characters

The most obvious gender stereotyping in many games
comes from the nature of the characters' bodies or avatars.
A 2007 content analysis of images of video game characters
from top-selling American gaming magazines showed that male
characters (83%) are more likely than female characters (62%)
to be portrayed as aggressive; however, female characters are
more likely to be sexualized (60 vs 1%) and scantily clad (39 vs
1%) (Dill & Thill, 2007, p. 851–864). Even female characters that are
considered strong or dominant in personality (such as Morgainn
in *Dragon Age: Origins* or Sheva in *Resident Evil 5*) routinely
dress in tops that are essentially strips of fabric and skin-tight
leather pants. In fact, the reward for beating *Resident Evil 5* is
that you get to dress the avatar Sheva in a leopard-print bikini.

In *Gender Inclusive Game Design*, S. G. Ray (2003)
outlined the physical traits seen between male and female
avatars: females are characterized by "exaggerated sexual
features such as large breasts set high on their torso, large
buttocks, and a waist smaller than her head" (pp. 102–104).
Dickerman, Christensen, and Kerl-McClain (2008) found
similar qualities. Analyzing characters in 60 video games,
Downs and Smith (2010) found that women were more likely
to be "hypersexualized" then men, depicted with unrealistic
body proportions, inappropriate clothing, and other qualities
(p. 728).

Even nonhuman females receive this treatment. Game
designer J. Rubenstein (2007) questions why females of

Citation with page number for direct quotation.

First heading.

Paragraph 4 starts to develop the first main point.

Paragraph 5 summarizes research related to the first main point.

Author and date are included in sentence, so only page numbers are in parentheses.

Paragraph 6 extends the first main point.

continued >>

WOMEN IN VIDEO GAMES   5

nonhuman races in the popular game *World of Warcraft* are so

much smaller and more feminine than their male counterparts.

Of one species she notes, "The male is massive: tall with

unnaturally large muscles and equally large hooves. . . . It

would not be unreasonable to expect the female of the species

to be similar." Apparently in *World of Warcraft's* earliest

designs, the genders were far more similar; however, when

screened to a pool of test gamers, complaints that the females

were "ugly" resulted in their being changed to their current

form. One scholar notes, "Since gamers and the like have been

used to video representations of scantily-clad females and

steroid-enhanced males," it is understandable that they would

design nonhuman races in a similar way (Bates, 2005, p. 13).

Gender and Character Behavior

The personalities of the characters also demonstrate

the gender bias in many games. Dietz's 1998 study of 33

games found that most did not portray women at all. Even

ten years later, 86% of game characters were male (Downs

& Smith, 2010). Only five of the games in Dietz's study

portrayed women as heroes or action characters. The second

most common portrayal in this study was as "victim or as

the proverbial 'Damsel in Distress'" (Dietz, 1998, pp. 434–435).

Examples of vulnerable women stretch from the 1980s to

today, from Princess Peach (Nintendo's *Mario*) and Princess

Zelda (Nintendo's *The Legend of Zelda*) to Alice Wake (Remedy

Entertainment's *Alan Wake*), Ashley Graham (Capcom's

Resident Evil 4), and Alex Roivas (Nintendo's *Eternal Darkness:

Sanity's Requiem*). The helpless woman, simply put, is a video

game staple, as college students overwhelmingly recognized

in one study (Ogletree & Drake, 2007).

Marginal annotations:

If the source had page numbers, a page reference would appear in parentheses.

Direct quotation embedded in a sentence.

Second heading.

Topic sentence of paragraph 7 announces the second main point.

In-text citation for a source by two authors.

No page number because examples are names of video games.

continued >>

WOMEN IN VIDEO GAMES 6

A different staple role gaining popularity is that of the aggressive but sexy woman who will seduce you at night and then shoot you in the morning. Bayonetta, Jill Valentine (in *Resident Evil 3* and *Resident Evil 5*) and, of course, Lara Croft of the *Tomb Raider* series are all examples of this archetype. There is some debate as to whether these examples are evidence of new female power and liberation or simply a new form of exploitation. Dill and Thill (2007) argue that an aggressive female is not necessarily a liberated one and that "many of these images of aggressive female video game characters glamorize and sexualize aggression." Eugene Provenzo agrees, pointing out the contradiction between "the seeming empowerment of women, while at the same time . . . they're really being exploited in terms of how they're shown, graphically" (as cited in Huntemann, 2000).

Lara Croft is perhaps the epitome of the energetic, aggressive character as an over-exaggerated sexual object. Lead graphic artist Gard went through five designs before arriving at her final appearance, and he began with the desire to counter stereotypical female characters, which he describes as "either a bimbo or a dominatrix" (as cited in Yang, 2007). Gard's inspirations included Swedish pop artist Neneh Cherry and comic book character Tank Girl, both feminist icons. Croft's original incarnation was as the South American woman Lara Cruz. Gard disavows accusations of sexism in the design, and insists that the character's iconic breasts were a programming accident that the rest of the team fought to keep (McLaughlin, 2008).

The Treatment of Women Gamers

Video game culture reinforces negative gender roles for female players. Many multiplayer games encourage players

---

Paragraph 8 introduces a slightly different aspect of the second main point.

Ellipses dots show that the writer has removed language from the quotation.

Paragraph 9 provides a specific example.

Third heading.

Topic sentence of paragraph 10 explains third main point.

continued >>

WOMEN IN VIDEO GAMES   7

to use headsets and microphones, a gender-revealing practice that is intended for easy strategizing. However, it often leads to sexual harassment and lewd commentary that also carries over to message boards, comments sections, and internet forums.

Specific examples illustrate the point.

Technology blogger Kathy Sierra was forced to abandon her website after multiple misogynistic comments and e-mails. Ailin Graef, who has made millions in the 3D chat-platform Second Life, was "swarmed by flying pink penises" during an interview in that virtual world (McCabe, 2008).

Paragraph 11 provides more examples of how women players are sometimes treated.

A study by psychologists at Nottingham Trent University in England determined that 70% of female players in massively multiplayer online games chose to "construct male characters when given the option," presumably in an attempt to avoid such actions as female posters on gaming message boards being asked to post pictures of their breasts or "get the f*** off" (McCabe, 2008). Women gamers are considered so rare (which is surprising, given that they makes up 40% of players) that it's a common occurrence for male gamers to respond with a degree of shock any time a female shows up in a game—even if that shock is complimentary or respectful. Sarah Rutledge, a 25-year-old female med student, said of her gaming on *World of Warcraft*,

Because this source was a personal interview and is not retrievable by others, student cites it only in the text, not in her References.

> On the one hand, you get a lot of help and attention from guys playing the game, which can be helpful. You get invitations to join groups. But it's clear this has less to do with my ability than the fact I'm that curious creature: a woman. (personal communication, April 29, 2011)

Explains different treatments of men and women matter.

One team of researchers found significant differences between men and women game players in gaining positive effects from gaming. They found males more likely than females to

continued >>

WOMEN IN VIDEO GAMES   8

develop leadership, teamwork, and communicative skills, and
they suggest this demonstrates games' biases toward males
(Thirunarayanon, Vilchez, Abreau, Ledesma, & Lopez, 2010, p. 324).

Gradual Changes in Gender Roles and Gaming

In recent years gender roles have somewhat shifted.
Often role-playing games permit the user to choose various
characteristics of the Player Character, including making her
female. Aside from appearance and responses from Non-Player
Characters, the gender rarely affects a character's actual skills
or attributes. More games have been released with females as
the sole protagonists, including *Silent Hill 3* (Heather Mason),
No One Lives Forever (Cate Archer), *Mirror's Edge* (Faith), and
Heavenly Sword (Nariko). Jade, the protagonist of *Beyond
Good and Evil* (released in 2003), has been praised for being
strong and confident without being overtly sexualized. So have
characters like Alyx Vance (co-protagonist of 2004's *Half-Life 2*)
and Chell (protagonist of *Portal*, 2007, and *Portal 2*, 2011).

Chell in particular was heralded as a massive step
forward in gender dynamics. People were surprised that "as the
player, you're never even aware that you're a woman until you
catch a glimpse of yourself in the third person" (iVirtua, 2007). In
this way, Chell echoes the "original" feminist character Samus
Aran of Nintendo's 1986 *Metroid*; one only discovers that Aran
is female when she removes her bulky robot armor during the
ending scene, after twenty-plus hours of first-person gameplay.
Portal, despite being an indie game produced by students as
their thesis, became a hit, was wildly acclaimed by critics, and
won multiple awards.

These developments don't satisfy all fans. Some argue
that a more all-inclusive focus actually threatens the quality of

Margin notes:

Fourth heading.

Topic sentence in paragraph 12 explains the fourth (and final) main point.

Paragraph 13 provides more detail about an example mentioned in the previous paragraph.

Paragraph 14 explains some fans' responses.

continued >>

WOMEN IN VIDEO GAMES 9

experience for stereotypically straight male gamers. Bioware, a Canada-based gaming company, came under fire during the releases of two major titles for featuring romance and dialogue options that cater not only to women, but to gays and lesbians. The release of *Dragon Age 2* in 2011 caused an uproar on its own message boards for allowing romantic options to be bisexual. One fan, "Bastal" (2011), protested that

> the overwhelming majority of RPG gamers are indeed straight and male.... That's not to say there isn't a significant number of women who play Dragon Age and that BioWare should forego the option of playing as a women altogether, but there should have been much more focus on making sure us male gamers were happy.

He and others then go on to propose a mode, which, if activated, would force male companions to flirt only with female PCs, and vice versa. However, such views disturb game creators like Gaider (2010), who argued that people like Bastal are

> so used to being catered to that they see the lack of catering as an imbalance.... The person who says that the only way to please them is to restrict options for others is, if you ask me, the one who deserves it least.

"If we just continue to cater to existing (male) players, we're never going to grow," says Beth Llewellyn, senior director of corporate communications for Nintendo (as cited in Kerwick, 2007). Video game companies have begun producing a new generation of games that give women the opportunity to grab a laser gun or broadsword and duke it out in billion-dollar franchises like *Halo*, *Fallout*, *Mass Effect*, *World of Warcraft*,

Quotations longer than 40 words are set off block style, with no quotation marks. They're both from online sources with no page numbers; other source information appears in the sentences introducing the quotations.

Concluding paragraph.

Key quotation begins the concluding paragraph based on idea in previous paragraph.

continued >>

WOMEN IN VIDEO GAMES 10

and *Guild Wars*. However, depicting women more accurately and favorably in games reaches a goal more important than mere entertainment. "Video-simulated interfaces" are being used to train people for various professions (Terlecki et al., 2010, p. 30), and it is crucial that these environments are suitable for all. The promising news is that while there is still extensive gender stereotyping (in both the gaming and the real world), game makers are taking giant strides—in both boots and heels.

Sentence helps answer the "so what?" question.

Because there are more than 6 authors for this citation, student uses the first author and "et al."

continued >>

WOMEN IN VIDEO GAMES 11

References

Bastal. (2011, March 22). Bioware neglected their main demographic: the straight male gamer [Online discussion posting]. Retrieved from http://social.bioware .com/forum/1/topic/304/index/6661775&lf=8 (Topic 304, Msg. 1)

Bates, M. (2005). *Implicit identity theory in the rhetoric of the massively multiplayer online role-playing game (MMORPG)* (Doctoral Dissertation, Pennsylvania State University.) Available from ProQuest Dissertations and Theses database. (AAT 3172955)

Dickerman, C., Christensen, J., & Kerl-McClain, S. B. (2008). Big breasts and bad guys: Depictions of gender and race in video games. *Journal of Creativity in Mental Health, 3*(1), 20–29. doi: 10.1080/15401380801995076

Dietz, T. L. (1998). An examination of violence and gender role portrayals in video games: Implications for gender socialization and aggressive behavior. *Sex Roles, 38*, 433–435.

Dill, K. E., & Thill, K. P. (2007, October 17). Video game characters and the socialization of gender roles: Young people's perceptions mirror sexist media depictions. *Sex Roles, 57*, 861–864.

Downs, E., & Smith, S. L. (2010). Keeping abreast of hypersexuality: A video game character content analysis. *Sex Roles, 62*, 721–733. doi: 10:1007/s11199-009-9637-1

Dragon Age: Origins. (2009). [Video game]. Edmonton, Canada: Bioware Studios.

Begin References on a new page, with hanging indent.

Dissertation from a database, with accession number.

Journal article online, with document object identifier (doi).

Journal article in print.

Video game.

continued >>

WOMEN IN VIDEO GAMES   12

Entertainment Software Association. (2011). *Essential facts about the computer and video game industry 2010: Sales, demographic and usage data.* Washington, DC: Author. Retrieved from http://www.theesa.com/

Gaider, D. (2011, April 2). Re: Bioware neglected their main demographic. [Online forum comment]. Retrieved May 3, 2011, from http://social.bioware.com/forum/1/topic/304 /index/6661775&lf=8 (Topic 304, Msg. 2)

Huntemann, N. (Producer & Director). (2000). *Game over: Gender, race & violence in video games.* [Video file]. USA: Media Education Foundation. Retrieved from http://www.mediaed.org/

iVirtua Editorial Team. (2007, December 9). Portal is a feminist masterpiece. London, England: iVirtua Media Group. Retrieved from http://www.ivirtuaforums.com/portal-is-a-feminist-masterpiece-great-read-media-studies-t14-61

Kerwick, M. (2007, May 13). Video games now starring strong female characters. *The Record.* Retrieved from http://www.popmatters.com/female-characters

McCabe, J. (2008, March 6). Sexual harassment is rife online: No wonder women swap gender. *The Guardian*, p. G2. Retrieved from http://www.guardian.co.uk/

McLaughlin, R. (2008). The history of Tomb Raider. IGN Entertainment, Inc. Retrieved from http://m.ign.com /articles/058183.

Ogletree, S. M., & Drake, R. (2007). College students' video game participation and perceptions: Gender differences and implications. *Sex Roles, 56,* 537–542. doi: 10.1007 /s11199-007-9193-5

Report available online. Because the author is the same as the publisher, the publisher is listed as "Author."

Comment in an online discussion.

Online video.

Newspaper article available online.

continued >>

WOMEN IN VIDEO GAMES   13

Book. Ray, S. G. (2003). *Gender inclusive game design: Expanding the
          market*. Hingham, MA: Charles River Media.

Rubenstein, J. (2007, May 26). Idealizing fantasy bodies. *Iris
          Gaming Network*. Retrieved from http://theirisnetwork.org/

Selwyn, N. (2007). Hi-tech = Guy-tech? An exploration of
          undergraduate students' gendered perceptions of
          information and communication technologies. *Sex
          Roles, 56*, 525–536. doi: 10.1007/s11199-007-9191-7

Terlecki, M., Brown, J., Harner-Steciw, L., Irvin-Hannum, J.,
          Marchetto-Ryan, N., Ruhl, L., & Wiggins, J. (2011). Sex
          differences and similarities in video game experience,
          preferences, and self-efficacy: Implications for the
          gaming industry. *Current Psychology, 30*, 22–33. doi:
          10.1007/s12144-010-9095-5

Thirunarayanon, M. O., Vilchez, M., Abreu, L., Ledesma, C.,
          & Lopez, S. (2010). A survey of video game players in a
          public, urban research university. *Educational Media
          International, 47*, 311–327. doi: 10.1080/09523987-2010.535338

Wong, D. (2010, May 24). Five reasons it's still not cool to admit
          you're a gamer. *Cracked*. Retrieved April 20, 2011, from
          http://www.cracked.com/article_18571

Yang, R. (2007). The man behind Lara. [Interview]. *GameDaily*.
          Retrieved from http://gamedaily.com/articles/features
          /the-man-behined-lara

30 CM-Style Documentation

Quick Points   You will learn to

➤ Cite your sources according to CM guidelines.

30A   What is CM-style documentation?

The Chicago Manual of Style (CM) endorses two styles of documentation. One CM STYLE is an author-date style, similar to the APA STYLE of IN-TEXT CITATIONS (Ch. 27), that includes a list of SOURCES usually titled "Works Cited" or "References."

The other CM style uses a BIBLIOGRAPHIC NOTE SYSTEM. This system gives information about each source in two places: (1) in a *footnote* (at the bottom of a page) or an *endnote* (in a separate page following your paper) and (2), if required, in a BIBLIOGRAPHY that begins on a separate page. We present this style here because it's often used in such humanities courses as art, music, history, philosophy, and sometimes English. Within the bibliographic note system, there are two substyles: "full" and "short."

■ The full bibliographic note system in CM style

The CM full bibliographic note system requires you to give complete information, in a footnote or an endnote, the first time you cite a source. Because you're giving full information, you don't need to include a bibliography page. If you cite a source a second time, you provide shortened information that includes the last name(s) of the author(s) and the key words in the work's title. The following example uses the full bibliographic note system.

> **TEXT**
>
> Ulrich points out that both Europeans and Native Americans told war stories, but with different details and different emphases.[3]

> **FULL FOOTNOTE (SAME PAGE) OR ENDNOTE (SEPARATE PAGE FOLLOWING TEXT)**
>
> 3. Laurel Thatcher Ulrich, *The Age of Homespun: Objects and Stories in the Creation of an American Myth* (New York: Knopf, 2001), 269.

> **SECOND CITATION OF THIS SOURCE**
>
> 6. Ulrich, *Age of Homespun*, 285.

313

■ The short bibliographic note system, plus bibliography, in CM style

In the abbreviated bibliographic note system, even your first endnote or footnote provides only brief information about the source. You provide complete information in a bibliography, which appears as a separate page at the end of the paper. Following is an example of using the full bibliographic note system.

TEXT

Ulrich points out that both Europeans and Native Americans told war stories, but with different details and different emphases.[3]

ABBREVIATED FOOTNOTE (SAME PAGE) OR ENDNOTE (SEPARATE PAGE FOLLOWING TEXT)

3. Ulrich, *Age of Homespun*, 269.

BIBLIOGRAPHY (SEPARATE PAGE AT END OF THE PAPER)

Ulrich, Laurel Thatcher. *The Age of Homespun: Objects and Stories in the Creation of an American Myth.* New York: Knopf, 2001.

! Alert: Ask your instructor which style he or she prefers. Remember that CM style requires a separate bibliography only when you use the short notes style, but your instructor may prefer one with the full style, too. ●

Quick Box 30.1 provides guidelines for compiling CM-style bibliographic notes.

Quick Box 30.1   ■ ■ ■ ■ ■ ■ ■ ■ ■

Guidelines for compiling CM-style bibliographic notes

TITLE AND PLACEMENT OF NOTES
If you're using endnotes, place them all on a separate page, before your bibliography. Center the heading "Notes," without using italics, underlining, or quotation marks, an inch from the top of the page. If you're using footnotes, place them at the bottom of the page on which the source needs to be credited. Never use a title above a note at the foot of the page. CM generally uses blank space (not a line) to divide the footnote(s) from the body text.

TITLE AND PLACEMENT OF BIBLIOGRAPHY
The abbreviated notes style requires a bibliography, which begins on a separate page at the end of the paper, following the endnotes page. An inch from

continued >>

the top of the page, center the heading "Bibliography" or "Works Cited" (either is acceptable in CM style). Don't underline the heading or put it in quotation marks.

FORMAT FOR ENDNOTES AND FOOTNOTES

Include an endnote or a footnote every time you use a source. Number notes sequentially throughout your paper whether you're using endnotes or footnotes. Use superscript (raised) arabic numerals for the footnote or endnote numbers in your paper. Position note numbers after any punctuation mark except the dash. The best position is at the end of a sentence, unless that position would be so far from the source material that it would be confusing. Don't use raised numbers in the endnote or footnote itself. Place the number, followed by a period, on the same line as the content of the note. Double-space both within each note and between notes. Indent each note's first line, but place subsequent lines flush left at the margin.

SPACING AFTER PUNCTUATION

A single space follows all punctuation, including the period.

AUTHORS' NAMES

In endnotes and footnotes, give the name in standard (first-name-first) order, with names and initials as given in the original source. Use the word *and* before the last author's name if your source has more than one author. If the source has four or more authors, in the note give only the first and use *et al.* for the rest.

In the bibliography, invert the name: last name, first name. If a work has two or more authors, invert only the first author's name. Give all authors' names in bibliography entry.

CAPITALIZATION OF SOURCE TITLES

Capitalize the first and last words and all major words.

SPECIAL TREATMENT OF TITLES

Use italics for titles of long works, and use quotation marks around the titles of shorter works. Omit *A, An,* and *The* from the titles of newspapers and periodicals. For an unfamiliar newspaper title, list the city (and state, in parentheses, if the city isn't well known): *Newark* (NJ) *Star-Ledger,* for example. Use postal abbreviations for states.

PUBLICATION INFORMATION

For a full note citing a book, put the publication information in parentheses. Use a colon and one space after the city of publication. Give complete publishers' names or abbreviate them according to standard abbreviations in

continued >>

Quick Box 30.1 (continued)

Books in Print. Omit *Co., Inc.,* and so on. Spell out *University* and *Press.* Don't abbreviate months.

PAGE NUMBERS
For inclusive page numbers, give the full second number for 2 through 99. For 100 and beyond, give the full second number only if a shortened version would be ambiguous: 243–47, 202–6, 1296–308. List all discontinuous page numbers. (See "First Endnote or Footnote: Book" toward the end of this box.) Use a comma to separate parenthetical publication information from the page numbers that follow it. Use the abbreviations *p.* and *pp.* with page numbers only for material from newspapers, for material from journals that do not use volume numbers, and to avoid ambiguity.

CONTENT NOTES
Try to avoid using content notes. If you must use them, use footnotes, not endnotes, with symbols rather than numbers: an asterisk (*) for the first note on that page and a dagger (†) for a second note on that page.

FIRST ENDNOTE OR FOOTNOTE: BOOK
For books, include the author, title, publication information, and page numbers when applicable. Do not include state if publisher's name makes it clear.

1. Becky Bradway, *Pink Houses and Family Taverns* (Bloomington: University of Indiana Press, 2002), 23.

FIRST ENDNOTE OR FOOTNOTE: ARTICLE
For articles, include the author, article title, journal title, volume number, year, and page numbers.

1. D. D. Cochran, W. Daniel Hale, and Christine P. Hissam, "Personal Space Requirements in Indoor versus Outdoor Locations," *Journal of Psychology* 117 (1984): 132–33.

SECOND MENTION IN ENDNOTES OR FOOTNOTES
Later citations of the same source can be brief. See 30B, examples 1 and 16.

30B What are CM guidelines for bibliographic notes?

The following directory corresponds to the sample bibliographic note forms that follow it. In a few cases, we give sample Bibliography forms as well. If you need a model that isn't here, consult *The Chicago Manual of Style*, 16th ed. (Chicago: University of Chicago Press, 2010).

Directory for CM Bibliographic Notes System

PERIODICALS

1. Article in a Scholarly Journal: Print

1. Bronwyn T. Williams. "Seeking New Worlds: The Study of Writing beyond Our Classrooms." *College Composition and Communication* 62, no. 1 (2010): 131.   [Full note]

2. Williams, "Seeking New Worlds," 131.   [Short note]

In a note, the author's name appears in regular order. Commas separate elements except for the page number, which follows a colon. In a full note, the volume number comes one space after the journal title. If there is an issue number, precede it with "no."

Bibliography

Williams, Bronwyn T. "Seeking New Worlds: The Study of Writing beyond Our Classrooms." *College Composition and Communication* 62, no. 1 (2010): 127–46.

In the bibliography entry needed for the short note version, the author's name appears inverted, last name first. Periods separate the elements.

2. Article in Scholarly Journal: Online with a DOI

1. Regan Gurung and Kristin Vespia, "Looking Good, Teaching Tell? Linking Liking, Looks, and Learning," *Teaching of Psychology* 34, no. 1 (2007): 7, doi: 10.1207/s15328023top3401_2. [full note]

2. Gurung and Vespia, "Looking Good," 7. [short note]

Bibliography

Gurung, Regan, and Kristin Vespia. "Looking Good, Teaching Tell? Linking Liking, Looks, and Learning." *Teaching of Psychology* 34, no. 1 (2007): 5–10. doi: 10.1207/s15328023top3401_2.

For an explanation of Digital Object Identifiers (DOI), see 28B. See examples 1 and 2 for short note and full note forms.

3. Article in a Scholarly Journal: Online with a URL

1. Richard A. Bryant, "Disentangling Mild Traumatic Brain Injury and Stress Reactions," *New England Journal of Medicine* 358, no. 5 (2008): 527, http://www.nejm.org/doi/full/10.1056/NEJMe078235.

2. Bryant, "Disentangling," 527.

Bibliography

Bryant, Richard A. "Disentangling Mild Traumatic Brain Injury and Stress Reactions." *New England Journal of Medicine* 358, no. 5 (2008): 525–527. http://www.nejm.org/doi/full/10.1056/NEJMe078235

4. Article in a Scholarly Journal: From a Database

1. Bronwyn T. Williams, "Seeking New Worlds: The Study of Writing beyond Our Classrooms," *College Composition and Communication* 62, no.1 (2010): 143, ProQuest.

2. Williams, "Seeking New Worlds," 143.

Bibliography

Williams, Bronwyn T. "Seeking New Worlds: The Study of Writing beyond Our Classrooms." *College Composition and Communication* 62, no. 1 (2010): 127–46. ProQuest.

For articles from library or commercial databases, include as much information as possible about any print version. List the name of the database at the end of the entry (ProQuest, in the example above). If the article has a stable URL (a unique URL that is permanently associated with it), provide it, as in the following example:

3. Michael Harker, "The Ethics of Argument: Rereading *Kairos* and Making Sense in a Timely Fashion," *College Composition and Communication* 59, no. 1 (2007): 77–97, http://www.jstor.org/stable/20456982.

5. Article in a Weekly or Biweekly Magazine: Print

1. Rana Foroohar, "Why the World Isn't Getting Smaller," *Time*, June 27, 2011: 20.

2. Foroohar, "Why the World," 20.

Bibliography

Foroohar, Rana. "Why the World Isn't Getting Smaller." *Time*, June 27, 2011.

CM recommends citing magazine articles by the date only. If there is no author given, begin with the title of the article.

3. "The Price Is Wrong." *Economist*, August 2, 2008: 58–59.

6. Article in a Weekly or Biweekly Magazine: Online with a URL

1. Rana Foroohar, "Why the World Isn't Getting Smaller," *Time*, June 19, 2011, http://www.time.com/time/magazine/article/0,9171,2078119,00.html

2. Foroohar, "Why the World."

Bibliography

Foroohar, Rana. "Why the World Isn't Getting Smaller." *Time*, June 19, 2011. http://www.time.com/time/magazine/article/0,9171,2078119,00.html.

The online version of this article did not list page numbers.

7. Article in a Monthly or Bimonthly Magazine: Print

1. Thomas Goetz, "The Feedback Loop," *Wired*, July 2011: 127.

8. Article in a Monthly or Bimonthly Magazine: Online

1. Thomas Goetz, "Harnessing the Power of Feedback Loops," *Wired*, July 2011, http://www.wired.com/magazine/2011/06/ff_feedbackloop/.

9. Article in a Newspaper: Print

1. Monica Hesse, "Love Among the Ruins," *Washington Post*, April 24, 2011, F1.

Page numbers for newspapers are usually not included, but we've shown above how to include one if your instructor requires. If no author is listed, begin with the title of the article:

2. "Prepping for Uranium Work," *Denver Post*, June 18, 2011.

10. Article in a Newspaper: Online

1. Monica Hesse, "Falling in Love with St. Andrews, Scotland," *Washington Post*, April 24, 2011, http://www.washingtonpost.com/lifestyle/travel /falling-in-love-with-st-andrews-scotland/2011/04/18/AFWZuoPE_story.html.

11. Editorial

1. "Primary Considerations," *Washington Post*, January 27, 2008: B6.

2. "Garbage In, Garbage Out," *Los Angeles Times*, February 2, 2008, http://www.latimes.com/news/printedition/la-ed-payroll2feb02,0,7684087.story.

12. Letter to the Editor

1. Lester Goldstein, letter to the editor, *Sierra*, May/June 2011, 2.

CM style does not include any title that might be given for a letter to the editor.

13. Review

1. David Shenk, "Toolmaker, Brain Builder," review of *Beyond Deep Blue: Building the Computer That Defeated the World Chess Champion*, by Feng-Hsiung Hsu, *American Scholar* 72 (Spring 2003): 150–52.

14. Article in a Looseleaf Collection of Reprinted Articles: Print

1. Thomas Hayden, "The Age of Robots," *US News and World Report*, April 23, 2001. Reprinted in *Applied Science 2002*, ed. Eleanor Goldstein (Boca Raton, FL: SIRS, 2002), art. 66.

Give the citation for the original publication first, followed by the citation for the collection.

15. Abstract: Print

1. Hazel R. Marcus and Shinobu Kitayamo, "Culture and the Self: Implications for Cognition, Emotion, and Motivation," *Psychological Abstracts* 78 (1991), item 23878.

BOOKS

16. Book by One Author: Print

1. Sherry Turkle, *Alone Together: Why We Expect More from Technology and Less from Each Other* (New York: Basic Books, 2011), 43.   [full note]

2. Turkle, *Alone Together*, 43.   [short note]

Bibliography

Turkle, Sherry. *Alone Together: Why We Expect More from Technology and Less from Each Other*. New York: Basic Books, 2011.

17. Book by One Author: E-Reader

1. Sherry Turkle, *Alone Together: Why We Expect More from Technology and Less from Each Other* (New York: Basic Books, 2011), Kindle edition, chap. 2.   [full note]

2. Turkle, *Alone Together*, chap. 2.   [short note]

Because electronic books often don't have page numbers, listing a chapter helps readers locate the citation.

Bibliography

Turkle, Sherry. *Alone Together: Why We Expect More from Technology and Less from Each Other*. New York: Basic Books, 2011. Kindle edition.

18. Book by One Author: Online

1. Sherry Turkle, *Alone Together: Why We Expect More from Technology and Less from Each Other* (New York: Basic Books, 2011), 43, http://books.google.com/.   [full note]

2. Turkle, *Alone Together*, 43.   [short note]

Bibliography

Turkle, Sherry. *Alone Together: Why We Expect More from Technology and Less from Each Other*. New York: Basic Books, 2011. http://books.google.com/.

19. Book by Two or Three Authors

1. Kathryn Edin and Maria Kefalas, *Promises I Can Keep: Why Poor Women Put Motherhood before Marriage* (Berkeley: University of California Press, 2005), 28.

2. Edin and Kefalas, *Promises*, 28.

Bibliography

Edin, Kathryn, and Maria Kefalas. *Promises I Can Keep: Why Poor Women Put Motherhood before Marriage*. Berkeley: University of California Press, 2005.

Include the names of two or three authors in notes. In the bibliography, invert the name of only the first author. For e-books, adapt this model to example 17. For a book accessed online, see example 18. See examples 16–18 for short note and full note forms.

20. Book by More Than Three Authors

1. Wendy Saul et al., *Beyond the Science Fair: Creating a Kids' Inquiry Conference* (Portsmouth, NH: Heinemann, 2005), 74.   [full note]

2. Saul et al., Beyond the Science Fair, 74.   [short note]

Bibliography

Saul, Wendy, Donna Dieckman, Charles R. Pearce, and Donna Neutze. *Beyond the Science Fair: Creating a Kids' Inquiry Conference*. Portsmouth, NH: Heinemann, 2005.

In notes, give only the first author's name, followed by the phrase *et al.* (abbreviated from the Latin *et alii*, meaning "and others"). In the bibliography list all names in full in the order in which they appear on the title page.

21. Two or More Works by the Same Author(s)

Bibliography

Jenkins, Henry. *Convergence Culture: Where Old and New Media Collide*. New York: New York University Press, 2006.

---. *Fans, Bloggers, and Gamers: Exploring Participatory Culture*. New York: New York University Press, 2006.

In the second and subsequent entries, use three hyphens and a period to stand for the same author name(s). If the person served as editor or translator, put a comma and *ed.* or *trans.* following the three hyphens. Arrange the works in alphabetical order by book title.

22. Book by a Group or Corporate Author

1. American Psychological Association, *Publication Manual of the American Psychological Association*, 6th ed. (Washington, DC: APA, 2010).

23. Book with No Author Named

1. *The Chicago Manual of Style*, 16th ed. (Chicago: University of Chicago Press, 2010), 711.

24. Book with an Author and an Editor

1. Harriet Beecher Stowe, *Uncle Tom's Cabin*, ed. Elizabeth Ammons (New York: Norton, 2010), 272.

2. Stowe, *Uncle Tom's Cabin*, 272.

Bibliography

Stowe, Harriet Beecher. *Uncle Tom's Cabin*. Edited by Elizabeth Ammons. New York: Norton, 2010.

If your paper refers to the work of the editor, put the editor's name first.

Ammons, Elizabeth, ed. *Uncle Tom's Cabin*. By Harriet Beecher Stowe. New York: Norton, 2010.

25. Translation

1. Jo Nesbo, *The Leopard*, trans. Don Bartlett (New York: Vintage, 2011), 7.

26. Work in Several Volumes or Parts

1. Ronald Chrisley, ed., *Artificial Intelligence: Critical Concepts* (London: Routledge, 2000), 4:25.

Give the volume number followed by a colon and the page number.

Bibliography

Chrisley, Ronald, ed. *Artificial Intelligence: Critical Concepts*. Vol. 4. London: Routledge, 2000.

27. Anthology or Edited Book

1. John L. Purdy and James Ruppert, eds., *Nothing but the Truth: An Anthology of Native American Literature* (Upper Saddle River, NJ: Prentice, 2001), 12.

2. Purdy and Ruppert, *Nothing but the Truth*, 12.

Bibliography

Purdy, John L., and James Ruppert, eds. *Nothing but the Truth: An Anthology of Native American Literature*. Upper Saddle River, NJ: Prentice, 2001.

Use this model if you are citing an entire anthology.

28. Selection from an Anthology or an Edited Book

1. Laura Trujillo, "Balancing Act," in *Border-Line Personalities: A New Generation of Latinas Dish on Sex, Sass, and Cultural Shifting*, ed. Robyn Moreno and Michelle Herrera Mulligan (New York: Harper, 2004), 62.

2. Trujillo, "Balancing Act," 62.

Bibliography

Trujillo, Laura. "Balancing Act." In *Border-Line Personalities: A New Generation of Latinas Dish on Sex, Sass, and Cultural Shifting*, edited by Robyn Moreno and Michelle Herrera Mulligan, 61–72. New York: Harper, 2004.

29. More Than One Selection from the Same Anthology or Edited Book

Bibliography

Bond, Ruskin. "The Night Train at Deoli." In Chaudhuri, *Vintage Book*, 415–18.

Chaudhuri, Amit, ed. *The Vintage Book of Modern Indian Literature*. New York: Vintage, 2004.

Vijayan, O.V. "The Rocks." In Chaudhuri, *Vintage Book*, 291–96.

When you cite more than one selection from the same anthology, you can list the anthology as a separate entry with all of the publication information. Also list each selection from the anthology by author and title of the selection, but give only the name(s) of the editor(s) of the anthology, a short title, and the page number(s) for each selection.

30. Article in a Reference Work

1. *Encyclopedia Britannica*, 15th ed., s.v. "Ireland."

If you're citing a widely used reference work, give only the edition and year of publication. In this case, *s.v.* means *sub vero* ("under the word"), which indicates looking up "Ireland" alphabetically in the source.

If the articles in the book are alphabetically arranged, you don't need to give volume and page numbers. If no author is listed, begin with the title of the article. For references with more substantial articles, cite them as you would chapters in a book (see item 28).

31. Second or Later Edition

1. *MLA Handbook for Writers of Research Papers*, 7th ed. (New York: MLA, 2009).

If a book is not a first edition, the edition number is on the title page. Place the abbreviated information (*2nd ed., 3rd ed.*, etc.) between the title and the publication information. Give only the latest copyright date for the edition you are using.

32. Introduction, Preface, Foreword, or Afterword

1. Doug Hesse, foreword to *The End of Composition Studies*, by David W. Smit (Carbondale: Southern Illinois University Press, 2004), xi.

2. Hesse, foreword, xi.

Bibliography

Hesse, Doug. Foreword to *The End of Composition Studies*, by David W. Smit, ix–xiii. Carbondale: Southern Illinois University Press, 2004.

Give first the name of the writer of the part you're citing and then the name of the cited part, without italics or quotation marks. When the introduction, preface, foreword, or afterword has a title, include it before the section name:

Fox-Genovese, Elizabeth. "Mothers and Daughters: The Ties That Bind." Foreword to *Southern Mothers*, iv–xviii. Edited by Nagueyalti Warren and Sally Wolff. Baton Rouge, LA: Louisiana State University Press, 1999.

33. Unpublished Dissertation or Essay

1. Gina Anne Stuart, "Exploring the Harry Potter Book Series: A Study of Adolescent Reading Motivation," (PhD diss, Utah State University, 2006), ProQuest (AAT 3246355).

Give a descriptive label (such as *Diss.* or *Unpublished essay*), followed by the degree-granting institution (for dissertations), and the date. Treat published dissertations as books. In the preceding example, "ProQuest" is the database containing the dissertation, and the number in parentheses is the accession number.

34. Reprint of an Older Book

1. Robert Coover, *A Night at the Movies, Or, You Must Remember This* (Champaign, IL: Dalkey Archive, 2007). First published 1987 by William Heinemann Ltd.

35. Book in a Series or Scholarly Project

1. Jean Hastings Ardell, *Breaking into Baseball: Women and the National Pastime*, Writing Baseball Series (Carbondale: Southern Illinois University Press, 2005).

36. Book with a Title within a Title

1. Robert M. Lumiansky and Herschel Baker, eds, *Critical Approaches to Six Major English Works: "Beowulf" through "Paradise Lost"* (Philadelphia: University of Pennsylvania Press, 1968).

Set the normally independent titles within quotation marks and italicize them.

37. Bible or Sacred Text

Bibliography

Bhagavad Gita. Translated by Juan Mascaro. Rev. ed. New York: Penguin, 2003.

The Holy Bible: New International Version. New York: Harper, 1983.

The Qur'an. Translated by M.A.S. Abdel Haleem. New York: Oxford University Press, 2004.

38. Government Publication

Bibliography

US Senate. Select Committee on Intelligence. *Report on the U.S. Intelligence Community's Prewar Intelligence Assessment of Iraq.* 108th Cong., 1st sess. Washington, DC: Government Printing Office, 2004.

For government publications that name no author, start with the name of the government or government body. Then name the government agency. Then include the title, any series information and publication information. If there is an author, begin with the author's name:

Wallace, David Rains. *Yellowstone: A Natural and Human History; Yellowstone National Park, Idaho, Montana, and Wyoming.* Interior Dept. National Park Service. Official National Park Handbook 150. Washington, DC: Government Printing Office, 2001.

39. Published Proceedings of a Conference

1. Luis Mateus Rocha, ed., *Artificial Life X: Proceedings of the Tenth International Conference on the Simulation and Synthesis of Living Systems* (Cambridge, MA: MIT Press, 2006).

Treat published proceedings as you would chapters in a book.

IMAGES, AUDIO, FILM, AND VIDEO

The Chicago Manual of Style, 16th Edition, includes no examples of notes or bibliographic entries for photographs, illustrations, graphs, or other images. When such materials are reproduced in a paper, CM recommends including a caption beneath the image, with source information included at the end of the caption. However, because student papers often refer to images as sources or discuss them as examples, we have provided some examples here, in CM style.

40. Photograph, Painting, Drawing, Illustration, etc. (Original)

1. Carl Mydans, *General Douglas MacArthur Landing at Luzon, 1945,* photograph displayed at Soho Triad Fine Art Gallery, New York (October 21–November 28, 1999).

2. Mydans, *General Douglas MacArthur.*

Bibliography

Mydans, Carl. *General Douglas MacArthur Landing at Luzon, 1945.* Photograph
displayed at Soho Triad Fine Art Gallery, New York. October 21–November
28, 1999.

Give the name of the image's maker, if known, the title or caption of the
image, the type of image, where you viewed the image, and when. If the image
has no title, provide a brief description.

41. Photograph, Painting, Drawing, Illustration, etc. in a Periodical: Print

1. Herb Greene, *Grace Slick,* photograph, *Rolling Stone,* September 30,
2004: 102.

2. Greene, *Grace Slick,* 102.

Bibliography

Greene, Herb. *Grace Slick.* Photograph. *Rolling Stone* September 30,
2004: 102.

42. Photograph, Painting, Drawing, Illustration, etc. in a Periodical: Online

1. Christopher Morris, *Man in Camouflage,* photograph, *The Atlantic,*
July/August 2011, http://www.theatlantic.com/magazine/archive/2011/07
/invisible-inc/8523/.

2. Morris, *Man in Camouflage.*

Bibliography

Morris, Christopher. *Man in Camouflage.* Photograph. *The Atlantic.* July/
August 2011. http://www.theatlantic.com/magazine/archive/2011/07
/invisible-inc/8523/.

43. Photograph, Painting, Drawing, Illustration, etc. in a Book

Bibliography

"The World's Most Populous Countries." Illustration in *Maps of the
Imagination: The Writer as Cartographer,* by Peter Turchi, 116–17.
San Antonio, TX: Trinity University Press, 2004.

44. Comic or Cartoon

Bibliography

Sutton, Ward. "Ryan's a Late Adopter." Cartoon. *New Yorker,*
May 2, 2011.

45. Slide Show or Photo Essay: Online

Bibliography

Nachtwey, James. *Crime in Middle America. Time,* December 2, 2006.
   Accessed May 4, 2011, http://www.time.com/time/photogallery
   /0,29307,1947522,00.html.

46. Image from a Service or Distributor

Bibliography

World Perspectives. *Launching of the Space Shuttle Columbia, Florida, USA,
   1998.* Photograph. Accessed March 3, 2011, from http://gettyimages.com.
   Getty Images (#AT3775-001).

In this example, the photographer was listed as "World Perspectives." Include
the name of the service or distributor, and the item number or other identifier, if any.

47. Online Map, Chart, or Other Graphic

Bibliography

"Hurricane Rita." Graphic from *New York Times Online,* September 24,
   2005. http://www.nytimes.com/packages/html/national
   /20050923_RITA_GRAPHIC/index.html.

48. Audio Book

   1. Sherry Turkle, *Alone Together: Why We Expect More from Technology
and Less from Each Other,* read by Laural Merlington, Tantor Media,
2011, CD.

49. Sound Recording

Verdi, Giuseppe. *Requiem.* Chicago Symphony Orchestra and Chorus. Ricardo
   Muti. CSO Resound B003WL7EJE, 2010. 2 compact discs.

Put first the name most relevant to what you discuss in your paper (performer, conductor, work performed). Include the recording's title, other
information (performer, composer, conductor), the name of the issuer,
the date the work was issued, the medium, and any additional recording
information.

Radiohead. "Jigsaw Falling into Place." From *In Rainbows.* Radiohead, 2007.
   MP3 file.

50. Podcast

Blumberg, Alex and Adam Davidson. "The Giant Pool of Money." *This
   American Life.* Podcast audio. May 9, 2008. http://www.thisamericanlife
   .org/radio-archives/episode/355/the-giant-pool-of-money.

51. Film, Videotape, or DVD

It Happened One Night. Directed and produced by Frank Capra. 1934; Culver
   City, CA: Sony Pictures, 1999. DVD.

Give the title first, and include the director, the distributor, and the year. For
films that were subsequently released on tape or DVD, provide the original
release date of the movie. Other information (writer, producer, major actors)
is optional but helpful.

   For video downloads, include the download date and the source.

It Happened One Night. Directed and produced by Frank Capra. 1934;
   Accessed December 15, 2010, from Netflix.

52. Video or Film: Online

"Challenger Disaster Live on CNN." YouTube video. Posted by CNN, January
   27, 2011. http://www.youtube.com/watch?v=AfnvFnzs9ls.

53. Television or Radio Program

Include at least the title of the program (in italics), the network, the local
station and its city, and the date of the broadcast.

*Not for Ourselves Alone: The Story of Elizabeth Cady Stanton and Susan B.
   Anthony.* By Ken Burns. Perf. Julie Harris, Ronnie Gilbert, and Sally
   Kellerman. Prod. Paul Barnes and Ken Burns. PBS. WNET, New York.
   8 Nov. 1999.

The Madeleine Brand Show. KPCC, Pasadena. 20 June 2011.

54. Television or Radio Program: Online

   1. "Bill Moyers," *The Daily Show,* with Jon Stewart, Comedy Central, June 1,
2011, http://www.thedailyshow.com/watch/wed-june-22-2005/bill-moyers.

   2. "The Disappearing Incandescent Bulb," *The Madeleine Brand Show,*
KPCC, June 20, 2011, http://www.scpr.org/programs/madeleine-brand/2011/06/20
/the-disappearing-incandescent-bulb/.

OTHER ONLINE SOURCES

55. Entire Web Site

WebdelSol.Com. Ed. Michael Neff. Accessed August 4, 2011.
   http://www.webdelsol.com.

Association for the Advancement of Artificial Intelligence. Accessed October 17,
   2011. http://www.aaai.org/home.html.

56. Page from a Web Site

American Psychological Association. "Think Again: Men and Women Share
   Cognitive Skills." Last modified January 18, 2006. http://www.apa.org
   /research/action/share.aspx.

Provide as much information as you can, starting with the author, if available, and the title of the page, followed by the site information.

57. Online Discussion or Electronic Mailing List Posting

1. Richard Haswell to WPA-L mailing list, October 17, 2005, "A New Graphic/Text Interface," http://lists.asu.edu/archives/wpa-l.html.

58. Chat or Real-Time Communication

Bibliography

Berzsenyi, Christyne. Online discussion of "Writing to Meet Your Match: Rhetoric, Perceptions, and Self-Presentation for Four Online Daters." *Computers and Writing Online*. AcadianaMoo, May 13, 2007. Accessed March 3, 2012. http//acadianamoo.com.

Glenn, Maria. Chat. *Facebook*, September 9, 2010. Accessed September 9, 2010.

Give the name of the speaker or writer, a title for the event (if any), the forum, date, publication medium, access date, and URL if needed.

59. E-Mail Message

1. Tara Martin, "Visit to Los Alamos," e-mail message to author, July 25, 2010.

60. Posting on a Blog

1. Matthew Phillips, "Need to Go to the ER? Not Until the Game's Over," *Freakonomics.com* (blog), June 15, 2011, http://www.freakonomics.com/2011 /06/15/need-to-go-to-the-er-not-until-the-games-over/.

Bibliography

Freakonomics.com (blog), http://www.freakonomics.com/.

61. Wiki

1. *NASCAR Wiki*, s.v. "NASCAR Sprint Cup Series," last modified January 11, 2011, http://nascarwiki.com.

OTHER SOURCES

62. Published or Unpublished Letter

Irvin, William. William Irvin to Lesley Osburn, December 8, 2011.

Williams, William Carlos. William Carlos Williams to his son, March 13, 1935. In *Letters of the Century: America 1900–1999*, edited by Lisa Grunwald and Stephen J. Adler, 225–26. New York: Dial, 1999.

63. Microfiche Collection of Articles

Wenzell, Ron. "Businesses Prepare for a More Diverse Work Force." *St. Louis Post Dispatch*, February 3, 1990: 17. Microform. *NewsBank: Employment* 27 (1990): fiche 2, grid D12.

64. Legal Source

1. Brown v. Bd. of Education, 347 U.S. 483 (1954).

Include the name of the case, the number of the case, the name of the court deciding the case, and the date of the decision. Legal sources can frequently be accessed through a database:

2. Brown v. Bd. of Education, 347 U.S. 483 (1954) LexisNexis Academic.

65. Interview

1. Randi Friedman, telephone interview by author, August 30, 2008.

2. Caro Pope, interview by Amy Standen, Salon.com, April 29, 2002, http://www.salon.com/people/interview/2002/04/29/carlpope.

Note the type of interview, for example "telephone" or "personal" (face-to-face). For a published interview, give the name of the interviewed person first, identify the source as an interview, and then give details as for any published source. Follow the citation format for a periodical, book, or online source, as appropriate.

66. Lecture or Speech

1. Jennifer Katz, "Spiral Galaxies" (lecture in Astronomy 1000, University of Denver, Denver, CO, February 7, 2011).

Bibliography

Katz, Jennifer. "Spiral Galaxies." Lecture in Astronomy 1000, University of Denver, Denver, CO, February 7, 2011.

King, Martin Luther. "I Have a Dream." Speech presented at the Lincoln Memorial, Washington, DC, August 28, 1963. MP3 on American Rhetoric Top 100 Speeches. http://www.americanrhetoric.com/speeches/mlkihaveadream.htm.

If citing only the original, the entry would end after "1963." This entry goes on to cite an online version.

67. Live Performance

Miller, Arthur. *All My Sons*. Directed by Calvin McLean. Performed at the Center for the Performing Arts, Normal, IL, September 27, 2005.

Nelson, Willie. *Country Throwdown Tour*. Performed at Red Rocks Amphitheater, Denver, CO, June 22, 2011.

68. Musical Score

1. Franz Schubert, *Symphony in B Minor (Unfinished)*, ed. Martin Cusid. New York: Norton, 1971.

69. Advertisement

1. Southwest Airlines, advertisement, ABC television, August 24, 2010.

2. Canon Digital Cameras, advertisement, *Time*, June 2, 2003, 77.

3. Budget Truck Rental, advertisement, *Huffington Post*, August 2, 2011, http://www.huffingtonpost.com.

70. Video Game or Software

The Island: Castaway. Computer game. N.p: Awem Studio, 2010.

"N.p." indicates that the place of publication is unknown.

31 CSE-Style Documentation

■ ■ ■ ■ ■ ■ ■

Quick Points You will learn to

➤ Cite your sources according to CSE guidelines.

31A What is CSE-style documentation?

View
the Model
Document

The Council of Science Editors, or CSE, produces a manual called *Scientific Style and Format* to guide publications in the mathematics, the life sciences, and the physical sciences. The information in this chapter adheres to the style guidelines in the seventh edition of that manual. For up-to-date information, go to the organization's Web site at http://www.councilscienceeditors.org.

CSE STYLE has two components: (1) citations within the text, called "in-text references," tied to (2) a bibliography, called "end references," at the end of the text. However, CSE offers three different options for in-text references: the citation-sequence system, the name-year system, and the citation-name system. In this chapter we explain the citation-name system, which the CSE most strongly endorses.

In the citation-name system, the in-text references use numbers to refer to end references that are arranged alphabetically. In other words, first complete the list of end references, arranging them alphabetically by author. Then, number each reference; for example, if you were documenting references by Schmidt, Gonzalez, Adams, and Zurowski, in your end references, they would be arranged:

1. Adams . . .

2. Gonzalez . . .

3. Schmidt . . .

4. Zurowski . . .

Finally, use superscript (raised) numbers for source citations in your sentences that correspond to the numbered author names in the end references. (Numbers in parentheses are also acceptable.)

IN-TEXT REFERENCES—CITATION-NAME

Sybesma[2] insists that this behavior occurs periodically, but Crowder[1] claims never to have observed it.

END REFERENCES—CITATION-NAME

1. Crowder W. Seashore life between the tides. New York: Dodd, Mead; 1931. New York: Dover Reprint; 1975. 372 p.

2. Sybesma C. An introduction to biophysics. New York: Academic; 1977. 648 p.

Quick Box 31.1 gives guidelines for compiling a References list. Especially pay attention to the arrangement of entries in a citation-name system.

When you're citing more than one reference at a time, list each source number in numeric order, followed by a comma with no space. Use a hyphen to show the range of three or more numbers in sequence, and put all in superscript:[2,5-7,9]

Quick Box 31.1 ■ ■ ■ ■ ■ ■ ■ ■ ■

Guidelines for compiling a CSE-style Cited References list

TITLE
Use "Cited References" or "References" as the title (no underlining, no italics, no quotation marks).

PLACEMENT OF LIST
Begin the list on a separate page at the end of the research paper. Number the page sequentially with the rest of the paper.

CONTENT AND FORMAT OF CITED REFERENCES
Include all sources that you quote, paraphrase, or summarize in your paper. Center the title one inch from the top of the page. Start each entry on a new line. Put the number, followed by a period and a space, at the regular left margin. If an entry takes more than one line, indent the second and all other lines under the first word, not the number. Double-space each entry and double-space between entries.

SPACING AFTER PUNCTUATION
CSE style specifies no space after date, issue number, or volume number of a periodical, as shown in the models in 31B.

continued >>

Quick Box 31.1   (continued)

ARRANGEMENT OF ENTRIES
Sequence the entries in alphabetical order by author, then title, etc. Number the entries. Put the number, followed by a period and a space, at the regular left margin.

AUTHORS' NAMES
Reverse the order of each author's name, giving the last name first. For book citations, you can give first names or use only the initials of first and (when available) middle names; for journal citations, use only initials. However, CSE style recommends you use only initials. Don't use a period or a space between first and middle initials. Use a comma to separate the names of multiple authors identified by initials; however, if you use full first names, use a semicolon. Don't use *and* or & with authors' names. Place a period after the last author's name.

TREATMENT OF TITLES
Never underline titles or enclose them in quotation marks. Capitalize a title's first word and any proper nouns. Don't capitalize the first word of a subtitle unless it's a proper noun. Capitalize the titles of academic journals. If the title of a periodical is one word, give it in full; otherwise, abbreviate the title according to recommendations established by the International Organization for Standardization (ISO). Capitalize a newspaper title's major words, giving the full title but omitting *A, An,* or *The* at the beginning.

PLACE OF PUBLICATION
Use a colon after the city of publication. If the city name could be unfamiliar to readers, add in parentheses the postal abbreviation for the US state or Canadian province. If the location of a foreign city will be unfamiliar to readers, add in parentheses the country name, abbreviating it according to ISO standards. Find ISO abbreviations at http://un.org/Depts/cartographic /english/geoinfo/geoname.pdf.

PUBLISHER
Give the name of the publisher, followed by a semicolon. Familiar names can be abbreviated. For example, *John Wiley & Sons, Ltd.* can be shortened to *Wiley*.

PUBLICATION MONTH
Abbreviate all month names longer than three letters to their first three letters, but do not add a period.

continued >>

Quick Box 31.1 (continued)

INCLUSIVE PAGE NUMBERS
Give complete page numbers in ranges: 233–234, 1056–1072.

DISCONTINUOUS PAGE NUMBERS
Give the numbers of all discontinuous pages, separating successive numbers or ranges with a comma: 54–57, 60–66.

TOTAL PAGE NUMBERS
When citing an entire book, give the total number of book pages, followed by the abbreviation *p* and a period, at the end of the citation.

FORMAT FOR CITED REFERENCES ENTRIES: BOOKS
Citations for books usually list author(s), title, publication information, and pages (either total pages when citing an entire work or inclusive pages when citing part of a book). Each unit of information ends with a period.

1. Primrose SB, Twyman RM, Old RW. Principles of gene manipulation. London: Blackwell; 2002. 390 p.

FORMAT FOR CITED REFERENCES ENTRIES: ARTICLES
Citations for articles usually list author(s), article title, and journal name and publication information, each section followed by a period. Abbreviate a journal's name only if it's standard in your scientific discipline. For example, *Exp Neurol* is the abbreviated form for *Experimental Neurology*. In the following example, the volume number is 184, and the issue number, in parentheses, is 1. Notice the lack of a space after the semicolon, before the parentheses, and after the colon.

1. Ginis I, Rao MS. Toward cell replacement therapy: promises and caveats. Exp Neurol. 2003;184(1):61–77.

31B What are CSE guidelines for sources in a list of references?

The directory that follows corresponds to the sample references that follow it. If you need a model not included in this book, consult *Scientific Style and Format*, 7th ed. (2006).

Directory: CSE Style for a Cited References List

BOOKS AND PARTS OF BOOKS

1. Book by One Author

1. Hawking SW. <mark>Black holes and baby universes and other essays.</mark> New York: Bantam; 1993. 320 p.

Use one space but no punctuation between an author's last name and the initial of the first name. Don't put punctuation or a space between first and middle initials (*Hawking SW*).

2. Book by More Than One Author

1. Wegzyn S, Gille JC, Vidal P. <mark>Developmental systems: at the crossroads of system theory, computer science, and genetic engineering.</mark> New York: Springer-Verlag; 1990. 595 p.

3. Book by a Group or Corporate Author

1. Chemical Rubber Company. <mark>Handbook of laboratory safety.</mark> 3rd ed. Boca Raton (FL): CRC; 1990. 1352 p.

4. Anthology or Edited Book

1. Heerrmann B, Hummel S, editors. <mark>Ancient DNA: recovery and analysis of genetic material from paleontological, archeological, museum, medical, and forensic specimens.</mark> New York: Springer-Verlag; 1994. 1020 p.

5. Selection or Chapter in an Anthology or Edited Book

1. Basov NG, Feoktistov LP, Senatsky YV. Laser driver for inertial confinement fusion. In: Bureckner KA, editor. Research trends in physics: inertial confinement fusion. New York: American Institute of Physics; 1992. p. 24–37.

6. Unpublished Dissertation or Thesis

1. Baykul MC. Using ballistic electron emission microscopy to investigate the metal-vacuum interface [dissertation]. [Orem (UT)]: Polytechnic University; 1993. 111 p. Available from: UMI Dissertation Express; http:// tls.il.proquest.com/hp/Products/DisExpress.html, Document 9332714.

7. Published Article from Conference Proceedings

1. Tsang CP, Bellgard MI. Sequence generation using a network of Boltzmann machines. In: Tsang CP, editor. Proceedings of the 4th Australian Joint Conference on Artificial Intelligence; 1990 Nov 8–11; Perth, AU. Singapore: World Scientific; 1990. p. 224–33.

PRINT ARTICLES FROM JOURNALS AND PERIODICALS

8. Article in a Journal

1. Ginis I, Rao MS. Toward cell replacement therapy: promises and caveats. Exp Neurol. 2003;184(1):61–77.

Give both the volume number and the issue number (here, *184* is the volume number and *1* is the issue number). Note that there is no space between the year and the volume, the volume and the issue, or the issue and the pages.

9. Journal Article on Discontinuous Pages

1. Richards FM. The protein folding problem. Sci Am. 1991;246(1):54–57, 60–66.

10. Article with Author Affiliation

1. DeMoll E, Auffenberg T (Department of Microbiology, University of Kentucky). Purine metabolism in *Methanococcus vannielii*. J Bacteriol. 1993;175:5754–5761.

11. Entire Issue of a Journal

1. Whales in a modern world: a symposium held in London, November 1988. Mamm Rev. 1990 Jan;20(9).

The date of the symposium, November 1988, is part of the title of this issue.

12. Newspaper Article

1. Kilborn PT. A health threat baffling for its lack of a pattern. New York Times (Final ed.). 2003 Jun 22;Sect. A:14 (col. 2).

Sect. stands for *section*. Note that there is no space between the date and the section.

CSE
31B

13. Editorial or Review

1. Leshner AI. "Glocal" science advocacy [editorial]. Science. 2008;319(5865):877.

2. Myer A. Genomes evolve, but how? Nature. 2008;451(7180):771. Review of Lynch M, The Origins of Genome Architecture.

CSE allows "notes" after the page number(s) that will help readers understand the nature of the reference.

ELECTRONIC SOURCES ON THE INTERNET

In general, CSE style requires that you cite electronic sources by including the author's name, if available; the work's title; the type of medium, in brackets, such as [*Internet*] or [*electronic mail on the Internet*]; the title of the publication if there's a print version or, if not, the place of publication and the publishing organization; the date the original was published or placed on the Internet; the date you accessed the publication, preceded by the word *cited* enclosed in brackets; and the address of the source, if from the Internet or a database. Omit end punctuation after an Internet address.

14. Books on the Internet

1. Colwell R, editor. MENC handbook of musical cognition and development [Internet]. New York: Oxford University Press; c2006 [cited 2011 Feb 4]. Available from: http://books.google.com/books/

15. Articles with Print Versions on the Internet

1. Pollard R. Evidence of a reduced home field advantage when a team moves to a new stadium. J Sport Sci [Internet]. 2002 [cited 2010 Nov 5]; 20(12):969–974. Available from: http://0-find.galegroup.com.bianca.penlib.du.edu:80/itx /start.do?prodId=AONE

16. Articles Available Only on the Internet

1. Overbye D. Remembrance of things future: the mystery of time. The New York Times on the Web [Internet]. 2005 Jun 28 [cited 2009 Dec 11]. Available from: http://www.nytimes.com/2005/06/28/science/28time.html

17. Web Pages

Begin with author, if available; otherwise, begin with title.

1. Think again: men and women share cognitive skills [Internet]. Washington (DC): American Psychological Association; 2006 [cited 2011 Jan 17]. Available from: http://www.psychologymatters.org/thinkagain.html

2. Welcome to AAAI [Internet]. Menlo Park (CA): Association for the Advancement of Artificial Intelligence; c2008 [cited 2011 Mar 17]. Available from: http://www.aaai.org

18. Videos or Podcasts

1. Wesch M. Web 2.0 . . . the machine is us/ing us [Internet]. 2007 Jan 31 [cited 2010 Dec 14]. Available from: http://www.youtube.com /watch?v=6gmP4nk0EOE

OTHER SOURCES

19. Map

1. Russia and post-Soviet republics [political map]. Moscow: Mapping Production Association; 1992. Conical equidistant projection: 40 × 48 in., color, scale 1:8,000,000.

20. Video Recording

1. Nova—The elegant universe [DVD]. Boston: WGBH; 2004. 2 DVDs: 180 min., sound, color.

21. Presentation Slides

1. Beaudoin E. Fruit fly larvae [PowerPoint slides]. Denver (CO): University of Denver; 2010 Oct 17. 49 slides.

Tab 8
Grammar Basics

■ ■ ■ ■ ■ ■ ■ ■ ■

Tab 8 Grammar Basics

MyCompLab® Visit mycomplab.com for the eText and for resources and exercises on grammar basics.

Parts of Speech and Parts of Sentences

■ ■ ■ ■ ■ ■ ■ ■

Quick Points   You will learn to

➤ Identify the parts of speech.
➤ Identify the parts of sentences (pp. 349–357).

PARTS OF SPEECH

To identify a word's part of speech, see how the word functions in the sentence. Sometimes the same word functions differently in sentences.

Watch
the Video

● We ate **fish**.

   Fish is a NOUN.* It represents a thing.

● We **fish** on weekends.

   Fish is a VERB. It represents an action.

32A   What is a noun?

A **noun** names a person, place, thing, or idea: *student, college, textbook, education*. Quick Box 32.1 (p. 342) lists types of nouns.

Watch
the Video

🌐 **ESOL Tips:** (1) Speakers of languages other than English find it helpful to know whether nouns are count nouns or noncount nouns. We cover this topic in Chapter 60.

(2) Nouns often appear with words that tell how much, how many, whose, which one, and similar information. These words include ARTICLES (*a, an, the*), ADJECTIVES, and other DETERMINERS, which we discuss in Chapters 60–62.

(3) Words with the SUFFIXES (word endings) *-ance, -ence, -ment, -ness*, and *-ty* are usually nouns. We discuss the spelling of suffixes in 46B. ●

32B   What is a pronoun?

A **pronoun** replaces or refers to a noun. The words a pronoun replaces are its **antecedents** (see 35A). Quick Box 32.2 (p. 343) lists types of pronouns.

Watch
the Video

---

* Words printed in SMALL CAPITAL LETTERS are discussed elsewhere in the text and are defined in the Terms Glossary at the back of the book.

Quick Box 32.1 ■ ■ ■ ■ ■ ■ ■ ■ ■ ■

Types of nouns

PROPER	names of specific people, places, or things (first letter is always capitalized)	*Will Smith, Paris, Buick*
COMMON	general things, places, or people	*singer, city, car*
CONCRETE	things experienced through the senses: sight, hearing, taste, smell, and touch	*landscape, pizza, thunder*
ABSTRACT	qualities, states, or ideas	*freedom, shyness*
COLLECTIVE	groups	*family, team*
NONCOUNT	"uncountable" things	*beef, dirt*
COUNT	countable items (singular or plural)	*lake (lakes), minute (minutes)*

Note: Some nouns are more than one type. *Love* is both common and abstract.

- **Sonya** is an architect. [noun]
- **She** is an architect. [pronoun]
- The interior designer needs to consult **her**.

  The pronoun *her* refers to its antecedents, *Sonya* in the first sentence and *she* in the second.

 ESOL Tip: Pronouns and nouns are covered in Chapters 59, 60, 62, and 63. ●

32C What is a verb?

👁 Watch the Video **Verbs** are of two types: main verbs and AUXILIARY VERBS (Ch. 64). **Main verbs** express action, occurrence, or state of being (see Chs. 33 and 64).

- You **danced**.
- The audience **grew** silent.
- Your dancing **was** awesome.

❗ **Alert:** When you're not sure if a word is a verb, try putting it into a different TENSE. If the sentence still makes sense, the word is a verb. (For help with verb tenses, see 33E.)

  NO He is a **changed** person. He is a **will change** person.

  YES The store **changed** owners. The store **will change** owners. ●

Chapters 33 and 64 cover verbs in more detail.

Quick Box 32.2

Types of pronouns

PERSONAL *I, you, they, her, its, ours,* and others	refers to people or things	I saw **her** take a book to **them**.
RELATIVE *who, which, that*	introduces certain NOUN CLAUSES and ADJECTIVE CLAUSES	The book **that** I lost was valuable.
INTERROGATIVE *who, whose, what, which,* and others	introduces a question	**Who** called?
DEMONSTRATIVE *this, these, that, those*	points out the antecedent	Whose books are **these**?
REFLEXIVE, INTENSIVE *myself, themselves,* and other *-self* or *-selves* words	refers to or intensifies the antecedent	They claim to support **themselves**. I **myself** doubt it.
RECIPROCAL *each other, one another*	refers to individual parts of a plural antecedent	We respect **each other**.
INDEFINITE *all, anyone, each,* and others	refers to nonspecific persons or things	**Everyone** is welcome here.

32D What is a verbal?

Verbals are verb forms that function as nouns, adjectives, or ADVERBS. Quick Box 32.3 (p. 344) lists types of verbals.

ESOL Tips: The word *to* has several functions, as discussed in Chapters 62–64. (1) As part of the INFINITIVE *to eat,* the word *to* modifies (limits) the PRONOUN *nothing.*

- He has nothing **to eat**.

(2) *To* can be part of a MODAL AUXILIARY VERB, such as *have to,* which means "must" (see 64B).

- He **has to eat** something.

(3) *To* is also a preposition that must be followed by a noun, pronoun, or gerund OBJECT—in this example, the word *eating* (see 63A).

- He is **accustomed to eating** at noon.

Quick Box 32.3

Types of verbals and functions they perform

INFINITIVE *to* + SIMPLE FORM of verb	1. NOUN: represents an action, state, or condition	**To eat** soon is our goal.
	2. ADJECTIVE or ADVERB: describes or modifies	Still, we have nothing **to eat**.
PAST PARTICIPLE *-ed* form of REGULAR VERB or equivalent for IRREGULAR VERB	ADJECTIVE: describes or modifies	**Boiled, filtered** water is usually safe to drink.
PRESENT PARTICIPLE *-ing* form of verb	1. ADJECTIVE: describes or modifies	**Running** water may not be safe.
	2. NOUN: represents an action, state, or condition*	**Drinking** contaminated water is dangerous.

*A present participle functioning as a noun is called a GERUND.

32E   What is an adjective?

Watch
the Video

Adjectives modify—describe or limit—nouns, pronouns, and word groups that function as nouns.

- I saw a **green** and **leafy** tree.

  Green and *leafy* modify the noun *tree*.

Descriptive adjectives, such as *green* and *leafy*, can show levels of intensity: *green, greener, greenest; leafy, more leafy, most leafy* (36D). **Proper adjectives** emerge from PROPER NOUNS: *American, Victorian*. In addition, words with these suffixes (word endings) are usually adjectives: *-ful, -ish, -less*, and *-like*. (For more about suffixes, see 46B.)

Determiners, sometimes called *limiting adjectives* because they "limit" nouns, tell whether a noun is general (**a** *tree*) or specific (**the** *tree*). Determiners also tell which one (**this** *tree*), how many (**twelve** *trees*), whose (**our** *tree*), and similar information. Quick Box 32.4 lists types of determiners.

🌐 **ESOL Tip:** To provide more help for multilingual writers, we discuss articles extensively in Chapter 60. ●

Quick Box 32.4

Types of determiners

ARTICLES *a, an, the*	**A** reporter working on **an** assignment is using **the** telephone.
DEMONSTRATIVE *this, these, that, those*	**Those** students rent **that** house.
INDEFINITE *any, each, few,* and others	**Few** films today have complex plots.
INTERROGATIVE *what, which, whose*	**What** answer did you give?
NUMERICAL *one, first, two, second,* and others	The **fifth** question was tricky.
POSSESSIVE *my, your, their,* and others	**My** dog is older than **your** cat.
RELATIVE *what, which, whose, whatever,* and others	He is the instructor **whose** course I enjoyed.

32F What is an adverb?

An **adverb** modifies—describes or limits—verbs, adjectives, other adverbs, and CLAUSES.

Watch the Video

- Chefs plan meals **carefully**.

  Carefully modifies the verb *plan*.

- Vegetables provide **very** important vitamins.

  Very modifies the adjective *important*.

- Those french fries are **too** heavily salted.

  Too modifies the adverb *heavily*.

- **Fortunately**, people realize that salt can do harm.

  Fortunately modifies the entire sentence.

Descriptive adverbs show levels of intensity, often by adding *more* (or *less*) and *most* (or *least*): *more happily, least clearly.* Many descriptive adverbs are formed by adding *-ly* to adjectives: *sadly, loudly, normally.* Some adverbs don't end in *-ly: very, always, not,* and *well* are some. Some *-ly* words look like adverbs but are really adjectives: *brotherly, lovely.* (For more on adverbs, see Chapter 36.)

Quick Box 32.5

Conjunctive adverbs and relationships they express

Relationship	Adverbs
ADDITION	*also, furthermore, moreover, besides*
CONTRAST	*however, still, nevertheless, conversely, nonetheless, instead, otherwise*
COMPARISON	*similarly, likewise*
RESULT OR SUMMARY	*therefore, thus, consequently, accordingly, hence, then*
TIME	*next, then, meanwhile, finally, subsequently*
EMPHASIS	*indeed, certainly*

Relative adverbs begin adjective clauses with words like *where, why,* and *when.*

Conjunctive adverbs modify by creating logical connections to express relationships as shown in Quick Box 32.5.

32G What is a preposition?

Watch
the Video
Prepositions are common words that show relationships: *The professor walked into the classroom before the students.* Some common prepositions are *on, in, at, by, for, during, after, over,* and *above.*

Prepositions combine with other words to form PREPOSITIONAL PHRASES. These phrases often express relationships in time or space: *in April, at home.*

🌐 **ESOL Tip:** Prepositions play an important role in PHRASAL VERBS, which multilingual writers need to study closely. We discuss them in Chapter 62. ●

32H What is a conjunction?

A **conjunction** connects words, phrases, or clauses. **Coordinating conjunctions**, which express the types of relationships listed in Quick Box 32.6, join two or more grammatically equivalent structures.

● We hike **and** camp every summer.

And joins two verbs.

● I love the outdoors, **but** my family does not.

But joins two INDEPENDENT CLAUSES.

Quick Box 32.6

■ ■ ■ ■ ■ ■ ■ ■ ■ ■

Coordinating conjunctions and relationships they express

Relationship	Coordinating Conjunction
ADDITION	*and*
CONTRAST	*but, yet*
REASON OR CAUSE	*for*
RESULT OR EFFECT	*so*
CHOICE	*or*
NEGATIVE CHOICE	*nor*

Correlative conjunctions function in pairs. They include *both . . . and, either . . . or, neither . . . nor, not only . . . but (also),* and *whether . . . or.*

● **Not only** students **but also** businesspeople should study a second language.

Subordinating conjunctions introduce DEPENDENT CLAUSES. They show that dependent clauses are less important than the independent clauses.

● **Because** it snowed, the school superintendent canceled all classes.

The important part is that the superintendent canceled classes.

Quick Box 32.7 shows the various relationships subordinating conjunctions express.

Quick Box 32.7

■ ■ ■ ■ ■ ■ ■ ■ ■ ■

Subordinating conjunctions and relationships they express

Relationship	Subordinating Conjunction
TIME	*after, before, once, since, until, when, whenever, while*
REASON OR CAUSE	*as, because, since*
RESULT OR EFFECT	*in order that, so, so that, that*
CONDITION	*if, even if, provided that, unless*
CONTRAST	*although, even though, though, whereas*
LOCATION	*where, wherever*
CHOICE	*rather than, than, whether*

321   What is an interjection?

An **interjection** expresses surprise or strong emotion. When it stands alone, punctuate an interjection with an exclamation point: *Hooray!* As part of a sentence, set off an interjection with a comma or commas: *Hooray, you got the promotion.* Use interjections sparingly, if at all, in ACADEMIC WRITING.

● **EXERCISE 32-1**   Identify the part of speech of each numbered and underlined word. Choose from noun, pronoun, verb, adjective, adverb, preposition, coordinating conjunction, correlative conjunction, and subordinating conjunction. For help, consult 32B through 32I.

The Mason-Dixon line <u>primarily</u>[1] marks the <u>boundary</u>[2] between Pennsylvania and Maryland. It was surveyed in the <u>eighteenth</u>[3] century by Charles Mason and Jeremiah Dixon, who had <u>previously</u>[4] worked together on a <u>scientific</u>[5] expedition to South Africa.

In 1760, the Calverts of Maryland and the Penns of Pennsylvania <u>hired</u>[6] Mason and Dixon to settle a <u>boundary</u>[7] dispute between their parcels <u>of</u>[8] land. Mason and Dixon <u>marked</u>[9] their line every <u>five</u>[10] miles using <u>stones</u>[11] shipped from England, which are called crownstones. These markers were decorated with two coats-of-arms and can still be found scattered <u>throughout</u>[12] this part of the country.

<u>Even though</u>[13] Mason <u>and</u>[14] Dixon were British, <u>they</u>[15] had very different backgrounds. Mason was the son of a baker and trained in astronomy. Dixon was a Quaker, and <u>he</u>[16] specialized in surveying.

The line they drew in America eventually <u>became</u>[17] a <u>symbolic</u>[18] division <u>between</u>[19] free states and slave states <u>until</u>[20] the end of the Civil War. <u>Because of</u>[21] the line's importance, <u>it</u>[22] has been the focus of <u>both</u>[23] literature and music, such as the <u>song</u>[24] "Sailing to Philadelphia" by Mark Knopfler. ●

PARTS OF SENTENCES

32J What are subjects and predicates?

A sentence consists of two basic parts: a **subject** and a **predicate**.

A **simple subject** is the word (or words) that acts, is described, or is acted on: *The **telephone** rang.* A **complete subject** is the subject and all its MODIFIERS: ***The red telephone*** *rang.*

The **simple predicate** consists of the verb: *The telephone **rang**.* The **complete predicate** is the verb and all its modifiers: *The telephone **rang loudly**.* Quick Box 32.8 explains three subject and predicate sentence patterns.

🌐 **ESOL Tip:** Never add a PERSONAL PRONOUN to repeat a stated SUBJECT.

NO   **My grandfather he** lived to be eighty-seven.

YES   **My grandfather** lived to be eighty-seven. ●

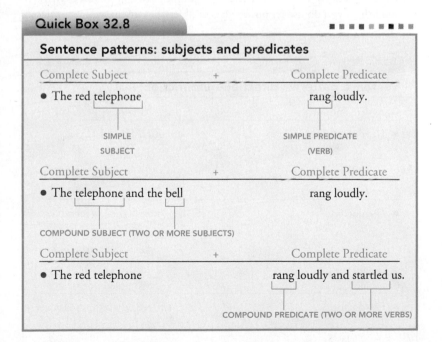

Quick Box 32.8

Sentence patterns: subjects and predicates

Complete Subject	+	Complete Predicate
● The red telephone		rang loudly.

SIMPLE SUBJECT · SIMPLE PREDICATE (VERB)

Complete Subject	+	Complete Predicate
● The telephone and the bell		rang loudly.

COMPOUND SUBJECT (TWO OR MORE SUBJECTS)

Complete Subject	+	Complete Predicate
● The red telephone		rang loudly and startled us.

COMPOUND PREDICATE (TWO OR MORE VERBS)

32K What are direct and indirect objects?

A **direct object** completes the meaning of TRANSITIVE VERBS. To find a direct object, ask *whom?* or *what?* about the verb: *Keisha bought* [what?] **a sweater**. To find an **indirect object**, ask *to whom?* or *for whom?* after the verb: *Keisha bought* [for whom?] **me** *a sweater*. Quick Box 32.9 illustrates direct and indirect objects.

ESOL Tips: (1) In sentences with indirect objects that follow the word *to* or *for*, always put the direct object before the indirect object.

NO   Will you please give **to** John this letter?

YES   Will you please give this letter **to** John?

(2) When a pronoun works as an indirect object, some verbs that go with the pronoun require *to* or *for* before the pronoun.

NO   Please explain **me** the rule.

YES   Please explain the rule **to me**.

(3) Even if a verb doesn't require *to* before an indirect object, you may use *to* if you wish. If you do use *to*, put the direct object before the indirect object.

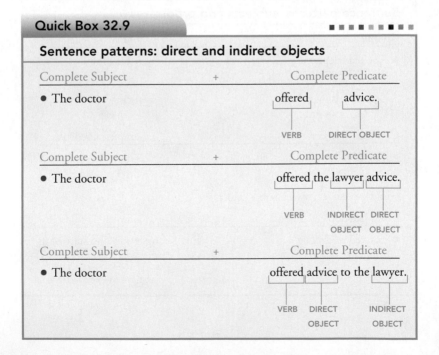

Quick Box 32.9

Sentence patterns: direct and indirect objects

Complete Subject   +   Complete Predicate

• The doctor   offered   advice.

                                     VERB   DIRECT OBJECT

Complete Subject   +   Complete Predicate

• The doctor   offered the lawyer advice.

                    VERB   INDIRECT   DIRECT
                              OBJECT   OBJECT

Complete Subject   +   Complete Predicate

• The doctor   offered advice to the lawyer.

                    VERB   DIRECT   INDIRECT
                              OBJECT   OBJECT

NO   Please give **to me** that book.

YES   Please give that book **to me**.

(4) When both the direct object and the indirect object are pronouns, put the direct object first, and use *to* with the indirect object.

NO   He gave **me it**.

YES   He gave **it to me**. ●

32L   What are complements, modifiers, and appositives?

■ Recognizing complements

A **complement** renames or describes a subject or an object in the predicate of a sentence. A **subject complement** is a noun, a pronoun, or an adjective after a LINKING VERB. An **object complement** is a noun or an adjective after a DIRECT OBJECT. We illustrate both complements in Quick Box 32.10.

■ Recognizing modifiers

A **modifier** is a word or words that function as an adjective or adverb.

● The **large red** telephone rang **loudly**.

   The adjectives *large* and *red* modify the noun *telephone;* the adverb *loudly* modifies the verb *rang*.

● The person **on the telephone** was **extremely** upset.

   The prepositional phrase *on the telephone* modifies the noun *person;* the adverb *extremely* modifies the adjective *upset*.

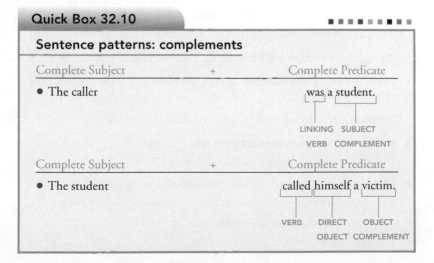

Quick Box 32.10   ■ ■ ■ ■ ■ ■ ■ ■

Sentence patterns: complements

Complete Subject	+	Complete Predicate
● The caller		was a student.

LINKING   SUBJECT
VERB   COMPLEMENT

Complete Subject	+	Complete Predicate
● The student		called himself a victim.

VERB   DIRECT   OBJECT
OBJECT   COMPLEMENT

- **Because the lawyer's voice was calm**, the caller felt reassured.

  Because the lawyer's voice was calm is a single ADVERB CLAUSE; it modifies the independent clause *the caller felt reassured.*

■ Recognizing appositives

An **appositive** renames the noun or pronoun that comes before it.

- The student's story, **a tale of broken promises**, was complicated.

  A tale of broken promises is an appositive that renames the noun *story.*

- The lawyer consulted an expert, **her law professor**.

  Her law professor is an appositive that renames the noun *expert.*

For details about commas with appositives see 47F.

32M What is a phrase?

Watch the Video

A **phrase** is a group of related words not containing both a subject and a predicate. A phrase can never stand alone as a sentence.

A **noun phrase** functions as a noun.

- **The modern population census** started in the seventeenth century.

A **verb phrase** functions as a verb.

- Two military censuses **are mentioned** in the Bible.

A **prepositional phrase**, which starts with a PREPOSITION and contains a noun or pronoun, functions as a modifier.

- William the Conqueror conducted a census **of landowners in 1086**.

  Two prepositional phrases come in a row, beginning with *of* and *in.*

An **absolute phrase** is a noun phrase that modifies the entire sentence.

- **Censuses being the fashion**, Quebec and Nova Scotia took sixteen counts between 1665 and 1754.

A **verbal phrase** is a word group that contains a VERBAL.

- In 1624, Virginia began **to count** its citizens in a census.

  The INFINITIVE PHRASE functions as a direct object.

- **Going from door to door**, census takers interview millions of people.

  The participial phrase functions as an adjective modifying *census takers.*

- **Going from door to door** takes many hours.

  The gerund phrase functions as the subject.

Although both gerund phrases and participial phrases use the *-ing* form of a verb, a **gerund phrase** functions only as a *noun*, whereas a **present-tense participial phrase** functions only as a *modifier*.

● **EXERCISE 32-2**   Combine each set of sentences into a single sentence by converting one sentence into a phrase—a noun phrase, verb phrase, prepositional phrase, absolute phrase, verbal phrase, or gerund phrase. You can omit, add, or change words. Identify which type of phrase you created.

Explore
the
Exercise

You can combine most sets in several correct ways, but make sure the meaning of your finished sentence is clear. For help, consult 32O.

EXAMPLE

Large chain stores often pose threats to local independent retailers. Smaller store owners must find innovative ways to stay in business.

With large chains posing threats to local independent retailers, smaller store owners must find innovative ways to stay in business. (prepositional phrase)

1. Independent stores develop creative marketing strategies to compete with chain stores. Independent stores figure out ways to offer special features.
2. One independent children's bookstore attracted new customers. It did that by bringing live animals into the store.
3. Animals are popular with children. The store purchased two pet chickens, plus tarantulas, rats, cats, and fish.
4. This children's bookstore did not need to lower prices to draw customers. The store could survive by owning animals that appeal to youngsters.
5. Other sorts of independent stores sometimes take a slightly different approach. They compete by offering better service than the large chain stores can.
6. For example, independent hardware and housewares stores can be service oriented and customer friendly. They sometimes can thrive financially doing this.
7. Many independent hardware and housewares store owners have begun to offer home-repair and decorating advice as well as to recommend house calls from staff members. They do this to attract and hold customers.
8. These store owners also feature high-end items that chains do not carry. They feature in-store displays and advertise heavily about their high-end items.
9. Independent hardware and housewares stores often stock fine items such as expensive lawn ornaments, costly brand-name paints, and rare Italian tiles. These stores tend to attract wealthier customers. ●

> ### Quick Box 32.11
>
> #### Sentence patterns: independent clauses
>
> | Complete Subject | + | Complete Predicate |
> |---|---|---|
> | ● The telephone | | rang. |

32N What is a clause?

Watch the Video

A **clause** is a group of words that contains both a subject and a predicate.

▪ Recognizing independent clauses

An **independent** or **main clause** can be a sentence, as in Quick Box 32.11.

▪ Recognizing dependent clauses

A **dependent** or a **subordinate clause** contains both a subject and a predicate, but it cannot stand alone as a sentence (see Quick Box 32.7).

Dependent clauses that start with *subordinating conjunctions* are called **adverb clauses**. They function as adverbs, usually answering one of these questions about the independent clause: *How? Why? When? Under what circumstances?*

- **If the bond issue passes**, the city will install sewers.

  The adverb clause modifies the verb *will install*, explaining under what circumstances.

- They are drawing up plans **as quickly as they can**.

  The adverb clause modifies the verb *are drawing up*, explaining how.

- The homeowners rejoice **because flooding will be controlled**.

  The adverb clause modifies the independent clause, explaining why.

🛈 **Alert:** When an adverb clause comes before its independent clause, the clauses are usually separated by a comma (see 47B). ●

Adjective clauses that are dependent clauses start with RELATIVE PRONOUNS (*who, whom, which, whose,* and *that*) or occasionally with RELATIVE ADVERBS such as *when* or *where*.

- The car **that Jack bought** is practical.

  The adjective clause describes the noun *car*.

- The day **when I can buy my own car** is getting closer.

  The adjective clause modifies the noun *day*.

Quick Box 32.12

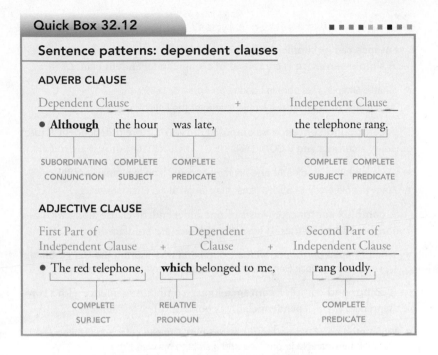

Sentence patterns: dependent clauses

ADVERB CLAUSE

Dependent Clause			+	Independent Clause	
• **Although**	the hour	was late,		the telephone rang,	
SUBORDINATING CONJUNCTION	COMPLETE SUBJECT	COMPLETE PREDICATE		COMPLETE SUBJECT	COMPLETE PREDICATE

ADJECTIVE CLAUSE

First Part of Independent Clause	+	Dependent Clause	+	Second Part of Independent Clause
• The red telephone,		**which** belonged to me,		rang loudly.
COMPLETE SUBJECT		RELATIVE PRONOUN		COMPLETE PREDICATE

Quick Box 32.12 illustrates adverb and adjective clauses.

Noun clauses usually begin with *that, who,* or *which,* but they can also start with *whoever, whichever, when, where, whether, why, what,* or *how.*

- **What politicians promise** is not always dependable.
- Often voters do not know **the truth**.
- Often voters do not know **that the truth is being manipulated**.

Remember, a noun clause is a subject, an object, or a COMPLEMENT; an adjective clause *modifies* a subject, object, or complement.

- Alert voters decide **whom they can trust**.

  Whom they can trust is a noun clause; *whom* has no antecedent.

- Politicians **who make promises** get voters' attention.

  Who make promises is an adjective clause describing *politicians,* the antecedent of *who.*

🛑 **Alert:** A noun clause functioning as a subject takes a *singular* verb: *What most politicians need **is** new careers. How we vote **matters**.* ●

32O What are sentence types?

A **sentence** can be simple, compound, complex, or compound-complex.

Watch
the Video

A **simple sentence** is composed of a single independent clause.

- Charlie Chaplin was born in London on April 16, 1889.
- As a mime, he was famous for his character the Little Tramp.

A **compound sentence** is composed of two or more independent clauses joined by a comma and a COORDINATING CONJUNCTION or just a semicolon.

- Chaplin's father died early, **and** his mother spent time in mental hospitals.
- Many people enjoy Chaplin's films; they laugh at his characters.

A **complex sentence** consists of one independent clause along with one or more dependent clauses. (Dependent clauses are boldfaced.)

- **When Chaplin performed with a troupe that was touring the United States**, he was hired by Mack Sennett, **who owned the Keystone Comedies**.

A **compound-complex sentence** joins a compound sentence with a complex sentence. (The dependent clause is boldfaced.)

- **When studios could no longer afford him**, Chaplin cofounded United Artists, and then he was able to produce and distribute his own films.

● **EXERCISE 32-3** Use subordinate conjunctions and relative pronouns from the following list to combine each pair of sentences. You may use words more than once, but try to use as many different ones as possible. Some sentence pairs may be combined in several ways. Create at least one elliptical construction.

Explore
the
Exercise

since	which	if	after	when	as
although	so that	unless	because	even though	that

EXAMPLE

Bluegrass music is associated with the American South. It has roots in Irish and Scottish folk music.

Even though it has roots in Irish and Scottish folk music, bluegrass is associated with the American South.

1. Certain aspects of jazz seem to have influenced bluegrass. It involves players of an instrumental ensemble improvising around a standard melody.
2. However, the instruments used in jazz are very different than those played in bluegrass. This style of music usually uses a banjo, fiddle, mandolin, and dobro.

3. The singing in bluegrass involves tight harmonies and a tenor lead singer. People who listen closely to the vocal arrangements can hear this.

4. Bill Monroe, the founder of bluegrass, added banjo player Earl Scruggs to his band, the Blue Grass Boys. This allowed him to produce a fuller sound.

5. The Blue Grass Boys went into the studio in 1945 to record some songs for Columbia Records. They hit the charts with "Kentucky Waltz" and "Footprints in the Snow."

6. They began touring America with their own large circus tent. They then became one of the most popular acts in country music.

7. Lester Flatt and Earl Scruggs left Bill Monroe's band. They formed their own group called the Foggy Mountain Boys.

8. A famous Flatt & Scruggs song is considered one of the most popular and difficult to play on the banjo. This song is called "Foggy Mountain Breakdown."

9. Most banjo players cannot play "Foggy Mountain Breakdown" at the same speed that Earl Scruggs plays it. Very skilled players can.

10. Bluegrass must continue to attract new and young fans. Otherwise, it will fade into obscurity. ●

33 Verbs

Quick Points You will learn to

➤ Explain the functions and forms of verbs.
➤ Use verb tenses to express time (pp. 363–366).

33A How do verbs function?

A **verb** expresses an action (*Many people* **overeat** *on Thanksgiving*), an occurrence (*Mother's Day* **fell** *early this year*), or a state of being (*Memorial Day* **is** *tomorrow*). Verbs also convey other information.

Watch the Video

Quick Box 33.1

Types of verbs

MAIN VERB	The word in a PREDICATE that says something about the SUBJECT: *She **danced** for the group.*
AUXILIARY VERB	A verb that combines with a main verb to convey information about TENSE, MOOD, or VOICE (see 33C). The verbs *be, do,* and *have* can be auxiliary verbs or main verbs. The verbs *can, could, may, might, should, would, must,* and others are MODAL AUXILIARY VERBS (see Ch. 64). They add shades of meaning such as ability or possibility to verbs: *She **might dance** again.*
LINKING VERB	A verb that links a subject to a **complement**, a word or words that rename or describe the subject: *She **was** happy dancing. Be* is the most common linking verb; sometimes sense verbs (*smell, taste*) or verbs of perception (*seem, feel*) function as linking verbs. (For a sentence pattern with a linking verb, see Quick Box 32.10.)
TRANSITIVE VERB	A verb followed by a DIRECT OBJECT that completes the verb's message: *They **sent** her a fan letter.* (For sentence patterns with objects, see Quick Box 32.9.)
INTRANSITIVE VERB	A verb that does not require a direct object: *Yesterday she **danced.***

PERSON	First person (the speaker: *I dance*), second person (the one spoken to: *you dance*), or third person (the one spoken about: *the pop star dances*).
NUMBER	Singular (one) or plural (more than one).
TENSE	Past (*we **danced***), present (*we **dance***), or future (*we **will dance***); see 33E.
MOOD	Moods are indicative (*we dance*), imperative (commands and polite requests: *Dance*), or subjunctive (speculation, wishes: *if we were dancing*); see 33F.
VOICE	Active voice or passive voice; see 33G.

Types of verbs vary as listed in Quick Box 33.1.

33B What are the forms of main verbs?

Watch
the Video

The **simple form** expresses an action, occurrence, or state of being in the present (*I laugh*) or, with an AUXILIARY VERB, in the future (*I will laugh*).

The **past-tense form** represents an action, occurrence, or state completed in the past (*I laughed*). Regular verbs add *-ed* or *-d* to the simple form. Irregular verbs vary as listed in Quick Box 33.2.

The **past participle** uses the same form as the past tense for regular verbs. Irregular verbs vary (see Quick Box 32.2). To function as a verb, a past participle must combine with one or more auxiliary verbs: *I have laughed.* Used alone, past participles function as ADJECTIVES: *crumbled cookies.*

The **present participle** is formed by adding *-ing* to the simple form (*laughing*). To function as a verb, a present participle must combine with one or more auxiliary verbs (*I was laughing*). Used alone, present participles function as NOUNS (*Laughing is healthy*) or as adjectives (*my laughing friends*).

Quick Box 33.2

Common irregular verbs

Watch
the Video

Simple Form	Past Tense	Past Participle
awake	awoke *or* awaked	awaked *or* awoken
be	was, were	been
become	became	become
begin	began	begun
break	broke	broken
bring	brought	brought
build	built	built
buy	bought	bought
catch	caught	caught
choose	chose	chosen
cost	cost	cost
deal	dealt	dealt
dive	dived *or* dove	dived
do	did	done
drink	drank	drunk
drive	drove	driven
eat	ate	eaten
fall	fell	fallen
fight	fought	fought
find	found	found
freeze	froze	frozen

continued >>

Quick Box 33.2 (continued)

Simple Form	Past Tense	Past Participle
get	got	got *or* gotten
give	gave	given
go	went	gone
grow	grew	grown
have	had	had
hear	heard	heard
keep	kept	kept
know	knew	known
lay	laid	laid
lead	led	led
lie	lay	lain
lose	lost	lost
make	made	made
read	read	read
ring	rang	rung
run	ran	run
say	said	said
see	saw	seen
send	sent	sent
sing	sang	sung
sink	sank	sunk
sit	sat	sat
sleep	slept	slept
speak	spoke	spoken
stand	stood	stood
steal	stole	stolen
swim	swam	swum
take	took	taken
teach	taught	taught
throw	threw	thrown
wear	wore	worn
write	wrote	written

■ Using regular verbs

Regular verbs form the past tense and past participle by adding *-ed* or *-d* to the simple form: *enter, entered; fix, fixed; smile, smiled.*

■ Using irregular verbs

More than two hundred English verbs are *irregular*, meaning that they form their past tense and past participle in unusual ways. Memorizing the most common **irregular verbs**, listed in Quick Box 33.2, can save you time.

■ Using the -s form of verbs

The *-s* form of a verb is used only in the third-person singular of the present tense. The *-s* ending attaches to the simple form (*laugh, laughs; teach, teaches*).

! **Alert:** Only the verbs *be* and *have* have irregular forms for the third-person singular of the present tense: *is* and *has*. They are the standard third-person singular forms to use in EDITED AMERICAN ENGLISH.

> **NO** Jasper be studying hard because he have to win a scholarship.

> **YES** Jasper **is** studying hard because he **has** to win a scholarship. ●

33C What are auxiliary verbs?

Listen
to the
Podcast

Auxiliary verbs, also called **helping verbs,** combine with MAIN VERBS to make VERB PHRASES.

- Clothing prices **have** [auxiliary verb] **soared** [main verb] recently.

  Have soared is a verb phrase.

- Leather shoes **can** [auxiliary verb] **be** [main verb] expensive.

  Can be is a verb phrase.

Modal auxiliary verbs include *can, could, may, might, must, shall, should, will, would,* and others. Modals communicate meanings of ability, permission, obligation, advisability, necessity, or possibility.

⊕ ESOL Tip: Modal auxiliary verbs can challenge multilingual writers, so we discuss them in detail in Chapter 64. ●

The three frequently used auxiliary verbs *be*, *do*, and *have* vary widely in form.

FORMS OF *BE, DO,* AND *HAVE*

	Be	**Do**	**Have**
SIMPLE FORM	be	do	have
PAST TENSE	was, were	did	had
PAST PARTICIPLE	been	done	had
-S FORM	is	does	has
PRESENT PARTICIPLE	being	doing	having

ESOL Tips: (1) Write with edited American English forms of *be*.

- The gym **is** a busy place. [meaning "it is always that way"]

- The gym **is filling** with young athletes. [meaning "it is happening right now"]

(2) If you use an auxiliary verb with a main verb, the auxiliary verb (not the main verb) often changes to an *-s* form to agree with a third-person singular subject.

- **Does** the gym **close** [*not* closes] at midnight?

33D Should I use *lie* or *lay*?

Listen to the Podcast

Many people confuse the forms of the irregular verbs *lie* ("to recline") and *lay* ("to place something down"). *Lie* is intransitive, so a direct object can *never* follow it. *Lay* is transitive, so a direct object *must* follow it.

	Lie	**Lay**
SIMPLE FORM	lie	lay
PAST TENSE	lay	laid
PAST PARTICIPLE	lain	laid
-S FORM	lies	lays
PRESENT PARTICIPLE	lying	laying

- The hikers are ~~laying~~ *lying* down to rest.
- Yesterday, the hikers ~~laid~~ *lay* down to rest.
- The hikers took off their gear and ~~lay~~ *laid* it on the rocks.

33E What are verb tenses?

The **tenses** of a verb express time. To do this, main verbs change form and combine with auxiliary verbs. **Simple tenses** divide time into the past, the present, and the future. **Progressive forms** show ongoing actions or conditions.

Watch the Video

SIMPLE TENSES

		Progressive Forms
PRESENT	I talk.	I am talking.
PAST	I talked.	I was talking.
FUTURE	I will talk.	I will be talking.

PERFECT TENSES

		Progressive Forms
PRESENT PERFECT	I have talked.	I have been talking.
PAST PERFECT	I had talked.	I had been talking.
FUTURE PERFECT	I will have talked.	I will have been talking.

■ Using the simple present tense

The simple **present tense** describes (1) what is happening now, (2) what is true at the moment, (3) what is generally or consistently true, or (4) what event will take place at a fixed time in the future.

- The tourists **are** on vacation.
- They **enjoy** the sunshine.
- Ocean voyages **make** them seasick.
- Their ship **departs** at midnight.

❶ Alert: Use the present tense to discuss action in literature.

- In *Romeo and Juliet*, Juliet's father **wants** Juliet to marry Paris.
- Shakespeare's play **depicts** the tragedy of ill-fated love. ●

⊕ ESOL Tip: In a dependent clause that begins with *if, when, before, after, until,* or *as soon as,* use the simple present in that clause; use *will* with the verb in the INDEPENDENT CLAUSE.

> **NO** After they **will arrive**, the meeting **will begin**.
>
> **YES** After they **arrive**, the meeting **will** begin. ●

■ **Using tense sequence accurately**

The sequence of verb tenses communicates different time relationships. Accurate sequence becomes an issue only when your sentence contains both an independent clause and a dependent clause. Quick Box 33.3 shows how the **tense sequence** communicates when something is happening, has happened, or will happen.

Quick Box 33.3   ■ ■ ■ ■ ■ ■ ■ ■ ■ ■

Sequence of verb tenses with independent and dependent clauses

Tense in the Independent Clause	Tense to Use in the Dependent Clause
PRESENT	Use *present tense* to show same-time action:
	● I **avoid** shellfish because I *am allergic* to it.
	Use *past tense* to show earlier action:
	● I **am sure** that I *deposited* the check.
	Use *present perfect tense* to show (1) a period of time extending from some point in the past to the present or (2) an indefinite time in the past:
	● They **say** that they *have lived* in Canada since 1979.
	● I **believe** that I *have seen* this movie before.
	Use *future tense* for action to come:
	● The book **is** open because I *will be reading* it later.
PAST	Use *past perfect tense* to show earlier action:
	● The sprinter **knew** that she *had broken* the record.
	Use *present tense* to state a general truth:
	● Columbus **determined** that the world *is* round.
PRESENT PERFECT OR PAST PERFECT	Use *past tense:*
	● The bread **has become** moldy since I *purchased* it.
	● Sugar prices **had** already **declined** when artificial sweeteners first *appeared*.

continued >>

Quick Box 33.3 (continued)

FUTURE	Use *present tense* to show action happening at the same time: • You **will be** rich if you **win** the prize. Use *past tense* to show earlier action: • You **will have** a good chance of winning if you **remembered** to send in your entry form.
FUTURE	Use *present perfect tense* to show future action occurring sooner than the action of the verb in the independent clause: • The river **will flood** again next year unless we **have built** a better dam by then.
FUTURE PERFECT	Use *present tense* or *past perfect tense:* • Dr. Chang **will have delivered** five thousand babies by the time she **retires**. • Dr. Chang **will have delivered** five thousand babies by the time she **has retired**.

● **EXERCISE 33-1** Underline the correct verb in each pair of parentheses that best suits the sequence of tenses. Be ready to explain your choices. For help, consult 33E.

Explore
the
Exercise

EXAMPLE

When he (is, <u>was</u>) seven years old, Yo-Yo Ma, possibly the world's greatest living cellist, (moves, <u>moved</u>) to the United States with his family.

1. Yo-Yo Ma, who (had been born, was born) in France to Chinese parents, (lived, lives) in Boston, Massachusetts, today and (toured, tours) as one of the world's greatest cellists.
2. Years from now, after Mr. Ma has given his last concert, music lovers still (treasure, will treasure) his many fine recordings.
3. Mr. Ma's older sister, Dr. Yeou-Cheng Ma, was nearly the person with the concert career. She had been training to become a concert violinist when her brother's musical genius (began, had begun) to be noticed.
4. Even though Dr. Ma eventually (becomes, became) a physician, she still (had been playing, plays) the violin.
5. The family interest in music (continues, was continuing), for Mr. Ma's children (take, had taken) piano lessons.
6. Although most people today (knew, know) Mr. Ma as a brilliant cellist, he (was making, has made) films as well.

7. One year, while he (had been traveling, was traveling) in the Kalahari Desert, he (films, filmed) dances of southern Africa's Bush people.

8. Mr. Ma first (becomes, became) interested in the Kalahari people when he (had studied, studied) anthropology as an undergraduate at Harvard University.

9. When he shows visitors around Boston now, Mr. Ma has been known to point out the Harvard University library where, he claims, he (fell asleep, was falling asleep) in the stacks when he (had been, was) a student.

10. Indicating another building, Mr. Ma admits that in one of its classrooms he almost (failed, had failed) German. ●

33F What are indicative, imperative, and subjunctive moods?

Mood conveys an attitude toward the action in a sentence. The **indicative mood** expresses statements about real things (*The door **opened***) or highly likely ones (*She **seemed** lost*). Questions about real events and facts are also expressed in the indicative (***Do** you **need** help?*).

The **imperative mood** expresses commands and direct requests (*Please **shut** the door. **Watch** out!*). If the subject is omitted in an imperative sentence, the subject is understood to be *you*.

The **subjunctive mood** expresses conditions that are not literally true or do not currently exist, such as wishes, recommendations, demands, indirect requests, and speculations: *If I **were** you, I **would** ask for directions.*

■ Using the subjunctive with *if, as if, as though,* and *unless* clauses

Many CLAUSES introduced by *if, as if, as though*, and *unless* require the subjunctive, but some don't. Use the subjunctive only when such clauses describe a speculation or condition contrary to fact.

> INDICATIVE   If she **leaves** late, I **will drive** her to the party.
>
> This is a fact, not speculation.
>
> SUBJUNCTIVE   If she **were** [*not* was] **going to leave** late, I **would drive** her to the party.
>
> SUBJUNCTIVE   If it **were** [*not* was] sunny, people **would go out**.

■ Using the subjunctive in *that* clauses

When *that* clauses express wishes, indirect requests, recommendations, and demands, use the subjunctive.

● I wish **that** this party **were** [*not* was] scheduled for tomorrow.

● I requested **that** the birthday cake **be ready** [*not* is ready] at noon.

33G What is "voice" in verbs? .

Voice indicates how the subject relates to the action of the verb. In the **active voice**, the subject performs the action. In the **passive voice**, the subject is acted upon.

Watch the Video

> ACTIVE **Svetlana considers** clams a delicacy.
>
> The subject, *Svetlana*, performs the action.
>
> PASSIVE **Clams are considered** a delicacy by Svetlana.
>
> The subject, *clams*, is acted on by Svetlana.

The active voice—which is usually more direct, concise, and dramatic than the passive voice—emphasizes the doer of an action. The passive voice, however, is appropriate when who or what did the action is unknown or unimportant.

- The lock **was broken** sometime last night.

  The doer of the action is unknown.

- The formula **was discovered** years ago.

  The doer of the action is unimportant.

ESOL Tip: The passive voice works only with TRANSITIVE VERBS. Many English verbs are not transitive, so if you're not certain, check a dictionary. ●

Do not use the passive voice to make your writing seem "lofty."

> NO An experiment **was conducted by me** to demonstrate the existence of carbon.
>
> This is pointless passive that is trying to sound lofty.
>
> YES I **conducted** an experiment to demonstrate the existence of carbon.

● **EXERCISE 33-2** First, determine which sentences are in the active voice and which the passive voice. Second, rewrite each sentence in the other voice, and then decide which voice better suits the meaning. Be ready to explain your choice. For help, consult 33G.

Explore the Exercise

EXAMPLE

In the West African country of Ghana, a few woodcarvers are creating coffins that reflect their occupants' special interests. (*active; change to passive*)

In the West African country of Ghana, *coffins that reflect their occupants' special interests are being created by a few woodcarvers.*

1. A coffin in the shape of a green onion was chosen by a farmer.
2. A hunter's family buried him in a wooden coffin shaped like a leopard.

3. A dead chief was carried through his fishing village by friends and relatives bearing his body in a large pink wooden replica of a fish.
4. The family of a wealthy man who greatly admired cars buried him in a coffin shaped like a Mercedes car.
5. Although a few of these fantasy coffins have been displayed in museums, most of them end up buried in the ground. ●

34 Subject–Verb Agreement
■ ■ ■ ■ ■ ■ ■ ■

Quick Points   You will learn to

➤ Match subjects and verbs in person and number.

34A What is subject–verb agreement?

Watch
the Video

Subject–verb agreement means that SUBJECTS and their VERBS match in **number** (singular or plural) and **person** (see 33A). **Singular** subjects require singular verbs, **plural** subjects require plural verbs, and third-person singular subjects require the -*s* form of present-tense verbs and AUXILIARIES.

The examples in Quick Box 34.1 show how the -*s* ending works in most cases.

Quick Box 34.1   ■ ■ ■ ■ ■ ■ ■ ■ ■

Subject-verb agreement

● The **student**   **works** long hours.
      SINGULAR   SINGULAR
      SUBJECT   VERB

● The **students**   **work** long hours.
      PLURAL   PLURAL
      SUBJECT   VERB

ESOL Tip: Although some spoken versions of English don't observe rules of agreement, for ACADEMIC WRITING, you'll want to observe these rules.

34B Can I ignore words between a subject and its verb?

For subject-verb agreement, you can ignore words between a subject and verb.

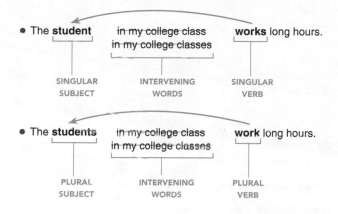

- The **student**   in my college class   **works** long hours.
  in my college classes

  SINGULAR SUBJECT   INTERVENING WORDS   SINGULAR VERB

- The **students**   in my college class   **work** long hours.
  in my college classes

  PLURAL SUBJECT   INTERVENING WORDS   PLURAL VERB

NO   The **winners** in the state competition **goes** to the national finals.

Winners is the subject, so the verb must agree with it. *In the state competition* is a PREPOSITIONAL PHRASE that comes before the verb, and it does not alter subject-verb agreement.

YES   The **winners** in the state competition **go** to the national finals.

To locate the subject of a sentence, first eliminate any PREPOSITIONAL PHRASES. What remains usually makes the subject stand out.

NO   The **moon**, as well as the stars, **are** visible in the night sky.

Moon is the subject, so the verb needs to agree with it. *Are* does not agree with *moon*.

YES   The **moon**, as well as the stars, **is** visible in the night sky.

■ Using *one of the*

The subject *one of the* takes a singular verb to agree with the word *one*. (This is not true of the construction *one of the . . . who;* see 34G.)

● **EXERCISE 34-1**   Use the subject and verb in each set to write two complete sentences—one with a singular subject and one with a plural subject. Keep all verbs in the present tense. For help, consult 34A and 34B.

Explore the Exercise

EXAMPLE

bird, sing

SINGULAR SUBJECT: When a *bird sings*, you will know spring is here.

PLURAL SUBJECT: When *birds sing*, you will know spring is here.

1. chair, rock
2. leaf, fall
3. river, flow
4. clock, tick
5. singer, sing
6. girl, laugh
7. hand, grab
8. loaf, rise ●

34C How do verbs work when subjects are connected by *and*?

👁 Subject joined by *and* are plural and require a plural verb.

Watch the Video

● **The student and the instructor**   **work** long hours.

COMPOUND SUBJECT (USES *AND*)   PLURAL VERB

● **The Cascade Diner and Joe's Diner have** [*not* has] fried catfish today.

However, use a singular verb for subjects joined by *and* that refer to a single person or thing.

● **Spaghetti and meatballs is** [*not* are] the special tomorrow.

▪ Using *each* and *every*

Each and *every* are singular PRONOUNS and always require singular verbs.

● **Each** human hand and foot **leaves** a distinctive print.
● **Every** human hand and foot **leaves** a distinctive print.

34D How do verbs work when subjects are connected by *or*?

When *or*, *nor*, or *but* join subjects, the verb agrees only with the subject nearest it.

Either the instructor or / Either the instructors or → **the student** | **knows** the answer

SINGULAR SUBJECT — SINGULAR VERB

Either the instructor or / Either the instructors or → **the students** | **know** the answer.

PLURAL SUBJECT — PLURAL VERB

34E How do verbs work with indefinite pronouns?

Indefinite pronouns refer to nonspecific people or things. They are usually singular, so they usually take singular verbs.

))•
Listen
to the
Podcast

COMMON INDEFINITE PRONOUNS

another	each	everything	nothing
anybody	either	neither	somebody
anyone	every	nobody	someone
anything	everyone	no one	something

- **Neither** of these directions **seems** [*not* seem] simple.
- **Everything** about these roads **is** [*not* are] dangerous.
- **Each** of the roads **has** [*not* have] to be resurfaced.

A few indefinite pronouns—*none, some, more, most, any,* and *all*—can be either singular or plural, depending on the meaning of the sentence.

- **Some** of our streams **are** polluted; **some** pollution **is** reversible, but **all** pollution **is** a threat to the balance of nature.

  The first *some* refers to the plural *streams*, so the plural verb *are* agrees with it; the second *some* and *all* refer to the singular word *pollution*, so the singular verb *is* agrees with them.

34F How do verbs work with *who*, *which*, and *that*?

When *who, which,* or *that* is the subject of a CLAUSE, the verb agrees with the noun or pronoun to which *who, which,* or *that* refers (its ANTECEDENT).

- Each of us **who are** graduating knows our distinguished director well.
- David Pappas is the student **who assists** our director.
- It is David **who is** introducing her.

34G How do verbs work with *one of the . . . who?*

Use a plural verb following the phrases *one of the . . . who, one of the . . . that,* and *one of the . . . which.*

- Here is **one of the books that are** [*not* is] recommended.
- Its author is **one of the experts who are** [*not* is] addressing us today.
- Music file sharing is **one of the topics which are** [*not* is] featured.

However, always follow the phrase *the only one of the* with a singular verb to agree with *the only one.*

- He is **the only one of the authors who is** [*not* are] speaking today.
- Music file sharing is **the only one of the topics which is** [*not* are] featured today.

34H How do verbs work in other complicated types of subject–verb agreement?

■ Finding the subject in inverted word order

Inverted word order (*In walked the mayor*) reverses the order of subject and verb but has no effect on subject–verb agreement. In statements and questions (which are often inverted), verbs and subjects agree.

- Across the street **stand** [*not* stands] many **protestors**.
- **Are they** serious about their demands?

■ Finding the subject with an expletive

It and *there* form **expletives** when they introduce a verb that precedes its subject. The expletive *it* requires a singular verb; after the expletive *there*, subjects and verbs agree.

- **It is** astronomers who study the planets.
- There **are** nine **planets** in our solar system.
- There **is** probably no **life** on eight of them.

■ Agreeing with the subject, not the subject complement

A verb agrees with its subject, not the SUBJECT COMPLEMENT, the NOUN or ADJECTIVE that follows a LINKING VERB.

| NO | The worst **part** of owning a car **are** the bills. |

The verb *are* agrees with the subject complement *bills.*

YES   The worst **part** of owning a car **is** the bills.

Now singular *part* agrees with singular *is*.

YES   **Bills are** the worst part of owning a car.

The sentence is rewritten to make the plural noun *bills* the subject, so the plural verb *are* is correct.

■ Making verbs agree with collective nouns

Listen
to the
Podcast

A **collective noun** names a group of people or things, such as *family, group, audience, class,* or *number*. When the group acts as one unit, use a singular verb. When the members of the group act individually, use a plural verb.

- The senior **class has** [*not* have] 793 people in it.

Here, *class* operates as one unit, so the singular verb *has* agrees with it.

- The senior **class were** [*not* was] **fitted** for their graduation robes today.

Here, *class* means the people in the class acting as individual members within the group, so the plural verb phrase *were fitted* agrees with it.

① **Alert:** Notice that the pronouns also agree with the nouns to which they refer (*it* agrees with *class, their* agrees with *class*). ●

■ Making verbs agree with subjects that specify amounts

Use a singular verb with a subject that specifies an amount of money, time, weight, or distance considered as one unit.

- **Ninety cents is** the current bus fare.
- **Two miles passes** quickly for a serious jogger.

In contrast, when a subject refers to units of measurement, each of which is considered individually rather than as a unit, use a plural verb.

- **Eighteen inches are** marked off on that ruler.
- **Fifty percent** of these peaches **are** rotten.

■ Making verbs agree with singular subjects in plural form

A few subjects look plural, particularly those naming fields of study (*statistics, mathematics, economics, physics*). These take singular verbs when they mean the field of study, but they are plural when they refer to items of data. Some other subjects (*news, measles, gallows*) look plural but are always singular.

- **Statistics is** an especially demanding major.
- **Statistics show** that a recession is inevitable.
- This **news is** making voters nervous.

Some other nouns that end in *-s* may be singular or plural, as shown by their meaning in the sentence.

- Six new television **series are** beginning this week.
- A **series** of setbacks **has** plagued their debut.
- One **means** to fame **is** producing a successful television show.
- *Jersey Shore*'s **means** to high ratings **include** sex appeal and shock behavior.

■ Using singular verbs with titles, terms, and plural words representing a single unit

The title of a work or a series of words used as a term is a single unit. Therefore, use a singular verb, even when the title or term contains plural words.

- *Cats* **was** [*not* were] a popular musical.
- **"Protective reaction strikes" is** a euphemism for bombing.

  The entire expression *"protective reaction strikes"* acts as a single unit; it therefore calls for the singular verb *is*.

Used alone, the word *states* is always plural. However, the name *United States* refers to a single country, so it takes a singular verb.

- **The United States has** [*not* have] a large television industry.

Explore the Exercise

● **EXERCISE 34-2** This exercise covers all of subject–verb agreement (34A through 34H). Supply the correct form of the verb in parentheses.

EXAMPLE

Of the thirty thousand plant species on earth, the rose (to be) <u>is</u> the most universally known.

1. Each plant species (to invite) _____ much discussion about origins and meanings, and when talk turns to flowers, the rose is usually the first mentioned.
2. More fragrant and colorful (to be) _____ other types of flowers, yet roses (to remain) _____ the most popular worldwide.
3. Each of the types of roses (to symbolize) _____ beauty, love, romance, and secrecy.
4. There (to be) _____ more than two hundred pure species of roses and thousands of mixed species, thirty-five of which (to flourish) _____ in the soil of North America.

5. It's impossible to determine exactly where or when the first rose (to be) _____ domesticated, because roses have existed for so many centuries; one of the earliest references dates back to 3000 BC.

6. One myth from Greek mythology (to suggest) _____ that the rose first appeared with the birth of the goddess Aphrodite.

7. Another myth, which focuses on the rose's thorns, (to say) _____ that an angry god shot arrows into the stem to curse the rose forever with arrow-shaped thorns.

8. While theories of this kind (to explain) _____ the significance and evolution of the rose, few people can explain the flower's enduring popularity.

9. Even today, a couple (to demonstrate) _____ love by purchasing red roses.

10. Of all flowers, the best seller (to remain) _____ the rose. ●

35 # Pronouns: Agreement, Reference, and Case
■ ■ ■ ■ ■ ■ ■ ■

Quick Points   You will learn to

➤ Match pronouns with their antecedents.
➤ Use pronouns with clear reference (pp. 379–381).
➤ Use the proper pronoun case (pp. 382–387).

PRONOUN–ANTECEDENT AGREEMENT

35A   What is pronoun–antecedent agreement?

Pronoun–antecedent agreement means that a PRONOUN must match the grammatical form of the word or words it refers to (the pronoun's ANTECEDENT). For example, if an antecedent is third-person singular, the pronoun that refers to it needs to be third-person singular, too (see Quick Box 35.1).

Watch the Video

Quick Box 35.1 ■ ■ ■ ■ ■ ■ ■ ■ ■

Pronoun-antecedent agreement

● Loud **music** has **its** harmful side effects.

SINGULAR   SINGULAR
ANTECEDENT PRONOUN

● The **musicians** damaged **their** auditory nerves.

PLURAL   PLURAL
ANTECEDENT PRONOUN

35B How do pronouns work when *and* connects antecedents?

Watch
the Video

Two or more antecedents joined by *and* require a plural pronoun, even if each antecedent is itself singular.

● **Chris and Pat** homeschool **their** children.

One exception occurs when *each* or *every* comes before singular NOUNS joined by *and*. In such cases, a singular pronoun is correct.

● **Every car and truck** that comes through the border station has **its** [*not* their] contents inspected.

Each car and truck is separate.

Another exception occurs when singular nouns joined by *and* refer to a single person or thing. In such cases, a singular pronoun is correct.

● Our **guide and translator** told us to watch out for traffic as **she** [*not* they] helped us off the tour bus.

The guide is the same person as the translator.

35C How do pronouns work when *or* connects antecedents?

Some antecedents are joined by the word *or* or *nor*. In addition, CORRELATIVE CONJUNCTIONS such as *either . . . or* and *not only . . . but (also)* can join anteced-ents. These antecedents can mix masculine and feminine as well as SINGULAR and PLURAL. However, for the purposes of agreement, ignore everything before the final antecedent.

Either the speakers or the **microphone** needs **its** wiring repaired.

SINGULAR ANTECEDENT — SINGULAR PRONOUN

Either the microphone or the **speakers** need **their** wiring fixed.

PLURAL ANTECEDENT — PLURAL PRONOUN

35D How do pronouns work when their antecedents are indefinite pronouns?

INDEFINITE PRONOUNS point to no particular person, thing, or idea (see 34E). They are generic and take on meanings according to the sentence they're in.

Indefinite pronouns are usually singular: *Anyone who knows the answer should raise **his or her** hand.* Some indefinite pronouns can be either singular or plural (*none, some, more, most, any, all*), depending on the meaning of the sentence.

- **None** fear that **they** will fail.

  All in the group expect to pass; the plural pronoun *they* shows this meaning.

- **None** fears that **he or she** will fail.

  No one expects to fail; the singular pronouns *he or she* show this meaning.

The pronouns *each* and *every* are singular, no matter what words follow.

- **Each** of the students handed in ~~their~~ _{his or her} final term paper.
- **Every** student in my classes is studying ~~their~~ _{his or her} hardest.

Be especially careful about agreement when you use the words *this* (singular) and *these* (plural): *This kind of hard work has **its** advantages. These kinds of difficult jobs have **their** advantages.*

! **Alert:** The expression *he or she* operates as a single unit and therefore calls for a singular antecedent. Generally, however, try to avoid this awkward expression by switching to plural forms. ●

35E How do pronouns work when antecedents are collective nouns?

A COLLECTIVE NOUN names a group of people or things, such as *family, group, audience, class,* or *number* (see 34H). When the group acts as one unit, a singular pronoun can refer to it. However, when the members of the group act individually, a plural pronoun should be used.

● The **audience** cheered as **it** rose to applaud.

The singular pronoun *it* conveys that the audience is acting as one unit.

● The **audience** put on **their** coats and walked to the exits.

The plural pronoun *their* conveys that audience members are acting as many individuals.

Explore the Exercise

● **EXERCISE 35-1** Underline the correct pronoun in parentheses. For help, consult 35A through 35E.

EXAMPLE

Many wonder where inventors like Benjamin Franklin get (his or her, <u>their</u>) creative energy.

1. Many so-called Founding Fathers are famous for one or two of (his, his or her, their) accomplishments, but anyone who knows (his, her, his or her, their) history knows that Franklin is known for many things, including (his, her, his or her, their) inventions.
2. The armonica is not one of his well-known inventions, but (its, their) design is ingenious.
3. Also called the glass harmonica, the armonica required a person to place (himself, herself, himself or herself) in front of the instrument and to rotate (its, their) glass bowls.
4. The lightning rod and the Franklin stove established his reputation as an inventor, but (it, they) remained in public domain because Franklin refused to secure patents for his inventions.
5. An inventor like Franklin does not limit (his, her, his or her, their) imagination to one field of science.
6. (He, She, He or she, They) can instead pursue many questions and the challenges (they, it) pose.
7. All scientists who study electricity should know that Ben Franklin provided the names (he, she, he or she, they) still use today for positive and negative electrons.
8. Franklin also named the Gulf Stream and mapped (their, its) current.
9. Franklin formed the first public lending library in America, which allowed people to borrow (its, their) books and read them at (his, her, his or her, their) leisure.

10. His public service record also includes the reform of the postal system and the establishment of The Academy and College of Philadelphia, which later merged (their, its) students with those of the State of Pennsylvania to become the University of Pennsylvania. ●

PRONOUN REFERENCE

35F How can I avoid unclear pronoun reference?

In sentences that contain more than one logical antecedent, meaning can get muddled.

UNCLEAR PRONOUN REFERENCE	In 1911, Roald Amundsen reached the South Pole just thirty-five days before Robert F. Scott arrived. **He** [*Amundsen or Scott?*] had told people that he was going to sail north to the Arctic, but then **he** [*Amundsen or Scott?*] turned south for the Antarctic.
REVISED	In 1911, Roald Amundsen discovered the South Pole just thirty-five days before Robert F. Scott arrived. Amundsen had told people that he was going to sail north to the Arctic, but then he turned south for the Antarctic.

In addition, when too much material comes between a pronoun and its antecedent, readers often lose track of the meaning.

● Alfred Wegoner, a German meteorologist and professor of geophysics at the University of Graz, was the first to suggest that all the continents on earth were originally part of one large landmass. According to his theory, the supercontinent broke up long ago and the fragments drifted apart. Slowly, these fragments formed the pattern of landmasses and oceans that we know today. Although they do so slowly over centuries, the landmasses are continuing to move. H̲e̲ named this supercontinent Pangaea.

(Wegener inserted above "He")

Wegener, the antecedent of *he*, may be too distant for readers. Remember to keep your pronouns and antecedents close.

35G How do pronouns work with *it*, *that*, *this*, and *which*?

Too often writers use the words *it*, *that*, *this*, and *which* carelessly, making it difficult for readers to understand what's being referred to.

NO	Comets usually fly by the earth at 100,000 mph, whereas asteroids sometimes collide with the earth. **This** interests scientists.
	This could refer to the speed of comets, comets flying by the earth, or asteroids colliding with the earth.

> **YES**   Comets usually fly by the earth at 100,000 mph, whereas asteroids sometimes collide with the earth. **This difference** interests scientists.

In ACADEMIC WRITING, avoid imprecise statements such as "It said on the news . . ." or "In Washington, they say . . ."

> **NO**   In California, **they say** that no one feels a minor earthquake.
>
> Who are *they?*
>
> **YES**   **Residents of California say** that no one feels a minor earthquake.

35H   When do I use *you* for direct address?

Reserve *you* for **direct address**, writing that speaks directly to the reader. Avoid using *you* in generalizations referring to people, situations, or occurrences.

> **NO**   Prison uprisings often happen when you allow overcrowding.
>
> The reader did not allow the overcrowding.
>
> **YES**   Prison uprisings often happen when prisons are overcrowded.

35I   When do I use *who, which,* and *that?*

Who refers to people and animals mentioned by name.

- **Theodore Roosevelt, who** served as the twenty-sixth U.S. president, inspired the creation of the stuffed animal called the teddy bear.
- **Lassie, who** was known for her intelligence and courage, was actually played by a series of male collies.

Which and *that* refer to animals, things, and sometimes anonymous or collective groups of people. Quick Box 35.2 shows how to choose *that* or *which.* (For help in using commas with *that* and *which,* see 47F.)

Explore the Exercise

● **EXERCISE 35-2**   Revise so that each pronoun refers clearly to its antecedent. Either replace pronouns with nouns or restructure the material to clarify pronoun reference. For help, consult 35F through 35I.

EXAMPLE

People who return to work after years away from the corporate world often discover that business practices have changed. They may find fiercer competition in the workplace, but they may also discover that they are more flexible than before.

HERE IS ONE POSSIBLE REVISION: *People who return to work after years away from the corporate world often discover that business practices have changed. Those people may find fiercer competition in the workplace, but they may also discover that business practices are more flexible than before.*

Most companies used to frown on employees who became involved in office romances. They often considered them to be using company time for their own enjoyment. Now, however, managers realize that happy employees are productive employees. With more women than ever before in the workforce and with people working longer hours, they have begun to see that male and female employees want and need to socialize. They are also dropping their opposition to having married couples on the payroll. They no longer automatically believe that they will bring family matters into the workplace or stick up for each other at the company's expense.

One departmental manager had doubts when a systems analyst for research named Laura announced that she had become engaged to Peter, who worked as a technician in the same department. She told her that either one or the other might have to transfer out of the research department. After listening to her plea that they be allowed to work together on a trial basis, the manager reconsidered. She decided to give Laura and Peter a chance to prove that their relationship would not affect their work. The decision paid off. They demonstrated that they could work as an effective research team, right through their engagement and subsequent marriage. Two years later, when Laura was promoted to assistant manager for product development and after he asked to move also, she enthusiastically recommended that Peter follow Laura to her new department. ●

Quick Box 35.2 ■ ■ ■ ■ ■ ■ ■ ■ ■

Choosing between *that* and *which*

In informal writing, you can use either *that* or *which* in a restrictive clause (a clause that is essential to the sentence's meaning), as long as you do so consistently in each piece of writing. However, in academic writing, your instructor and peers usually expect you to use *that*.

● The zoos **that most children like** display newborn and baby animals.

The clause *that most children like* is essential to the meaning of the sentence; if you remove it, the meaning changes substantially.

Use *which* in a NONRESTRICTIVE CLAUSE (a clause that isn't essential to the sentence's meaning).

● Zoos, **which most children like**, attract more visitors if they display newborn and baby animals.

The clause *which most children like* is not essential to the meaning of the sentence; if you remove it, the meaning of the sentence doesn't change substantially.

PRONOUN CASE

Watch
the Video

35J What is pronoun case?

Case shows the relationship (subject, object, possession) of nouns and pronouns to other words in a sentence. Pronouns use different forms in different cases (subjective, objective, possessive). Nouns change form only in the possessive case. (For use of the apostrophe in the possessive, see Chapter 50.)

35K What are personal pronouns?

Personal pronouns refer to persons or things. Quick Box 35.3 shows the case forms of personal pronouns (subjective, objective, and possessive) in both the singular and the plural.

Most questions about pronoun case concern *who/whom* and *whoever/whomever*. For a full discussion, see 35P.

Watch
the Video

35L How can I select the correct case?

When you're unsure whether to use the SUBJECTIVE CASE or the OBJECTIVE CASE, try the three-step test shown in Quick Box 35.4.

35M Which case is correct when *and* connects pronouns?

When *and* connects more than one noun, one pronoun, or a noun and a pronoun, it forms a **compound subject** or a compound object. Compounding doesn't affect pronoun case—use the same case for all the pronouns.

COMPOUND PRONOUN SUBJECT	**He and I** saw the solar eclipse.
COMPOUND PRONOUN OBJECT	That eclipse astonished **him and me**.

Quick Box 35.3 ■ ■ ■ ■ ■ ■ ■ ■ ■

Case forms of personal pronouns

	Subjective	Objective	Possessive
SINGULAR	I, you, he, she, it	me, you, him, her, it	mine, yours, his, hers, its
PLURAL	we, you, they	us, you, them	ours, yours, theirs

Quick Box 35.4   ■ ■ ■ ■ ■ ■ ■ ■ ■

Using the "QA case test"

((•
Listen
to the
Podcast

These examples use pronouns. The test also works with nouns.

Step 1   Write the sentence twice, once using the subjective case and once using the objective case. Then cross out enough words to isolate the element you're questioning.

Janet and me learned about the moon.

Janet and I learned about the moon.

Step 2   Omit the crossed-out words and read both sentences aloud to see which one sounds right.

Me learned about the moon. [No, this doesn't sound right.]

I learned about the moon. [This sounds right.]

Step 3   Select the correct version and restore what you crossed out.

Janet and I learned about the moon.

Whenever you're unsure of whether to use pronouns in the subjective or objective case, use the QA case test in Quick Box 35.4 to get the answer.

- **She and I** [*not* Her and me, She and me, *or* Her and I] work as a team.
- He trained **her and me** [*not* she and I, her and I, *or* she and me] well.

🚫 Alert: As objects of PREPOSITIONS, PRONOUNS are in the objective case.

NO   Mrs. Parks gave an assignment to Sam and I.

YES   Mrs. Parks gave an assignment to **Sam and me**.

NO   Mrs. Parks divided the work between **he and I**.

YES   Mrs. Parks divided the work between **him and me**.●

35N   How can I match case in appositives?

Match an APPOSITIVE to the same case as the word or words it renames. If you're uncertain which case to use, see the QA case test in Quick Box 35.4 to help you determine the answer.

- **We** [*not* Us] tennis players practice hard.

  The subjective pronoun *we* renames the subject *tennis players*.

- The winners **she and I** [*not* her and me] advanced to the finals.

  The subjective pronouns *she and I* rename the subject *winners*.

- The coach trains **us** [*not* we] tennis players to practice hard.

  The objective pronoun *us* renames the object *tennis players*.

- The crowd cheered the winners, **her and me** [*not* she and I].

  The objective pronouns *her and me* rename the object *winners*.

350 How does the subjective case work after linking verbs?

A pronoun that comes after a LINKING VERB either renames the SUBJECT or shows possession. In such cases, always use a pronoun in the subjective case.

- The contest winner was **I** [*not* me].

  I renames the subject, which is the noun *contest winner*, so the subjective-case *I* is correct.

- The prize was **mine**.

  Mine shows possession, so the possessive-case *mine* is correct.

35P When do I use *who*, *whoever*, *whom*, and *whomever*?

Listen to the Podcast

The pronouns *who* and *whoever* are in the subjective case. The pronouns *whom* and *whomever* are in the objective case.

Whenever you're unsure of whether to use the subjective-case *who* and *whoever* or the objective-case *whom* and *whomever*, use a variation of the QA case test in Quick Box 35.4. For *who* and *whoever*, substitute *he, she,* or *they*. For *whom* and *whomever*, substitute *him, her,* or *them*.

- **Who/Whom** is coming to your party?

  He/She are coming to your party, so *who* is correct.

- Will you let **whoever/whomever** into the house?

  You will let *him/her* into the house, so *whomever* is correct.

In sentences with more than one CLAUSE, isolate the clause with the pronoun (shown in **boldface**), and apply the test.

- Give the package to **whoever/whomever is at the door**.

  He is at the door, so *whoever* is correct.

- Invite those guests **who/whom you can trust**.

  You believe you can trust *them*, so *whom* is correct.

- I will invite **whoever/whomever I wish to come**.

  I wish *them* to come, so *whomever* is correct.

- I will invite **whoever/whomever pleases me**.

  He pleases me so *whoever* is correct.

- I will not invite strangers **who/whom show up at the house**.

  They show up at the house, so *who* is correct.

- Don't Twitter people **who/whom I did not invite**.

  I did not invite *them*, so *whom* is correct.

- If uninvited guests arrive, I will tell the police **who/whom they are**.

  They are *they* (not *them*), so *who* is correct.

Remember that *who* and *whoever* can function only as SUBJECTS or SUBJECT COMPLEMENTS in clauses. If the person(s) you refer to perform some action or are linked to a subject, *who/whoever* is correct.

35Q What case do I use after *than* and *as*?

When a pronoun follows *than* or *as*, choose its case according to the meaning you want to convey. These two sentences convey very different messages.

> SENTENCE 1   My sister loved that dog more than **me**.
> SENTENCE 2   My sister loved that dog more than **I**.

Sentence 1 means "My sister loved that dog more than she loved me" because the pronoun *me* is in the objective case. Sentence 2 means "My sister loved that dog more than I loved it" because the pronoun *I* is in the subjective case.

To make sure that your sentences using *than* or *as* deliver the message you intend, mentally fill in the implied words.

35R What case do I use with infinitives and *-ing* words?

When you use INFINITIVES, make sure that your pronouns are in the objective case. This rule holds whether the pronoun is the subject or the object of the infinitive.

- Our tennis coach expects **me *to serve***.

  Me is the subject of the infinitive *to serve*.

- Our tennis coach expects **him *to beat* me**.

  Me is the object of the infinitive *to beat*.

With *-ing* words, the POSSESSIVE CASE can change a sentence's meaning entirely. For example, the following two sentences convey very different messages simply because of the change in case of the noun *man*. The same distinction applies to both nouns and pronouns.

SENTENCE 1   The detective noticed the **man** staggering.

Man is in the objective case.

SENTENCE 2   The detective noticed the **man's** staggering.

Man's is in the possessive case.

Sentence 1 means that the detective noticed the *man*. In contrast, sentence 2 means that the detective noticed the *staggering*. The same differences exist for the following two sentences, which use pronouns.

SENTENCE 3   The detective noticed **him** staggering.

SENTENCE 4   The detective noticed **his** staggering.

35S What case do I use for *-self* pronouns?

Pronouns that end in *-self* (singular) or *-selves* (plural) usually refer to the subject of the sentence. They have a limited number of case forms.

FIRST PERSON	myself; ourselves
SECOND PERSON	yourself; yourselves
THIRD PERSON	himself, herself, itself; themselves

-Self pronouns are called **reflexive pronouns** when they refer to the subject. They cannot be subjects.

- She freed **herself** from a difficult situation.
- They allowed **themselves** another break from work.
- He is not **himself** today.
- Their new business can't possibly pay for **itself**.

Never use a reflexive pronoun in place of a subject or an object.

NO   The detective and **myself** had a long talk. He wanted my partner and **myself** to help him.

The reflexive pronoun *myself* does not refer to the subject; it is the subject.

YES   The detective and **I** had a long talk. He wanted my partner and **me** to help him.

-Self pronouns are called **intensive pronouns** when they provide emphasis by intensifying the meaning of a nearby word: *The detective felt that his **career itself** was at risk.*

● **EXERCISE 35-3** Underline the correct pronoun of each pair in parentheses. For help, consult 35J through 35S.

Explore
the
Exercise

EXAMPLE

Ricky Jay holds the world's record for card throwing; no one can throw a playing card faster than (he/him).

(1) Many magicians agree that no one is better at sleight-of-hand magic than (he/him). (2) Younger magicians often say that Ricky Jay influenced (their/them) to become professional performers. (3) In addition to (him/his) being a respected sleight-of-hand artist, Jay is also a scholar and historian. (4) His interest in strange performers led (him/he) to write *Learned Pigs and Fireproof Women*, which discusses unusual acts and begins with (him/his) explaining their appeal to audiences. (5) Jay's acting career has involved (his/him) performing in several different movies and TV shows. (6) In the James Bond film *Tomorrow Never Dies*, few could have played a villain as well as (he/him). (7) Other roles include (him/his) narrating the introduction to the movie *Magnolia*. (8) Overall, few performers have had such as varied and interesting career as (him/he). ●

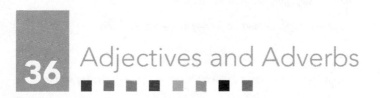

36 Adjectives and Adverbs

■ ■ ■ ■ ■ ■ ■ ■

Quick Points   You will learn to

➤ Distinguish between adjectives and adverbs.
➤ Use adjectives and adverbs properly (pp. 388–392).

36A   What are the differences between adjectives and adverbs?

Both **adjectives** and **adverbs** are MODIFIERS. Modifiers describe other words. Adjectives and adverbs, however, modify very different parts of speech.

Watch
the Video

WHAT ADJECTIVES MODIFY

| NOUNS | The *busy* lawyer rested. |
| PRONOUNS | **She** felt *tired*. |

WHAT ADVERBS MODIFY

VERBS	The lawyer **spoke** *quickly*.
ADVERBS	The lawyer spoke *very* **quickly**.
ADJECTIVES	The lawyer was *extremely* **busy**.
INDEPENDENT CLAUSES	*Undoubtedly*, **the lawyer needed a rest**.

Many adverbs end in *-ly* (*run **swiftly***), but some do not (*run **often***). Also, some adjectives end in *-ly* (***friendly*** *dog*). Therefore, never depend entirely on an *-ly* ending to identify a word as an adverb.

36B What's wrong with double negatives?

👁
Watch
the Video

A **double negative** is nonstandard. STANDARD ENGLISH requires only one negative (for example, *no, not, never, none, nothing,* or *hardly*) in a sentence.

NO The union members did **not** have **no** money in the reserve fund.

Two negatives, *not* and *no*, are used in the same sentence, contrary to the rules of standard English.

YES The union members did **not** have **any** money in the reserve fund.

Only one negative, *not*, is in this sentence.

YES The union members had **no** money in the reserve fund.

36C Do adjectives or adverbs come after linking verbs?

LINKING VERBS use adjectives as COMPLEMENTS. ACTION VERBS use adverbs.

- Anne **looks** *happy*.

  Here *looks* functions as a linking verb, so the adjective *happy* is correct.

- Anne **looks** *happily* at the sunset.

  Here *looks* functions as an action verb, so the adverb *happily* is correct.

■ Using *bad* and *badly*

🔊
Listen
to the
Podcast

Never substitute *badly* (adverb) for *bad* (adjective) after linking verbs such as *feel, smell,* and *taste.*

NO The student **felt** *badly*, so he went home.

Here *felt* links the adverb *badly* to *student*, a noun subject.

YES The student **felt** *bad*, so he went home.

Here *felt* links the adjective *bad* to *student*, a noun subject.

■ Using *good* and *well*

Good is always an adjective. *Well* is an adjective only when it is referring to health; otherwise, *well* is an adverb.

● You look **well**.

This means "You look to be in fine health." *Well* functions as an adjective.

● You write **well**.

This means "You write skillfully." *Well* functions as an adverb.

● **EXERCISE 36-1** Underline the correct uses of negatives, adjectives, and adverbs by selecting between the choices in parentheses. For help, consult 36A through 36C.

Explore the Exercise

EXAMPLE

Because she was only five when her father died, Bernice King, Martin Luther King's youngest child, (barely, bare) remembers the details of her father's (solemnly, solemn) funeral, yet her father's image lives (strong, strongly) within her.

1. Although she did feel (badly, bad) about her father's death when she was younger, King's daughter has managed to put his influence on her to good use by speaking (passionately, passionate) about issues her father first introduced.
2. In her (widely, wide) acclaimed book of sermons and speeches, titled *Hard Questions, Hard Answers*, Bernice King strives to deal with the (intensely, intense) topic of race relations.
3. Bernice King believes, as did her father, that all people must connect (genuinely, genuine), or they won't (never, ever) manage to coexist.
4. Bernice King decided to enter the ministry after she heard a (deeply, deep) voice within her directing her to this (extremely, extreme) (spiritually, spiritual) profession.
5. Bernice King entered the public eye when she gave a (locally, local) televised Martin Luther King Day sermon at her father's church, and since then she has lived (happily, happy) in her home in Atlanta with memories of her father that are (peacefully, peaceful) recollections. ●

36D What are correct comparative and superlative forms?

When adjectives and adverbs show comparisons, most forms are regular.

Listen to the Podcast

■ Regular forms of adjectives and adverbs

In the **comparative**, used to compare two items, regular adjectives and adverbs add either an *-er* ending or the word *more* or *less*. In the **superlative**, used to compare three items or more, regular forms add either an *-est* ending or the word *most* or *least*.

Positive [1]	Comparative [2]	Superlative [3+]
green	greener	greenest
early	earlier	earliest
selfish	less selfish	least selfish
beautiful	more beautiful	most beautiful

[1] That tree is **green**.

[2] That tree is **greener** than this tree.

[3+] That tree is the **greenest** tree on the block.

The number of syllables in the adjective or adverb usually determines whether you use *-er* or *more* (comparative) or *-est* or *most* (superlative).

- Add *-er* and *-est* to one-syllable adjectives and adverbs: *large, larger, largest* (adjective); *far, farther, farthest* (adverb).
- Use *more* and *most* for adverbs with two or more syllables: for example, *easily, more easily, most easily*.
- Use either the *-er* and *-est* endings or *more* and *most* for two-syllable adjectives. The only way to know which forms are correct is to check the dictionary. The forms vary greatly.
- Add *more* and *most* to adjectives and adverbs with three or more syllables: *protective, more protective* [*not* "protectiver"], *most protective* [*not* "protectivest"].

🚫 **Alert:** Never use *more* or *most* together with the *-er* or *-est* ending. For example, *more louder* and *most soonest* are incorrect forms. ●

■ Irregular forms of adjectives and adverbs

Few adjectives and adverbs are irregular in the comparative and superlative.

Positive [1]	Comparative [2]	Superlative [3+]
good [adjective]	better	best
well [adverb]	better	best
well [adjective]		
bad [adjective]	worse	worst
badly [adverb]	worse	worst

Positive [1]	Comparative [2]	Superlative [3+]
many	more	most
much	more	most
some	more	most
little	less	least

[1]   The Millers had **little** trouble finding jobs.

[2]   The Millers had **less** trouble finding jobs than the Smiths did.

[3+]   The Millers had the **least** trouble finding jobs of everyone.

⓵ **Alert:** Use *less* to refer to NONCOUNT NOUNS and *fewer* to refer to numbers and COUNT NOUNS: *They consumed **fewer calories** by using **less sugar.*** ●

36E   Why do I avoid using too many nouns as modifiers?

Nouns sometimes modify other nouns: *truck driver, train track, security system.* Usually, these combinations don't trouble readers. However, when you string together too many nouns in a row as modifiers, you challenge readers to distinguish nouns that are modifying from nouns that are being modified. You can revise such sentences in several ways.

SENTENCE REWRITTEN

NO   The traffic accident vehicle description form instructions are clear.

YES   The form for descriptions of vehicles in traffic accidents has clear instructions.

NOUN REVISED TO POSSESSIVE CASE

NO   Some students might take the **US Navy engineering training examination**.

YES   Some students might take the **US Navy's examination** for **engineering training**.

NOUN REVISED TO PREPOSITIONAL PHRASE

NO   Our **student adviser training program** has won merit awards.

YES   Our **training program for student advisers** has won merit awards.

This revision also requires the plural *advisers*. Plural nouns are generally changed to singular when used as modifiers.

ESOL Tips: (1) Never add *-s* to an adjective, even when it modifies a plural noun.

> **NO**   The instructor taught us **hards lessons**.
>
> **YES**   The instructor taught us **hard lessons**.

(2) Never put an adverb between a VERB and a DIRECT OBJECT.

> **NO**   He drank **quietly** the cola.
>
> **YES**   He **quietly** drank the cola.
>
> **YES**   He drank the cola **quietly**. ●

Explore
the
Exercise

● **EXERCISE 36-2**   Underline the better choice in parentheses. For help, consult this entire chapter.

EXAMPLE

Alexis, a huge and powerful six-year-old Siberian tiger, (curious, <u>curiously</u>) explores her new zoo home together with five other tigers.

1. The new tiger home at the world-famous Bronx Zoo is a (special, specially) designed habitat, planted with (dense, denser) undergrowth so that it (close, closely) imitates the tigers' natural wilderness.

2. Like tigers in the wild, the six tigers in this habitat, which (more, many) experts consider the (more authentic, most authentic) of all artificial tiger environments in the world, will face some of the physical challenges and sensory experiences that keep them happy and (healthy, healthier).

3. Research shows that tigers feel (bad, badly) and fail to thrive in zoos without enrichment features placed in (good, well) locations to inspire tigers to stalk (stealthy, stealthily) through underbrush, loll (lazy, lazily) on heated rocks, or tug (vigorous, vigorously) on massive pull toys.

4. Wildlife zoologists think that the new Tiger Mountain exhibit will also serve zoo visitors (good, well) by allowing them to observe and admire the amazing strength, agility, and intelligence of a (rapid, rapidly) dwindling species.

5. Today, (fewer, less) than 5,000 Siberian tigers remain in the wild, which makes it imperative for zoos to raise people's awareness of the (great, greatest) need to prevent the extinction of these big cats that are considered among the (more, most) powerful, beautiful animals in the world. ●

Tab 9
Sentences and Words

CHAPTERS
37–46

Tab 9 Sentences and Words

MyCompLab® Visit mycomplab.com for the eText and for resources and exercises on sentences and words.

37 Sentence Fragments

■ ■ ■ ■ ■ ■ ■ ■

Quick Points You will learn to

➤ Identify sentence fragments.
➤ Correct sentence fragments (pp. 395–398).
➤ Use intentional sentence fragments when appropriate (p. 398).

37A How can I recognize sentence fragments?

A **sentence fragment** is a written error because it looks like a sentence but isn't one. Even though it starts with a capital letter and ends with a period, it's not a sentence. If you avoid the four types of sentence fragments listed in Quick Box 37.1, your sentences will be complete.

Watch
the Video

Quick Box 37.1

■ ■ ■ ■ ■ ■ ■ ■ ■

How to recognize four types of sentence fragments

Watch
the Video

1. If a word group starts with a SUBORDINATING CONJUNCTION,* such as *when*, without being joined to a complete sentence, it's a sentence fragment (see 37B).

   FRAGMENT When winter comes early.

   CORRECT When winter comes early, ice often traps whales in the Arctic Ocean.

   CORRECT Winter comes early.

2. If a word group includes no VERB and ends with a period, it's a sentence fragment.

   FRAGMENT Whales in the Arctic Ocean.

   CORRECT Whales **live** in the Arctic Ocean.

   Note that a VERBAL (the ones ending in *-ing* or *-ed*) is not a verb unless it teams up with an AUXILIARY VERB, such as *is* or *are* (see 37C).

   ──── **continued >>** ────

---

* Words printed in SMALL CAPITAL LETTERS are discussed elsewhere in the text and are defined in the Terms Glossary at the back of the book.

393

> **Quick Box 37.1**   (continued)
>
> Verbals beginning with *to*, called INFINITIVES, remain as verbals. Auxiliary verbs have no effect on them.
>
> **FRAGMENT**   **Whales living in the Arctic Ocean**.
>
> **CORRECT**   Whales **are living** in the Arctic Ocean.
>
> 3. If a word group lacks a SUBJECT and ends with a period, it's a sentence fragment (see 37D).
>
> **FRAGMENT**   **Were trapped by the solid ice**.
>
> **CORRECT**   The whales **were trapped by the solid ice**.
>
> 4. If a word group is the second half of a COMPOUND PREDICATE and stands alone ending in a period, it's a sentence fragment. Compound predicates always start with one of the seven COORDINATING CONJUNCTIONS (*and, but, so, yet, for, or, nor;* see 37E).
>
> **FRAGMENT**   The whales panicked in the confines of the ice. **And thrashed about, bumping into each other**.
>
> **CORRECT**   The whales panicked in the confines of the ice **and thrashed about, bumping into each other**.

Explore the Exercise

● **EXERCISE 37-1**   Identify each word group as either a complete sentence or a fragment. If the word group is a sentence, circle its number. If it's a fragment, tell why it's incomplete. For help, see Quick Box 37.1.

EXAMPLE

Although antibacterial soaps have become popular. [Starts with a subordinating conjunction (*although*), which creates dependence, and lacks a full sentence to complete the thought.]

1. Because antibacterial soaps do not provide protection against viruses.
2. Viruses responsible for a variety of common health problems.
3. Regular soap often successfully eliminates bacteria, viruses, and dirt.
4. Indicate that antibacterial soaps may wash away useful bacteria.
5. Eliminates most of the harmful bacteria as effectively as regular soap.
6. Careful hand washing cannot be stressed enough.
7. To work efficiently, antibacterial soaps, even those purchased in health food stores.
8. Most studies show that antibacterial soaps do not lead to resistant bacteria.
9. Although many people still believe they should not use antibacterial soaps.
10. Bacteria from overuse of antibiotics. ●

37B How can I correct a fragment that starts with a subordinating word?

First, you want to become entirely familiar with the list of SUBORDINATING CONJUNCTIONS (complete list appears in section 32H). If a word group starts with a subordinating conjunction without being joined to a complete sentence, it's a sentence fragment.

FRAGMENT **Because the ship had to cut through the ice.**

CORRECT **Because the ship had to cut through the ice**, the rescue effort took time.

The sentence fragment starts with the subordinating conjunction *because* and ends in a period, so it's a word group, not a complete sentence. Attaching the fragment to the start of an added complete sentence corrects the error.

CORRECT The rescue effort took time **because the ship had to cut through the ice**.

Attaching the fragment to the end of an added complete sentence corrects the error.

CORRECT **The ship had to cut through the ice**.

Dropping the subordinating conjunction *because* from the fragment corrects the error.

Unless they start a question, the subordinating words *who* or *which* create a special type of sentence fragment.

FRAGMENT **Who feared the whales would die without enough space for air.**

CORRECT The ship's noisy motor worried the crew, **who feared the whales would die without enough space for air.**

Attaching the *who* sentence fragment at the end of the complete sentence, where it makes sense, corrects the error.

FRAGMENT **Which sent booming sound waves through the water.**

CORRECT The ship's noisy motor, **which sent booming sound waves through the water**, worried the crew.

Placing the *which* fragment in the middle of the complete sentence, where it makes sense, corrects the error.

CORRECT The ship's noisy motor, **which sent booming sound waves through the water**, worried the crew, **who feared the whales would die without enough space for air.**

Combining both the *who* and *which* sentence fragments with the complete sentence creates a richly textured message.

37C How can I correct a fragment that lacks a verb?

If a word group includes no VERB and ends with a period, it's a sentence fragment. In looking for a verb, don't mistake a verbal for a complete verb. Verbals ending in *-ing* or *-ed* become verbs only when teamed up with an AUXILIARY VERB. Verbals beginning with *to*, called INFINITIVES, remain as verbals; auxiliary verbs have no effect on them.

> **FRAGMENT** The sailors **debating** whether **to play** classical music over the ship's sound system.

> **CORRECT** The sailors **were debating** whether **to play** classical music over the ship's sound system.

> Adding the auxiliary verb *were* to *debating* creates a complete verb, which corrects the error. *To play* doesn't change.

An APPOSITIVE is a descriptive word group that lacks a verb, so it can't stand alone as a sentence. An appositive needs to be placed within a sentence immediately next to what it describes.

> **FRAGMENT** **An enormously powerful icebreaker**. The ship arrived to free the whales.

> **CORRECT** **An enormously powerful icebreaker**, the ship arrived to free the whales.

> **CORRECT** The ship, **an enormously powerful icebreaker**, arrived to free the whales.

> The appositive placed immediately next to "the ship" within the sentence corrects the error.

If a TRANSITIONAL EXPRESSION (complete list in Quick Box 7.3) starts a word group that lacks a verb, it's a sentence fragment.

> **FRAGMENT** **Such as Bach's sonatas for flute**.

> **CORRECT** The ship's crew chose Bach's sonatas for flute.

> **CORRECT** The crew wanted to play high-pitched music, **such as Bach's sonatas for flute**.

> The sentence fragment revised into a complete sentence or attached to a nearby sentence corrects the error.

37D How can I correct a fragment that lacks a subject?

If a word group lacks a SUBJECT and ends with a period, it's a sentence fragment.

> **FRAGMENT** **Had heard recordings of the high-pitched calls whales make**.

CORRECT	Some crew members **had heard recordings of the high-pitched calls whale make**.

Inserting the subject *Some crew members* at the start of the fragment corrects the error.

37E How can I correct a fragment that's a part of a compound predicate?

Many types of COMPOUND PREDICATES occur in sentences. One type contains two or more verbs connected by a COORDINATING CONJUNCTION (*and, but, for, or, nor, yet, so*). When a compound predicate isn't attached to the end of its companion sentence, it is a sentence fragment.

FRAGMENT	With a flute concerto playing loudly on its speakers, the ship finally reached the whales. **And led them to freedom**.

CORRECT	With a flute concerto playing loudly on its speakers, the ship finally reached the whales **and led them to freedom**.

Joining the compound predicate to the end of the complete sentence corrects the error.

CORRECT	With a flute concerto playing loudly on its speakers, the ship finally reached the whales. **The ship led them to freedom**.

Dropping *and* and inserting a subject "the ship" corrects the error.

● **EXERCISE 37-2** Revise this paragraph to eliminate all sentence fragments. In some cases, you can combine word groups to create complete sentences; in other cases, you must supply missing elements to revise word groups. Some sentences may not require revision. In your final version, check not only the individual sentences but also the clarity of the whole paragraph. Refer to 37A through 37E for help.

Explore the Exercise

(1) The English games cricket and rounders. (2) Are the forerunners of the American game baseball. (3) Which became popular in America in the nineteenth century. (4) According to the *New York Morning News*, in an article from 1845. (5) Members of the New York Knickerbockers Club played the first reported baseball game. (6) Taking place at Elysian Fields in Hoboken, New Jersey. (7) Creating one of baseball's first teams, and writing "20 Original Rules of Baseball." (8) Alexander Cartwright is often called The Father of Baseball. (9) By scholars and historians of the game. (10) His new rules, which became known as Knickerbocker Rules. (11) Changed baseball in a number of ways. (12) Such as giving each batter three strikes and each inning three outs. (13) The first game, therefore. (14) That used the Knickerbocker Rules was played on June 19, 1846, in New Jersey. (15) Acting as umpire for this

game. (16) Cartwright charged six-cent fines for swearing. (17) The Knicker-bockers lost this game by 22 points to a team. (18) That was known as "The New York Nine." ●

37F What are intentional fragments?

Professional writers sometimes intentionally use sentence fragments for empha-sis and effect. Today, such fragments are not unusual in popular magazines and in written advertisements. A writer's ability to judge the difference between acceptable and unacceptable sentence fragments comes from much experience writing as well as exposure to the works of skilled writers. Some instructors consider a sentence fragment an error in ACADEMIC WRITING. Other teachers occasionally accept well-placed intentional fragments after a student has shown the consistent ability to write well-constructed complete sentences. Therefore, if you'd like to use a fragment for emphasis and effect, we advise that you either inquire about your teacher's stance ahead of time or write a footnote in your essay that says you're using a sentence fragment intentionally for effect.

Comma Splices and Run-On Sentences

38

Quick Points   You will learn to

➤ Identify comma splices and run-on sentences.
➤ Correct comma splices and run-on sentences (pp. 400–402).

38A What are comma splices and run-on sentences?

Comma splices and run-on sentences are errors that incorrectly join two INDE-PENDENT CLAUSES. A **comma splice** is created when only a comma separates independent clauses. A **run-on sentence** is created when no punctuation at all separates independent clauses (see Quick Box 38.1).

COMMA SPLICE   The storm **intensified, it** turned toward land.

RUN-ON SENTENCE   The storm **intensified it** turned toward land.

Quick Box 38.1

■ ■ ■ ■ ■ ■ ■ ■ ■

How to identify and correct comma splices and run-on sentences

1. Watch out for a second independent clause that starts with a PERSONAL PRONOUN.

👁
Watch
the Video

COMMA SPLICE	Thomas Edison was a productive **inventor, he held** more than 1,300 American and foreign patents.
RUN-ON SENTENCE	Thomas Edison was a productive **inventor he held** more than 1,300 American and foreign patents.
CORRECT	Thomas Edison was a productive **inventor. He held** more than 1,300 American and foreign patents.

2. Watch out for a CONJUNCTIVE ADVERB that joins two sentences.

COMMA SPLICE	Thomas Edison was a brilliant **scientist, however,** he spent only three months in school.
RUN-ON SENTENCE	Thomas Edison was a brilliant **scientist however,** he spent only three months in school.
CORRECT	Thomas Edison was a brilliant **scientist; however,** he spent only three months in school.

3. Watch out for a TRANSITIONAL EXPRESSION that joins two sentences.

COMMA SPLICE	Thomas Edison invented the **microphone, in addition, he created** a superior storage battery.
RUN-ON SENTENCE	Thomas Edison invented the **microphone in addition, he created** a superior storage battery.
CORRECT	Thomas Edison invented the **microphone. In addition, he created** a superior storage battery.

4. Watch out when a second independent clause explains or gives an example of the information in the first independent clause.

COMMA SPLICE	Edison created **many inventions,** his best known include the phonograph and the incandescent lamp.
RUN-ON SENTENCE	Edison created **many inventions** his best known include the phonograph and the incandescent lamp.
CORRECT	Edison created many **inventions.** His best known include the phonograph and the incandescent lamp.

! Alert: Occasionally, experienced writers use a comma to join short, contrasting independent clauses: *Mosquitoes do not **bite, they** stab.* Your teacher may consider this punctuation an error, so check before you use it. ●

38B How can I correct comma splices and run-on sentences?

Watch the Video

To correct comma splices and run-on sentences, you can use punctuation or a coordinating conjunction, or you can revise one of the two incorrectly joined sentences into a DEPENDENT CLAUSE.

■ Using punctuation

You can use a period or a semicolon to separate independent clauses in a comma splice or run-on sentence.

COMMA SPLICE	A shark's skeleton is all **cartilage, the shark** does not have a bone in its body.
RUN-ON SENTENCE	A shark's skeleton is all **cartilage the shark** does not have a bone in its body.
CORRECT	A shark's skeleton is all **cartilage. The shark** does not have a bone in its body.

■ Using a coordinating conjunction

If the ideas in your independent clauses relate closely in meaning and are grammatically equivalent, you can connect them with a comma followed by a coordinating conjunction (*and, but, for, or, nor, yet, so*).

COMMA SPLICE	Every living creature sends a weak electrical charge in **water,** a shark can detect these signals.
RUN-ON SENTENCE	Every living creature sends a weak electrical charge in **water** a shark can detect these signals.
CORRECT	Every living creature sends a weak electrical charge in **water, *and*** a shark can detect these signals.

■ Revising an independent clause into a dependent clause

If one of two independent clauses expresses information that can be logically subordinated to the other independent clause, start it with a subordinating word and join it correctly to the independent clause.

COMMA SPLICE	Costa Rica's Cocos Island harbors more sharks than anywhere else on **earth, it is** paradise to underwater filmmakers.

RUN-ON SENTENCE	Costa Rica's Cocos Island harbors more sharks than anywhere else on **earth it is** paradise to underwater filmmakers.
CORRECT	***Because*** Costa Rica's Cocos Island harbors more sharks than anywhere else on **earth, it is** paradise to underwater filmmakers.
	Because makes the first clause dependent.
COMMA SPLICE	Some sharks have large, triangular **teeth, these** teeth can tear flesh.
RUN-ON SENTENCE	Some sharks have large, triangular **teeth these** teeth can tear flesh.
CORRECT	Some sharks have large, triangular **teeth *that*** can tear flesh.
	That makes the second clause dependent.

When a conjunctive adverb (such as *however, therefore, also, next, then, thus, furthermore,* or *nevertheless*) or a transitional expression (such as *for example* or *for instance*) falls between spliced or run-on independent clauses, you need to use a period or a semicolon to correct the error.

COMMA SPLICE	Some sharks cannot **bite, for example**, the whale shark filters plants through its tiny mouth.
RUN-ON SENTENCE	Some sharks cannot **bite for example**, the whale shark filters plants through its tiny mouth.
CORRECT	Some sharks cannot **bite. For example**, the whale shark filters plants through its tiny mouth.
CORRECT	Some sharks cannot **bite; for example**, the whale shark filters plants through its tiny mouth.

● **EXERCISE 38-1** Working individually or with your peer-response group, identify and then revise the comma splices and run-on sentences. Circle the numbers of correct sentences. For help, consult 38A and 38B.

Explore the Exercise

EXAMPLE

COMMA SPLICE	Artists occasionally need a catalyst to set them on the road to their careers, for B. B. King, a tractor acted as that catalyst.
RUN-ON SENTENCE	Artists occasionally need a catalyst to set them on the road to their careers for B. B. King, a tractor acted as that catalyst.
CORRECT	Artists occasionally need a catalyst to set them on the road to their **careers; for** B. B. King, a tractor acted as that catalyst.

(1) B. B. King, the great blues guitarist and singer, born Riley B. King in Itta Bena, Mississippi, began his working life as a sharecropper and tractor driver, he earned one dollar a day at a plantation owned by Johnson Barrett in

Indianola, Mississippi. (2) As a side venture to his farm work, King sang with the excellent St. John's Gospel Singers he wanted the group to leave Mississippi to find riches and recognition in the music world. (3) In 1946, King left the group, he had tried very hard to urge them to go with him. (4) King was working hard all day in Mr. Barrett's fields, driving a tractor, he always returned to the barn at the end of the day, jumping off the tractor to the ground. (5) One day, the sudden movement made the tractor charge ahead and break off its exhaust stack King had already turned off the engine. (6) A terrified young King, fearing his boss's anger over the damaged tractor, ran away to Memphis with his guitar and $2.50, his fear kept him there for many months. (7) After a year of unsuccessfully pursuing a music career, King became discouraged and returned to Indianola he went back to work for Johnson Barrett. (8) By 1948, King had saved enough money as a tractor driver, sharecropper, and street musician to try his luck again making a living as a musician and singer, he returned to Memphis and finally found recognition and fortune, not only in that city but internationally. (9) By 1999, B. B. King had been nominated for twenty Grammy Awards, he won his ninth in that year for *Blues on the Bayou*, in the category of the Best Traditional Blues Recording. (10) In 1998, B. B. King was installed in the Grammy Hall of Fame, after having received the Grammy Lifetime Achievement Award in 1987, among his most dramatic honors were honorary PhDs granted by Yale University and the University of Mississippi. ●

Problems with Sentence Shifts

39 ■ ■ ■ ■ ■ ■ ■ ■

Quick Points   You will learn to

➤ Write sentences that have consistent grammatical forms.

Shifts are mismatched grammatical forms that cloud your meaning and baffle your readers. To avoid writing sentence shifts, be consistent in using the grammatical forms covered in 39A–39D.

Watch
the Video

39A   How can I be consistent in person and number?

Person indicates who or what performs or receives action. FIRST PERSON (*I, we*) is the writer or speaker; SECOND PERSON (*you*) is someone written or spoken to; THIRD PERSON (*he, she it, they*) is someone or something written or spoken about. Unintended shifts in person shifts blur your meaning.

Watch
the Video

NO   I enjoy reading financial forecasts, but **you** wonder which are accurate.

First person *I* shifts unnecessarily to second person *you*.

YES   I enjoy reading financial forecasts, but **I** wonder which are accurate.

! Alert: All NOUNS and many PRONOUNS are always in third person. ●

Number refers to SINGULAR (one) or PLURAL (more than one). Don't mix singular and plural unless your meaning calls for it.

NO   Because **people** are living longer, **an employee** now retires later.

The plural *people* shifts to the singular *employee*.

YES   Because **people** are living longer, **employees** now retire later.

! Alerts: (1) Watch for shifts from nouns to the second-person pronoun *you*.

●   By the year 2020, **most people** will live longer, and ~~you~~ *they* will have to work longer, too.

(2) Watch for shifts between singular and plural in the third person.

●   The longer ~~a person stays~~ *people stay* in the workforce, the more competition they will face from younger job seekers. ●

39B   How can I be consistent in subject and voice?

A needless shift in SUBJECT can cause your writing to lose its emphasis.

NO   **I realize** the dangers of sugary, high-fat foods, but **donuts are often** my breakfast.

The subject needlessly shifts from *I* to *donuts*.

YES   **I realize** the dangers of sugary, high-fat foods, but **I often eat donuts** for breakfast.

VOICE tells whether the subject acts (ACTIVE VOICE) or is acted upon (PASSIVE VOICE). In addition shifts in voice also necessitate shifts in subject.

NO   The officers **confronted** me, and **I was accused** of the crime.

The sentence shifts from active voice *confronted* to passive voice *was accused*.

YES   The officers **confronted** me and **accused** me of a crime.

YES   **I was confronted** by the officers and **accused** of a crime.

39C How can I be consistent in mood?

MOOD tells what the writer wishes to convey in a verb: a statement or question (INDICATIVE MOOD), a command or request (IMPERATIVE MOOD), a condition or supposition (SUBJUNCTIVE MOOD). Shifts in mood perplex your readers.

> **NO** Students **should bring** identification to the exam, and **don't be** late.
>
> The verb switches from the indicative *should bring* to the imperative *don't be.*

> **YES** Students **should bring** identification to the exam and **arrive** on time.

> **YES** **Bring** your identification to the exam and **be** on time.

39D How can I be consistent in verb tense?

To be consistent in verb tense, remain in the same tense unless a shift is necessary to show time passing (see Quick Box 33.3).

> **NO** She **stared** at the exam and **wonders** about her grade in this class.
>
> The verb tense shifts from past tense *stared* to present tense *wonders.*

> **YES** She **stared** at the exam and **wondered** about her grade in this class.

> **YES** She **stares** at the exam and **wonders** about her grade.

39E How can I be consistent in direct and indirect discourse?

Direct discourse repeats someone's words exactly, with quotation marks enclosing them. **Indirect discourse** reports, rather than repeats exactly, someone's words without using quotation marks. Shifts between these two disrupt the smoothness of your sentence.

> **NO** She asked me was I going out.
>
> This sentence shifts from indirect to direct discourse. Direct discourse requires quotation marks and changes in language.

> **YES** She asked me whether I was going out.

> **YES** She asked me, "Are you going out?"

39F What happens in sentences with mixed parts?

A sentence with mixed parts starts in one direction but confusingly goes off in a different direction. To revise such errors, think through exactly what you want to say.

■ Avoiding mixed clauses

In a sentence containing a DEPENDENT CLAUSE and an INDEPENDENT CLAUSE, the clauses are clear when they carry meaning in one direction, not two directions.

NO When we lost first prize motivated us to train harder.

The second part of the sentence *motivated us to train harder* has no subject.

YES When we lost first prize, we became motivated to train harder.

YES Losing first prize motivated us to train harder.

■ Avoiding mixed constructions

If a group of words contains a PHRASE and only part of an independent clause, it forms a **mixed construction** that makes no sense.

NO By tweeting her fans creates much excitement.

This sentence opens with a phrase *by tweeting her fans* then moves to the verb *creates*.

YES Tweeting her fans creates much excitement.

Dropping the preposition *by* focuses the sentence's meaning.

YES Tweeting her fans, she creates much excitement.

The subject *she* and the verb *creates* are logically and grammatically related.

■ Avoiding faulty predication

Faulty predication results when the subject and PREDICATE of a sentence don't make sense together. You can avoid the error by revising either part.

NO The purpose of television was invented to entertain.

The subject of the sentence *purpose* doesn't make sense with the predicate *was invented to entertain*.

YES **Television** was invented to entertain.

YES The purpose of television **was to entertain**.

39G How do elliptical constructions and comparisons work?

An **elliptical construction** deliberately leaves out one or more words that appear earlier in a sentence. An elliptical sentence is correct only when it omits exactly the same words as have been used previously in the same sentence.

- In 1920s Chicago, cornetist Manuel Perez ~~was leading~~ *led* one outstanding jazz group, Tommy and Jimmy Dorsey another.

The singular verb *was leading* cannot take the place of *were leading* in the second part of the sentence. *Led* works because it goes with both the singular *Perez* and the plural *Tommy and Jimmy Dorsey*.

- The period of the big jazz dance bands began *in* and lasted through World War II.

Began needs to be followed by *in*, because *through* doesn't work after both *began* and *lasted*.

In writing a comparison, you can omit words as long as the reader can clearly tell what the missing words are.

- High achievers make better business executives. *than low achievers do*

Better implies a comparison, but none is stated, so the revision corrects the problem.

- Most stockholders value high achievers more than *they value* risk takers.

The revised sentence states clearly who values whom. Another revision, *Most stockholders value high achievers more than risk takers do*, changes the meaning.

- A risk taker's ability to manage long-term growth is very different *from that of a high achiever*.

Different from what? When the comparison expresses both items, it succeeds.

> ⓘ **Alert:** When you write *as much as*, *as . . . as . . . than* (for example, *as tall as*, *if not taller than*), and similar comparisons, be sure to state the second *as*.

- High achievers value success as much, *as* if not more than, high salary. ●

Explore the Exercise

● **EXERCISE 39-1**   Revise this paragraph to create correct elliptical constructions, to complete comparisons, and to insert any missing words. For help, see 39G.

(1) A giant tsunami is as destructive and even larger than a tidal wave. (2) The word *tsunami* is Japanese for "harbor wave," for this kind wave appears suddenly in harbor or bay. (3) A tsunami begins with rapid shift in ocean floor caused by an undersea earthquake or volcano. (4) The wave this produces in the open sea is less than three feet high, but it can grow to a height of a hundred feet as it rushes and strikes against the shore. (5) For this reason, tsunamis are much more dangerous to seaside towns than ships on the open sea. (6) In 1960, a huge tsunami that struck coasts of Chile, Hawaii, and Japan killed total of 590 people. (7) In 2004, a huge tsunami that struck coasts of Indonesia, Thailand, Malaysia, and other countries killed total 275,000 people. (8) In 2011, tsunami struck the coast of Japan and caused more than 20,000 deaths. ●

Quick Points   You will learn to

➤ Place modifiers carefully so that your intended meaning is clear.

A MODIFIER is a word, PHRASE, or CLAUSE that describes or limits other words, phrases, or clauses. When you write, place modifiers carefully so that your intended meaning is clear.

Watch
the Video

40A How can I correct misplaced modifiers?

The correct placement for a modifier is almost always next to the word that it modifies. If you misplace the modifier, the sentence becomes confusing.

MISPLACED MODIFIER   Nicholas Cugnot built the first self-propelled vehicle, determined to travel without horses.

> Because the modifier *determined to travel without horses* is positioned next to *vehicle*, the sentence says the *vehicle* was determined to travel without horses, not Nicholas Cugnot.

CORRECT   Determined to travel without horses, Nicholas Cugnot built the first self-propelled vehicle.

Carefully place ADVERBS such as *only, just, almost, hardly, scarcely,* and *simply* to say precisely what you mean. For example, notice how various positions of *only* influence the meaning of the sentence *Professional coaches say that high salaries motivate players.*

- **Only** professional coaches say that high salaries motivate players.
  No one else says that.

- Professional coaches **only** say that high salaries motivate players.
  The coaches don't believe it.

- Professional coaches say that **only** high salaries motivate players.
  The coaches think nothing else works.

- Professional coaches say that high salaries motivate **only** players.
  No one else is motivated by high salaries.

407

40B How can I correct squinting modifiers?

A misplaced **squinting modifier** can modify both the words before it and after it. The writer needs to put the modifier near the word it modifies to communicate the meaning clearly.

NO   Witnesses claimed **furiously** the driver bolted from the scene.

Which happened furiously: *witnesses claimed* or *the driver bolted?*

YES   Witnesses claimed the driver bolted **furiously** from the scene.

40C How can I correct split infinitives?

A misplaced **split infinitive** occurs when words separate *to* from the verb that completes the infinitive. I want *to boldly design.* Often, the effect is awkward.

NO   The student tried **to in some way pacify** his instructor.

In some way is misplaced because it splits *to pacify.*

YES   The student tried **to pacify** his instructor in some way.

YES   In some way, the student tried **to pacify** his instructor.

40D How can I keep modifiers from disrupting a sentence?

Avoid writing complex descriptive phrases or clauses that separate the SUBJECT and VERB of a sentence. Such modifiers make a sentence overly complicated, disturbing its smooth flow.

- ~~The invention of the automobile,~~ If we consider the complete history of people
  working independently in different countries, the invention of the automobile should probably be credited to

  Nicholas Cugnot in 1769.

Also, interrupting a VERB PHRASE with modifiers disturbs sentence flow. Follow the general rule to put modifiers next to the word they modify.

- Karl Benz has ~~by most automobile historians~~ by most automobile historians been given credit for the invention
  of the automobile.

● **EXERCISE 40-1** Revise these ten sentences to correct misplaced modifiers, split infinitives, and other splits. If a sentence is correct, circle its number. For help, consult 40A through 40D.

Explore the Exercise

EXAMPLE

The city of Deadwood is known for its many notorious residents **made popular by** a TV show including Wild Bill Hickok and Calamity Jane.

Made popular by a TV show, the city of Deadwood is known for its many notorious residents, including Wild Bill Hickok and Calamity Jane.

1. Deadwood, because of its location near the Deadwood Gulch and the Black Hills of South Dakota, was named for the dead trees found in that canyon.
2. The city's founding, during a gold rush that attracted a quarter of a million miners to the area, was in 1876.
3. The main source of revenue for the city was gambling, which was outlawed in 1905 but reinstated in 1989.
4. Today, tourists who visit Deadwood often gamble and enjoy the historical reenactments of the town's famous events.
5. Deadwood nearly was the home to a dozen of famous characters from the Old West.
6. Serving as the sheriff of Hays City and Abilene, Wild Bill Hickok worked to with an iron fist tame the lawless towns of the frontier.
7. Hickok moved to Deadwood after he without much success performed in a Wild West show.
8. During a poker game at Nuttall & Mann's saloon, Jack McCall shot for unknown reasons Wild Bill.
9. The cards Hickok was holding included a pair of black aces, a pair of black eights, and an unknown fifth card now known as the dead man's hand.
10. The legends of Deadwood and Wild Bill in the stories of fiction writers and TV shows continue to grow. ●

40E How can I correct dangling modifiers?

A **dangling modifier** is an introductory phrase that hangs (or dangles) helplessly because the NOUN it modifies isn't the intended subject. Introductory phrases attach their meaning to the first noun after the phrase—the sentence's subject. If some other word falls in that position, the result is confusing.

NO **Approaching the island, a mountainous rock wall** was terrifying.

This sentence suggests that the mountainous wall was approaching the island.

YES Approaching the island, **we** saw a foreboding mountainous wall.

YES   As we approached the island, **we** saw a frightening mountainous wall.
       Both revised sentences include the subject *we*.

NO   To ease our fears, our ship swerved around the island.
       This sentence suggests that our ship eased our fears.

YES   To ease our fears, the pilot steered our ship around the island.

Explore
the
Exercise

● **EXERCISE 40-2**   Using each list of words and phrases, create all the possible logical sentences. Insert commas as needed. Explain differences in meaning among the alternatives you create. For help, consult 40A through 40E.

EXAMPLE

exchange students
learned to speak French
while in Paris
last summer

A.   Last summer,/exchange students/learned to speak French/while in Paris.
B.   While in Paris,/exchange students/learned to speak French/last summer.
C.   Exchange students/learned to speak French/while in Paris/last summer.
D.   Exchange students/learned to speak French/last summer/while in Paris.

1. chicken soup
   according to folklore
   helps
   cure colds

2. tadpoles
   instinctively
   swim
   toward
   their genetic relatives

3. the young driver
   while driving
   in the snow
   skidded carelessly

4. climbed
   the limber teenager
   a tall palm tree
   to pick a ripe coconut
   quickly

5. and cause mini-avalanches
   ski patrollers
   set explosives
   often
   to prevent
   big avalanches ●

41 Conciseness

■ ■ ■ ■ ■ ■ ■ ■

Quick Points You will learn to

➤ Write concisely.

Conciseness is desirable because it makes writing direct. **Wordiness** uses empty, unnecessary, words and PHRASES that contribute nothing to meaning.

41A How can I write concisely?

You can write concisely by deleting all words not necessary for delivering your message clearly. Get rid of the unneeded words listed in Quick Box 41.1 (p. 412) and similar expressions.

41B How can I avoid redundant writing?

Redundant writing is undesirably repetitious writing that duplicates a message that has already been stated. Unlike intentional repetition, which can create powerful rhythms, redundant writing is sloppy and burdensome to readers.

Watch
the Video

- ~~People who are~~ anesthetized ~~for surgery~~ can remain semiconscious during surgery but nevertheless feel no pain.

  A   *people*

  Surgery is used twice unnecessarily. The word *anesthetized* carries the concept of surgery. The revision is not redundant.

- The cell phone was red ~~in color~~ and rectangular ~~in shape~~.

  Red includes the concept of color; *rectangular* includes shape.

- Concise writing in college is a ~~required~~ necessity.

  The concept *necessity* includes the concept *required*.

● **EXERCISE 41-1** Working individually or with a group, revise the sentences on page 413 in two steps. First, underline all words that interfere with conciseness. Second, revise each sentence to make it more concise. (You'll need to drop words and replace or rearrange others.)

Explore
the
Exercise

Quick Box 41.1

Deleting unneeded words

Empty Words	Wordy Examples Revised
as a matter of fact the fact of the matter	~~As a matter of fact,~~ ^M^many marriages end in divorce.
at the present time	The bill is being debated ~~at the present time~~^now^.
because of the fact that, in light of the fact that, due to the fact that	Because ~~of the fact that~~ a special exhibit is scheduled, the museum is open late.
factor	The project's final cost was ~~an~~ essential ~~factor~~ to consider.
that exists	The crime rate ~~that exists~~ is unacceptable.
for the purpose of	A work crew arrived ^to^~~for the purpose of~~ fixing the pothole.
in a very real sense	~~In a very real sense,~~ ^D^drainage problems persist.
in the case of	~~In the case of~~ ^T^the proposed tax ^angered^residents ~~were angry~~.
in the event that	~~In the event that~~ ^If^you are late, I will buy our tickets.
it seems that	~~It seems that~~ ^T^the union struck over wages.
manner	The hikers looked at the snake ~~in a fearful manner~~^fearfully^.
nature	The review was ~~of a~~ markedly sarcastic ~~nature~~.
the point that I am trying to make	~~The point that I am trying to make is that~~ ^N^news reporters often invade people's privacy.
what I mean to say	~~What I mean to say is that~~ I expect a bonus.
type of, kind of	Gordon took a relaxing ~~type of~~ vacation.

EXAMPLE

It seems that most North Americans think of motor scooters as vehicles that exist only in European countries.

1. <u>It seems that</u> most North Americans think of motor scooters as <u>vehicles that exist</u> only in European countries.
2. Most North Americans think of motor scooters as only European vehicles.

1. As a matter of fact, in the popular imagination, motor scooters are the very essence of European style.
2. Today, over one million scooters are purchased by people in Europe each year, compared with a number that amounts to only 70,000 buyers in the United States.
3. In fact, Europeans have long used fuel-efficient, clean-running scooters for the purpose of getting around in a manner that is relatively easy in congested cities.
4. The use of these brightly colored, maneuverable scooters allows city dwellers to zip through traffic jams and thereby to save time and to save gas.
5. However, sales of scooters, it might interest you to know, are in the process of increasing in North America.
6. What I am trying to say is that motor scooters use much less gasoline than cars, and that as a matter of fact the cost factor is about one-fourth that of an inexpensive new car.
7. In addition, many motor scooters, it is pleasing to note, run on electricity, which in fact makes them noise and emission free.
8. A scooter running by means of electrical power amounts to a cost in the neighborhood of 25 cents to travel 50 miles at 30 miles per hour.
9. Members of many different population groups, from college students to retired persons, have begun to be finding this type of vehicle to be of a useful nature in a very real sense.
10. Traveling by means of an agile, snappy scooter makes getting around a college campus or doing errands in a city neighborhood quick and easy. ●

41C How can I avoid wordy sentence structures?

Expletive constructions and the passive voice frequently cause wordiness.

■ Avoiding expletive constructions

An EXPLETIVE CONSTRUCTION places *it* or *there* and a form of *be* before the subject of the sentence. To make such sentences more concise, revise them to eliminate the expletive.

- ~~It is necessary for~~ students *need* to fill out both registration forms.

- ~~There are three majors offered by~~ the computer science department *offers three majors*.

■ Using the passive voice appropriately

The PASSIVE VOICE is generally less lively and concise than the ACTIVE VOICE (see 33G). Unless your meaning calls for the passive voice, write in the active voice.

> **PASSIVE**　　Volunteer work **was done by me** for extra credit.
>
> Here the passive voice is unnecessary. The writer, who is doing the action of volunteer work, needs to be the subject of this sentence.
>
> **ACTIVE**　　**I did** volunteer work for extra credit.
>
> **ACTIVE**　　**Volunteer work earned me** extra credit.
>
> Here, *Volunteer work*, the subject, performs the action *earned*.

41D　How can combining sentence elements help me be concise?

Sometimes you can combine sentences to save words. Look at two sentences at a time to see if words in one sentence can be included in another.

👁
Watch
the Video

- ~~The Titanic was discovered~~ seventy-three years after being sunk by an iceberg. *Titanic* ~~The liner~~ was located under the water by a team of French and American scientists.

Sometimes you can shorten longer structures to a phrase or a word.

- The *Titanic*, ~~which was~~ a huge ocean liner, sank in 1911.

- The scientists who discovered the *Titanic* held a memorial service for the passengers and crew ~~members who had died.~~ *dead*

~~Loaded with luxuries,~~ the liner was thought to be unsinkable. *luxury*

41E　How do action verbs improve conciseness?

Action verbs are strong verbs. Weak verbs, especially forms of *be* and *have*, usually lead to wordy sentences.

> **WEAK VERB**　　The plan before the city council **has to do with** tax rebates.
>
> **STRONG VERB**　　The plan before the city council **proposes** tax rebates.

Alert: Revise phrase patterns such as *be aware of* and *be capable of* to make them more concise. Often action verbs have greater impact than these wordy phrases. Here are some examples: I *envy* [not *am envious of*] your self-confidence. We *support* [not *are supportive of*] your cause. ●

When you revise to use strong VERBS, turn nouns that end with *-ance*, *-ment*, and *-tion* into verbs to write more concisely.

NO The **accumulation** of old newspapers went on for seven years.

YES The old newspapers **accumulated** for seven years.

● **EXERCISE 41-2** Working individually or with a group, revise this paragraph in two steps. First, underline all words that interfere with conciseness. Second, revise the paragraph to make it more concise. (You'll need to drop words and replace or rearrange others.)

Explore the Exercise

EXAMPLE

1. <u>Within a matter of</u> minutes after <u>the completion of</u> a championship game, the winning team's players <u>are enabled to put on</u> caps <u>that have been</u> embroidered with their team's name, the year, <u>as well as</u> the word "champions."

2. Minutes after completing a championship game, the winning team's players receive caps embroidered with their team's name, the year, and the word "champions."

(1) At the present time, caps for sports teams are manufactured in factories located primarily in Asian countries such as China, Korea, and Taiwan. (2) Championship caps are quickly produced and shipped by factories wherever they are needed for both of the two teams playing in a final game or series. (3) The very moment the game ends, a trucking company delivers the caps to the winning team's locker room, and it then immediately and instantly burns the losing team's caps so as to prevent embarrassing anyone. (4) Companies that produce all types of sports apparel know that in most cases there is only a short period of time available for making and earning high profits from merchandise connected to a winning team. (5) Within barely a day or two, they flood the market with all sorts of every kind of t-shirts, jackets, caps, coffee mugs, in addition to banners showing and presenting the winning team's championship information. ●

42 Coordination and Subordination

■ ■ ■ ■ ■ ■ ■ ■

Quick Points You will learn to

➤ Use coordination and subordination so that your intended meaning is clear.

Watch
the Video

Coordination and *subordination* are two ways of arranging ideas to communicate relationships. Many experienced writers use both to convey meaning and achieve variety in their writing styles.

TWO IDEAS	The sky grew cloudy. The wind howled.
COORDINATION	The sky grew cloudy, **and** the wind howled.
	Here, the *sky* and *wind* get equal emphasis.
SUBORDINATION 1	**As** the sky grew cloudy, the wind howled.
	Here, the *wind* is the main focus.
SUBORDINATION 2	**As** the wind howled, the sky grew cloudy.
	Here, the *sky* is the main focus.

42A How does coordination show that ideas are equivalent?

Coordination is an arrangement of ideas of approximately equal importance. A COMPOUND SENTENCE joins independent clauses either by a semicolon or by a comma (47C) and a COORDINATING CONJUNCTION (*and, but, for, or, nor, yet, so*).

- The sky turned brighter, **and** the wind calmed down.
- The sky turned brighter; the wind calmed down.

42B How can I avoid problems with coordination?

First, be sure to join logically related and equivalent ideas with a coordinating conjunction.

NO	Computers came into common use in the 1970s, and they sometimes make costly errors.
	The ideas aren't logically connected, so they can't be coordinated.
YES	Computers came into common use in the 1970s, and now they are indispensable business tools.

416

Second, be sure not to bundle more than two or three ideas together with coordinating conjunctions (*and, but, for, or, nor, yet, so*).

NO Dinosaurs could have disappeared for many reasons, **and** one theory holds that the climate suddenly became cold, **and** another suggests that a sudden shower of meteors and asteroids hit the earth, **so** the impact created a huge dust cloud that caused a false winter. The winter lasted for years, **and** the dinosaurs died.

YES Dinosaurs could have disappeared for many reasons. One theory holds that the climate suddenly became cold, **and** another suggests that a sudden shower of meteors and asteroids hit the earth. The impact created a huge dust cloud that caused a false winter. The winter lasted for years, killing the dinosaurs.

● **EXERCISE 42-1** Working individually or with a group, revise these sentences to eliminate illogical or overused coordination. If you think a sentence needs no revision, explain why. For help, consult sections 42A and 42B.

Explore
the
Exercise

EXAMPLE

Fencing, once a form of combat, has become a competitive sport worldwide, and today's fencers disapprove of those who identify fencing with fighting.

Fencing, once a form of combat, has become a competitive sport worldwide, *but* today's fencers disapprove of those who identify fencing with fighting.

1. As depicted in movies, fencing sometimes appears to be reckless swordplay, and fencing requires precision, coordination, and strategy.
2. In the 1800s, fencing became very popular, and it was one of the few sports included in the first modern Olympic Games in 1896, and fencing has been part of the Olympics ever since.
3. Fencing equipment includes a mask, a padded jacket, a glove, and one of three weapons—a foil, épée, or saber—and a fencer's technique and targets differ depending on the weapon used and the fencer's experience.
4. Generally, a fencer specializes in one of the three weapons, but some competitors are equally skilled with all three.
5. The object of fencing is to be the first to touch the opponent five times, and a "president," who is sometimes assisted by a number of judges, officiates at competitions. ●

42C How does subordination work to express nonequivalent ideas?

Subordination is an arrangement of ideas of unequal importance within a sentence. Effective subordination places the more important idea in an INDEPENDENT CLAUSE and the less important, subordinate idea in a DEPENDENT

CLAUSE. Let your own meaning decide which of your ideas is most important, and subordinate other ideas to it.

> **NO** In 1888, two cowboys had to fight a dangerous Colorado snowstorm. They were looking for cattle. They came to a canyon. They saw outlines of buildings through the snow. Survival then seemed certain.
>
> The sentences are disconnected because no idea is emphasized.

> **YES** In 1888, <u>two cowboys had to fight a dangerous Colorado snowstorm</u> **while** they were looking for cattle. **When** they came to a canyon, <u>they saw outlines of buildings through the snow</u>. Survival then seemed certain.
>
> The two underlined independent clauses get the emphasis; the other clauses are now dependent clauses.

To subordinate successfully, use a SUBORDINATING CONJUNCTION to start the clause. Subordinating conjunctions (see Quick Box 42.1) start ADVERB CLAUSES. RELATIVE PRONOUNS, such as *who, which*, and *that* (see 32B), and RELATIVE ADVERBS, such as *where, why,* and *when* (see 32F), start ADJECTIVE CLAUSES.

Quick Box 42.1   ■ ■ ■ ■ ■ ■ ■ ■ ■

Subordination patterns

SENTENCES WITH ADVERB CLAUSES

ADVERB CLAUSE AT BEGINNING
- **After the sky grew dark**, the wind died suddenly.

ADVERB CLAUSE AT END
- Birds stopped singing, **as they do during an eclipse.**
- The stores closed **before the storm began**.

SENTENCES WITH ADJECTIVE CLAUSES

RESTRICTIVE ADJECTIVE CLAUSE* AT END
- Weather forecasts warned of a storm **that might bring a thirty-inch snowfall.**

NONRESTRICTIVE ADJECTIVE CLAUSE* AT END
- Spring is the season for tornadoes, **which may develop wind speeds over 220 miles per hour.**

RESTRICTIVE ADJECTIVE CLAUSE* BETWEEN PARTS OF THE INDEPENDENT CLAUSE
- Anyone **who lives through a tornado** remembers the experience.

NONRESTRICTIVE ADJECTIVE CLAUSE* BETWEEN PARTS OF THE INDEPENDENT CLAUSE
- The sky, **which had been clear,** turned greenish black.

*For RESTRICTIVE (essential) and NONRESTRICTIVE (nonessential) CLAUSES, see 47F.

42D How can I avoid problems with subordination?

First, be sure your subordinating conjunctions communicate a logical relationship between your clauses. (For the relationships subordinating conjunctions express, see Quick Box 32.7.)

> **NO** **Because** he was injured in the sixth inning, he remained in the game.
>
> *Because* is illogical here; it says that his injury caused him to remain.

> **YES** **Although** he was injured in the sixth inning, he remained in the game.
>
> *Although* is logical here; it says that he remained despite his injury.

Second, be sure not to overuse subordination. Your readers lose track of your message because you crowd too many ideas together.

> **NO** A new technique for eye surgery, **which** is supposed to correct nearsightedness, **which** previously could be corrected only by glasses, has been developed, **although** many doctors disapprove of the new technique **because** it can create unstable vision.

> **YES** A new technique for eye surgery, which is supposed to correct nearsightedness, has been developed. Previously, nearsightedness could be corrected only by glasses. However, many doctors disapprove of the new technique because it can create unstable vision.
>
> In this revision, one long sentence is broken into three sentences, making the relationships among ideas clearer.

● **EXERCISE 42-2** Working individually or in a group, use subordination and coordination to combine these sets of short, choppy sentences. For help, consult all sections of this chapter.

Explore
the
Exercise

EXAMPLE

Owls cannot digest the bones and fur of the mice and birds they eat. They cough up a furry pellet every day.

Because owls cannot digest the bones and fur of the mice and birds they *eat, they* cough up a furry pellet every day.

1. Owl pellets are a rich teaching tool in biology classrooms around the country. The pellets provide an alternative to dissecting frogs and other animals.
2. Inside the pellet are the remains of the owl's nightly meal. They include beautifully cleaned hummingbird skulls, rat skeletons, and lots of bird feathers.
3. The owl-pellet market has been cornered by companies in New York, California, and Washington. These companies distribute pellets to thousands of biology classrooms all over the world.

4. Company workers scour barns and the ground under trees where owls nest to pick up the pellets. The pellets sell for $1 each.
5. The owl-pellet business may have a short future. The rural areas of the United States are vanishing. Old barns are being bulldozed. All the barns are torn down. The owls will be gone, too. ●

43 Sentence Style

Quick Points You will learn to

➤ Use parallel structures to give rhythm and grace to your writing.
➤ Use a variety of sentence patterns to give interest to your writing (pp. 422–423).

43A What is parallelism?

Watch
the Video

When words, PHRASES, or CLAUSES within a sentence grammatically match, the result is **parallelism**. Parallelism serves to emphasize information or ideas. Also, balance and rhythm in parallel structures add style and grace to your writing.

PARALLEL WORDS	Recommended exercise includes **running**, **swimming**, and **cycling**.
PARALLEL PHRASES	Exercise helps people **maintain healthy bodies** and **handle mental pressures**.
PARALLEL CLAUSES	Many people exercise **because they want to look healthy, because they need to increase stamina**, and **because they hope to live longer**.

43B How can I avoid faulty parallelism?

You can avoid faulty parallelism by checking that you always use the same grammatical form for words, phrases, or clauses.

NO   The strikers had tried **shouting**, **threats**, and **pleading**.

The list incorrectly mixes *-ing* forms and a plural.

YES   The strikers had tried **shouting**, **threatening**, and **pleading**.

The three words are all in *-ing* form.

YES   The strikers had tried **shouts**, **threats**, and **pleas**.

The three words are all plural nouns.

NO   The strikers **read** the offer, **were discussing** it, and the unanimous **decision was to reject** it.

Two verbs mix forms; the third switches to the PASSIVE VOICE.

YES   The strikers **read, discussed**, and **rejected** the offer.

All three verbs are in the past tense.

43C   How should I use parallelism with conjunctions?

Items joined with COORDINATING CONJUNCTIONS (*and, but, for, or, nor, yet, so*) deliver their message clearly and concisely when written in parallel form.

- You can cook a chicken by **roasting**, **grilling**, or **broiling** it.

Similarly, use parallel forms when you link sentence elements with COR-RELATIVE CONJUNCTIONS (such as *either . . . or* and *not only . . . but also*).

- **Either** you attend classes **or** you fail the course.

43D   How does parallelism strengthen my message?

Parallelism—which calls for deliberate but controlled repetition of word forms, word groups, and sounds—creates a rhythm that intensifies a sentence's message.

> You can fool some of the people all of the time and all of the people some of the time, but you cannot fool all of the people all of the time.
>
> —Abraham Lincoln

Another parallel structure that intensifies ideas is the balanced sentence. **Balanced sentences** consist of two short, contrasting independent clauses.

> **By night**, the litter and desperation disappeared as the city's glittering lights came on; **by day**, the filth and despair reappeared as the sun rose.
>
> —Jennifer Kirk, student

● **EXERCISE 43-1**   Working individually or with a group, revise these sentences by putting appropriate information in parallel structures. For help, consult sections 43A through 43D.

Explore
the
Exercise

EXAMPLE

Difficult bosses affect not only their employees' performances but their private lives are affected as well.

Difficult bosses affect not only their employees' performances *but their private lives as well.*

1. According to the psychologist Harry Levinson, the five main types of bad boss are the workaholic, the kind of person you would describe as bullying, a person who communicates badly, the jellyfish type, and someone who insists on perfection.

2. As a way of getting ahead, to keep their self-respect, and for survival purposes, wise employees handle problem bosses with a variety of strategies.

3. To cope with a bad-tempered employer, workers can both stand up for themselves and reasoning with a bullying boss.

4. Often, bad bosses communicate poorly or fail to calculate the impact of their personality on others; being a careful listener and sensitivity to others' responses are qualities that good bosses possess.

5. Employees who take the trouble to understand what makes their bosses tick, engage in some self-analysis, and staying flexible are better prepared to cope with a difficult job environment than suffering in silence like some employees. ●

43E What is sentence variety?

Watch the Video

Writers use sentence variety when they vary the length and structure of their sentences in relation to each other.

■ Revising strings of short sentences

Sometimes several short sentences in a row create impact. Be careful, however, to avoid strings of short sentences that don't intensify your ideas; they tend to make reading dull.

NO There is a problem. It is widely known as sick-building syndrome. It comes from indoor air pollution. It causes the suffering of office workers. They have trouble breathing. The workers develop rashes that are painful. Their heads ache badly. Their eyes burn.

YES Widely known as sick-building syndrome, indoor air pollution causes office workers to suffer. They have trouble breathing. They have painful rashes. Their heads ache. Their eyes burn.

Here a long sentence introduces the interaction of indoor air pollution and its victims. Then a series of short sentences emphasizes each problem the victims suffer. The revision also reduces forty-two words to twenty-seven.

■ Revising for a mix of sentence lengths

You can emphasize one idea by expressing that idea in a sentence noticeably different in length or structure from sentences surrounding it. The "yes" example just shown illustrates the graceful impact of one long sentence among shorter ones. Here's an example of one short sentence among longer ones.

> Today is one of those excellent January partly cloudies in which light chooses an unexpected landscape to trick out in gilt, and then shadow sweeps it away. **You know you are alive.** You take huge steps, trying to feel the planet's roundness arc between your feet.
>
> —Annie Dillard, *Pilgrim at Tinker Creek*

43F How does a sentence's subject affect emphasis?

Because the SUBJECT establishes the sentence's focus, always choose for the sentence's subject what you want to emphasize. Notice how changing the subject (and VERB, as needed) in the following sentences affects each sentence's meaning and emphasis.

- **Our study** showed that 25 percent of college freshmen gain weight.
  Focus is on the study.

- **College freshmen** gain weight 25 percent of the time, our study shows.
  Focus is on the freshmen.

- **Weight gain** hits 25 percent of college freshmen, our study shows.
  Focus is on the weight gain.

- **Twenty-five percent** of college freshmen gain weight, our study shows.
  Focus is on the percentage.

43G How does adding modifiers affect writing style?

You can add richness, variety, and focus to your writing with MODIFIERS.

BASIC SENTENCE	The river rose.
ADJECTIVE	The **swollen** river rose.
ADVERB	The river rose **dangerously**.
PREPOSITIONAL PHRASE	**In April**, the river rose **above its banks**.
PARTICIPIAL PHRASE	**Swelled by melting snow**, the river rose, **flooding the farmland**.
ABSOLUTE PHRASE	**Trees swirling away in the current**, the river rose.
ADVERB CLAUSE	**Because the snows had been heavy that winter**, the river rose.
ADJECTIVE CLAUSE	The river, **which runs through vital farmland**, rose.

Explore
the
Exercise

● **EXERCISE 43-2** Working individually or with a group, expand each sentence by adding each kind of modifier illustrated in section 43G.

1. We bought a house.
2. The roof leaked.
3. I remodeled the kitchen.
4. Neighbors brought food.
5. Everyone enjoyed the barbeque. ●

43H How does inverting standard word order affect emphasis?

Standard word order, common in English sentences, places the subject before the verb: *The mayor* [subject] *walked* [verb] *into the room.*

When used sparingly, **inverted word order**, which places the verb before the subject, produces emphasis.

> STANDARD   The mayor walked into the room.
> INVERTED   Into the room walked the mayor.

44 Word Meanings and Word Impact

■ ■ ■ ■ ■ ■ ■ ■

Quick Points You will learn to

➤ Choose the precise word to convey your meaning.
➤ Use words to create the appropriate effect in a piece of writing (pp. 427–430).

44A How can I learn about words and their meanings?

Watch
the Video

Three fine dictionaries, which tell you the meaning and use of words, are *Webster's New World Dictionary, Merriam-Webster's Collegiate Dictionary,* and the *American Heritage Dictionary of the English Language.* For students whose native language is not English, we recommend the *American Heritage English as a Second Language Dictionary.* Each dictionary's introductory pages describe the information found in word entries.

44B   How can I choose exact words?

Exact words are words that express your meaning precisely and unmistakably. Your **diction**, the words you use to offer your message, affects the meaning and impact of your message. To strengthen your diction, be alert to the distinctions between denotation and connotation, and between general and specific words.

■ Distinguishing between denotation and connotation

Denotation is a word's literal dictionary definition. But even SYNONYMS can have subtle differences. For example, Steve Jobs was *famous*, which means "widely known and favorably spoken of." Al Capone, however, was *notorious*, which means "unfavorably known and spoken of."

In addition, some words convey connotations. **Connotation** refers to the ideas suggested by a word. For example, the word *home* suggests more than its dictionary definition, its denotation, which is "a house or dwelling place." For some people, *home* suggests warmth, security, and family togetherness. For others, *home* connotes abusive experiences.

● **EXERCISE 44-1**   Working individually or with a group, look at each list of words and divide the words among three headings: "Positive" (good connotations); "Negative" (bad connotations); and "Neutral" (no connotations). If you think that a word belongs under more than one heading, you can assign it more than once, but be ready to explain your thinking. For help, consult a good dictionary and 44B.

Explore
the
Exercise

EXAMPLE

grand, big, bulky, significant, oversized
Positive: grand, significant; *Negative:* bulky, oversized; *Neutral:* big

1. harmony, sound, racket, shriek, melody, music, noise, pitch, voice
2. talkative, articulate, chattering, eloquent, vocal, verbose, gossipy, fluent, gabby
3. decorative, beautiful, modern, ornate, overelaborate, dazzling, flashy, elegant, sparkling
4. long, lingering, enduring, continued, drawn-out, stretched, never-ending, unbreakable, incessant
5. calculating, shrewd, crafty, ingenious, keen, sensible, sly, smooth, underhanded ●

■ Using specific and concrete language

Specific words identify individual items in a group (*Jeep, Honda*). General words relate to an overall group (*car*). Concrete words identify persons and things that can be perceived by the senses (*black padded vinyl dashboard*).

Abstract words denote qualities, concepts, relationships, acts, conditions, and ideas (*justice*).

Concrete, specific words enliven abstract, general words. You strengthen your diction and clarify your message when your writing balances the general with the specific and the concrete with the abstract.

GENERAL   SPECIFIC   SPECIFIC   SPECIFIC
- My **car**, a **220-horsepower Maxi Armo**, accelerates **from 0 to 50**

  SPECIFIC   SPECIFIC   SPECIFIC
miles per hour in **6 seconds** but gets only **18 miles per gallon**.

       SPECIFIC   GENERAL
In contrast, the **Gavin Motors' Bobcat** gets **very good** gas mileage,

  SPECIFIC   GENERAL   SPECIFIC   SPECIFIC
about **35 mpg** in **highway driving** and **30 mpg** in **stop-and-go traffic**.

- **EXERCISE 44-2** Revise this paragraph by providing specific and concrete words and phrases to explain and enliven the ideas presented here in general and abstract language. You may revise the sentences to accommodate your changes in language. For help, consult 44B.

Explore the Exercise

> I hope to get a job as an administrative assistant in the company. At the interview, the person who would be my supervisor was pleasant. We seemed to get along well. The other assistants in the division appeared to be nice. My college courses clearly have prepared me for the position. I think the job would teach me a great deal more. The salary is a bit less than I had hoped for, but the Human Resources representative promised me raises at regular intervals if my work is good. Also, my trip to work would not take too much time for me. If my interviewer calls to offer me the job, I will accept it. •

44C How can I increase my vocabulary?

All people have an **active vocabulary**, words that come to mind easily. Everyone also has a **passive vocabulary**, words people don't use actively yet recognize and understand. The larger your vocabulary, the more you understand what you read and hear—and the more skillfully you can speak and write.

Choosing What Words to Learn

- Move words you already know passively into your active vocabulary.
- Select unfamiliar words as you read them and create a file of them to study.
- Use context clues to figure out definitions.
- Use **prefixes**, syllables added to the front of a word that modify its meaning (for example, *intend* and *pretend*).

- Use **suffixes**, syllables added to the end of a word that modify its meaning (for example, *excitable* and *excitement*).

- Listen closely to speakers who know the language well. Jot down new words.

- Find the words in a dictionary, and then write them down to study.

Studying New Vocabulary Words

- Select eight to ten words to study each week.

- Write each new word and its meaning on an index card, in a notebook, or on a computer list.

- Set aside time each day to study your selected words. (Carry your cards, notebook, or computer printout to study in spare moments.)

- Try **mnemonics**—memory-jogging techniques—to help you memorize words. (For example, *desert*, spelled with one *s*, is filled with *sand;* in contrast, *dessert*, spelled with two *s*'s, could stand for *strawberry shortcake*.

- Push these words from your passive to your active vocabulary.

44D What is suitable language for writing?

■ Using appropriate language

Appropriate language matches your diction to your AUDIENCE and PURPOSE. Obscene, profane words, for example, don't belong in ACADEMIC WRITING. Similarly, medical JARGON doesn't belong in a magazine for the general public.

Watch the Video

■ Being aware of levels of formality

Choose the **level of formality**—formal, semiformal, or informal—appropriate to your audience and your purpose. Informal language works in an e-mail to a "pal." Formal language suits speeches at ceremonial occasions or at official events. Semiformal writing uses standard vocabulary (for example, someone is *angry*, not *mad*) and conventional sentence structure. Your level of formality has an impact on the style and tone of your writing; see 6E.

■ Using edited American English

Edited American English conforms to established rules of grammar, sentence structure, punctuation, and spelling. Academic writing uses edited American English—the forms of written language that we use in this handbook—since it addresses a college audience.

■ Using slang, colloquialisms, and regionalisms

Slang consists of new words (*phat* meaning "very good") or existing words that have new meanings (*sick* meaning "awesome"). Slang is appropriate only in very informal situations.

Colloquial language is characteristic of casual conversation and informal writing: *The student flunked* [instead of *failed*] *chemistry.* Regional language (also called **dialect**) is specific to a particular geographic area: *They have nary a cent.* Slang, colloquial, and regional language are not substandard or illiterate, but they're usually inappropriate for academic writing.

44E What is figurative language?

Figurative language consists of words that carry other meanings along with their literal meaning. There are various kinds of figurative language.

Analogy compares similar traits shared by dissimilar things. You can develop an analogy in one, several, or many sentences.

- A **cheetah sprinting across the dry plains** after its prey, the **base runner dashed** for home plate, cleats kicking up dust.

Irony uses words to suggest the opposite of their usual sense.

- Told that a minor repair to her home would cost $2,000 and take two weeks, she said, **"Oh, how nice!"**

Metaphor compares otherwise dissimilar things. A metaphor doesn't use the word *like* or *as* to make a comparison.

- Rush-hour **traffic** in the city **bled out through major arteries** to the suburbs.

Avoid **mixed metaphors**, the combining of two or more inconsistent images in one sentence or expression.

- The violence of the hurricane reminded me of a train ride.

A train ride is not violent, stormy, or destructive.

Personification involves assigning a human trait to something not human.

- The **book begged** to be read.

Overstatement (also called **hyperbole**) exaggerates to emphasize.

- If this paper is late, **the professor will kill me**.

Simile compares dissimilar things using the word *like* or *as*.

- Langston Hughes observes that a deferred dream dries up **"like a raisin in the sun."**

Understatement emphasizes by using deliberate restraint.

- **It only begins to feel warm** when the temperature reaches 105 degrees.

44F What is a cliché?

A **cliché** is an overused, worn-out expression that has grown trite from overuse: *dead as a doornail, gentle as a lamb, lap of luxury.* Such clichés are *similes* (comparisons using *like* or *as*) that have become corny. Refresh or delete a cliché, such as "living happily ever after."

> **NO**   Needing to travel five hundred miles before dark, we left **at the crack of dawn**.

> **YES**   Needing to travel five hundred miles before dark, we left **at dawn**.

44G What is the effect of tone in writing?

TONE refers to *how* you convey a message, not to the message itself. Consider the difference between "Today's meeting was genuinely useful" and "Today's party was awesome!" Academic writing uses a reasonable tone. It avoids the misuses explained next.

■ Avoiding slanted language

SLANTED LANGUAGE attempts to bias readers with words containing emotionally charged connotations (see 44B). Referring to a group of protestors as a *mob* or as *concerned citizens* elicits different reader responses. Avoid slanted language in ACADEMIC WRITING.

■ Avoiding pretentious language

Pretentious language draws attention to itself with big, unusual words and overly complex sentence structures. Such overblown language obscures your message and damages your credibility with your readers.

> **NO**   The **raison d'être** for my **matriculation** at this **institution of higher learning** is the **acquisition** of an education.

> **YES**   My reason for being in college is to get an education.

■ Avoiding jargon

Jargon is common in every field—the professions, academic disciplines, business, and sports—because each field has its own specialized vocabulary. Specialized language, including jargon, allows people who share technical vocabularies to understand each other quickly. When your readers are members of the general public, however, you can't assume that they will know what you mean. Therefore, if you absolutely can't avoid a specialized term when writing for such an audience, define it in simpler terms.

■ Avoiding euphemisms

Euphemisms attempt to avoid unpleasant truths by substituting "tactful" words for more direct, perhaps harsh-sounding words. When the truth is "Our leader tells many lies," you don't want to be overly indirect by writing "Our leader has a wonderfully vivid imagination." Of course, a euphemism is not only acceptable but also expected in certain social situations. When offering condolences, for example, you may use *passed away* instead of *died*.

● **EXERCISE 44-3** Working individually or with a group, revise these examples of pretentious language, jargon, and euphemisms. For help, consult 44D through 44G.

Explore
the
Exercise

1. Allow me to express my humble gratitude to you two benefactors for your generous pledge of indispensable support on behalf of the activities of our Bay City's youngsters.
2. No lateral transfer applications will be processed before an employee's six-month probation period terminates.
3. She gave up the ghost shortly after her husband kicked the bucket.
4. Creating nouns in positions meant for verbs is to utter ostentatious verbalizations that will lead inexorably to further obfuscations of meaning.
5. After his operation, he would list to port when he stood up and list to starboard when he sat down. ●

45 Using Inclusive Language
■ ■ ■ ■ ■ ■ ■ ■

Quick Points You will learn to

➤ Use gender-neutral language.

45A What is gender in the English language?

Gender classifies nouns and some pronouns as masculine, feminine, common, or neuter. Only a few words in English (such as *man, woman, he, her, princess, uncle*) have gender-specific meanings, all based on actual physical identity.

45B What is gender-neutral language?

Gender-neutral language, also called *nonsexist language*, uses terms that do not draw unnecessary attention to a person's gender. **Sexist language** unfairly discriminates against both sexes. For example, it assumes that nurses and homemakers are female (calling them *she*) and physicians and engineers are male (calling them *he*).

Watch
the Video

When you write, use gender-neutral language. For example, use *police officer* instead of *policeman*, *representative* instead of *congressman*, and *salesperson* instead of *salesgirl*. Also, avoid the use of masculine PRONOUNS in sentences where gender is unknown or irrelevant. Revise the sexist sentence *Each tourist must carry his passport* to ***Tourists** must carry **their** passports*. Follow the guidelines in Quick Box 45.1.

Some writers avoid sexist language by using *he or she* (or *him or her*) to refer to singular nouns. Overuse of these phrases is awkward. Use plural nouns and *they* or *them* when possible.

In ACADEMIC WRITING, treat both sexes equally. For example, if you describe a woman by her looks, clothes, age, or marital status, do the same for a man in that context. If you call one member of a partnership by first name only, do the same for the other member—and if you use a title for one, such as *Mr.*, *Dr.*, or *Mrs.*, use a title for the other.

NO   Mr Tyrone Stevens and his wife June are both lawyers.

YES   Tyrone and June Stevens are both lawyers.

YES   Mr. and Mrs. Stevens are both lawyers.

● **EXERCISE 45-1**   Working individually or with a group, revise these sentences by changing sexist language to gender-neutral language. For help, consult this chapter.

Explore
the
Exercise

1. Dogs were one of the first animals to be domesticated by mankind.
2. Traditionally, certain breeds of dogs have helped men in their work.
3. On their long shifts, firemen often kept Dalmatians as mascots and companions, whereas policemen preferred highly intelligent and easily trained German shepherds.
4. Another breed, the Newfoundland, accompanied many fishermen on their ocean voyages, and the Newfoundland has been credited with rescuing many a man overboard.
5. Breeds known as hunting dogs have served as the helpers and companions of sportsmen. ●

Quick Box 45.1

■ ■ ■ ■ ■ ■ ■ ■ ■

Avoiding sexist language

Avoid using masculine pronouns to refer to both men and women.

- Use a pair of pronouns.

  or her
  - A doctor has little time to read outside his specialty.
                                                      ^

- Use the plural.

  S   s   they have
  - A successful doctor knows that he has to work hard.
      ^   ^   ^

- Omit gender-specific pronouns.

          to
  - Everyone hopes that he will win the scholarship.
                     ^

- Avoid stereotyping jobs and roles by gender.
  supervisor [*not* foreman]
  businessperson, business executive [*not* businessman]
  poet, actor [*not* poetess, actress]

- Avoid expressions that exclude one sex.
  person [*not* man]
  humanity, people [*not* mankind]
  the average person [*not* the common man]
  superstitions [*not* old wives' tales]

- Avoid demeaning and patronizing labels.
  nurse [*not* male nurse]
  professional, executive, manager [*not* career girl]
  My assistant will help you *or* Ida Morea will help you
  Not My girl will help you.

46 Spelling

■ ■ ■ ■ ■ ■ ■ ■

Quick Points You will learn to

➤ Use spelling rules to improve your spelling.
➤ Distinguish between homonyms and other easily confused words
  (pp. 436–438)

You might be surprised to learn that fine writers aren't always good spellers. Still, they check their spelling while EDITING their work, either by using a spelling checker program on the computer or by looking words up in a dictionary (see 6H). How do you look a word up in a dictionary when you can't spell it? If you know the first few letters, find them and then browse for the word. Try a thesaurus to look up an easier-to-spell synonym, and see if it's in the list. You can avoid many misspellings in your writing by learning a few common spelling rules and troublesome words.

46A How are plurals spelled?

- **Adding -s or -es:** Plurals of most words are formed by adding -s, including words that end in "hard" *ch* (sounding like *k*): *leg, legs; shoe, shoes; stomach, stomachs.* Words ending in *s, sh, x, z,* or "soft" *ch* (as in *beach*) add -es to form the plural: *lenses, wishes, taxes, coaches.*

- **Words ending in *o*:** Add -s if the *o* is preceded by a vowel: *radio, radios; cameo, cameos.* Add -es if the *o* is preceded by a consonant: *potato, potatoes.* A few words can be made plural either way: *cargo, volcano, tornado, zero.*

- **Words ending in *f* or *fe*:** Some *f* and *fe* words are made plural by adding -s: *belief, beliefs.* Others require changing *f* or *fe* to *ves: life, lives; leaf, leaves.* For words ending in *ff* or *ffe*, simply add -s: *staff, staffs; giraffe, giraffes.*

- **Compound words:** For most compound words, add -s or -es at the end of the last word: *checkbooks, player-coaches.* Sometimes, the first word is plural: *sister-in-law, sisters-in-law; attorney general, attorneys general.* (For guidelines on hyphens and compound words, see Quick Box 54.2.)

- **Internal changes and endings other than -s:** A few words change internally or add endings other than -s as plurals: *foot, feet; man, men; mouse, mice; crisis, crises; child, children.*

- **Foreign words:** Many Latin words ending in *um* become plural by changing *um* to *a: curriculum, curricula; datum, data; medium, media; stratum,*

433

strata. Latin words that end in *us* often change to *i* in plural: *alumnus, alumni; syllabus, syllabi*. Greek words that end in *on* usually form the plural by changing *on* to *a*: *criterion, criteria; phenomenon, phenomena*.

- **One-form words:** Some words have the same form in both the singular and the plural: *deer, elk, fish, quail*.

46B How are suffixes spelled?

Watch
the Video

A SUFFIX is an ending added to a word to change the word's meaning or its grammatical function. For example, adding the suffix *-able* to the verb *depend* creates the adjective *dependable*.

- **Words ending in *y*:** If the letter before the final *y* is a consonant, change the *y* to *i* and add the suffix: *fry, fried*. If, however, the suffix begins with an *i*, keep the *y*: *fry, frying*. If the letter before the *y* is a vowel, keep the final *y*: *employ, employed, employing*. These rules do not apply to irregular verbs (see Quick Box 33.2).

- **Words ending in *e*:** Drop a final *e* when the suffix begins with a vowel unless this would cause confusion: *be + ing* does not become *bing*, but *require, requiring; like, liking*. Keep the final *e* when the suffix begins with a consonant: *require, requirement; like, likely*. Exceptions include *argument, judgment*, and *truly*.

- **Words that double a final letter:** If the final letter is a consonant, double it only if it passes all three of these tests: (1) Its last two letters are a vowel followed by a consonant. (2) It has one syllable or is accented on the last syllable. (3) The suffix begins with a vowel: *drop, dropped; begin, beginning; forget, forgettable*.

- **Words ending in *cede*, *ceed*, or *sede*:** Only one word in the English language ends in *sede*: *supersede*. Three words end in *ceed*: *exceed, proceed, succeed*. All other words with endings that sound like "seed" end in *cede*: *concede, intercede, precede*.

- **Adding *-ally* and *-ly*:** The suffixes *-ally* and *-ly* turn ADJECTIVES into ADVERBS. For all words ending in *ic* except *public*, add *-ally*: *logically, statistically*. Otherwise, add *-ly*: *quickly, sharply*.

46C What is the *ie, ei* rule?

The old rhyme for *ie* and *ei* is usually true: I before *e* [believe, field, grief] except after *c* [ceiling, conceit]; or when sounded like "ay" as in *neighbor* and *weigh* [eight, vein].

You'll want to memorize (sorry!) these exceptions: For *ie*, conscience, financier, science, species. For *ei*, either, neither, leisure, seize, counterfeit, foreign, forfeit, sleight (*as in* sleight of hand), weird.

46D How are commonly confused words and homonyms spelled?

English is rich with **homonyms**—words that sound alike but have different meanings and spellings: *hear, here; to, too, two; elicit, illicit; accept, except.* See Quick Box 46.1 to distinguish these and other commonly confused words.

Watch
the Video

46E What else leads to spelling errors?

"Swallowed pronunciation," which occurs when speakers blur word endings, often leads to spelling errors: *use* for *used; suppose* for *supposed.* Mispronunciation may also cause misspellings in phrases like *all right* (not *alright*), *a lot* (not *alot*) and *should've* (not *should of*).

Watch
the Video

● **EXERCISE 46-1** Circle the correct homonym or commonly confused word of each group in parentheses.

Explore
the
Exercise

   Imagine that you (are, our) standing in the middle of a busy sidewalk, with a worried look on (your, you're, yore) face. In your hand (your, you're, yore) holding a map, (which, witch) you are puzzling over. If that happened in (real, reel) life, (its, it's) almost certain that within (to, too, two) or three minutes a passerby would ask if you (where, were) lost and would offer you (assistance, assistants). That helpful passerby, (buy, by) taking a (personal, personnel) interest in your problem, is displaying a quality known as empathy—the ability (to, too, two) put oneself in another person's place. Some researchers claim that empathy is an instinct that (human, humane) beings share with many other animals. Other scientists wonder (weather, whether) empathy is instead a (conscience, conscious) (moral, morale) choice that people make. ●

Quick Box 46.1

Homonyms and other commonly confused words

ALL READY	fully prepared
ALREADY	by this time
ALL TOGETHER	all in one place
ALTOGETHER	thoroughly
ASCENT	the act of rising or climbing
ASSENT	consent [NOUN, VERB]
BARE	nude, unadorned
BEAR	carry [VERB]; an animal [NOUN]
BUY	purchase
BY	next to, through the agency of
CAPITAL	major city; money
CAPITOL	government building
COUNCIL	governing body
COUNSEL	advice [NOUN]; advise [VERB]
DESERT	abandon [VERB]; dry, usually sandy area [NOUN]
DESSERT	final, sweet course in a meal
DEVICE	a plan; an implement
DEVISE	create
DIE	lose life (dying) [VERB]; one of a pair of dice [NOUN]
DYE	change the color of something (dyeing)
DOMINANT	commanding, controlling
DOMINATE	control
EMINENT	prominent
IMMANENT	living within; inherent
IMMINENT	about to happen
ENSURE	guarantee, protect
INSURE	buy or give insurance
FORMALLY	conventionally, with ceremony
FORMERLY	previously
FORTH	forward
FOURTH	number four in a series

continued >>

Quick Box 46.1 (continued) ■ ■ ■ ■ ■ ■ ■ ■

GORILLA	animal in the ape family
GUERRILLA	soldier conducting surprise attacks
HOLE	opening
WHOLE	complete [ADJECTIVE]; an entire thing [NOUN]
ITS	POSSESSIVE form of *it*
IT'S	CONTRACTION for *it is*
LEAD	heavy metal substance [NOUN]; guide [VERB]
LED	PAST TENSE of *lead*
LIGHTENING	making lighter
LIGHTNING	storm-related electricity
LOOSE	unbound, not tightly fastened
LOSE	misplace
MAY BE	might be [VERB]
MAYBE	perhaps [ADVERB]
PASSED	PAST TENSE of *pass*
PAST	at an earlier time
PATIENCE	forbearance
PATIENTS	people under medical care
PLAIN	simple, unadorned [ADJECTIVE]; area of level land [NOUN]
PLANE	shave wood [VERB]; aircraft [NOUN]
PRECEDE	come before
PROCEED	continue
PRESENCE	being at hand; attendance at a place or in something
PRESENTS	gifts
PRINCIPAL	foremost [ADJECTIVE]; school head [NOUN]
PRINCIPLE	moral conviction, basic truth
RAIN	water that falls to earth [NOUN]; fall like rain [VERB]
REIGN	rule
REIN	strap to guide or control an animal [NOUN]; guide or control [VERB]
RESPECTFULLY	with respect
RESPECTIVELY	in that order

continued >>

Quick Box 46.1 (continued)

RIGHT	correct; opposite of *left*
RITE	ritual
WRITE	put words on paper
SCENE	place of an action; segment of a play
SEEN	viewed
SENSE	perception, understanding
SINCE	from that time; because
STATIONARY	standing still
STATIONERY	writing paper
THAN	in comparison with; besides
THEN	at that time; next; therefore
THEIR	POSSESSIVE form of *they*
THERE	in that place
THEY'RE	CONTRACTION for *they are*
TO	toward
TOO	also; excessively
TWO	number following *one*
WEATHER	climatic conditions
WHETHER	if
WERE	PAST TENSE of *be*
WHERE	in which place
WHICH	one of a group
WITCH	female sorcerer
WHO'S	CONTRACTION for *who is*
WHOSE	POSSESSIVE form of *who*
YORE	long past
YOUR	POSSESSIVE form of *you*
YOU'RE	CONTRACTION for *you are*

Tab 10
Punctuation and Mechanics

Tab 10 Punctuation and Mechanics

MyCompLab® Visit mycomplab.com for the eText and for resources
and exercises on punctuation and mechanics.

47 Commas

■ ■ ■ ■ ■ ■ ■

Quick Points You will learn to

➤ Use commas correctly.

47A When do I use commas?

Watch the Video

The comma separates sentence parts for greater clarity. Use commas as listed in "When to Use Commas" in Quick Box 47.1. For more about each rule in the chart, go to the chapter section given in parentheses.

47B How do I use a comma to set off introductory words?

When introductory words come before an INDEPENDENT CLAUSE,* usually place a comma after the introductory material unless it is very short.

- **When the topic is dieting,** many people say sugar craving is their worst problem.

  An introductory DEPENDENT CLAUSE (in bold) is followed by a comma.

- **Between 1544 and 1689,** sugar refineries appeared in New York.

  An introductory PREPOSITIONAL PHRASE is followed by a comma.

- **Beginning in infancy,** we develop lifelong tastes for sweet foods.

  An introductory PARTICIPIAL PHRASE is followed by a comma.

- **Sweets being a temptation for many adults,** candy sells well.

  An introductory ABSOLUTE PHRASE is followed by a comma.

- **For example,** fructose comes from fruit, but it is still sugar.

  An introductory TRANSITIONAL EXPRESSION is followed by a comma.

- **Nevertheless,** many people think fructose is not harmful.

  An introductory CONJUNCTIVE ADVERB is followed by a comma.

---

* Words printed in SMALL CAPITAL LETTERS are discussed elsewhere in the text and are defined in the Terms Glossary at the back of the book.

Quick Box 47.1

When to use commas

COMMAS AFTER INTRODUCTORY ELEMENTS (see 47B)

- **Although most postcards cost only a quarter,** one recently sold for thousands of dollars.
- **On postcard racks,** several designs are usually available.
- **For example,** animals are timeless favorites for postcards.
- **However,** most postcards show local landmarks.

COMMAS WITH COORDINATING CONJUNCTIONS LINKING INDEPENDENT CLAUSES (see 47C)

- Postcards are ideal for brief greetings, **and** they are sometimes miniature works of art.

COMMAS WITH ITEMS IN SERIES (see 47D)

- **Places, paintings, and people** appear on postcards.
- The illustrations on postcards—**places, paintings, people, animals**—are chosen for their wide appeal.

COMMAS WITH COORDINATING ADJECTIVES (see 47E)

- Some postcards feature **breathtaking, dramatic** scenes.

NO COMMAS WITH CUMULATIVE ADJECTIVES (see 47E)

- Other postcards feature **famous historical** scenes.

COMMAS WITH NONRESTRICTIVE ELEMENTS (see 47F)

- **Four years after the first postcard appeared,** the US government began to issue prestamped postcards.
- The Golden Age of postcards, **which lasted from about 1900 to 1929,** yielded many especially valuable cards.
- Collectors attend postcard shows, **which are similar to baseball card shows.**

NO COMMAS WITH RESTRICTIVE ELEMENTS (see 47F)

- Collectors **who attend these shows** may specialize in a particular kind of postcard.

continued >>

Quick Box 47.1 (continued)

COMMAS WITH QUOTED WORDS (see 47G)

- One collector told me, **"Attending a show is like digging for buried treasure."**

- **"I always expect to find a priceless postcard,"** he said.

- **"Everyone there,"** he joked, **"believes a million-dollar card is hidden in the next stack."**

◼ Exception

When an introductory element is short, some writers omit the comma. However, in ACADEMIC WRITING, you'll never be wrong if you use the comma.

YES In 1992, the Americans with Disabilities Act was passed. [preferred]

YES In 1992 the Americans with Disabilities Act was passed.

47C How do I use a comma before a coordinating conjunction?

When you link independent clauses, place a comma before a COORDINATING CONJUNCTION (*and, but, for, or, nor, yet, so*).

- The sky turned black, **and** the wind blew fiercely.

  A comma and *and* link two independent clauses.

- The sky began to brighten, **but** the wind continued blowing strongly.

  A comma and *but* link two independent clauses.

- Soon high winds would start, **or** snow would begin.

When commas are already part of one or both independent clauses, use a semicolon to link them.

- With temperatures below freezing, the snow did not melt**; and** people, gazing at the white landscape, wondered when they would see grass again.

  Each of the two independent clauses contains one or more commas. Therefore, a semicolon with *and* does the linking of the independent clauses.

❗ **Alerts:** (1) Never put a comma *after* a coordinating conjunction that joins independent clauses.

> **NO** A house is renovated in two weeks **but,** an apartment takes a week.
>
> **YES** A house is renovated in two weeks, **but** an apartment takes a week.

(2) Never use a comma when a coordinating conjunction links only two words, phrases, or dependent clauses.

> **NO** Habitat for Humanity depends on volunteer **labor, and donations** for its construction projects.
>
> **YES** Habitat for Humanity depends on volunteer **labor and donations** for its construction projects.

(3) Never use a comma between independent clauses unless you also use a coordinating conjunction. (If you make this error, you create a COMMA SPLICE.)

> **NO** Five inches of snow fell in two **hours, driving** was hazardous.
>
> **YES** Five inches of snow fell in two **hours, and driving** was hazardous. ●

● **EXERCISE 47-1** Insert commas before coordinating conjunctions that link independent clauses. Some sentences may be correct.

Explore the Exercise

1. England, Scotland, and Wales are located on the same island.
2. Wales is located on the western peninsula of the island and England and Scotland occupy the rest of it.
3. It is bounded on the east by the North Sea and on the south by the English Channel.
4. The Teutonic invaders of the fifth century had to struggle with native Britons for possession of the island for the Romans had virtually abandoned the island by that time.
5. Britain is the proper name of the whole island but England is the political name of the part conquered by the Angles.
6. Neither the Jutes nor the Saxons moved north for they chose to settle in what is today Kent or moved on to Sussex, Wessex, and Essex. ●

47D How do I use commas with a series?

Listen to the Podcast

A *series,* which always calls for commas, consists of three or more elements with the same grammatical form.

> **WORDS** The earliest clothing fabrics were made from natural fibers such as **cotton, silk, linen,** and **wool.**

PHRASES	Fabrics today are made **from natural fibers, from synthetic fibers,** and **from natural and synthetic fiber blends.**
CLAUSES	**Natural fibers are durable as well as absorbent, synthetic fibers resist wrinkling as well as fading,** and **blends of the two fibers offer the advantages of both.**

Although some professional writers omit the comma before a final coordinating conjunction in a series, most instructors prefer that you use that comma. The comma helps readers understand the sentence.

Items in a series often appear as numbered or lettered lists within a sentence. In such cases, use commas or semicolons exactly as you would if the numbers or letters were not there.

- Three synthetic fibers predominate in clothing manufacturing: **(1) rayon, (2) polyester,** and **(3) acrylic.**

- Three popular fabrics for blouses are **(a) cotton, a natural fiber; (b) rayon, a synthetic fiber;** and **(c) ramie, a natural fiber.**

🛇 Alerts: (1) Never use a comma before the first item or after the last item in a series, unless another rule makes it necessary.

NO	We used**, red, white,** and **blue** ribbons for the Fourth of July.
NO	We used **red, white,** and **blue,** ribbons for the Fourth of July.
YES	We used **red, white,** and **blue** ribbons for the Fourth of July.

(2) Never use a comma when only two items are linked by a coordinating conjunction.

NO	Everyone enjoyed **the parade,** and **the concert.**
YES	Everyone enjoyed **the parade** and **the concert.** ●

47E When do I use a comma between adjectives?

Use a comma between **coordinating adjectives** (adjectives that carry equal weight when modifying a noun) unless a coordinating conjunction (such as *and* or *but*) already links them.

In contrast, never use a comma between **cumulative adjectives,** which do not carry equal weight in modifying a noun. The role of cumulative adjectives is to build up—accumulate—meaning as they move toward the noun.

To determine whether adjectives are carrying equal weight in a sentence, use the tests in Quick Box 47.2, p. 444.

((••

Listen
to the
Podcast

Quick Box 47.2 ■ ■ ■ ■ ■ ■ ■ ■ ■

Tests for coordinating and cumulative adjectives

If the answer to either of the following questions is yes, the adjectives are coordinating and need commas.

1. Can the order of the adjectives be changed without changing the sentence's meaning or creating nonsense?

   - The **large, restless, noisy** crowd wanted the concert to start.

     The order of adjectives can be changed (*noisy, restless, large*) and the sentence still makes sense, so these are *coordinating adjectives that need commas.*

   - The concert featured **several familiar backup** singers.

     Several familiar backup cannot be changed to *backup familiar several* and make sense, so these are *cumulative adjectives, which do not need commas.*

2. Can *and* be inserted between the adjectives without changing the meaning or creating nonsense?

   - The **large,ˆrestless,ˆnoisy** crowd wanted the concert to start.
     and   and

     Inserting *and* does not change the meaning of the sentence. Therefore, the adjectives are *coordinating and the commas are correct.*

   - The concert featured **severalˆfamiliarˆbackup** singers.
     and   and

     Inserting *and* creates nonsense. Therefore, the adjectives are *cumulative adjectives and do not need commas.*

47F How do commas work with nonrestrictive and restrictive elements?

A **restrictive element** pinpoints, narrows, or restricts the meaning of its ANTECEDENT to a particular person or class: *Don't eat tomatoes **that are canned.*** A **nonrestrictive element** describes but does not pinpoint, narrow, or restrict the meaning of its antecedent: *Berries, **which sweeten your breakfast,** are highly nutritious.*

Use commas to separate nonrestrictive elements from the rest of a sentence. Do not use commas to separate restrictive elements from their antecedents. Simply stated:

- Restrictive element—do not use commas.
- Nonrestrictive element—use commas.

NO Someone**, named Princess,** canceled the concert.

Named Princess narrows who *someone* is to Princess; it is restrictive. Commas are unnecessary.

YES Someone **named Princess** canceled the concert.

A restrictive, pinpointing element requires no comma.

NO Princess **who writes all her material** is suing her promoter.

Who writes all her material is descriptive and does not pinpoint Princess; it is nonrestrictive. Commas are required.

YES Princess**, who writes all her material,** is suing her promoter.

A nonrestrictive element needs to be set off by commas.

NO Princess started playing on a piano**, that was out of tune.**

That was out of tune is restrictive because it identifies the piano. No comma is necessary.

YES Princess started playing on a piano **that was out of tune.**

A restrictive, pinpointing clause requires no comma.

NO **A prolific artist** Princess is on her way to fame and fortune.

A prolific artist is a descriptive, nonrestrictive element, so it requires a comma.

YES **A prolific artist,** Princess is on her way to fame and fortune.

A nonrestrictive element requires a comma.

● **EXERCISE 47-2** Using your knowledge of restrictive and nonrestrictive elements, insert commas as needed. If a sentence is correct, explain why. For help, consult 47F.

Explore
the
Exercise

EXAMPLE

During the summer when butterflies are most active gardeners can attract them by planting the right flowers.

During the summer, when butterflies are most active, gardeners can attract them by planting the right flowers.

1. In spring as birds and bees look for water and food certain plants and trees provide those needs and thus attract the greatest number of airborne visitors.
2. Gardeners who learn to attract birds may find they have fewer problems with insects and other unwelcome pests.
3. During suburban sprawl when cities eat up more and more land birds have to adapt by putting their nests in buildings.

4. Birds are attracted to pines and evergreens where they can find food and shelter.

5. Hungry birds who are not picky will enjoy a feeder stocked with black oil sunflower seeds.

6. Birds also need to eat insects which provide a higher protein content than seeds.

7. Some common plants such as butterfly weed and lantana are ideal for attracting butterflies.

8. Because they have the nectar that butterflies want these plants enhance any butterfly garden.

9. As butterflies pass by a garden looking for bright colors and strong fragrances they will notice flowers planted in large clumps.

10. Gardens that are favorable to birds and butterflies will also invite honeybees and other pollinators. ●

47G How do I use commas with quoted words?

Use a comma to set off quoted words from explanations in the sentence.

- The poet William Blake wrote, "Love seeketh not itself to please."

- "I love you," Mary told John, "but I cannot marry you."

- "My love is a fever," declared William Shakespeare.

However, when you use *that* to introduce a quotation, never use a comma whether you write a DIRECT QUOTATION or an INDIRECT QUOTATION.

NO	Mary claims, that "our passion is strong."
NO	Mary claims that, "our passion is strong."
YES	Mary claims that "our passion is strong."

❶ Alert: When the quoted words end with an exclamation point or a question mark, retain that original punctuation, even if explanatory words follow.

QUOTED WORDS	*"O Romeo! Romeo!"*
NO	"O Romeo! Romeo!," whispered Juliet from her window.
NO	"O Romeo! Romeo," whispered Juliet from her window.
YES	"O Romeo! Romeo!" whispered Juliet from her window. ●

47H What other word groups do I set off with commas?

Additional word groups that call for a comma to set them off include transitional expressions, conjunctive adverbs, asides, contrasts, words addressed directly to a reader or listener, and **tag questions** (such as *isn't it?* or *don't you think?*).

TRANSITIONAL EXPRESSIONS

- **For example,** California is a major food producer.
- California, **for example,** is a major food producer.
- California is a major food producer, **for example.**

CONJUNCTIVE ADVERBS

- **However,** the Midwest is the world's breadbasket.
- The Midwest, **however,** is the world's breadbasket.
- The Midwest is the world's breadbasket, **however.**

ASIDES

- Most large growers, **I imagine,** hope to export food.
- Most large growers hope to export food, **I imagine.**

CONTRASTS

- Food, **not technology,** tops the list of US exports.

WORDS ADDRESSED DIRECTLY TO READER

- **All you computer majors,** perhaps the future lies in soybeans rather than software.
- Perhaps the future, **all you computer majors,** lies in soybeans rather than software.
- Perhaps the future lies in soybeans rather than software, **all you computer majors.**

TAG QUESTIONS

- You know, **don't you,** what tag questions are?
- You know what tag questions are, **don't you?**

47I How do I use commas in dates, names, places, addresses, letter format, and numbers?

■ Punctuating dates

Use a comma between the day and the month. In addition, use a comma between a day of the week and the month.

- July 20, 1969
- Sunday, July 20, 1969

When you use month-day-year order for dates, use a comma after the day and the year.

- Everyone watched television on July 20, 1969, to see the moon landing.

When you use day-month-year order for dates, never use commas.

- Everyone watched television on 20 July 1969 to see the moon landing.

Never use a comma between only a month and year, only a month and day, or only a season and year.

- The major news story in July 1969 was the moon landing; news coverage was especially heavy on July 21. Many older people will always remember summer 1969.

■ Punctuating names, places, and addresses

When an abbreviated academic degree (*MD, PhD*) comes after a name, use a comma between the name and the title (see 57B). When a sentence continues after a name and title, also use a comma after the title.

- Rosa Gonzales, MD, was the principal witness for the defense.

However, don't place a comma before or after *Jr., Sr., II,* or *2nd* (57C).

- Ron Gonzales Jr. was the defendant.

Use a comma between the last and first names in an inverted name.

- Troyka, David

Use a comma between a city and state. When a sentence continues after a city and state, also use a comma after the state.

- Philadelphia, Pennsylvania, is home to the Liberty Bell.

When a sentence includes a complete address, use a comma to separate all of the items in the address except the ZIP code (see 67E). The ZIP code follows the state after a space and no comma.

- I wrote to Mr. Hugh Lern, 10-01 Rule Road, Classgate, NJ 07632, for the instruction manual.

■ Punctuating letter openings and closings

Use a comma after the opening of an informal letter or e-mail. Use a colon after the opening of a formal letter.

- Dear Betty,   - Dear Ms. Renshaw:

After the closing of a formal or informal letter, use a comma.

- Sincerely yours,
- Love,

■ Punctuating numbers

In numbers more than four digits long, put a comma after every three digits, counting from the right.

- 150,567,066
- 72,867

In four-digit numbers, a comma is optional for money, distance, amounts, and most other measurements. Be consistent in each piece of writing.

- $1776 $1,776
- 1776 miles   1,776 miles
- 1776 potatoes 1,776 potatoes

Use a comma to separate the act and scene numbers in plays. In addition, use a comma to separate a page reference in any SOURCE from a line reference.

- act ii, scene iv [or act 2, scene 4]
- page 120, line 6

47J How can a comma prevent a misreading?

Use a comma to clarify the meaning of a sentence, even if no other rule calls for one.

NO People who can practice many hours a day.

YES People who can, practice many hours a day.

● **EXERCISE 47-3** Working individually or with a group, insert commas to prevent misreading. For help, consult 47J.

Explore
the
Exercise

EXAMPLE
For scientists tracking and measuring hurricanes is still an inexact science.
For scientists, tracking and measuring hurricanes is still an inexact science.

1. Lasting for thirteen days in August 1992 Hurricane Andrew after 2005's Katrina was the second most expensive hurricane.
2. Andrew was rated a category four smaller than 2005's Katrina when it made landfall in south Florida.
3. The highest gust officially recorded 164 miles per hour at 130 feet above the ground occurred before Andrew shut down the National Hurricane Center's measuring devices.

4. The thousands of vortexes within Andrew as with many high-intensity storms are what caused the worst damage.

5. Andrew difficult to measure accurately was upgraded from a category four to a category five hurricane ten years after it occurred. ●

47K How can I avoid other comma errors?

In explaining comma rules in this chapter so far, we've covered the errors associated with those rules. Here are a few helpful tips for using commas.

1. Never put a comma in a number in an address or in a page reference.

   ● 11263 Dean Drive   ● see page 1338

2. Never put a comma in years expressed in four figures. If the year is expressed in five or more figures, use a comma. If you list years in a sentence, separate them with a comma.

   ● 1995, 2002   ● 25,000 BCE

3. Never put a comma after *such as.*

   NO   The Wright brothers were fascinated by other vehicles, **such as,** bicycles and gliders.

   YES   The Wright brothers were fascinated by other vehicles, such as bicycles and gliders.

4. Never put a comma before *than* in a comparison.

   NO   The 1903 airplane sustained its flight longer**, than** any other engine-powered aircraft had.

   YES   The 1903 airplane sustained its flight longer **than** any other engine-powered aircraft had.

5. Never put a comma before an opening parenthesis. When a comma is required, put it *after* the closing parenthesis.

   NO   Because aviation enthralls many of us**, (especially children)** a popular spot to visit is Kitty Hawk's flight museum.

   YES   Because aviation enthralls many of us **(especially children),** a popular spot to visit is Kitty Hawk's flight museum.

6. Never put a comma after a PREPOSITION.

   NO   People expected more damage **from,** the high winds.

   YES   People expected more damage **from** the high winds.

7. Never put a comma after a SUBORDINATING CONJUNCTION.

   NO   **Although,** winds exceeded fifty miles an hour, little damage occurred.

   YES   **Although** winds exceeded fifty miles an hour, little damage occurred.

8. Never put a comma between a SUBJECT and its VERB. (A pair of commas, however, is acceptable.)

   NO   Orville and Wilbur Wright, made their first successful airplane flights in 1903.

   YES   Orville and Wilbur Wright made their first successful airplane flights in 1903.

   YES   Orville and Wilbur Wright, on a beach in North Carolina, made their first successful airplane flights in 1903.

9. Never put a comma between a verb and its OBJECT.

   NO   These inventors tackled, the problems of powered flight.

   YES   These inventors tackled the problems of powered flight.

10. Never put a comma between a verb and its COMPLEMENT.

   NO   Flying has become, an important industry and a popular hobby.

   YES   Flying has become an important industry and a popular hobby.

● **EXERCISE 47-4** Some commas have been deliberately misused in these sentences. Delete misused commas. If a sentence is correct, explain why. For help, consult all parts of this chapter, especially 47J and 47K.

Explore
the
Exercise

EXAMPLE
The Harlem Renaissance was a cultural and artistic movement, that began around 1919 and lasted until the early 1930s.

The Harlem Renaissance was a cultural and artistic movement that began around 1919 and lasted until the early 1930s.

1. Although, this movement is named for Harlem, its impact spread to urban areas throughout the country, and the world.
2. During the Harlem Renaissance, artists in many fields found new ways to express the different facets, of black life in America.
3. The migration of millions of African Americans from the rural South to the urban North in the early twentieth century, helped make the Harlem Renaissance possible.
4. W. E. B. Du Bois played an important role in the Harlem Renaissance, for he edited the magazine, that became the official publication of the NAACP.

5. Furthermore, Du Bois rose to prominence by becoming, the first African American to receive a PhD from Harvard University.
6. The music, of the Harlem Renaissance, became a vital tool for expressing and celebrating, the culture of those who lived there.
7. In particular, many people listened to jazz after, musicians from the South moved north and began playing it in clubs, theaters, and private homes.
8. The Harlem Renaissance produced diverse, original, writers, and they created everything from plays to poems.
9. For example, Claude McKay wrote novels that those in, literary studies, still study today.
10. The political and cultural gains achieved by African Americans during this time paved, the way for future generations. ●

48 Semicolons

Quick Points   You will learn to

➤ Use semicolons correctly.

48A When can I use a semicolon instead of a period between independent clauses?

Watch
the Video

You can choose whether to use a semicolon to replace a period, but do so only between two closely related INDEPENDENT CLAUSES; using a semicolon creates one sentence.

NO   After she walked out the door; I never saw her again.

After she walked out the door is not an independent clause; a comma should be used.

YES   She walked out the door; I never saw her again.

YES   She walked out the door; later, I never saw her again.

The semicolon separates the two closely related independent clauses. In the second example, a CONJUNCTIVE ADVERB (*later, then*) introduces the second independent clause.

48B When do I need to use a semicolon to replace a comma?

A semicolon replaces a comma when you use a COORDINATING CONJUNCTION to link independent clauses that already contain commas.

> Because Death Valley is the hottest place in North America, some people think that no animals live there**; but** visitors, especially, are amazed to see many tiny and a few larger animals emerge at night, when the temperatures drop, to find food.

In addition, when individual items in a series (see 47D) contain commas, use a semicolon instead of a comma to separate the items.

> The animals in Death Valley include **spiders,** such as black widows and tarantulas**; snakes,** such as coral snakes and sidewinders; and **small mammals,** such as kangaroo rats, which can convert seeds into water, and trade rats, which nest around cactus.

🚫 Alert: Use a colon, never a semicolon, to introduce a list of items.

NO Predators live in Death Valley; spiders, snakes, and some mammals.

YES Predators live in Death Valley: spiders, snakes, and some mammals. ●

● **EXERCISE 48-1** Combine each set of sentences into one sentence so that it contains two independent clauses. Use a semicolon correctly between the two clauses. You may add, omit, revise, and rearrange words. Try to use all the patterns in this chapter, and explain the reasoning behind your decisions. More than one revision may be correct. For help, consult all sections of this chapter.

Explore the Exercise

EXAMPLE
Although not as well known as Thomas Edison, the inventor Nikola Tesla was a revolutionary and important scientist. One biographer calls him "the man who invented the twentieth century."

Although not as well known as Thomas Edison, the inventor Nikola Tesla was a revolutionary scientist; one biographer calls him "the man who invented the twentieth century."

1. Tesla was born in what is now Croatia and studied at the Technical University at Graz, Austria. He excelled in physics, mechanical engineering, and electrical engineering.
2. Tesla's accomplishments include inventing alternating current. He also contributed to the fields of robotics, computer science, and wireless technology. And he helped increase knowledge of nuclear physics, ballistics, and electromagnetism.
3. The Italian inventor Guglielmo Marconi and Tesla both claimed to have invented the radio. However, the US Supreme Court, in 1943, upheld Tesla's radio patent and officially credited him as the device's inventor.

4. In 1901, Tesla began construction of a tower that he claimed would create a global network of wireless communication and be able to control the weather. Unfortunately, Tesla soon lost funding and never finished the project.

5. At his lab in Colorado Springs, he was able to produce artificial lightning. This scene was vividly portrayed in the 2006 film *The Prestige.* ●

49 Colons

Quick Points   You will learn to

➤ Use colons correctly.

49A   How do I use a colon with a list, an appositive, or a quotation?

Watch
the Video

Use a colon after an INDEPENDENT CLAUSE to introduce a list, an APPOSITIVE, or a QUOTATION. Some lead-in words, such as *the following* and *as follows,* are followed by a colon. Other lead-ins (*such as, like,* and *including*) aren't.

LISTED ITEMS

● The students demanded the following: an expanded menu in the cafeteria, improved janitorial services, and more up-to-date textbooks.

APPOSITIVE

● Museums in New York and Florida own the best-known works from Louis Tiffany's studio: those wonderful stained-glass windows.

Stained-glass windows is an appositive that renames *best-known works.*

QUOTATION

● The little boy in *E.T.* did say something neat: "How do you explain school to a higher intelligence?"

—George F. Will, "Well, I Don't Love You, E.T."

🛇 **Alert:** If an incomplete sentence introduces a DIRECT QUOTATION, use a comma, not a colon (see 47G).●

49B When can I use a colon between sentences?

When one sentence introduces the next, you can use a colon between the two.

- I'll say it again: Snakes are lovable.

Alerts: (1) Never use a colon when a DIRECT OBJECT consists of a series or list of items.

NO We bought: eggs, milk, cheese, and bread.

YES We bought eggs, milk, cheese, and bread.

(2) Never separate a DEPENDENT CLAUSE from an independent clause with a colon. Use a comma instead.

NO After the drought ended: water restrictions were lifted.

YES After the drought ended, water restrictions were lifted.

(3) Capitalizing the word after a colon is optional. Simply be consistent. ●

49C What conventional formats call for colons?

BETWEEN TITLE AND SUBTITLE

- *Literature: An Introduction to Critical Reading*

BETWEEN HOURS AND MINUTES AND MINUTES AND SECONDS

- The runner passed the halfway point at 1:23:02.

BETWEEN NUMBERS IN RATIOS

- a proportion of 7:1   ● a 3:5 ratio

AFTER WORDS IN MEMO HEADINGS

- To: Dean Kristen Joy

- From: Professor Daniel Black

- Re: Student work-study program

AFTER FORMAL LETTER OPENINGS

- Dear Ms. Carter:

BETWEEN BIBLE CHAPTERS AND VERSES

- Psalm 23:1–3

! **Alert:** In MLA STYLE, a period comes between chapter and verse in Bible references: *Ps. 23.1–3.* See Ch. 24 for other MLA rules. ●

● **EXERCISE 49-1** Insert colons where needed and delete any not needed. If a sentence is correct, explain why. For help, consult all sections of this chapter.

Explore
the
Exercise

EXAMPLE
The twentieth century saw a flowering of Irish literature, W. B. Yeats, G. B. Shaw, Samuel Beckett, and Seamus Heaney all won the Nobel Prize for Literature.

The twentieth century saw a flowering of Irish literature: W. B. Yeats, G. B. Shaw, Samuel Beckett, and Seamus Heaney all won the Nobel Prize for Literature.

1. People who work the night shift are typically deprived of essential sleep, an average of nine hours a week.
2. The Iroquois of the Great Lakes region lived in fortified villages and cultivated: corn, beans, and squash.
3. Five nations originally formed the Iroquois Confederacy: the Mohawk, the Oneida, the Onondaga, the Cayuga, and the Seneca.
4. Later, these five Iroquois nations were joined by: the Tuscarora.
5. Shouting: "Come back!" Adam watched the vehicle speed down the highway.
6. When a runner breaks through that unavoidable wall of exhaustion, a very different feeling sets in; an intense sense of well-being known as the "runner's high."
7. However: the "runner's high" soon disappears.
8. Two new nations were born on the same day in 1947, India and Pakistan achieved their independence from Britain at midnight on August 15.
9. Date   December 8, 2012
   To   English 101 Instructors
   From   Dean of Instruction
   Re   Classroom Assignments
10. Only a hurricane could have kept Lisa from meeting Nathaniel at 800 p.m.; unfortunately, that night a hurricane hit.
11. George's interests were typical of a sixteen-year-old's, cars, music, and dating.
12. Like many people who have never learned to read or write, the woman who told her life story in *Aman; The Story of a Somali Girl* was able to remember an astonishing number of events in precise detail. ●

50 Apostrophes

■ ■ ■ ■ ■ ■ ■ ■

Quick Points You will learn to

➤ Use apostrophes correctly.

50A How do I use an apostrophe to show that a noun is possessive?

The **possessive case** shows possession or ownership (*the writer's pen*) or other relationships (*the writer's parent*). To indicate possession in NOUNS, you can choose to use *-'s* (*the instructor's comments*), which calls for an apostrophe; or a PHRASE beginning with *of* (*the comments of the instructor*), which doesn't call for an apostrophe. Here are some applications of this general rule.

1. Add *-'s* to nouns not ending in *s*.

   - She felt a **parent's** joy.

   - We care about our **children's** education.

2. Add *-'s* to singular nouns ending in *s*.

   - The **business's** system for handling complaints is inefficient.

   - Lee **Jones's** car insurance is expensive.

3. Add only an apostrophe to plural nouns ending in *s*.

   - The two **boys'** eyewitness statements helped solve the crime.

   - The **workers'** contracts permit three **months'** maternity leave.

4. Add *-'s* to the last word in compound words and phrases.

   - His **mother-in-law's** company makes scuba gear.

5. Add *-'s* to each noun in individual possession.

   - **Avery's and Jimmy's** houses are next to each other.

6. Add *-'s* to only the last noun in joint or group possession.

   - **Lindsey and Ryan's** house has a screened porch.

🛈 Alerts: (1) Never use an apostrophe at the end of a nonpossessive noun ending in *s*.

Watch the Video

Listen to the Podcast

NO	The circus' has dropped all its animal acts.
YES	The circus has dropped all animal acts.

(2) Never use an apostrophe with a nonpossessive plural noun.

NO	**Team's** of doctors are researching the effects of cholesterol.
	Teams is a plural noun that ends in *s*, but the sentence expresses no possession.
YES	**Teams** of doctors are researching the effects of cholesterol. ●

50B How do I use an apostrophe to show that an indefinite pronoun is possessive?

INDEFINITE PRONOUNS refer to general or nonspecific persons or things: *someone, somebody, anyone, anything, no one, else.* (For a complete list of types of pronouns, see Quick Box 32.2, p. 343.) To indicate possession in an indefinite pronoun, add *-'s.*

- I need **someone's** help to prepare for the test.

- Are **anyone else's** directions more accurate than mine are?

  When one indefinite pronoun follows another (*anyone else*), the second one takes the possessive *-'s.*

50C Do I ever use an apostrophe with *hers, his, its, ours, yours,* and *theirs*?

Never use an apostrophe with **possessive pronouns:** *hers, his, its, ours, yours,* and *theirs.* As possessive pronouns, they already carry possessive meaning.

NO	Because cholesterol has been widely publicized, **it's** role in heart disease is well known.
YES	Because cholesterol has been widely publicized, **its** role in heart disease is well known.

🚫 **Alert:** Never confuse *its,* the possessive pronoun, with the contraction *it's,* which stands for *it is.* A similar confusion arises between *you're* and *your, who's* and *whose,* and *they're* and *their.* ●

50D Do I ever add an apostrophe to a verb that ends in -s?

Never add an apostrophe to a VERB that ends in *s.*

NO	Exercise **play's** a key role in longevity.
YES	Exercise **plays** a key role in longevity.

50E How do I use apostrophes in contractions?

In **contractions**, an apostrophe indicates that one or more letters have been omitted from a word or a term: *can't, don't, I'm, isn't, it's, let's, they're, wasn't, weren't, we've, who's, won't, you're.*

Listen
to the
Podcast

- **It's** [not Its] still snowing.

 Alert: Many college instructors believe that contractions aren't appropriate in ACADEMIC WRITING. Indeed, the seventh edition of the *MLA Handbook* says they are "rarely acceptable in research papers" (74). ●

50F Do I use an apostrophe with letters, numerals, symbols, and terms?

Use an apostrophe before the *s* to form the plurals of single letters, numbers written as figures, symbols, and words used as terms.

LETTERS	Printing **w's** is hard for some first graders.
NUMBERS IN FIGURES	The address includes six **2's**.
SYMBOLS	The use of **#'s** is now common on Twitter.
WORDS USED AS TERMS	All the ***for*'s** were misspelled *four.*

 Alert: When you use letters as letters or words as words, you can choose to underline them or put them in italics, or enclose them in quotation marks (see 51E). Whatever you choose, be consistent in each piece of writing. ●

● **EXERCISE 50-1** Rewrite these sentences to insert *'s* or an apostrophe alone to make the words in parentheses show possession. (Delete the parentheses.) For help, consult this chapter.

Explore
the
Exercise

EXAMPLE
All boxes, cans, and bottles on a (supermarket) shelves are designed to appeal to (people) emotions.

All boxes, cans, and bottles on a *supermarket's* shelves are designed to appeal to *people's* emotions.

1. A (product) manufacturer designs packaging to appeal to (consumers) emotions through color and design.
2. Marketing specialists know that (people) beliefs about a (product) quality are influenced by their emotional response to the design of its package.

3. Circles and ovals appearing on a (box) design supposedly increase a (product user) feelings of comfort, while bold patterns and colors attract a (shopper) attention.

4. Using both circles and bold designs in (Arm & Hammer) and (Tide) packaging produces both effects in consumers.

5. (Heinz) ketchup bottle and (Coca-Cola) famous logo achieve the same effects by combining a bright color with an old-fashioned, "comfortable" design.

6. Often, a (company) marketing consultants will custom-design products to appeal to the supposedly "typical" (adult female) emotions or to (adult males), (children), or (teenagers) feelings.

7. One of the (marketing business) leading consultants, Stan Gross, tests (consumers) emotional reactions to (companies) products and their packages by asking consumers to associate products with well-known personalities.

8. Thus, (test takers) responses to (Gross) questions might reveal that a particular brand of laundry detergent has (Russell Crowe) toughness, (Oprah Winfrey) determination, or (someone else) sparkling personality.

9. Manufacturing (companies) products are not the only ones relying on (Gross) and other corporate (image makers) advice.

10. (Sports teams) owners also use marketing specialists to design their (teams) images, as anyone who has seen the angry bull logo of the Chicago Bulls basketball team will agree. ●

51 Quotation Marks

■ ■ ■ ■ ■ ■ ■ ■

Quick Points   You will learn to

➤ Use quotation marks correctly.

51A How do I use quotation marks with short direct quotations?

Watch the Video

Quotation marks are most often used to enclose a **direct quotation**—a speaker or writer's exact words. Use quotation marks to enclose short direct quotations, which in MLA style means a quotation of fewer than four typed lines of prose or three typed lines of poetry.

- Remarked director Fritz Lang of his masterpiece *Siegfried*, "Nothing in this film is accidental" (228).

For MLA in-text citation style with quotations, see Chapter 24; for APA style, see Chapter 27.

■ Using double quotation marks (" ")

Use double quotation marks to enclose a short quotation.

- Edward T. Hall explains the practicality of close conversational distances: **"If you are interested in something, your pupils dilate; if I say something you don't like, they tend to contract"** (47). Some cultures prefer arm's length for all but the most intimate conversations.

- As W. H. Auden wittily defined personal space, **"Some thirty inches from my nose / The frontier of my person goes"** (539).

■ Using single quotation marks (' ')

Use single quotation marks in short quotations only to replace any double quotation marks that appear in the original source.

ORIGINAL SOURCE

He has also said that he does not wish to be the arbiter for what is or is not an **"official"** intelligence.

—Thomas Hoerr, "The Naturalistic Intelligence," p. 24

EXAMPLE FROM A RESEARCH PAPER

As Thomas Hoerr reports, Gardner "does not wish to be the arbiter for what is or is not an **'official'** intelligence" (24).

🛈 **Alerts:** (1) Use a slash to signal a break between lines of poetry (2) Capitalize and punctuate poetry you quote exactly as in the original. ●

51B How do I use quotation marks with long direct quotations?

In MLA style, a **long quotation** runs five or more lines of prose or more than three lines of poetry. A long quotation starts on a new line and is indented, or *displayed,* as a whole block of words, 1 inch from the left margin in MLA style (see Chs. 24–26).

Because a block indentation signifies quoted material, don't use quotation marks to enclose block quotations. If, however, words in the original are in quotation marks, punctuate exactly as in the original. The following passage demonstrates such usage.

> As Desmond Morris explains, personal space varies among cultures:
>
> > When you are talking to someone in the street or in any open space, reach out with your arm and see where the nearest point on his body comes. If you hail from western Europe, you will find that he is at roughly fingertip distance from you. In other words, as you reach out, your fingertips will just about make contact with his shoulder. If you come from eastern Europe, you will find you are standing at "wrist distance." If you come from the Mediterranean region you will find that you are much closer to your companion. (23)

! Alert: In MLA style, at the end of a long quotation, place the page number or the author's name and the page number (only if you don't mention the author's name in the sentence that leads into the quotation) in parentheses. Put the period that ends the sentence before the parentheses, never after them. ●

51C How do I use quotation marks to indicate spoken words?

Spoken words are called DIRECT DISCOURSE. Use quotation marks when you quote direct discourse or write dialogue. Start a new paragraph—that is, indent the first line—each time the speaker changes.

> "I don't know how you can see to drive," she said.
>
> "Maybe you should put on your glasses."
>
> "Putting on my glasses would help you to see?"
>
> "Not me; you," Macon said. "You're focused on the windshield instead of the road."
>
> —Ann Tyler, *The Accidental Tourist*

If the same speaker's words continue for more than one paragraph, use opening quotation marks only at the start of each paragraph. Use closing quotation marks only when you come to the final paragraph of the dialogue.

! Alert: Never enclose INDIRECT DISCOURSE (see 39D) in quotation marks.

● The mayor said that he was tired.

> This indirect discourse needs no quotation marks. As a direct quotation, this sentence would read *The mayor said, "I am tired."* ●

● **EXERCISE 51-1**   Working individually or with a group, decide whether each sentence that follows is direct or indirect discourse, and then rewrite each sentence in the other form. Make any changes needed for grammatical correctness. With direct discourse, put the speaker's words wherever you think they belong in the sentence. For help, consult 51A through 51C.

Explore the Exercise

EXAMPLE
A school counselor told Betty, a senior at Whatsamatta U, that she needed to take one more three-unit elective to graduate in May.

A school counselor told Betty, a senior at Whatsamatta U, "You need to take one more three-unit elective to graduate in May."

1. "Betty, would you be interested in taking an introductory electronics course?" asked the counselor.
2. Betty asked why she would take such a course when she was a nursing major.
3. The counselor looked Betty straight in the eye and said, "Some knowledge of electronics may not be part of your major, but it's a very important modern subject, nevertheless."
4. Betty wondered whether it might give her a greater understanding of all the electronics used in medical diagnosis and treatment today. But she also asked if there wasn't another elective that might do more to enhance her nursing career.
5. The counselor was quiet for a moment and then declared, "And don't forget, electronics is something you can always fall back on, Betty. And the more you have to fall back on, the softer the landing." ●

51D   How do I use quotation marks with titles?

Use quotation marks around the titles of short published works: poems, short stories, essays, articles from periodicals, song titles, and individual episodes of a television or radio series. Use italics (or underlining) for longer works. See Chapter 56 for more on italics.

51E   How do I use quotation marks to indicate terms, language translations, and irony?

You can choose either quotation marks or italics (or underlining) to indicate words that are technical terms; words in another language; translated words; and words meant ironically. Simply be consistent in your choice.

TECHNICAL TERM	"Plagiarism"—the unacknowledged use of another person's words or ideas—is a serious offense. Plagiarism by students can result in expulsion.
	Once the term has been introduced it needs no further quotation marks.
TRANSLATED WORDS	My grandfather usually ended arguments with an old saying: *de gustibus non disputandum est* ("there is no arguing about tastes").
IRONIC WORD	The tax "reform" is actually a tax increase.

51F When are quotation marks wrong?

Never use quotation marks around CLICHÉS, SLANG, or other language that is inappropriate in ACADEMIC WRITING. Use appropriate, alternative wording.

NO   They "eat like birds" in public and "stuff their faces" in private.

YES   They nibble in public and gorge themselves in private.

Never enclose a word in quotation marks merely to call attention to it.

NO   Remember, the "customer" matters to your business.

YES   Remember, the customer matters to your business.

Never enclose indirect discourse in quotation marks.

NO   The College Code of Conduct points out that "plagiarism can result in expulsion."

The original words are "Grounds for expulsion include plagiarism." Here, the quotation is indirect, so quotation marks are wrong.

YES   The College Code of Conduct points out that plagiarism can result in expulsion.

Never use quotation marks around the title of your own paper, unless your title includes another title of a short work (see Quick Box 56.1, on p. 486).

NO   "The Elderly in Nursing Homes: A Case Study"

YES   The Elderly in Nursing Homes: A Case Study

NO   Sentence Structure in Emerson's Essay Self-Reliance

YES   Sentence Structure in Emerson's Essay "Self-Reliance"

51G How do I use quotation marks with other punctuation?

1. Put commas and periods inside closing quotation marks.

   - After we read Poe's poem "The Raven," we sought out his other works.
   - Edward T. Hall coined the word **"proxemics."**

2. Put colons and semicolons *outside* closing quotation marks.

   - We try to discover **"how close is too close"**: We do not want to invade others' personal space.
   - The sign read **"Dead Man's Hill"**; we knew we were in San Francisco.

3. Put question marks, exclamation points, and dashes outside quotation marks unless they are part of the original quotation.

   - **"Did I Hear You Call My Name?"** was the winning song.
   - They shouted, **"We won the lottery!"**

   If a question mark, an exclamation point, or a dash punctuates words not enclosed in quotation marks, put it outside the closing quotation mark.

   - Have you read Nikki Giovanni's poem **"Knoxville, Tennessee"**?
   - Edward T. Hall's coined word **"proxemics"**—a term based on the noun **"proximity"**—can now be found in dictionaries.

Explore the Exercise

● **EXERCISE 51-2** Correct any errors in the use of quotation marks and other punctuation with quotation marks. If you think a sentence is correct, explain why. For help, consult 51D through 51G.

1. Dying in a shabby hotel room, the witty writer Oscar Wilde supposedly said, "Either that wallpaper goes, or I do".

2. Was it the Russian novelist Tolstoy who wrote, "All happy families resemble one another, but each unhappy family is unhappy in its own way?"

3. In his poem A Supermarket in California, Allen Ginsberg addresses the dead poet Walt Whitman, asking, Where are we going, Walt Whitman? The doors close / in an hour. Which way does your beard point tonight?

4. Toni Morrison made this reply to the claim that "art that has a political message cannot be good art:" She said that "the best art is political" and that her aim was to create art that was "unquestionably political" and beautiful at the same time.

5. Benjamin Franklin's strange question—"What is the use of a newborn child?—" was his response to someone who doubted the usefulness of new inventions. ●

52

Periods, Question Marks, and Exclamation Points

■ ■ ■ ■ ■ ■ ■ ■

Quick Points   You will learn to

➤ Use periods, question marks, and exclamation points correctly.

52A   When should I use a period?

Watch the Video

A period is used after a statement, a mild command, or an **indirect question**, which reports a question that someone asks. (For help with periods in abbreviations, see Chapter 57.)

STATEMENT	Mountain climbers enjoy the outdoors.
MILD COMMAND	Pack warm clothes for the climb.
INDIRECT QUESTION	I asked if they wanted to climb Mount Ross.

52B   When should I use a question mark?

A question mark is used after a **direct question** (which asks a question outright), a directly quoted question (which needs quotation marks), a series of questions, or a polite request. Use a question mark after each question in a series, whether or not you choose to capitalize the first word.

DIRECT QUESTION	Have you ever climbed a mountain?
DIRECTLY QUOTED QUESTION	I asked, "Do you want to climb Mount Everest?"
SERIES OF QUESTIONS WITH CAPITALS	The mountain climbers debated what to do: Turn back? Move on? Rest?
SERIES OF QUESTIONS WITH LOWERCASE	The mountain climbers debated what to do: turn back? move on? rest?

To end a polite request, you can choose a question mark or a period.

● Would you please send me the report.

This version emphasizes the politeness more than the request.

● Would you please send me the report?

This version emphasizes the request more than the politeness.

To convey IRONY or sarcasm, depend on words, not a question mark in parentheses, to communicate your message.

NO Having altitude sickness is a **pleasant (?)** experience.

YES Having altitude sickness is **as pleasant as having a terrible case of the flu.**

52C When should I use an exclamation point?

An exclamation point is used after a strong command (*Look out!*); an emphatic declaration (*Those cars are going to crash!*); or an INTERJECTION, a word that conveys surprise or other emotion (*Oh! I'm terrified of heights!*). In ACADEMIC WRITING, reserve exclamation points for dialogue. Use words with sufficient impact for forceful messages.

NO Each day in Nepal, we tried to see Mount Everest. Each day we failed! The summit remained shrouded! Clouds defeated us!

YES Each day in Nepal, we tried to see Mount Everest. Each day we failed. The summit remained shrouded. Clouds defeated us!

To convey amazement or sarcasm, use precise words, not an exclamation point in parentheses.

NO At 29,035 feet **(!)**, Everest is the world's highest mountain.

YES Everest, the world's highest mountain, **soars** at 29,035 feet.

● **EXERCISE 52-1** Insert needed periods, question marks, and exclamation points. For help, consult all sections of this chapter.

Explore
the
Exercise

Weather experts refer to a rise in surface temperature of the Pacific Ocean as El Niño, but La Niña refers to a drop in ocean temperature What effects can these changes cause In the spring of 1998, the cold water of La Niña surfaced quickly and produced chaotic and destructive weather In the American Northeast, rainfall amounts for June were three times above normal But no one expected the strangest consequence: snow in June Can you imagine waking up on an early summer morning in New England to snow Throughout the summer, most New England states failed to experience a single heat wave, which requires more than three days of 90 degree weather During that winter, the Great Lakes experienced record warmth, but California suffered from disastrously cold air A citrus freeze caused $600 million of damage That's more than half a billion dollars. ●

53

Other Punctuation Marks
■ ■ ■ ■ ■ ■ ■ ■

Quick Points   You will learn to

➤ Use dashes, parentheses, brackets, and ellipses correctly.

53A   When should I use a dash?

The dash, typed as two unspaced hyphens, injects a thought within a sentence—in the middle or at the end—for special emphasis or commentary. You can set off EXAMPLES, DEFINITIONS, APPOSITIVES, contrasts, and asides with dashes.

> Two of the strongest animals in the jungle are vegetarians—the elephant and the gorilla. [examples]
>> —Dick Gregory, *The Shadow That Scares Me*

> Although the emphasis at the school was mainly language—speaking, reading, writing—the lessons always began with an exercise in politeness. [definition]
>> —Jade Snow Wong, *Fifth Chinese Daughter*

> The caretakers—the helpers, nurturers, teachers, mothers—are still systematically devalued. [appositive]
>> —Ellen Goodman, "Just Woman's Work"

> Tampering with time brought most of the house tumbling down, and it was this that made Einstein's work so important—and controversial. [contrast]
>> —Banesh Hoffman, "My Friend, Albert Einstein"

> I live on an income well below the poverty line—although it does not seem like poverty when the redbud and dogwood are in bloom together—and when I travel I have to be careful about expenses. [aside]
>> —Sue Hubbell, *Beekeeper*

🛑 Alerts: (1) If the words within a pair of dashes are a complete sentence and call for a question mark or an exclamation point, place such punctuation *before* the second dash:

- *A first love—do you remember?—stays in the memory forever.*

(2) Never use commas, semicolons, or periods next to dashes. Revise your writing to avoid these types of double punctuation. ●

53B When should I use parentheses?

Like dashes (see 53A), parentheses let you interrupt a sentence's structure to add information. Parentheses tend to de-emphasize whatever they enclose; dashes tend to call attention to whatever they set off.

■ Using parentheses to add information

Parentheses can enclose the same kind of material that dashes can, such as explanations, definitions, examples, contrasts, and asides.

> In division (also known as partition), a subject commonly thought of as a single unit is reduced to its separate parts. [definition]
>
> —David Skwire, *Writing with a Thesis*

> Though other cities (Dresden, for instance) had been utterly destroyed in World War II, never before had a single weapon been responsible for such destruction. [example]
>
> —Lawrence Behrens and Leonard J. Rosen, *Writing and Reading Across the Curriculum*

> The sheer decibel level of the noise around us is not enough to make us cranky, irritable, or aggressive. (It can, however, affect our mental and physical health, which is another matter.) [aside]
>
> —Carol Tavris, *Anger: The Misunderstood Emotion*

■ Using parentheses to enclose numbers or letters

Conventional uses for parentheses include enclosing numbers or letters of listed items: *The topics to be discussed are (1) membership, (2) fund-raising, and (3) networking.* Another conventional use occurs in business writing when parentheses sometimes enclose a number written as a figure immediately after its spelled-out version: *We shipped **fifteen (15)** cartons yesterday.*

■ Using parentheses with other punctuation

A parenthetical complete sentence inserted within the body of another sentence does not start with a capital letter or end with a period. (It would, however, end with a question mark or exclamation point if one is required.) A complete parenthetical sentence standing alone follows regular rules of punctuation, as the previous sentence highlights.

NO If you decide to join us (We hope you do.), bring your dog also.

YES If you decide to join us (we hope you do), bring your dog also.

YES   If you decide to join us, bring your dog also. (We hope you do.)

YES   Your dog (isn't Rex his name?) will delight all my other guests.

As in the preceding examples, place a required comma outside your closing parenthesis unless you're using commas to set off a numbered list.

53C   When should I use brackets?

Use brackets to feature an insert, such as an additional word or a brief definition, added by you to material that you are quoting.

ORIGINAL SOURCE

For a variety of reasons, the system attempts to maintain stability and resist temporal change.

—Peter Bonner, "Travel Rhythms," *Sky Magazine,* p. 72

SOURCE IN A QUOTATION

In "Travel Rhythms," Bonner explains that **"maintain[ing]** stability and **resist[ing]** temporal change" are natural goals for human beings.

Brackets are used to fit the quotation's wording into the rest of the sentence structure.

ORIGINAL SOURCE

In the future, a trip to the doctor may well involve an evaluation of such environmental components of our health.

—Winifred Gallagher, *The Power of Place,* p. 19

SOURCE IN A QUOTATION

Gallagher points out that a doctor visit may soon include "an evaluation of such environmental components **[the air we breathe and water we drink]** of our health."

Brackets indicate words inserted by the writer, not the original author, Gallagher.

🛈 **Alert:** Use the bracketed term [*sic*] when you've found an error in something you're quoting—perhaps a wrong date or an error of fact. Adding [*sic*] tells the reader, "It is this way in the original." In MLA STYLE, use regular (roman) type, not italics or underlining, for sic. When this term falls within a sentence, use brackets around it, but use parentheses when the term falls at the end of a sentence, and place punctuation after them. In APA STYLE, italicize the term *sic* between roman brackets. ●

53D   When should I use ellipsis points?

Use **ellipsis points** (or ellipses) to indicate you've intentionally omitted words—even a sentence or more—from the source you're quoting.

◼ Using ellipses in prose quotations

Use three spaced periods (. . .) to show where you have omitted a portion of the quoted material. If ellipsis points appear in the original source, include them. Never split ellipsis points between the end of a line and the beginning of the next.

ORIGINAL SOURCE

For over a century, twins have been used to study how genes make people what they are. Because they share precisely the same genes but live in different surroundings under different influences, identical twins reared apart are helping science sort out which qualities of body and mind are shaped by our genes and which by upbringing. Researchers needn't worry about running out of subjects: according to the Twins Foundation, there are approximately 4.5 million twin individuals in the United States alone, and about 70,000 more are born each year.

—Sharon Begley, "Twins," p. 84

MLA STYLE

According to Begley, "identical twins reared apart are helping science sort out which qualities of body and mind are shaped by our genes and which by upbringing" (84).

Ellipses are unnecessary; quotation has been worked into a sentence.

Begley says, "Because they share precisely the same genes . . . , identical twins reared apart are helping science sort out which qualities of body and mind are shaped by our genes and which by upbringing" (84).

Ellipses show that the writer has omitted words from the middle of the quoted sentence or a longer passage.

Begley says, "Because they share precisely the same genes but live in different surroundings under different influences, identical twins reared apart are helping science . . . " (84).

Ellipses show that the writer has omitted words from the end of the quoted sentence or a longer passage.

Begley says, "For over a century, twins have been used to study how genes make people what they are.... Researchers needn't worry about running out of subjects" (84).

Ellipses points between sentences show that one or more sentences have been omitted from the quoted material.

APA STYLE

Begley says, "Because they share precisely the same genes ..., identical twins reared apart are helping science sort out which qualities of body and mind are shaped by our genes and which by upbringing" (p. 84).

Ellipses show that the writer has omitted words from the middle of the quoted sentence.

Begley says, "Identical twins reared apart are helping science sort out which qualities of body and mind are shaped by our genes and which by upbringing" (p. 84).

Omission of words from the beginning of the quoted sentence doesn't require use of ellipses. Also, APA style permits a writer to change a lowercase letter at the start of a quotation to a capital letter.

Begley says, "Because they share precisely the same genes but live in different surroundings under different influences, identical twins reared apart are helping science" (p. 84).

APA style does not require ellipses to show that words have been omitted from the end of the quoted sentence.

Begley says, "For over a century, twins have been used to study how genes make people what they are.... Researchers needn't worry about running out of subjects" (p. 84).

Ellipsis points between sentences show that one or more sentences have been omitted from the quoted material.

■ Using ellipses in quotations from poetry

Omission of words within a line of poetry is indicated with ellipsis points exactly as for prose. Omission of an entire line or more of poetry is indicated with a row of spaced periods in MLA style.

ORIGINAL SOURCE
Fear no more the heat o' the sun
Nor the furious winter's rages;

Though thy worldly task has done,
Home art gone, and ta'en thy wages;
Golden lads and girls all must,
As chimney-sweepers, come to dust.

—William Shakespeare, *Cymbeline*

MLA STYLE

Ultimately, however, as Shakespeare reminds us, "Golden lads and girls all must / . . . come to dust."

Short poetry quotation with a few words omitted

Fear no more the heat o' the sun
Nor the furious winter's rages;
. . . .
Golden lads and girls all must
. . . come to dust.

Long poetry quotation with lines and words omitted

APA STYLE

Ultimately, however, as Shakespeare reminds us, "Golden lads and girls all must . . . come to dust."

Short poetry quotation with a few words omitted

Fear no more the heat o' the sun
Nor the furious winter's rages; . . .
Golden lads and girls all must
. . . come to dust.

Long poetry quotation with lines and words omitted

53E When should I use a slash?

When quoting three or fewer lines of poetry, use a slash to divide one line from the next. Leave a space on each side of the slash.

Consider the beginning of Anne Sexton's poem "Words": "Be careful of words, / even the miraculous ones."

To type numerical fractions (2/3, 1/16) or mixed numbers (12 1/2, 3 1/8), use a slash to separate the numerator from the denominator, leaving no space before or after the slash.

Revise a sentence to avoid word combinations like *and/or* when writing in the humanities. Where the use of word combinations is acceptable, separate the two words with a slash, leaving no space before or after it.

Explore the Exercise

● **EXERCISE 53-1** Supply needed dashes, parentheses, brackets, ellipses, and slashes. If a sentence is correct as written, circle its number. In some sentences, when you can use either dashes or parentheses, explain your choice. For help, consult all sections of this chapter.

EXAMPLE
Two tiny islands in the English Channel Jersey and Guernsey have breeds of cows named after them.
Two tiny islands in the English Channel—Jersey and Guernsey—have breeds of cows named after them.

1. In *The Color Purple* a successful movie as well as a novel Alice Walker explores the relationships between women and men in traditional African American culture.
2. W. C. Fields offered two pieces of advice on job hunting: 1 never show up for an interview in bare feet, and 2 don't read your prospective employer's mail while he is questioning you about your qualifications.
3. A series of resolutions was passed 11–0 with one council member abstaining calling on the mayor and the district attorney to improve safety conditions and step up law enforcement on city buses.
4. All the interesting desserts ice cream, chocolate fudge cake, pumpkin pie with whipped cream are fattening, unfortunately.
5. Thunder is caused when the flash of lightning heats the air around it to temperatures up to 30,000°F 16,666°C.
6. Christina Rossetti wonders if the end of a life also means the end of love in a poem that opens with these two lines: "When I am dead, my dearest, Sing no sad songs for me."
7. After the internationally famous racehorse Dan Patch died suddenly from a weak heart, his devoted owner, Will Savage, died of the same condition a mere 32 1/2 hours later.
8. In his famous letter from the Birmingham jail on April 16, 1963, Martin Luther King Jr. wrote: "You the eight clergymen who had urged him not to hold a protest deplore the demonstrations taking place in Birmingham."
9. The world's most expensive doll house sold for $256,000 at a London auction contains sixteen rooms, a working chamber organ, and a silver clothes press but no toilet.

10. The person renting this apartment agrees to pay seven hundred fifty dollars $750 per month in rent.

11. Railroad entrepreneur George Francis Train his real name! dreamed of creating a chain of great cities across the United States, all connected by his Union Pacific Railroad.

12. Patients who pretend to have ailments are known to doctors as "Munchausens" after Baron Karl Friedrich Hieronymus von Münchhausen he was a German army officer who had a reputation for wild and unbelievable tales. ●

● **EXERCISE 53-2**   Follow the directions for each item. For help, consult all sections of this chapter.

Explore
the
Exercise

EXAMPLE
Write a sentence about getting something right using a dash.
I tried and failed, I tried and failed again—and then I did it.

1. Write a sentence that quotes only three lines of the following sonnet by William Shakespeare:

   Let me not to the marriage of true minds
   Admit impediments. Love is not love
   Which alters when it alteration finds,
   Or bends with the remover to remove.
   O, no! it is an ever-fixèd mark
   That looks on tempests and is never shaken;
   It is the star to every wand'ring bark,
   Whose worth's unknown, although his height be taken.
   Love's not Time's fool, though rosy lips and cheeks
   Within his bending sickle's compass come;
   Love alters not with his brief hours and weeks,
   But bears it out even to the edge of doom.
   If this be error, and upon me proved,
   I never writ, nor no man ever loved.

2. Write a sentence using parentheses to enclose a brief example.
3. Write a sentence using dashes to set off a definition.
4. Write a sentence that includes four numbered items in a list.
5. Quote a few sentences from any source you choose. Omit words without losing meaning or use brackets to insert words to maintain meaning or grammatical structure. Use ellipses to indicate the omission, and place the parenthetical reference where it belongs. ●

Hyphens

■ ■ ■ ■ ■ ■ ■

Quick Points   You will learn to

➤ Use hyphens correctly.

54A   When should I hyphenate at the end of a line?

Listen
to the
Podcast

Always set the default on your word processing program to avoid hyphenation. In handwritten reports, keep in mind the following procedures: (1) Wherever possible, avoid dividing words with hyphens at the end of a line; (2) If a division is necessary, divide longer words by syllable and between consonants if possible (*omit-ting, ful-ness, sep-arate*); (3) Never divide for one or two letters or for any one-syllable words (like *wealth* or *screamed*).

54B   When should I hyphenate prefixes and suffixes?

Prefixes and **suffixes** are syllables attached to words—prefixes at the beginning and suffixes at the end. A few prefixes and suffixes call for hyphens, but most don't (see Quick Box 54.1).

54C   When should I hyphenate compound words?

You can write a **compound word**—two or more words combined to express one concept—in one of three ways: as separate words (*night shift*), as hyphenated words (*tractor-trailer*), or as one word (*handbook*). Follow the rules in Quick Box 54.2, p. 478.

54D   When should I hyphenate spelled-out numbers?

For help in deciding when to use numerals and when to spell out numbers, see Chapter 58. Quick Box 54.3, p. 478, shows how to hyphenate spelled-out numbers.

Quick Box 54.1

Hyphenating prefixes and suffixes

Use hyphens after the prefixes *all-, ex-,* and *self-.*

all-inclusive, self-reliant

Never use a hyphen when *self* is a root word onto which a suffix is attached.

selfishness, selfless, selfhood

Use a hyphen to avoid a distracting string of repeated letters.

anti-intellectual, bell-like

Use a hyphen between a prefix and the first word of a compound word.

anti-gun control

Use a hyphen to prevent confusion in meaning or pronunciation.

re-dress ("dress again"), un-ionize ("remove the ions")

redress ("set right"), unionize ("form a union")

Use a hyphen when two or more prefixes apply to one root word.

pre- and postwar eras

Use a hyphen before the suffix *-elect.*

president-elect

Use a hyphen when a prefix comes before a number or before a word that starts with a capital letter.

post-1950, pro-American

Alert: Use figures for fractions that require more than two words in their spelled-out form. If you do spell out a fraction in three or more words, use a hyphen between words in the numerator or the denominator; use a space (but no hyphen) to separate the numerator from the denominator.

- 2/100 *or* two one-hundredths

- 33/10,000 *or* thirty-three ten-thousandths ●

Quick Box 54.2 ■ ■ ■ ■ ■ ■ ■ ■ ■

Hyphenating compound words

Use a hyphen for most compound modifiers that precede the noun. Never use a hyphen for compound modifiers *after* the noun.

> well-researched report; two-inch clearance [before the noun]

> report is well researched; clearance of two inches [after the noun]

Use a hyphen between compound nouns joining two units within a measure.

> light-year, kilowatt-hour, foot-pound

Never use a hyphen when a compound modifier starts with an adverb ending in *ly*.

> happily married couple

Use a hyphen for most compound modifiers in the comparative (*-er*) or superlative (*-est*) form. Never use a hyphen when the compound modifier includes *more/most* or *less/least*.

> better-fitting shoe, best-known work

> more significant factor, least welcome guest

Never use a hyphen when a compound modifier is a foreign phrase.

> post hoc fallacies

Never use a hyphen with a possessive compound modifier.

> a full week's work, eight hours' pay

Quick Box 54.3 ■ ■ ■ ■ ■ ■ ■ ■ ■

Hyphenating spelled-out numbers

- Use a hyphen between two-word numbers from twenty-one through ninety-nine.

  > thirty-five, two hundred thirty-five

- Use a hyphen in a compound modifier formed from a number and a word.

  > fifty-minute class [also 50-minute class]

  > three-to-one odds [also 3-to-1 odds]

- Use a hyphen between the numerator and the denominator of a two-word fraction.

  > one-half, two-fifths, seven-tenths

● **EXERCISE 54-1** Provide the correct form of the words in parentheses, according to the hyphenation rules in this chapter. Explain your reasoning for each.

Explore the Exercise

1. The tiger is (all powerful) _____ in the cat family.
2. (Comparison and contrast) _____ studies of tigers and lions show that the tiger is the (more agile) _____ and powerful.
3. Male tigers and lions look similar except for their hair length: Tigers have (ultra short) _____ hair and male lions have (extra long) _____ hair in their manes.
4. The tiger's body is a (boldly striped) _____ yellow, with a white (under body) _____.
5. The Bengal tiger, the largest of the family, is aggressive and (self confident) _____.
6. In India, where the Bengal tiger is called a (village destroyer) _____, it goes (in to) _____ villages to hunt for food.
7. Entire villages have been temporarily abandoned by (terror stricken) _____ people who have seen a Bengal tiger nearby.
8. Villagers seek to protect their homes by destroying tigers with traps, (spring loaded) _____ guns, and (poisoned arrows) _____.
9. Bengal tigers are also called (cattle killers) _____, although they attack domestic animals only when they cannot find wild ones.
10. Many people who do not live near a zoo get to see tigers only in (animal shows) _____, although (pro animal) _____ activists try to prevent tigers from being used this way. ●

55 Capitals
■ ■ ■ ■ ■ ■ ■

Quick Points You will learn to

➤ Use capitals correctly.

55A When should I capitalize a "first" word?

Capitalize the first word in a sentence.

Watch the Video

 ● Four inches of snow fell last night.

When a complete sentence follows a colon, choose consistently either a capital or lowercase letter in each piece of writing. If what follows your colon is not a complete sentence, don't capitalize the first word.

YES   The question remains: What will the jury decide?

YES   The question remains: what will the jury decide?

NO   The jury is considering all the evidence: Motive, means, opportunity.

YES   The jury is considering all the evidence: motive, means, opportunity.

If a series of questions imply, but are not themselves, complete sentences, you can choose capitals or not. Simply be consistent in each piece of writing.

- Whose rights does voter fraud deny? Mine? Yours? Or everyone's?

- Whose rights does voter fraud deny? mine? yours? or everyone's?

When a sentence itemizes other sentences, capitalize and punctuate the items as complete sentences.

- The bank robbers made demands: (1) They wanted money. (2) They wanted hostages. (3) They wanted transportation.

When the items are not complete sentences, use commas between them unless the items contain commas. When they do, use semicolons between items. Use the word *and* before the last item if there are three or more nonsentence items.

- The bank robbers made demands: (1) money, (2) hostages, and (3) transportation.

A complete sentence enclosed in parentheses may stand alone or fall within another sentence. If it stands alone, capitalize the first word and use an appropriate ending punctuation (a period, a question mark, or an exclamation point). If it falls within a sentence, don't capitalize the first word. Use ending punctuation *only* if your sentence in parentheses ends with a question mark or an exclamation point, not with a period.

I didn't know till years later that they called it the Cuban Missile Crisis. But I remember Castro. (We called him Castor Oil and were awed by his beard—beards were rare in those days.) We might not have worried so much (what would the Communists want with our small New Hampshire town?) except that we lived 10 miles from an air base.

—Joyce Maynard, *An 18-Year-Old Looks Back on Life*

Explore the Exercise

- **EXERCISE 55-1** In the following paragraph, sort out sentences and their meanings, placing capital letters where they belong.

drugs are one of the techniques of western therapy of which we are most proud. however, drugs are used by healers in other cultures as well. rauwulfia root, for example, which was introduced into western psychiatry in the 1950s as reserpine, a major tranquilizer, has been used in india for centuries as a tranquilizer and has also been in wide use in west africa for many years. another example is shock therapy. when electric shock therapy was introduced by cerletti in the 1930s, he was not aware that it had been used in some cultures for up to 4,000 years. the technique of applying electrical eels to the head of a patient is referred to in the writings of aristotle, pliny, and plutarch. what kinds of results do therapists in other cultures—witch doctors—achieve? a canadian psychiatrist, dr. raymond prince, spent 17 months studying 46 nigerian witch doctors and judged that the therapeutic results were about equal to those obtained in north american clinics and hospitals.

—Edwin Fuller Torrey, *The Mind Game* ●

55B How should I capitalize quotations?

Capitalize the first word in a prose QUOTATION.

- Encouraging students to study in other countries, Mrs. Velez says, "**Y**ou will absorb a good accent with the food."

When you interrupt quoted words, never capitalize the continued part of the quoted words.

- "**Y**ou will absorb a good accent," says Mrs. Velez, "**w**ith the food."

If the quoted words form part of your own sentence, never capitalize the first quoted word unless it is a PROPER NOUN. Phrases such as *writes **that**, thinks **that**,* and *says **that*** usually signal this kind of quotation.

- Mrs. Velez believes that "**y**ou will absorb a good accent with the food" if you study in another country.

When you quote poetry in your writing, use capital and lowercase letters exactly as they appear in the original SOURCE. (If you need help using quotation marks, see Chapter 51.)

55C When should I capitalize nouns and adjectives?

Capitalize **proper nouns** (*Mexico, Arthur*) and **proper adjectives** (*a Mexican diplomat, the Arthurian legend*). Capitalize certain **common nouns** when you add specific names or titles to them: For example, *We visit a **lake** every summer. This summer we went to **Lake Seminole**.* See Quick Box 55.1.

❶ Alerts: (1) Never capitalize DETERMINERS and other words just because they accompany proper nouns or proper adjectives: *Here is a Canadian penny* [not *A Canadian penny* or *a Canadian Penny*].

(2) Be aware that some proper nouns and proper adjectives become so common that they lose their capital letters: *french fries, italics, pasteurized.* ●

Quick Box 55.1

Capitalization guide

	Capitals	Lowercase Letters
NAMES	Mother Teresa [also when used as names: Mother, Dad, Mom, Pa]	my mother [relationship]
	Doc Holliday	the doctor [role]
TITLES	President Truman	the president
	Democrat [party member]	democrat [believer in democracy]
	Representative Harold Ford	the congressional representative
	Senator Edward M. Kennedy	the senator
	Queen Elizabeth II	the queen
GROUPS OF PEOPLE	Caucasian [race]	white, black [*also* White, Black]
	Korean [nationality]	
	Jew, Buddhist [religious affiliation]	
	Hispanic [ethnic group]	
ORGANIZATIONS	Congress	legislative branch of the US government
	Ohio State Supreme Court	state supreme court
	the Republican Party	the party
	National Gypsum Company	the company
	American Medical Association	professional group
	Sigma Chi	fraternity
	Alcoholics Anonymous	self-help group
PLACES	Los Angeles	the city
	the South [region]	turn south [direction]
	the West Coast	the states along the western seaboard
	Main Street	the street
	Atlantic Ocean	the ocean
	the Black Hills	the hills
BUILDINGS	the Capitol [in Washington, DC]	the state capitol
	Central High School	a high school
	Highland Hospital	a hospital

continued >>

Quick Box 55.1 (continued)

	Capitals	Lowercase Letters
SCIENTIFIC	Earth [as a planet]	the earth in the garden
	the Milky Way	the galaxy, the moon, the sun
	Streptococcus aureus	a streptococcal infection
	Gresham's law	the theory of relativity
LANGUAGES	Spanish, French, Chinese	foreign languages
SCHOOL COURSES	Chemistry 342	a chemistry course
	English 111	my English class
	Introduction to Photography	a photography class
NAMES OF SPECIFIC THINGS	the *Boston Globe*	the newspaper
	Time	the magazine
	Purdue University	the university
	Heinz ketchup	ketchup
SEASONS		spring, winter, autumn
HOLIDAYS	Halloween, New Year's Day	
HISTORICAL EVENTS AND DOCUMENTS	World War II	the war
	the Roaring Twenties	a decade
	the Great Depression	a depression
	the Paleozoic	an era, an age
	the Reformation	the eighteenth century
	the Bill of Rights	fifth-century manuscripts
RELIGIOUS TERMS	God	a god, a goddess
	Buddhism	a religion
	the Torah, the Koran, the Bible	
LETTER PARTS	Dear Ms. Kupperman:	
	Sincerely,	
	Yours truly,	
TITLES OF PUBLISHED AND RELEASED WORKS	"The Lottery"	[Capitalize the first letter of the first and last words and all other words except ARTICLES, short PREPOSITIONS, and COORDINATING CONJUNCTIONS.]
	A History of the United States to 1877	
	Jazz on Ice	
ACRONYMS AND INITIALISMS	NATO, FBI, AFL-CIO, UCLA, DNA, CD	

continued >>

Quick Box 55.1   (continued)

	Capitals	Lowercase Letters
COMPUTER TERMS	Microsoft Word, WordPerfect	computer software
	Netscape Navigator	a browser
	World Wide Web, the Web	
	Web site, Web page	a home page, a link
	the Internet	a computer network
PROPER ADJECTIVES	Victorian	biblical
	Midwestern	transatlantic
	Indo-European	alpine

Explore the Exercise

● **EXERCISE 55-2** Individually or with a group, add capital letters as needed. See 55A through 55C for help.

1. The state of california is best known as the golden state, but other nicknames include the land of milk and honey, the el dorado state, and the grape state.

2. Most people think of san Francisco as northern california, but the city of Eureka, from the greek word meaning "I have found it," is 280 miles north of san Francisco, and the state line is another 90 miles north of eureka.

3. South of san Francisco on the california coast is santa Barbara, which hosts the annual Dickens Universe, a weeklong series of studies and celebrations of the famous writer charles dickens.

4. The highest point in the contiguous United States is mt. Whitney at 14,495 feet high, and the lowest place in the contiguous United States is bad Water in death valley at 282 feet below sea level, both located in california.

5. Having approximately 500,000 detectable seismic tremors per year, california rocks, literally.

6. Because the tehema county fairgrounds are located in red bluff, california hosts the largest three-day rodeo in the united States.

7. Numerous songs have been written about california, including "california girls" by the beach boys and the theme of the tv show *the beverly hillbillies.*

8. san Bernardino county with almost three million acres is the largest county in the united states.

9. Hollywood and movie stars are what many people associate california with, and well they might because two of California's governors, ronald reagan and arnold schwarzenegger, were actors before they became governors.

10. When told all these fantastic facts about california, a stereotypical valley girl would respond, "whatever." ●

Italics (Underlining)

■ ■ ■ ■ ■ ■ ■ ■

Quick Points   You will learn to

➤ Use italics (underlining) correctly.

Most printed material is set in roman type. Type that slants to the right is called *italic type*. Italics and underlining mean the same thing. MLA style requires italics, not underlining, in all documents (see Chapters 24–26).

ITALIC TYPE	*Great Expectations*
HANDWRITTEN AND UNDERLINED	<u>Great Expectations</u>

56A   How do I choose between italics and quotation marks?

Generally, use italics for titles of long works or works that contain subsections. Use quotation marks for titles of shorter works or titles of subsections within a larger work. Consult Quick Box 56.1 for specifics.

56B   When should I use italics for emphasis?

Use italics sparingly for emphasis. Instead, use language for emphasis.

* The pain from my injury was *totally severe*.

* The pain from my injury was so severe that I could not breathe.

   That I could not breathe emphasizes with words, not with italics.

● **EXERCISE 56-1**   Edit these sentences for correct use of italics (or underlining), quotation marks, and capitals. For help, consult this chapter and Chapter 55.

Explore
the
Exercise

1. The article "the Banjo" in the Encyclopaedia Britannica calls the Banjo "America's only national instrument" because it combines the traditional mbanza (an instrument native to certain southern areas of africa) and some European stringed instruments.
2. The writer of a humor column at a newspaper called The "Globe and Mail" has described an imaginary newspaper called The mop and pail, where things are more ridiculous than in Real Life.

Quick Box 56.1

■ ■ ■ ■ ■ ■ ■ ■ ■ ■

Italics, quotation marks, or nothing

	Italicize	Quotations Marks or Nothing
TITLES	*The Bell Jar* [a novel]	title of student essay
	Death of a Salesman [a play]	act 3
	Collected Works of O. Henry [a book]	"The Last Leaf" [a story in the book]
	Simon & Schuster Handbook for Writers [a book]	"Verbs" [a chapter in the book]
	The Prose Reader [a collection of essays]	"Putting in a Good Word for Guilt" [title of an essay]
	The Iliad [a book-length poem]	"Nothing Gold Can Stay" [a short poem]
	Almost Famous [a film]	
	the *Los Angeles Times** [a newspaper]	"Supreme Court Judge Steps Down" [a headline]
	Scientific American [a magazine]	"The Molecules of Life" [an article in a magazine]
	Aida [an opera]	
	Symphonie Fantastique [a long musical work]	Concerto in B-flat Minor [a musical work identified by form, number, and key]
	The Twilight Zone [a television series]	"Terror at 30,000 Feet" [an episode of the television series]
	The Best of Bob Dylan [an album or CD]	"Mr. Tambourine Man" [one cut on an album or CD]
	the USS *Intrepid* [a ship]	aircraft carrier [a class of ship]
	Voyager 2 [specific aircraft, spacecraft, satellites]	Boeing 787 [names shared by classes of aircraft, spacecraft, or satellites]
OTHER WORDS	*semper fidelis* [words in a language other than English]	burrito, chutzpah [widely understood non-English words]
	What does *our* imply? [a word referred to as such]	
	the *ABC*s; confusing *3*'s and *8*'s [letters and numerals referred to as such]	

*Even if *The* is part of the title printed on a newspaper, don't capitalize it and don't italicize it in the body of your paper. In MLA-style documentation, omit the word *The* entirely. In APA-style documentation, retain *The* as part of the title.

3. "Porgy and Bess," a Folk Opera by George and ira Gershwin and Du Bose Heyward, introduced the beautiful, haunting song *Summertime.*
4. Marlon Brando persuaded the Director of *The Godfather* to cast him as the Elderly don Corleone by auditioning with cotton-stuffed cheeks and mumbling hoarsely.
5. When the name of a Small Business begins with the letter a repeated many times, as in AAAAAbc "Auto Body," we know its marketing plan includes being listed First in the telephone directory. ●

57 Abbreviations

Quick Points   You will learn to

➤ Use abbreviations correctly.

The guidelines in this chapter apply to writing in the humanities. Guidelines in other disciplines vary. For disciplines outside the humanities, check your college dictionary for capitalization, spacing, and use of periods.

Watch
the Video

⚠ **Alerts:** (1) Place only one period after a sentence that ends with an abbreviated word: *At the picnic, we hosted Mr. John Janes Jr.*

(2) Place a question mark or an exclamation point after the abbreviation's period at the end: *Do we have paper plates, plastic forks, etc.?* ●

57A   What abbreviations can I use with times and amounts?

With exact times, use abbreviations (*a.m.* or *A.M.* and *p.m.* or *P.M.*), including the periods. Choose consistently capital or lowercase letters for these.

- 7:15 a.m.
- 3:47 p.m.
- 7:15 A.M.
- 3:47 P.M.

Use capital letters without periods for abbreviations for eras.

BC (meaning *before Christ*)—place after the year number: *1200 BC.*

BCE (meaning *before the Common Era*), which is a more inclusionary, contemporary form—place after the year: *1200 BCE.*

AD (Latin for *anno Domini,* which means *in the year of the Lord*)—place before the year: *AD 977.*

CE (meaning *Common Era*), a more contemporary form—place after the year: *1507 CE.*

In tables, you can abbreviate amounts and measurements (such as *in., mi., cm, km, gal., ml, lb., kg*) when you use them with exact numbers. You can also abbreviate days and months (*Mon., Jan., Aug.*).

Use the symbol *$* with exact amounts of money expressed in numerals or numerals and words.

- $4.95
- $34 million

As a rule, let common sense and clarity guide your use of symbols. If measurements like temperatures appear only once or twice in your paper, spell them out: *sixty degrees Fahrenheit, minus seven degrees Celcius.* If your work uses temperatures throughout, use numbers and symbols: *60°F, –7°C.*

57B How should I use abbreviations with people's names?

Use *Mr., Mrs., Ms.,* and *Dr.* with either full names or last names only.

- Dr. Anna Freud
- Dr. Freud
- Mr. Daljit Singh
- Mr. Singh

When you follow a person's name with the abbreviation of a professional or academic degree, use no periods. Also, never use in the same context both a title of address before a name and an abbreviated degree after a name.

NO Dr. Jill Sih, **MD**

YES Jill Sih, **MD**

YES **Dr.** Jill Sih

Follow the official military title abbreviations for each branch of the US armed forces (you can find the most up-to-date ones on the Internet). Today these abbreviations are almost always in all capital letters, and they use no periods.

- **ADM** admiral
- **CPO** chief petty officer
- **CO** Commanding officer
- **COL** colonel
- **ENS** ensign
- **GEN** general

57C How do I use *Jr., Sr., II, III, 2nd,* and *3rd*?

Indications of birth order apply only to males, not to females, as below:

1. End only the birth order indicators *Jr.* and *Sr.* with a period.

2. Never use a comma before or after *Jr.* or *Sr.* unless another rule calls for one.

- Under the pseudonym James Tiptree **Jr.**, Alice B. Sheldon wrote outstanding science fiction.

  A comma is correct here because *Jr.* ends an introductory phrase.

- The James Tiptree **Jr.** Memorial Award honors Alice B. Sheldon.

  No comma appears after *Jr.* because no other rule calls for one.

- Douglas Young **III** is a physical therapist.

  Neither a period nor a comma is required.

- Douglas Young **III**, a physical therapist, specializes in geriatrics.

  Commas are necessary to set off the appositive, *a physical therapist.*

- Douglas Young **III, PT, MA**

  Use commas between multiple titles.

3. Never use a birth-order abbreviation with a last name only: not *Syms Jr.* If you add initials to the last name, however, you can use it: *I. J. Syms Jr.*

57D When can I abbreviate names of countries, organizations, and government agencies?

Spell out the names of countries as a sign of respect. You can abbreviate *United States* without a period only as an adjective (*the US Constitution*). Never abbreviate *United States* as a noun (*Constitution of the United States*).

When you refer to an organization, spell the full name the first time you use it and then, immediately afterward, put the abbreviation in parentheses. Thereafter, you can use the abbreviation alone.

- Spain voted to continue as a member of the **North Atlantic Treaty Organization (NATO),** to the surprise of other **NATO** members.

57E What abbreviations can I use in addresses?

You can use abbreviations for addresses such as *St.* for *Street* and *Blvd.* for *Boulevard.* You can also use abbreviations for *North (N.), South (S.), East (E.),* and *West (W.).* In the United States, use the two-letter postal abbreviations for state names in addresses: CA for California, IL for Illinois, and so on.

If you include a full address in a sentence, spell out all words except the two-letter postal abbreviation. Otherwise, spell out the name of the state.

> I wrote to Mr. Hugh Lern, 7 Rule Road, Summit, **NJ** 07901, for the handbook. Unfortunately, he had already moved to Flagstaff, **Arizona.**

57F When can I use *etc.* and other Latin abbreviations?

Avoid *etc.,* Latin for "and the rest," in ACADEMIC WRITING. Instead, use substitutes *and the like, and so on*—or use a more concrete description.

Explore the Exercise

● **EXERCISE 57-1** Working individually or with a group, revise these sentences for correct use of abbreviations. For help, consult this chapter.

1. Originally named the Geo. S. Parker Company, located in Salem, Mass., the toy co. changed its name to Parker Bros. when Chas. joined the business in 1888.
2. Sev. of their games have become quite famous, esp. Monopoly and Clue, both of which were released in the 20th cent.
3. The obj. of the game Monopoly (meaning "dominating the mkt.") is to get the most $ by purchasing, renting, & selling real est.
4. Clue, another pop. brd. game, is a murder mys. in which players move from 1 rm. to another, making accusations to reveal the i.d. of the murderer, the weapon used, and the room where the crime took place.
5. On a cold day in Jan., when the snow is 3 ft. deep and it's dark by early eve., passing the hrs. with your fam. and friends playing a board game is great fun. ●

58 Numbers ■ ■ ■ ■ ■ ■ ■ ■

Quick Points You will learn to

➤ Use spelled out numbers and numerals correctly.

58A When should I spell out numbers in words?

Watch the Video

If numbers occur often in your humanities paper, spell out *one* through *nine;* use numerals (*1, 9*) for all others. If numbers occur rarely in your paper, use words.

❗ **Alert:** Use a hyphen in the two-word numbers *twenty-one* through *ninety-nine.* ●

Spell out a number at the beginning of a sentence, or revise the sentence.

ACCEPTABLE   Six hundred forty-six dollars buys a Gucci tote.

BETTER   A Gucci tote costs $646.

Never mix spelled-out numbers and figures when they refer to the same thing. In the following example, all numbers referring to bids are in figures, but *four* is spelled out because it refers to days, not bids.

- In the past four days, $5 bids increased from 5 to 8 to 17 to 233.
- On Saturday morning, 59 bids arrived from 22 districts.

58B How should I write dates, addresses, times, and other numbers?

After plural numbers, use the singular form of *hundred, thousand,* and *million.* Add *-s* only when no number comes before those words.

- **Five hundred** books were damaged in the flood.
- **Hundreds** of books were damaged in the flood.

Quick Box 58.1, p. 492, models numbers in some common forms.

● **EXERCISE 58-1** Revise these sentences so that the numbers are in correct form, either spelled out or as figures. For help, consult this chapter.

Explore the Exercise

1. At five fifteen p.m., the nearly empty city streets filled with 1000's of commuters.
2. A tarantula spider can survive without food for about two years and 3 months.
3. By the end of act one, scene five, Romeo and Juliet are in love and at the mercy of their unhappy fate.
4. Sound travels through air at a speed of 1,089 feet per second, but in water it travels four hundred and fifty percent faster, at four thousand, eight hundred fifty-nine feet per second.
5. 21 years old and unhappily married, Cleopatra met middle-aged Julius Caesar in forty-eight BCE.
6. An adult blue whale, which can weigh one hundred tons—the combined weight of 30 elephants—has gained over seven-point-five pounds an hour since infancy.
7. On the morning of August thirteen, nineteen hundred thirty, 3 huge meteorites smashed into the Amazon jungle.
8. 2 out of every 5 people who have ever lived on earth are alive today, according to 1 estimate.

Quick Box 58.1
■■■■■■■■■

Using numbers

DATES	August 6, 1941 1732–1845 34 BCE to AD 230
ADDRESSES	237 North Eighth Street [*or* N. 8th St.] Export Falls, MN 92025
TIMES	8:09 a.m., 4:00 p.m. [*but* four o'clock, *not* 4 o'clock; 4 p.m. *or* four in the afternoon, *not* four p.m. *or* 4 in the afternoon]
CHAPTERS AND PAGES	Chapter 27, page 245
ACT, SCENE, AND LINE	act 2, scene 2 (or act II, scene ii) lines 75–79
SCORES AND STATISTICS	a 6–0 score a 5-to-3 ratio [*or* a 5:3 ratio] 29 percent
IDENTIFICATION NUMBERS	93.9 on the FM dial call (212) 555-3930
MEASUREMENTS	2 feet 67.8 miles per hour 1.5 gallons, 3 liters 8-by-10-inch photograph
TEMPERATURES	–5°F, 3°C, 43° Celsius
MONEY	$1.2 billion $3.41 25 cents
DECIMALS AND FRACTIONS	5.55 98.6 3.1416 7/8 12 1/4 3/4 (three-quarters *but not* 3-quarters)

9. The house at six hundred and fifty-three Oak Street—the 1 that children think is haunted—has been empty for 8 years, waiting for a buyer willing to pay its price of $ six million, forty-nine thousand dollars.

10. The 1912 sinking of the *Titanic,* in which one thousand five hundred and three people drowned, is widely known, but few people remember that more than three thousand people lost their lives aboard the ferryboat *Doña Paz* when it hit an oil tanker in the Philippines in nineteen eighty-seven. ●

Tab 11
Tips for Multilingual Writers

CHAPTERS
59–64

11

Tips for Multilingual
Writers

Tab 11 Tips for Multilingual Writers

Tips for Multilingual Writers 493–516

MyCompLab® Visit mycomplab.com for the eText and for resources and exercises on grammar.

A Message to Multilingual Writers

Depending an how, when, and where you began learning English, you migh feel very comfortable with spoken English but not written American English. Or you might understand English grammar quite well, but you might struggle with idioms, slang, and sentence structure. You might be an international student just learning the expectations of ACADEMIC WRITING* in American English, or you might be a bilingual student who went to high school in the United States. You might be an adult returning to school encountering academic writing for the first time, or you might be a student who received an advanced degree in another country but must now master written American English.

The process of learning to write American English is like learning to play a musical instrument. Few people can play fluently without first making many errors. If you're among the multilingual writers who become frustrated about the errors that they make in written English, we encourage you to realize that such mistakes demonstrate that you're moving normally through the stages of second-language development. As with your progress in speaking, listening, and reading in a new language, developing writing skills—including absorbing the rules of American English grammar—takes time.

What can help you advance as quickly as possible? If you attended school elsewhere before coming to the United States, we recommend that you recall how you were taught to present ideas in your written native language. Chances are you encountered quite a different system, especially when presenting information or mounting an argument and then when supporting your topic with specific details. Compare your native system to how writing American English works. Becoming conscious of the similarities and differences can help you understand typical writing strategies in American English.

For example, most college essays and research papers in the United States use a direct tone and straightforward structure. Typically, the THESIS STATE-MENT (the central message of the piece of writing) is expected at the end of the first paragraph; in a longer piece of writing, at the end of the second paragraph. Each paragraph that follows, known as a BODY PARAGRAPH, relates in content directly to the essay's thesis statement, and each body paragraph usually starts with a TOPIC SENTENCE that contains the main point of that paragraph. The rest of each body paragraph supports the main point made in the topic sentence. The final paragraph of an essay brings the content to a reasonable conclusion that grows out of what has been written in the prior paragraphs.

We urge you always to honor your culture's writing traditions and structures. They reflect the richness of your heritage. As you continue practicing your writing in American English, we suggest that you look for possible interesting ways to blend the traditions and structures of writing in your first language with the conventions of academic writing in the United States. We

---

* Words printed in SMALL CAPITAL LETTERS are discussed elsewhere in the text and are defined in the Terms Glossary at the back of the book.

493

suggest, too, that you get to know *The American Heritage English as a Second Language Dictionary* because it includes many English idioms as well as sample sentences and phrases that show how American English operates. If your college library doesn't own a few copies, ask your professor to request that the reference librarian purchase some for students like you to consult. You can also check the Merriam-Webster Learner's Dictionary online at www.learnersdictionary.com.

Our *Quick Access* offers special features we've designed specifically for you as a multilingual learner. Chapters 32 through 46 focus on the most challenging grammar issues that you face as you learn to write English. The chapters in the "ESOL" section that follow this letter address major grammar issues that often trouble multilingual writers. Also, in various chapters throughout the book, ESOL Tips offer you specific helpful hints about non-USA cultural references and grammar issues.

As individuals, we two authors greatly enjoy discovering the rich variations in the writing traditions of our students from many cultures of the world. As U.S. writing teachers, however, our responsibilities require that we explain what you need to do as writers in the United States. If you were in one of our classes, we would say "Welcome!" and ask you to teach us about writing in your native language. Using your knowledge of writing in your first language, we want to help you learn how to approach writing effectively in American English so that you can succeed as a writer in the United States. You bring a richness of experience in communicating in more than one language that most U.S. students have never had, and we hope you're always proud of that experience.

Lynn Quitman Troyka
Doug Hesse

59 Singulars and Plurals

■ ■ ■ ■ ■ ■ ■ ■

Quick Points   You will learn to

> Distinguish between count and noncount nouns.
> Use the proper determiners with singular and plural nouns (p. 496).

59A What are count and noncount nouns?

Count nouns represent items that can be counted: *radio, fingernail, street, idea.* **Noncount nouns** represent things that cannot be counted: *knowledge, rain, traffic.*

Watch
the Video

Count nouns can be SINGULAR (*radio, street*) or PLURAL (*radios, streets*), so they may use singular or plural VERBS. Noncount nouns (see Quick Box 59.1) are used in singular form only, so they use only singular verbs.

❶ Alert: If you're not sure whether a noun is count or noncount, look it up in a learner's dictionary such as the *American Heritage English as a Second Language Dictionary.* ●

Some nouns can be count or noncount, depending on their meaning in a sentence. Most of these nouns represent things that can be meant either individually or as "wholes" made up of individual parts (see Quick Box 59.1).

COUNT	**Two hairs** were on his collar.
NONCOUNT	**His hair** was cut very short.

Quick Box 59.1

Uncountable items represented by noncount nouns

- Groups of similar items making up "wholes": *clothing, equipment, furniture, luggage, mail, money*
- Abstractions: *equality, fun, health, ignorance, knowledge, peace, respect*
- Liquids: *blood, coffee, gasoline, water*
- Gases: *air, helium, oxygen, smog, smoke, steam*
- Materials: *aluminum, cloth, cotton, ice, wood*
- Food: *beef, bread, butter, macaroni, meat, cheese*
- Collections of particles or grains: *dirt, dust, hair, rice, salt, wheat*
- Languages: *Arabic, Chinese, Japanese, Spanish*
- Fields of study: *biology, computer science, history, physics, literature, math*
- Natural phenomena: *electricity, heat, moonlight, sunshine, thunder*

When EDITING your writing, make sure you haven't added the plural *-s* ending to any noncount nouns, which are always singular in form.

🚫 **Alert:** Use a singular verb with any noncount noun that functions as a SUBJECT in a CLAUSE. •

59B Which determiners should I use with singular and plural nouns?

DETERMINERS, including expressions of quantity, are used to tell *which, how much,* or *how many* about NOUNS. You choose the correct determiner to use with a noun, depending on whether the noun is noncount or count. For count nouns, you also need to decide whether the noun is singular or plural (see Quick Box 59.2 on p. 497).

🚫 **Alerts:** (1) *Many, most,* and *some* require *of the* before a noun that is specific but not before a noun that is a generalization.

- **Most** supervisors are well qualified. [general]
- **Most of the** supervisors **here** are well qualified. [specific]

(2) The phrases *a few* and *a little* convey the meaning "some": *I have a few rare books* means "I have *some* rare books." *They are worth a little money* means "They are worth *some* money." Without the word *a,* the meaning of *few* and *little* is "almost none": *I have few* [or *very few*] *books* means "I have *almost no* books." *They are worth* [*very*] *little money* means "They are worth *almost no* money."

(3) A phrase with *one of the* always has a plural noun as the OBJECT of the PREPOSITION *of.* The verb agrees with *one,* not with the plural noun, so it is always singular: *One of the most important inventions of the twentieth century is* [not *are*] *television* (see 34G). •

59C What forms are correct for nouns used as adjectives?

Some words that function as nouns can also function as ADJECTIVES. In English, adjectives don't have plural forms. If you use a noun as an adjective, don't add *-s* or *-es* to the adjective, even when the noun or PRONOUN it modifies is plural.

- Many American students are basketball fans.
- My nephew likes to look at picture books.

Quick Box 59.2 ■ ■ ■ ■ ■ ■ ■ ■ ■

Using determiners with count and noncount nouns

GROUP 1: DETERMINERS FOR SINGULAR COUNT NOUNS
With singular count nouns, use any of the determiners on the left.

a, an, the	**a** house; **an** egg; **the** house, **the** egg
one, any, some, every, each, either,	**any** book; **each** person;
neither, another, the other	**another** year
my, our, your, his, her, its, their,	**your** father; **its** cover;
nouns with *'s* or *s'*	**Connie's** car
this, that	**this** week; **that** desk
one, no, the first, the second,	**one** example; **no** reason;
and so on	**the fifth** chair

GROUP 2: DETERMINERS FOR PLURAL COUNT NOUNS
All of the following determiners can be used with plural count nouns.
Plural count nouns can also be used without determiners (see 60B).

the	**the** bicycles; **the** rooms; **the** ideas
some, any, both, many, most, few,	**some** people; **many** jobs;
fewer, the fewest, a number of,	**all** managers
other, several, all, all the, a lot of	
my, our, your, his, her, its, their,	**our** coats; **her** books;
nouns with *'s* or *s'*	**students'** grades
these, those	**these** days; **those** computers
no; two, three, four, and so on;	**no** exceptions; **four** students;
the first, the second, the third,	**the first** month
and so on	

GROUP 3: DETERMINERS FOR NONCOUNT NOUNS
All of the following determiners can be used with noncount nouns (which are always singular). Noncount nouns can also be used without determiners (see 60B).

the	**the** rice; **the** electricity
some, any, much, more, most, other,	**enough** snow; **a lot of** equipment;
the other, little, less, the least,	**more** food
enough, all, all the, a lot of	
my, our, your, his, her, its, their,	**their** fame; **India's** heat; **your**
nouns with *'s* or *s'*	leader's smile
this, that	**this** sugar; **that** fog
no, the first, the second, the best,	**no smoking; the first** rainfall;
and so on	**the best** vocabulary

Explore
the
Exercise

● **EXERCISE 59-1** Consulting all sections of this chapter, select the correct choice from the words in parentheses and write it in the blank.

EXAMPLE

At the beginning of every school year, all (student, students) <u>students</u> can expect (homework, homeworks) <u>homework</u> that teaches them about the toll-free No Bully hot line.

1. One of the main (reason, reasons) _____ for such a hot line is the change in tempers and violent capacities of (American, Americans) _____ students.
2. Because students are often bullied by a fellow classmate when outside the classroom, it is important that they receive (information, informations) _____ about how to react when confronted by such a threat.
3. Many a child in the (United State, United States) _____ is in danger not only of being teased and taunted by others but also of being the victim of a crime in which (blood, bloods) _____ is spilled, such as from assault or robbery.
4. Because (many, much) _____ classrooms are unsupervised after school, this (time, times) _____ becomes especially dangerous.
5. In a moment of danger, (ignorance, ignorances) _____ can be deadly, so the No Bully hot line was set up to give students (advice, advices) _____ on how to handle bullying and other threatening situations. ●

60 Articles

Quick Points You will learn to

➤ Use articles correctly.

Watch
the Video

The words *a, an,* and *the* are **articles**. Articles are one type of DETERMINER. They signal that a NOUN will follow and that any MODIFIERS between the article and the noun refer to that noun (see Quick Box 60.1 on p. 499).

● **a** chair, **the** computer

Quick Box 60.1

Using articles: *the, a,* and *an*

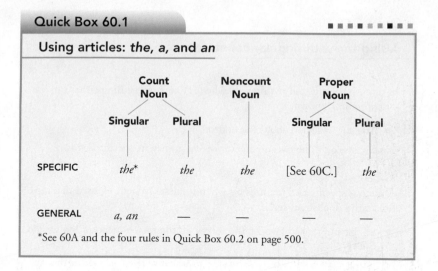

	Count Noun		Noncount Noun	Proper Noun	
	Singular	Plural		Singular	Plural
SPECIFIC	*the**	*the*	*the*	[See 60C.]	*the*
GENERAL	*a, an*	—	—	—	—

*See 60A and the four rules in Quick Box 60.2 on page 500.

60A How should I use articles with singular count nouns?

When you use a singular COUNT NOUN (see Quick Box 60.2 on p. 500), you need to use a determiner, as shown for Group 1 in Quick Box 59.2 on page 497. If you have to choose between *a, an,* and *the,* decide whether the noun is specific or nonspecific. A noun is specific when a reader can understand from the context exactly and specifically what the noun is referring to. Quick Box 60.2 can help you decide when a singular count noun is specific and requires *the.*

Alerts: (1) One common exception affects rule 3 in Quick Box 60.2. A noun may still require *a* or *an* after the first use if one or more descriptive adjectives come between the article and the noun: *I bought a sweater today. It was a* [not *the*] **red** *sweater.*

(2) *An* is used before words that begin with a vowel sound; *a* is used before words that begin with a consonant sound. Sound, not spelling, is the key. Words that begin with *h* or *u* can have either a vowel or a consonant sound; check your dictionary. Choose *a* or *an* based on the sound of the first word after the article, even if that word is not the noun.

- **an** idea, **a** good idea
- **an** umbrella, **a** useless umbrella
- **an** honor, **a** history book ●

Quick Box 60.2

▪ ▪ ▪ ▪ ▪ ▪ ▪ ▪ ▪ ▪

Using *the* with singular count nouns

RULE 1
A noun is specific and requires *the* when it names something either unique or commonly known.

- **The** sun has risen above **the** horizon.

  Because only one *sun* and one *horizon* exist, they are specific nouns.

RULE 2
A noun is specific and requires *the* when it names something used in a representative or abstract sense.

- Benjamin Franklin favored **the** turkey as **the** national bird of the United States.

  Because *turkey* and *national bird* are representative references rather than references to a particular turkey or bird, they are specific nouns in this context.

RULE 3
A noun is specific and requires *the* when it names something that is defined elsewhere in the same sentence or in an earlier sentence.

- **The** ship *Savannah* was the first steam vessel to cross **the** Atlantic Ocean.

  Savannah names a specific ship, and *Atlantic Ocean* is a specific ocean.

- **The** carpet in my bedroom is new.

  In my bedroom defines exactly which carpet is meant, so *carpet* is a specific noun in this context.

- I have a computer and a fax machine in my office. **The** computer is often broken.

  Computer is introduced in the first sentence, so it uses *a*. *Computer* has been made specific by the first sentence, so the second sentence uses *the* to refer to the same noun.

RULE 4
A noun is specific and requires *the* when it represents something that can be inferred from the context.

- **I need an expert to fix the problem.**

  If you read this sentence after the example about a computer in Rule 3, you understand that *problem* refers to the broken computer, and so *problem* is specific in this context. Here the word *the* is similar to the word *this*.

60B How should I use articles with count and noncount nouns?

Like singular count nouns, plural count nouns and NONCOUNT NOUNS that are *specific* usually use *the* according to the rules in Quick Box 60.2 (p. 500). When a noun has a *general* meaning, it usually does not use *the*.

Using articles with plural count nouns

● Geraldo planted tulips and roses this year. **The** tulips will bloom in April.

The plural count noun *tulips* is used in a general sense in the first sentence, without *the*. Therefore, the second sentence refers to them specifically as *the tulips*. This example is related to rule 3 in Quick Box 60.2.

Using articles with noncount nouns

● Kalinda served rice and chicken to us. She flavored **the** rice with curry.

Rice is a noncount noun. By the second sentence, *rice* has become specific, so *the* is used. This example is related to rule 3 in Quick Box 60.2.

Generalizing with plural and noncount nouns

Omit *the* in generalizations using plural or noncount nouns.

● ~~The~~ tulips are the flowers that grow from the bulbs.

Compare this sentence to a generalization with a singular count noun.

● **A** tulip is **a** flower that grows from **a** bulb.

60C How should I use *the* with proper nouns?

Proper nouns represent specific people, places, or things. Most proper nouns do not require articles: *We visited Lake Mead* [not *the Lake Mead*] *with Asha and Larry.* However, certain types of proper nouns do require *the*.

Nouns with the pattern *the . . . of . . .* : *the United States of America, the president of Mexico* [not the Mexico]

Plural proper nouns: *the Johnsons, the Chicago Bulls, the United Arab Emirates*

Collective proper nouns (nouns that name a group): *the Society of Friends, the AFL-CIO*

Some, but not all, geographical features: *the Amazon, the Gobi Desert, the Indian Ocean*

Explore
the
Exercise

● **EXERCISE 60-1** Consulting all sections of this chapter, decide which of the words in parentheses is correct and write it in the blank. If no article is needed, leave the blank empty.

EXAMPLE

For (a, an, the) _____ years, people have worked under (a, an, the) <u>the</u> assumption that (a, an, the) <u>the</u> best remedy for (a, an, the) <u>a</u> burn is butter.

1. This kind of treatment seems to be (a, an, the) _____ good idea because butter looks and feels like ointment, but butter doesn't contain (a, an, the) _____ antibacterial property like ointment does.
2. In using butter to treat (a, an, the) _____ burns, you are coating (a, an, the) _____ skin with debris that must be removed later to keep it from interfering with (a, an, the) _____ healing process.
3. In actuality, cold water without ice will not only ease (a, an, the) _____ pain but also prevent scarring and further damage.
4. In fact, (a, an, the) _____ person who keeps the finger submerged for at least several minutes and as long as half an hour will have (a, an, the) _____ least painful or scarred burn, according to doctors.
5. However, if (a, an, the) _____ burn is serious, (a, an, the) _____ first person to be consulted should be a doctor. ●

61 Word Order
■ ■ ■ ■ ■ ■ ■ ■

Quick Points You will learn to

➤ Use appropriate English word order.
➤ Place adjectives and adverbs in the proper places in sentences (pp. 503–505).

61A What are standard and inverted word orders?

Standard word order is the most common sentence pattern in English. The SUBJECT comes before the VERB: *That book* [subject] *was* [verb] *heavy.*

Inverted word order, with a verb coming before the subject, is common for DIRECT QUESTIONS in English: *Was* [verb] *that book* [subject] *heavy? Were* [verb] *you* [subject] *close to it when it fell?*

A common way to form questions with MAIN VERBS other than *be* is to use inverted order with a form of the verb *do* as an AUXILIARY VERB before the subject and the SIMPLE FORM of the main verb after the subject: *Do you want me to put the book away?*

Use *do* with inverted order when a question begins with a question-forming word such as *what, why, when, where,* or *how:* ***Where does** the book belong?*

When a question has more than one auxiliary verb, put the subject after the first auxiliary verb: ***Would you** have replaced the book?*

🛑 **Alert:** Do not use inverted word order with INDIRECT QUESTIONS: *She asked where I saw the book* [*not* She asked where did I see the book]. ●

Verb–subject word order is also required by certain ADVERBS at the beginning of a sentence.

- Only once **did she** ask my advice.
- Never **have I** seen such a mess!

Verb–subject word order rules also apply to emphatic exclamations: ***Was** that **book** heavy! **Did she** ever enjoy that book!*

61B Where should I place adjectives?

In English, an ADJECTIVE ordinarily comes directly before the NOUN it modifies. Quick Box 61.1, page 504, shows the most common order for positioning several adjectives that modify the same noun.

61C Where should I place adverbs?

ADVERBS and adverbial PHRASES modify verbs, adjectives, other adverbs, or whole sentences. They can go in three different places in a CLAUSE: first, middle, or last. ("Middle" usually means just after the auxiliary verb, if any.) See Quick Box 61.2 (page 505).

🛑 **Alert:** If a sentence begins with a negative adverb of frequency (*never, rarely, only once, seldom*), the subject–verb word order must be inverted (see 61A). This creates emphasis.

- **Never** has Nick been bitten by a dog. ●

Quick Box 61.1

Word order for adjectives

1. Determiner, if any: *a, an, the, my, your, Jan's, these,* and so on
2. Expressions of order, including ordinal numbers, if any: *first, second, next, last, final,* and so on
3. Expressions of quantity, including cardinal numbers, if any: *one, two, few, each, every, some,* and so on
4. Adjectives of judgment or opinion, if any: *smart, happy, interesting, sad, boring,* and so on
5. Adjectives of size or shape, if any: *big, small, short, round, rectangular,* and so on
6. Adjectives of age or condition, if any: *new, young, broken, dirty, shiny,* and so on
7. Adjectives of color, if any: *red, green, beige, turquoise,* and so on
8. Adjectives that can also be used as nouns, if any: *French, metal, Protestant, cotton,* and so on
9. The noun

1	2	3	4	5	6	7	8	9
A		few		tiny		red		ants
The	last	six					Thai	drums
My			fine		old		oak	table

● **EXERCISE 61-1** Consulting all sections of this chapter, find and correct any errors in word order.

Explore the Exercise

1. A beautiful few flowers began to bloom in my garden this week.
2. A neighbor asked me, "You did grow all these yourself?"
3. "Yes," I replied, "the roses are my favorite husband's, but the tulips are my favorite."
4. My neighbor, who extremely was impressed with my gardening efforts, decided to grow some flowers of her own.
5. Weeks later, as I strolled by her house, I saw her planting happily seeds from her favorite type of plant—petunias. ●

Quick Box 61.2

Types and positions of adverbs

ADVERBS OF MANNER
Describe how something is done. Usual position: middle or last.

- Nick **carefully** groomed the dog.
- Nick groomed the dog **carefully.**

ADVERBS OF TIME
Describe when an event occurs or how long it lasts. Usual position: first or last.

- **First,** Nick shampooed the dog.
- Nick shampooed the dog **first.**

ADVERBS OF FREQUENCY
Describe how often an event takes place. Usual position: middle to modify a verb, first to modify an entire sentence.

- Nick has **never** been bitten by a dog.
- **Occasionally,** Nick is scratched while shampooing a cat.

ADVERBS OF DEGREE OR EMPHASIS
Indicate *how much* or *to what extent* about other modifiers. Usual position: directly before the word they modify.

- Nick is **rather** quiet around animals.
- Nick wears protection **only** when examining an exotic pet.

  See 40A on the placement of *only.*

SENTENCE ADVERBS
Modify an entire sentence. They include transitional words and expressions, as well as such words as *maybe, probably, possibly, fortunately,* and *incredibly.* Usual position: first.

- **Incredibly,** Nick was once asked to groom a squirrel.

62 Prepositions

Quick Points   You will learn to

➤ Use *in, at,* and *on* to show time and place.
➤ Use prepositions correctly (pp. 506–508).

Watch the Video

Prepositions and their OBJECTS form PREPOSITIONAL PHRASES. Such phrases often describe relationships in time or space. When prepositions are combined with certain VERBS, they are called **phrasal verbs** (see 62B). In some cases, phrasal verbs take on idiomatic meanings. A dictionary such as the *Longman Dictionary of Contemporary English* or the *Oxford Advanced Learner's Dictionary* is especially helpful for finding the correct preposition for certain **idioms.**

62A How should I use *in, at,* and *on* to show time and place?

To Show Time

- *in* a year or a month (*during* is also correct but less common): *in 1999, in May*
- *in* a period of time: *in a few months* (*seconds, days, years*)
- *in* a period of a day: *in the morning* (*afternoon, evening*), *in the daytime* but *at night*
- *on* a specific day: *on Friday, on my birthday, on May 12*
- *at* a specific time or period: *at noon, at 2:00, at dawn, at nightfall, at takeoff* (the time a plane leaves), *at breakfast* (the time a specific meal takes place)

To Show Place

- *in* a location surrounded by something else: *in the province of Alberta, in Utah, in downtown Bombay, in my apartment*
- *at* a specific location: *at your house, at the corner of Third Avenue and Main Street, at 376 Oak Street, at home*
- *on* a street: *on Oak Street, on Third Avenue, on the road*

62B How should I use prepositions in phrasal verbs?

Phrasal verbs are verbs that combine with prepositions to deliver their meaning. The meaning of many phrasal verbs is idiomatic, not literal; *pick on,* for example, means "annoy" or "tease" rather than anything associated with either

506

pick or *on*. Also, many phrasal verbs are informal and are therefore more appropriate for conversation than for ACADEMIC WRITING. For a research paper, for example, *propose* or *suggest* is a better choice than *come up with*.

In some phrasal verbs, the verb and the preposition must always stay together, without being separated by other words: **Look at** *the moon* [not **Look** *the moon* **at**].

In other phrasal verbs, called *separable phrasal verbs*, words can separate the verb and the preposition without interfering with meaning: *I* **threw away** *my homework* [or *I* **threw** *my homework* **away**].

When a separable phrasal verb has a PRONOUN object, that object should be positioned between the verb and the preposition: *I* **threw** *it* **away** [not *I* **threw away** *it*]. Object PHRASES or CLAUSES with more than four or five words are usually positioned after the preposition: *I* **threw away** *the homework that was assigned last week.*

Here's a list of some common phrasal verbs. The ones that can't be separated are marked with an asterisk (*).

SELECTED PHRASAL VERBS

ask out	fill up	keep up with*	make up
break down	find out	leave out	run across*
call back	get along with*	look after*	speak to*
call off	get back	look around*	speak with*
drop off	get off*	look into*	throw out
figure out	go over*	look out for*	turn down
fill out	hand in	look over	

● **EXERCISE 62-1** Consulting the preceding sections of this chapter and using the list of phrasal verbs in 62B, write a one- or two-paragraph description of a typical day at work or school in which you use at least five phrasal verbs. After checking a dictionary, revise your writing, substituting for the phrasal verbs any more formal verbs that might be more appropriate for academic writing. ●

Explore
the
Exercise

62C How should I use prepositions with the passive voice?

VERBS used in the PASSIVE VOICE usually follow the pattern *be* + PAST PARTICIPLE + *by*: *The child* **was frightened by** *a snake.* However, many passive constructions require other prepositions instead of *by*: *The child* **is afraid of** *snakes.* Here's a list of some of these passive expressions with their prepositions. Look in a dictionary for others. (See 63A on using GERUNDS after some of these expressions.)

SELECTED VERBS AND PREPOSITIONS
USED IN PASSIVE CONSTRUCTIONS

be accustomed to	be interested in
be acquainted with	be known for
be composed of	be located in
be concerned about	be made of (*or* from)
be disappointed with (*or* in)	be married to
be discriminated against	be prepared for
be done with	be satisfied with
be excited about	be tired of (*or* from)
be finished with	be worried about

62D How should I use prepositions in expressions?

Different prepositions convey great differences in meaning in many common expressions. For example, with the verb *agree,* four different prepositions create different meanings: *agree **to**, agree **about**, agree **on**,* and *agree **with**.* Check a dictionary if you're unsure of the precise differences.

Many adjectives also require certain prepositions: *afraid of, familiar with, famous for, friendly toward* (or *with*), *guilty of, patient with, proud of.*

63 Gerunds and Infinitives
■ ■ ■ ■ ■ ■ ■ ■

Quick Points   You will learn to

➤ Use gerunds correctly.
➤ Use infinitives correctly (pp. 509–511).

GERUNDS and INFINITIVES are types of verbals. **Verbals** are VERB forms that function as NOUNS or MODIFIERS. Like all nouns, gerunds and infinitives can be DIRECT OBJECTS. Some verbs call for gerund objects to follow them; other verbs must be followed by infinitive objects. Still other verbs can be followed by either gerund or infinitive objects. A few verbs change meaning depending on whether a gerund object or an infinitive object is used.

63A What verbs use a gerund, not an infinitive, object?

Certain VERBS cannot be followed by infinitives as direct objects; they require gerunds: *Yuri considered **calling*** [not *to call*] *the mayor.*

VERBS THAT USE GERUND OBJECTS

acknowledge	delay	have trouble	recall
admit	deny	imagine	recommend
advise	detest	include	resent
anticipate	discuss	insist on	resist
appreciate	dislike	keep (on)	risk
avoid	dream about	mention	suggest
cannot help	enjoy	mind	talk about
complain about	escape	object to	tolerate
consider	evade	postpone	understand
consist of	favor	practice	
contemplate	finish	put off	
defer from	give up	quit	

◾ Using a gerund after *go*

Although *go* is usually followed by an infinitive object (*We can **go to see*** [not *go seeing*] *a movie*), *go* is followed by a gerund in such phrases as *go swimming, go fishing, go shopping,* and *go driving: I will **go swimming*** [not *go to swim*] *tomorrow.*

◾ Using gerunds after *be* + complement + preposition

A COMPLEMENT often follows a form of *be*. Some complements require certain PREPOSITIONS (see 62C).

SELECTED *BE* + COMPLEMENT + PREPOSITION EXPRESSIONS

be (get) accustomed to	be prepared for	be tired of (*or* from)
be angry about	be responsible for	be (get) used to
be bored with	be capable of	be worried about
be excited about	be committed to	
be interested in	be concerned about	

- We are excited about **voting** [not *to vote*] in the election.
- They were interested in **hearing** [not *to hear*] the candidates' debate.

❶ **Alert:** Always use a gerund, not an infinitive, as the object of a preposition. Be especially careful when the word *to* is functioning as a preposition in a PHRASAL VERB (see 62B): *We are committed to **saving*** [not *committed to save*] *the elephants.* ●

63B What verbs use an infinitive, not a gerund, object?

Certain verbs cannot be followed by gerunds as direct objects; they can be followed by infinitives: *Three people decided **to question*** [not *decided questioning*] *the speaker.*

VERBS THAT USE INFINITIVE OBJECTS

afford to	claim to	intend to	refuse to
agree to	consent to	know how to	seem to
aim to	decide to	learn to	struggle to
appear to	decline to	like to	tend to
arrange to	demand to	manage to	threaten to
ask to	deserve to	mean to	try to
attempt to	expect to	offer to	volunteer to
be able (unable) to	fail to	plan to	wait to
be left to	give permission to	prepare to	want to
beg to	hesitate to	pretend to	would like to
care to	hope to	promise to	

▣ Using infinitives after *be* + some complements

- We are eager **to go** [*not* going] to the mountains.
- I am ready **to sleep** [*not* sleeping] in a tent.

▣ Using unmarked infinitive objects

Be careful not to overuse the word *to* in an unmarked infinitive, which is a verb in its SIMPLE FORM without the word *to*. Common verbs followed by unmarked infinitives are *feel, have, hear, let, listen to, look at, make* (meaning "compel"), *notice, see,* and *watch.* In the following examples, the first shows *take* as an unmarked infinitive, while the second shows *take* as a marked infinitive.

- Please **let** me **take** [*not* to take] you to lunch.

  Take is an unmarked infinitive because it's used after *let.*

- I want **to take** you to lunch.

  To take is a marked infinitive because it's used after *want.*

63C How does meaning change if an infinitive object or a gerund follows *stop, remember,* or *forget?*

Here are some examples of what happens when a verb is followed by either a gerund or an infinitive. Followed by a gerund, *stop* means "finish, quit": *We stopped eating* means "We finished our meal." However, followed by an infinitive, *stop* means "stop or interrupt one activity to begin another": *We stopped to eat* means "We stopped doing something [such as driving or painting the house] to eat."

Followed by a gerund, *remember* means "recall a memory": *I remember talking to you last night.* However, followed by an infinitive, *remember* means "not to forget to do something": *I must remember to talk with Isa.*

Followed by a gerund, *forget* means "do something and not recall it": *I forget having put my keys in the refrigerator.* However, followed by an infinitive, *forget* means "not do something": *If you forget to put a stamp on that letter, it will be returned.*

63D Do sense verbs change meaning with a gerund or an infinitive object?

Sense verbs such as *see, notice, hear, observe, watch, feel, listen to,* and *look at* usually don't change meaning whether a gerund or an infinitive is used as an object. *I saw the water rising* and *I saw the water rise* (unmarked infinitive—see 63B) both deliver the same message.

● **EXERCISE 63-1** Write the correct form of the verbal object (either a gerund or an infinitive) for each verb in parentheses. For help, consult 63A through 63D.

Explore
the
Exercise

EXAMPLE

People like (think) <u>to think</u> that they have a good memory, but everybody shows signs of forgetfulness from time to time.

1. Think about (ride) _____ the railroad to work on a rainy Monday morning.
2. The comfortable reclining seats let passengers (take) _____ a relaxing nap on the way to work.
3. Because of the rain, commuters are forced (bring) _____ an umbrella and a raincoat, along with their usual traveling items.
4. Once they reach their destination, passengers forget that they need their umbrellas and raincoats (walk) _____ the few blocks to work.
5. (Step) _____ out into the rain makes the passengers suddenly realize that they've left their umbrellas and raincoats on the train, which has already left the station. ●

63E How should I choose between -*ing* and -*ed* forms of adjectives?

Deciding whether to use the -*ing* form (PRESENT PARTICIPLE) or the -*ed* form (PAST PARTICIPLE of a REGULAR VERB) as an ADJECTIVE in a specific sentence can be difficult. For example, *I am amused* and *I am amusing* are both correct in English, but their meanings are very different.

- **I am amused** at the circus.

  I experience amusement.

- **I am amusing** at the circus.

  I cause the amusement of other people.

To make the right choice, decide whether the modified NOUN or PRONOUN is causing or experiencing what the participle describes.

Use a present participle (-*ing*) to modify a noun or pronoun that is the cause of the action. This meaning is in the ACTIVE VOICE.

- Mica explained your **interesting** plan.

  The noun *plan* caused interest, so *interesting* is correct.

- I find your plan **exciting**.

  The noun *plan* causes excitement, so *exciting* is correct.

Use a past participle (-*ed* on regular verbs) to modify a noun or pronoun that experiences or receives whatever the MODIFIER describes. This meaning is in the PASSIVE VOICE.

- An **interested** committee wants to hear your plan.

  The noun *committee* experiences interest, so *interested* is correct.

- **Excited** by your plan, I called a board meeting.

  The pronoun *I* experiences excitement, so *excited* is correct.

Here's a list of some frequently used participles that can be used as adjectives. To choose the right form, decide whether the noun or pronoun *experiences* or *causes* what the participle describes.

annoyed, annoying	frightened, frightening
appalled, appalling	insulted, insulting
bored, boring	offended, offending
confused, confusing	pleased, pleasing
depressed, depressing	reassured, reassuring
disgusted, disgusting	satisfied, satisfying
fascinated, fascinating	shocked, shocking

● **EXERCISE 63-2**   Choose the correct participle from each pair in parentheses. For help, consult 63E.

EXAMPLE

It can be a (satisfied, satisfying) <u>satisfying</u> experience to learn about the lives of artists.

1. The artist Frida Kahlo led an (interested, interesting) _____ life.
2. When Kahlo was eighteen, (horrified, horrifying) _____ observers saw her (injured, injuring) _____ in a streetcar accident.
3. A (disappointed, disappointing) _____ Kahlo had to abandon her plan to study medicine.
4. Instead, she began to create paintings filled with (disturbed, disturbing) _____ images.
5. Some art critics consider Kahlo's paintings to be (fascinated, fascinating) _____ works of art, though many people find them (overwhelmed, overwhelming) _____. ●

64 Modal Auxiliary Verbs

■ ■ ■ ■ ■ ■ ■ ■

Quick Points   You will learn to

➤ Use modal auxiliary verbs to help main verbs convey information.

Modal auxiliary verbs convey meaning about ability, necessity, advice, possibility, and other conditions. These verbs include *can, could, had better, may, might, must, should, ought, will,* and *would.* Like the auxiliary verbs *be, do,* and *have,* modal auxiliary verbs help MAIN VERBS convey more information than those verbs can alone.

64A   How do modal auxiliary verbs differ from *be, do,* and *have*?

Modal auxiliary verbs are always followed by the SIMPLE FORM of a main verb: *I **might go** tomorrow.*

One-word modal auxiliary verbs usually do not have an -*s* ending in the third-person singular: *She **could** go with me, you **could** go with me,* and *they **could** go with me.*

Two modals that have forms that end in -*s* are *have to* and *need to* in the third-person singular: *She **has** to stay; he **needs** to smile more.*

64B Which modal auxiliary verbs express ability, necessity, advisability, or probability?

■ Expressing ability

The modal auxiliary verb *can* means "ability in the present." The modal auxiliary verb *could* sometimes means "ability in the past." These words deliver the meaning of "able to."

● You **can work** late tonight.

This means "You are able to work late tonight."

● I **could play** the piano when I was younger.

This means "I was able to play the piano when I was younger."

The modal auxiliary verb *could* often expresses some condition that is required to be fulfilled before another condition.

● If you **could** come early, we can start on time.

This means "We can't start on time unless you come early."

● I **could** have gone to bed at 10:00 if I had finished my homework.

This means "I couldn't go to bed at 10:00 because I had not finished my homework."

Adding *not* between a modal auxiliary verb and the main verb makes the sentence negative: *I could **not** work late last night.*

■ Expressing necessity

The modal auxiliary verbs *must, have to,* and *need to* express a requirement to do something. *Must* implies only future action. *Have to* and *need to* imply action in all verb tenses.

● You **must leave** before midnight. She **has to leave** when I leave.
● We **needed to be** with you last night. You **will need to be** here before dark tonight.

■ Expressing advice or the notion of a good idea

The modal auxiliary verbs *should* and *ought to* mean that doing the action of the main verb in the present or future is a good idea. The PAST-TENSE FORMS are *should have* and *ought to have;* they are followed by the PAST PARTICIPLE.

- You **should call** your dentist tomorrow. I **ought to have** gone to my dentist last week.

The modal *had better* expresses the meaning of good advice or warning or threat.

- You **had better see** a doctor before your cough gets worse.

◼ Expressing probability

The modal auxiliary verbs *may, might, could,* and *must* usually express probability, possibility, or likelihood.

((**•**

Listen
to the
Podcast

- We **might** see a tiger in the zoo. We **could** go this afternoon.

The past-tense forms for the modal auxiliary verbs *may, might, could,* and *must* add *have* and the main verb's past participle to the modals.

- I'm hungry; I **must have neglected** to eat breakfast.

64C Which modal auxiliary verbs express preference, plan, or past habit?

◼ Expressing preferences

Would rather (present tense) and *would rather have* (past tense) express a preference. In the past tense, the modal is also followed by a past participle.

- We **would rather see** a comedy than a mystery. We **would rather have seen** a movie last night.

◼ Expressing a plan or obligation

A form of *be* followed by *supposed to* and the simple form of a main verb, in both present and past tense, means something planned or an obligation.

- I **was supposed to meet** them at the bus stop.

The word *supposed* may be omitted with no change in meaning.

- I **was to meet** them at the bus stop.

◼ Expressing past habit

The modal auxiliary verbs *used to* and *would* mean that something happened repeatedly in a time that has passed.

- I **used to hate** getting a flu shot. I **would dread** the injection for weeks beforehand.

❗ Alert: Both the modal auxiliary verbs *used to* and *would* can be used for repeated actions in the past, but the modal auxiliary verb *would* cannot be used for a situation that lasted for a period of time in the past.

> used to
> I ~~would~~ live in Arizona. ●
> ^

Explore the Exercise

● **EXERCISE 64-1** Select the correct choice from the words in parentheses and write it in the blank. For help, consult 64A through 64C.

EXAMPLE

When I was younger, I (would, used to) <u>used to</u> love to go bicycle riding.

1. You (ought to have, ought have) _____ called yesterday as you had promised you would.
2. Judging by the size of the puddles in the street outside, it (must be rained, must have rained) _____ all night long.
3. Ingrid (must not have, might not have been) _____ as early for the interview as she claims she was.
4. After all the studying he did, Pedro (should have, should have been) _____ less frightened by the exam.
5. I have to go home early today, although I really (cannot, should not) _____ leave before the end of the day because of all the work I have to do. ●

Tab 12
Specific Writing Situations, Glossaries, Index

■ ■ ■ ■ ■ ■ ■ ■ ■

CHAPTERS
65–72

Tab 12 Specific Writing Situations, Glossaries, Index

MyCompLab® Visit mycomplab.com for the eText and for resources on special writing situations.

An Overview of Writing Across the Curriculum

65

Quick Points You will learn to

> Adapt your writing to various college courses.
> Use cue words to tell what your college writing needs to accomplish.

65A What is writing across the curriculum?

Watch
the Video

Writing across the curriculum refers to the writing you do in college courses beyond first-year composition. (A related term is "writing in the disciplines," which usually refers to writing that is specific to individual majors.) Good writing in courses as different as history, biology, and psychology has many common features. However, there are also important differences. A lab report for a chemistry course, for example, differs from a paper for a literature course. Quick Box 65.1 summarizes different types of writing across the curriculum

Quick Box 65.1

Comparing the disciplines

Discipline	Types of Assignments	Primary Sources	Secondary Sources	Usual Documentation Styles
HUMANITIES history, languages, literature, philosophy, art, music, theater	essays, response statements, reviews, analyses, original works such as stories, poems, autobiographies	literary works, manuscripts, paintings and sculptures, historical documents, films, plays, photographs, artifacts from popular culture	reviews, journal articles, research papers, books	MLA, CM
SOCIAL SCIENCES psychology, sociology, anthropology, education	research reports, case studies, reviews of the literature, analyses	surveys, interviews, observations, experiments, tests and measures	journal articles, scholarly books, literature reviews	APA

continued >>

Quick Box 65.1   (continued)

Discipline	Types of Assignments	Primary Sources	Secondary Sources	Usual Documentation Styles
NATURAL SCIENCES biology, chemistry, physics, mathematics	reports, research proposals and reports, science reviews	experiments, field notes, direct observations, measurements	journal articles, research papers, books	often CSE but varies by discipline

65B How do audience and purpose work across the curriculum?

The AUDIENCE for ACADEMIC WRITING consists of scholars, professors, and students in particular fields. As a result, you need to use the kind of sources and follow the kinds of conventions that are expected in each discipline. Conventions include format and organization, types of evidence, tone and style, and documentation style. They can vary considerably from writings for more general and popular readers. We suggest you study examples of the kinds of writing you've been asked to produce.

PURPOSES can vary widely. Some tasks mainly require explaining information you acquire from readings or other data. Other tasks require making an argument supported by evidence and reasoning. Most assignments contain **cue words** that tell what your writing needs to accomplish. Quick Box 65.2 presents some common cue words.

Quick Box 65.2   ■ ■ ■ ■ ■ ■ ■ ■ ■

Some common cue words

Cue Word	Meaning
ANALYZE	Separate into parts and discuss each, often including how it contributes to a meaning or implication.
CLASSIFY	Arrange in groups based on shared characteristics or functions.
CRITICIZE	Give your opinion and explain why you approve or disapprove of something.
COMPARE	Show similarities and differences.

continued >>

Quick Box 65.2	(continued)

Cue Word	Meaning
DEFINE	Tell what something is to differentiate it from similar things.
DISCUSS	Explain and comment on, in an organized way, the various issues or elements involved.
EXPLAIN	Make clear a complex thing or process that needs to be illuminated or interpreted.
INTERPRET	Explain the meaning or significance of something.
REVIEW	Evaluate or summarize critically.
SUMMARIZE	Lay out the major points of something.
SUPPORT	Argue in favor of something.

66 Writing About the Humanities

Quick Points   You will learn to

➤ Understand the different types of papers in the humanities.

66A What are the humanities?

Disciplines in the humanities seek to represent and understand human experience, creativity, thought, and values. These disciplines include literature, languages, philosophy, and history, although some colleges group history with the social sciences. Also, many colleges include the fine arts (music, art, dance, theater, and creative writing) as part of the humanities.

66B What are types of writing in the humanities?

Because the humanities cover an impressively broad range of knowledge, writing in the humanities covers many types and purposes.

■ Summaries

Occasionally your instructor will request an objective summary of a text; you might need to tell the plot of a novel or present the main points of an article (see Chapter 15). Generally, however, a summary is a means to a greater end. For example, writing an interpretation often requires you to summarize parts of the source so that your points about it are clear.

■ Syntheses

SYNTHESIS relates several texts, ideas, or pieces of information to one another (see Chapter 17). For example, you might read several accounts of the events leading up to the Civil War and then write a synthesis that explains what caused that war. Or you might read several philosophers' definitions of morality and write a synthesis of the components of a moral life.

■ Responses

In a response, you give your personal reaction to a work, supported by explanations of your reasoning (see 17C). For example, do you think Hamlet's behavior makes sense? Do you agree with Peter Singer's philosophical arguments against using animals in scientific experiments? Before you write a response, clarify whether your instructor wants you to justify it with references to a text. (See also Chapter 14 and section 67B.)

■ Interpretations

An interpretation explains the meaning or significance of a particular text, event, or work of art (see Quick Box 66.1). For example, what does Plato's *Republic* suggest about the nature of a good society? What was the significance of the 9/11 tragedy for Americans' sense of security? Your reply isn't right or wrong; rather, you present your point of view and explain your reasoning. The quality of your reasoning determines how successfully you convey your point.(See also Quick Box 67.1 in section 67B.)

■ Narratives

When you write a narrative, you construct a coherent story out of separate facts or events. In a history class, for example, you might examine news events, laws, diaries and journals, and related materials to create a chronological version of what happened. You might do the kind of work that a biographer does by gathering information about isolated events in people's lives, interviews with those people or others who knew them, letters or other writings, and related SOURCES, all to form a coherent story of their lives. (See also Chapter 9.)

Quick Box 66.1

Selected analytical frameworks used in the humanities

RHETORICAL	Explores how and why people use LOGICAL, EMOTIONAL, and ETHICAL APPEALS to create desired effects on specific audiences, in specific situations (see 3B).
CULTURAL OR NEW HISTORICAL	Explores how social, economic, and other cultural forces influence the development of ideas, texts, art, laws, customs, and so on. Also explores how individual texts or events provide broader understandings of the past or present.
DECONSTRUCTIONIST	Assumes that the meaning of any given text is not stable or "in" the work. Rather, meaning always depends on contexts and the interests of the people in power. The goal of deconstruction is to produce multiple possible meanings of a work, usually to undermine traditional interpretations.
FEMINIST	Focuses on how women are presented and treated, concentrating especially on power relationships between men and women.
FORMALIST	Centers on matters of structure, form, and traditional literary devices (plot, rhythm, imagery, symbolism, and others; see Quick Box 67.2).
MARXIST	Assumes that the most important forces in human experience are economic and material ones by focusing on power differences between economic classes of people and the effects of those differences.
READER-RESPONSE	Emphasizes how the individual reader determines meaning. The reader's personal history, values, experiences, relationships, and previous reading all contribute to how he or she interprets a particular work or event.

Some writing assignments in the humanities may ask you to write about your memories or experiences (see Chapter 9). Generally, such writings involve not only effectively telling a story but also some reflection on or analysis of that story.

■ Textual analyses

Chapter 11 explains common features of textual analysis. The humanities use a number of analytical frameworks, or systematic ways of investigating a work. Quick Box 66.1, on page 521, summarizes some common analytical frameworks used, most notably in literary analysis. Nearly all writing in the humanities depends on analysis to some extent.

66C What documentation styles are common in the humanities?

Most fields in the humanities use the Modern Language Association (MLA) documentation style (see Chapters 24 through 26). Some disciplines in the humanities use *Chicago Manual* (CM) style (see Chapter 30). A few have begun to use the American Psychological Association (APA) documentation style (see Chapters 27–29).

67 Writing About Literature

■ ■ ■ ■ ■ ■ ■ ■ ■

Quick Points   You will learn to

➤ Understand the different types of literature papers.
➤ Identify the major elements to analyze in literary works.

67A What is literature?

Literature encompasses fiction (novels and stories), drama (plays, scripts, and some films), and poetry (poems and lyrics), as well as nonfiction with artistic qualities (memoirs, personal essays, and so on).

Writing effective papers about literature involves more than summarizing the plot. It involves CRITICAL THINKING and SYNTHESIS. In such papers, you state a CLAIM (an observation or a position about the work of literature) and convince your readers that your thesis is reasonable. To be effective, a paper needs to be thorough, and its claims have to be well supported. For support, you make direct references to the work itself, by summarizing, paraphrasing, and quoting specific passages (see Chapter 15) and by explaining precisely *why* and *how* the selected passages support your interpretation. Use MLA documentation style for literature papers.

67B What are different types of papers about literature?

■ Writing a personal response

A personal response paper is an essay in which you explain your reaction to a literary work or some aspect of it. You might discuss whether situations in the work are similar to your personal experiences, explain whether you agree or disagree with the author's point of view and why, or answer a question or explore a problem that the work raised for you (see Chapters 11 and 14). As with all effective papers about literature, you need to explain your response by discussing specific passages or elements from the text.

■ Writing an interpretation

An interpretation explains the message or viewpoint that you think the work conveys (see Chapter 11). Most works of literature are open to more than one interpretation. Your task is not to discover a single "right answer." Instead, you determine a possible interpretation and provide an argument that supports it. The questions in Quick Box 67.1 (referring to the complete poem on pp. 526–527) can help you write an effective interpretation paper.

Quick Box 67.1   ■ ■ ■ ■ ■ ■ ■ ■

Questions for an interpretation paper

1. What is a central theme of the work? For example, in the poem "Blackberries," a central theme might be shame.

2. How do particular parts of the work relate to the theme? In "Blackberries," the smirking children in the car make the boy shamefully aware of his stained hands.

3. Why might the work end as it does?

4. If patterns exist in the work, what might they mean? Patterns include repeated images, situations, and words. In "Blackberries," the words *consecrated, garland of thorns,* and *forgiveness* form a pattern.

5. What meaning does the author create through the elements listed in Quick Box 67.2?

■ Writing a formal analysis

A formal analysis explains how elements of a literary work function to create meaning or effect (see Chapter 11). Your instructor may ask you to concentrate on one of these elements (for example, "How does the point of view in the story contribute to its meaning?") or to discuss how a writer develops a theme through several elements (for example, "How do setting, imagery, and symbolism reveal the author's viewpoint?"). The paper by student Michael Choi (see 67E) is an example of an interpretation based on a formal analysis. Quick Box 67.2 describes some of the major literary elements that you might expect to use in formal analyses.

Quick Box 67.2   ■ ■ ■ ■ ■ ■ ■ ■ ■

Major elements to analyze in literary works

PLOT	Events and their sequence
THEME	Central idea or message
STRUCTURE	Organization and relationship of parts to each other and to the whole
CHARACTERIZATION	Traits, thoughts, and actions of the people in the work
SETTING	Time and place of the action
POINT OF VIEW	Perspective or position from which a narrator or a main character presents the material
STYLE	Word choice and sentence structures that author uses: the "how," not the "what."
IMAGERY	Descriptive language that creates mental pictures for the reader
TONE	Attitude toward the subject of the work—and sometimes toward the reader as shown by author—as expressed through choice of words, imagery, and point of view
FIGURES OF SPEECH	Unusual use or combination of words, such as METAPHOR or SIMILE, for enhanced vividness or effect
SYMBOLISM	Using a specific object or event to represent a deeper, often abstract, meaning or idea
RHYTHM	Beat, meter
RHYME	Repetition of similar sounds for their auditory effect

Quick Box 67.3

Major topics for cultural analyses

GENDER	How does a work portray women or men and define or challenge their roles in society?
CLASS	How does a work portray relationships among the upper, middle, and lower classes? How do characters' actions or perspectives result from their wealth and power—or from their poverty and powerlessness?
RACE AND ETHNICITY	How does a work portray the influences of race and ethnicity on the characters' actions, status, and values?
HISTORY	How does a work reflect—or challenge—past events and values in a society?
AUTOBIOGRAPHY	How did the writer's life experiences influence his or her work?
GENRE	How is the work similar to or different from other works of its type (for example, plays, sonnets, mysteries, comic novels, memoirs)?

■ Writing a cultural analysis

A cultural analysis relates a literary work to broader historical, social, cultural, or political situations. Instructors might ask you to explain how events or prevailing attitudes influenced the writing of a work or the way readers understand it. Quick Box 67.3 lists some common topics appropriate for a cultural analysis.

67C What special rules apply to writing about literature?

■ Using correct verb tenses

Always use the PRESENT TENSE when you describe or discuss a literary work or any of its elements: *Walter* [a character] ***makes*** *a difficult decision when he* ***turns down*** *Linder's offer to buy the house.* In addition, always use the present tense for discussing what an author has done in a specific work: *Lorraine Hansberry, author of* A Raisin in the Sun, ***explores*** *not only powerful racial issues but also common family dynamics.* Always use a PAST-TENSE VERB to discuss historical events or biographical information: *Lorraine Hansberry's* A Raisin in the Sun ***was*** *the first play by an African American woman to be produced on Broadway.*

Watch
the Video

■ Using your own ideas and using secondary sources

Watch
the Video

Some assignments call only for your own ideas about a literary work. Other assignments call for you to use SECONDARY SOURCES. Secondary sources include books and articles in which experts discuss some aspect of the literary text or other material related to your topic. You can locate secondary sources by using the research process explained in Chapter 20.

67D A student's essay about literature

■ Working on the assignment

View
the Model
Document

Michael Choi, a student in first-year English, fulfilled an assignment to write an interpretation of the images and metaphors in Yusef Komunyakaa's poem "Blackberries." When Michael first read the poem, several images puzzled him. He wondered how they connect to an apparently simple scene of a boy picking, eating, and selling blackberries. In the process of writing his essay, Michael came to understand how those previously puzzling images and metaphors shape the poem's deeper meaning. Here is his final draft.

■ Learning about the poet, Yusef Komunyakaa

Yusef Komunyakaa is an African American poet who was born in 1947 and raised in Louisiana. His father was a carpenter. Komunyakaa was educated at the University of Colorado, at Colorado State University, and at the University of California–Irvine. He served a tour of duty in Vietnam and was awarded the Bronze Star. In 1994, he won the Pulitzer Prize for poetry—one of the most prestigious honors a poet can receive in the United States—for his book *Neon Vernacular*. Here is his poem "Blackberries."

BLACKBERRIES

Yusef Komunyakaa

They left my hands like a printer's
Or thief's before a police blotter
& pulled me into early morning's
Terrestrial sweetness, so thick
The damp ground was consecrated   5
Where they fell among a garland of thorns.
Although I could smell old lime-covered
History, at ten I'd still hold out my hands
& berries fell into them. Eating from one
& filling a half gallon with the other,   10
I ate the mythology & dreamt
Of pies & cobbler, almost

Needful as forgiveness. My bird dog Spot
Eyed blue jays & thrashers. The mud frogs
In rich blackness, hid from daylight.   15
An hour later, beside City Limits Road
I balanced a gleaming can in each hand,
Limboed between worlds, repeating *one dollar.*
The big blue car made me sweat.
Wintertime crawled out of the windows.   20
When I leaned closer I saw the boy
& girl my age, in the wide back seat
Smirking, & it was then I remembered my fingers
Burning with thorns among berries too ripe to touch.

Student's essay about literature

Choi 1

Michael Choi

Professor May

English 100

4 Mar. 2012

Images, Metaphors, and Meaning in "Blackberries"

In Yusef Komunyakaa's poem "Blackberries," the poet
describes himself as "limboed between worlds" (line 18). At
that moment, he is a boy standing beside City Limits Road—a
symbolic line between the city and the country—selling berries
that he has just picked. Yet the boy is also caught between his
familiar natural world and a world of wealth and privilege.
One of the poem's key issues is whether the boy is responsible
for his situation. Komunyakaa uses a rich set of images and
metaphors to suggest the boy's complicated position.

Some plain and direct images connect the boy to the world
of nature. As he picks blackberries, the poet describes the "bird
dog Spot" watching blue jays and thrashers (13-14), and he

continued >>

Choi 2

mentions "mud frogs" hiding in the dark (14-15). Readers form
an impression of a rustic boy trying to earn some money from a
countryside that is familiar and comfortable to him. He eats as
he fills "gleaming" half-gallon cans (17) and dreams of "pies &
cobbler" (12). The day is "thick" with "terrestrial sweetness" (4),
and the atmosphere is peaceful, almost sleepy.

When the boy moves beyond the country to the City
Limits Road to sell his harvest, however, his pleasant
morning is shattered. After a customer drives up, the boy
says, "The big blue car made me sweat" (19). Partly, he
sweats because the car's air-conditioning makes him aware
of heat that had not bothered him until that very moment.
Komunyakaa uses the strong image that "Wintertime crawled

out of the windows" to
heighten the contrast
between the artificial
environment of the
car and the natural
environment of the
boy (20). Even more
important, the boy
sweats because he is
suddenly self-conscious. He feels uncomfortable at the gap
between himself and "the boy / & girl my age, in the wide
back seat" (21-22). The emphasis on the air-conditioning and
the width of the seat makes clear that these children come
not only from the city but also from wealthier circumstances.
When they smirk at him, he remembers his berry-stained
fingers. Those stained hands are a metaphor for how

continued >>

Choi 3

different he is from the children in the car, both socially and economically. He feels ashamed.

Should he feel this way? Several complicated images and metaphors in the poem make this question difficult to answer. For example, at the beginning, the poet says that the berries "left my hands like a printer's" (1). This image not only calls attention to the inky stains on his hands but also likens berry picking to printing. Both are forms of honest manual labor. Furthermore, picking ripe berries is similar to the messy job of shedding ink-saturated type from a printing press—the typesetting method used before computers. This printing metaphor suggests a subtle connection between the boy's work and the poet's work. Komunyakaa immediately complicates the first image with a second that compares the boy's hands to a "thief's before a police blotter" (2). The common element between the two metaphors is the ink, which in the second is used for fingerprinting.

Note that the person whose fingerprints are being taken by the police is not simply a suspect but a thief (2). The person is already guilty of a crime. Has the boy been stealing berries that do not belong to him, and does he feel guilty when he is caught? This possible interpretation does not completely fit the encounter with the big blue car. The "smirking" response of the children in the car seems snobbish (20). Rather than accusing him of being a thief, the children make fun of him for getting dirty while picking berries, which they can buy in cool comfort. For his efforts, which even involve his "fingers / Burning with thorns" (23-24), the boy receives ridicule. The reader's sympathies lie with

continued >>

Choi 4

the boy selling the berries. Even if he did steal the berries, his crime does not seem that great.

Another set of metaphors, more mythic in nature, suggests an answer to the question of whether the boy should feel guilty. The boy reports that he "could smell old lime-covered / History" as he picks and eats (7-8). While lime might refer to a bright shade of green or to the citrus fruit, another meaning seems to apply here. The chemical substance lime has two uses. Farmers use it to reduce acidity in soil, where it serves as a kind of fertilizer. Alternatively, quicklime spread over the bodies of dead animals speeds their decomposition. To cover history in lime, therefore, means either to cultivate it or to bury it. Later, the boy states that he "ate the mythology & dreamt / Of pies & cobbler" (11-12). Obviously, no one can literally eat mythology. This metaphor suggests that the boy is consuming the berries with little thought of any deeper significance his actions might have. There is a mythic dimension to picking blackberries, but the boy focuses on pleasant physical sensations and, eventually, the chance to make some money. Similarly, history is something to consume or ignore. If the boy is a criminal (which seems unlikely), maybe he is unaware that he is doing anything wrong. Furthermore, perhaps no one owns the berries, and he is merely "stealing" from nature.

The poem's most profound images and metaphors have religious overtones. The poet describes the ground beneath the berry bushes as "consecrated" (5). This powerful word choice characterizes the ground as holy. The berries do not fall simply among thorns but among "a garland of thorns" (6). The image of a

continued >>

garland suggests the crown of thorns placed on the head of Jesus after his trial, and these images draw out the deepest meaning of the poet's being "limboed between worlds" (18). In some religious traditions, limbo is a place where souls temporarily go before entering heaven or where innocent but unbaptized babies permanently dwell. In addition to standing between the world of wealth and status that is represented by the car and the simpler world of bird dogs and mud frogs, the boy stands outside paradise. He has left and knows that he cannot go back.

Although mythic and religious elements are present in "Blackberries," Komunyakaa's poem ultimately supports interpretations on several levels. The poet uses religious images to give depth to the boy's situation. When the boy picks the berries, he is in a peaceful, natural environment that is almost sacred, even if he does not realize it. When he sells the berries, he encounters a foreign world of wealth and privilege. Because of his background, he cannot easily join that world. Yet he cannot easily go back to his familiar ways because he now sees his actions differently. He perceives that there may be something wrong with picking blackberries. Whether or not he should feel guilty, he does feel guilty. The poet is truly limboed between worlds.

Work Cited

Komunyakaa, Yusef. "Blackberries." *Pleasure Dome: New and Collected Poems.* Middletown: Wesleyan UP, 2001. 280–81. Print.

68 Writing in the Social Sciences

Quick Points You will learn to

➤ Understand the different types of papers in the social sciences.

68A What are the social sciences?

The social sciences focus on the behavior of people as individuals and in groups. This includes disciplines such as economics, education, geography, political science, psychology, sociology, and sometimes history. In the social sciences, PRIMARY SOURCES include surveys and questionnaires, observations, interviews, and experiments. Surveys and questionnaires systematically gather information from a representative number of individuals. To prepare a questionnaire, use the guidelines in Quick Box 19.1 on p. 167. For advice on collecting information through observation, see 19C, where we also explain interviewing strategies, especially in Quick Box 19.2. on p. 168.

The social sciences sometimes use data from experiments as a source. For example, if you want to learn how people react in a particular situation, you can set up that situation artificially and bring individuals (known as "subjects") into it to observe their behavior. With all methods of inquiry in the social sciences, you are required to treat subjects fairly and honestly, not in ways that could harm their body, mind, or reputation.

Use APA documentation style for papers in the social sciences.

68B What are different types of papers in the social sciences?

The social sciences often involve the same kinds of writing as in the humanities (see 66C). Four additional types of papers are case studies, ethnographies, research reports, and research papers (or reviews of the literature).

■ Case studies

A **case study** is an intensive study of one group or individual. Case studies are important in psychology, social work, education, medicine, and similar fields in which it's useful to form a comprehensive portrait of people to understand them and, in some cases, to help them. For example, if you learn that a certain teaching style is effective, you might do a case study of a student to understand how it works in a particular instance.

A case study's specific parts and their order vary. Most case studies contain the following components:

1. Basic identifying information about the individual or group
2. A history of the individual or group
3. Observations of the individual's or group's behavior
4. Conclusions and perhaps recommendations as a result of the observations

■ Ethnographies

Ethnographies are comprehensive studies of people interacting in a particular situation. Ethnographies commonly are written in courses in business, education, or the social sciences, with anthropology and sociology being prime examples. A sociologist might compose an ethnography of a classroom, for instance, to understand the interactions and relationships among students. The level of details needed in ethnographies has been described by anthropologist Clifford Geertz as "thick description." The more details you have, the better because you can't be sure which ones will be important until you analyze and reflect on the information.

■ Research reports

Research reports explain your own original research based on PRIMARY SOURCES. These may result from interviews, questionnaires, observations, or experiments. Research reports in the social sciences often follow a prescribed format:

1. Statement of the problem
2. Background, sometimes including a review of the literature
3. Methodology
4. Results
5. Discussion of findings

■ Research papers (or reviews of the literature)

Very often social science research requires you to summarize, analyze, and synthesize SECONDARY SOURCES (see 19B). These sources are usually articles and books that report or discuss the findings of other people's primary research. To prepare a review of the literature, comprehensively gather and analyze the sources that have been published on a specific topic. *Literature* in this sense simply means "the body of work on a subject." Sometimes a review of the literature is a part of a longer paper, usually in the "background" section of a research report. Other times the entire paper might be an extensive review of the literature.

69 Writing in the Natural Sciences

Quick Points You will learn to

➤ Understand the different types of papers in the natural sciences.

69A What are the natural sciences?

The natural sciences include disciplines such as astronomy, biology, chemistry, geology, and physics. The sciences seek to describe and explain natural phenomena. The *scientific method,* commonly used in the sciences to make discoveries, is a procedure for gathering information related to a specific hypothesis. Quick Box 69.1 gives guidelines for using this method.

Documentation styles differ among the various sciences. A common style is that of the Council of Science Editors (CSE), described in Chapter 31.

69B What are different types of papers in the natural sciences?

Two major types of papers in the sciences are reports and reviews.

Quick Box 69.1

Watch
the Video

Guidelines for using the scientific method

1. Formulate a tentative explanation (a *hypothesis*) for a scientific phenomenon.
2. Read and summarize previously published information related to your hypothesis.
3. Plan a method of investigation to test your hypothesis.
4. Experiment, following exactly the investigative procedures you have outlined.
5. Observe closely the results of the experiment, and write notes carefully.
6. Analyze the results. Do they confirm the hypothesis?
7. Write a report of your research. At the end, you can suggest additional hypotheses that might be investigated.

Quick Box 69.2

Parts of a science report

1. **Title.** Precisely describes your report's topic.

2. **Abstract.** Provides a short overview of the report to help readers decide whether or not your research is of interest to them.

3. **Introduction.** States the purpose behind your research and presents the hypothesis. Any needed background information and a review of the literature appear here.

4. **Methods and materials.** Describes the equipment, material, and procedures used.

5. **Results.** Provides the information obtained from your efforts. Charts, graphs, and photographs help present the data in a way that is easy for readers to grasp.

6. **Discussion.** Presents your interpretation and evaluation of the results. Did your efforts support your hypothesis? If not, can you suggest why not? Use concrete evidence in discussing your results.

7. **Conclusion.** Lists conclusions about the hypothesis and the outcomes of your efforts, paying particular attention to any theoretical implications that can be drawn from your work. Be specific in suggesting further research.

8. **List of references.** Presents references cited in the review of the literature, if any. Its format conforms to the requirements of the DOCUMENTATION STYLE in the particular science that is your subject.

■ Science reports

Science reports tell about observations and experiments. When they describe laboratory experiments, as is often true in academic settings, they're usually called lab reports. Formal reports feature the eight elements identified in Quick Box 69.2. Less formal reports, which are sometimes assigned in introductory college courses, might not include an abstract or a review of the literature. Ask your instructor which sections in Quick Box 69.2 to include in your report.

■ Science reviews

A science review discusses published information on a scientific topic. The purpose of the review is to summarize for readers all the current knowledge about the issue. Sometimes the purpose of a science review is to synthesize to present a new interpretation of previously published material. In such a review, the writer presents EVIDENCE to persuade readers that the new interpretation is valid. In a science review, you want to

1. Choose a very limited scientific issue currently being researched

2. Use information that is current—the more recently published the articles, books, and journals you consult, the better

3. Accurately paraphrase and summarize material (see Chapter 15)

4. Document your sources

If your review runs longer than two or three pages, you might want to use headings to help readers understand your paper's organization and idea progression.

70 Making Presentations

Quick Points   You will learn to

➤ Adjust your presentation to fit your audience and purpose.
➤ Organize your presentation.
➤ Use multimedia in your presentation.

70A What are presentations?

Presentations—speeches often supported with multimedia tools—are common not only in academic disciplines across the curriculum but also in work and public settings. Preparing a presentation and drafting a paper involve similar processes (see Chapters 5–7). This chapter provides additional information for preparing presentations and using multimedia tools.

70B How does my situation focus my presentation?

You need to adjust presentations to fit PURPOSES, AUDIENCES, roles, and any special considerations. Consider three different situations.

• You want to address a group of students to inform them about a film club you're starting.

• You need to persuade a management group at work to adopt a new set of procedures for making purchasing decisions.

Quick Box 70.1

■ ■ ■ ■ ■ ■ ■ ■ ■ ■

Adapting a presentation to your audience

UNINFORMED AUDIENCE	Start with the basics and then move to a few new ideas. Define new terms and concepts and avoid unnecessary technical terms. Use visual aids and give examples. Repeat key ideas—but not too often.
INFORMED AUDIENCE	Never give more than a quick overview of the basics. Devote most of your time to new ideas and concepts.
MIXED AUDIENCE	In your introduction, acknowledge the more informed audience members who are present. Explain that you're going to review the basic concepts briefly so that everyone can build from the same knowledge base. Move as soon as possible toward more complex concepts.

- You plan to give a toast at a friend's wedding to express your feelings and to entertain the wedding guests.

Different approaches will be successful in each instance because your purpose and audience are different.

Adapting your presentation to your listeners means holding their interest and being responsive to their viewpoints. Consult the strategies for analyzing AUDIENCES in Quick Box 5.6 on p. 42. Especially consider your listeners' prior knowledge of your topic. Are they *uninformed, informed,* or *mixed?* Quick Box 70.1 suggests how to adapt your message to each type of audience.

70C How do I organize my presentation?

As with essays, an oral presentation has three parts: introduction, body, and conclusion. Within the body, you present your major points, with support for each point. Drafting a SENTENCE OUTLINE (see 5H) gets you close to your final form and forces you to sharpen your thinking.

■ Introducing yourself and your topic

All audiences want to know three things about a speaker: Who are you? What are you going to talk about? Why should I listen? To respond effectively to these unasked questions, try these suggestions.

- Grab your audience's attention with an interesting question, quotation, or statistic; a bit of background information; a compliment; or an anecdote. If it is necessary to establish your credibility—even if someone has introduced you—briefly and humbly mention your qualifications as a speaker about your topic.
- Give your audience a road map of your talk: Tell where you're starting, where you're going, and how you intend to get there. Your listeners need to know that you won't waste their time.

■ Following your road map

Listening to a presentation is very different from reading an essay. Audiences generally need help following the speaker's line of reasoning. Try these strategies:

- Signal clearly where you are on your road map by using cue word transitions such as *first, second,* and *third; subsequently, therefore,* and *furthermore;* or *before, then,* and *next.*
- Define unfamiliar terms and concepts, and follow up with strong, memorable examples.
- Occasionally tell the audience what you consider significant, memorable, or especially relevant and why. Do so sparingly, at key points.
- Provide occasional summaries at points of transition. Recap what you've covered, and say how it relates to what's coming next.

■ Wrapping up your presentation

To demonstrate that you haven't let key points simply float away, try ending with these suggestions.

- Never let your voice volume fall or your clarity of pronunciation falter because the end is in sight.
- Do not introduce new ideas at the last minute.
- Signal that you are wrapping up your presentation using verbal cues, such as "In conclusion" and "Finally." When you say "finally," mean it!
- Make a dramatic, decisive statement; cite a memorable quotation; or issue a challenge. Allow a few seconds of silence, and then say "thank-you."
- Use body language, such as stepping slightly back from the podium, and then sit down.

70D How do I use multimedia in presentations?

Multimedia elements such as visual aids, sound, and video can reinforce key ideas in your presentation by providing illustrations or concrete images for the audience. See also Chapter 8 for ideas about designing documents.

■ Using traditional visual aids

Various types of visual aids can enhance your presentation. Always make the text or graphics large enough to be read easily at a distance.

- **Posters** can dramatize a point, often with color or images.
- **Dry-erase boards** are preferable to chalkboards because colors on them are visually appealing. Use them to roughly sketch an illustration or to emphasize a technical word.
- **Handouts** are useful when the topic calls for a longer text or when you want to give your audience something to refer to later. Short, simple handouts work best during a presentation, but longer, more detailed ones are more effective at the end. Remember to wait until everyone has one before you begin speaking about it. Always include DOCUMENTATION information for any SOURCES used in preparing the handout. A handout can be an all-important backup in case other technologies are missing or broken.

■ Using presentation software

PowerPoint, the most widely used presentation software, can create digital slides. (A similar program, "Impress," is free from www.openoffice.org.) These slides can contain words, images, or combinations of both (see Figure 70.1). To project your slides during a presentation, you need an LCD projector to connect to your computer and a large screen.

View the Model Document

Never present so much information that your audience spends more time reading than listening to you. Also, never simply read large amounts of text from your slides; your audience will quickly—and rightfully—become bored. People have coined the phrase "death by PowerPoint" in despair at presenters who simply repeat what's written on slides. For advice on designing presentation slides, see Quick Box 70.2 on p. 540.

■ Using sound or video clips

A brief sound file (for example, a sentence or two from a speech) or a video clip (perhaps 20 to 30 seconds of footage from an event) can occasionally help you illustrate a point. Always keep them brief, and be absolutely sure that your audience will recognize immediately that they enhance your message and aren't just for show.

Figure 70.1 A sample PowerPoint slide.

Quick Box 70.2

Guidelines for designing PowerPoint or similar presentation slides

- **Keep slides simple.** Use only a few very short lines of text on each slide. (Use the old rule "six by six": no more than six lines, each with no more than six words.

- **Keep slides readable.** Make sure text and images are large enough to be read by everyone in the room (find out in advance the room size). Contrast is important, so use black or very dark colors for text on a white background, or use white text on a very dark background.

- **Keep slides interesting.** A single well-chosen image can enhance a slide. Sometimes a slide that consists only of an image (a photograph, a chart, or other graphic) can be quite effective.

- **Keep slides few.** It's far more effective to have five well-chosen and designed slides for a short talk than to have twenty. "Death by PowerPoint" results mainly from endless streams of slides.

■ Planning for multimedia in your presentation

Few things are more frustrating for you or annoying to your audience than technical problems during a presentation. Beforehand, make sure all your visual aids and multimedia will work well—and have a backup plan at hand in case they fail. Rehearse carefully with technology so that you can use it seamlessly during your presentation.

70E What presentation styles can I use?

Presentation style is the way you deliver what you say. You may memorize your talk, read it, use notes, or speak without notes. Memorized talks often sound unnatural unless you've mastered the material well enough to recite it in a relaxed way. Reading your presentation aloud can bore your audience. If you have no choice but to read, avoid speaking in a monotone and vary your pace and pitch. In general, always use notes until you have considerable experience giving speeches, unless otherwise instructed by your professor or supervisor. Notes can be an outline or key words.

Your body language can either add to or detract from your message. Eye contact is your most important nonverbal communication tool because it communicates confidence and shows respect for your listeners. Smile or nod at your audience as you begin. If you use a podium, stand squarely behind it before you begin speaking. When gestures aren't needed, rest your hands on the podium—don't wave your hands, scratch your head, dust your clothing, or fidget.

70F How do I collaborate for a presentation?

Group presentations are common in academic, business, and public settings. Here are some guidelines to follow.

- Choose a topic or a position about an issue that most members of your group are familiar with.
- Lay out clearly each member's responsibilities for preparing the presentation.
- Agree on firm time limits for each person who speaks. Usually each gets an equal amount of time. If not everyone is required to speak, people who enjoy public speaking can take responsibility for delivery, while others can do more of the preparatory work.

- Allow enough time for practice. Plan at least two whole group complete run-throughs of your presentation, using multimedia elements if
you have them. Though each member can practice his or her own part
alone, always schedule practice sessions for the entire group together.
This helps you work on transitions, make sure the order of presenters is
effective. Clock the length of the presentation, and cut or expand material
accordingly.

Writing for Digital Environments

71

Quick Points   You will learn to

> Understand how to write for blogs and wikis.
> Use video and sound.

71A   What is writing for digital environments?

Writing for digital environments means producing texts that can best—or
perhaps that can only—be read through computers, generally online. Examples
include blogs, wikis, videos, podcasts, and photo essays. Digital composing,
sometimes called "multimodal writing," opens possibilities that are difficult or
impossible in traditional print papers. Digital environments:

- allow writers easily to incorporate photographs, images, and colorful
graphics, without the expense of printing

- allow writers to create or incorporate recordings, either sound or visual

- allow links to other sources available online, to enrich the content of a text

- allow instant publication so that readers far and wide can read texts online,
reaching real audiences

- allow interactions, so that readers can share comments on what they've
read or even collaborate in different times and places to compose a text
together

Digital environments can also present challenges or complications that you
need to avoid.

- They require so much time and energy designing that they take attention away from writing.

- They raise copyright or ownership concerns by circulating found images without getting proper permission.

- They allow work to be made public that isn't of the highest quality, potentially hurting its author's reputation.

The one problem you cannot prevent is people posting inappropriate or reckless comments on other peoples' work.

71B How do I write for a blog?

A Web log, or **blog,** is a Web site that displays a series of posts, or items. Posts are usually diarylike entries or observations, but may also be images, videos, audio files, and links. Blogs generally focus on a particular topic.

Watch
the Video

Most blogs have a similar design. The main content, a post about a particular topic, is in the center of the screen. The most recent post appears at the top of a page, followed by previous ones as a reader scrolls down. Many blogs contain a comment feature that allows others to respond to the original blog post. Some blogs also have a blogroll, which is a list of links to other blogs that focus on similar topics. Figure 71.1 shows a typical blog design.

Figure 71.1   Typical blog design.

Quick Box 71.1

Guidelines for writing your own blog

- **Pick a unique title for your blog.** People and Internet search engines will recognize your blog if it has a good title.

- **Decide whether to use your own name or a made-up username.** You can protect your privacy to some degree if you have a pseudonym (literally, a "false name") or username. Especially if you're writing about controversial topics or taking controversial positions, you might not want employers, instructors, or even relatives to know your identity. Of course, an anonymous username doesn't give you license to be irresponsible or unethical. On the other hand, the advantage of your real name is that you get credit (and, we suppose, blame) for your writings. Think carefully about this decision.

- **Link, show, and share.** Include links in your posts to other, similar posts or items from the Web. Post images, videos, or audio files, but do respect copyrights. And share your posts and blog with others through the use of a blogroll or by participating on other blogs.

Many instructors require students to contribute to a class blog. This is like having students write in journals as a regular way of writing about course content with the twist that other class members are required to read and comment on each person's postings. If you're assigned to write on a course blog, follow your instructor's specific directions.

If you'd like to create your own blog, decide on a type and PURPOSE. You need to find an AUDIENCE who cares about your perspective. You might participate in blogs and network with others, eventually gaining the attention of people who are interested in what you have to say. Most important, have something interesting to say. Easily available software allows you to start blogging almost immediately with little trouble. For example, Blogger (blogger.com) is a popular online community that gets you started with only a few mouse clicks. Quick Box 71.1 contains guidelines for writing for a blog.

71C How do I write for a wiki?

A wiki is a technology that allows anybody to change the content of a Web page without using special Web writing or uploading software. *Wiki* is a Hawaiian word meaning "fast," and the name refers to how quickly people using this technology can collaborate and revise information. One of the more popular wiki applications is the online encyclopedia, Wikipedia.

Quick Box 71.2

Guidelines for writing in a wiki

- **Revise with respect for others.** The strength of a wiki is its ability to allow people to share their expertise, so try to maintain what others have said. Instead of deleting material, you might add qualifications, for example, words like "possibly" or phrases such as "in some cases" or "some have argued." You might add a section entitled "opposing arguments" (see 12C) that suggests an alternative viewpoint.

- **Cite your sources whenever possible.** Whenever possible, cite your sources, and in some cases, find corroborating sources. Any addition to a wiki entry that contains references to reputable sources is less likely to be deleted or revised later, making your influence more lasting.

- **Post images, videos, and audio files.** Include links and references from other sources on the Web, but in every case, respect copyrights.

Wikis can be useful tools for collaborative writing projects because group members can all view a draft at the same time. Individuals can easily make contributions and changes. However, as you can imagine, this can also lead to complications. If you're using a wiki for a college project, you'll want to review strategies for writing with others. If you want to create a new wiki, setting one up is fairly easy. Simple software like Pbwiki (http://pbwiki.com/education.wiki) will allow you quickly to do so without worrying about server space. Quick Box 71.2 offers guidelines for writing for a wiki.

71D How do I create video and sound recordings?

As you probably know from YouTube, short online videos can be an excellent source of entertainment (or, depending on your point of view, a major waste of time). However, videos and sound recordings, such as radio essays or podcasts, can be effective ways to deliver information or even make arguments. Also, videos often present complicated how-to directions more effectively than words alone. Documentaries, such as Ken Burns's famous series on baseball, the Civil War, the national park system, or jazz, vividly convey the sights and sounds of people and places.

Watch the Video

Despite their advantages video and sound projects can take considerable time and expertise to do well. Just like written texts, they require planning, drafting, and revising, using technologies so make sure you have sufficient time before you take one on. Quick Box 71.3 offers guidelines for recordings.

Quick Box 71.3

■ ■ ■ ■ ■ ■ ■ ■ ■ ■

Guidelines for producing sound and video recordings

- **Plan your recording.** A good video or podcast has a beginning, middle, and end. Decide what elements you need to record for each.

- **Create and practice a script.** If your project has a narrator, write a script that contains what the person needs to say, what will be shown when someone is speaking, and what music or sound effects you'll need. Practice the script with whomever is involved before you record.

- **Create a storyboard for visual projects.** A storyboard is a series of rough sketches (you can use stick people, for example) that show the major scenes or elements in your video. It helps to plan the sequence and keep track of what shots you need to make.

- **Arrange to interview and record people** who will appear in your recording. Set up a time and place to record or film people. Have anyone appearing in your work sign a release, which is a form you can create that gives you permission to circulate their voice and images.

- **Find an appropriate place to record.** Unless you're trying to capture a real atmosphere such as the crowd at a ball game or a protest, find a quiet place with good acoustics and no background noise, especially for narrations or interviews.

- **Use the best equipment available.** A dedicated video camera will generally produce better quality than a regular digital camera that has video capacity, for example. A dedicated microphone records better than a laptop's built-in microphone. Your college may have equipment you can borrow.

- **Edit what you've recorded or shot.** The real work of producing an effective recording comes in editing the raw footage. To get the best result, you'll need to shorten some elements and move them around. You'll need to add transitions. You may even need to shoot new material that you don't find you need until you're in the middle of the project. Learn how to use free or cheap sound editing programs like Audacity (audacity.sourceforge.net/) or video editing programs like MovieMaker or iMovie.

Figure 71.2 shows the opening to a documentary video that student Siena Pinney created about a forest fire in Colorado.

Figure 71.2 Opening shot of documentary video.

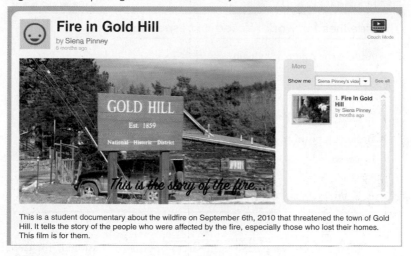

This is a student documentary about the wildfire on September 6th, 2010 that threatened the town of Gold Hill. It tells the story of the people who were affected by the fire, especially those who lost their homes. This film is for them.

72 Writing for Work

■ ■ ■ ■ ■ ■ ■ ■

Quick Points   You will learn to

➤ Identify the unique features of workplace writing

72A   Who writes in the workplace and why?

If you're working in an office, chances are good that you will need to write often. Writing infuses most workplaces, from corporate offices and health care facilities to farms and factories. People write to coworkers, customers, vendors, or service providers. Even people who work independently (such as consultants, therapists, artists, and craftspeople) keep records, correspond with customers, and advertise their services.

72B   What are features of work-related correspondence?

Correspondence is the general name for written communications, such as e-mails, memos, and letters, that you send to specific individuals. Your goal is to communicate plans, procedures, or purchases; share or ask for information; request specific actions; or influence decisions.

Quick Box 72.1

Guidelines for work-related correspondence

- Address the recipient by name.
- Use GENDER-NEUTRAL LANGUAGE.
- Announce the PURPOSE of your communication at the outset.
- Be clear, concise, and specific.
- Be honest, positive, and natural, using a personal touch.
- Never spread gossip, personal opinion, put-downs, jokes, or chain letters.
- Edit ruthlessly for CONCISENESS and correctness.

Work-related correspondence needs to appear professional, focused, and well informed. Avoid slang, abbreviations, informal words, or informal expressions. Use standard EDITED AMERICAN ENGLISH grammar, spelling, and punctuation. Remember, too, that when a business document takes on legal significance, even your most casually written messages can become official evidence in court. Write all your business materials, therefore, with such a possibility in mind. Quick Box 72.1 provides general guidelines for writing work-related correspondence.

ESOL Tip: In some cultures, work-related correspondence is often sprinkled with elaborate language, many descriptive details, and even metaphors. Most American organizations, however, prefer correspondence that is clear and gets to the point quickly. ●

72C How do I write work-related e-mail?

View
the Model
Document

Business e-mail has purposes and AUDIENCES quite different from those of the informal e-mail messages you exchange with friends and family. In work settings, avoid slang or abbreviations like LOL (laughing out loud) or BTW (by the way).

The "cc" or "Copies" space is for the e-mail addresses of other people who need to see your message, even when they aren't expected to respond. When you use the "Bcc" (blind copy) space, you're sending a copy to someone without your primary recipients' knowing about it. Often, it's rude to send blind copies, but some situations might call for it. For example, you might choose to blind-copy a long list of e-mail addresses to protect their privacy and so that your recipients don't have to scroll through lots of names.

In the body of your e-mail, single-space the text, and double-space between paragraphs and before your complimentary closing. Start paragraphs flush left at the margin. When you need to include a separate document with your e-mail, such as a report, compose it as a separate document in your word processing program, and attach it to your e-mail using the "Attachments" function. Figure 72.1 is an example of a professional e-mail.

Know your workplace's policy covering issues such as use of business e-mail accounts for personal purposes, the length and tone of most e-mail, your legal responsibilities concerning your e-mail, and restrictions on visiting WEB SITES unrelated to work. Increasingly, businesses monitor their employees' e-mail.

Quick Box 72.2 summarizes some key points about writing business e-mail.

Figure 72.1 Professional e-mail.

To:	sherrel. ampadu@jpltech.com
From:	Chris Malinowitz <cmalinowitz@chateauby.com>
Subject:	Confirming Meeting Arrangements
Cc:	dmclusky@chateauby.com
Bcc:	
Attached:	C:\Documents and Settings\Desktop\Chateau Menus.doc

Dear Ms. Ampadu:

I am writing to confirm the final arrangements for your business meeting on June 17, 2012, at our conference center.

As you directed, we will set the room in ten round tables, each seating six. We will provide a podium and microphone, an LCD projector and screen, and a white board with markers. I understand that you will be bringing your own laptop. Our technician can help your set up.

You indicated that you would like to provide lunch and refreshments at two breaks. Attached please find our menus. You will need to make your lunch selections at least 48 hours in advance.

If you have any questions or wish to make any changes, I would be pleased to accommodate your needs. Thank you for choosing The Chateau at Brickyard.

Sincerely,

Chris Malinowitz
Catering Director, The Chateau at Brickyard

Quick Box 72.2

■■■■■■■■■

Guidelines for writing business e-mail

- Write a specific, not general, topic on the Subject line.
- Start your e-mail with a sentence that tells what your message is about.
- Put the details of your message in the second paragraph. Supply any background information that your recipients may need.
- Conclude your e-mail by asking for certain information or a specific action, if such is needed, or by restating your reason for writing.
- Never write in all capital letters or all lowercase letters. Not only are they annoying to read, but all capital letters are considered the written equivalent of shouting. All lowercase letters suggest laziness and a lack of respect.
- Keep your message brief and your paragraphs short.
- Be cautious about what you say in a business e-mail. After all, the recipient can forward any e-mail to others without your permission, even though this practice is considered unethical.
- Forward an e-mail message only if you've asked the original sender for permission.
- At the end of your message, before your full name and position, use a commonly accepted complimentary closing, such as *Sincerely, Cordially,* or *Regards.*

72D How do I format and write memos?

View the Model Document

Memos are usually exchanged internally (that is, within an organization or business). Today e-mail takes the place of most memos, unless the correspondence requires a physical record or signature. The guidelines for writing e-mail (see 72C) also pertain to memos. The appropriate form of communication—paper memos or e-mail—depends on what's customary in your work environment.

The standard format of a memo includes two major parts: the headings and the body.

To: [Name your audience—a specific person or group.]

From: [Give your name and your title, if any.]

Date: [Give the date on which you write the memo.]

Re: [State your subject as specifically as possible in the "Subject" or "Re" line.]

Here are some guidelines for preparing a memo.

- **Introduction:** State your purpose for writing and why your memo is worth your reader's attention. Either here or at the conclusion, mention whether the recipient needs to take action.

- **Body:** Present the essential information on your topic. If you write more than three or four paragraphs, use headings to divide the information into subtopics (see 8D).

- **Conclusion:** End with a one- to two-sentence summary, a specific recommendation, or what action is needed and by when. Finish with a "thank-you" line.

72E How do I format business letters?

E-mail has generally taken the place of business letters; however, letters are sometimes still used for formal and contractual correspondence when you want to establish a physical record of your communications. Cover letters (also called "letters of transmittal") accompany resumes, packages, reports, or other documents. Here are guidelines for the format and content of your business letters.

View the Model Document

- **Paper:** Use 8½-by-11-inch paper. The most suitable color is white. Fold your business letters horizontally into thirds to fit into a standard number 10 business envelope (9½ by 4 inches).

- **Letterhead:** Use the official letterhead stationery (name, address, and logo, if any) of the business where you're employed. If no letterhead exists, center your full name, address, and phone number at the top of the page, and use a larger font than you use for the content of your letter. Keep it simple.

- **Format:** Without indents, use single spacing within paragraphs and double spacing between paragraphs, which is called **block style.** Figure 72.2 shows a job application letter in business format.

- **Recipient's name:** Use the full name of your recipient whenever possible. If you can't locate a name, either through a phone call to a central switchboard or on the Internet, use a specific category—for example, "Dear Billing Department," placing the key word "Billing" first (not "Department of Billing"). Always use gender-neutral language (see 45B).

Figure 72.2 Sample job application letter.

Monica A. Schickel
1817 Drevin Avenue
Denver, CO 80208

Cell phone: (303) 555-7722
E-mail: mnsschl@wordnet.com
Professional portfolio: www.schickelgraphics.net

May 3, 2012

Jaime Cisneros
Publications Director
R.L. Smith Consulting
2000 Wabash Avenue
Chicago, IL 60601

Dear Mr. Cisneros:

Please consider my application for the graphic designer position currently being advertised on your company's Web site. I believe that my professional experiences, education, and skills prepare me well for this opportunity.

I am currently completing a paid internship at Westword, a weekly features and entertainment magazine in Denver, CO, where I have worked as an effective member of a creative team. My responsibilities have included designing advertisements, laying out sections, and editing photographs. Other related experience includes commissions as an illustrator and photographer. My professional portfolio demonstrates the range and quality of my work. As the enclosed resumé notes, I have additional experience in business environments.

Next month I will earn a BA in graphic design from The University of Denver, where my course of study has included extensive work in graphic design, photography, drawing, and illustration. Simultaneously, I will complete a minor in digital media studies that has included courses in Web design, video editing, and sound editing. I have expertise in all the standard software applications that would be relevant to your position.

I would be pleased to provide further information and to interview at your convenience. The opportunities at R.L. Smith closely match my background and goals, and the prospect of joining your team in Chicago is exciting. I look forward to discussing how I can contribute to your publications department.

Sincerely,

Monica A. Schickel
Monica A. Schickel

72F How do I write a resume?

A resume details your accomplishments and employment history. Its purpose is to help a potential employer determine whether you'll be a suitable candidate. To make a favorable impression, follow the guidelines for writing a resume in Quick Box 72.3. Today, many employers have applicants upload their resumes to an employment Web site or send them as an e-mail attachment. Sometimes employers use software to scan electronic resumes, looking for keywords. See page 555 for a sample resume (Figure 72.3).

View
the Model
Document

Quick Box 72.3

Guidelines for writing a traditional, scannable, or plain-text resume

- At the beginning, include your name, address, e-mail address, and telephone number.

- Make the resume easy to read. Label the sections clearly, and target the resume to the position you want. Help employers see your most significant attributes quickly and easily.

- Adjust your resume to fit your PURPOSE. For example, if you're applying for a job as a computer programmer, you'll want to emphasize different facts than you would if you were applying for a job selling computers in an electronics store.

- Use headings to separate blocks of information. Include headings, as appropriate: "Position Desired" or "Career Objective"; "Education"; "Experience"; "Licenses and Certifications"; "Related Experience"; "Honors and Awards"; "Publications and Presentations"; "Activities and Interests"; and "Special Abilities, Skills, and Knowledge."

- Place your most recent job first when you list your work experience; when listing education, place your most recent degrees, certificates, or enrollments first.

- Do not mention your religion or marital status (such details are sometimes expected by cultures outside the United States).

- Write telegraphically. Start with verb phrases, not with the word *I,* and omit *a, an,* and *the.*

- Include only relevant information.

- Tell the truth. Even if you get the job, an employer who discovers you lied will likely fire you.

continued >>

Quick Box 72.3   (continued)

- Include references, or state that you can provide them on request.
- Start every line of text at the left margin.
- Try to fit all of the information on one page. If you need a second page, make sure the most important information is on the first page.
- Proofread carefully; even one spelling error or one formatting error can eliminate you from consideration.
- Use high-quality paper that is white or off-white for print resumes.
- Be aware that scannable resumes are designed to be scanned by machines that digitize their content. This means that sophisticated software searches the content to match key terms to position requirements. As a result, scannable resumes need a very simple design: don't use columns, different fonts, lines, graphics, or bold or italic fonts. Choose a clean sans serif font such as Arial or Geneva in a 10–12 point size. Include keywords that the computer can match to the job. Here is the keyword list Monica Schickel created for her scannable resume in Figure 72.3:

SAMPLE OF KEYWORDS

Publications experience, graphic design, editing, photography, supervisor, editing, customer service, digital media, excellent Spanish, Adobe creative suite, Photoshop, InDesign, Quark, CSS, Dreamweaver, Web design, illustrator, proofreader, Excel, Access, Publisher, newspaper, layout, sales, willing to relocate

- Use the same standards for scannable resumes as for plain-text resumes pasted into e-mails or sent to application databases.

72G How do I write a job application letter?

View the Model Document

A job application letter always needs to accompany your resume. Avoid repeating what's already on the resume. Instead, connect the company's expectations to your experience by emphasizing how your background has prepared you for the position. Your job application letter, more than your resume, reflects your energy and personality. Today, many employers have applicants upload letters to an application Web site, send them as e-mail attachments, or even send them as e-mails themselves. See Figure 72.2 for a sample letter and Quick Box 72.4, p. 556, for guidelines.

Figure 72.3 Sample resume.

MONICA A. SCHICKEL

1817 Drevin Avenue
Denver, CO 80208
Cell phone: (303) 555-7722
E-mail: mnsschl@wordnet.com
Professional portfolio: www.schickelgraphics.net

OBJECTIVE: Entry level position as a graphic designer or publications assistant

EXPERIENCE

9/12 – present   **Publications Intern** (half-time; paid), *Westword* (Denver, CO)
            • Design advertisements
            • Prepare photographs for publications
            • Lay out the "Tempo" section
            • Fact-check, edit, and proofread articles

6/10 - 8/12   **Customer Service Representative,** Wells Fargo Bank (Aurora CO).
            • Sold accounts to customers; made all sales goals
            • Created promotional posters

4/07 - 8/09   **Evening Assistant Manager,** McDonalds Restaurant (Longmont, CO).
            • Supervised 7 cooks and counter workers
            • Assured food and service quality

EDUCATION

8/11 – present   Bachelor of Arts, The University of Denver, expected June 2013
                Major: Graphic Arts; Minor: Digital Media Studies

8/09 – 5/11   AA General Education, Front Range Community College, May 2011

SKILLS AND SELECTED EXPERIENCES

        • Expert in complete Adobe Creative Suite
        • Expert in complete Microsoft Office Suite
        • Excellent Spanish language skills
        • Illustrator and photographer; have completed several commissions
(see portfolio, above)
        • Vice President, Student Residence Halls Association
        • Cartoonist and Designer, *The DU Clarion* (campus newspaper)
        • Excellent customer service skills

REFERENCES: Available on request

Quick Box 72.4

Guidelines for writing a job application letter

- Use one page only.

- Think of your letter as a polite sales pitch about yourself and what benefits you can bring to the company. Don't be shy, but don't exaggerate.

- Use the same name, content, and format guidelines as for a business letter (see 72E).

- Address the letter to a specific person. To try to find a name, telephone or send an e-mail to the company to which you're sending a letter or e-mail. State your reason for making contact, and ask for the name of the person to whom you need to address your letter. If you can't discover a name, use a gender-neutral title. Address men as "Mr." and women as "Ms.," unless you're specifically told to use "Miss" or "Mrs." If your recipient goes by another title, such as "Dr." or "Professor," use it.

  NO   Dear Sir: [sexist]   Dear Sir or Madam: [sexist for both genders]

  YES   Dear Human Resources Officer: Dear Sales Manager:

- Open your letter by identifying the position for which you're applying.

- Mention your qualifications not to repeat your resume, but to explain how your background will meet the job requirements.

- Make clear that you're familiar with the company or organization; your research will impress the employer.

- End by being specific about what you can do for the company. If the job will be your first, give your key attributes—but make sure they're relevant. For instance, you might state that you're punctual, self-disciplined, eager to learn, and hardworking.

- State when you're available for an interview and how the potential employer can reach you.

- Edit and proofread the letter carefully. If you have to hand-correct even one error, print the letter again.

TERMS GLOSSARY

Words printed in SMALL CAPITAL LETTERS in your *Quick Access Reference for Writers* indicate important terms that are defined in this glossary. The parenthetical references with each definition tell you the handbook sections where each term is most fully discussed. If you can't find a term's definition in this glossary, look for the term in the Index.

absolute phrase A phrase containing a subject and a participle that modifies an entire sentence: *The semester* [subject] *being* [present participle of *be*] *over, the campus looks deserted.* (32M)

academic writing The writing people do for college courses and as scholarship published in print and online journals. (7A)

action verb A verb that describes an action or occurrence done by or to the subject. (41E)

active reading Annotating reading to make connections between your prior knowledge and the author's ideas. (4C)

active voice When a verb shows that its action or the condition expressed is done *by* the subject. The *active voice* stands in contrast with the *passive voice*, which conveys that the verb's action or condition is done *to* the subject. (33G)

adjective A word that describes or limits (modifies) a noun, a pronoun, or a word group functioning as a noun: *silly* joke, *three* trumpets. (32E, Ch. 36)

adjective clause A dependent clause, also known as a *relative clause*, that modifies a noun or pronoun that comes before it. An adjective clause begins with a relative word (such as *who, which, that,* or *where*). Also see *clause*. (32N)

advanced searches Also called *guided searches*. Allow you to search by entering information in a form online. (20D)

adverb A word that describes or limits (modifies) verbs, adjectives, other adverbs, phrases, or clauses: *loudly, very, nevertheless, there.* (32F, Ch. 36)

adverb clause A dependent clause beginning with a subordinating conjunction that establishes the relationship in meaning between itself and its independent clause. An adverb clause can modify an independent clause's verb or an entire independent clause. (32N)

agreement The concept of matching number and person of a subject and verb (Ch. 34) and of a pronoun and its antecedent (35A–35E). See also *antecedent.*

analogy An explanation of the unfamiliar in terms of the familiar, often comparing things not usually associated with each other. Analogy is a rhetorical strategy useful for developing a paragraph (7F). Unlike a simile, which uses *like* or *as* in making a comparison, an analogy does not use such words. (44E)

analysis A process of critical thinking, sometimes called *division*, that divides a whole into its component parts that shows how the parts interrelate. Analysis is a rhetorical strategy useful for developing paragraphs. (7F)

annotated bibliography Bibliography in which listed sources are accompanied by summaries of, or comments about, each source. (19H)

annotating Brief summaries or comments about a reading, perhaps in the margins, on a separate page, or in a computer file. (4C)

antecedent The noun or pronoun to which a pronoun refers. (Ch. 35)

APA style *APA* is the abbreviation for the American Psychological Association. APA style specifies the format and the form of citation and documentation used in source-based papers in many academic disciplines, especially psychology and most other social sciences. (Chs. 27–29)

appositive A word or group of words that renames the noun or noun phrase coming immediately before or after it: *my favorite month,* **October**. (32L)

argumentative writing Using rhetorical strategies to convince one's readers to agree with the writer's position about a topic open to debate. (Ch. 12)

articles Also called *determiners* or *noun markers*, the words *a, an*, and *the*. *A* and *an* are indefinite articles; *the* is a definite article. Also see *determiner*. (Ch. 60)

assertion A statement that expresses a point of view about a topic. Often used by writers to develop a thesis statement. (5G)

audience The readers to whom a written document is primarily directed. (1E, 5E)

auxiliary verb Also known as a *helping verb*, a form of *be, do, have*, or one of the modal verbs. Auxiliary verbs combine with main verbs to express tense, mood, and voice. Also see *modal auxiliary verbs*. (33C)

balanced sentences Sentences consisting of two short independent clauses that serve to compare or contrast. (43D)

bias Material that is slanted toward beliefs or attitudes and away from facts or evidence. (Ch. 4)

bibliographic note system Documentation system used by the *Chicago Manual of Style*. (30A)

bibliography A list of sources with their authorial and publication facts. (20H)

blog Shortened form of "Web log," an online journal usually updated on a fairly regular basis. (71B)

body paragraphs Paragraphs in an essay or other document that come between the introductory and concluding paragraphs. (7F)

book catalog Database that lists all books and bound volumes owned by a particular library. (Ch. 20)

Boolean expressions Words such as *AND, OR*, and *NOT* that researchers can use in a search engine to create keyword combinations that narrow and refine their searches. (20D)

brainstorming Listing all ideas that come to mind on a topic, and then grouping the ideas by whatever patterns emerge. (5E)

browser Software that allows people to connect to the Internet. Common examples are Microsoft Internet Explorer and Mozilla Firefox.

call number Identification number, usually according to the Dewey Decimal System, used to store and retrieve an individual book or other library material. (20F)

case The form of a noun or pronoun that shows whether it's functioning as a subject, an object, or a possessive in a particular context. Nouns change form in the possessive case only (*city* can be a subject or object; *city's* is the possessive form). Also see *pronoun case*. (35J–35S, 50A)

case study Research that relies on the careful, detailed observation and analysis of one person or a small group of people. (68B)

catalog Also called a *card catalog*, often in digitized form an extensive and methodically organized list of all books and other bound volumes in a library. (20F)

cause and effect The relationship between outcomes (effects) and the reasons for them (causes), which is a rhetorical strategy for developing paragraphs. (7F)

citation Information that identifies a source referred to in a piece of writing. Also see *documentation*. (Chs. 24 and 27)

claim States an issue and then takes a position on a debatable topic related to the issue, supported with evidence and reasons. (5G)

classical argument An argument with a structure consisting of introduction, thesis statement, background, evidence and reasoning, response to opposing views, and conclusion. (12A)

classification A rhetorical strategy that organizes information by grouping items according to their underlying shared characteristics. (7F)

clause A group of words containing a subject and a predicate. A clause that delivers full meaning is called an *independent* (or *main*) *clause*. A clause that lacks full meaning by itself is called a *dependent* (or *subordinate*) *clause*. Also see *adjective clause, adverb clause, nonrestrictive element, noun clause, restrictive element*. (32N)

cliché An overused, worn-out phrase that has lost its capacity to communicate effectively: *soft as a kitten, lived to a ripe old age*. (44F)

close reading The practice of reading carefully, analytically, and critically. (4C)

clustering Also called *mapping*, it is an invention technique based on thinking visually about a topic and drawing attached balloons for its increasingly specific subdivisions. (5F)

CM style *CM*, the abbreviation for *Chicago Manual* style, is a form of citation and documentation used in many academic disciplines, including history and the arts. (Ch. 30)

coherence The written or spoken progression from one idea to another using transitional expressions, pronouns, selective repetition, and/or parallelism to make connections between ideas explicit. (7E)

collective noun A noun that names a group of people or things: *family, committee*. (34H)

colloquial language Casual or conversational language. (44D)

comma splice Sometimes called a *comma fault*, the error that occurs when a comma alone connects two independent clauses. (Ch. 38)

common noun A noun that names a general group, place, person, or thing: *dog, house*. (32A)

comparative The form of a descriptive adjective or adverb that expresses a different degree of intensity between two things: *bluer, less blue; more easily, less easily*. Also see *positive, superlative*. (36D)

comparison and contrast A rhetorical strategy for organizing and developing paragraphs by discussing a subject's similarities (by comparing them) and differences (by contrasting them). (7F)

complement A grammatical element after a verb that completes the predicate, such as a direct object after an action verb or a noun or adjective after a linking verb. Also see *object complement* and *subject complement*. (32L, 33A)

complete predicate See *predicate*.

complete subject See *subject*.

complex sentence See *sentence*.

compound-complex sentence See *sentence*.

compound predicate See *predicate*.

compound sentence See *sentence*.

compound subject See *subject*.

compound word Two or more words placed together to express one concept, such as "fuel-efficient" or "proofread." (54C)

conciseness Writing that is direct and to the point. Its opposite, which is undesirable, is *wordiness*. (Ch. 41)

concluding paragraph Final paragraph of an essay, report, or other document. (7G)

conjunction A word that connects or otherwise establishes a relationship between two or more words, phrases, or clauses. Also see *coordinating conjunction, correlative conjunction, subordinating conjunction*. (32H)

conjunctive adverb An adverb that expresses a relationship between words, such as addition, contrast, comparison, and the like. (32F)

connotation Ideas implied, not directly stated, by a word giving emotional overtones. (44B)

content notes Notes researchers write to record information about what each source they've found says—along with publication information so that the researcher can find the source again if needed. (19I)

contraction A word in which an apostrophe takes the place of one or more omitted letters: *can't, don't, I'm, isn't, it's, let's, they're, we've, won't,* and others. (50E)

coordinating adjectives Two or more adjectives that carry equal weight in modifying a noun (*big, friendly dog*). The order of coordinating adjectives can be changed without changing the meaning. Also see *cumulative adjectives.* (47E)

coordinating conjunction A conjunction that joins two or more grammatically equivalent structures: *and, or, for, nor, but, so, yet.* (32H)

coordination The use of grammatically equivalent forms to show a balance in, or sequence of, ideas. (42A)

correlative conjunction A pair of words that joins equivalent grammatical structures: *both . . . and; either . . . or; not only . . . but also.* (32H)

count noun A noun that names items that can be counted: *radio, street, idea, fingernail.* (60A)

critical reading A parallel process to critical thinking in which readers think about what they are reading during and after reading. (4A)

critical thinking A form of thinking in which you take control of your conscious thought processes by judging evidence, considering assumptions, making connections, and analyzing implications. (3A)

CSE style *CSE,* the abbreviation for the Council of Science Editors, is a form of citation and documentation used in the natural sciences. (Ch. 31)

cue words Words that tell what an assignment suggests that students accomplish in their writing. (65B)

cumulative adjectives Adjectives that build up meaning from word to word as they get closer to the noun (*familiar rock tunes*). The order of cumulative adjectives cannot be changed without destroying the meaning. Also see *coordinating adjectives.* (47E)

dangling modifier A modifier that illogically attaches its meaning to the rest of its sentence, either because it is closer to another noun or pronoun than to its true subject or because its true subject is not expressed in the sentence. (40E)

database An electronic collection of citations and, frequently, articles or documents on a particular subject matter or field, or about a specific body of sources. (20C)

definition A rhetorical strategy that defines or gives the meaning of terms or ideas. (7F)

deliberate repetition A writing technique that uses the conscious repetition of a word, phrase, or other element to emphasize a point or to achieve a specific effect on readers. (7E)

denotation The dictionary definition of a word. (44B)

dependent clause Also called *subordinate clause,* a subordinate clause can't stand alone as an independent grammatical unit. If it tries to, it is a sentence fragment. Also see *adjective clause, adverb clause, noun clause.* (32N)

description A statement that paints a picture in words. (7F)

descriptive adjective An adjective that describes the condition or properties of the noun it is modifying and (except for a very few words, such as *dead* and *unique*) has comparative and superlative forms: *flat, flatter, flattest.* (32E)

descriptive adverb An adverb that describes the condition or properties of whatever it is modifying and has comparative and superlative forms: *happily, more happily, most happily.* (32F)

descriptive writing Paints a picture in words. (7F)

determiner A word or word group, traditionally identified as an *adjective*, that limits a noun by telling whether a noun is general (**a** noun) or specific (**the** tree). (32E and Quick Box 32.4)

dialect Also called *regional language.* Language that is specific to a particular geographic area. (44D)

diction Word choice. (44B)

direct address Words naming a person or group being spoken to: *"The solution, my friends, is in your hands."* (35H)

direct discourse Words that repeat speech or conversation exactly, always enclosed in quotation marks. Also see *indirect discourse.* (39E, 51C)

direct object A noun, pronoun, or group of words functioning as a noun that receives the action (completes the meaning) of a transitive verb. (32K)

direct question A sentence that asks a question and ends with a question mark: *Are you going to the concert?* (52B)

direct quotation See *quotation.*

documentation The acknowledgment of a source's words and ideas being used in any written document by giving full and accurate information about the source of the words used and about where those words can be found. Also see *documentation style.* (24A, 27A)

documentation style Any of various systems for providing information about the source of words, information, and ideas that a writer quotes, paraphrases, or summarizes from any source other than the writer. Documentation styles discussed in this handbook are MLA (Chs. 24–26), APA (Chs. 27–29), CM (Ch. 30), and CSE (Ch. 31).

document design The arrangement of words, images, graphics, and space on a page or screen. (8A)

double negative A nonstandard structure that uses two negative modifiers rather than one. (36B)

drafting The part of the writing process in which writers compose ideas in sentences and paragraphs, thereby creating *drafts.* A *discovery draft* is what some writers call an early, rough draft. (6A)

edited American English Written usage of the American English language, expected in academic writing, that conforms to mainstream rules of grammar, sentence structure, punctuation, spelling, and mechanics. Sometimes it is referred to as *standard English,* but given the diversity of dialects in the United States today, the term *standard* is less descriptive than it once was. (44D)

editing The part of the writing process in which writers check a document for the technical correctness in edited American English of its grammar, sentence structure, punctuation, spelling, and mechanics. (6F)

ellipsis points Group of three or four spaced periods to help fit quotations smoothly into your sentences. Ellipsis points indicate that words have been omitted from the original source. When used, you want to be sure that the remaining words accurately reflect the source's meaning and that your sentences flow smoothly. (53D)

elliptical construction A sentence structure that deliberately omits words that can be filled in because they repeat words already in the sentence. (39G)

emotional appeal Rhetorical strategy intended to evoke empathy and compassion. Its Greek name is *pathos.* (3B, 12B)

ethical appeal Rhetorical strategy intended to evoke confidence in your credibility, reliability, and trustworthiness. Its Greek name is *ethos.* (3B, 12B)

euphemism Language that attempts to blunt certain realities by speaking of them in "nice" or "tactful" words. (44G)

evaluation Examining new ideas independently and fairly, avoiding biases and prejudices that you might have accepted without question before. (3A)

evidence Facts, data, and examples used to support a writer's assertions and conclusions. (23E)

example Specific incident or instance provided to illustrate a point. (7F)

expletive construction The phrase *there is (are), there was (were), it is (was)* at the beginning of a clause, which postpones the subject: *It is Mars that we hope to reach* (a better version would be *We hope to reach Mars*). (34H)

expletives Words or phrases, such as *there are* or *it is*, that postpone the subject. (34H)

fact Information or data widely accepted as true. (4B)

faulty predication A grammatically illogical combination of subject and predicate: *The purpose of television was invented to entertain.* (39F)

field research Primary research that involves going into, and taking notes on, real-life situations to observe, survey, interview, or be part of some activity. (19C)

figurative language Words that carry other meanings in addition to their literal meanings, sometimes by making unusual comparisons. Also see *analogy, irony, metaphor, personification, overstatement, simile, understatement*. (44E)

first person See *person*.

focused freewriting Freewriting that start with a set topic or build on one sentence taken from earlier freewriting. (5E)

formal outline An outline that lays out the topic levels of generalities or hierarchies and marks them with roman numerals, letters, and numbers indented in a carefully prescribed fashion. (5H)

frame Guides that suggest how to develop or structure an essay or assignment. (Ch. 9)

freewriting Writing nonstop for a period of time to generate ideas by free association of thoughts. (5E)

future perfect progressive tense The form of the future perfect tense that describes an action or condition ongoing until some specific future time: *I will have been talking when you arrive.* (33E)

future perfect tense The tense indicating that an action will have been completed or a condition will have ended by a specified point in the future: *I will have talked to him by the time you arrive.* (33E)

future progressive tense The form of the future tense showing that a future action will continue for some time: *I will be talking when you arrive.* (33E)

future tense The form of a verb, made with the simple form and either *shall* or *will*, expressing an action yet to be taken or a condition not yet experienced: *I will talk.* (33E)

gender The classification of words as masculine, feminine, or neuter. In English, a few pronouns show changes in gender in third-person singular: *he, him, his; she, her, hers; it, its, its;* also few nouns that define roles change form to show gender difference (*prince, princess*), but most no longer do (*actor, police officer, chairperson*). (45A)

gender-neutral language Nonsexist language. Also see *sexist language*. (45B)

general databases Include sources from a broad range of periodicals and books, both popular and scholarly. (20C)

generalization A broad statement without details. (7C)

general reference work The starting point for many college researchers that help identify keywords useful in searching for subject headings and catalogs— and for finding examples and verifying facts. (20H)

gerund A present participle functioning as a noun: *Walking is good exercise.* Also see *verbal*. (32D, Quick Box 32.3, Ch. 63)

gerund phrase A gerund, along with its modifiers and/or object(s), which functions as a subject or an object: ***Walking the dog*** *can be good exercise.* See also *gerund.* (32M)

helping verb   See *auxiliary verb.*

homonyms   Words spelled differently that sound alike: *to, too, two.* (46D)

idiom   A word, phrase, or other construction that has a different meaning from its usual or literal meaning: *He lost his head. She hit the ceiling.* (Ch. 62)

illustration   Provides support for the main idea of a paragraph by giving several examples, often ones that call on the five senses to picture them. (7F)

imperative mood   The grammatical form that expresses commands and direct requests, using the simple form of the verb and almost always implying but not expressing the subject: *Watch out.* (33F)

indefinite pronoun   A pronoun, such as *all, anyone, each,* and others, that refers to a nonspecific person or thing. (34E, 35D)

independent clause   A clause that can stand alone as an independent grammatical unit. (32N)

index   List of main terms used in a text and the page(s) on which each term can be found. (20A)

indicative mood   The grammatical form of verbs used for statements about real things or highly likely ones: *I think Grace will be arriving today.* (33F)

indirect discourse   Reported speech or conversation that does not use the exact structure of the original and so is not enclosed in quotation marks. (39E, 51C)

indirect object   A noun, pronoun, or group of words functioning as a noun that tells to whom, or for whom, the action expressed by a transitive verb was done. (32K)

indirect question   A sentence that reports a question and ends with a period, not a question mark: *I asked if you are going.* (52A)

indirect quotation   A quotation that reports a source's words without quota-

tion marks, unless any words are repeated exactly from the source. It requires documentation of the source to avoid plagiarism. Also see *indirect discourse.* (47G)

inference   What is implied, not stated, by words. (4B)

infinitive   A verbal made of the simple form of a verb and usually, but not always, preceded by the word *to.* It functions as a noun, an adjective, or an adverb. (33B, Ch. 62)

infinitive phrase   An infinitive, with its modifiers and/or object, which functions as a noun, an adjective, or an adverb. (32M)

informal outline   Outline that doesn't follow the rules of a *formal outline.* (5H)

intensive pronoun   A pronoun that ends in *-self* and that intensifies its antecedent: *Vida **himself** argued against it.* Also see *reflexive pronoun.* (35S)

interjection   An emotion-conveying word that is treated as a sentence, starting with a capital letter and ending with an exclamation point or a period: *Oh! Ouch.* (32I)

in-text citation   Source information placed in parentheses within the body of a research paper. Also see *citation, parenthetical documentation.* (Chs. 24 and 27)

intransitive verb   A verb that does not take a direct object. (33A)

introductory paragraph   Opening paragraph of document that orients readers and generates interest in the topic or ideas that follow. (7B)

inverted word order   In contrast to standard order, the main or auxiliary verb comes before the subject in a sentence: *In **walks** [verb] the president [subject].* Most questions and some exclamations use inverted word order: *Did [verb] you [subject] see the circus?* (43H)

irony   Using words to imply the opposite of their usual meaning. (44E)

irregular verb   A verb that forms the past tense and past participle other than by adding *-ed* or *-d.* (33B)

jargon Specialized vocabulary of a particular field or group that is not familiar to a general reader. (44G)

keywords Main words in a source's title, or that the author or an editor has identified as central to that source. Sometimes keywords are called *descriptors* or *identifiers*. (20D)

levels of formality The degrees of formality of language, reflected by word choice and sentence structure. A formal level is used for ceremonial and other occasions when stylistic flourishes are appropriate. A semiformal level, which is neither too formal nor too casual, is acceptable for most academic writing. (Ch. 6, 44D)

linking verb A main verb that links a subject with a subject complement that renames or describes the subject. Linking verbs convey a state of being, relate to the senses, or indicate a condition. (Quick Box 33.1, 34H)

literal meaning What is stated "on the line" explicitly by words. (4B)

logical appeal Rhetorical strategy that intends to show readers that the argument depends on formal reasoning, including providing evidence and drawing conclusions from premises. Its Greek name is *logos*. (12E)

logical fallacies Flaws in reasoning that lead to illogical statements that need to be rejected in logical arguments. (12A)

long quotation A direct quotation that in an MLA-style source-based paper occupies, if it is prose, more than four lines of type, and if it is poetry, more than three lines of the poem. In an APA-style source-based paper, if it is more than forty words of prose. Long quotations are block indented on the page. Also see *short quotation*. (51B)

main clause See *independent clause*.

main verb A verb that expresses action, occurrence, or state of being and that shows mood, tense, voice, number, and person. (32C)

mechanics Conventions governing the use of capital letters, italics, abbreviations, and numbers. (Chs. 55–58)

memo Commonly shortened term for *memorandum*. A brief form of business correspondence with a format that is headed with lines for "To," "From," "Date," and "Subject" (or "Re") and uses the rest of its space for its message. (72D)

metaphor A comparison implying similarity between two things: *a mop of hair*. A metaphor does not use the words *like* or *as*, which are used in a simile to make a comparison explicit: *hair **like** a mop*. (44E)

misplaced modifier Describing or limiting words that are wrongly positioned in a sentence so that their message either is illogical or relates to the wrong word(s). (Ch. 40)

mixed construction A sentence that unintentionally changes from one grammatical structure to another incompatible grammatical structure, so that the result is garbled meaning. (39F)

mixed metaphor Inconsistent metaphors in a single expression: *You'll get into hot water skating on thin ice*. (44E)

MLA style *MLA*, the abbreviation for the Modern Language Association, specifies the format and the form of citation and documentation in source-based papers in English and some other humanities courses. (Chs. 24–26)

modal auxiliary verb A group of auxiliary verbs that communicate possibility, likelihood, obligation, permission, or ability: *can, might, would*. (33C)

modifier A word or group of words functioning as an adjective or adverb to describe or limit (modify) another word or word group. (32L)

mood The attribute of verbs showing a writer's orientation to an action by the way the verbs are used. English has three moods: imperative, indicative, and subjunctive. Also see *imperative mood, indicative mood, subjunctive mood*. (33F)

narrative writing Writing that tells a story. (7F)

noncount noun A noun that names "uncountable" things: *water, time.* (60A)

nonrestrictive clause A clause that is not essential to the sentence's meaning. (Quick Box 35.2, 47F)

nonrestrictive element A descriptive word, phrase, or dependent clause that provides information not essential to understanding the basic message of the element it modifies; it is therefore set off by commas. Also see *restrictive element.* (47F)

nonsexist language See *sexist language.*

noun A word that names a person, place, thing, or idea. Nouns function as subjects, objects, or complements. (33A)

noun clause A dependent clause that functions as a subject, object, or complement. (32N)

noun phrase A noun along with its modifiers functioning as a subject, object, or complement. (32M)

number The attribute of some words indicating whether they refer to one (singular) or more than one (plural). (34A, 35A, 39A)

object A noun, pronoun, or group of words that receives the action of the verb (*direct object;* 32K); tells to whom or for whom something is done (*indirect object;* 32K); or completes the meaning of a preposition (*object of a preposition;* 32G).

object complement A noun or adjective renaming or describing a direct object after certain verbs, including *call, consider, name, elect,* and *think:* Some *call* daily *joggers* [object] *fanatics* [object complement]. (32L)

objective case The case of a noun or pronoun functioning as a direct object, an indirect object, an object of a preposition, or a verbal. A few pronouns change form to show the objective case (for example, *him, her, whom*). Also see *case.* (35J)

opinion A statement open to debate. (4B)

outline A technique for laying out ideas for writing in an orderly fashion that shows levels of generality. An outline can be formal or informal. (5H)

overstatement Deliberate exaggeration for emphasis; also called *hyperbole.* (44E)

paragraph A group of sentences that work together to develop a unit of thought. (7A)

paragraph development Rhetorical strategies for arranging and organizing paragraphs using specific, concrete details (RENNS) to support a generalization in the paragraph. (7A, 7D)

parallelism The use of equivalent grammatical forms or matching sentence structures to express equivalent ideas: *singing* and *dancing.* (7E, 43A)

paraphrase A restatement of a source's ideas in language and sentence structure different from that of the original. (15B)

parenthetical documentation Citation of source information enclosed in parentheses that follows quoted, paraphrased, or summarized material from another source. Such citations alert readers that the material comes from a source other than the writer. Parenthetical documentation and a list of bibliographic information at the end of a source-based paper together document the writer's use of sources. (Chs. 24 and 27)

participial phrase A phrase that contains a present participle or a past participle and any modifiers and that functions as an adjective. Also see *verbal.* (32M, 43G)

participle A verb form that indicates the present tense (*-ing* ending) or the past tense (*-ed, -d, -n,* or *-t* ending). A participle can also function as an adjective or an adverb. Also see *present participle, past participle.* (Chs. 32–33)

parts of speech The names and definitions of types of words that give you a vocabulary for identifying words and understanding how language works to create meaning. (32A–32I)

passive voice The *passive voice* emphasizes the action, in contrast to the *active voice*, which emphasizes the doer of the action. If the subject is mentioned in the sentence, it usually appears as the object of the preposition *by: I was frightened by the thunder* (the active voice form is *The thunder frightened me*). (33G)

past participle The third principal part of a verb, the past participle is formed in regular verbs by adding *-d* or *-ed* to the simple form to create the past tense. In irregular verbs, past and past participle formation varies by adding a letter or two to the simple form: *break, broke, broken*. The past participle functions as a verb only with an auxiliary verb as its partner. (33B)

past perfect progressive tense The past-perfect-tense form that describes an ongoing condition in the past that has been ended by something stated in the sentence: *Before the curtains caught fire, I had been talking*. (33E)

past perfect tense The tense that describes a condition or action that started in the past, continued for a while, and then ended in the past: *I had talked to him before*. (33E)

past progressive tense The past-tense form that shows the continuing nature of a past action: *I was talking when you walked in*. (33E)

past-tense verb The second principal part of a verb. In regular verbs, the past tense is formed by adding *-d* or *-ed* to the simple form. In irregular verbs, the formation of the past tense varies from merely adding a letter or two to the simple form: *break, broke; see, saw*. (33B)

peer-response group Groups of students in your class who gather together to read and constructively react to each other's writing. (5E)

perfect tenses The three tenses—the present perfect (*I have talked*), the past perfect (*I had talked*), and the future perfect (*I will have talked*)—that help to show complex time relationships between two clauses. (33E)

periodicals Magazines, newspapers, and journals published on a regular basis. (20G)

person The attribute of nouns and pronouns showing who or what acts or experiences an action. *First person* is the one speaking (*I, we*); *second person* is the one being spoken to (*you*); and *third person* is the person or thing spoken about (*he, she, it, they*). All nouns are third person. (34A, 39A)

personal pronoun A pronoun that refers to people or things: *I, you, them, it*. (35K)

personification Assigning a human trait to something not human. (44E)

phrasal verb A verb that combines with one or more prepositions to deliver its meaning: *ask out, look into*. (62B)

phrase A group of related words that does not contain a subject and predicate and thus cannot stand alone as an independent grammatical unit. A phrase can function as a noun, a verb, or a modifier. (32M)

plagiarism A writer's presenting another person's words or ideas without giving credit to that person. Writers use documentation systems to give proper credit to sources in standardized ways recognized by scholarly communities. Plagiarism is a serious offense, a form of intellectual dishonesty that can lead to course failure or expulsion from an institution. (Chs. 15, 16)

planning Early part of the writing process in which writers gather ideas. (5A)

plural See *number*.

possessive case The case of a noun or pronoun that shows ownership or possession. Also see *case*. (35J, 50A)

possessive pronoun A pronoun that shows ownership: *his, hers*, and so on. (50C)

predicate The part of a sentence that contains the verb and tells what the subject is doing or experiencing or what is being done to the subject. A *simple predicate* contains only the main verb and any auxiliary verb(s). A *complete predicate* contains the verb, its modifiers, objects, and other related words. A *compound predicate* contains two or more verbs, modifiers, objects, and other related words. (32J)

prefix Letters added at the beginning of a root word to create a new word: *pretest*. (44C, 54B)

preposition A word that conveys a relationship, often of space or time, between the noun or pronoun following it and other words in the sentence: *under, over, in, out*. The noun or pronoun following a preposition is called the *object of the preposition*. (32G, Ch. 62)

prepositional phrase A group of words beginning with a preposition and including a noun or pronoun, which is called the *object of the preposition*. (32M)

present participle A verb's *-ing* form: *talking, singing*. Used with auxiliary verbs, present participles function as main verbs. Used without auxiliary verbs, present participles function as nouns or adjectives. (33B)

present perfect progressive tense The present-perfect-tense form that describes something ongoing in the past that is likely to continue into the future: *I have been talking for a while*. (33E)

present perfect tense The tense indicating that an action or its effects, begun or perhaps completed in the past, continue into the present: *I had talked to her before you arrived*. (33E)

present progressive tense The present-tense form of the verb that indicates something taking place at the time it is written or spoken about: *I am talking right now to her*. (33E)

present tense The tense that describes what is happening, what is true at the moment, and/or what is consistently true. It uses the simple form (*I talk*) and

the *-s* form in the third-person singular (*he talks, she talks, it talks*). (33E)

present-tense participial phrase A verbal phrase that uses the *-ing* form of a verb and functions only as a modifier (whereas a gerund phrase functions only as a noun). (32M)

primary sources Also called *primary evidence*, these sources are "firsthand" work such as written accounts of experiments and observations by the researchers who conducted them; taped accounts, interviews, and newspaper accounts by direct observers; autobiographies, diaries, and journals; and expressive works such as poems, plays, fiction, and essays. They stand in contrast to *secondary sources*. (19B)

process writing Presents instructions, lays out steps in a procedure, explains how objects work, or describes human behaviors. (7F)

progressive forms Verb forms made, in all tenses, with the present participle and forms of the verb *be* as an auxiliary. Progressive forms show that an action, occurrence, or state of being is ongoing: *I am singing; he was dancing*. (33E)

pronoun A word that takes the place of a noun and functions in the same ways that nouns do. Types of pronouns are demonstrative, indefinite, intensive, interrogative, personal, reciprocal, reflexive, and relative. (32B)

proofreading Carefully scrutinizing your final draft to fix typing errors and missing/repeated small words. (6H)

pronoun–antecedent agreement The match required between a pronoun and its antecedent in number and person, including personal pronouns and their gender. (35A)

pronoun case The way a pronoun changes form to reflect its use as the agent of action (*subjective case*), the thing being acted upon (*objective case*), or the thing showing ownership (*possessive case*). (35J–35S)

pronoun reference The relationship between a pronoun and its antecedent. (35F–35I)

proper adjective An adjective formed from a proper noun: *Victorian, American.* (32E)

proper noun A noun that names specific people, places, or things; it is always capitalized: *Tom Thumb, Buick.* (55C)

purpose Purposes for writing vary: to narrate, give information, analyze a text, argue or persuade, and evaluate. (5D)

quotation Repeating or reporting another person's words. *Direct quotation* repeats another's words exactly and encloses them in quotation marks. *Indirect quotation* reports another's words without quotation marks except around any words if they are repeated exactly from the source. Both direct and indirect quotation require documentation of the source to avoid plagiarism. (15B)

References The title of a list of sources at the end of a research paper or scholarly article or other written work used in many documentation styles, especially that of APA. (Chs. 27–29)

reflexive pronoun A pronoun that ends in *-self* and that reflects back to its antecedent: *They claim to support **themselves**.* (35S)

regular verb A verb that forms its past tense and past participle by adding *-ed* or *-d* to the simple form. Most English verbs are regular. (33B)

relative adverb An adverb that introduces an adjective clause: *The garage **where** I usually park my car was full.* (32F)

relative clause See *adjective clause.*

relative pronoun A pronoun—such as *who, which, that, whom, whoever,* and a few others—that introduces an adjective clause or sometimes a noun clause. (32N)

RENNS A memory aid for the specific, concrete details used to support a topic sentence in a paragraph: reasons, examples, names, numbers and the five sentences. (7D)

research A systematic process of gathering information to answer a question. (18A)

research log A diary of your research process; useful for keeping yourself organized and on track. (19E)

research or term paper A paper written using the results of research. (18A)

research question A question that provides a clear focus for your research and a goal for your writing process. (18C)

response essay Provides a summary of a source and gives your opinion—supported by reasons—about the source's ideas or quality. (17C)

restrictive clause A dependent clause that gives information necessary to distinguish whatever it modifies from others in the same category. In contrast to a nonrestrictive clause, a restrictive clause is not set off with commas. (47F)

restrictive element A word, phrase, or dependent clause that provides information essential to the understanding of the element it modifies. In contrast to a nonrestrictive element, a restrictive element is not set off with commas. Also see *nonrestrictive clause.* (47F)

revising A part of the writing process in which writers evaluate their rough drafts and, on the basis of their assessments, rewrite by adding, cutting, replacing, moving, and often totally recasting material. (9C)

rhetoric The art and skill of speaking and writing effectively. (7F)

rhetorical strategies Various techniques for presenting ideas to deliver a writer's intended message with clarity and impact, including logical, ethical, and emotional appeals. (3B) Rhetorical strategies involve stylistic techniques such as parallelism and planned repetition as well as patterns for organizing and developing writing such as illustration, description, and definition. (7F)

Rogerian argument An argument technique using principles developed by Carl Rogers in which writers strive to find common ground and thus assure readers who disagree with them that they understand others' perspectives. (12C)

run-on sentence A sentence in which independent clauses run together without the required punctuation that marks them as complete units. Also known as a *fused sentence*. (Ch. 38)

search strategy A systematic way of finding information on a certain topic. (19A)

secondary source A source that reports, analyzes, discusses, reviews, or otherwise deals with the work of someone else. It stands in contrast to a primary source, which is someone's original work or firsthand report. A reliable secondary source must be the work of a person with appropriate credentials, must appear in a respected publication or other medium, must be current or historically authentic, and must reflect logical reasoning. (19B)

second person See *person.*

sentence A group of words, beginning with a capitalized first word and ending with a final punctuation mark, that states, asks, commands, or exclaims something. A sentence must consist of at least one *independent clause*. A *simple sentence* consists of one independent clause. A *complex sentence* contains one independent clause and one or more dependent clauses. A *compound sentence* contains two or more independent clauses joined by a coordinating conjunction. A *compound-complex sentence* contains at least two independent clauses and one or more dependent clauses. (32J–32O)

sentence fragment A portion of a sentence that is punctuated as though it were a complete sentence. (Ch. 37)

sentence outline A type of outline in which each element is a sentence. (5H)

sexist language Language that unfairly or unnecessarily assigns roles or characteristics to people on the basis of gender. Language that avoids gender stereotyping is called *gender-neutral* or *nonsexist language*. (45B)

shift An unnecessary change within a sentence in person, number, voice, tense, or other grammatical framework that makes a sentence unclear. (Ch. 39)

short quotation A direct quotation that occupies no more than four lines of type in an MLA-style source-based paper (for prose) or no more than three lines of poetry. In an APA-style source-based paper, a short quotation has no more than forty words of prose. Short quotations are enclosed in quotation marks. (51A)

simile A comparison, using *like* or *as*, of otherwise dissimilar things. (44E)

simple form Part of a verb, the simple form shows action, occurrence, or state of being taking place in the present. It is used in the singular for first and second person and in the plural for first, second, and third person. Simple forms divide time into past, present, and future. (33B, 33E)

simple predicate See *predicate.*

simple sentence See *sentence types.*

simple subject See *subject.*

simple tenses The present, past, and future tenses, which divide time into present, past, and future. (33E)

singular See *number.*

slang Coined words and new meanings for existing words, which quickly pass in and out of use. Slang is inappropriate for most academic writing except when used intentionally as such. (44D)

slanted language Language that tries to manipulate the reader with distorted facts. (12H)

source A print or online book, article, document, CD, other work, or person providing information in words, music, pictures, or other media. (19B)

specialized database A database of sources covering a specific discipline or topic. (20C)

specialized reference work A reference work (such as a dictionary, encyclopedia, biographical compendium) covering a specific discipline or topic. (20H)

split infinitive One or more words coming between the two words of an infinitive. (40C)

squinting modifier A modifier that is considered misplaced because it isn't clear whether it describes the word that comes before it or the word that follows it. (40B)

standard English See *edited American English*.

standard word order The most common sentence pattern in English, which places the subject before the verb. (43H, Ch. 61)

subject The word or group of words in a sentence that acts, is acted upon, or is described by the verb. A *simple subject* includes only the noun or pronoun. A *complete subject* includes the noun or pronoun and all its modifiers. A *compound subject* includes two or more nouns or pronouns and their modifiers. (32J)

subject complement A noun or adjective that follows a linking verb, renaming or describing the subject of the sentence. (32L)

subject directories Lists of topics or resources and services, with links to sources on those topics and resources. An alternative to keyword searches. (20E)

subjective case The case of the noun or pronoun functioning as a subject. Also see *case*. (35J)

subject–verb agreement The required match in number and person between a subject and a verb. (Ch. 34)

subjunctive mood The verb orientation that expresses wishes, recommendations, indirect requests, speculations, and conditional statements: *I wish you were here.* (33F)

subordinate clause See *dependent clause*.

subordinating conjunction A conjunction that introduces a dependent clause and expresses a relationship between the word and the idea in the independent clause. (32H)

subordination The use of grammatical structures to reflect the relative importance of ideas in a sentence. The most important information falls in the independent clause, and less important information falls in the dependent clause or phrases. (42C)

suffix Letters added at the end of a root word to change function or meaning: *useless*. (44C, 54B)

summary A critical thinking activity to extract the main message or central point of a passage or other discourse. (Quick Box 3.2, 15D)

superlative The form of an adjective or adverb that expresses the greatest degree of quality among three or more things: *bluest; most easily*. (36D)

synonym A word that is close in meaning to another word. (6A)

synthesis A component of critical thinking in which material that has been summarized, analyzed, and interpreted is connected to what one already knows (one's prior knowledge) from reading or experiences. (17E)

tag question An inverted verb–pronoun combination added to the end of a sentence and creating a question that "asks" the audience to agree with the assertion in the first part of the sentence: *You know what a tag question is, **don't you?*** A tag question is set off from the rest of the sentence with a comma. (47H)

tense The time at which the action of the verb occurs: in the present, the past, or the future. (33E)

tense sequence In sentences that have more than one clause, the sequencing of verb forms to reflect logical time relationships. (33E)

thesis statement A statement of an essay's central theme that makes clear the main idea, the writer's purpose, the focus of the topic, and perhaps the organizational pattern. (5G)

third person See *person*.

tone The writer's attitude toward his or her material and sometimes to the reader, especially as reflected by word choice. (6E)

topic outline An outline in which items are listed as words or phrases, not full sentences. (5H)

topic sentence The sentence that expresses the main idea of a paragraph. (7C)

transition The word or group of words that connects one idea to another in discourse. Useful strategies for creating transitions include transitional expressions, conjunctive adverbs, parallelism, and planned repetition of key words and phrases. (7E)

transitional expressions Words and phrases that signal connections among ideas and create coherence. (7E, Quick Box 7.3)

transitive verb A verb that must be followed by a direct object. (Ch. 33)

understatement Figurative language in which the writer uses deliberate restraint for emphasis. (44E)

unity The clear and logical relationship between the main idea of a paragraph and the evidence supporting the main idea. As a design principle, the term refers to whether the elements (color, text, images) work together visually. (8B)

URL *URL* is the abbreviation for *Universal* (or *Uniform*) *Resource Locator*. It is the online address of a site or page on the Web. (20C)

verb A word that shows action or occurrence, or that describes a state of being. Verbs change form to show time (tense), attitude (mood), and role of the subject (voice). Verbs occur in the predicate of a clause. Verbs can be parts of verb phrases, which consist of a main verb, any auxiliary verbs, and

any modifiers. Verbs can be described as transitive or intransitive, depending on whether they take a direct object. (32C, Ch. 33)

verb phrase A main verb, along with any auxiliary verb(s) and any modifiers. (32M)

verbal A verb form that functions as a noun, adjective, or adverb. (32D, Quick Box 32.3)

verbal phrase A group of words that contains a verbal (an infinitive, participle, or gerund) and its modifiers. (35M)

voice Attribute of verbs showing whether the subject acts (active voice) or is acted upon (passive voice). (36G)

warrants The writer's underlying assumptions, which are often implied rather than stated, that connect reasons to claims. (12B)

Web site A collection of related files online that may include documents, images, audio, and video. Web sites typically have a *home page* that provides links to this content. (20C)

wordiness Writing that is full of words and phrases that don't contribute to meaning. The opposite of *conciseness*. (Ch. 41)

word order The order in which words fall in most English sentences. Usually, the subject comes before the predicate. Inverted word order can bring emphasis to an idea. Multilingual writers are often accustomed to word orders in sentences other than those used in English. (Ch. 61, 43H)

working bibliography A preliminary annotated list of useful sources in research writing with a brief summary of each source. (19F)

Works Cited In MLA documentation style, the list of standardized information about all sources drawn upon in a research paper or other scholarly written work. (Ch. 25)

writing process Stages of writing in which a writer plans, drafts, revises, edits, and proofreads. The stages often overlap. (5A, Quick Box 5.1)

writing situation Elements for writers to consider at the beginning of the writing process: their writing topic, purpose, audience, context, role, and special requirements. (5B, Quick Box 5.2)

USAGE GLOSSARY

This usage glossary explains the customary manner of using particular words and PHRASES. As used here, *informal* and *colloquial* indicate that words or phrases occur commonly in speech but should be avoided in ACADEMIC WRITING. *Nonstandard* indicates that words or phrases should not be used in either standard spoken English or writing.

All grammatical terms mentioned here are defined in the Terms Glossary at the back of the book. Also consult the commonly confused words listed in Quick Box 46.1.

a, an Use *a* before words that begin with a consonant (*a dog, a grade, a hole*) or a consonant sound (*a one-day sale, a European*). Use *an* before words or acronyms that begin with a vowel sound or a silent *h* (*an owl, an hour, an MRI*). American English uses *a*, not *an*, before words starting with a pronounced *h*: *a* [*not* an] *historical event.*

accept, except The verb *accept* means "agree to, receive." As a preposition, *except* means "leaving out." As a verb, *except* means "exclude, leave out."

> The workers were ready to **accept** [verb] management's offer **except** [preposition] for one detail: They wanted the no-smoking rule **excepted** [verb] from the contract.

advice, advise *Advice*, a noun, means "recommendation." *Advise*, a verb, means "recommend, give advice."

> I **advise** [verb] you to follow your car mechanic's **advice** [noun].

affect, effect As a verb, *affect* means "cause a change in, influence." (*Affect* also functions as a noun in the discipline of psychology.) As a noun, *effect* means "result or conclusion"; as a verb, it means "bring about."

> Loud music **affects** people's hearing for life, so some bands have **effected** changes to lower the volume. Many fans, however, don't care about the harmful **effects** of high decibel levels.

aggravate, irritate *Aggravate* is used colloquially to mean "irritate." In formal writing, use *aggravate* to mean "intensify, make worse." Use *irritate* to mean "annoy, make impatient."

> The coach was **irritated** by her assistant's impatience, which **aggravated** the team's inability to concentrate.

ain't *Ain't* is a nonstandard contraction. Use *am not, is not,* or *are not* instead.

all right *All right* should be written as two words, never one (*not* alright).

allusion, illusion An *allusion* is an indirect reference to something. An *illusion* is a false impression or idea.

> The applicant's casual **allusions** to many European tourist attractions created the **illusion** that he had seen them himself.

a lot *A lot* is informal for *a great deal* or *a great many;* avoid it in academic writing. Write it as two words (*not* alot) when you do use it.

a.m., p.m. These abbreviations may also be written as A.M., P.M. Use them only with numbers, not as substitutes for *morning, afternoon,* or *evening.*

> We will arrive **in the afternoon** [*not* in the p.m.], and we have to leave no later than **8:00 a.m.**

among, amongst, between Use *among* for three or more items and *between* for two items. American English prefers *among* to *amongst.*

> My three roommates discussed **among** [*not* between or amongst] themselves the choice **between** staying in school and getting full-time jobs.

amount, number Use *amount* for uncountable things (*wealth, work, corn, happiness*). Use *number* for countable items.

> The **amount** of rice to cook depends on the **number** of dinner guests.

an See *a, an.*

and/or This term is appropriate in business and legal writing when either or both of two items can apply: *The process is quicker if you have a wireless connection and/or a fax machine.* In the humanities, writers usually express the alternatives in words: *This process is quicker if you have a wireless connection, a fax machine, or both.*

anyplace *Anyplace* is informal. Use *any place* or *anywhere* instead.

anyways, anywheres *Anyways* and *anywheres* are nonstandard. Use *anyway* and *anywhere* instead.

apt, likely, liable *Apt* and *likely* are used interchangeably. Strictly, *apt* indicates a tendency or inclination. *Likely* indicates a reasonable expectation or greater certainty than *apt. Liable* denotes legal responsibility or implies unpleasant consequences.

> Alan is **apt** to leave early on Friday. I will **likely** go with him to the party. Maggy and Gabriel are **liable** to be angry if we do not show up.

as, as if, as though, like Use *as, as if,* or *as though,* but not *like,* to introduce clauses.

> This hamburger tastes good, **as** [*not* like] a hamburger should. It tastes **as if** [*or* as though *but not* like] it were barbequed over charcoal.

Both *as* and *like* can function as prepositions in comparisons. Use *as* to indicate equivalence between two nouns or pronouns. Use *like* to indicate similarity but not equivalence.

> Beryl acted **as** [*not* like] the moderator in our panel.

> Mexico, **like** [*not* as] Argentina, belongs to the United Nations.

assure, ensure, insure *Assure* means "promise, convince." *Ensure* and *insure* both mean "make certain or secure," but *insure* is reserved for financial or legal certainty, as in insurance.

> The agent **assured** me that he could **insure** my roller blades but that only I could **ensure** that my elbows and knees would outlast the skates.

as to   *As to* is nonstandard. Use *about* instead.

awful, awfully   Do not use *awful* or *awfully* in place of *terribly, extremely,* or *very.*

a while, awhile   As two words, *a while* (an article and a noun) can function as a subject or object. As one word, *awhile* is an adverb; it modifies verbs. In a prepositional phrase, the correct form is *a while: for a while, in a while, after a while.*

> The seals basked **awhile** in the sun after they had played for **a while** in the sea.

backup, back up   As a noun, *backup* is a copy of electronic data. *Backup* can also be used as an adjective to mean "alternative." *Back up* is a verb phrase.

> Many people recommend that you **back up** even your **backup** files.

bad, badly   *Bad* is an adjective; use it after linking verbs. (Remember that verbs like *feel* and *smell* can function as either linking verbs or action verbs.) *Badly* is an adverb and is nonstandard after linking verbs (see 36C).

> Farmers feel **bad** because a **bad** drought has **badly** damaged the crops.

beside, besides   *Beside* is a preposition meaning "next to, by the side of."

> She stood **beside** the new car, insisting that she would drive.

As a preposition, *besides* means "other than, in addition to."

> No one **besides** her had a driver's license.

As an adverb, *besides* means "also, moreover."

> **Besides,** she owned the car.

better, had better   Used in place of *had better, better* is informal.

> We **had better** [*not* We better] be careful.

between   See *among, amongst, between.*

bring, take   Use *bring* to indicate movement from a distant place to a near place or to the speaker. Use *take* to indicate movement from a near place or from the speaker to a distant place.

> If you **bring** a leash to my house, you can **take** the dog to the vet.

but, however, yet   Use *but, however,* or *yet* alone, not in combination with each other.

> The economy is strong, **but** [*not* but yet *or* but however] unemployment is high.

can, may   *Can* signifies ability or capacity; *may* requests or grants permission. In negations, however, *can* is acceptable in place of *may.*

> When you **can** get here on time, you **may** be excused early.

can't hardly, can't scarcely   These double negatives are nonstandard (see 36B).

censor, censure   The verb *censor* means "delete objectionable material, judge." The verb *censure* means "condemn or reprimand officially."

> The town council **censured** the mayor for trying to **censor** a report.

chairman, chairperson, chair   Many prefer the gender-neutral terms *chairperson* and *chair* to *chairman; chair* is more common than *chairperson.*

complement, compliment   Each term functions as both a noun and a verb. As a noun, *complement* means "something that goes well with or completes." As a noun, *compliment* means "praise, flattery." As a verb, *complement* means "bring to perfection, go well with; complete." As a verb, *compliment* means "praise, flatter."

> The president's **compliment** was a fine **complement** to our celebration.
> When the president **complimented** us, her praise **complemented** our joy.

comprise, include   See *include, comprise.*

conscience, conscious   The noun *conscience* means "a sense of right and wrong." The adjective *conscious* means "aware or awake."

> To live happily, be **conscious** of what your **conscience** tells you.

continual(ly), continuous(ly)   *Continual* means "occurring again and again." *Continuous* means "occurring without interruption."

> Intravenous fluids were given **continuously** for three days after surgery, so nurses were **continually** hooking up new bottles of saline solution.

could care less   *Could care less* is nonstandard; use *couldn't care less* instead.

could of   *Could of* is nonstandard; use *could have* instead.

couple, a couple of   These terms are informal. Use *a few* or *several* instead.

> Rest for **a few** [*not* a couple *or* a couple of] minutes.

criteria, criterion   A *criterion* is "a standard of judgment." *Criteria* is the plural form of *criterion.*

> Although charisma is an important **criterion** for political candidates to meet, voters must also consider other **criteria**.

data   This is the plural of *datum*, a rarely used word. Informally, *data* is commonly used as a singular noun requiring a singular verb. In academic or professional writing, it is more acceptable to treat *data* as plural.

> The researchers' **data** suggest that some people become addicted to e-mail.

different from, different than   *Different from* is preferred for formal writing, although *different than* is common in speech.

> Please advise the council if your research produces data **different from** past results.

don't   *Don't* is a contraction for *do not* but not for *does not* (use *doesn't*).

> She **doesn't** [*not* She don't] like crowds.

effect   See *affect, effect.*

elicit, illicit   The verb *elicit* means "draw forth or bring out." The adjective *illicit* means "illegal."

> The government's **illicit** conduct **elicited** mass protest.

emigrate (from), immigrate (to) *Emigrate* means "leave one country to live in another." *Immigrate* means "enter a country to live there."

> My great-grandmother **emigrated** from the Ukraine in 1890. After a brief stay in Germany, she **immigrated** to Canada in 1892.

ensure See *assure, ensure, insure.*

etc. *Etc.* is the abbreviation for the Latin *et cetera,* meaning "and the rest." For writing in the humanities, avoid using *etc.* outside parentheses. Acceptable substitutes are *and the like, and so on,* and *and so forth.*

everyday, every day The adjective *everyday* means "daily." *Every day* is an adjective-noun combination that can function as a subject or an object.

> Being late for work has become an **everyday** occurrence. **Every day** that I am late brings me closer to being fired.

everywheres Nonstandard for *everywhere.*

except See *accept, except.*

explicit, implicit *Explicit* means "directly stated or expressed." *Implicit* means "implied, suggested."

> The warning on cigarette packs is **explicit**: "Smoking is dangerous to health." The **implicit** message is "Don't smoke."

fewer, less Use *fewer* for anything that can be counted (with count nouns): *fewer dollars, fewer fleas, fewer haircuts.* Use *less* with collective or other non-count nouns: *less money, less scratching, less hair.*

finalize Academic audiences prefer *complete* or *make final* instead of *finalize.*

> After intense negotiations, the two nations **completed** [*not* finalized] a treaty.

former, latter When two items are referred to, *former* signifies the first one and *latter* signifies the second. Avoid using *former* and *latter* in a context with more than two items.

> Brazil and Ecuador are South American countries. Portuguese is the most common language in the **former**, Spanish in the **latter**.

go, say *Go* is nonstandard when used for forms of *say.*

> After he stepped on my hand, he **said** [*not* he goes], "Your hand was in my way."

gone, went *Gone* is the past participle of *go; went* is the past tense of *go.*

> They **went** [*not* gone] to the concert after Ira **had gone** [*not* had went] home.

good and This phrase is an informal intensifier; omit it from writing.

> They were **exhausted** [*not* good and tired].

good, well *Good* is an adjective. Using it as an adverb is nonstandard. *Well* is the equivalent adverb.

> **Good** maintenance helps cars run **well**.

hardly See *can't hardly, can't scarcely.*

have, of Use *have*, not *of*, after such verbs as *could, should, would, might,* and *must*.

> You **should have** [*not* should of] called first.

have got, have to, have got to Avoid using *have got* when *have* alone delivers your meaning.

> I **have** [*not* have got] two more sources to read.

Avoid using *have to* or *have got to* for *must*.

> I **must** [*not* have got to] finish this assignment today.

he/she, s/he, his, her To avoid sexist language, use *he or she* or *his or her*. A less wordy solution is to use plural pronouns and antecedents.

> Every mourner bowed **his or her** head [*not* his head *or* their head].
>
> The **mourners** bowed **their** heads.

humanity, humankind, humans, mankind To avoid sexist language, use *humanity, humankind,* or *humans* instead of *mankind*.

> Some people think computers have influenced **humanity** more than any other twentieth-century invention.

i.e. This abbreviation refers to the Latin term *id est*. In formal writing, use the English translation *that is*.

if, whether At the start of a noun clause, use either *if* or *whether*.

> I don't know **if** [*or* whether] I want to dance with you.

In conditional clauses, use *whether* (*or* whether or not) when alternatives are expressed or implied.

> I will dance with you **whether or not** I like the music. I will dance with you **whether** the next song is fast or slow.

In a conditional clause that does not express or imply alternatives, use *if*.

> **If** you promise not to step on my feet, I will dance with you.

illicit See *elicit, illicit*.

illusion See *allusion, illusion*.

immigrate See *emigrate, immigrate*.

imply, infer *Imply* means "hint at or suggest." *Infer* means "draw a conclusion." A writer or speaker implies; a reader or listener infers.

> When the governor **implied** that she would not seek reelection, reporters **inferred** that she was planning to run for vice president.

include, comprise The verb *include* means "contain or regard as part of a whole." The verb *comprise* means "to be composed of."

inside of, outside of These phrases are nonstandard when used to mean *inside* or *outside*.

> She waited **outside** [*not* outside of] the dormitory.

In time references, avoid using *inside of* to mean "in less than."

> I changed clothes **in less than** [*not* inside of] ten minutes.

insure   See *assure, ensure, insure.*

irregardless   *Irregardless* is nonstandard. Use *regardless* instead.

is when, is where   Avoid these constructions in giving definitions.

Defensive driving **requires that** [*not* is when] drivers stay alert.

its, it's   *Its* is a possessive pronoun. *It's* is a contraction of *it is.*

The dog buried **its** bone.

It's a hot day.

kind, sort   Use *this* or *that* with these singular nouns; use *these* or *those* with the plural nouns *kinds* and *sorts.* Also, do not use *a* or *an* after *kind of* or *sort of.*

Drink **these kinds of** fluids [*not* this kind of fluids] on **this sort of** [*not* this sort of a] day.

kind of, sort of   These phrases are colloquial adverbs. In formal writing, use *somewhat* instead.

The campers were **somewhat** [*not* kind of] dehydrated after the hike.

lay, lie   *Lay* (*laid, laid, laying*) means "place or put something, usually on something else" and needs a direct object. *Lie* (*lay, lain, lying*), meaning "recline," does not take a direct object (see 32K). Substituting *lay* for *lie* is nonstandard.

Lay [*not* Lie] the blanket down, and then **lay** the babies on it so they can **lie** [*not* lay] in the shade.

leave, let   *Leave* means "depart"; *let* means "allow, permit." *Leave* is nonstandard for *let.*

Let [*not* Leave] me use your car tonight.

less   See *fewer, less.*

lie   See *lay, lie.*

like   See *as, as if, as though, like.*

likely   See *apt, likely, liable.*

lots, lots of, a lot of   These are colloquial usages. Use *many, much,* or *a great deal* instead.

mankind   See *humanity, humankind, humans, mankind.*

may   See *can, may.*

maybe, may be   *Maybe* is an adverb; *may be* is a verb phrase.

Maybe [adverb] we can win, but our team **may be** [verb phrase] too tired.

may of, might of   *May of* and *might of* are nonstandard. Use *may have* and *might have* instead.

media   This word is the plural of *medium,* yet colloquial usage now pairs it with a singular verb.

The **media** saturates us with information about every fire.

morale, moral   *Morale* is a noun meaning "a mental state relating to courage, confidence, or enthusiasm." As a noun, *moral* means an "ethical lesson implied or taught by a story or event"; as an adjective, *moral* means "ethical."

> One **moral** to draw from corporate downsizings is that overstressed employees suffer from low **morale**. Unhappy employees with otherwise high **moral** standards may steal from their employers.

most   *Most* is nonstandard for *almost: Almost* [*not* Most] *all the dancers agree. Most* is correct as the superlative form of an adjective (*some, more, most*): *Most dancers agree.* It also makes the superlative form of adverbs and some adjectives: *most suddenly, most important.*

Ms.   *Ms.* is a women's title free of reference to marital status, equivalent to *Mr.* for men. For a woman who does not use *Dr.* or another title, use *Ms.* unless she requests *Miss* or *Mrs.*

must of   *Must of* is nonstandard. Use *must have* instead.

nowheres   Nonstandard for *nowhere.*

number   See *amount, number.*

of   Use *have* instead of *of* after the following verbs: *could, may, might, must, should,* and *would.*

OK, O.K., okay   All three forms are acceptable in informal writing. In academic writing, try to express meaning more specifically.

> The weather was **suitable** [*not* OK] for the picnic.

outside of   See *inside of, outside of.*

plus   *Plus* is nonstandard as a substitute for *and, also, in addition,* or *moreover.*

> The band will give three concerts in Hungary, **and** [*not* plus] it will tour Poland for a month. **Also** [*not* Plus], it may perform once in Vienna.

precede, proceed   *Precede* means "go before." *Proceed* means "advance, go on; undertake; carry on."

> **Preceded** by elephants and tigers, the clowns **proceeded** into the tent.

pretty   *Pretty* is an informal qualifying word; in academic writing, use *rather, quite, somewhat,* or *very.*

> The flu epidemic was **quite** [*not* pretty] severe.

principal, principle   *Principle* means "a basic truth or rule." As a noun, *principal* means "chief person; main or original amount"; as an adjective, *principal* means "most important."

> During the assembly, the **principal** said, "A **principal** value in this society is the **principle** of free speech."

proceed   See *precede, proceed.*

quotation, quote   *Quotation* is a noun; *quote* is a verb. Do not use *quote* as a noun.

> The newspaper **quoted** the attorney general, and the **quotations** [*not* quotes] quickly showed up in public health messages.

raise, rise   *Raise (raised, raised, raising)* means "lift" and needs a direct object. *Rise (rose, risen, rising)* means "go upward" and does not take a direct object (see 32K). Using these verbs interchangeably is nonstandard.

If the citizens **rise** [*not* raise] up in protest, they may **raise** the flag of liberty.

real, really   *Real* is nonstandard as an intensifier, and *really* is almost always unnecessary; leave it out.

reason is because   This phrase is redundant; use *reason is that* instead.

One **reason** we moved **is that** [*not* is because] we changed jobs.

regardless   See *irregardless.*

respective, respectively   The adjective *respective* relates the noun it modifies to two or more individual persons or things. The adverb *respectively* refers to a second set of items in a sequence established by a preceding set of items.

After the fire drill, Dr. Pan and Dr. Moll returned to their **respective** offices [that is, each to his or her office] on the second and third floors, **respectively**. [Dr. Pan has an office on the second floor; Dr. Moll has an office on the third floor.]

right   *Right* is a colloquial intensifier; use *quite, very, extremely,* or a similar word for most purposes.

You did **very** [*not* right] well on the quiz.

rise   See *raise, rise.*

scarcely   See *can't hardly, can't scarcely.*

seen   The past participle of *see (see, saw, seen, seeing), seen* is a nonstandard substitute for the past-tense form, *saw.* As a verb, *seen* must be used with an auxiliary verb.

Last night, I **saw** [*not* seen] the show that you **had seen** in Florida.

set, sit   *Set (set, set, setting)* means "put in place, position, put down" and must have a direct object. *Sit (sat, sat, sitting)* means "be seated" and does not take a direct object (see 32K). Using these verbs interchangeably is nonstandard.

Susan **set** [*not* sat] the sandwiches beside the salad, made Spot **sit** [*not* set] down, and then **sat** [*not* set] on the sofa.

should of   *Should of* is nonstandard. Use *should have* instead.

sit   See *set, sit.*

sometime, sometimes, some time   The adverb *sometime* means "at an unspecified time." The adverb *sometimes* means "now and then." *Some time* is an adjective–noun combination meaning "an amount or span of time."

Sometime next year we have to take qualifying exams. I **sometimes** worry about finding **some time** to study for them.

sort of   See *kind of, sort of.*

such *Such* is an informal intensifier; avoid it in academic writing unless it precedes a noun introducing a *that* clause.

> The play got **terrible** [*not* such terrible] reviews. It was **such** a dull drama **that** it closed after one performance.

supposed to, used to The final *d* is essential in both phrases.

> We were **supposed to** [*not* suppose to] leave early. I **used to** [*not* use to] wake up as soon as the alarm rang.

sure *Sure* is nonstandard as a substitute for *surely* or *certainly*.

> I was **certainly** [*not* sure] surprised at the results.

sure and, try and Both phrases are nonstandard. Use *sure to* and *try to* instead.

than, then *Than* indicates comparison; *then* relates to time.

> Please put on your gloves, and **then** put on your hat. It is colder outside **than** inside.

that there, them there, this here, these here These phrases are nonstandard. Use *that, them, this*, and *these*, respectively.

that, which Use *that* with restrictive (essential) clauses only. *Which* can be used with both restrictive and nonrestrictive clauses; many writers, however, use *which* only for nonrestrictive clauses and *that* for all restrictive clauses (see 47F).

> The house **that** [*or* which] Jack built is on Beanstalk Street, **which** [*not* that] runs past the reservoir.

their, there, they're *Their* is a possessive. *There* means "in that place" or is part of an expletive construction (see 34H). *They're* is a contraction of *they are*.

> **They're** going to **their** accounting class in the building **there** behind the library. **There** are twelve sections of Accounting 101.

theirself, theirselves, themself These are nonstandard. Use *themselves* instead.

them Use *them* as an object pronoun only. Do not use *them* in place of the adjective *these* or *those*.

> Buy **those** [*not* them] strawberries.

then See *than, then*.

till, until Both are acceptable; except in expressive writing, avoid the contracted form *'til*.

to, too, two *To* is a preposition. *Too* is an adverb meaning "also; more than enough." *Two* is the number.

> When you go **to** Chicago, visit the Art Institute. Go **to** Harry Caray's for dinner, **too**. It won't be **too** expensive because **two** people can share an entrée.

try and, sure and See *sure and, try and*.

type *Type* is nonstandard when used to mean *type of*.

> Use that **type of** [*not* type] glue on plastic.

unique   *Unique* is an absolute adjective; do not combine it with *more, most,* or other qualifiers.

> Solar heating is **uncommon** [*not* somewhat unique] in the Northeast. A **unique** [*not* very unique] heating system in one Vermont home uses hydrogen for fuel.

used to   See *supposed to, used to.*

utilize   Academic writers prefer *use* to *utilize.*

> The team **used** [*not* utilized] all its players to win the game.

way, ways   When referring to distance, use *way* rather than *ways.*

> He is a long **way** [*not* ways] from home.

well   See *good, well.*

where   *Where* is nonstandard when used for *that* as a subordinating conjunction.

> I read **that** [*not* where] Bill Gates is the richest man alive.
> **Where** is your house? [*not* Where is your house at?]

whether   See *if, whether.*

which   See *that, which.*

who, whom   Use *who* as a subject or a subject complement. Use *whom* as an object (see 32K).

who's, whose   *Who's* is a contraction of *who is. Whose* is a possessive pronoun.

> **Who's** willing to drive? **Whose** truck should we take?

would of   *Would of* is nonstandard. Use *would have* instead.

your, you're   *Your* is a possessive. *You're* is the contraction of *you are.*

> **You're** generous to volunteer **your** time at the elementary school.

CREDITS

INDEX

Where can I find what I need to know about . . . ?